Ecoto Organizations

Economic Approaches to Organizations

Sytse Douma
Tilburg University, the Netherlands

Hein Schreuder
Vlerick Business School, Belgium

PEARSON

Harlow, England • London • New York • Boston • San Francisco • Toronto • Sydney
Auckland • Singapore • Hong Kong • Tokyo • Seoul • Taipei • New Delhi
Cape Town • São Paulo • Mexico City • Madrid • Amsterdam • Munich • Paris • Milan

PEARSON EDUCATION LIMITED

Edinburgh Gate
Harlow CM20 2JE
United Kingdom
Tel: +44 (0)1279 623623
Web: www.pearson.com/uk

First published 1991 (print)
Second edition published 1998 (print)
Third edition published 2002 (print)
Fourth edition published 2008 (print)
This edition published 2013 (print and electronic)

© Prentice Hall Europe 1991, 1998 (print)
© Pearson Education Limited 2002, 2008, 2013 (print and electronic)

The rights of Sytse Douma and Hein Schreuder to be identified as authors of this work have been asserted by them in accordance with the Copyright, Designs and Patents Act 1988.

The print publication is protected by copyright. Prior to any prohibited reproduction, storage in a retrieval system, distribution or transmission in any form or by any means, electronic, mechanical, recording or otherwise, permission should be obtained from the publisher or, where applicable, a licence permitting restricted copying in the United Kingdom should be obtained from the Copyright Licensing Agency Ltd, Saffron House, 6-10 Kirby Street, London EC1N 8TS.

The ePublication is protected by copyright and must not be copied, reproduced, transferred, distributed, leased, licensed or publicly performed or used in any way except as specifically permitted in writing by the publishers, as allowed under the terms and conditions under which it was purchased, or as strictly permitted by applicable copyright law. Any unauthorised distribution or use of this text may be a direct infringement of the author's and the publishers' rights and those responsible may be liable in law accordingly.

All trademarks used herein are the property of their respective owners. The use of any trademark in this text does not vest in the author or publisher any trademark ownership rights in such trademarks, nor does the use of such trademarks imply any affiliation with or endorsement of this book by such owners.

Pearson Education is not responsible for the content of third-party internet sites.

The Financial Times. With a worldwide network of highly respected journalists, *The Financial Times* provides global business news, insightful opinion and expert analysis of business, finance and politics. With over 500 journalists reporting from 50 countries worldwide, our in-depth coverage of international news is objectively reported and analysed from an independent, global perspective. To find out more, visit www.ft.com/pearsonoffer.

ISBN: 978-0-273-73529-8 (print)
      978-0-273-78561-3 (PDF)
      978-0-273-78082-3 (eText)

British Library Cataloguing-in-Publication Data
A catalogue record for the print edition is available from the British Library

Library of Congress Cataloging-in-Publication Data
Douma, S. W.
  Economic approaches to organizations/Sytse Douma, Hein Schreuder.–5th ed.
     p. cm.
  Includes bibliographical references and index.
  ISBN 978-0-273-73529-8 (pbk.)
  1. Managerial economics. I. Schreuder, H.   II. Title.
  HD30.22.D69 2013
  338.5024'658–dc23
                         2012031862

10 9 8 7 6 5 4 3
16 15 14

Print edition typeset in 9.5/12.5 pt Stone Serif by 71
Print edition printed and bound in Great Britain by Ashford Colour Press, Gosport, Hants

NOTE THAT ANY PAGE CROSS REFERENCES REFER TO THE PRINT EDITION

Contents

Lecturer Resources

For password-protected online resources tailored to support the use of this textbook in teaching, please visit **www.pearsoned.co.uk/doumaschreuder**

ON THE WEBSITE

Preface

This is the fifth edition of a book originally published in 1991. In the meantime, it has been translated into five languages – Chinese, Danish, Japanese, Korean and Spanish.

It has been gratifying to witness the success of the book, but to us it has been even more satisfying to work on its evolution from one edition to the other. In the fourth edition, we expanded the conceptual framework of our book and added three new chapters on applications of economic approaches to organizations. Positive feedback from the users of this book has led us to maintain this format. In this fifth edition, we have however split the chapter on economic approaches to strategic management in two separate chapters, dealing with business strategy and corporate strategy respectively. This allows us to delineate the distinctive strategic tasks at the business and corporate level of larger, diversified organizations in a more focused approach. In addition, many chapters have been updated with new developments and examples.

There has been no lack of theoretical developments and demonstrations of the relevance of economic policies and approaches in recent years. Since the publication year of our fourth edition (2008), the world has experienced a severe financial crisis, triggered by the collapse of Lehman Brothers in the USA. This has led to severe pressures on the banking systems of many countries. The term 'moral hazard' which may have been a rather arcane, technical term in the first edition of our book has become very familiar to those reading newspaper coverage of the bail out of banks and large corporations that were deemed 'too large to fail'. The financial crisis has also exacerbated the plight of companies with unsuccessful strategies to cope with rapid technological change (Kodak) or globalization of markets (Volvo). Other companies have thrived in these circumstances (Apple, BMW). As a result, we have had no difficulty at all in coming up with about 50 new Boxes illustrating the applicability of the economic concepts and approaches covered in this book.

This book is intended for students of organization and management – an important area of study for students of business administration, economics, sociology and organizational psychology. There is no shortage of textbooks on organization and/or management, but most do not include even a short introduction to the various economic approaches to organizations that have been developed in recent decades. This book takes a different approach: it has been designed as an introductory text on the analysis of organizations from an economic perspective. The book has been used successfully as a main text on organization and management courses in many universities and business schools with an emphasis on economic aspects of management (such as finance, marketing and accounting). In other settings, the book can be used as a supplementary text in conjunction with a more conventional textbook on organization and/or (strategic) management.

No prior knowledge of economics is assumed. The economic background needed to understand the arguments made in the text is explained in the text itself, mainly in Chapter 2.

Students of economics will also find this book useful. Most textbooks in microeconomics devote little attention to the field of organization and management. This book offers students in economics a view from their own discipline into a related but usually unknown field.

The book starts by comparing markets and organizations. Why do organizations exist at all? Why are not all economic decisions coordinated by the market mechanism? Conversely, why do markets exist at all? Why is not all production carried out by one large firm?

Our answer is that information requirements play a crucial role in understanding why markets and organizations coexist. Markets and organizations offer different solutions to the information problems that are inherent in many situations. Understanding these differences leads to insights where markets are most appropriate and where we should expect organizations to perform better. The different advantages of markets and organizations also explain why we often find that a mix of market and organizational coordination is the optimal solution from an economic point of view.

The book consists of three parts. In Part I, Chapters 1 to 5, we lay the foundations for the economic approaches to organizations that are discussed in Part II. In Chapter 1, we build, step by step, a conceptual framework to explain the fundamental economic approach to organizations. In that framework, information is a concept of vital importance.

Chapters 2 and 3 explain how markets and organizations work. In particular, these chapters explain how decisions are coordinated by various mechanisms, such as the price mechanism, direct supervision, mutual adjustment and standardization. Chapter 4 then focuses on the information requirements of different types of coordinating mechanisms. How players can coordinate their decisions in different information settings is also the central theme of the discussion of game theory in Chapter 5. The first five chapters, which form Part I, thus explain the fundamental concepts and methods underlying the economic approaches to organizations.

As the title of this book suggests, there are several different but related economic approaches to organizations. These approaches are discussed and compared in Part II, which consists of Chapters 6 to 12. The approaches are:

- behavioural theory, which sees the firm as a coalition of groups of participants, each with its own interests;
- agency theory, which focuses on delegating decision making to an agent, while the boss (or principal) can only partly observe the agent's behaviour;
- transaction cost economics, which focuses on the sum of transaction costs and production costs as determinants of organizational forms;
- economic contributions to strategic management from the field of industrial organization and game theory, with applications in the areas of business strategy and corporate strategy

- evolutionary approaches to organizations, which direct our attention to the development of organizational forms in the context of their interaction with their environments.

Chapter 12 compares and evaluates these different approaches.

Part III describes three areas of the application of the theories and approaches discussed in Part II. Chapter 13 describes how managers involved in mergers and acquisitions cope with problems of information asymmetry. Chapter 14 discusses several hybrid organization forms, such as joint ventures, business groups and franchising using theories and approaches discussed in Part II. Chapter 15 treats the subject of corporate governance as a special case of the framework developed in earlier chapters.

The chapters in Part III each focus on a highly relevant practical issue and highlight that issue in relation to the framework developed in the earlier chapters of the book. The main differences between this fifth edition and the previous edition are that:

- it has two chapters in the economic contributions to strategic management, one on business level strategy and one on corporate level strategy;
- more explicit attention has been given to behavioural economics by adding sections in Chapter 2 and 6;
- the number of real world illustrations of theoretical ideas has been increased substantially by adding new boxes.

The field of economic approaches to organizations has been growing substantially since 1991 and this book has been growing as well. The first edition consisted of 185 pages, while this fifth edition has increased to 14 pages. Nevertheless, our ambition has remained the same throughout these years: to present the economic approaches to organizations in a way that we hope is concise, illuminating and appealing. We welcome the feedback of users whether we have achieved that ambition and any comments or suggestions you may have to improve this book further. For this purpose, we provide an email link below.

An instructor's manual containing answers to end-of-chapter questions, suggestions for further reading for each chapter, additional open questions with answers, multiple choice questions and true/false statements with answers, items for further discussion in the class room, as well as copies of many of the figures found in this edition, is available at no extra cost to lecturers adopting this book as a textbook. The manual is available in hard copy on application to the publishers. An electronic version is available to download at **www.booksites.net/douma**.)

Sytse Douma
Hein Schreuder
douma.schreuder@gmail.com

Visit the Companion Website at **http://www.pearsoned.co.uk/douma** to find valuable Lecturer Resources including:

- complete, downloadable Instructor's Manual.
- Powerpoint slides that can be downloaded.

Acknowledgements

No book can be written without the assistance of others. We wish to thank first of all our fellow economists who developed and continue to develop the exciting field of economic approaches to organizations. We owe a heavy debt to all contributors to this new literature. Their names can be found in the References section. We owe special thanks to Rejie George for his important contribution to Section 13.4 on business groups and to Louis Mulotte, Marco Furlotti, Elena Golovko, and Wolfgang Sofka for their contributions to the website accompanying this book. Further, we wish to express our thanks to the anonymous referees of the subsequent editions of this book and to Kate Brewin and Priyadharshini Dhanagopal from Pearson Education for their support.

Publisher's acknowledgements

We are grateful to the following for permission to reproduce copyright material:

Figures

Figure 8.4 from *Organization Theory: From Chester Barnard to the present and beyond*, Oxford University Press (Williamson, O. E. 1995) p. 213; Figure 9.3 reprinted with the permission of The Free Press, a Division of Simon & Schuster, Inc., from (*Competitive Strategy: Techniques for analyzing industries and competitors*) by Michael E. Porter. Copyright © 1980, 1998 by The Free Press. All rights reserved.

Text

Box 1.4 from 'Why do firms exist?', *The Economist* © The Economist Newspaper Limited, London (16/12/2010); Box 1.5 from 'Electronic glue', *The Economist* © The Economist Newspaper Limited, London (31/05/2001); Box 1.6 from 'The new tech bubble', *The Economist*, © The Economist Newspaper Limited, London (12/05/2011); Box 1.7 from *Globalization and Its Discontents*, Penguin (Stiglitz, J. 2002); Box 1.8 from http://ec.europa.eu/information_society/activities/roaming/tariffs/index_en.htm; Box 1.9 from 'Li & Fung: Link in the global chain' *The Economist* © The Economist Newspaper Limited, London (02/06/2012); Box 2.1 from *The Economist* © The Economist Newspaper Limited, London (12/02/1996); Box 3.7 from 'ÍCANN can be independent', *The Economist* © The Economist Newspaper Limited, London (26/09/2009); Box 5.5 from 'The price is right', *The Economist* © The Economist Newspaper Limited, London (29/07/2000); Box 8.7 from 'The machine that ran too hot',

The Economist © The Economist Newspaper Limited, London (27/02/2010); Box 8.12 from 'Economics focus: reality bites', *The Economist* © The Economist Newspaper Limited, London (17/10/2009); Boxes 10.3, 10.4 from http://www.berkshirehathaway.com/letters/2010ltr.pdf, The material is copyrighted and used with permission of the author; Box 11.6 after 'The last Kodak moment?', *The Economist* © The Economist Newspaper Limited, London (14/01/2012); Box 13.6 after 'Ebbers Rex', *The Wall Street Journal*, 22/03/2005 (Cools, K.); Box 13.7 after 'Hubris, overarching vanity and how one man's ego brought banking to the brink', *Daily Mail*, 20/01/2009; Box 14.5 after *The Economist* © The Economist Newspaper Limited, London (17/03/2012); Box 14.6 from 'In praise of rules: a survey of Asian business', *The Economist* © The Economist Newspaper Limited, London (07/04/2012); Box 15.1 from 'Seeing the forest for the trees', *The Economist* © The Economist Newspaper Limited, London (04/02/2012)

Part I

Foundations

1 Markets and organizations

1.1 The economic problem

Imagine a world of abundance – perhaps a tropical island where you are basking in the sun, with lots of food and a tribe of friendly islanders as your companions. Would you have any economic problems on this island? Well, 'No', you may say, 'I can't imagine *any* problem on such an island, let alone an economic problem.'

Many people associate economic problems with money. As money would be either absent or abundant on our imaginary island, they would think there would be no economic problems. An economist, however, would not be content with this reasoning. She would enquire further, asking, for example, whether you felt you had enough time to enjoy all the pleasures of your island or if your needs for housing, education, culture, friendship and so on had been met. The point is

Economic problem
that an economist would identify an **economic problem** in any situation where needs would not be met as a result of scarcity of resources – 'resources' being quite broadly conceived as meaning all factors that may contribute towards the satisfaction of human needs. So, yes, you may not have an economic problem on your fantasy island, but only if you could truly say that all your needs would be met.

Time to return to the real world, where economic problems abound, whether we apply a narrow definition or the broader one presented above. We do not have enough land to meet all our needs for cultivation as well as ecological preservation. We do not manage to feed the world's population properly. Many raw materials are in limited supply. Talent is always scarce and so is time. Most people, even in rich countries, do not earn enough money to buy everything that they would like to buy. In short, scarcity is a fact of life in the real world. Given this predicament, the economic problem may be rephrased as the problem of how to make the best use of the available resources. Alternatively, in economic

Optimal allocation
jargon, what is the **optimal allocation** of the scarce resources over the alternative uses that can be made of them? Resources that are optimally allocated are said

Efficiency
to be used with **efficiency.**

This book is concerned with economic approaches to organizations. Now, economics might not be the first discipline you think of when trying to understand organizational phenomena. Indeed, it will be argued later that economics had for a long time hardly any contribution to make to the study of organizations. The approaches that we present in this book have been developed relatively recently, although in some cases their origins are much older. So, you are quite justified in wondering what insights economics has to offer. Our answer is that economic approaches to organizations are fruitful whenever the problem to be studied has an **economic aspect** – that is to say, whenever part of the problem deals with the (optimal) allocation of scarce resources.

Note that we have carefully specified that economics deals with parts and aspects of problems. We believe that there are hardly any 'purely economic' problems. Similarly, there are hardly any purely legal, sociological or psychological problems. All these social sciences deal with aspects of real-world phenomena. All illuminate a part of social reality. Whoever believes that economics can explain entirely the 'marriage market' or, for that matter, organizational phenomena is guilty of 'economism' (which, we are informed, is a contraction of economics and colonialism). There is an equal danger of legalism, sociologism or psychologism, too, whenever the explanatory power of one discipline is exaggerated. Having said that, we do believe economics has an important contribution to make to the understanding of organizations. From the perspective outlined above, two points follow:

- Economic approaches to organizations focus specifically on the economic problem of optimal allocation of scarce resources (broadly conceived).
- The economic contribution to our understanding of an organizational problem increases when the economic problem forms a greater part of the organizational problem that we are trying to understand.

In this book, we present the major strands of the current economic approaches to organizations. In addition, we illustrate some of the applications of those approaches to organizational problems. In doing so, we shall avoid technical expositions and, instead, concentrate on the basic concepts involved. Our aim is to provide a conceptual introduction to these approaches. By focusing on the basic concepts, we hope also to present a more coherent picture of organizational economics than has been provided before. In this first chapter, we build, step by step, the basic conceptual framework that we use to explain the fundamental economic approach to organizations. This framework is shown in Figure 1.1. The framework will clarify the crucial role of information and the various ways in which information can be mediated. This central role of information will be elaborated further in Chapter 4, where we argue that this is the glue that binds the various economic approaches to organizations together.

1.2 The division of labour

Adam Smith is usually credited as the founding father of modern economics. In his book *An Inquiry into the Nature and Causes of The Wealth of Nations* (1776), he accords great importance to the division of labour: 'The greatest improvement in the productive powers of labour, and the greater part of the skill, dexterity, and judgment with which it is anywhere directed, or applied, seem to have been the effects of the division of labour.'

His famous example is that of a pin factory. He showed that a tremendous increase in the productivity of the work of pin-makers could be achieved by

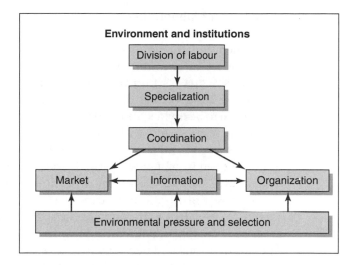

Figure 1.1 The basic concepts

splitting this work up into distinct tasks and having each worker perform one specific task rather than making entire pins (see Box 1.1).

Box 1.1 The pin factory

To take an example, therefore, from a very trifling manufacture; but one in which the division of labour has been very often taken notice of, the trade of the pin-maker; a workman not educated to this business (which the division of a labour has rendered a distinct trade), nor acquainted with the use of the machinery employed in it (to the invention of which the same division of labour has probably given occasion), could scarce, perhaps, with his utmost industry, make one pin in a day, and certainly could not make twenty. But in the way in which this business is now carried on, not only the whole work is a peculiar trade, but it is divided into a number of branches, of which the greater part are likewise peculiar trades. One man draws out the wire, another straights it, a third cuts it, a fourth points it, a fifth grinds it at the top for receiving the head; to make the head requires two or three distinct operations; to put it on, is a peculiar business, to whiten the pins is another; it is even a trade by itself to put them into the paper; and the important business of making a pin is, in this manner, divided into about eighteen distinct operations, which, in some manufactories, are all performed by distinct hands, though in others the same man will sometimes perform two or three of them. I have seen a small manufactory of this kind where ten men only were employed, and where some of them consequently performed two or three distinct operations. But though they were very poor, and therefore but indifferently accommodated with the necessary machinery, they could, when they exerted themselves, make among them about twelve pounds of pins in a day. There are in a pound upwards of four thousands pins of a middling size. Those ten persons, therefore, could make among them upwards of forty-eight thousand pins in a day. Each person, therefore, making a tenth part of forty-eight thousand pins, might be considered as making four thousand eight hundred pins in a day. But if they had all wrought separately and independently, and without any of them having been educated to this particular business, they certainly could not each of them have made twenty, perhaps not one pin in a day; that is certainly, not the two hundred and fortieth, perhaps not the four thousand eight hundredth part of what they are at present capable of performing, in consequence of a proper division and combination of their different operations.

Source: http://ec.europa.eu/information_society/activities/roaming/tariffs/index_en.htm

Division of labour, therefore, refers to the splitting of composite tasks into their component parts and having these performed separately. It is a pervasive phenomenon in modern societies.

Our primeval ancestors were much more self-supporting. They built their own houses, grew or hunted their own food, made their own tools, defended themselves from various threats and so on. Since then, gradually, these tasks have come to be divided into separate sectors in society (such as the private and the public sectors), and, within those sectors, further divided into separate entities (such as government agencies, industries and firms). An economic system has developed in which we normally buy these goods or services in exchange for money. Most of us work in organizations where we earn our money. Looking inside those organizations we can see that the division of labour occurs there as well. We usually perform but a small part of an entire organization's task. In order to accomplish its task the organization itself is split into different parts (such as divisions and departments), levels and functions. As a result, we need organization charts (see Box 1.2) as maps to guide us through the organizational territory. These charts are one reflection of the division of labour within organizations.

Box 1.2 Brill Organization Chart – May 2011

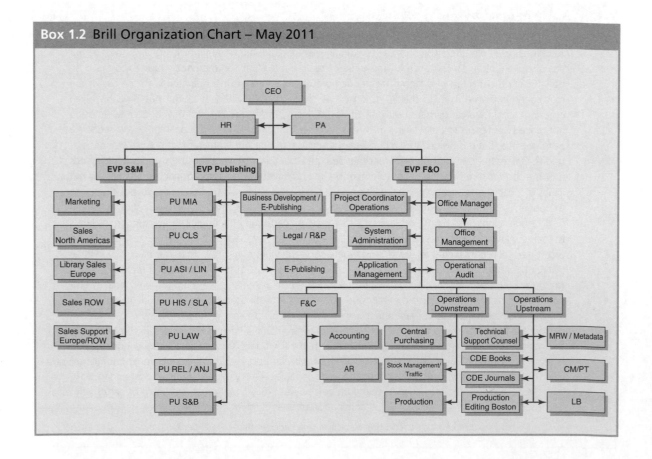

It was Adam Smith's contention that the progressive division of labour led to productivity increases that constituted the main source of the increasing 'wealth of nations'. In the next section we shall see what the basis for this contention was. Here we want to conclude by emphasizing that we take the division of labour as a fact of life in our kind of society. No matter what position we occupy, every time we interact with others to obtain goods or services we need, we may be reminded of this fact. This is what forms the starting point for our conceptual framework, which is outlined in Figure 1.1.

1.3 Specialization

Why would an increasing division of labour lead to such great productivity increases and, thus, to a growth in 'the wealth of nations'? Smith gave the following explanation:

> This great increase in the quantity of work, which, in consequence of the division of labour, the same number of people are capable of performing, is owing to three different circumstances; first, to the increase of dexterity in every particular workman; secondly, to the saving of the time which is commonly lost in passing from one species of work to another; and lastly, to the invention of a great number of machines which facilitate and abridge labour, and enable one man to do the work of many.

Economies of specialization

In our present economic terminology we say that there are **economies of specialization** to be gained. In the specialized pin factory the same amount of output can be produced with less labour effort than in the unspecialized factory. Conversely, a greater amount of output can be achieved with the same level of labour input (ten men), as Smith showed. Specialized production is thus more *efficient* than unspecialized production.

Among the reasons for this being true are the ones mentioned in the quotation above. Essentially, when work is split into specific tasks, we may select one that particularly suits our own needs and capabilities. When we specialize in that task, we can devote all our attention to improving our performance of that task. We can learn from more experience and we can use that experience to devise methods and instruments to further improve our execution of the task. For all these reasons, a specialized economic system is usually more efficient than an unspecialized one. Division of labour thus leads to specialization, which allows for efficiency gains (Figure 1.2).

This is a pervasive phenomenon in society. Let us consider some examples. In the family, household work is usually split into different tasks and the members of the family specialize in distinct tasks (while others may be shared). They become good at those tasks but not at others. Some know exactly where to shop for particular goods and get the best value for money. Some know how to operate the household appliances; perhaps others know how to fix them. Some have specialist skills in filling out the tax forms; others perhaps in monitoring the budget. Whatever the particular distribution of tasks, some degree of

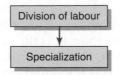

Figure 1.2 Division of labour leads to specialization

specialization is present in all families and, in most families, the efficiency of running the household is seriously disturbed when members have to switch to unfamiliar tasks. In that sense, there is a cost to specialization.

Similarly, in sports, specialization leads to higher performance, but comes at a cost. An individual cannot compete, let alone excel, in all sports. Choices have to be made and long, specialized training has to be undertaken. Once specialized, high performance is necessarily restricted to a narrow range of options. Even an admirable sportsman such as Rafael Nadal is restricted to playing professional tennis. Specialization, building on a unique talent, has allowed him to reach the top in playing tennis, but even Nadal would not be able to compete at the highest level in two sports (for example, in tennis and golf). In team sports such as hockey or soccer, it is usually very unproductive to switch goalkeepers and field players. Good teams make the best use of their members' specializations. Specialized skills are scarce. Good teams allocate those with these skills in an optimal manner to the tasks to be executed and, thus, are organized efficiently.

In many fields, such as medicine or transportation, it would even be disastrous to switch specialists. However much we favour variety of work, we are not willing to enter hospitals or board aircraft where the specialists take turns doing each other's work.

For the individual, then, specialization has the advantage of allowing higher levels of performance to be reached, but the disadvantage of restricting choice. At the individual level, the limits of specialization are reached when the satisfaction gained from higher performance (and the consequent rewards) is outweighed by the dissatisfaction from too narrow an area of application of one's skills (with the resulting boredom and frustration). As many organizations have learned over time, the gains from further specialization are easily offset by the costs of dissatisfaction when those individual limits are exceeded. The conveyor belt, for instance, enabled great gains in productivity, but only to the extent that the workers accepted the range of activities required of them. If such a range becomes too narrow, the gains are offset and a restructuring of activities (for example, into semi-autonomous workgroups) is called for. Individual limits are thus one boundary to increasing specialization, but there is also another boundary, which is the subject of the next section.

1.4 Coordination

In the previous paragraphs we have seen that division of labour and specialization are pervasive phenomena in society. As a result, hardly any people are economically self-reliant, in the sense that they produce all the goods and services they wish to consume. In order to obtain those goods and services, they have to acquire them from other specialized people.

Exchange

In economic terminology we say that **exchange** has to take place. Goods and services are exchanged whenever the right to use them is transferred. Much exchange takes place through markets. In a market, the right to use particular goods and services is bought (and, of course, sold at the same time). When I buy a piece of soap in my local store, I acquire the right to use the soap, while the storeowner acquires the right to use the money I have paid for it.

Exchange of goods is usually beneficial to both parties to the exchange. For example, a painter should paint and a cook should cook. They can both specialize when they exchange their products. A nice example is given in Box 1.3.

Box 1.3 Exchange of art for food

John Kay tells the story how the French hotel and restaurant Colombe d'Or acquired an extensive collection of modern art:

> For two hundred years European artists have been attracted to the bright light and brilliant scenery of the south of France. The walled village of Saint-Paul de Vence still houses a community of artists. Paul Roux, who bought a small hotel and restaurant at the entrance of the village in 1919, offered food and lodging to artists in return for examples of their work. Today, the Colombe d'Or's collection of modern French art is the envy of many galleries.
>
> Mr Roux was a talented cook and his visitors talented painters. It therefore made sense for Paul Roux to cook and for Georges Braque, one of the artists he encouraged, to paint. The exchange of food for paintings benefited both parties. It is common to think of exchange as a process in which one party wins at the expense of another, or one party makes a mistake. But the exchange between Braque and Roux, like most economic exchanges, was characterized by mutual gains from trade.
>
> The division of labour between Braque and Roux made these gains possible. By getting together each obtained a mixture of food and art. The two individuals had different capabilities. But these capabilities were, in themselves, insufficient for their needs. Braque needed to eat, and Roux did not wish to live by bread alone. Whenever there are differences in talent and a mutual desire for variety, there is the possibility of a division of labour and mutually beneficial exchange.

Source: Kay (2003)

Exchange, though, is broader than just market exchange. First, the goods involved need not be only goods that are marketable. Economists speak of goods whenever scarce resources are involved. We can indeed also exchange favours as they are very scarce and can be used to get things done. Similarly, we exchange information as soon as the right to use the information has been transferred. Second, the transfer of rights need not be mutual. When I offer you some of my time, I am offering you the right to use a scarce resource. An economist would regard your use of my time as an example of exchange, whether or not you reciprocate in any way.

Transaction

Whenever exchange takes place, we speak of an (economic) **transaction**. Owing to the division of labour and to specialization, innumerable transactions have to occur in society. As, on the one hand, we are all specialized ourselves

Figure 1.3 Specialization entails coordination

and, on the other hand, need the specialized goods and services of others, a vast network of exchange is necessary to allocate the available goods and services. How is that accomplished? How do the parties who are willing to engage in a transaction find each other? Phrased in economic terminology, how is the

Coordination

coordination achieved within an economic system?

Specialization leads to a need for coordination (Figure 1.3). Essentially, we shall submit, there are two types of coordination: transactions may take place either across markets or within organizations. The next section will discuss this distinction further.

1.5 Markets and organizations

Consider the stock market. Each day on the major stock markets of the world, millions of shares and bonds are exchanged. On the New York Stock Exchange alone, as many as 5 million transactions may be carried out on an average trading day, involving more than a billion shares with a total value of more than $40 billion. Buyers and sellers are not only American, but include private and institutional investors from all over the world.

How do all those parties find each other to sort out the opportunities for transactions? How, for instance, does a Japanese buyer find out who (from the USA, Germany or Hong Kong) wants to sell the stocks in which he is interested? The answer is, he does not.

He does not because the stock market comes close to that ideal type of market in which it is not necessary for buyers and sellers to have any kind of personal

Price system

contact. The reason is that the **price system** is the coordinating device that takes care of allocation.

Suppose you are a potential buyer or seller of IBM stock. All you have to do is inform yourself of the current price of IBM shares, make up your mind whether or not you want to transact at that price level and, if so, instruct your bank or broker to carry out the transaction. You will never know the party with whom you exchanged the stock. It is not necessary to know the other party. The price contains all the information you need to base your transaction on: it is a

Sufficient statistic

sufficient statistic (Hayek, 1945).

No wonder economists marvel at the functioning of these types of markets. Through the interlinked system of stock exchanges in the world, all potential buyers and sellers of, in our example, IBM stock are connected with each other.

What is more, if, globally, there are more potential buyers than sellers, the price goes up. This has the effect that some buyers are discouraged at that price level and some new sellers are interested in entering the market. This goes on until demand and supply of stock is in equilibrium. At that point, we can say that an optimal allocation of that stock has been achieved, as the buyers who are most interested in that stock have been satisfied, while the sellers who were least interested have sold. This optimal allocation obtains without any personal contact being made between the transacting parties.

There are a number of such markets. Markets for raw materials often approximate ideal markets. Let us borrow an example from Hayek (1945) to emphasize how efficiently such markets operate:

> Assume that somewhere in the world a new opportunity for the use of some raw material, say tin, has arisen, or that one of the sources of the supply of tin has been eliminated. It does not matter for our purpose – and it is very significant that it does not matter – which of these two causes has made tin more scarce. All that the users of tin need to know is that some of the tin they used to consume is now more profitably employed elsewhere, and that in consequence they must economize tin. There is no need for the great majority of them even to know where the more urgent need has arisen, or in favor of what other needs they ought to husband the supply. If only some of them know directly of the new demand, and switch resources over to it, and if the people aware of the new gap thus created in turn fill it from still other sources, the effect will rapidly spread throughout the whole economic system and influence not only all the uses of tin, but also those of its substitutes and the substitutes of these substitutes, the supply of all the things made of tin, and their substitutes, and so on; and all this without the great majority of those instrumental in bringing about these substitutions knowing anything at all about the original cause of these changes.

Again, the adjustment of the price levels of tin and its substitutes is sufficient for a worldwide communication of all the necessary information to all relevant parties. As if led by the famous 'invisible hand' of Adam Smith, the individual decisions made by these parties will lead to new aggregate equilibrium levels of the supply and demand of tin.

Assuming you are now convinced of the efficiency properties of ideal markets, we may proceed to ask, why is not all exchange executed across markets? In fact, this is a rather old question. It was raised most effectively by Coase in 1937, who put it this way:

> If a workman moves from department Y to department X, he does not go because of a change in relative prices, but because he is ordered to do so ... The example given above is typical of a large sphere in our modern economic system ... But in view of the fact that it is usually argued that co-ordination will be done by the price mechanism, why is such organization necessary?

Coase went on to provide an answer along the following lines. Contrary to the standard assumptions for ideal markets, Coase maintained that usually there is a *cost* associated with using the price system. First of all, there is usually a cost (if only time) involved in finding out what the relevant prices are. Next, when important, a *contract* is usually drawn up to provide the basis for a market transaction. For instance, in the labour market, employment contracts are necessary to specify the conditions under which most exchanges take place. It is costly to draw up those contracts. Finally, there may be conditions under which it is hardly possible (or extremely costly) to reach a contractual agreement that may serve as a basis for market exchange. In those cases, too, *organization* may provide an alternative.

Therefore, Coase posited markets and organizations as alternatives for the execution of transactions. For markets, the price system is the coordinating device. Within organizations, the price system is, in Coase's view, replaced by authority as a coordinating mechanism. The question remains as to the circumstances under which the market will be employed for exchange transactions and the conditions under which organizations will be preferred. Coase's answer was that it is determined by the relative cost of transacting under these two alternatives. Transactions will typically be executed at the lowest cost. As a consequence, transactions will shift between markets and organizations as a function of the *transaction costs* under those two alternatives.

This last answer was taken up much later by Williamson (1975) to establish 'transaction cost economics', as we shall see in Chapter 8. Here we conclude by noting that Coase's analysis (1937) allowed standard economic reasoning to be employed in analyzing both the nature and the size of the firm:

> When we are considering how large a firm will be, the principle of marginalism works smoothly. The question always is, will it pay to bring an extra exchange transaction under the organizing authority? At the margin the cost of organizing within the firm will be equal either to the cost of organizing in another firm or to the costs involved in leaving the transaction to be 'organized' by the price mechanism.

The important contribution made by Coase was largely ignored for a very long time, but eventually recognized by by most economists (see Box 1.4).

Box 1.4 Why do firms exist? The contribution of Ronald Coase

Ronald Coase celebrated his 100th birthday on the 29th of December 2010. On that occasion *The Economist* offered the following observations:

> The economics profession was slow to recognize Ronald Coase's genius. He first expounded his thinking about the firm in a lecture in Dundee in 1932, when he was just 21 years old. Nobody much listened. He published "The Nature of the Firm" five years later. It went largely unread.
>
> But Mr Coase laboured on regardless: a second seminal article on "The Problem of Social Cost" laid the intellectual foundations of the deregulation revolution of the 1980s. Eventually, Mr Coase acquired an army of followers, such as Oliver Williamson, who fleshed out his ideas.
>
> His central insight was that firms exist because going to the market all the time can impose heavy transaction costs. You need to hire workers, negotiate prices and enforce contracts, to name but three time-consuming activities. A firm is essentially a device for creating long-term contracts when short-term contracts are too bothersome. But if market are so inefficient, why don't firms go on getting bigger for ever? Mr Coase also pointed out that these little planned societies impose transaction costs of their own, which tend to rise as they grow bigger. The proper balance between hierarchies and

markets is constantly recalibrated by the forces of competition: entrepreneurs may choose to lower transaction costs by forming firms but giant firms eventually become sluggish and uncompetitive. Mr Coase's theory continues to explain some of the most puzzling problems in modern business.

In 1991, aged 80, Ronald Coase was awarded a Nobel prize. Far from resting on his laurels, he published the book *How China Became Capitalist,* together with Ning Wang, in 2012.

Source: 'Why do firms exist? *The Economist,* 16 December 2010

We adopt Coase's original distinction between markets and organizations as two ideal types of coordination for exchange transactions. In the next section we argue that markets and organizations differ most essentially in the way that information is communicated between the transacting parties. The argument developed above entails that an **ideal market** is characterized by the fact that prices act as 'sufficient statistics' for individual decision making. If we adopt this characterization, **ideal organizations** can be characterized as all those forms of coordination of transactions that do *not* use prices to communicate information between the transacting parties. In fact, we argue in Chapter 3 that most transactions in the real world are governed by hybrid forms of coordination. Most markets are to some extent 'organized'. Most organizations do use prices (such as transfer prices) to communicate information within the organization. As a summary of the argument so far, we may present the conceptual framework in its present stage of development, in Figure 1.4.

Ideal market

Ideal organizations

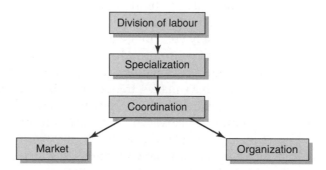

Figure 1.4 There are two types of ideal coordination: market and organization

1.6 Information

We now arrive at a decisive step in the development of our conceptual framework. We have seen that the division of labour, leading to economies of specialization, necessitates the coordination of transactions. We have seen that there are two ideal types of coordination: market and organization. We shall now

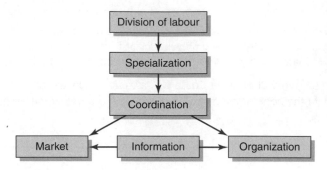

Figure 1.5 The market/organization mix depends on the particular information requirements of the situation

argue that the actual (mix of) coordination mechanism(s) that we will observe in any situation will depend mainly on the information requirements that are inherent in that situation. Thus we present *information* as the crucial concept in our framework, explaining how coordination will take place (Figure 1.5). We introduce this concept below and elaborate on its significance in Chapter 4.

Recall that ideal markets are characterized by the operation of prices as sufficient statistics – that is to say, the price contains all the information needed for the coordination of transactions. The price mechanism is, therefore, a perfect channel of information to all parties potentially interested in transacting. In situations where the price mechanism is applicable as a coordination device, it is, therefore, hard to beat its efficiency properties. However, we have also argued that in many situations the price mechanism is complemented or substituted by organizational coordination mechanisms. There are many situations in which the price cannot absorb all the information necessary to enable the execution of transactions. When Volkswagen buys ignition systems for the Audi A6, it will probably use a long-term contract containing many details with respect to quality and quantities with one or a few suppliers. In such a situation – where Volkswagen buys ignition systems rather than making ignition systems itself – we still have market transactions, but we cannot say that price is a sufficient statistic. Rather, we have a situation in which the price mechanism (which is still important: Volkswagen will try to buy from the cheapest source) is supplemented by a form of planning not unlike the planning used within organizations.

There are also many situations in which the price mechanism is totally incapable of performing its coordination function. In Chapter 4, we delve into the reasons for this. We show there are fundamental information problems that cannot be resolved by the price system. A number of these problems can, however, be dealt with by means of organizational coordination. Thus, from the perspective developed in this book, *organizations arise as solutions to information problems.* Organizations are more suited to dealing with certain information problems than are markets.

As Figure 1.5 indicates, the market/organization mix depends on the particular information requirements of the situation. Information and communication costs determine, to a large extent, the relative efficiency of the two broad coordination mechanisms (markets and organizations). This is also illustrated in Box 1.5.

Box 1.5 Organizations and the Internet

We argue in this book that organizations arise as solutions to information problems. A similar line of reasoning was followed by *The Economist* when analysing the effects that the rise of the Internet and other new communication technologies may have on the shape of firms:

> A prime reason why economic activity is organized within firms rather than in open markets is the cost of communication. The costlier it is to process and transmit information, the more it makes sense to do things in firms; the cheaper communication becomes, the more efficient (relatively) markets will be. Because the Internet and other inventions have cut the cost of communication so much, firms ought to be able to do less in-house and to outsource more. In 1999, General Motors, a byword for vertical integration, spun off Delphi Automotive Systems, one of its supply divisions, for instance.

In Chapter 10 we shall discuss vertical integration and show that more factors are involved in General Motors' decision than just the cost of communication. However, the basic reasoning in *The Economist* is sound and well in line with the approach taken in this book:

- Markets and organizations represent alternative ways to coordinate transactions.
- Information will determine their relative efficiency.

Source: 'Electronic glue', *The Economist,* 2 June 2001

1.7 The environment and institutions

Finally, we want to add the *context* in which the trade-offs between market and organizational coordination are made. Broadly speaking, we will call this context the *environment.* The broad concept of the environment includes many dimensions. They are not only economic in nature, but may also be social, political, cultural or institutional. As we will show in this section, economists have particularly highlighted the importance of the institutional dimension (see Figure 1.6).

In Chapter 11 we will discuss evolutionary approaches to organizations. In those evolutionary approaches, attention is paid to the fact that organizations not only adapt to their environment, but are also shaped by pressures from the environment and may also be selected by their environment. We can best see such environmental pressures operating when we take a somewhat longer time horizon.

Consider, for instance, how environmental pressures have shaped organizations with respect to their labour practices (such as the abolition of child labour), waste management (such as reductions in carbon emissions) or internationalization (as a result of the international trade agreements negotiated by the World Trade Organization, for example).

Consider also how rapidly changing environmental conditions allowed, first, the creation of many new companies during the 'dot-com bubble' (see Box 1.6) of the late nineties and then the rapid selection of the few companies that survived and have become successful (such as Amazon and eBay), while others have

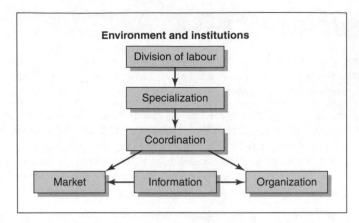

Figure 1.6 Environment as context for the market/organization mix

perished. Who remembers today such companies as Boo.com, Kozmo.com or Webvan? These examples illustrate that organizations do not operate in a vacuum, but live in an *environment* that:

- provides the conditions for particular organizations to be created;
- shapes all organizations by exerting economic, social, political and other pressures;
- is also the ultimate *selection mechanism* for determining which organizations can survive and be successful (while other organizations are 'selected out' and perish).

Box 1.6 The dot-com bubble and a new tech bubble?

The 'dot-com bubble' was a speculative bubble covering roughly 1995–2000 during which stock markets in Western nations saw their value rise rapidly from growth in the new Internet sector and related fields. The period was marked by the founding (and in many cases, spectacular failure) of a group of new Internet-based companies commonly referred to as *dot-coms*. A combination of rapidly increasing stock prices, individual speculation in stocks, and widely available venture capital created an exuberant environment in which many of these businesses dismissed standard business models, focusing on increasing market share without much regard to the bottom line. The bursting of the dot-com bubble marked the beginning of a relatively mild yet rather lengthy recession in Western nations.

In 2011, *The Economist* warned that irrational exuberance had returned to the internet world:

Some time after the dotcom boom turned into a spectacular bust in 2000, bumper stickers began appearing in Silicon Valley imploring: "Please God, just one more bubble." That wish has now been granted…Facebook and Twitter are not listed, but secondary-market trades value them at some $76 billion (more than Boeing or Ford) and $7.7 billion respectively. This week LinkedIn, a social network for professionals, said it hoped to be valued at up to $3.3 billion in an initial public offering (IPO). The next day Microsoft announced its purchase of Skype, an internet calling and video service, for a frothy-looking $8.5 billion – ten times its sales last year and 400 times its operating income….some bets on start-ups now will pay off. But investors should take a great deal of care when it comes to picking firms to back: they cannot just rely on somebody else paying even more later. And they might want to put another bumper sticker on their cars: "Thanks, God. Now give me the wisdom to sell before it's too late.".

Source: 'The new tech bubble', *The Economist*, 14 May 2011

Not only organizations but also markets are shaped and selected by environments. In 'centrally planned economies', such as the Soviet Union used to have, many markets were non-existent because the government attempted to coordinate economic activity by administrative rule. In 'market economies' too, governments have a fundamental influence on which markets are allowed to exist and how they function. Consider, for example, the government monopoly on military force, the prohibition of commercial markets for human organs for transplantation or the strict regulations on gambling. In all these cases, the government (as an important actor in the environment) determines which markets can come into being and shapes the rules by which such markets must function.

The functioning of markets will also be affected by other actors in the environment, such as trade unions, which have an impact on labour markets in many countries, or environmental pressure groups, which attempt to set standards of acceptable eco-behaviour in many markets. Moreover, markets are susceptible to more subtle environmental pressures, of social and cultural origin, for instance. In the United States of America, the market for chief executive officers of large corporations allows for them to receive much higher levels of compensation than in similar markets in Europe, where the American salary levels for CEOs are generally regarded as 'excessive'.

Finally, new markets come into being as a result of environmental developments, such as advancing technology (the market for online gaming) or ecological needs (the markets for renewable energy and resources). At the same time, 'old markets' shrink or disappear for such reasons – the market for fixed telephones or Freon (the traditional cooling agent for refrigerators, that was banned for ecological reasons). As such examples show, markets do not function in a vacuum either. Markets operate in an environment that:

- provides the conditions for particular markets to be created;
- shapes all markets by exerting economic, social, political and other pressures;
- is also the ultimate *selection mechanism* for determining which markets can survive and be successful (while other markets are 'selected out' and perish).

Economists have paid particular attention to the environmental dimension that we call *institutional*. Institutions have been defined by Douglass North (1990), one of the most prominent 'institutional economists', as follows:

Institutions are the rules of the game in a society, or more formally, are the humanly devised constraints that shape human interaction.

This definition includes both formal and informal rules of the game and the way those are enforced in a society. Formal rules are written laws, constitutions, regulations and the like. Informal rules are norms of behaviour, conventions and internally imposed rules of conduct–those in a company culture, for example. Enforcement of the rules can also be formal (such as through the legal courts) or informal (through peer pressure and social sanctions).

In most countries, the role of formal rules and enforcement has increased over time. As explained by Douglass North (2005b, p. 27) himself:

> Throughout most of history, exchange has been based on personal knowledge of the other party. Reputation and repeat dealings have been the basis for confidence that the exchange would be lived up to in terms of both the quantity and the quality of the good or service exchanged and that the agreement would be executed in accordance with the understanding of both parties. Transaction costs in such cases were small. But, also, markets were necessarily small.
>
> As long-distance trade expanded in the Middle Ages, the difficulties of exchange between parties that did not know each other posed fundamental transaction problems. At the champagne fairs in France in the twelfth century, one merchant was designated to collect information on the reliability of the merchants attending the fair; when contemplating an exchange that was not instantaneous, a merchant would seek advice from the designated merchant on the reliability of the other party. But extending personal knowledge by such devices has limits with respect to the size of markets. And Adam Smith, the patron saint of economists, was unequivocal in his assertion that specialization, division of labour, and the size of the markets are the source of the wealth of nations. Everything economists have learned since then reinforces this assertion.
>
> Impersonal exchange – exchange between parties with no knowledge of each other and occurring over time and space – not only runs counter to innate genetic features that evolved of the several million years that humans were hunters/gatherers; it is also simply an open invitation to fraud, cheating and corrupt practices. In fact, in the absence of the essential institutional safeguards, impersonal exchange does not exist, except in cases where strong ethnic or religious ties make reputation a viable underpinning.
>
> What is required is a political institutional structure that will put in place the rule of law and the necessary enforcement structure. Such a framework must substitute effectively for the 'trust' that comes with personal exchange. The failure to create the essential institutional base is the central problem of economic development.

Indeed, the creation of appropriate institutions has not only been the central problem of economic development in historical times but also remains so today. Box 1.7 illustrates this for the recent development of Russia. In Chapter 15, Corporate Governance, we will provide modern-day examples of the importance of institutions.

Box 1.7 The importance of institutions

Consider the problems facing Russia (or the other countries) in 1989. There were institutions in Russia that had names similar to those in the West, but they did not perform the same functions. There were banks in Russia, and the banks did garner savings; but they did not make decisions about who got loans, nor did they have the responsibility for monitoring and making sure that the loans were repaid. Rather, they simply provided the 'funds,' as dictated by the government's central planning agency.

There were firms, enterprises producing goods in Russia, but the enterprises did not make decisions: they produced what they were told to produce, with inputs (raw material, labour, machines) that were allocated to them. The major scope for entrepreneurship lay in getting around problems posed by the government: the government would give enterprises quotas on output, without necessarily providing the inputs needed, but in some cases providing more than necessary. Entrepreneurial managers engaged in trades to enable themselves to fulfill their quotas, in the meanwhile getting a few more perks for themselves than they could have enjoyed on their official salaries. Those activities – which had always been necessary to make the Soviet system merely function – led to the corruption that would only increase as Russia moved to a market economy. Circumventing what laws were in force, if not breaking them outright, became part of the way of life, a precursor to the breakdown of the 'rule of law' which was to mark the transition.

As in a market economy, under the Soviet system there were prices, but the prices were set by government fiat, not by the market. Some prices, such as those for basic necessities, were kept artificially low – enabling even those at the bottom of the income distribution to avoid poverty. Prices for energy and natural resources also were kept artificially low – which Russia could only afford because of its huge reservoirs of these resources.

Old fashioned economics textbooks often talk about market economics as if it had three essential ingredients: prices, private property and profits. Together with competition, these provide incentives, coordinate economic decisionmaking, ensuring that firms produce what individuals want at the lowest possible cost. But there has also long been a recognition of the importance of institutions. Most important are legal and regulatory frameworks, to ensure that contracts are enforced, that there is an orderly way of resolving commercial disputes, that when borrowers cannot repay what is owed there are orderly bankruptcy procedures, that competition is maintained, and that banks that take depositors are in a position to give the money back to depositors when they ask. That framework of laws and agencies helps ensure securities markets operate in a fair manner, managers do not take advantage of shareholders nor majority shareholders of minority shareholders. In the nations with mature market economies, the legal and regulatory frameworks had been built up over a century and a half, in response to problems encountered in unfettered market capitalism. Bank regulation came into place after massive bank failures; securities regulation after major episodes in which unwary shareholders were cheated. Countries seeking to create a market economy did not have to relive these disasters: they could learn from the experiences of others. While the market reformers may have mentioned this institutional infrastructure, they gave it short shrift. They tried to take a short cut to capitalism, creating a market economy without the underlying institutions, and institutions without the underlying institutional infrastructure. Before you set up a stock market, you have to make sure there are real regulations in place. New firms need to be able to raise new capital, and this requires banks that are real banks, not the kinds of banks that characterized the old regime, or banks that simply lend money to government. A real and effective banking system requires strong banking regulations. New firms need to be able to acquire land and that requires a land market and land registration.

Source: Stiglitz (2002)

If we regard institutions as the rules of the game, imposed by the environment, then we can see how the economic 'game' played is fundamentally shaped by the institutional framework of a particular country. The government is, of course, a particularly important actor in the environment of markets and organizations. Market processes may, by themselves, leave many people with too few resources to survive. In countries that have been most successful, government has stepped in and compensated for such 'market failures', providing a safety net for the poor. Governments provided a high-quality education to all and furnished much of the institutional infrastructure, such as the legal system, which is required for markets to work effectively. They regulated the financial sector, ensuring that capital markets worked more in the way that they were supposed to. They fought against fraud and corruption. They promoted technology, for example, by setting up technological institutes and public research programmes. Sometimes they intervene directly in the operation of markets, as Box 1.8 illustrates for the market of mobile phone calls in Europe.

Box 1.8 Market intervention by the European Union

The European Commission has imposed price caps on what it describes as 'excessive roaming charges'. This is a significant intervention by the EU in the market and came despite fierce opposition from operators such as Vodafone. Thanks to EU roaming rules, the cost of making and receiving calls when abroad in the EU is now 73% cheaper than in 2005, when the EU first started to tackle excessive roaming charges. Under the revised roaming rules, the maximum roaming charges would be 35 cents per minute for calls made and 11 cents for calls received while abroad. In addition, price caps for SMS were introduced in 2009, which reduced the cost of sending roaming text messages by 60%. Measures to tackle "bill shocks" for consumers surfing the internet through a mobile connection while abroad were also adopted. From 1 July 2010, travellers' data-roaming limit is automatically set at €50 excluding VAT (unless they have chosen another limit-higher or lower). Operators have to send users a warning when they reach 80% of their data-roaming bill limit. The operator has to cut off the mobile internet connection once the limit has been reached, unless the customer has indicated they want to continue data roaming that particular month.

Source: from http://ec.europa.eu/information_society/activities/roaming/tariffs/index_en.htm © European Union, 1995–2012

There is much debate about the appropriate roles of government and the desirable extent of a government's reach in the economy. Among economists, however, there is 'broad agreement that government has a role in making any society, any economy, function efficiently – and humanely' (Stiglitz, 2002, p. 218).

Next to the government, many other actors and factors play a role in shaping economic activities in markets and firms. Think of the legal system, trade unions, consumer groups, non-governmental organizations (NGOs), often acting as pressure groups for specific causes, and so on. Add to this the many informal institutional rules that countries develop over time – traditions, norms of (non-)acceptable behaviour – and specific codes of conduct.

Together, all such actors and factors constitute the specific environmental context and institutional framework in which economic activity is carried out in organizations and markets. Given the many different choices that can be made in those dimensions in different countries, the context will also vary from country to country.[1] We will highlight some such differences in forthcoming chapters – for instance, in Section 14.4, Business groups, and Chapter 15, Corporate Governance.

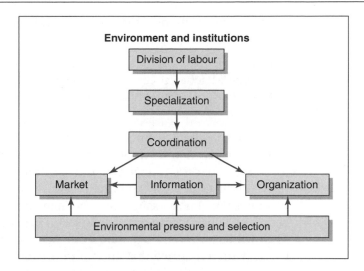

Figure 1.7 Environmental pressure and selection codetermines market/organization mix

All in all, it should be clear by now that we have to complete our basic conceptual framework by showing how markets and organizations are embedded in an environmental context and, particularly, an institutional framework. Environmental and institutional factors co-determine which markets and organizations are allowed to exist and also exert pressure on how they function. Those factors are not static, but evolve over time as governments change, laws are amended, social norms develop, and new issues and challenges have to be addressed by societies.

For the economic problems in society, markets and organizations are appropriate responses. The choices between these two coordination mechanisms will be driven primarily by the information requirements of the situation, but will also, to some extent, depend on the environmental and institutional context in which the choice is made.

That concludes the basic conceptual framework we use to explain the economic approaches to organizations. We take the division of labour in society as our starting point, leading to specialization, which allows efficiency gains. However, with increasing specialization, there is a corresponding need for coordination. Coordination can be achieved via markets or organizations. Information is a crucial element in the trade-off between market and organizational coordination. In this section, we have shown that the trade-offs between markets and organizations are not made in a vacuum, but are embedded in an environment that shapes and selects the market/organization mix in various ways, particularly through the institutional context (see Figure 1.7).

1.8 Historical perspective

One may wonder why the economic approaches to organizations have been only fairly recently developed. Why did it take so long, for instance, to pick up on the fundamental question raised by Coase in 1937 – why do we observe so many organizations if markets are so efficient? The main reasons, as we see them, are summarized by the following two statements:

- Until recently, most (but not all) economists focused their attention on how the market achieves coordination *between* organizations (and individuals).
- Most (but not all) organization theorists studied coordination *within* organizations.

We shall briefly illustrate these statements below.

The older economic writers, such as Adam Smith and Alfred Marshall, had a lot to say about the functioning of organizations. However, over time, economists' fascination with the functioning of markets led them to study market coordination almost exclusively. The mainstream economists of the twentieth century elaborated a theory of markets. That theory is now highly developed. Meanwhile, however, there were some exceptional economists, such as Ronald Coase, who recognized that an important and growing share of the economic transactions within society were executed not across markets but within organizations. It was only fairly recently that more economists became interested in these economic processes and the resulting allocation within organizations, such as business firms. One of the reasons was that new theoretical approaches were developed that were more satisfactory than the older ones. It is the purpose of this book to introduce these approaches.

Organization theory, on the other hand, was interested primarily in what goes on within organizations. The first writers on organization focused on 'scientific management' – that is, discovering principles of work organization that would enhance productivity. Many of these early writers had a technical or engineering background and management experience to draw on. Later on, social and psychological considerations were introduced by writers in the 'human relations' school. Many of the early contributions to the field of organization studies attempted to formulate the 'one best way to organize'. Only since the 1950s and 1960s has it been recognized that the best way to organize is dependent on the particular situation the organization is in. The 'contingency theories' of organization were developed. These theories emphasized the technological and environmental factors that were important in shaping the organization. Still later, since the 1970s, organization studies have become even more multidisciplinary. Some would maintain that the subject has become increasingly fragmented. Diverse perspectives and approaches coexist. Contributions are made from the disciplines of sociology, psychology, political science, management, anthropology and so on. Since organizations have so many facets it may be inevitable that they are studied from many different angles and backgrounds.

Since the 1970s, an economic perspective has been added to these various contributions. Initially, this occurred because economists became interested in organizations and exported their newly developed theories into the field of organization studies. As such, the economic perspective simply came to coexist alongside the other disciplinary perspectives on organizations. Organization theorists, however, became interested in these new theories, too.

One reason for their interest was that some of the economic approaches incorporated concepts that had been borrowed by economists from earlier work within organization theory. Transaction cost economics, for example, makes extensive use of the concept of *bounded rationality,* developed in organization theory. Through such common use of concepts the integration of economic theories within organization studies is facilitated. Another reason for the growing interest in economic perspectives on organizations is that they allow the analysis of organizational problems that are different from those studied in the other disciplines. As mentioned in Section 1.1, these problems always deal with the economic aspect of organizations – how to allocate the scarce organizational resources efficiently.

We conclude this section with a final introductory observation: there is currently a *family* of economic approaches to organizations. The family is bound together by their focus on the economic aspect of organizations. This identifies them as *economic* theories of organization. Within this common family resemblance, however, the various theories to be introduced differ in many respects. They differ, for instance, in the problems identified and in their basic modes of analysis, as will become clear when they are introduced. In the following chapters, therefore, the differences within the family may stand out more clearly than the similarities. In Chapter 12, we return to this observation and discuss the question of how tightly knit the family currently is and what the prospects are for its members' future development.

1.9 Summary: the conceptual framework of this book

This chapter has introduced the basic conceptual framework we use to explain the fundamental economic approach to organizations (Figure 1.1). The framework takes the division of labour in society as its starting point. The division of labour leads to specialization, which allows efficiency gains to be made. With increasing specialization, however, there is a corresponding need for coordination. Coordination is necessary in order to arrange the vast network of exchange between specialized economic actors. This is illustrated in a modern, international context in Box 1.9.

Box 1.9 Globalization, specialization and coordination: the case of Li & Fung

In this chapter we have used Adam Smith's original example of a pin factory as an illustration of the concepts of division of labour, specialization and coordination. These forces play not only at the local level of a factory, however, but also at the global level. This is shown by the case of Li & Fung, a Chinese firm that was called 'a surprising world leader in supply-chain management' by *The Economist:*

> Li & Fung used to introduce Western retailers of clothes, toys and the like to the sweatshops of China. As such, it was no different from countless Chinese firms … But when Victor and William Fung, the brothers who today run the family business, sat down to think about globalization and what it means for Asia, they came up with a winning new strategy for their company.

To them, globalization meant above all specialization, and specialization brings complexity. If supply chains of companies once consisted of five links, they might soon have dozens, or even hundreds, they surmised. 'Somebody's got to pick up the pieces and bring them back together' says William Fung, the younger brother – which is what Li & Fung is now doing, to all appearances better than its rivals in the West.

It works like this. Say, a European clothes retailer wants to order a few thousand garments. The optimal division of labour might be for South Korea to make the yarn, Taiwan to weave and dye it, and a Japanese-owned factory in Guangdong Province to make the zippers. Since China's textiles quota has already been used up under some country's import rules, Thailand may be the best place to do the sewing. However, no single factory can handle such bulk, so five different suppliers must share the order. The shipping and letters of credit must be seamless, and the quality assured. Coordinating all this is the challenge of globalization ... And this requires knowledge. Village women with sewing machines in Bangladesh are not on the Internet. Finding the best suppliers at any given time, therefore, takes enormous research – so much, indeed, that companies are increasingly deciding that it no longer pays to do it in-house. Instead, they outsource the knowledge gathering to Li & Fung, which has an army of 3600 staff roaming 37 countries ('a machete in one hand, a laptop in the other', as Victor Fung likes to caricature them) for the purpose. In this sense, Li & Fung is itself a product of specialization. A company that focuses entirely on optimizing supply chains for other companies is a recent phenomenon.

Source: 'Li & Fung: Link in the global chain' *The Economist,* 2 June 2001

We have argued that there are two ideal types of coordination of exchange transactions: markets and organizations. Markets use the price system as the coordinating device, while organizations use non-price systems, such as authority. In practice, both ideal types of coordination are usually mixed. We have argued that the actual mix found in any situation will depend mainly on the information requirements of that situation. Markets and organizations are different solutions to information problems that are inherent in (economic) transactions. From an economic perspective, they have different efficiency properties. They are efficient coordination mechanisms for different sets of transactions, depending on the information requirements involved.

Finally, we have argued that markets and organizations are embedded in an environmental context and an institutional framework. Therefore, environmental and institutional factors will codetermine the trade-off between market and organizational coordination. This basic perspective is further elaborated and illustrated in this book.

1.10 Outline of the book

This first chapter has introduced some basic concepts in a preliminary way. They will be elaborated in Chapters 2 to 11. Equipped with this further knowledge, we return to the common perspective in Chapter 12. There we discuss it more thoroughly and contrast various ways of highlighting the similarities and the differences in the economic approaches to organizations. Finally, we apply the economic concepts to the topics of mergers and acquisitions, hybrid forms and corporate governance in Chapters 13 to 15. These chapters illustrate the broad range of the applicability of the approaches introduced in this book.

In Chapters 2 to 4, the general ideas introduced so far are explored in more depth. Chapter 2 focuses on markets. Standard microeconomic theory is used to explain how coordination is achieved in an (ideal) market. This theory illustrates the role of the price mechanism in equating demand and supply for goods and services. The chapter serves two purposes: first, to introduce some basic economic concepts and modes of analysis and, second, to serve as a benchmark against which other economic approaches can be measured. If you are already familiar with standard microeconomics, you can either glance quickly through Chapter 2 or skip it entirely.

To conclude this introductory chapter, we borrow from the economist A. C. Pigou (1920) the following quotation: 'When a man sets out upon any course of inquiry, the object of his search may be either light or fruit – either knowledge for its own sake or knowledge for the sake of good things to which it leads.' On your 'course of inquiry' through this book, we wish you occasional light and fruit, as well as some fun along the way. To this end, Box 1.10 introduces you to some typical fun that economists enjoy – light-bulb jokes.

Box 1.10 A Russian light-bulb

There are many light-bulb jokes in economics, including these:

Q: How many economists does it take to change a light-bulb?
A: Two: one to assume the existence of a ladder and one to change the bulb!

An alternative answer to this question is:

A: Eight: one to change the bulb and seven to hold everything else constant!

John McMillan tells the following version from Russia.
In Russia in 1992, amid the ruins of communism, the State abruptly ceased controlling the economy. A few years later, when the country's progress toward a market economy had bogged down and the country was in a sorry state, a joke circulated on the streets of Moscow:

Q: 'How many people does it take to change a light-bulb under communism?'
A: 'Five: one to hold the light-bulb, four to rotate the table he is standing on.'
Q: 'Under capitalism, how many does it take?'
A: 'None, the market will take care of it.'

The Russian sarcasm underlines a key point. While markets can do a lot, they do not work automatically. Unaided, the market will not take care of things.

Source: McMillan (2002, p. 14)

Questions

1 Suppose you are a Saudi prince and studying economics at Oxford University in the UK. Your family sends you a very large monthly allowance to cover tuition and other expenses. In fact, this allowance is more than ten times the average allowance of the other students. Do you think that you would still have an economic problem? Why?

2 Suppose you are an American student and you are about to obtain your MBA and start looking for a job. An economist would say that you are about to enter the job market. Compare this market with the tin market that is described in the text. Is the job market for MBAs also an example of an ideal market? Is price a sufficient statistic for this market? Discuss the latter question from the point of view of both employers and those seeking employment.

3 What might be the economic aspect of partner matching in the 'marriage market'?

4 Box 1.9 describes the success of a company named Li & Fung. What exactly is Li & Fung's business? Who are Li & Fung's customers? After having read Chapter 1, including Box 1.9, what do you think is the main point that the case brings forward?

5 In Box 1.5, it is argued that the rise of the Internet has cut the cost of communication so much that firms will be inclined to outsource more than before. Do you think this is true? Do you see an implicit assumption, made by the journalists of The Economist, that is highly relevant but which is not mentioned in Box 1.5? Discuss.

Note

1   On the other hand, such differences have likely become smaller in recent decades as globalization and economic integration of the world has progressed (see Stiglitz, 2002).

2 Markets

2.1 Introduction

When the weather is bad in the summer, the price for foreign holiday breaks goes up, but domestic hotels start cutting their prices. When political tensions rise in the Middle East, the price of oil increases, but the cost of purchasing a used car that consumes a lot of petrol decreases. Governments in many countries try to discourage drinking and smoking by slapping hefty taxes on alcohol and cigarettes. At the same time, many governments would like to create a market for 'emission trading rights' to combat climate change.

What do these examples have in common? They all refer to situations where:

1 there is demand and supply for certain goods or services
2 a market can match demand and supply at a certain price.

In this chapter we examine how standard microeconomic theory explains the functioning of such markets.

Standard microeconomic theory focuses on how economic decisions are coordinated by the market mechanism. Economic decisions have to be made by both consumers and producers. Consumers can choose from a large number of goods. For each good, they must decide how much they are going to consume. Producers must decide how much they are going to produce and how they are going to produce. Consumers and producers meet each other in the market. Coordination between the total quantity demanded by consumers and the total quantity supplied by producers is achieved through interaction in the market. Thus, the quantity of tomatoes shipped to London on a certain day is determined not by a planning authority but by **the process of market interaction** (see Box 2.1). This process of market interaction is explained in Section 2.2. In competitive markets, prices are determined by the process of market interaction, not by individual buyers or sellers.

The process of market interaction

Box 2.1 The London vegetable market

In rich countries, markets are too familiar to attract attention. Yet a certain awe is appropriate. When Soviet planners visited a vegetable market in London during the early days of *perestroika*, they were impressed to find no queues, shortages, or mountains of spoiled and unwanted vegetables. They took their hosts aside and said: 'We understand, you have to say it's all done by supply and demand. But can't you tell us what's really going on? Where are your planners, and what are their methods?'

Source: The Economist, 17 February 1996

How does an individual consumer choose between different goods when the prices of those goods are given? That is the central question of the theory of demand that we discuss in Section 2.3. How does an individual producer decide how much to produce? How does the producer decide how to produce that quantity? Those are the central questions of the theory of production that we discuss in Section 2.4. In Section 2.5 we summarize how choices made independently by producers and consumers lead to market coordination: the exact quantity demanded by all consumers is produced without any central coordination. We also point out that, in a competitive market, no producer will make a profit although every producer maximizes profit. This is the 'paradox of profit' discussed in Section 2.6. Having thus outlined the main characteristics of standard microeconomic theory, Section 2.7 offers a number of comments on the theory. Here we highlight important assumptions underlying the models of standard microeconomics and give a preview as to which of these assumptions will be relaxed in subsequent chapters. Section 2.8 focuses on one particular important assumption of standard micro economic theory: the assumption that human beings are rational decision makers, who act in their own self-interest only. Section 2.9 provides a summary.

2.2 Market interaction: analysis of demand and supply

The total demand for a certain good depends on the price for that good. Take, for example, TV sets. When the price of a TV set is €500, total demand in the European Union (EU) market may be 10 million sets annually. If the price of TV sets goes down (and nothing else changes), some families that now have only one set may decide to buy a second one. Other families may decide to replace their existing set with a new one. Hence, we would expect total demand to go up if the price goes down. This is the **law of demand**. The relation between price and quantity demanded is shown in Figure 2.1. The **demand curve** D in Figure 2.1 is presented as a straight line only for the purposes of simplicity – there is no reason to expect a linear relationship between price and quantity demanded. From the demand curve we can read, for every price, the quantity demanded. For a price of €500, the quantity demanded is 10 million sets.

Television sets are supplied to the market by TV manufacturers. The total quantity supplied also depends on the price. If prices go up (and everything else remains the same), then TV manufacturers will find it more profitable to make TV sets and they will supply more sets in order to take advantage of increased profit opportunities. Therefore we expect supply to go up as the price goes up. This is the **law of supply**. The **supply curve** S in Figure 2.2 depicts the relationship between price and quantity supplied. For example, if the price is €500, all manufacturers will together produce 24 million sets. The supply curve need not be a straight line, as it is shown in the figure.

Law of demand

Demand curve

Law of supply

Supply curve

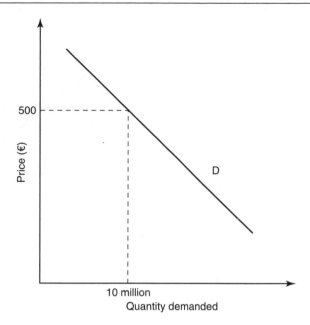

Figure 2.1 Demand for TV sets within the EU

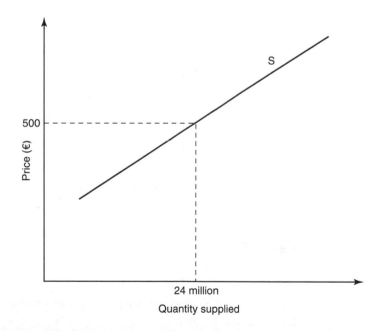

Figure 2.2 Supply of TV sets to the EU market

Market equilibrium

Market equilibrium occurs where the demand curve D and the supply curve S intersect. The equilibrium price is €400 per set (see Figure 2.3). At that price, total supply is 14 million sets, while total demand is also 14 million sets. At the equilibrium price of €400 per set, all sets manufactured by producers are sold to

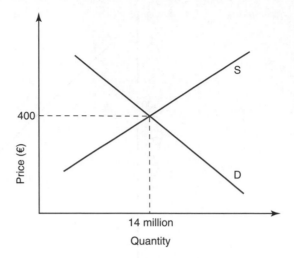

Figure 2.3 Supply and demand

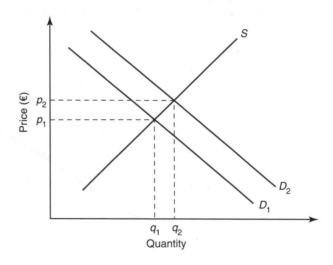

Figure 2.4 An increase in the demand for TV sets

consumers. Moreover, all consumers who want to buy at €400 per set actually buy a set.

Suppose there is an increase in the demand for TV sets in the EU. This may occur as a result of population growth or because of an increase in per capita income. As a result the whole demand curve will shift upwards, as in Figure 2.4.

The shift of the demand curve gives a new market equilibrium: the price of a TV set increases from p_1 to p_2 and the quantity demanded (and sold) increases from q_1 to q_2.

2.3 The theory of demand

How does an individual consumer choose between the goods he or she can buy? Suppose a consumer is confronted with several different baskets of goods. Standard microeconomic theory assumes that each person can rank these baskets in the order that reflects their preferences. These preference rankings are assumed to be **transitive**. This means that if a person prefers basket A to basket B and prefers basket B to basket C, then he also prefers basket A to basket C. Finally, it is assumed that each person prefers more of a certain good to less of it.

With these assumptions about consumers' preferences it is possible to represent the preferences of a certain consumer by a set of **indifference curves**. Figure 2.5 shows the indifference curves for a consumer who can choose between baskets containing different Quantities of apples and pears.

The consumer, whose preferences are depicted in Figure 2.5, is indifferent about baskets B_1 and B_2. Basket B_1 means having X_1 kilograms of apples per week and Y_1 kilograms of pears per week; basket B_2 means having X_2 kilograms of apples and Y_2 kilograms of pears per week. Points B_1 and B_2 lie on curve U_1. A curve like U_1 is called an indifference curve: this consumer is indifferent about the baskets represented by points on U_1. He is not indifferent about baskets B_1 and B_3: on the contrary, he prefers B_3 over B_1. This is represented in Figure 2.5 by the fact that B_3 lies on an indifference curve that is further from the origin. This consumer prefers all baskets represented by points on indifference curve U_2 to all points on indifference curve U_1.

The satisfaction that consumers derive from having goods is usually called **utility** by economists. Instead of saying that a consumer is indifferent about baskets B_1 and B_2, we can say that this consumer derives the same utility from both basket B_1 and basket B_2. Thus, an indifference curve is a curve that represents

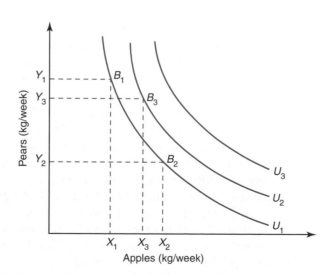

Figure 2.5 Indifference curves

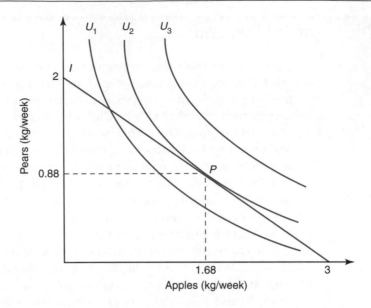

Figure 2.6 A model of consumer choice: a budget line and a set of indifference curves

points with the same level of utility. Curve U_2 represents all points that give our consumer a level of utility equal to U_2, whereas curve U_1 indicates all points that give him a level of utility U_1.

It is not possible to measure utility. Standard microeconomic theory assumes only that consumers can rank different baskets of goods. Therefore the assumption is that our consumer can indicate that he prefers basket B_3 to basket B_1, but not that he can indicate how great the difference in utility is between these two baskets.

The amounts of apples and pears that our consumer will buy depend not only on his preferences as given by his set of indifference curves, but also on his budget. Suppose that this consumer has €3.00 per week available for buying fresh fruit and that apples are €1.00 per kg and pears €1.50 per kg (for simplicity, assume that it is possible to buy every quantity you want, such as 0.683 kg).

The quantities of apples and pears that our consumer can buy with this

Budget line budget are given by line *l* in Figure 2.6. Line *l* is called the **budget line**.

We assume that every consumer wants to maximize his level of utility, so our consumer will choose the point on line *l* that gives him the highest possible level of utility. This is point *P* on line *l*, where line *l* is tangential to indifference curve U_2. Point *P* represents a basket of 1.68 kg of apples and 0.88 kg of pears.

Looking at the set of indifference curves, we see that some indifference curves (such as U_1) intersect with line *l*, while other indifference curves (such as U_3) do not. There is one, and only one, indifference curve that is tangential to the budget line: it is U_2. The point of tangency indicates the basket that the consumer will actually buy, given the budget constraint set out above. This basket provides him with the highest attainable utility.

2.4 The theory of production

How does a producer of a certain good decide *how much* she is going to produce? How does she decide *how* she is going to produce that quantity? These are the two main questions of the theory of production in standard microeconomic theory. In order to answer them we need a description of the firm.

Objective function

In standard microeconomics the firm is described as an entity that maximizes an **objective function**. The objective function of a firm describes the goal(s) that the firm pursues (usually profit or the value of the firm on the stock market). The objective function can be maximized only within the constraints given to the firm by its production function.

Here, we shall first describe the concept of a production function, then discuss how the firm, in trying to maximize profits, decides how much and how to produce.

2.4.1 The production function

Production function

A **production function** describes the relationship between any combination of inputs and the maximum output that a firm can produce with those inputs. As an example, consider a firm producing pencils. In order to make pencils, the firm needs machines, labour and raw materials. Assume, for the sake of simplicity, that the firm needs only one kind of machine, only one kind of labour and only one kind of raw material. This assumption is not very realistic, but it has no influence at all on what follows. Standard microeconomic theory can easily handle several kinds of machine, several kinds of labour and several kinds of raw materials – it just makes the mathematics a little bit more complicated.

Let K be the amount of capital, L the amount of labour and M the amount of raw material the firm has at its disposal. K may be measured as the number of machines, L as the number of labour hours per period (number of employees times the number of hours worked per period) and M as the volume or weight of raw material. Let Q be the maximum quantity of pencils that the firm can produce for a given combination of K, L and M. The production function is the relationship between Q and K, L, M and is expressed as:

$$Q = Q(K, L, M)$$

The production function describes how much output can be achieved with any combination of inputs. For given values of K and M, Q generally increases when L is increased. This implies that, for a factory with a given number of machines and a given amount of raw materials, output can be increased by hiring more employees or working overtime. However, output cannot be increased indefinitely in this way: either the amount of raw materials available per period or the amount of capital goods will prevent a further increase in production by adding more and more labour.

To increase or decrease the inputs that are available for production takes time. It is useful to make a distinction between the *short-run* and the *long-run*. In the short-run, only some inputs can be varied. In the long-run, all inputs can be varied.

In most cases it is fairly easy to vary the amounts of raw materials that the firm buys per period. This means that M can be varied in the short run. To build a new factory usually takes more time, so it seems reasonable to assume that K can vary only in the long run. Labour may fall somewhere between, depending on how easily employees can be hired and fired or induced to work overtime. Whether or not it is possible to vary the amount of labour may also depend on the type of labour: perhaps it is easier to hire and fire unskilled workers at short notice than highly skilled workers.

The distinction between input factors that can be varied in both the short run and the long run and input factors that can be varied only in the long run is an important one. In fact, we need only two kinds of input to develop the theory further:

■ those inputs that can be varied in the short run as well as in the long run;
■ those inputs that can vary only in the long run.

It is customary to denote input factors that can be varied in the short run by L and input factors that can be varied only in the long run by K, so, from now on, L stands for all input factors that can vary both in the short run and in the long run, such as raw materials and perhaps certain kinds of labour, while K stands for all inputs that can vary only in the long run, such as capital goods and other kinds of labour. Despite this new interpretation of L and K we shall still refer to L as labour and to K as capital, so labour now means those inputs that can be varied in the short run as well as in the long run, while capital means those inputs that can be varied only in the long run.

The production function with two inputs is:

$$Q = Q(K,L)$$

This production function is depicted in Figure 2.7.

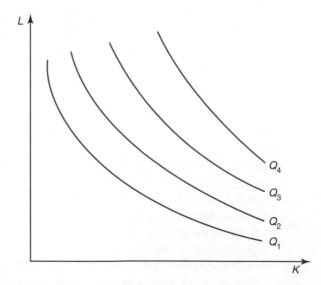

Figure 2.7 An isoquant map as a graphical representation of a production function

The curve Q_1 in Figure 2.7 represents all possible combinations of K and L that the firm can choose from, if it wants to produce quantity Q_1. The points on Q_1 thus represent combinations of K and L leading to the same volume of output. The curves Q_1, Q_2, Q_3 and Q_4 are called **isoquants.** In Figure 2.7 the four isoquants are such that $Q_4 > Q_3 > Q_2 > Q_1$.

Isoquants

2.4.2 Profit maximization in competitive markets

Suppose we have a firm with a given production function. How does this firm decide how and how much to produce? In order to answer these questions we need to make an assumption about the firm's objective function. In standard microeconomics it is usually assumed that the firm wants to maximize profits.

How can a firm with a given production function maximize profits? It depends on whether or not the firm has some freedom to determine the price of its products. In a competitive market – that is, a market with many sellers and buyers and with free entry and exit of firms – the firm cannot set its own prices. In competitive markets, prices are determined by the process of market interaction. The price resulting from this process is then given for each individual firm. In what follows, we discuss only profit maximization in competitive markets.

We first need a definition of profit. *Profit* is defined as revenue minus total cost, or:

$$\pi = p.Q - c.K - w.L$$

where:

π = profit
p = market price of the firm's product
Q = quantity produced (and sold)
pQ = total revenue
c = cost of a unit of capital
K = amount of capital used
w = cost of a unit of labour
L = amount of labour used
$cK + wL$ = total cost

Here, Q is a function of K and L (remember that profit can be maximized only within the constraint of the firm's production function), $Q = Q(K,L)$.

We now have all that we need in order to discuss the two main questions of the theory of production: how much to produce and how to produce. How much to produce means choosing a value for Q. How to produce means choosing values for K and L. The two questions are not independent as $Q = Q(K,L)$. So, the firm cannot choose Q, K and L independently: it can choose only two of those three variables independently. The third variable is then determined by $Q = Q(K,L)$. We shall assume that K and L are the two decision variables and Q is then determined by $Q = Q(K,L)$.

In the *short run*, K is fixed, so the firm can choose only L. By choosing a value for L (with a fixed value for K), Q is also determined by $Q = Q(K, L)$. This

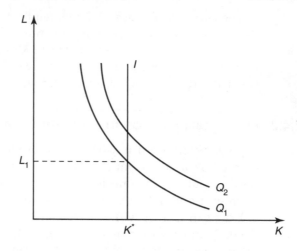

Figure 2.8 In the short run, K is fixed. By choosing a level of L, the firm also chooses a level Q

is illustrated in Figure 2.8. Here K^* is the amount of capital that the firm has installed. In the short run it cannot add or scrap capital goods, so it can choose only values for K and L that lie on the vertical line l. If the firm chooses a value for L, say L_1, then it has also decided to produce quantity Q_1 (Q_1 is the isoquant through point (K^*, L_1)).

We can now formulate the problem of short-run profit maximization in mathematical terms. Total profit as a function of L is:

$$\pi = p.Q(KL) - cK - wL$$

For a maximum, the first-order derivative with respect to L must equal zero, so we have:

$$P\frac{dQ}{dL} - w = 0$$

or, alternatively: $\dfrac{dQ}{dL} = \dfrac{w}{p}$

Solving this equation gives a value for L. Quantity Q is then determined by $Q = Q(K,L)$. This procedure can be illustrated by an example.

Suppose, that the firm is producing pencils. The market price of pencils is 25 cents per item and the rate of pay is $20.00 per hour. So, we have $p = 0.25$ and $w = 20$.

Suppose, further, that the production function is such that its first-order derivative with respect to L is a decreasing function of L. In Figure 2.9 we have sketched dQ/dL, which is called the **marginal productivity of labour,** as a function of L. The economic interpretation of dQ/dL is the additional quantity of pencils that the firm can produce if it adds one hour of labour.

Marginal productivity of labour

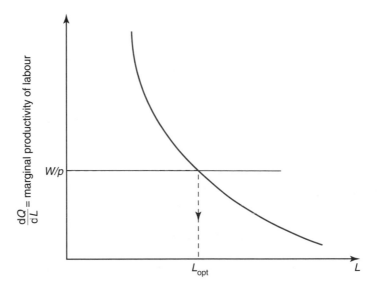

Figure 2.9 How the firm chooses L in short-run profit maximization

Given this interpretation, it is quite reasonable to assume that dQ/dL is a decreasing function of L. In our example, the firm will choose that value of L for which:

$$\frac{dQ}{dL} = \frac{w}{p} = \frac{20}{0.25} = 80$$

This is L_{opt} in Figure 2.9.

We can summarize this discussion on profit maximization in the short run as follows. In the short run, the firm can choose only L. By choosing a value for L, Q is also determined. The firm will choose L such that the marginal productivity of labour (dQ/dL) is equal to w/p.

In the *long run,* however, both K and L can be varied. The problem of profit maximization now is one of working out how to maximize the expression

$$\pi = pQ(K,L) - cK - wL$$

with respect to both the decision variables K and L.

For a maximum, both partial derivatives $\partial\pi/\partial K$ and $\partial\pi/\partial L$ must equal zero. This gives:

$$\frac{p\partial Q}{\partial K} - c = 0$$

or, alternatively:

$$\frac{\partial Q}{\partial K} = \frac{c}{p}$$

and:

$$\frac{p\partial Q}{\partial L} - w = 0$$

or, alternatively:

$$\frac{\partial Q}{\partial L} = \frac{w}{p}$$

Solving these two equations gives the optimal values for K and L. With $Q = Q(K,L)$, Q is also determined. The firm will choose K and L such that the marginal productivity of capital, $\partial Q/\partial K$, is equal to the ratio c/p, and the marginal productivity of labour, $\partial Q/\partial L$, is equal to the ratio w/p. The interpretation of this result is analogous to the interpretation given above for the short run case.

We can summarize these results as follows:

- In the short run, the firm can only decide how much labour to use. This is equivalent to deciding how much to produce. Once L and, thus, Q have been determined, the firm has no freedom left. So, the firm can, in the short run, decide only how much to produce, not how to produce. It decides how much to produce by choosing L, such that the marginal productivity of labour equals w/p.
- In the long run, the firm can decide how much to produce *and* how to produce. This is equivalent to choosing both K and L independently. It will choose K and L such that the marginal productivity of capital equals c/p and the marginal productivity of labour equals w/p.

2.5 Market coordination

This, then, is how market coordination works: a producer maximizes her profits; for any given price she calculates the amount that maximizes profits. In the short run producers can only adjust L, K is fixed. This results for all firms in an industry in a supply curve such as depicted in Figure 2.2. A consumer maximizes his utility. For any given price he calculates the amount he is going to buy. For all consumers this results in the demand curve sketched in Figure 2.1. Supply equals demand for one price only: at the intersection of the supply curve and the demand curve (Figure 2.3). This results in a price that is a given for both producers and consumers. Now every producer knows how much she is going to produce and every consumer know how much he is going to buy.

If there is a shift in demand (for example because new consumers enter the market, the price goes up (Figure 2.4). Producers will now produce more. In the short run they will increase L only; if they do so they will stay on the same supply curve (Figure 2.4). If price remains high, producers will in the long run increase K too. This will lead to an upward shift in the supply curve.

In the oil industry demand for oil has been rising fast between 1999 and 2008, due to a rapidly expanding world economy. Oil prices have gone up and down as a result of changes in supply and demand. But the long run growth of demand and oil prices has resulted in substantial investments in exploration and new technologies that allow oil companies to produce more oil. This is the long run effect, described above. For details see Box 2.2.

Box 2.2 Oil prices and the pace of new discoveries

Oil prices have been quite volatile in recent decades, ranging from below $20 per barrel (in early 1999) to above $120 in early 2008, down to $30 in late 2008 and back again to above $100 in 2011. The *New York Times* reported on the effects of such price swings in 2009 as follows:

The oil industry has been on a hot streak this year, thanks to a series of major discoveries that have rekindled a sense of excitement across the petroleum sector, despite falling prices and a tough economy. These discoveries, spanning five continents, are the result of hefty investments that began earlier in the decade when oil prices rose, and new technologies that allow explorers to drill at greater depths and break tougher rocks.

"That's the wonderful thing about price signals in a free market – it puts people in a better position to take more exploration risk" said James T. Hackett, chairman and chief executive of Andarko Petroleum. More than 200 discoveries have been reported so far this year in dozens of countries, including northern Iraq's Kurdish region, Australia, Israel, Iran, Brazil, Norway, Ghana and Russia. They have been made by international giants, like Exxon Mobil, but also by industry minnows, like Tullow Oil.

While recent years have featured speculation about a coming peak and subsequent decline in oil production, people in the industry say there is still plenty of oil in the ground, especially beneath the ocean floor, even if finding and extracting it is becoming harder. They say that prices and the pace of technological improvement remain the principal factors governing oil production capacity.

Source: The New York Times, 24 September 2009. See also Box 5.7.

2.6 The paradox of profits

In a competitive market (that is, a market with large numbers of sellers and buyers and with free entry and exit of firms) the firm can earn no economic profit in the long run. Here, economic profit means profit in excess of normal profit, where normal profit is defined as the profit that a firm needs to make in order to stay in business. Normal profit is equal to the opportunity cost[1] of the equity capital provided by the owner(s) of the firm. If profit is lower than the opportunity cost of equity capital, the owners will decide to take their capital out of this firm and employ it elsewhere (in a competitive market there is free – that is, costless – exit). In the long run, no firm can earn an economic profit in a competitive market. It is easy to see why this is true: if there were economic profits, entry would occur, supply would increase, price would go down and economic profits would vanish. This then is the paradox of profits; while each firm tries to earn an economic profit, no firm can do so in the long run.

2.7 Comments on standard microeconomic theory

The model of a competitive market is an important benchmark for understanding how markets operate. It shows how coordination between quantities demanded by buyers and quantities supplied by sellers is achieved by the price mechanism. It introduces some basic concepts and techniques of economic analysis. It also shows that, although every firm has maximization of profits as its objective, no firm can earn an economic profit in the long run.

If all industries were adequately described by the model of perfect competition, we should live in a maximally efficient world. The result of free competition would then be an allocation of resources in the economy that is called Pareto-optimal. A **Pareto-optimal allocation of resources** is such that no one can be made better off by changing the allocation of resources without anyone becoming worse off. It does not mean that everyone's wants are satisfied to the same extent. Some people may be able to buy many more goods than others, depending on the initial distribution of wealth and talents. A Pareto-optimal allocation of resources means only that there is no other allocation of resources that can make someone better off while making no one worse off.

Pareto-optimal allocation of resources

This result of the model of competitive markets has led economists and policymakers alike to the conclusion that competition between firms should be encouraged. This is the general idea behind antitrust policy.

Perfect competition

While recognizing the importance of the model of **perfect competition,** we should also point out some of its limitations. We should start by summarizing the basic assumptions on which the model of perfect competition is based. There are three assumptions that, when relaxed, lead to other models within the context of standard microeconomics:

- There is a *large number of small buyers and sellers.* That is, each seller and each buyer is so small that their decisions do not affect the market price. This assumption is relaxed in other models of standard microeconomics, such as models of monopoly and oligopoly (industry consisting of a few large companies).
- There is *free entry and exit of firms.* That is, there are no barriers to entry and no barriers to exit. This assumption is also relaxed in other models of standard microeconomics, such as models of monopoly and oligopoly.
- Each industry is characterized by *standardized products.* That is, consumers do not care whether they buy from firm A or firm B. The products of firms A and B are perfect substitutes in the eyes of the consumer. This assumption is relaxed in the model of monopolistic competition. This is another extension of standard microeconomics.

We shall not discuss these other models of standard microeconomics here. If you would like to know more about them, you should consult a textbook on microeconomics. Instead, we want to point out five other assumptions underlying all models of standard microeconomics:

Holistic entities

- Firms are viewed as **holistic entities**. This means that a firm is considered to be a single unified entity. There is, in fact, no difference in standard microeconomics between the concept of a producer (one person working alone) and a firm (several people cooperating to produce outputs). When, for example, profit maximization is the firm's objective, then it is assumed that everyone inside the firm makes all decisions solely with that objective in mind. In standard microeconomics, the firm is really no more than a production function with an objective function (profit maximization). When the purpose of the analysis is to explain how competitive markets work, this may be an adequate description of a firm. When, however, the purpose of the analysis is to explain how a firm makes decisions to coordinate the work of its employees, we need another description of the firm.

Single objective

■ Firms are supposed to have a **single objective.** Standard microeconomics assumes that this is so. Usually it is assumed that the objective is to maximize either profits or the value of the firm on the stock market. Now, imagine a firm having two objectives: to maximize profits *and* maximize employee satisfaction. Suppose it is impossible to measure profits and employee satisfaction with the same yardstick: there is no common *numéraire,* no unit for expressing both objectives. In standard microeconomics this situation can be handled in one of two ways: one can assume that the firm's objective is to maximize profits and introduce a minimum level of employee satisfaction as an additional constraint *or* one can assume that the firm's objective is to maximize employee satisfaction and introduce a minimum profit level as an additional constraint. Suppose now, for the sake of argument, that all producers are able to say, 'for me, every unit of employee satisfaction is worth €3.00 of profits'. It would then be possible to combine both objectives into one single objective: profits in € + units of employee satisfaction × €3.00. Standard microeconomics can handle firms with two objectives only when these two objectives can be combined into a single one. With objectives such as maximization of profits and maximization of employee satisfaction, this seems unlikely.

Perfect information

■ There is **perfect information.** Another important assumption of standard microeconomics is that everyone has perfect information: everyone knows everything. Here, 'everything' means everything that is relevant to making decisions about how much and how to produce (producers) and how much to buy of each finished consumer good (consumers). Hence, each producer is assumed to know the production functions of all goods and prices of all finished consumer goods, component parts, raw materials, wages and capital goods, while all consumers are supposed to know all the prices of all consumer goods. In modern microeconomics, that assumption of perfect information is relaxed. In Section 4.2 we illustrate this by discussing the market for health insurance. Here, an individual considering whether or not to take out a policy has more information about his risk profile than the insurance company does. We show that such a market cannot exist (that is, no transactions in health insurance policies can take place) unless there is a solution to this information problem. Another example is the market for the services of a travelling salesperson. Here, the salesperson has more information about the level of effort exerted than does the boss back in the office. As we explain in Section 4.3, the problem now is how to write a contract that gives the travelling salesperson a strong incentive to put in a real effort without allocating all the risk to him. This is an example of an agency relation. Agency theory is discussed in Chapter 7.

Maximizing behaviour

- Behaviour of producers and consumers is described as **maximizing behaviour.** Producers are assumed to maximize profit, consumers are assumed to maximize utility. This implies that producers and consumers are rational decision makers. This is a very strong assumption that has been questioned by psychologists and economists alike. In Section 2.6 we discuss if and when this assumption matters. Another important assumption is that producers know all the alternatives (for example, they know the complete isoquant map we saw in Figure 2.7), such that they are able to compare all the alternative decisions and choose the one that maximizes the objective function. For some types of decision, such as how much to produce in the short run, that assumption may not be very unrealistic. For other types of decision, for example decisions concerning which new products to develop, it does seem unrealistic. Such decisions can be so complex that it is difficult or costly to fully evaluate even one alternative. Moreover, ideas for new products do not all come along at the same time. Firms have to decide on one idea without knowing what other ones may come up the next day. Therefore, not all the alternative decisions may be known at the time a decision must be made.

Markets function in isolation

- Finally, standard microeconomics examines markets as if they **function in isolation** – 'on their own' – disregarding the environmental context. However, as we argued in Chapter 1, markets function in an environment. They are shaped by their social, political, cultural and institutional context. Markets are 'embedded' in that context. Standard microeconomics abstracts from that environmental context to focus on the functioning of markets as such. It is useful as an analytical approach. To understand the functioning of markets in the real world, however, it will often be necessary to add the environmental factors. We will return to this theme in subsequent chapters as well.

2.8 Economic Man (*homo economicus*) and his further development

The preceding sections have illustrated how, in standard microeconomic theory, individual consumers and producers make their decisions. Consumers base their decisions on their utility functions which express the satisfaction they will derive from consumption of particular goods and services. They are also able to compare different goods and services as expressed by an indifference curve. Similarly, producers (individuals and firms) have an objective function expressing the goal(s) pursued. Consumers strive to maximize their utility and producers strive to maximize their objective(s), usually profit or the value of the firm on the stock market. The price mechanism establishes the equilibrium price at which demand meets supply and the market is 'cleared'.

Underlying this standard microeconomic model we thus find a view of human decision-making which is sometimes expressed as *homo economicus*. This view is characterized by rationality of decisionmaking and by maximizing behavior. Further simplifying assumptions are that Economic Man is exclusively interested in his own well-being and that he possesses perfect information about the decision context at hand. In models with different time periods, Economic Man is also able to allocate consumption (or production) over time, based on a rate of time preference.

How should we look at these assumptions about human decisionmaking? One way to look at them is to evaluate them as **simplifying assumptions**, that allow the construction of models that are useful to explain and predict certain economic outcomes, like the market clearing price. Seen in this way, we should not focus on the realism of the assumptions but on the accuracy and usefulness of the explanations and predictions. An analogy would be with the science of physics, where we first construct models that use simplifying assumptions, like absence of friction or air resistance. For the explanation and prediction of some phenomena, like the pathway of a cannonball, such models are good enough. Only if the phenomena that interest us require further development of the model can we add more complex assumptions, like friction and air resistance. For instance, to explain the pathway of a falling feather this is necessary. The point is that all science uses simplifying assumptions that are to some degree unrealistic. It is usually impossible to model phenomena in all their intricate detail and based on entirely realistic assumptions. Viewed in this way *homo economicus* is just one manifestation of such simplifying assumptions.

However, one can also regard such simplification as inherently unsatisfactory, first of all in a descriptive sense ('this is not the way humans decide'). Therefore, economists and other social scientists have extensively studied human decisionmaking and have come up with a number of modifications of the simplified model. We will report in Chapter 5 the results of experiments like the Ultimatum Game and the Trust Game that show that many people go beyond their narrow self-interest in these decision settings. And we will encounter such modifications for instance in Chapter 6 when we discuss satisficing behaviour (instead of maximizing behaviour) and bounded rationality (instead of full rationality). We will then also note the many heuristics and biases that people use in their decisionmaking, leading to further limits on rationality. All in all, such further insights have led to the field of **Behavioural Economics**, which is based on more realistic, empirically validated assumptions on human decisionmaking.The view adopted in this book is that there is no harm in using *homo economicus* as a set of simplifying assumptions in the standard microeconomic models explaining market outcomes. For such aggregate phenomena complete realism of the underlying assumptions is not required. Care should be taken, however, if models are applied outside this sphere. Then a careful evaluation of the simplifications against the accumulated evidence of Behavioral Economics is in order. The latter becomes even more important when economic models are used to make policy prescriptions. We should not base such prescriptions on a too narrow view of human decision making.

Simplifying assumptions

Behavioural Economic

2.9 Summary: how economic decisions are coordinated by the market

In a competitive market, economic decisions are coordinated by the laws of supply and demand. The law of supply states that supply will increase as the price of a product goes up. The law of demand states that demand will decrease as the price of a product goes up. This means that there is only one price at which total demand equals total supply. This is the market (or equilibrium) price. The market price is determined by the point of intersection of the supply curve and the demand curve. Let us take another look at Figure 2.3. The supply curve for TV sets and the demand curve for TV sets intersect at a price of €400. At that price, all manufacturers of television sets in the EU will together produce exactly 14 million sets without any planning authority telling them how many to produce. Each manufacturer of television sets will take the price of €400 as given. Given this price, it will determine how many sets to produce. There are many manufacturers of TV sets in the EU. With a price of €400, total production by all these manufacturers is 14 million sets. Also, with a price of €400, total demand by all consumers in the EU is equal to 14 million sets. This means that all sets will be sold and that every consumer who wants to buy at €400 can do so. The quantity of sets to be produced is determined not by a planning authority but by the laws of supply and demand.

Consumers buy not only TV sets but also many other products. Consider a consumer who likes apples as well as pears. Given a certain budget, how many apples and how many pears will he buy?

That depends on his tastes and on the prices of apples and pears. In order to explain how a consumer makes this type of decision, economists use the rather abstract concept of utility. Consumers act as if they are maximizing their utility. This enables us to draw indifference curves like those in Figure 2.5. All points on the same indifference curve give the consumer the same level of utility. The concepts of utility and indifference curves belong to the standard toolbox of a microeconomist. These tools are used again in Chapter 7.

How does a manufacturer decide how much to produce? Here we have to make a distinction between the short run and the long run. In the short run (days or weeks), the manufacturer cannot add another assembly line or close one of the existing assembly lines. The firm can add labour, however, by, for example, working overtime or hiring temporary employees (perhaps students).

It is standard economic theory to assume that, as the firm adds more and more labour, the output will not increase linearly. That is because employees get tired if they work long hours and the factory becomes crowded as the number of employees increases. The additional output, as a result of an additional hour of labour, decreases as the firm adds more and more labour. In the language of economists, the marginal productivity of labour decreases as the amount of labour increases. Given a market price, the firm will choose the amount of labour in such a way that its profits are maximized.

In the long run, the firm can vary both capital *and* labour. For example, the firm can invest in additional assembly lines and hire additional employees. The firm has more freedom in the long run than in the short run. In the long run it can decide not only how much to produce but also how to produce it – that is, how much capital and labour to use in order to produce a given quantity.

The standard microeconomic theory that is explained in this chapter is based on five assumptions:

- *Firms are holistic entities* This means that a firm is assumed to be a single, unified entity. The result is that, in standard microeconomics, one does not consider what goes on inside the firm: it is as if the firm is simply a black box that we cannot look into. This first assumption is relaxed in more modern approaches that are discussed in subsequent chapters. It is quite obvious that, if we want to discuss organizations, we have to look inside them.
- *Firms have a single objective function* such as to maximize profit or the value of the firm. That assumption means the objectives of the owner(s) of the firm are the only objectives that matter. In later chapters, especially in Chapters 6 and 7, that assumption is relaxed.
- *Everyone has perfect information* That is a very important assumption underlying standard microeconomics. As we have stated in Chapter 1, however, organizations arise mainly as solutions to information problems. If we want to understand why not all economic decisions are coordinated by the price mechanism of standard microeconomics, then we have to relax that crucial assumption, which we do in all subsequent chapters.
- *The behaviour of producers and consumers can be described as maximizing behaviour* This assumption typifies the *homo economicus,* who knows everything and makes decisions solely on the basis of calculating the solution to some maximizing problem. This *homo economicus* reappears in Chapters 5 and 7. In several other chapters, however, we assume that human beings may try to maximize something, but they are unable to calculate the optimal solutions in all circumstances.
- *Standard microeconomics examines the market independent of its environmental context* While this is useful as an analytical approach, the functioning of many markets in the real world cannot be fully understood without including the environmental factors. In Chapter 1 we highlighted some of these factors and will continue to add illustrations in subsequent chapters.

Questions

1 Prove that two indifference curves can never intersect. *Hint:* sketch a situation in which two indifference curves do intersect and show that this leads to a contradiction.

2 Prove that two isoquants can never intersect.

3 In Chapter 1 we quoted Hayek (1945): 'Assume that somewhere in the world a new opportunity for the use of some raw material, say tin, has arisen....' A new opportunity

for the use of tin means an increase in the demand for tin. This results in a shift in the demand curve, as illustrated in Figure 2.4. As you can see in Figure 2.4, the quantity supplied increases (from q_1 to q_2) as a result of the shift in the demand curve. Does this contradict Hayek's conclusion that a new opportunity for the use of tin will cause existing users of tin to economize on the use of tin?

4 Consider Figure 2.9. This figure gives the marginal productivity of labour, dQ/dL, as a function of L. According to the text, the firm should choose L such that dQ/dL equals w/p, where w is the price of labour and p is the price of pencils. In the example given in the text, $w = \$20$ and $p = \$0.25$, so L must be chosen such that $dQ/dL = 80$.

Show that the firm can increase profits by adding labour when $dQ/dL > 80$. Also show that the firm can increase profits by reducing the amount of labour when $dQ/dL < 80$.

5 Consider a very large firm such as Royal Dutch/Shell. Do you think that it is realistic to treat such a firm as an holistic entity? Can you give an example of a situation in which conflicts between different parts of such a firm can arise?

Note

1   If you are unfamiliar with the notion of opportunity cost, consider the following example. Suppose a dentist decides to take a day off in order to fish. Suppose that, on a normal working day, he earns €1800. The opportunity cost of his day off is then €1800. To put it in more general terms, the opportunity cost of a resource (a dentist's day, an amount of capital) is equal to the revenue that could have been generated by the best alternative use.

3 Organizations

3.1 The world of organizations

We live in a world of organizations. Think about it for a moment. When you were born, it was perhaps in a hospital – a healthcare organization. Growing up, you attended school – an educational organization. In your adult life, you will probably earn your living in a work organization. You may be a member of one or more recreational organizations. You may belong to a religious organization. You buy the goods and services you need from a variety of organizations. You pay your taxes to government organizations. Culture is preserved in organizations such as museums and libraries. Communication is made possible by organizations such as publishers, television networks and telecom services. Discovery is enabled by research laboratories and universities. Resocialization is arranged in psychiatric hospitals and prisons. Finally, when you die, your funeral will probably be supervised by an undertaker's business.

A moment's reflection will make it clear that organizations are a pervasive phenomenon in the contemporary world. So pervasive are they that some people will be surprised (or even mildly shocked) by the realization of their ubiquity. Organizations perform many of the pleasant and unpleasant tasks that we usually take for granted in our societies. They are the main vehicles by which individuals can collaborate in the pursuit of specified goals. As a well-known sociologist has observed, 'the development of organizations is the principal mechanism by which, in a highly differentiated society, it is possible to "get things done", to achieve goals beyond the reach of the individual' (Parsons, 1960, p. 41).

If we state this in the terms introduced in our opening chapter, in a world characterized by a high level of division of labour, in which we are all specialized, organizations are the principal means by which we coordinate for collective action. We can hardly imagine a world in which individuals would have only the market mechanism to coordinate their actions. Even people working 'alone' from home, say as a 'power seller' on eBay, depend on organizations to get things done. They depend on eBay, of course, itself an organization, but they also depend on a Web-enabled, standardized (hence, organized) way of working with other people, as argued in Box 3.1. Also, finally, they depend on the Internet itself, which – contrary to popular belief – needs to be managed and organized as well (see Box 3.7 at the end of this chapter).

> **Box 3.1** Specialization and organization via the Internet
>
> The Internet allows people to work in what seems a quite individual way. It enables us to work from home or 'on the road'. However, behind this appearance of individuals working on their own is a reality of highly sophisticated interdependency. The internet has in fact spurred new, Web-enabled ways of working and organizing:
>
> > This, then, is a fundamental paradox at the heart of modern economies: the more highly educated and specialized we become, the more we need other people to perform. The Internet, which allows so many people to work as individual contributors and to think of themselves as free agents or independent professionals, underscores this interdependency but, ironically, also makes it less immediately apparent. We think we live in worlds of our own and can contribute as individuals, but this is only possible because some form of organization makes the specialized work we do productive.
>
> *Source:* Magretta (2002, p. 7)

How is organizational coordination achieved? How does it differ from market coordination by the price mechanism, as introduced in the previous chapter? That is the subject of the next section, where six coordination mechanisms will be identified. In Section 3.3, we build on this distinction to identify six ideal types of organization. Then we relax somewhat the sharp distinction between organizational and market coordination in Sections 3.4 and 3.5. In the concluding section, we summarize the argument so far.

3.2 Organizational coordination

Let us first examine what economists have had to say about organizational coordination. When Coase (1937) posited organizations and markets as alternative coordination devices, he assumed that, within organizations, **authority** directed the allocation of resources instead of the price mechanism:

Authority

> Outside the firm, price movements direct production, which is coordinated through a series of exchange transactions on the market. Within a firm, these market transactions are eliminated and in place of the complicated market structure with exchange transactions is substituted the entrepreneur/coordinator, who directs production ... We may sum up this section of the argument by saying that the operation of a market costs something and by forming an organization and allowing some authority (an 'entrepreneur') to direct the resources, certain marketing costs are saved.

Similarly, when Hayek (1945) praised the virtues of the market, he compared a market system with a central planning authority for an entire economic system:

> The various ways in which the knowledge on which people base their plans is communicated to them is the crucial problem for any theory explaining the economic process. And the problem of what is the best way of utilizing knowledge initially dispersed among all the people is at least one of the main problems of economic policy – or of designing an efficient economic system. The answer to this question is closely connected with that other question which arises here, that of *who* is to do

the planning. It is about this question that all the dispute about 'economic planning' centers. This is not a dispute about whether planning is to be done or not. It is a dispute as to whether planning is to be done centrally, by one authority for the whole economic system, or is to be divided among many individuals.

We show in this section that Hayek's problem diagnosis was right: the best use of dispersed knowledge is indeed one of the main problems in economic coordination. However, by comparing a market system with a central planning system, Hayek overlooked the fact that there are various other ways to communicate knowledge and coordinate economic activities than through prices or authority. It is to these alternatives that we now turn.

Mintzberg (1979, 1989) has synthesized the organizational literature on the structure of organizations. He has shown how the various elements of the structure of organizations (such as the size of its parts or the extent of decentralization) 'configure' with determinants of organizational structure (such as the type of environment). He has thus developed a typology of **organizational configurations**. This typology is described in the next section. For now, we focus on the basis of this typology: a distinction between various types of coordination mechanism. These six mechanisms are reproduced in Figure 3.1. Here is a description of each of them (based on Mintzberg, 1989, p. 101):

Organizational configurations

Mutual adjustment

Direct supervision

- **Mutual adjustment**, which achieves coordination by the simple process of informal communication (as between two operating employees).
- **Direct supervision**, in which coordination is achieved by having one person issue orders or instructions to several others whose work interrelates (as when a boss tells othevrs what is to be done, one step at a time).

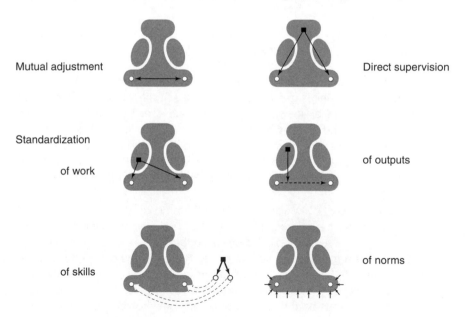

Figure 3.1 The co-ordinating mechanisms

Source: Mintzberg (1989, p. 102)

- **Standardization of work processes**, which achieves coordination by specifying the work processes of people carrying out interrelated tasks. The standards are developed in the technostructure, which is the part of the organization where staff outside the hierarchy who plan and control the work of others (such as work study analysts, schedulers, quality control engineers, budgeters, planners, and accountants) are located. The work processes are carried out in the operating core, as in the case of the work instructions that come out of time-and-motion studies – see Box 3.2 for an example of the standardization of work processes.

- **Standardization of outputs**, which achieves coordination by specifying the results of different work (again, usually developed in the technostructure, as in a financial plan that specifies subunit performance targets or specifications that outline the dimensions of a product to be produced).

- **Standardization of skills** (as well as *knowledge*), in which different pieces of work are coordinated by virtue of the related training the workers have received (as with medical specialists – say, a surgeon and an anaesthetist in an operating room – responding almost automatically to each other's standardized procedures).

- **Standardization of norms**, in which it is the norms determining the work that are controlled, usually for the entire organization, so that everyone functions according to beliefs (as in a religious order). See Box 3.3 for an example.

Box 3.2 Standardization of 'operating procedures' at Aravind Eye Hospital

India's Aravind Eye Hospital was founded in 1976 by a retired eye surgeon, Dr Govindappa Venkataswamy. He started small, with a 11-bed private, non-profit hospital. Today, Aravind has added 6 other hospitals and with 4000 beds has become the largest provider of eye surgery in the world. It handled 2,646,129 outpatient visits and performed 315,483 surgeries from April 2010 to March 2011. Two-thirds of the outpatient visits and three-fourths of the surgeries were serviced to the poor either free or at a steeply subsidized rate – yet it continues to operate profitably.

Dr V's vision and his methods owe a lot to Henry Ford. (Dr V himself credited McDonald's as his inspiration; the principles are the same). In India, millions of people suffer from blindness, for example due to cataracts. Most can be cured with a simple operation. The management challenge is to make that operation affordable. Dr V's dream, in a sense, was to build an eye hospital for the multitude.

Cataract surgery is Dr V's Model T. Aravind has designed an extraordinarily efficient, high-volume, assembly-line process to produce it. Every step has been standardized, from patient screening and registration to the surgery itself. The operating theatre is designed to maximize the productivity of the surgeons. The surgeon moves from one operating table to the other, focusing on just the procedure, while teams of two nurse-practitioners remain at each table and oversee the patient's care. When the first operation ends, the surgeon can turn immediately to start the next one, and so on, back and forth.

Yes, the surgeons have given up some autonomy in order to follow, step by step, a standardized operating procedure. However, through specialization and standardization Aravind is able to offer eye surgery at one-fiftieth of the cost in a typical United States hospital. Similarly, Narayana Hrudayalaya (NH) in Bangalore is one of the world's largest cardiac care centers, offering its services at typically one-thirtieth of the US level. These organizations are demonstrating that specialization and standardization still work miracles for productivity and cost control. They are now an inspiration to health organizations in the more developed economies, who may move more toward such business models as well.

Source: Magretta (2002), C.K. Prahalad (2005), *The Fortune at the Bottom of the Pyramid,* Wharton School Publishing C.K. Prahalad, (2006), 'The Innovation Sandbox', *Strategy + Business,* 44, Reprint No. 06306. http://www.aravind.org/aboutus/genesis.aspx

The six mechanisms listed above are all ways in which work is coordinated within organizations. They are thus also the ways in which people in organizations can communicate knowledge and expectations. Conversely, they are the ways in which people in the organization may learn from others what they need to know to carry out their tasks as well as what is expected from them. In short, all six mechanisms are alternatives to the price mechanism for communicating information and coordinating economic activities. Authority (direct supervision by an entrepreneur or a boss) is but one of these organizational coordinating mechanisms.

Only in relatively small organizations can authority be used as the primary coordination mechanism, as we emphasize in the next section. Almost all large organizations use a variety of coordination mechanisms, including mutual adjustment and standardization of work processes, skills, outputs and norms. Standardization of work processes, skills, outputs and norms may be fostered by training. Box 3.3 explains how Disney uses training of new employees at Disney University to standardize norms.

Box 3.3 Disney training: the standardization of norms

The Disney company is well known for the rigorous training it offers to every new employee. The courses are taught by the Disney Institute, the company's own training organization. The introductory course is called 'Disney Traditions' and is designed so that 'new members of the Disney team can be introduced to our traditions, philosophies, organization, and the way we do business' (company brochure). The trainers drill new employees with questions about Disney characters, history and mythology. They also constantly emphasize the values and norms that Disney holds dear:

Trainer: What business are we in? Everybody knows that McDonald's makes hamburgers. What does Disney make?

New hire: It makes people happy.

Trainer: Yes, exactly! *It makes people happy.* It doesn't matter who they are, what language they speak, what they do, where they come from, what colour they are, or anything else. We're here to make them happy…

In the Disney Institute textbooks the values and norms are reinforced:

At Disneyland we get tired, but never bored, and even if it's a rough day, we appear happy.
You've got to have an honest smile. It's got to come from within … If nothing else helps, remember that you get paid for smiling.

▶

The culture even comes with its own language, which is designed to convey that work at Disney should be seen as 'play', a theatrical performance:

- employees = cast members
- customers = guests
- a crowd = audience
- a work shift = performance
- a job = part
- a uniform = costume
- on duty = onstage
- off duty = backstage

Today, the Disney Institute offers training programs to other organizations who want to emulate the Disney company in building "an effective organizational culture founded in values-based leadership, where employees are recognized for their achievements, encouraged to work as a team and think creatively, and, in their consistent pursuit of excellence, continually break the confines of the status quo to surpass the expectations of the world."

Sources: Collins and Porras (1998); Tom Peters Group, *In Search of Excellence* – video and www.disneyinstitute.com

To illustrate how organizations use a variety of coordinating mechanisms, let us take an example from our own experience. When we have moved to new universities, we have learned, in various ways, how to coordinate our work with that of others. First, we received several rule books, such as the university's 'rules and regulations' administrative procedures, safety regulations and library instructions. These told us the formal rules that govern the coordination of work (standardization of work processes). However, although universities are definitely bureaucracies, they are not so bureaucratic that all work is coordinated 'by the book'. Some of the formal rules are not upheld (they might, for instance, be outdated and nobody has bothered to update them). Moreover, much coordination is not formalized, so we negotiated with co-workers how to work with each other (mutual adjustment). With our fellow professors we coordinated our courses, with the administrative staff we scheduled them and, with the secretaries, we negotiated to have them processed. In our research work we looked for co-workers who understood our type of work and had complementary knowledge or skills. On the doctoral courses, we taught the skills required of future colleagues (standardization of skills). Finally, we tried to find out what was regarded as really important at our new institutions: how important research was versus teaching, how important the fulfillment of administrative duties or the rendering of community service was, how sociable we were expected to be and so on (standardization of norms). In all of these ways and more we learned how to coordinate our work with that of our new colleagues.

Similar accounts could be given about learning to deal with other types of organization. The point is that each organization has an array of communication and coordination mechanisms available. Through these mechanisms, knowledge and information are transported. In certain types of organization, certain mechanisms dominate, but hardly any organization uses just one mechanism – and we shall see in the next section that it is only in relatively small, entrepreneurial organizations that authority (direct supervision) is dominant. Therefore, it is too simple a view to assume that authority is substituted for the price mechanism when markets give way to organizations. The price mechanism is certainly substituted when we move away from ideal markets, but the alternatives are manifold.

In concluding this section, let us restate what we indicated by way of a preview in Chapter 1. If we adopt the definition of an ideal market as the coordination device that uses the price mechanism *only,* then we may define ideal organizations as the coordination devices that do *not* use the price mechanism at all for (internal) coordination. This leaves, however, a number of organizational forms, each defined by which mechanism it uses primarily for coordination purposes. The next section is devoted to these forms.

3.3 Types of organizations

We have introduced six alternative coordination mechanisms to the price system. The descriptions of these six mechanisms are based on Mintzberg's (1979, 1989) work, which integrates much previous organizational research into a typology of organizational configurations. The purpose of this section is to introduce the organizational configurations that correspond to the dominant use of any one of these six mechanisms. As real organizations are often hybrid forms of these six 'pure' types, this section provides an overview of the variety of organizational forms we are dealing with that operate as alternatives to market coordination.

The six coordination mechanisms introduced in the previous section correspond with six organizational configurations, as presented in Figure 3.2. That is to say, when, for instance, direct supervision is the prime coordinating

Entrepreneurial organization

mechanism, we are dealing with a configuration called the **entrepreneurial organization**. This type corresponds well to the firm that Coase envisaged as substituting for market coordination. In this firm, an entrepreneur directs production and the allocation of resources. The firm is simple enough for the

CONFIGURATION	PRIME COORDINATING MECHANISM
Entrepreneurial organization	Direct supervision
Machine organization	Standardization of work processes
Professional organization	Standardization of skills
Diversified organization	Standardization of outputs
Innovative organization	Mutual adjustment
Missionary organization	Standardization of norms

Figure 3.2 The six configurations

entrepreneur to control personally the organizational activities through direct supervision. Its structure is thus flexible, informal and not elaborated. It operates in environments that are simple and dynamic – simple enough for one person at the top to be able to coordinate activities; dynamic enough to require organizational flexibility and not turn into a bureaucracy. Think of retail stores or young internet companies as good examples of this type.

Take Apple. In the early stages of its existence, it was an entrepreneurial organization under the direct supervision of Steve Jobs. Jobs was a charismatic leader with a clear vision of the company that he wanted Apple to be. Under his personal leadership and supervision, Apple developed the Macintosh and became a credible, aggressive player in the market for personal computers. As the company grew, however, coordination solely from the top became problematic – one man could no longer oversee all the operations. Choices had to be made about how to reshape Apple in order to allow it to develop further. Jobs appointed a manager, John Sculley. At first, the two sought solutions together, but, over time, their differences of opinion grew and, in 1985, Jobs was forced to leave the company (see Isaacson, 2011).

From a configuration point of view, the dilemmas could be described as follows. Apple had grown too large to be run as a simple entrepreneurial organization. Direct supervision was breaking down as the prime coordinating mechanism. The organization could have been taken through a transition phase in which one or more of the alternative coordinating mechanisms shown in Figure 3.2 would have become more prominent. Which one(s) would have depended on the circumstances. To the extent that Apple's environment had stabilized, standardization of work processes would have been feasible. If, for instance, technological developments had slowed down and basic technical designs had been developed, more routinization of production would have been possible than in the early stages when no one really knew what technological horse to bet on. Once production is routinized, other functions can be standardized, too. Standard products generate standard purchasing requirements, standard packaging instructions and so on. The more Apple standardized its work
Machine organization processes, the more it would turn into a **machine organization**.

This is not the only possibility, though. Also important is the amount of professional work in the company's operations. Professional work (such as R&D and systems design) cannot be standardized: all an organization can do is standardize the skills required for executing this work by, for instance, demanding a certain type of training. The more professional work an organization requires, the more it has to rely on well-trained individuals to execute their work with considerable discretion and coordinate it through the professional standards acquired during their long
Professional training. Universities and hospitals are examples of **professional organizations**,
organizations but certain parts of Apple would probably show these features as well.

Similarly, the other three coordinating mechanisms listed in Figure 3.2 could be employed. If the company wanted to diversify into other markets or market niches, it could aim for standardization of outputs, in terms of both product specifications and financial results of its divisions. It would then move towards
Diversified organization the **diversified organization**, which specifies the output expected from its divisions and then leaves them considerable autonomy as to how they attain these

goals. Many of the large corporations in the world, such as General Electric, Unilever and Mitsubishi, are diversified organizations, which operate on diverse markets with different families of products. Also Apple divisionalized its organization to some extent, for instance creating the Apple Macintosh division when it ventured into other products than computers.

It is important to remain innovative in the computer and consumer electronics markets, which requires the collaboration of hardware and software specialists, marketing and production people through mutual adjustment. Organizations that rely primarily on this coordination mechanism are called **Innovative organization** **innovative organizations.** As organizations grow larger, it becomes harder to retain mutual adjustment as the dominant coordination mechanism. This point is illustrated in Box 3.4 about Hewlett-Packard (HP). HP has found it difficult to maintain the entrepreneurial and innovative spirit that brought the company enormous growth and success. On the contrary, after his return to Apple in 1997 Steve Jobs has deliberately tried to maintain the innovative and collaborative (mutual adjustment) culture of Apple: 'One of the keys to Apple is that Apple is an incredibly collaborative company. We're organized like a startup. We're the biggest start up on the planet. (Source: http://edition.cnn.com/2011/TECH/innovation/08/24/steve.jobs.team/index.html)

Box 3.4 The HP Way

In 1939, Bill Hewlett and Dave Packard, two engineers aged 26, founded the Hewlett-Packard company in a garage in Palo Alto, California. That garage is regarded by many as the birthplace of Silicon Valley. The founders instilled an entrepreneurial, innovative spirit into their company. HP became a symbol of inventiveness. It also became well known for its business principles, encoded in 'the HP Way'. The HP way of doing business emphasized:

- making a technological contribution to society;
- respect and opportunity for its employees;
- being a responsible citizen in its communities;
- profitable growth as a means to achieve these other values and goals.

The HP Way brought the company enormous success. Its famous products included hand-held calculators and printers. By the end of the century, it was approaching $50 billion in revenue and employed 80,000 people. However, as our organizational framework predicts, HP had found it increasingly difficult to maintain its entrepreneurial and innovative spirit as it grew to this huge size. New product development was disappointing, growth was faltering and profitability was decreasing rapidly. Moreover, it had developed the image of a slow, stumbling giant and was dubbed the Gray Lady of Silicon Valley.

In 1999, the HP Board took the radical step of looking outside the company for a new president and CEO. It appointed Carly Fiorina, the first woman to head a company listed on the Dow Jones Industrial Average. She found a company that still lived up to 'the core values of the firm: respect, integrity, teamwork, contribution', but one that had also become 'a gentle bureaucracy of entitlement and consensus', consisting of 'a collection of tribes'. In order to revitalize this company, she launched the slogan 'preserve the best, reinvent the rest'. Reaching back to its origins, HP issued new 'Rules of the Garage', including the following.

- Believe you can change the world.
- Share tools, ideas. Trust your colleagues.

- No politics. No bureaucracy. (These are ridiculous in a garage.)
- Radical ideas are not bad ideas.
- Make a contribution every day. If it doesn't contribute, it doesn't leave the garage.
- Believe that together we can do anything.

Fiorina streamlined the company, slashing the number of product divisions from 83 to 16. In addition, she cut costs and jobs (5 per cent of the workforce) and reorientated the company to become a service-centred company rather than a hardware-centred company.

On 4 September 2001, Fiorina announced that HP would acquire Compaq, a large maker of personal computers, for $19 billion. 'For the first time in a very long time, IBM will have a competitor that is strong enough to take it head-on', she said. Analysts, however, dubbed this step 'a classical defensive move in a consolidating industry'. For the next few years, HP struggled to integrate Compaq well, Dell was still increasing its market share (see Box 10.6), HP's share price suffered and a bitter feud broke out between Fiorina and Walter Hewlett, the son of Bill and a board member of HP. In 2005, Fiorina was fired. HP continued to struggle making several unsuccessful acquisitions and changing CEO again in 2011. It was clear once again how difficult it is for successful firms to retain their success – a theme we shall return to in Chapters 11 and 12.

Based on Collins and Porras (1998); 'The HP Way forward', interview with Carly Fiorina in *Worldlink*, magazine of the World Economic Forum, Jan/Feb 2001; 'Rebuilding the HP way', *Information Week*, 23 July 2001; 'Hewlett-Packard and Compaq: sheltering from the storm', *The Economist*, 8 September 2001; 'Can anyone save HP?', *Business Week*, 21 February 2005

Smaller organizations, though, such as consultancy firms or architectural practices, can rely on mutual adjustment as the main coordination mechanism and thus maintain a spirit of innovation. For larger organization, such as Apple and HP, the challenge is to combine mutual adjustment – which is especially suited to bringing together specialists collaborating under dynamic and complex circumstances – with other coordination mechanisms.

Finally, Apple could rely on the standardization of norms (or ideology), to the extent that members of its workforce share a common system of values and beliefs that direct their activities. A strong sense of mission, *esprit de corps* or ideology, which individuals share, tells them how to act together and dispenses the need for other forms of coordination. Religious orders may depend to a large extent on standardization of norms – they are prime examples of **missionary organizations** – but other organizations often have their own cultures, too. If those cultures are strong and tell organizational members what to do in certain situations, they act as a coordination mechanism.

Missionary organizations

With the return of Steve Jobs in 1997, Apple held on to direct supervision as much as it could. For its innovative culture it stimulated mutual adjustment. There are strongly shared norms, for instance relating to the value of design. However, Apple also professionalized and divisionalized. Also, a company with more than $100 billion revenue in 2011, 60,000 employees and stores in more than 30 countries had to standardize its work processes as well. The example shows that – even with a charismatic leader like Steve Jobs – direct supervision cannot be used as the sole coordinating mechanism as a company grows. One or more other mechanisms have to be added. That is common – most organizations combine several types of coordination mechanisms. Another example is given in Box 3.5.

Box 3.5 An insurance brokerage firm

Real organizations are often a mixture of two or more of the six pure organizational configurations described above. As an example, consider an insurance brokerage firm. Such a firm is often a combination of a professional organization and a machine organization.

An important element that characterizes an insurance brokerage firm as a professional organization is the extensive training that insurance brokers receive before they are allowed to work independently. As a result, standardization of skills is an important coordinating mechanism in these firms.

Administrative procedures also tend to be very much standardized in an insurance brokerage firm. When a client requires a certain type of policy, all brokers within the firm use exactly the same administrative method and routing for that type of policy. This is an example of standardization of work processes and, as mentioned earlier, standardization of work processes is the prime coordinating mechanism for a machine organization.

Figure 3.3 summarizes the space available for organizational forms. The relatively pure configurations are located toward the corners of the pentagon. Within the pentagon, all kinds of hybrid forms are possible. What form a particular organization will tend to take is a complex issue. For a discussion of

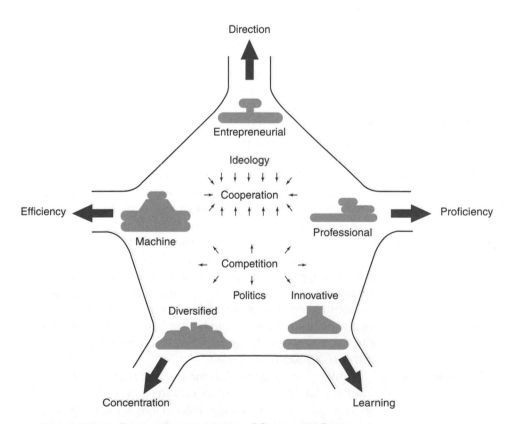

Figure 3.3 An integrating pentagon of forces and forms

Note: in this figure you do not see the missionary organization, whish is the organizational form relying primarily on the standardization of norms or ideology.

Source: Mintzberg (1989, p. 256)

the forces involved, you are referred to Mintzberg (1989). For our purposes, it is sufficient if the main point has come across: when markets are replaced by organizations, coordination by the price mechanism gives way to coordination by a set of other mechanisms. Organizations can take many forms and each one is specifically adapted to particular circumstances – it can handle different types of transactions. No wonder we see so many organizations and that such a large part of economic life is conducted within them.

3.4 Organizational markets

Until now, we have argued as though market coordination and organizational coordination were mutually exclusive – that is, as if these two types of coordination cannot be combined. We now take the argument one step further and show that markets may exist within organizations as well. In the next section, we briefly show that markets may be organized to some extent, too. Hence, in practice, market and organizational coordination may often be found in combination.

Take the example of a large, diversified organization such as Exxon. Within that organization, transactions between divisions may take place, such as when the oil division delivers oil to the petrochemical division, which processes it further into commodity chemicals. Within the petrochemical division, similar exchanges may occur, such as when the commodity chemicals are produced by one business unit and delivered to the next to be processed further into specialized chemicals. Often such transactions are effected against an internal price, the transfer price. In such a case, Exxon may be said to have an **internal market for goods**. Decisions on whether to sell or procure internally will be based on the transfer price as compared with external prices.

Internal market for goods

Similarly, Shell has an **internal capital market** as corporate management allocates its funds to the divisions on the basis of those divisional plans that fit best with corporate policy and generate the highest returns. Internally, Shell's corporate management takes over the function of the external capital market by directing financial resources to their best use. The internal and external capital markets remain linked. Management may decide not to invest all its available resources internally if the internal returns are insufficient. It may then seek temporary outside investment for its superfluous funds, perhaps in anticipation of the acquisition of another firm. Or it may give money back to its shareholders by increasing its dividend or buying back some shares. Alternatively, it may want to attract new (external) capital when it can meet the required external conditions and earn an additional profit.

Internal capital market

Similarly, an **internal labour market** may be said to exist where divisions compete for the best human resources and may also bid up their potential salaries.[1] Members of an organization may seek career advancement by applying internally for better positions with higher salaries. If the allocation of human resources is primarily an internal affair, the function of the external labour market is taken over by the organization. Again, the internal and external markets

Internal labour market

remain linked. New people enter the organization through its ports of entry. Others leave the organization and seek new employment in the external labour market.

Within organizations, then, several types of market may operate. This implies that market and organizational coordination may be mixed. It further implies that there is no sharp demarcation between markets and organizations. In our conceptual framework we distinguish between the two ideal types: 'pure' market coordination (solely by the price mechanism) and 'pure' organizational coordination (solely by other mechanisms). Most real cases fall between these two pure types and will be characterized by mixed coordination systems. This is shown below for the operation of most markets.

3.5 Organized markets

Pure market coordination – solely by means of the price mechanism – is an exceptional case. Let us return to the example of the stock market, discussed in Section 1.5, Chapter 1. That example was used because it conforms closely to the model of perfect competition. The numerous buyers and sellers of IBM stock individually have no effect on the stock price. IBM's common stock is standardized: there is no product variation. The market for IBM stock has no barriers to entry or exit. That market therefore meets the main assumptions specified in Chapter 2 for the operation of perfect competition.

Yet, when we look more closely at the operation of that market, we see at least two organizational coordination mechanisms operate as well. First, the market is regulated. It is regulated by both governments (through Securities Acts) and stock exchange boards (through conditions for listing). Those regulations specify the rules with which the various market parties must comply. For example, in most countries, buyers are prohibited from acquiring a controlling interest in listed firms without prior notification of their intentions. Similarly, IBM has to comply with a number of regulations and restrictions before it is permitted to issue new stock. Such regulations standardize the work processes of the market parties. The Securities Acts and the stock exchange regulations function just as operating manuals do in organizations. The market parties can use them to see what behaviour is required in particular situations. The stock market is organized in that sense. It is organized in the further sense, too, that direct supervision is operative. The stock markets are supervised by bodies such as the Securities and Exchange Commission in the USA and stock market boards. Those bodies have the power to interfere with free market interaction, for instance, by suspending the listing of a firm when there are strong indications of irregularities or misconduct. These examples illustrate that markets do not operate in isolation: they are embedded in an institutional environment that sets the 'rules of the game'. The fact that rules are really necessary became apparent during the debt crisis, even to Alan Greenspan, former chair of the FED and a fervent advocate of 'deregulation' (see Box 3.6).

Box 3.6 Greenspan 'shocked' that free markets are flawed

Alan Greenspan was the chairman of the Federal Reserve (the Fed), the central bank of the USA, for 18 years before stepping down in 2006. At the time, he was widely regarded as a very successful central banker who had brought inflation in the USA down and had contributed to economic growth with a low interest rate policy. He firmly believed in the self-regulating capacity of financial markets and therefore supported deregulation. In 2008 when the 'housing bubble' had burst and problems with low-quality ('subprime') mortgages had surfaced, he was subjected to a congressional hearing:

'For years, a congressional hearing with Alan Greenspan was a marquee event. Lawmakers doted on him as an economic sage. Markets jumped up and down depending on what he said. Politicians in both parties wanted the maestro on their side. But on Thursday, almost three years after stepping down as chairman of the Federal reserve, a humbled Greenspan admitted that he had put too much faith in the self-correcting power of free markets and had failed to anticipate the self-destructive power of wanton mortgage lending.

"Those of us who have looked to the self-interest of lending institutions to protect shareholders' equity, myself included, are in a state of shocked disbelief", he told the House Committee on Oversight and Government Reform. He noted that the immense and largely unregulated business of spreading financial risk widely, through the use of exotic financial instruments called derivatives, had gotten out of control and had added to the havoc of today's crisis. As far back as 1994, Greenspan staunchly and successfully opposed tougher regulation on derivatives.

Greenspan, along with most other banking regulators in Washington, also resisted calls for tighter regulation of subprime mortgages and other high-risk exotic mortgages that allowed people to borrow far more than they could afford. Greenspan said that he had publicly warned about the "underpricing of risk" in 2005 but that he had never expected the crisis that began to sweep the entire financial system in 2007.'

Source: *International Herald Tribune,* 23 October 2008

Let us take another of the six organizational coordination mechanisms: mutual adjustment. As explained above, this mechanism achieves coordination through the process of informal communication. Such informal communication is a common feature in many markets. One pernicious form of it is called **collusion** by economists. It refers, for example, to conspiracies by the few suppliers in oligopolistic markets to set prices higher than would result under free market interaction. Alternatively, informal cartels may divide markets between them and thus collude to restrain competition.

Collusion

Collusion may be rather overt or it may be tacit. **Tacit collusion** is a prime example of mutual adjustment as it involves the informal development of rules regulating market behaviour. One such rule may be that a particular supplier acts as price leader. If that supplier changes its price level, the other suppliers follow. No formal communication is required to organize an oligopolistic market in that way.

Tacit collusion

Finally, consider two examples of the influence of culture (standardization of norms) on the operation of markets. First, the Islamic prohibition on charging interest. The prohibition derives from the Koran. As a result, the Islamic banking system has to organize some of its transactions differently from those customary in the Western world. Second, take the common Asiatic practice of

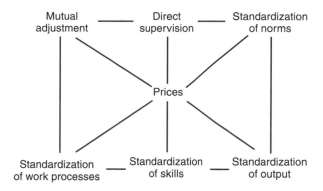

Figure 3.4 The seven coordinating mechanisms

charging a different price to the 'in group' of family, friends and long standing business associates from that charged to outsiders. These examples illustrate how economic transactions are embedded in cultural norms.[2]

If some foreign practices seem strange to us, we should realize that our norms, too, are standardized to allow us to engage in economic transactions with roughly the same expectations of what is fair and what is not. One illustration of this is provided by Stewart Macaulay (1963, p. 61):

> One purchasing agent expressed a common business attitude when he said, 'if something comes up, you get the other man on the telephone and deal with the problem. You don't read legalistic contract clauses at each other if you ever want to do business again. One doesn't run to lawyers if he wants to stay in business because one must behave decently.

These few examples suffice to show that combining market and organizational coordination is the rule rather than the exception. Analytically, it is necessary to distinguish carefully between the price system as the market coordination device and the six organizational mechanisms. We shall continue to do so in the following chapters. Only by means of a clear, analytical separation can we examine which device is most efficient under what circumstances. The foregoing discussion will have made it clear, however, that, when we move from the analytical world (with its sharp distinctions) to the messy real world, we often find bundles of coordination mechanisms operating together. This is illustrated in Figure 3.4.

3.6 Summary: how organizations achieve coordination

Market and organizational coordination are the two ideal types of coordination device for economic transactions. Pure market coordination is effected by the use of the price mechanism only. Pure organizational coordination is characterized by the use of non-price mechanisms only. In this chapter, we introduced six of those non-price mechanisms. All six mechanisms can communicate the knowledge necessary for organizational members to engage in economic transactions. All six may substitute for the price mechanism in coordinating economic action.

Associated with the dominant use of each of these six mechanisms are six pure types of organizational configuration, such as the entrepreneurial organization in which direct supervision is the prime coordinating mechanism. The entrepreneurial organization thus conforms closely to the type of organization that Coase had in mind when he posited authority as the alternative to the price mechanism in coordinating economic transactions. However, organizational theory shows that four types of standardization (of work processes, skills, outputs or norms) and mutual adjustment can act as coordinating mechanisms as well. If organizational coordination is dominated by one of these six mechanisms, we shall observe one of the relatively 'pure types' of organizational configuration. It was shown, however, that most organizations use a combination of those mechanisms. In the real world, therefore, we usually encounter hybrid types of organization. Moreover, it was shown that many organizations (such as business firms) also use the price mechanism to some extent for internal purposes. Within those firms, market and organizational coordination are then combined.

Finally, it was briefly shown that the opposite occurs frequently as well – that is, markets are often organized to some extent. Market coordination by the price mechanism is often combined with one or more of the organizational mechanisms. We conclude, therefore, that, in practice, we often find economic transactions are coordinated by a bundle of coordination mechanisms. It is the exception when one mechanism suffices; it is the rule where two or more are combined. Box 3.7 illustrates this for the Internet.

Box 3.7 Management and organization of the Internet

According to computer entrepreneurs Sharon Eisner Gillett and Mitchell Kapor (the founder of the software giant Lotus Development Corporation), 'Contrary to its popular portrayal as total anarchy, the Internet is actually managed.' It is not fully decentralized. While 99 per cent of the Internet's day-to-day operations, according to a guesstimate by Gillett and Kapor, are handled without any direction, central authorities are needed for the remaining 1 per cent, consisting of various non-routine activities. In addition, central authorities were needed to set up the system initially and continue to be needed to integrate new activities into it.

Some of the Internet's central decisions come from organizations run from the bottom up. Technical management and standard-setting is the responsibility of *ad hoc* voluntary groups such as the Internet Engineering Task Force, with open membership and democratic procedures. Self-regulation has not been the only form of central decisionmaking, however – the government has also played a role. The Internet did not arise spontaneously. It was built by the government. With the Internet, for once the government picked a winner.

Subsidies from the State got the Internet started: the US government spent about $125 million building the Internet's predecessors. In the 1960s and 1970s, the US military sponsored research into how to link computers so as to allow the sharing of data and that research led to a network of university computers. Crucial technological advances were also made at the European Laboratory for

Particle Physics (known by its French acronym CERN), a cooperative effort by European governments. The National Science Foundation, the US government's science agency, also provided substantial funding after it took over responsibility for the computer network from the military in the 1980s. It was not until 1995 that the US government ceased to have direct control over the Internet.

Not only was government funding crucial but so was government decisionmaking. The very fact that the Internet was so decentralized is, ironically enough, the result of a decision made centrally. The US military imposed the modular structure in the early 1980s for the sake of flexibility of use. Another decision by the military – the adoption of the Internet Protocol – solved the problem that, to be able to talk to each other, different kinds of computers needed a common language. Incompatibilities between networks could have arisen, otherwise making it hard to send documents and read web pages. Without a modicum of central management, the Internet would not have grown into the flexible, easy-to-use tool we experience now.

Some management continues to be needed – in particular regarding domain names or dot-com addresses. For the network to be able to function, each name must be unique, which could not be ensured without coordination. The domain name servers bring an unavoidable element of centralization. Each of these servers, one or a few for each address ending, for example, '.com' or '.edu', acts like a telephone directory, maintaining a master list of addresses and ensuring communications are routed accurately. The system of assigning names to Internet users is also unavoidably centralized. Names must be in step if they are to be usable.

Initially, the US government assigned names itself or through a subcontractor. In 1998, it established a private, non-profit corporation to do it – the Internet Corporation for Assigned Names and Numbers (ICANN). ICANN became controversial among those who saw the Internet as free and informal because it could prevent them from picking whatever domain names they felt like, but coordination of some sort was needed. 'Like it or not, you really do need a single root to make it all work,' says Vinton Cerf, an Internet pioneer who became chair of ICANN. 'There should be common ground rules. That's what ICANN strives to achieve.' In the meantime, it has signed a new agreement with the US government which basically gives ICANN the autonomy to run its own affairs. As of 2012 it will start authorizing domain names in non-Latin characters, like Arabic or Chinese, which will significantly change the face of the global internet.

For contracting and intellectual property protection, Internet commerce has relied on the existing State-supplied legal system. The regulatory apparatus of antitrust has shielded Internet firms from predatory competition, just as it has shielded traditional firms. The State prosecutes those who spread computer viruses.

The Internet offers us, then, a conflicting pair of lessons. Its vigour lies in its decentralization. The initiative and imagination of hundreds of thousands have pushed it forward. Decentralization has limits, however. A crucial aspect of the Internet's success lies in its central management.

Based on McMillan (2002, pp. 157–9), 'ICANN can be independent', *The Economist*, 26 September 2009 and http://en.wikipedia.org/wiki/ICANN

Questions

1 Did you see the film *A Few Good Men?* It is a film about an American élite corps of marines. What do you think is the main coordinating mechanism in such an élite unit? What other coordinating mechanisms will probably be employed?

2 Section 3.4 gave two examples of internal markets – an internal capital market and an internal labour market. Read the two examples again carefully. Do you feel that the

example of the internal labour market is a better example of an internal market than the internal capital market? Discuss the possible differences between the internal capital market and the internal labour market.

3 Linklaters is a large international law firm with more than 1900 lawyers, including 429 partners based in 26 offices in Europe, Asia and North and South America. The firm is headed by a senior partner, who is elected by the partners for a five-year term. Lawyers who are not (yet) partners work under the supervision of one of the partners, often as a member of a client team. The firm also has more than 20 key practice areas, such as competition and antitrust, litigation and arbitration, intellectual property and corporate and mergerr and acquisitions (M&A), as well as a number of business groups, drawing together lawyers from across the firm specializing in certain sectors of the economy.

Which type(s) of coordination mechanism(s) is/are likely to be used by Linklaters? Would you say that Linklaters corresponds closely to one of Mintzberg's six configurations or that it corresponds more closely to a hybrid form?

4 SNCF is the French, State-owned railway company, comprised of the parent company SNCF (organized in five divisions) and a number of consolidated subsidiaries. In 2010, it employed 241,000 employees, 65 percent of whom were working for the parent company. More than 70 per cent of its annual income is from the railway itself. SNCF's ambition is to become the model for public service companies in Europe. It is firmly committed to guaranteeing a high level of traffic safety, punctuality, reliability, security of people and goods and cleanliness.

Which type(s) of coordination mechanism(s) is/are likely to be used by SNCF? Would you say that SNCF corresponds closely to one of Mintzberg's six configurations or that it corresponds more closely to a hybrid form?

Notes

1 Interestingly, from an economist's perspective, internal labour markets are characterized by the existence of formalization (see Doeringer and Piore, 1971). However, given that we are dealing with markets that are internal to organizations and organizations are generally characterized by some degree of formalization, for an organization theorist, the distinguishing characteristic of internal markets is that competition is allowed, partly by price.

2 On the embeddedness of economic behaviour, see Granovetter (1985).

4 Information

4.1 Coordination and information

In Chapter 1, we developed a basic conceptual framework that represents a fundamental economic approach to organizations. This approach starts from the division of labour within society, which necessitates coordination between specialized economic entities. We have argued that there are two ideal types of coordination mechanism for economic transactions: markets and organizations. We have also indicated that the information requirements present in any situation will determine the actual (mix of) coordination mechanism(s) we observe in that situation.

In this chapter, we explore those information requirements, indicate some fundamental information problems and discuss how organizations may be seen as solutions to such problems. In the first section, we explore some differences between information requirements in various situations and show how they are related to market and organizational coordination. The purpose is to give you a feel for those situations. In the course of this chapter, we gradually use more precise language and distinctions, thus introducing the main concepts involved in the economic analysis of information problems.

Let us again take an ideal market as a point of departure. Hayek's example of the tin market (see Chapter 1) may come reasonably close. In the tin market, numerous buyers and sellers operate. Let us assume that each one of them has no appreciable effect on the market price for tin as all buyers and sellers are small. That is to say, their individual transactions will not have an effect on the market price as there is such a huge volume of transactions that no individual transaction can make a difference. Only the collective (in economic terms, aggregate) effect of all those individual transactions becomes noticeable as changes of the market price. As discussed in Chapter 2, we say that, under these circumstances, *perfect competition* exists. With perfect competition, each individual economic entity is necessarily a **price-taker:** it has to accept the prevailing market price and cannot hope to influence the price level. Only in such circumstances can we say prices act as sufficient statistics that convey all the necessary information to the market parties.

Prices act as sufficient statistics under conditions of perfect competition because the decisions that the economic entities can make are really very limited. Given the prevailing market price, each seller can only decide *how much* to (produce and) sell. Each buyer can only decide *how much* to buy. Hence, each

Price-taker

party can only make decisions as to *quantities* of tin. Under conditions of perfect competition, many other types of decision are irrelevant, owing to the assumptions that underlie the model of perfect competition. One of those assumptions is indeed that there are numerous buyers and sellers – so many, in fact, that we are always assured of a counterparty when we want to transact at the market price. Another crucial assumption is that we are dealing with a **homogeneous good** – a good that comes in only one standardized form. Therefore, we do not have to be concerned what variety of the good to make or buy. There are no quality differences: it does not matter to whom we sell or from whom we buy. Moreover, as buyers of those goods, we can easily observe if we have obtained what we expected as all we have to do is check the quantity delivered. As we shall see, such conditions (numerous buyers and sellers, homogeneous goods) are not met in most situations in the real world. As Samuelson (1976, p. 43) noted in his well-known introduction to economics:

Homogeneous good

> A cynic might say of perfect competition what Bernard Shaw said of Christianity: The only trouble with it is that it has never been tried.

The price mechanism, then, is a sufficient coordination mechanism only in circumstances where the economic entities involved have quite limited information requirements. Essentially, only when all the necessary information can be 'absorbed' in the price can we rely on the price mechanism as the sole communication device. Let us examine some situations in which the price mechanism is *not* sufficient to communicate all the necessary information, taking situations that are quite close to the model of perfect competition as a starting point.

First, let us have a look at retail markets – for instance, groceries and supermarkets. Have you ever wondered why the various products are displayed so differently? Some products are packaged, others are not. Some have brand names, others do not. Some can be inspected by the customer, others cannot. We submit that a major reason for these differences is the variation in *quality* that may be expected of these different goods. Sugar, for instance, is such a standardized product that most people are interested only in its price per kilo. They have no desire to inspect the product before purchasing it and do not care much about brand names. Now compare sugar with, for instance, fruit. Fruit is normally on display for customers. Often they are also able to inspect the fruit and even choose the particular pieces that they would like to buy. The major reason for this, we submit, is that fruit quality varies (with season, region, delivery time and so on). The customer wants to be able to form a first-hand judgment about its quality before purchase. The price is insufficient as a communication device to transmit the quality dimension. A higher price should reflect a higher quality, but not many of us trust the operation of that mechanism to be flawless.

For many retail products, an intermediate solution is to standardize quality as much as possible. Soup, for example, is a product that may also vary in quality. It is difficult, however, to give the potential buyers a first-hand experience of the product before purchase. The solution to that information problem is usually the creation of *brand names* that are supposed to reflect the quality class of particular soups. Through advertising, the accumulation of consumer experience and joint use of common brand names for different products (soups and sauces), we learn to identify certain brand names as signals of particular quality classes. We may rely on that signal as an accurate indicator of quality, at least for the first purchase of a particular soup. If our quality expectation is met, our confidence in the accuracy of the brand name signal is increased. Brand names can thus be seen as solutions to information problems. Those solutions are available to organizations that are willing to invest in the creation and maintenance of their brand name reputations. Box 4.1 illustrates the value (and the vulnerability) of brand name reputations in the car market.

Box 4.1 The Toyota brand name as a signal of quality

Toyota, the Japanese car company, has worked for decades to establish its brand name as a signal of quality and reliability. It pioneered 'The Toyota Way' of manufacturing, developing best practices like *kaizen* (continuous improvement) and *genchi genbutsu* (getting to the root cause of problems by investigating them on the shopfloor). Simultaneously, the Toyota Way incorporates principles of 'lean production', making it the most efficient car producer. Its relentless pursuit of quality and efficiency allowed it to become the largest automobile seller in the world with 8.6 million units produced in 2010.

However, in recent years its quality image has taken a beating. The story illustrates well the old saying that 'trust comes on foot and goes by horse'. It also demonstrates the potential consequences when customers lose faith in a brand name as a signal of quality:

It has been a brutal week for Toyota, long the gold standard for quality, reliability and efficiency in car manufacturing. On Friday, Akido Toyoda, company president and chief executive apologized for causing customers "worry" after a global recall ballooned into broader concerns over its vehicles' quality, its own integrity and the future of its business. Toyota has lost more than a fifth of its market value since January 21, when it announced a recall in the US of cars due to defective accelerator pedals that might stick. The recall widened to Europe and beyond.

Toyota's use of common parts across many models was one of the reasons behind the size of the latest recall, which affects 4.5 m vehicles, mostly in the US and Europe. This was separate from its earlier recall of 5.75 m cars whose floor mats risks jamming in the accelerator, though some models are subject to both recalls. Toyota said the recall and related sales and production freeze – it closed five US assembly lines temporarily last week – would cost it about $2bn, but that figure does not take into account the impact from lost future sales. Last month, Toyota saw its US sales drop 16 percent, while its top two rivals General Motors and Ford both reported big gains. Its rapid fall from favour contrasts sharply with its slow rise to the top as one of the industry's most valuable and trusted brands.

Mr Toyoda on Friday promised a return to the *genchi genbutsu* and "customer first principles".

Source: 'Toyota's long climb comes to an abrupt halt', *The Financial Times*, 5 February 2010

The above examples assume that there is one true quality of the product and the information problem is one of communicating the true quality to the consumer. Suppose, however, that the quality of the product is not yet known (to anyone). That might be the case for a supermarket wanting to be assured of a good supply of next year's crop of fruit. In such a situation, the supermarket might contemplate a long-term contract with a supplier. The quality of next year's crop, however, is dependent on the future weather, which is unknown to both the supermarket and the supplier. In that case, we say there is *uncertainty* as to the quality of the fruit.

Markets can deal with uncertainty, at least to some extent. In our example, the supermarket and the supplier will have difficulty agreeing on a contract that specifies only the quantities of fruit to be delivered next year (at a certain price). Both will want to feel assured that the price is fair given the quality of next year's fruit. They have opposing interests in setting a particular price level, given the uncertainty involved. They might agree, however, on a specification of quality levels and prices that are dependent on the actual quality levels of next year's fruit. Such a contract is called a **contingent claims contract**. The specific terms of the contract are made contingent on the uncertainty involved. Note, such a contract is possible only if there is a way to determine next year's fruit quality that is acceptable to both parties. If such quality measurement is not possible, the transaction will probably not come to pass.

Contingent claims contract

If parties can negotiate a contract covering all possible future contingencies, they can agree to that *complete contract*. However, in reality, we will often observe **incomplete contracting** in situations of uncertainty. Reasons for incomplete contracting include the following:

Incomplete contracting

- It is usually difficult to foresee and plan for all possible contingencies.
- It may be expensive to fully negotiate contracts. Parties may make a trade-off between such expenses and the risks of leaving contingencies (with a low probability of occurrence) open.
- Language limitations may prevent the totally unambiguous description of terms and situations. Thus, after-the-fact interpretations may remain necessary.

In such circumstances, we may see that incomplete contracts cover some, but not all, uncertainty. In Chapter 13 we will discuss further incomplete contracts in the M&A context.

While markets may handle some uncertainty in such ways, they are not able to handle very much of it. The simple reason is that it is not possible for human minds to juggle with very many uncertain factors simultaneously. That is why we are unable to write contingent claims contracts for situations with numerous uncertain factors.

Suppose the fruit supplier wants to research and develop a new strain of fruit – say, a cross between apples and pears: appearls. Imagine that to do so requires large sums in investment, for a laboratory and specialized biologists, for example. If the supplier wanted to cover part of that investment by offering the supermarket a contract for the delivery of appearls (for an advance payment), it is questionable whether the supermarket would take it.

The reason is that there are so many uncertain factors (the technology required, the mass production possibilities, consumers' tastes and so on) that it would be almost impossible to specify all the possible (combinations of) contingencies. Hence, the contract for it could not be written and the basis for the transaction would not be there.

One organizational solution might be vertical integration of the supermarket and the fruit supplier – the one taking over the other. That organizational solution would remedy the fact that the price mechanism and, hence, market coordination cannot absorb all the uncertainty involved (we return to this issue in Chapter 8).

Information asymmetry

Finally, let us explore the situation where information is available but it is unevenly distributed – there is an **information asymmetry.** Say the supplier has developed his appearls in the laboratory, but is unable to grow them on a scale large enough by himself. Then, there would be two routes he could follow. One would be to sell his knowledge in the market – for instance, to other suppliers. However, there is a fundamental difficulty here. Those other suppliers would want to know what exactly they were buying. How are appearls grown? What steps are to be followed in the appearl-growing process and which investments are necessary for each step? How sensitive are appearls to weather conditions? Are they resistant to the common apple and pear diseases? All such questions would have to be answered before potential buyers would be able to determine the value of the new appearl-growing recipe they were being offered. If, however, all these questions were answered, they would have all the information they would need to grow appearls themselves. That is the **fundamental paradox of information:** the value of information can only be realized by revealing it to another party, but such disclosure destroys its value.

Fundamental paradox of information

The second route the appearl-grower could take would also be an organizational route. He could, for example, enter into joint venture agreements with other producers. Such agreements can be efficient risk-sharing arrangements, as we discuss further in Section 7.6.

We have now discussed situations in which:

- the price cannot reflect all the dimensions of the good;
- uncertainty is present; and
- information asymmetries exist.

It is especially in situations where there are information asymmetries that all kinds of interesting problems occur. The reason is that such asymmetries may give rise to *opportunistic behaviour.* The notion of opportunistic behaviour (also called *strategic behaviour*) is more fully described in Chapter 8. Here, though, we shall illustrate it by means of an example derived from Milgrom and Roberts (1987, p. 184). The example also introduces the distinction between information (in)completeness, uncertainty and asymmetry:

> To get an idea of the role of informational asymmetries in strategic behavior, consider three simple card games. In the first, each player is dealt five cards face up, the players make any bets they want, and then the best hand wins. In the second, each player receives five cards, some of which are dealt face up and the rest face down. Without looking at their hole cards, the players make their bets, then the cards are turned face up and the best hand wins. Finally, the third game is like the second except that the players can look at their hole cards. Again there is betting, the hidden cards are revealed, and the best hand wins.
>
> The first game is one of complete (and perfect) information. Everyone knows everything, and as long as we assume that people prefer more money to less, it is fairly trivial to figure out what will happen: there will certainly be no betting, and probably no one will bother to play! ...
>
> The second game has uncertainty/informational incompleteness, but no information asymmetries ... Games of this sort are useful models for studying such issues as insurance, risky investments, and learning (especially if we revise the

game to have the hole cards revealed one at a time, with betting after each is shown). However, its play would not generate any interesting forms of strategic behavior.

The third game involves informational asymmetries: while there is some publicly available information, each player is privately informed of his or her hole cards ... The existence of this private information can obviously lead to interesting strategic play: bluffing, signaling, reputation building, etc. It is also the reason why poker is of enduring popularity.

In the next sections, we continue the exploration of the consequences of information problems, particularly of information asymmetries. From the examples above, we hope that you have gained the intuition that information problems might be significant in explaining the type of coordination that is appropriate for particular transactions.

All coordination requires information. When two parties wish to enter into a transaction, they must both be able to receive the necessary information. Markets and prices are able to transmit certain types of information, but often not all the necessary information. Through organizational coordination, other types of information can be communicated. In the following sections, we shall develop this basic notion further by introducing some concepts from the economics of information.

4.2 Hidden information

The economics of information is a young branch of economics. It studies the implications of information problems and characteristics for economic theory. Some of its main inspirations have come from the analysis of insurance problems. We shall use some of these classic examples to introduce the concepts of *hidden information* (or *adverse selection*) and *hidden action* (or *moral hazard*) below and in Section 4.3.

First, let us look at hidden information. To illustrate, imagine a country with no health insurance. Let us call the country Riskaria. You have emigrated to Riskaria and have determined that no health insurance coverage is yet available, so you decide to go into the insurance business to fill that market niche. How do you proceed? The normal course of action is to employ an actuary.[1] The actuary will determine the health risks of the population of Riskaria. She might come up with a bell-shaped curve (a normal distribution), as shown in Figure 4.1.

We can observe from Figure 4.1 that the population of Riskaria includes people with very low health risks (represented towards the left of the figure) as well as people with high risks (on the right). Older people will tend to be located on the right as health risks increase with age. Also, people with, for instance, hereditary health risks or who smoke will be located further to the right than one would expect just from their age. There will also be older people who are in good shape and thus represent lower health risks than is average for their age group. In Riskaria, most people know more or less what risk class they belong to.

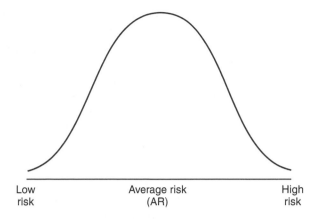

| Low risk | Average risk (AR) | High risk |

Figure 4.1 The health risks in the population of Riskaria

On the basis of risk distributions, such as Figure 4.1, an actuary can calculate the insurance rate you would have to set in order to be able to provide the specified coverage. Say this rate was calculated on the basis of Figure 4.1, which represents the entire population of Riskaria. In essence, the rate then reflects the average risk.

You now enter the market and offer your new product – a health insurance policy. Which members of the population of Riskaria will buy it? The prediction is that members of the population with higher than average risks will be particularly keen to take out a policy. The reason is simple: at a rate reflecting average risks, your product is attractive to those with higher risks. Very few people with lower-than-average risks will take out your insurance policy. For them, the required rate is unattractive.

Adverse selection

The phenomenon described is called **adverse selection** in insurance economics. It refers to the expected outcome of the above scenario, which is that you will end up with a set of clients in which the high-risk part of the population is over-represented. The high-risk clients have self-selected themselves in response to your product offer. They alone have been offered an attractive incentive to apply for health insurance.

As a consequence of such adverse (client) selection, you will be forced to raise your rates, but that has an adverse effect as well. At the higher rate, the insurance policy has become unattractive even to those in the average-risk group. They will cancel their policies and you will be left with an even worse selection of clients. Driven to the extreme, adverse selection could become a self-reinforcing mechanism that would make a health insurance policy an impossible product to offer in the market.

Before delving into the possible solutions to this problem, let us first consider the basic characteristics of the adverse selection phenomenon.

Hidden information

Essentially, adverse selection is a type of information asymmetry. It is a problem of **hidden information** (Arrow, 1985), which means that one party in a potential transaction (here, the population of Riskaria) is better informed about a relevant variable in the transaction (the individual member's health) than the other party (your insurance company). It is an information problem that already exists *before* the insurance contract is written. In the language of the economics of information, it is an ***ex ante* information problem.**

The problem for your insurance company is how to determine the actual risks that your potential clients represent: you will want to know whether your potential clients are indeed a fair representation of the Riskaria population. If not, you may want to adjust your rates or introduce risk-dependent rates (for instance, partly dependent on age). To some extent, the company can use available information, such as age, to determine such risks. Those seeking insurance, however, will still have better knowledge about risk factors, such as hereditary risks and smoking habits, than the insurance company. They have no *incentive* to reveal this knowledge truthfully, if it could be harmful to them. On the contrary, those who have private knowledge that they are higher risks than is observable have an incentive to both apply for the insurance *and* keep quiet about their private information. The company has hardly any means of finding out what this knowledge is without the cooperation of the potential clients.

In its information structure, this example corresponds with the third card game discussed in the previous section. The adverse selection phenomenon arises because one party has *private information* that is relevant to a potential transaction. That private information is unobservable to the other party. It is that *unobservability* of the private information which constitutes the essence of the information problem and introduces the risks for the other party.

Box 4.2 Blood donorship

In various parts of the world, there is a serious shortage of good quality blood that can be used for blood transfusion purposes. As a potential recipient of such blood, you can imagine that you want it to be of the best quality – that is, totally uncontaminated (by hepatitis or HIV viruses, for example). It would be very beneficial if more people could be convinced to donate uncontaminated blood. In principle, it could command a high price, yet we observe that most blood collection is still organized on a voluntary basis. The problem of increasing the blood supply, therefore, is one of finding more voluntary donors. Why do we not observe more commercial transactions? Why is blood collection not governed by the price mechanism?

One reason is the adverse selection problem introduced by offering money for blood. The incidence of hepatitis and HIV among drug addicts is high because they tend to infect one another by sharing needles. At the same time, their need for cash is high. For those individuals, then, 'cash for blood' is a particularly attractive offer.

Any attempt to purchase blood in the market, therefore, is likely to attract a relatively large proportion of carriers. Such adverse selection is unacceptable, if we cannot be 100 per cent certain that our blood testing procedures will capture all contaminations, including possible new strains of viruses.

Conversely, a voluntary system presents no incentive whatsoever to people who know or suspect that they are carriers to volunteer for blood donation (Titmuss, 1971). Another reason is given in Box 8.4. If you are interested in current practices regarding blood donation, including the screening for potential risks, see for example: http://www.fda.gov/BiologicsBloodVaccines/BloodBloodProducts/QuestionsaboutBlood/DonatingBlood/default.htm

Adverse selection problems abound in society. One example is given in Box 4.2. Another example comes from the market for used cars, as analysed by Akerlof (1970). Akerlof set out to explain why there is such a large price difference between brand new (that is, unregistered) cars and those that have just left the showroom. Suppose you have just bought a new car (say, a Ford) and have driven it for only a short time when you find out that you have won a Mercedes in a lottery. You decide to sell the Ford. Then you will normally have to accept a loss of up to 20 per cent of the original purchase price of the Ford. Why is this?

Akerlof's answer starts from the assumption that there are good cars and bad cars. The latter may have been assembled on a Monday morning. Such cars are referred to as 'lemons'. When buying a new car, we all run the risk of buying a 'lemon'. All parties involved are unaware which of the new cars is a lemon. Your Ford dealer was unaware whether he sold you a good car (the normal case) or a lemon (the exception). Similarly, you, as a buyer, cannot tell the difference after just one test drive. So, we all face the same probability of ending up with a new car that is a lemon.

After owning the car for some time, however, the owner can form a revised opinion about the quality of his automobile. He may have become aware of some (potential) problems. An information asymmetry develops: the sellers of used cars now have more knowledge about the true quality of their vehicles than the potential buyers. The buyers, however, have no way to discriminate between good and bad used cars. As they are unable to tell the difference, good cars and bad cars must sell at the same market price. However, at this price, there is little incentive for owners of good used cars to sell their vehicles. For owners of lemons, however, selling is attractive. As a consequence, the probability of buying a lemon is much higher in the used car market than the new car market. That risk is reflected in the market price. Even if your Ford has given you no problem at all, its selling price will reflect the higher probability of used cars being lemons.

Again, the basic problem is the unobservability of the true quality of the used cars for the buyers. Sellers have private information and they have no incentive to share bad news with the buyers. Bad risks self-select into the used car market. Buyers have few means at their disposal to identify bad risks. If there were no means at all, the market for used cars would conceivably not exist.

The 'lemon effect' can also occur in the labour market, as illustrated in Box 4.3, and even in the market for movies, as Box 4.4 shows.

Box 4.3 Layoffs and lemons

Suppose you are working for a company fiercely threatened by international competition. During the imminent company restructuring, about 10 per cent of all white-collar workers are to be fired. However, it is also possible that the company will go bankrupt and, if that happens, every worker will lose their job. Do you think that it will make any difference to you whether you lose your job as a result of a restructuring or a bankruptcy?

In a world of asymmetrical information, it is reasonable to assume that your current employer has better information on your productivity than potential future employers. If you were to be fired as a result of restructuring, then future employers would probably think that, in the opinion of your current employer, you belong to the 10 per cent of workers with the lowest productivity. It would not be easy for you to find a new job and you may be forced to accept a level of pay that is much lower than you currently earn. The fact that you have been fired is a negative signal to future employers. There is no such negative signal if the company goes bankrupt as all workers would then have to leave. So, it should be easier for you to find a job if the company were to go bankrupt, than if you were fired.

This effect has been confirmed in statistical research: the earnings of white-collar workers who have been displaced by lay-offs are significantly lower than those who have been displaced by plant closings. Also, white-collar workers displaced by lay-offs endure longer unemployment spells than those displaced by plant closings (Gibbons and Katz, 1991).

Hence, you are probably better off when you are fired as a result of bankruptcy rather than as a result of restructuring.

Box 4.4 Beware of Hollywood lemons

In some countries, investors are offered an opportunity to fund movies in return for a stake in the future revenues. In the USA there have even been attempts to set up a 'futures exchange' that will match buyers and sellers of future movie receipts. One such exchange (the Cantor exchange) was proposed by the investment bank Cantor Fitzgerald and approved in 2010 by the U.S. Commodity Futures Trading Commission (CFTC). Wharton professor of insurance and risk management Kent Smetters, however, warned for the risk of *adverse selection* on this new exchange:

Taking bets on the performance of individual contracts – in this case, specific movies – is often subject to the curse of "adverse selection" where only the bad quality product is actually offered for sale. The problem is not with futures exchanges themselves. Trillions of dollars are traded each year in future contracts for all sorts of commodities, including pork bellies, corn, oil, and exchange rates on currency. In theory, a movie exchange should allow a studio to also diversify its future risk by effectively selling some of its unpredictable future cash flow for guaranteed money today.

But a movie exchange fails to appreciate the economics behind a market for lemons. Whenever the product being offered for sale varies in quality – and the sellers have more information about its true value than buyers – the low quality variation is what tends to get sold. In other words, the Cantor Exchange could end up selling movies that studios know are real lemons based on internal market testing.

The reason why traditional commodity exchanges, like wheat or currency, work so well is that buyers and sellers have fairly equal information about the underlying risks. Moreover, the goods being traded are somewhat standardized, so that sellers can't pick off only the low quality product to sell. In fact, marketers commonly refer to the "commoditization" of a product to suggest that it has very little quality differentiation. But movies are not commodities. Indeed, studios have considerable private information about the quality of a movie before it is released…the new Cantor Exchange will likely encourage studios to simply "pump and dump" their lemons.

In the meantime, US Congress has enacted new legislation that bans box office receipts as the basis of any futures contract. Next to the concerns above, the Motion Pictures Association of America had voiced other worries, including other abuse of private information:

"Our coalition of film industry workers, creators, independent producers and distributors, business organisations and theatre owners, remains united in opposition to a risky online-wagering service that would be detrimental to the motion picture industry and the 2.4 m Americans whose livelihoods are based on this industry," it said in a statement. The coalition is opposed to the exchanges because it believes futures trading on box-office performance will be ripe for abuse and insider trading. Technicians or other production staff could exploit their knowledge about the quality and prospects of a particular film for financial gain in the markets.

Insider trading is illegal, whether you are on the staff of a movie company or not. So, perhaps the real objection of the movie industry was against the price signal that the Cantor exchange would have given about the expectations of 'the market' about the success of the traded movies?

Based on 'Betting on future movie receipts: beware the Hollywood lemons', Knowledge@Wharton, 28 April 2010; 'CTFC approves second Hollywood futures exchange', *The Financial Times,* 21 April 2010; and http://www.cantorexchange.com/Market-Overview/Market-Launch-Announcement.aspx

Fortunately, in many cases there are some solutions to the problems of hidden information, although they are often only partial solutions. As the essential problem is one of unobservability, we could try to increase its observability. In the case of health insurance, we may require applicants to undertake a medical examination. That would at least reveal already observable problems but it would not reveal hereditary risks. Similarly, a used car buyer may insist on an inspection of the vehicle. Such an inspection can be carried out by a qualified dealer, although he has some interest in an active used car market for his brand of cars. In some countries, automobile associations arrange for independent inspections. In these countries the consumers have thus organized to try and overcome the information problem. Even then, an inspection can reveal apparent problems, but still cannot guarantee that the car is not a lemon.

If we cannot directly improve the observability of the hidden information, perhaps we can do so in an indirect way. That is the idea behind the concept of **signalling,** pioneered by Michael Spence (1973) for job markets. Consider an employer looking to recruit a person who can absorb new information fast in a business context. Of course, all potential applicants will say that they possess this skill and only they will know their true level of skill. Thus, there is an information asymmetry between employer and applicants.

Signalling

Spence proposed that going to a business school and getting an MBA can serve as a *signal* of that skill. The reason is that, if the education signal is really correlated to the skill, employers are better off recruiting those who have invested in that (costly) signal. In our chapter on mergers and acquisitions we will look at the example of start-up firms using the costly process of filing for an initial public offering (IPO) to signal their credibility as acquisition targets.

There are other strategies for dealing with hidden information. A number of them aim at the risk involved. For the adverse selection problem in health insurance, one solution is to pool the risks. If the insurance policy can be made a collective one for *all* inhabitants of Riskaria, the asymmetry problem is dealt with as the actuarial rates would reflect the true risks of the population. That, of course, is the solution adopted in the case of mutual insurance companies or insurance provided by the State.

An alternative strategy is to redistribute the risks involved. In a used car transaction, all the risk that the car is a lemon is located with the buyer. Part of that risk can be relocated if the seller can provide a warranty specifying risks that will remain with the seller for some period of time. Often, garages will provide such a warranty. The credibility of that arrangement is strongly dependent on the type of organization that provides it. You will not believe the junkyard garage as easily as an approved dealer, which has more of a *reputation* to protect (we return to this subject and trust in Chapter 8).

Finally, risks can sometimes be *segmented* (if only crudely) and dealt with in separate ways. In many countries, health risks are segmented into one portion that is dealt with privately and another that is covered collectively (by social security). In the used car market, you indeed have a choice between buying from another individual, the junkyard garage or approved dealers. You know that the risk characteristics of these market segments as well as the terms of trade will differ from each other.

To conclude this section, it is probably useful to emphasize that hidden information is a problem that may be manifest across markets as well as within organizations. It can prevent the development of a market for health insurance as well as the establishment of a mutual insurance company. Private information, unobservable to other parties, may preclude transactions across markets as well as within organizations. It does not matter whether you, as an individual, are trying to sell your Ford to another individual or whether you are acting in your capacity as the head of a department trying to sell a car, a person or an idea to another department. Hidden information, or only the suspicion of it, may hinder all such transactions.

From the examples above, however, we hope you have gained the insight that markets and organizations do differ in the kinds of solution they may provide for particular problems of hidden information. For some types of problem, the market has an appropriate solution, such as market segmentation. For other types, we need organizations such as mutual insurance companies or consumer associations. Hence, problems of hidden information lead us to the basic perspective of this book: markets and organizations provide differential solutions for the information problems involved in economic transactions. Which (mix of) coordination mechanism(s) is most appropriate depends on the kinds of information problems involved and the kinds of solutions offered by both mechanisms. We develop this perspective further in the next section, which deals with problems of hidden action.

4.3 Hidden action

Hidden action

Hidden action (or moral hazard) is another kind of information asymmetry that can develop in both market and organizational settings. It is, however, not an *ex ante* but an *ex post* phenomenon. That is to say, it refers to actions that parties in a transaction may take *after* they have agreed to execute the transaction. If those actions are unobservable to the other party in the transaction and if they may harm that other party's interest, then they may prevent the successful completion of the transaction. Worse still, the *anticipation* that such hidden actions are possible may prevent the transaction altogether. We illustrate these ideas with some examples, first from the insurance field once again.

Take fire insurance. In the Netherlands, personal fire insurance policies used to extend to damage to personal belongings from contact with burning objects, such as cigars and cigarettes. The latter coverage has been terminated now. The reason is that the insurance companies were confronted with a rising tide of claims for such coverage. An increasing amount of damage to, for instance, clothes and furniture was claimed to be the result of accidental contact with cigarettes and so on. Interestingly, the clothes tended to be not brand new, but last year's models.

Here we have a typical problem of hidden action. Once insurance is provided for such accidents, there is an *incentive effect* on the behaviour of the insured. They may start to behave with less caution, perhaps with some sloppiness or, in extreme cases, even with malicious intent. Examples of this kind gave rise to the term **moral hazard.** For the insurance company, it is impossible to observe whether the damage has indeed been caused by uncontrollable accidents or whether the behaviour of the insured had something to do with the damage. When, as a result, the number of claims becomes too high, the coverage cannot be continued.

Moral hazard

Travel insurance is a similar case in point, which also indicates one type of organizational solution. Under travel insurance, we may claim personal belongings that we have lost while travelling abroad. Such claims have also risen enormously. It is hard to believe that we have collectively become much more accident prone. Some degree of deception and fraud must be present.

Apparently, a growing number of those insured try to finance their trip partly by making false travel insurance claims. In order to counter this trend, Dutch insurance companies have set up a joint venture that supervises a collective databank to register such claims. In addition, they have agreed on measures to take against possible fraud, such as joint exclusion of people who make an exceptionally high number of claims. Through a databank, they share information and may prevent some frauds, such as those involving one lost item being claimed twice under different policies and people with fraudulent behaviour going unnoticed as long as they 'hop' from one company to another. It will be clear that these organizational arrangements are (partial) countermeasures against the problem of the unobservability of hidden action.

When we leave the field of insurance, we find that problems of hidden action are plentiful elsewhere, too. Take the travelling salesperson as an example. One such person may be assigned by his company to a particular new region. Assume that he returns with a disappointing number of orders. Perhaps he has not put in enough effort and has chosen to pursue other interests. Perhaps, also, the competition is stiffer in that region, consumer tastes are different, the time of year is not right and so on. The point is that the company is unable to differentiate between these reasons because of a lack of observability. Box 4.5 discusses how McKinsey, a major consultancy firm, advises the use of 'ride-alongs' as one of the ways to tackle the lack of observability of the work of field service technicians.

Companies with large field service teams – for example, technicians who install telephone lines or cable-TV boxes – find it hard to raise their productivity. For one thing, managers can't easily observe the way these employees work. Besides, many companies don't know how to schedule their field technicians: they underestimate what can be done in a day and fail to recognize that cancellations generally outnumber new jobs.

What's the answer? For starters, giving teams more work in a shift than they could actually complete – that's right, the way airlines overbook – knowing that some customers will cancel. Companies can also dispatch teams in the field more flexibly by reassigning them on the fly as jobs are cancelled and new ones pop up. Finally, managers should appoint "ride-alongs" to observe teams at work and use the findings to raise their efficiency

Source: http://www.mckinseyquarterly.com/newsletters/chartfocus/2008_02.htm

One strategy to address hidden action, as discussed above, is to increase observability. Another strategy is to consider risk-sharing arrangements. If our salesman is paid a fixed salary, the risk is entirely on the company. Whatever amount of effort the salesman puts in, he always receives the same salary. So, he bears no risk in this transaction. At the same time, there is little incentive for him to put in the required effort, let alone that extra bit of work. As a consequence, the entire risk of disappointing outcomes is on the company. If, instead, the salesman is paid an entirely variable salary (say, on a percentage basis), all the risk is on him: no orders, no salary. That will probably not be acceptable to him. Hence, the company may negotiate a salary with him that contains fixed as well as variable elements. The mix of these elements determines the specific allocation of risks (and incentives). In Chapter 7 we return to these kinds of solutions when we discuss agency theory.

As a final example, assume that you cannot even determine whether or not actions are correct, even if you observe them. The relation between a physician and a patient is a case in point. The very basis of the relation is the superior knowledge of the physician in medical affairs. Even if the physician were to disclose every step she took when treating you as a patient, you would normally not be able to determine whether her actions were as diligent and as responsible as they could be. There is a fundamental information asymmetry owing to the existence of professional knowledge. You simply do not have the knowledge correctly to interpret the signals regarding the physician's actions. You will want some assurance that this asymmetry is not being exploited against your best interests: you want the best treatment possible. In this case, the medical associations try to provide you with some such assurance by the development of professional codes of conduct, requiring the continuous education of their members and reviewing complaints that are brought to their attention (with sanctions in case of professionally substandard behaviour). While those organizational arrangements may give you some assurance, they are not able to guarantee high performance in all cases. In the end, professional ethics and individual responsibility are the only solutions with regard to the considerable discretion that the doctor has as a consequence of this fundamental information asymmetry (Arrow, 1963, 1973).

To summarize this section, we may list some similarities and some differences between the concepts of hidden information (adverse selection) and hidden action (moral hazard). One basic similarity is that they are both a consequence of problems of unobservability. If, at any time, all parties in a transaction were able to observe all the information they needed to prepare and execute the transaction, both concepts would be irrelevant. A second similarity is that the information is unevenly distributed. One party has private information that is unobservable to the other party. That private information is valuable, in the sense that it could affect the terms of trade in the transaction. As the information is private, the owner can decide whether to disclose it or not. There is no incentive to do so when disclosure would harm the owner's private interest. A final similarity is that both problems may occur in both market and organizational settings. However, markets and organizations offer different solutions for these problems, albeit often partial ones.

Hidden information

Hidden action

Differences between both concepts are the following. **Hidden information** is an *ex ante* concept – it refers to private information that exists before parties agree on a transaction. **Hidden action** is an *ex post* concept – it pertains to private information that may develop during the execution of a transaction. Moreover, it denotes a particular type of private information – information about the unobservable behaviour of one of the parties in the transaction. Again, the behaviour is valuable in the sense that it affects the terms of trade in the transaction. If an insurance company knows negligence or fraud is involved, it will provide no coverage. There is no incentive for the insured party to disclose such information. The similarity and the differences between the concepts of moral hazard and adverse selection are also illustrated in Box 4.6. Both concepts are extensively applied in Chapter 13 on mergers and acquisitions.

Box 4.6 An insurer's worst nightmare

Insurance can reduce the devastating financial fallout from accidents, but it can also increase the risk of them happening, as *The Economist* argued using the following examples:

Aeroplane crashes, oil spills and product failures are generally unpredictable events, but they are not totally random. Their occurrence can sometimes be influenced by human actions, and, although insurance can help to protect people from the financial impact of accidental misfortune, it may also inadvertently make them more accident-prone.

Insurance works on the principle of pooling risks and charging each customer a premium based only on the average risk of the pool. This approach has much appeal, but it also presents two problems, which economists call 'adverse selection' and 'moral hazard'.

Customers who have the greatest incentive to buy insurance are likely to be those who pose the worst risk for insurers, hence adverse selection. A person will be keener to buy health insurance, for example, if he is already ill. This increases the odds that insurers will have to pay out claims and so may drive up premiums for healthier people. It should not, however, increase a society's total risk.

Moral hazard does increase society's risk. The term describes the temptation for a customer, once he has bought insurance, to take greater risks than he otherwise might have done. Moral hazard can take different forms. A customer might, for instance, increase the chances that he will incur a loss, so somebody with car insurance may drive more recklessly than he would if he were uninsured. Even though an insured person may try to reduce the odds of a mishap, he may do so in a way that increases the size of the potential loss. A firm that discovers it has a defective product, for example, may withhold its findings to avoid early lawsuits it has to settle itself, while raising the risk of a huge later payout that falls on its insurance company.

Source: The Economist, 29 July 1995

Moral hazard played an important role in the financial crisis of 2007-2011 as big banks took on too much risk in the expectation they were simply too big to fail (see Box 4.7). If a risky investment turns out well bank executives receive large bonuses. If cumulative losses threaten the bank's survival, the tax payer foots the bill. Note that moral hazard occurs in this case even if there is no formal contract between the bank and the government obliging the government to bail out the bank.

Box 4.7 Too big to fail: banking on kicking the ball into someone else's court?

Some organizations can grow so large that they are deemed 'too big to fail'. Prime examples can be found in the banking industry. Some banks are so large that their potential default would endanger the whole financial system, not only of their home country but of the world at large. This problem came to the fore in the financial crisis of 2007–2011. While the investment bank Lehmann Brothers was allowed to fail, sparking the financial crisis, many other banks were rescued from potential default (bailed out) by the governments of their home countries. Examples are Citigroup and Bank of America in the USA, Commerzbank in Germany, Royal Bank of Scotland in the UK, ING in The Netherlands and Dexia in Belgium.

Essentially, 'too big to fail' is a problem of moral hazard. When an organization perceives that it is too big to fail, excessive risk-taking is encouraged. A bank may, for instance, invest in high risk assets in the implicit belief that it will be bailed out by the government if the cumulative losses would ever threaten its financial solidity. Private risk-monitoring by those institutions may also be less strict than if they would operate solely for their own risk and benefit. In other words: there is an *incentive effect* to behave differently if the rewards for risk-taking are private (the famous bonuses for bankers) while the penalties may become public if they become too large (taxpayers footing the bill of bail-outs).

While banking is surely the industry where this problem is most significant, it is certainly not the only industry where 'too big to fail' is present. General Motors, the American car company, was bailed out by the US government at a cost of over $50 billion in 2008–2009. And many football clubs around the world also consider themselves 'too big to fail':

No big soccer club disappears under its debts. No matter how much money clubs waste, someone will always bail them out. This is what is known in finance as "moral hazard": when you know you will be saved however much money you lose, you are free to lose money.

In 2011, Manchester City announced the biggest loss in English football history, £197 million for the most recent financial year. It eclipsed the previous biggest loss ever made, £141 million by Chelsea in 2005. In these cases the losses were bankrolled by the clubs oil-rich owner's, Sheikh Mansour bin Zayed al-Nahyan and Roman Abramovich respectively. In total, top-level European soccer clubs' losses widened by 36 per cent to €1.6 billion ($2.1 billion) in the 2010 fiscal year, according to an audit of 665 teams by the sport's regional governing body UEFA. The teams had debts of €8.4 billion.

Source: S. Kuper & S. Szymanski, *Soccernomics,* New York, NY: Nation books, 2009 and http://www.bloomberg.com/news/2012-01-25/european-soccer-clubs-losses-widen-36-to-2-1-billion-in-2010-uefa-says.html

Assuming that these concepts have now been sufficiently clarified by the use of examples, we proceed to introduce the basic concepts in the economics of information somewhat more formally. This will help to define their exact meaning and will also allow us to use them in subsequent chapters in these precise terms.

4.4 The value of information

In a world where everybody knew everything, the economics of information would have no place. Information would not be scarce, so economics would have nothing to say about it. The *economic aspect* of information pertains to its scarcity and the value that scarce information may have.

We illustrate this first with the example of an individual decisionmaker who has to choose an action in the face of uncertainty. In the language of game theory (the subject of the next chapter) this is the situation of an individual playing against Nature. In this section we show how the value of information can be determined in such a game.

You are the marketing manager of Standard Breakfast Corporation. A new product has been developed and you have to decide whether or not to introduce it. If the new product is a success, you gain 8 (million dollars). If it is a failure you lose 2 (unfortunately also million dollars). Your estimate that the new product will be a success is 0.3, that it will be a failure 0.7. What do you decide? Figure 4.2 summarizes the situation.

		STATES OF NATURE	
		Success	Failure
ACTS	Introduce	8	−2
	Do not introduce	0	0
	Probabilities of states	0.3	0.7

Figure 4.2 An individual decision under uncertainty: whether or not to introduce a new product

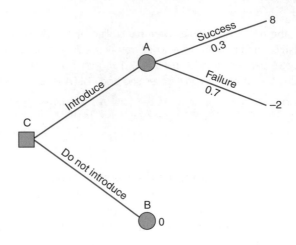

Figure 4.3 Decision tree: introducing a new product

If you are risk-neutral, you should simply calculate the expected value of introducing the new product:

$$0.3 \times 8 + 0.7 \times (-2) = 1 \text{ (million dollars)}$$

The result is positive, so you should introduce the new product.

Decision tree   Another way to describe the situation is by using a **decision tree** (Figure 4.3). A decision tree may have two kinds of node: nodes where an individual has to choose an act (represented by squares) and nodes where Nature chooses her moves by means of a random process (represented by circles). Working backwards (that is, from right to left), we can calculate the expected value for each node. In Figure 4.3, the expected value for node A is:

$$0.3 \times 8 + 0.7 \times (-2) = 1$$

For node B it is 0. Therefore, in node C you will choose A rather than B. The expected value for node C is 1 (million dollars). That is the expected value of this game against Nature.

Now, suppose that you could do test marketing. Suppose, first, that test **Complete information**   marketing gives you **complete information**. By complete information we mean information that removes all uncertainty. So, by test marketing first, you will know for sure whether or not the new product will be a success.

How valuable is complete information in this case? There is a probability of 0.3 that test marketing will tell you the new product will be a success (see Figure 4.2). As you now know for sure that it will be successful, you introduce the new product. Without test marketing, you also introduce the new product. So, there is a probability of 0.3 that test marketing will not alter your decision. There is a probability of 0.7 that test marketing will show the product to be a failure. You then decide not to introduce the new product, in which case you save 2 (million dollars). So, by test marketing you have a 0.7 probability of saving 2. The value of the information from test marketing is:

$$0.3 \times 0 + 0.7 \times 2 = 1.4 \text{ (million dollars)}$$

THE NEW PRODUCT WILL REALLY BE

		a success	a failure
TEST MARKETING IS	a success	0.8	0.2
	a failure	0.1	0.9

Figure 4.4 Incomplete information from test marketing

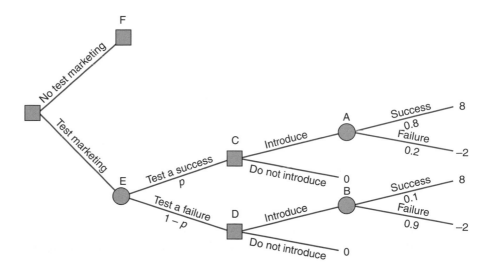

Figure 4.5 Decision tree: introducing a new product with test marketing

If test marketing costs you less than that amount, it is rational to test market your product.

In practice, test marketing seldom gives you complete information. In most cases there will be some uncertainty left. For example, if test marketing is successful, your estimate that the new product will really be a success may be revised to 0.8. If test marketing is a failure, your estimate that the new product will really be a failure may be 0.9. The situation is summarized in Figure 4.4. The information in the figure would be complete if the first and the second row each contained one 1 and one 0. As it is, the information is incomplete.

In order to determine the expected value of this incomplete information, consider Figure 4.5. Working backwards, we calculate the expected value for each node as follows. For node A, the expected value is:

$$0.8 \times 8 + 0.2 \times (-2) = 6$$

In node C, you will choose A, so the expected value for node C is also 6. For node B the expected value is:

$$0.1 \times 8 + 0.9 \times (-2) = -1$$

In node D, you decide not to introduce, so the expected value for node D is 0.

To find the expected value in node E, we need the probability, *p,* that test marketing will be successful. We can calculate *p* as follows. The probability that the new product will really be a success is equal to:

$$p \times 0.8 + (1 - p) \times 0.1$$

This expression must be equal to 0.3, which is the known probability that the new product will be a success. So, we have:

$$p \times 0.8 + (1 - p) \times 0.1 = 0.3$$

Hence:

$$p = 2/7$$

The expected value in node E is $2/7 \times 6 = 12/7$.

The value of information from test marketing can now be calculated by comparing the expected value in node E with the expected value in node F, which we know is 1. So, the value of the information from test marketing is:

$$12/7 - 1 = 5/7 \text{ (million dollars)}$$

which is about $714,000. Again, if test marketing costs you less than this amount, you should test market your product.

4.5 Summary: information problems for markets and organizations

In this chapter, information has been examined from an economic viewpoint. It has been shown how information can be seen as an economic good, deriving its value from its scarcity.

The chapter took an ideal market with perfect competition as its point of departure. Under perfect competition, prices act as sufficient statistics for conveying all the necessary information to the market parties. It was shown that perfect competition can work only under conditions of very limited information requirements. If goods are not homogeneous, for instance, it may be necessary to signal a quality dimension to potential buyers. The price mechanism is often insufficient for conveying such information. Also, under conditions of uncertainty, the price mechanism may break down as a coordination device. Particular attention has been paid to situations of information asymmetry. In such situations, information is unevenly distributed. This introduces the risk that some economic players will use their informational advantage to gain an economic advantage in executing transactions.

In the economics of information, a fundamental distinction is made between *ex ante* and *ex post* information problems. Adverse selection (or hidden information) is an *ex ante* information problem. It arises when one party has private information that is relevant to a potential transaction. Private information is unobservable to the other party. In the case of adverse selection, the private information already exists *before* parties agree to execute a transaction. We have used the examples of setting up health insurance in Riskaria and selling used cars to illustrate the concept. Hidden information, or only the suspicion of it, may hinder transactions across markets as well as within organizations. Markets and organizations offer different solutions, however, to the information problems inherent in adverse selection.

Moral hazard (or hidden action) can also develop in both market and organizational settings. This concept refers to an *ex post* information problem. It applies *after* parties have agreed to execute a transaction. Hidden information and hidden action both pertain to private information that one of the parties in a transaction may possess. In the case of hidden action, this information concerns unobservable behaviour of one of the parties in executing the transaction. This information is valuable as it would affect the terms of the trade, if the other party were aware of it. However, the party with private information has no incentive to disclose it. Again, markets and organizations offer different solutions for overcoming the problem of hidden action.

Finally, we illustrated one approach to determining the value of information. It was shown how we should distinguish between decisions where complete information can be obtained (removing all uncertainty) and decisions under conditions of remaining uncertainty (with incomplete information). In both cases we made use of a decision tree to sketch the decision context. The decision tree depicted a game of one individual playing against Nature. In the next chapter, we explore more complicated games, involving two or more players.

Questions

1 There are many jokes about the laziness of civil servants. Do you think that those jokes contain an element of truth? Let us, for the sake of argument, suppose that government officials are lazier than employees working for a business firm. Can you explain this phenomenon by using the concepts of hidden information and hidden action?

2 Section 4.2 discussed the market for 'lemons'. The large price difference between new (unregistered) cars and ones that have just left the showroom can be explained by the information asymmetry between buyers and sellers of used cars: the seller knows if the car is a 'lemon' but the buyer does not. Do you see another explanation for the large price difference between new cars and cars that have just left the showroom?

3 Suppose you are the negotiator for I.G. Metall, an important union in Germany. You expect that, in the next four years, many companies will have to reduce their labour force substantially. You know that if a company fires 10 per cent of its employees, there might be a 'lemon effect'. What would you demand from employers in order to eliminate that effect?

4 Mutual insurance companies exist in most European countries, together with insurance companies owned by investors. Most mutual insurance companies were founded by farmers and many today still have close ties with the agricultural sector. In the eighteenth century a class of very small farmers emerged in continental Europe. These farmers owned their farms (in previous centuries many farms had been owned by the nobility), but farmers were quite poor. They produced their own food and sold the rest in local markets. Their farmhouses were usually thatched with straw or hay. Fire brigades did not exist in the countryside. If a farm caught fire, the farmer lost everything he owned, including his means of subsistence. Investor owned insurance companies existed in those days, but most refused to insure these small farms. Can you explain why mutual fire insurance companies arose in those days in the agricultural sector?

5 In baseball, there is a 'designated hitter' rule that allows a team to designate a player to bat instead of its pitcher. Designated hitters (who are good at batting) substitute for pitchers (who are not so good) to increase the chance that pitches will be hit and runs will be scored. Interestingly, the rule applies in the American League (AL) of baseball in the USA, but not in the National League (NL). In the AL, pitchers hit batsmen more often with their pitches than in the NL. Bradbury & Drinen (2006) argue that this may be due to 'moral hazard'. Would you be able to formulate an argument why this could be true?

Note

1   An actuary is an expert in the determination of insurance risks. A well-known alternative description of an actuary is 'someone who found life as an accountant too exciting'.

5 Game theory

5.1 Introduction

In the previous chapter we discussed the value of information. As an example, we used the decisionmaking process involved in choosing whether or not to introduce a new product. As we saw in Section 4.4, that situation can be modelled as a game against Nature. We saw how an individual can make up his mind what to do in the face of uncertainty.

In this chapter, we introduce game theory. Game theory is concerned with situations in which there are two or more players. Moreover, these players have to make interdependent decisions. By that we mean any player in the game is affected by what the others do. Each player in making their decision has to take into account the other players' decisions. We assume in Sections 5.2 to 5.5 that players are rational decision makers who act only in their own interest. Moreover, we assume that each player knows that other players are rational. These are the assumptions of 'classical' game theory. In Section 5.6, we move on to 'evolutionary' game theory, which studies the development of populations rather than the rational decision making of individuals.

There are several types of games. Two important characteristics of games are the number of:

- players involved;
- stages in the game.

Combining these two characteristics in Figure 5.1, we can distinguish the types of game we discuss in this chapter.

	2 players	N players ($N > 2$)
1 stage	Coordination game (Section 5,2) Single-stage prisoner's dilemma (Section 5.5.1)	Auctions (Section 5.4)
M stages ($M > 1$)	Entry game (Section 5.3)	Iterated prisoner's dilemma for many players (Section 5.5.2) Evolutionary game theory (Section 5.6)

Figure 5.1 Six types of games in this chapter

The purpose of this chapter is to acquaint you with some important insights from game theory. Game theory has become an increasingly important tool in a number of sciences, including economics. By introducing game theory here, we hope to give you a feel for the different types of setting in which economic decisions can be made. An important message in this chapter is that different settings (different structures of games) provide different incentives for players and allow different strategies of play. It is, therefore, important to discern the basic features of any economic game in theory or practice.

5.2 The coordination game

Coordination game

Simultaneous and sequential games

We start with an example of a game between two players. The game is played in one stage. The main point to note in this game is how players can coordinate their actions. Therefore, we call it the **coordination game.** The coordination game introduces the important distinction between **simultaneous and sequential games.**

There are many situations in which two or more players have to coordinate their decisions in order to reach the outcome that is best for all of them. An example is the standardization of a new technology. Suppose that Philips and Sony have to decide on the standard specifications of a new piece of electronic technology – say, a combination of video and compact disc technology called VIDISC (see also Box 5.1). Both have been working on this breakthrough.

There are two types of system both can choose. If they choose the same type of system, the pay-offs for each of them will be larger than if they choose different systems. The reason is that, with different systems, they have to compete not only in terms of the brand chosen by consumers, but also in terms of the system chosen. The VI technology (video technology with added CD facilities) promises larger pay-offs for both than the DISC technology (CD technology with added video facilities). VI is twice as attractive for both players as DISC. Figure 5.2 gives a handy summary of the main game theory features of this story.

The numbers in Figure 5.2 indicate the pay-offs to both players. The first number always gives the pay-off for the row player (Philips in this example), the second, the pay-off to the column player. The pay-off is the reward enjoyed by a player at the end of the game. For example, if Philips and Sony both choose VI,

		SONY	
		VI	DISC
PHILIPS	VI	4, 4	−2, −2
	DISC	−2, −2	2, 2

Figure 5.2 Philips and Sony with the VIDISC technology

they would both gain $400 million. If both choose DISC, they would both gain $200 million. The worst situation would be if one company chooses VI while the other chooses DISC. In that case both would incur a loss of $200 million. Which of these results will come about?

Box 5.1 Philips, Sony, Toshiba and video disc in the real world

The example of VIDISC technology was included in the first edition of this book, which appeared in 1991. Meanwhile, it has become clear that the 'game' of video disc technology has played out in the real world as well. Here are some of the features of this real-world game:

- More players were involved than just Sony and Philips. At least ten electronics firms had an interest in setting the standard for digital video discs (DVDs). DVDs have a much higher data storage capacity than CDs and were expected to replace them in the future.
- Initially, there were two camps of players, Philips/Sony versus Toshiba/Matsushita/Time Warner. Both camps tried to set the standard for DVDs on their own, thus risking a 'standards war', as observed for videos but not for CDs.
- In September 1995 the two camps reached an agreement to form one consortium in order to set a joint technology standard.
- However, within that consortium, the haggling over each other's contributions continued. This focused on the licence fees that individual players could require for their contributions to the common standard. The lengthy haggling could jeopardize a rapid and successful introduction of the new technology.
- In 1996, Philips and Sony threatened individually to sell their licences to other hardware and software firms interested in DVDs. That did not undermine the common standard, but required other interested firms to obtain the necessary licences from two separate camps again.
- In 1997, Philips, Sony and Pioneer (the three main DVD patent holders) announced their cooperation. Other firms wishing to produce DVDs would be required to pay a 3.5 per cent royalty fee (on the sales price) to these three firms.
- For the next generation of DVDs, however, a 'standards war' broke out again between Toshiba (High Definition DVD) and Sony (Blu-ray technology). This 'war' ended in 2008, when Toshiba announced it would no longer develop or manufacture HD DVD players and drives.

This real-world 'game' illuvstrates some features that we introduce in this chapter. We move from two-player to N(>2)-player games. We discuss the potential benefits of cooperation, such as in consortia or cartels, as well as some inherent difficulties. In particular, we show that, for individual players, the central question often is whether to cooperate or defect.

That depends on the way the game is played. If both players have to choose simultaneously, without any information on the other's preferences, no prediction can be made. The reason is that it is not clear what each player will assume the other player will do. If Philips, for example, expects Sony to choose DISC, Philips may be tempted to choose DISC, too. However, if one player is allowed to move *after* the other, we can predict that both companies will choose the same technology. That is because, for the second player, it is always the most advantageous choice to follow the first player's move.

Game tree

Suppose Philips has to move first and Sony can observe Philips' move. We can now represent the game by drawing a **game tree** (Figure 5.3). A game tree is similar to a decision tree, as introduced in Chapter 4, except that in a game tree there are two rational players acting in their own interests, while in a decision tree there is only one. At the end nodes of a game tree, two pay-offs are given. The first pay-off is for the player who moves first, the second pay-off for the other player.

Philips has to move first. What should Philips do? Assuming that the required information is available, the Philips manager who has to make the decision could look at the game tree in Figure 5.3. The Philips manager will see immediately that Sony will choose VI in node B and DISC in node C. So, the Philips manager sees that whatever she chooses, Sony will choose, too. So, Philips chooses VI and Sony follows. Both players receive $400 million.

In this game, it is important that one player be allowed to move first. In the sequential game, it is easy to coordinate the choices made by both players. In a simultaneous game, it is not at all obvious how coordination between the two players' choices can be obtained.

Simultaneous game

When is a game a **simultaneous game**? Is it really necessary that both players make their choices at exactly the same time? No, of course not. Both companies may make their choices at different dates. The point is that, when Sony has to make its choice, it does not know what Philips has chosen or will choose. It is that lack of information which distinguishes the simultaneous game from the sequential game.

In this game, it is in Philips' interest to tell Sony about its choice as soon as it has made a final decision. For Sony, there is no reason not to believe the message it receives from Philips. So, in this game, it is quite likely that reality is represented better by a sequential game than by a simultaneous game.

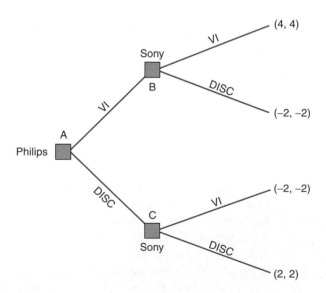

Figure 5.3 Game tree for the sequential coordination game

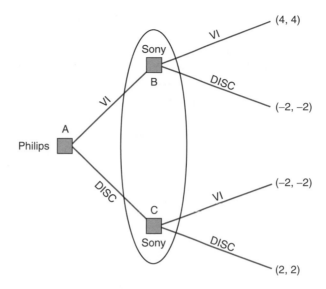

Figure 5.4 Game tree for the simultaneous coordination game

A sequential game can be represented by a matrix specifying the pay-offs or by a game tree. So, Figure 5.2 can represent both a simultaneous game and a sequential game. If the matrix represents a sequential game, we also need to know who moves first before we can draw the game tree.

A simultaneous game can be represented by a matrix giving the pay-offs and by a game tree. The game tree for the simultaneous coordination game is given in Figure 5.4. Figure 5.4 is quite similar to Figure 5.3, except for the oval around Sony's two decision nodes. That oval represents Sony's information set. It indicates the fact that Sony cannot distinguish between the two nodes at the time it has to make its decision. Sony's manager simply does not know whether he is in node B or in node C at the time he has to make his choice. Because of that lack of information, the game has no predictable outcome.

The coordination game is a very simple game. If there are only two players, the best solution is reached if the players can communicate (Philips and Sony will simply agree to choose VI). If the number of players is large, it may be necessary to establish a rule. An example is on which side of the road to drive.

In a country with only two car-owners, the government need not establish a rule – the two car-owners can simply agree to drive either on the right or on the left. If the number of car owners is very large, it is difficult and costly for all of them to make an agreement. In such a case we see that the government establishes a rule.

In a duet for violin and piano, the two players must play at the same tempo. The pay-off for both of them (in terms of their satisfaction or the number of CDs they sell) is zero if they play at different tempos. However, they can easily agree on the tempo to use. If the number of players becomes large, as in a symphony orchestra, it becomes much more difficult to agree on a tempo (that is one of the reasons for a symphony orchestra needing a conductor).

Philips and Sony, the two car-owners and the two musicians can reach the best solution to the coordination game through mutual adjustment (see Chapter 3). A large number of car owners or the members of a symphony orchestra, however, may need another coordination mechanism, such as standardization or direct supervision, to reach the best solution.

This section has illustrated two features of games that are important in the context of economic approaches to organizations: the distinction between simultaneous and sequential games. It was shown that in sequential games, where the moves of the first player can be observed by the second player, coordination is easily achieved. The second player has *information* to base a decision on. In contrast, simultaneous games lack such information and, hence, have no predictable outcome.

However, coordination between two (or a small number of) players can be achieved through mutual adjustment. Because of the interdependence of the players' decisions, however, this coordination mechanism breaks down as the number of players increases. It then has to be replaced with other coordination mechanisms (see Chapter 3).

5.3 The entry game

Two-stage games

In this section, we move from one-stage games to **two-stage games** by considering the entry game. The entry game is a sequential game between a monopolist and a potential entrant. Suppose, first, that the monopolist restricts output and keeps prices high. That gives a potential entrant the opportunity to enter the industry. We analyze that situation first as a one-stage game and then as a two-stage game.

Suppose that a telecommunications company – let us call it National Telecom – has a legal monopoly in the market for mobile telecommunications. The firm knows, however, that the legal protection it now enjoys will not last forever and predicts that, within a few years, other companies will be allowed to enter the market.

Suppose, next, that there is a potential entrant, Mobicom, which possesses the know – how and resources to enter that market. Will Mobicom enter the market? Is there anything National can do to prevent entry by Mobicom? These are the questions considered in the entry game.

In a sequential game like the entry game, it is known which player moves first. Let us suppose that Mobicom moves first. Mobicom has to decide whether or not to enter the market. It knows that National charges relatively high prices. Mobicom knows that it will make a nice profit if National maintains that price level after it enters the market. If National lowers its price substantially after entry, however, Mobicom will not be able to make a profit. What should Mobicom do? We suppose that Mobicom knows exactly what National will earn in each situation. The game tree representing the choices is given in Figure 5.5.

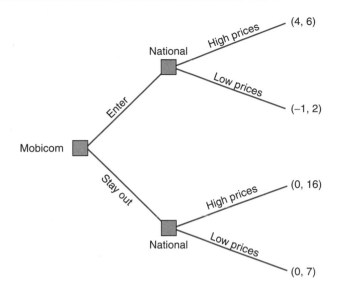

Figure 5.5 Game tree for an entry game

Mobicom's decision depends on the price level that National will choose after its entry. Mobicom will have to put itself into National's shoes in order to predict what National will do after its entry. It is quite easy to predict what National will do if Mobicom stays out. National's pay-off with high prices is 16; with low prices it is only 7. Therefore, National will choose high prices if Mobicom stays out.

Much more relevant for Mobicom is predicting what National will do after its entry. It is easy for Mobicom to see that, with high prices, National will earn 6 and with low prices only 2. Mobicom knows that National is a rational player, acting only in its own interest, so predicts that National will choose high prices after its entry. Thus, Mobicom enters and knows that it will earn a profit of 4. This illustrates an important principle for solving sequential games. It is the **principle of looking ahead and reasoning backwards**. By looking ahead and then reasoning backwards, Mobicom is able to predict that entry will be profitable.

Principle of looking ahead and reasoning backwards

Is there anything that National can do to deter entry? Suppose that, before Mobicom makes its decision, National threatens to choose low prices after its entry. If Mobicom believes that National will carry out its threat, it will not enter because, with low prices, it will incur a loss. It is quite likely, however, that Mobicom will not believe National will actually carry out its threat. After all, if entry has in fact occurred, it is no longer in National's interest to lower its prices.

Credible threat

National's threat is not a **credible threat**.

Suppose that National already has a large network in place before Mobicom makes its decision. The result of having that large network is that National faces higher fixed costs and, thus, earns a smaller profit. However, if entry occurs, National already has a large network in place. It can now lower its prices and attract many new customers for very low additional costs. Indeed, if

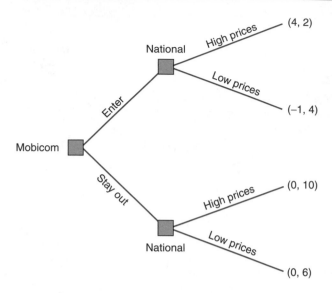

Figure 5.6 Game tree for another entry game

entry occurs, National is now better off with low prices than with high prices. Figure 5.6 shows the revised pay-offs that result from having that large network. Mobicom will now predict low prices if it enters. Mobicom knows that it will incur a loss in case of entry and decides not to enter. If National now threatens to lower prices after entry, Mobicom will believe this. National's threat is now a credible threat.

We have seen what happens if National has a small network and what happens if National has a large network. If National can choose first between having a small and a large network, which should it choose? It is a two-stage, sequential game in which National chooses first between a small and a large network, then Mobicom decides whether or not to enter and, finally, National chooses between high and low prices. The game tree for that sequence is given in Figure 5.7, which combines the two game trees in Figures 5.5 and 5.6 into one larger tree.

Should National choose a small or a large network? How should Mobicom react to National's choice concerning the size of its network? How should National react to Mobicom's decision? Those three questions can be answered by applying the principle of looking ahead and reasoning backwards through the two stages of the game tree. In nodes D and E, National will choose high prices. So, in node B, Mobicom will decide to enter. In node F, National will choose low prices and, in node G, it will choose high prices. Mobicom knows this, so, in node C, it decides to stay out. Now National knows that, with a small network, Mobicom will enter. The result for National is a profit of 6. It also knows that when it decides to build a large network, Mobicom will not enter. The result is that it will enjoy a profit of 10. So, National decides to build a large network in order to prevent Mobicom's entry.

The point of this example is that, by building a large network, National can commit itself to lower its prices if entry occurs. In the language of game theory, **commitment** is the process whereby a player irreversibly alters the pay-offs

Commitment

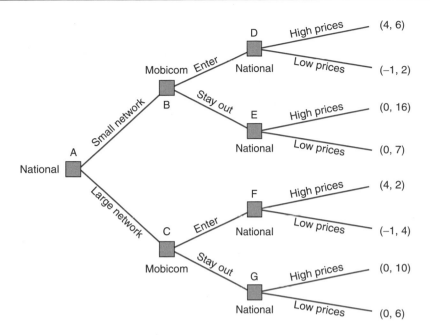

Figure 5.7 An entry game with commitment

in advance so that it will be in his own interest to carry out a threat. In this example, by building a large network, National alters the pay-offs in such a way that, after Mobicom's entry, it is in National's self-interest to carry out the threat of lowering prices. Hence, such commitment makes National's threat credible.

From this section you can infer the following:

- In a sequential game, you should anticipate your rival's response. You can do so by applying the principle of looking ahead and reasoning backwards through the game tree. If the game tree shows more than one stage, the principle also applies.
- A threat can be made credible by showing commitment. By undertaking actions that demonstrate commitment, one player can show another that it is in his own interest to carry out the threat. In order to be effective, commitments must be observable and credible. Box 5.2 illustrates the dangers of making threats that are not credible because they are not backed up by binding commitments.

Box 5.2 Commitment in labour negotiations

Labour negotiations can be viewed from the perspective of game theory as well. In any negotiation, one party may attempt to formulate a 'take it or leave it' offer at a certain stage. In order for such a strategy to be effective, the 'or leave it' part must be credible. If the other party does not believe that is the final offer, the negotiations may be seriously disturbed, as the following story illustrates.

For a time, General Electric in its labour negotiations used a strategy known as Boulwarism (named after Lemuel R. Boulware, the GE vice-president of employee and public relations who introduced it in

▶

the 1950s), under which its initial offer, chosen after careful research into wages and working conditions in GE and its competitors, was its final offer. Although this take-it-or-leave-it offer was intended to be fair and acceptable to the workers, the union strongly opposed this technique – understandably, given … the amount of bargaining power to be gained from commitment. One union response was likewise to present a set of demands and announce they were inflexible. Another was to behave disruptively during negotiations. Another was to strike. Yet another was to complain to the National Labor Relations Board, which found that GE was guilty of an unfair labour practice; the adjudicator considered the lack of real concessions by GE during negotiations as evidence that GE was not bargaining in good faith. By 1970, the union's opposition had induced GE to cease using the commitment strategy.

Source: McMillan (1991)

5.4 Auctions

We now turn to a situation involving more than two players in a single-stage game. A prototypical example is the auction.

Open auction

Sealed bid auction

Auctions come in various shapes and forms. An important distinction is between the **open auction**, in which the bids of all parties are observable, and the **sealed bid auction**, in which that is not the case. Again, we shall see that the observability of information plays a crucial role.

Imagine that, as a manager, you are attending the open auction of a piece of land that is adjacent to your factory. As you are contemplating an expansion that exceeds the boundaries of your current acreage, you are strongly interested in this additional piece of land. You think the land should be worth more to you than to competing bidders, but are not sure. Several people you do not know are attending the auction. What should your bidding strategy be? How should the seller set up the auction in order to extract the highest possible price from the audience? As we shall see, the answers to those questions are not unrelated.

If the seller sets up the auction as an 'increasing bid' competition, the optimal strategy for you as a potential buyer is straightforward. It is to remain in the bidding competition until the price rises to your own valuation of the land and drop out of the competition as soon as the price moves beyond your own valuation. If all bidders are rational and execute the same strategy, the land will be transferred to the buyer with the highest private valuation of the land. Note that during the bidding process you will also thus be informed of the other players' private valuations of the land. As the bidding process unfolds, you are able to observe what those private valuations are by noticing who remains in the competition and who drops out. The bidding process forces the players to reveal their preferences.

Such an increasing bid competition is, however, not entirely optimal from the seller's point of view. In order to grasp this point, imagine that you are among the last two bidders for the property. One of the two must have the highest private valuation – say it is you. However, the other player will then be the first to drop out of the competition. He drops out as soon as the price rises just beyond his own private valuation. That may still be far below your own private valuation, however. Hence, there is good news for you: you acquire the land at a price substantially below the level you were willing to pay. Conversely, it is bad news for the seller: her land could have fetched far more than it did.

There are several strategies the seller could employ to counter that risk. One of the most interesting is to use a **Dutch auction** instead of an increasing bid competition. In a Dutch auction, the auctioneer starts with a very high price (a price that is, in the auctioneer's opinion, well above the highest private value of all bidders). The auctioneer cries out loudly prices that slowly decrease. This process stops when one of the bidders cries out 'mine'.

In a Dutch auction you have to make your bid (that is, you have to cry out 'mine') without knowing what other bidders might be willing to bid. So, if the piece of land is worth $1 million to you and you estimate that it is worth $700,000 to the second highest bidder, then your best strategy would seem to be to cry out 'mine' when the price is $701,000. That, however, is risky because your estimate may be too low. If you think that the private value of the second highest bidder is somewhere between $650,000 and $750,000 with an expected value of $700,000 your best strategy is probably to cry out 'mine' at a price level somewhere between $751,000 and $701,000.

In a Dutch auction, the seller probably receives at least a part of the difference between the private values of the highest and the second highest bidders. For the seller there is also a risk, however. In an increasing bid auction the auctioneer can start with a minimum price. In a Dutch auction there is no such minimum.

In order to establish a minimum, the seller can convert the auction from a one-stage to a two-stage game. In the first stage, the game is played as an increasing bid competition. The winner of the first stage gets a financial reward (a fixed fee or a small percentage of his bid), but not the land. The land is subsequently auctioned in a second stage, which takes the form of a Dutch auction. If, in the second stage, no one cries out 'mine' before the first-stage price is reached, the winner of the first stage has to buy the land for the first-stage price. The bidders in the first stage are usually professional bidders who bid in order to obtain the fee for winning the first stage. They usually do not want the land for themselves.

Notice several interesting features of the open auction game:

- It is a game with private information: each bidder's valuation of the land is his own private information;
- In the increasing bid case most of this private information is revealed as the game is played: only the winner's private information can ultimately remain private;
- The design of the game determines the incentives for players to reveal their private information and by adding a second-stage Dutch auction, the seller attempts to induce the bidder with the highest private valuation to reveal her private information;
- The private information is valuable – the seller is prepared to pay the first-stage winner a price (the fee or percentage) in order to participate in this design.

Dutch auction

In a **sealed-bid (one-stage) auction,** all bidders have to submit their bids in a sealed envelope at the same time. The most striking difference between it and the open auction is that you do not learn about the private information of the other bidders during the auction process. You get only one chance to place your bid under conditions of uncertainty about the other players' private valuations.

What is a good strategy for bidders when sellers design the game as a sealed-bid, one-stage auction? To derive the answer, first consider the case where you, as a bidder, have full information on all the other bidders' valuations. If your valuation is the highest, what should you bid? It seems clear that you should bid just above the second highest valuation. If you bid lower than that, you risk losing the competition. However, bidding much higher makes no sense as you would pay more than needed (colloquially, you would leave money on the table).

The full information case gives a clue as to how to proceed in the more realistic case in which none of the bidders knows the competitors' valuations. Say you are contemplating submitting a bid for a business unit that is divested by its parent company. The parent has solicited the help of an investment banker to set up a one-stage sealed bid auction.

First, you have to determine the likely competition. Which other companies may be interested in acquiring that particular business unit? Which companies are bidding only because they think that they can run the business unit better (financial bidders)? Which other companies, in addition, believe that they could realize synergies by combining the business unit with their current operations (strategic bidders)?

As a potential bidder, you must determine that there is a reasonable chance your valuation is the highest of all (you are the most strategic bidder). If so, the prescription is to estimate what the second highest valuation is most likely to be and submit a bid slightly above that level.

To illustrate, assume that the value of the business unit on sale is €100 million at its current performance level. Assume further that this level of performance can already be raised on a standalone basis. If the performance level is raised to 'best practice level', the value increases to €120 million. That means €120 million represents the maximum amount the best financial bidder should be willing to submit. However, strategic bidders can go beyond that level if they can also raise the performance level of the unit and, in addition, realize synergy benefits. If the combined effects of those two factors are more than €20 million, then strategic bidders can win over financial bidders. If you are the most strategic bidder, the rule is to submit a bid just above the valuation level of your best competitor.

The example above highlights the fact that the value of the bid you, as the most strategic bidder, submit depends on a number of estimates:

- the performance level to which you can raise the acquired unit;
- the synergies to be gained by combining this unit with your own operations;
- the private valuation of your best competitor in the auction.

It is possible that you will make one or more mistakes in these various estimates, as it is highly unlikely all your estimates will be correct. Some will be too pessimistic; some too optimistic. In circumstances of intense competition by many bidders, however, it is quite likely that the winner turns out to have made the most optimistic estimates. If you are the winner, there may therefore be good news as well as bad news in that outcome. The good news is that you have acquired the business unit. The bad news may be that you have based your calculations on the most optimistic calculations of all the competitors. That phenomenon is called the **winner's curse** in game theory. It refers to situations where winners obtain the prize not because the value is truly highest for them, but because of their optimistic expectations.

Winner's curse

The main difference between open and sealed bid auctions pertains to the uncertainty about other players' private valuations. In an increasing bid open auction, most of the players' private valuations become observable as the process unfolds. Only the winner's private valuation remains unobservable. Sellers who wish to extract more value for their property may therefore wish to design the auction process differently – by for instance, adding a second stage Dutch auction. However, because of the open nature of the auction, a rational winner will never pay more than his private valuation. In sealed bid auctions the private valuations of all players remain unobservable. In situations of uncertainty regarding the true value of the auctioned object, all private valuations must be based on estimates (in our example of a divested business unit, on three estimates). In such situations, it is possible that the winner is inflicted with the 'winner's curse', obtaining the prize as a consequence of making the most optimistic estimates – Box 5.3 relates an example. We return to the winner's curse in Chapter 13, on mergers and acquisitions, where we also examine a potential cause of the phenomenon in the M&A context.

Box 5.3 The winner's curse in the classroom

To demonstrate the winner's curse, Bazerman and Samuelson (1983) held a series of auctions in an MBA classroom. The object was a glass jar filled with $8-worth of coins. The value of the jar was not revealed, but students could look at it and make their own estimates. Thereafter, they submitted their sealed bids.

Over a large number of such auctions, the average bid was $5.13, while the average winning bid was $10.01. On average, the winner therefore lost $2.01, a clear example of the winner's curse.

Source: Bazerman and Samuelson (1983)

While the winner's curse is a potential problem for buyers in an auction, there is also a potential problem for sellers: collusion between buyers. We encountered collusion in Chapter 3 as an example of mutual adjustment between economic actors – for instance, in cartels. It can also occur in auctions, particularly if there is only a small number of potential buyers (and it is known who these are). Buyers can secretly agree not to drive prices up. Alternatively, they can agree how to divide the auction's objects between them. Sometimes it is even possible for bidders in 'increasing bid' auctions to use the early rounds to signal their intentions. Box 5.4 gives an example. Needless to say, collusion between buyers may prevent the seller from obtaining the full value for the items in the auction.

Box 5.4 Signalling and collusion in auctions

Ascending bid auctions, particularly when they involve only a few bidders, are often susceptible to collusion, since participants can use early rounds to signal their intentions.

In 1999, Germany sold some mobile phone spectrums by auction, with one rule specifying that any new bid had to exceed the previous high bid by 10 per cent. Two serious bidders were involved.

One company bid 18.18 million marks on blocks 1 to 5 and 20 million on blocks 6 to 10. Why the difference? Note that 18.18 million plus 10 per cent is just about 20 million. The first company was sending the second a message: 'We think 20 million is the right price: let's not compete to push it up.' The signalling strategy worked: the auction ended after two rounds, and each bidder got half the blocks at the same low price.

Source: H. R. Varian, 'Tales of manipulation and design flaws from the crypt of auction history', *The New York Times,* 1 August 2002

In concluding this section, we want to stress that the way an auction is designed determines the result to a large extent. We have discussed only the most fundamental forms: a single stage increasing bid auction, a Dutch auction (also known as an open descending price auction), a two stage auction where the first stage is an increasing bid auction and the second stage a Dutch auction, and a single stage sealed bid auction. The outcome of an auction is further determined by the number of bidders, number of items to be sold and rules allowing or forbidding the formation of alliances. All these factors can have important consequences for the outcome of the auction, as illustrated in Box 5.5.

Box 5.5 The 3G mobile spectrum auctions in Europe

In 2000, many European governments were contemplating how to allocate a new and scarce good: third-generation (3G) mobile phone licences. 3G mobile phones would use the Universal Mobile Technology Standard (UMTS), which offers much more bandwidth than previously, allowing applications such as high speed Internet and video on your mobile phone. The governments owned the rights to the radio spectra necessary for UMTS. How should they allocate these rights to the interested telecom companies?

Some governments (Finland, Poland, Spain, Sweden) chose to distribute the 3G licences on the basis of a *beauty contest.* In such a contest, the interested parties compete by demonstrating their qualifications against criteria set by the government. An advantage of a beauty contest may be that governments can set any criteria they deem politically relevant. A disadvantage may be that this invites favouritism by the governments – for instance, towards the incumbent national telecom companies.

Economic theory suggests that an *auction* could allocate the new licences efficiently – that is, to those who value them most, not those whom regulators favour. Governments interested in obtaining the highest prices for the new licences should therefore consider using an auction.

In fact, the UK government was the first to use an auction in April 2000. There were nine telecom companies wishing to enter the UK market. Those new entrants bid strongly against the four incumbents to obtain one of the five available licences. As a result, the UK government collected an astonishing £22.5 billion. Finance ministers across Europe started grinning at the prospect of their own auctions.

The next auction was held in the Netherlands. There were five incumbents and five new licences available. The Dutch government anticipated that, again, many new entrants would compete. In fact, many of them formed alliances with the incumbents: BT-Telfort, KPN-NTT Docomo and Ben–Deutsche Telekom. On the morning before the auction, two of the three last new entrants withdrew from the auction, leaving only six players – the five incumbents and one weak new entrant, Versatel. As a result, the Dutch government collected only € 2.7 billion, less than a third of what they hoped on the basis of the UK experience.

Revenue from European 3G mobile spectrum auctions in 2000

	Euros per capita
Austria	100
Germany	615
Italy	240
Netherlands	170
Switzerland	20
UK	630

As the table illustrates, revenue from 3G auctions has varied widely. The revenue was high again in Germany, but very low in Austria and Switzerland. Reasons for these differences include the experience that players acquired over time and the changing market sentiment about the high sums paid initially. A comparison of the auctions shows that it has also been tremendously important how auctions were designed. Important design features include the following:

- Increasing bid only or also a second-stage Dutch auction?
- Were there incentives for new entrants to compete (such as a special lot reserved for them)?
- What were the rules for forming alliances and 'collusive behaviour' during the auction?

Many game theorists were employed by governments to advise on optimal auction design and by companies on optimal bidding strategies. They have had a spectacular opportunity to test their theories (see Klemperer, 2002, 2006). Moreover, the practical value of a good training in game theory was evident for many in the public sector and the business world. Indeed, *The Financial Times* quoted a telecoms analyst as saying, 'All these people who thought that they wasted their first year at university listening to boring game theory lectures are now running around the City feeling really grateful.'

Based on Klemperer (2002, 2004); 'Best bids guaranteed', *The Financial Times,* 8 November 2000; 'The price is right', *The Economist,* 29 July 2000; www.paulklemperer.org/index.htm

5.5 The prisoner's dilemma: single stage and iterated

We now introduce a famous class of games: the prisoner's dilemma. We start with the single stage prisoner's dilemma (for two players) to show its basic structure. We then proceed to play the prisoner's dilemma game repeatedly with two or more players in order to show the difference between single stage and iterated games.

5.5.1 The single stage prisoner's dilemma

Two men, Robber and Thief, are being accused of a bank robbery. They are interrogated separately. They know that, if they both confess, each will be sentenced to five years in prison. If neither of them confesses, each will be sentenced to three years for illegal possession of arms. However, if Robber confesses while Thief holds out, Robber will be sentenced for only one year and Thief will receive six years. If Thief confesses and Robber holds out, the situation will be reversed. The pay-offs for this game are given in Figure 5.8.

Robber will now reason as follows. If Thief holds out, then my best choice is to confess (one year in prison is better than three years). If Thief confesses, then my best choice is to also confess (six years in prison is worse than five years). So, whatever Thief does, my best choice is to confess.

Dominant strategy

In the language of game theory we say that Robber has a **dominant strategy** – that is, one which is best whatever the other player does. Robber's dominant strategy is to confess.

Thief will follow the same line of reasoning, so he will also confess. The result is that both will confess, while both would be better off if they were to hold out.

Suppose that Robber and Thief are allowed to communicate before being interrogated. Perhaps they have been held in the same cell, but they are now interrogated in separate rooms. Suppose Robber and Thief have promised each other not to confess. Will they stick to their promise?

If we suppose that each is completely selfish and rational, then we must predict that they will not. It is in Robber's interests to promise Thief that he, Robber, will cooperate (by not confessing) if Thief promises the same. Having made that promise, however, it is in Robber's interests to break that promise. Whether or not Thief keeps his promise, Robber will always be better off breaking his promise.

The problem is that, if the prisoners are dishonest and disloyal (as we would expect bank robbers to be), they cannot make binding commitments. Because they cannot make binding commitments, they have no way to achieve cooperation. If they could make binding commitments, cooperation could be achieved.

Looking at the dilemma in that way, it is logical to relabel the actions the players can choose as 'cooperate' (which for the prisoners is equal to 'do not confess') and 'defect' (which for the prisoners is the same as 'confess'). The general form of a prisoner's dilemma is given in Figure 5.9.

		THIEF	
		Do not confess	Confess
ROBBER	Do not confess	−3, −3	−6, −1
	Confess	−1, −6	−5, −5

Figure 5.8 The prisoner's dilemma

COLUMN PLAYER

		Cooperate	Defect
ROW PLAYER	Cooperate	R,R	N,T
	Defect	T,N	P,P

Key:
R = reward for cooperation
N = pay off for being naive
T = temptation to defect
P = penalty for mutual defection

Figure 5.9 General form of the prisoner's dilemma

The game represented in Figure 5.9 is a prisoner's dilemma if there are certain relations between the four pay-offs that each player can receive. Those relations are:

$$N < P < R < T$$

where

$N < P$ means that, for the row player, it is better to defect if the column player defects;

$P < R$ means that the pay-off for mutual defection is less than it is for mutual cooperation;

$R < T$ means that, if the other player cooperates, then it is better to defect (there is a temptation to defect).

Note that the pay-offs given in Figure 5.8 for the two prisoners satisfy these inequalities.

In Box 5.6 we offer an example of how government authorities may offer incentives to increase the temptation to defect for conspirators in a cartel.

Box 5.6 Leniency policy as an incentive to defect

The lessons of game theory can be applied in many contexts. One of them is the antitrust policy of governments, aimed at illegal secret (cartel) agreements between competitors to fix prices, restrict supply or divide up markets. The authorities have learned from the prisoner's dilemma that it can pay to increase the incentive for players to defect from such cartels. Increasingly, they have adopted a 'leniency policy' to stimulate companies to defect from cartels. Under the leniency policy of the EU, adopted in 2002, the first company to 'blow the whistle' on a cartel is granted immunity from the (rather stiff) fines that the European Commission can impose.

The leniency policy works well. For instance, the Swiss company ABB blew the whistle on a cartel for gas insulated switchgear (GIS) projects:

The Commission concluded that the companies had participated in an illegal cartel on the basis of numerous documents and corporate statements provided by the immunity applicant (including two detailed written agreements concluded in 1988), together with documents discovered by the Commission during on-site inspections ... From at least 1988, when a written agreement between the members was adopted, GIS suppliers informed each other of calls for tender for GIS and coordinated their bids in order to secure projects for the cartel members according to their respective cartel quotas.

▶

Alternatively, they would agree to respect minimum bidding prices. The companies agreed that the Japanese companies would not sell in Europe, and the European companies would not sell in Japan. European tenders were usually allocated according to the cartel rules and the European projects won by cartel members outside their home countries were counted into the agreed global cartel quotas. Thus the Japanese companies have also been fined, despite their nearly total absence from the market for GIS in Europe, because their agreement to abstain from bidding contributed directly to the restriction of competition on the EU market.

As a result, the European Commission imposed fines of, in total, €750 million on 10 members of the cartel, while ABB was granted immunity for its fine, which would otherwise have amounted to € 215 million. The largest fine was imposed on the German company Siemens (€396 million).

Source: http://europa.eu/rapid/PressReleasesaction.do?reference=IP/07/80&guiLanguage=en (IP/07/80), 24 January 2007

The fundamental problem in the prisoner's dilemma is that, for each player, the dominant strategy is to defect, while they would both be better off if they chose mutual cooperation.

There are many situations in which a prisoner's dilemma arises. Consider the following situation. Suppose there are only two oil-producing countries in the world. Let us call those countries Arabia and Russia. Both countries have to choose an output level. If each chooses a low output level, then oil prices will be high and both will make a profit of 3 (billion dollars). If each chooses a high output level, oil prices will be low and each will make a profit of 1 (billion dollars). If Arabia chooses a low output level and Russia a high output level, then oil prices will be moderately high. Now Russia, with its high output level, will make a large profit of 5 (billion dollars) while Arabia, with its low output level, will earn nothing. If Russia chooses a low output level and Arabia a high one, then the situation is reversed. The pay-offs for each country are given in Figure 5.10.

In this example, to cooperate means to choose a low output level and to defect means to choose a high output level. If oil-producing countries form a cartel, then each country promises to maintain a certain price level and restrict output. Having made such a promise, however, it is in each country's interest to produce and sell more oil than its quota, even at a slightly lower price. As each country will do this, the cartel will break down.

In reality, we see that OPEC was able to raise oil prices effectively in the 1970s (the oil crises), but has suffered from defection at other times. In particular,

	RUSSIA	
	Cooperate	Defect
ARABIA Cooperate	3,3	0,5
Defect	5,0	1,1

Figure 5.10 Two oil-producing countries facing a prisoner's dilemma

certain countries have repeatedly tried to benefit from the lack of observability of actual output levels, as illustrated in Box 5.7. Furthermore, availability of non-OPEC oil (which increases when oil prices are high) has helped to keep OPEC 'honest'.

That shows our model does not (yet) incorporate all the relevant aspects of reality. One important and relevant aspect in many prisoner's dilemmas in the real world is that the game is played many times instead of only once. In the next section we find that makes a big difference.

5.5.2 The iterated prisoner's dilemma for many players

Suppose that two selfish and rational players play the prisoner's dilemma many times. That is the iterated prisoner's dilemma.

In the iterated prisoner's dilemma, each player has to choose to either cooperate or defect in each round of the game. In making that choice, each player can take into account what the other player did in previous rounds. In the repeated game, a strategy is defined as a set of rules that specify what action to take given the history of the game so far. To illustrate the concept of a strategy for an iterated game, we give a few examples.

Box 5.7 Cheating in OPEC

Cheating has been a persistent problem in the OPEC cartel, regardless of whether the oil price has been high or low. After the oil shocks of the 1970s and 1980s, when oil prices reached levels of above $50, the price level had come down again to around $20. However, in the late 1990s, the oil price slid towards a level of $10, which caused a lot of turmoil within OPEC, with various members blaming each other:

> After criticising each other from afar for several weeks, Saudi and Venezuelan oil officials got into the same room and glared at each other: the Venezuelans blinked. As recently as early March, Erwin Jose Arrieta, Venezuela's energy minister, had declared that he was too busy to attend a proposed OPEC meeting and vowed not to cut production 'even by one barrel'. Coming from OPEC's biggest cheater, that attitude was regarded as unhelpful. Oil prices had dropped by 55% since January 1997, to hit a low of $11.27 a barrel, and had been sinking by 50 cents a week for months. Now, under a deal brokered by Mexico, its great non-OPEC rival in the hemisphere, Venezuela has agreed to cheat somewhat less flagrantly, and Saudi Arabia to match cuts by the two big Latin American producers. Ten other producers are having their arms twisted to follow suit. By removing between 1.1 m and 2 m barrels a day from world markets, the producers hope to 'stabilize' prices.

Oil prices recovered and, by the year 2000, they were above $30 again. High oil prices are a threat to economic growth in many regions, so the OPEC countries had, in principle, agreed to keep oil prices in a target band of $22–28. If the price remained above $28 for 20 trading days, the cartel was supposed to raise production by 0.5 million barrels a day. That 'automatic' increase did not happen in June 2000, however, when the price had sailed past the 20-day upper trigger. The Economist analysed the situation as follows:

> Various confused and contradictory explanations surfaced from ministers, but not the oil. Only at their next officially scheduled meeting did they come up with a meagre quota increase. Even if ministers

▶

agree to lift quotas by the magic 500,000 barrels per day (bpd) figure, very little oil may actually reach the markets. That is because this figure does not allow for cheating. At the moment, the cartel's official quotas total about 25.4m bpd, whereas its actual production last month topped 26m bpd. A quota increase of 500,000 bpd will serve merely to legitimize existing cheating. Countries will try to cheat once again on whatever new quotas are agreed.

Sources: The Economist, 28 March 1998 and 9 September 2000

Tit-for-tat

- **Tit-for-tat** is the strategy consisting of the following decision rules: in the first round, choose cooperate, in the following rounds choose whatever the other player did in the previous round.
- *Permanent retaliation:* in the first round, choose cooperate; if the other player defects in any round, choose defect in all subsequent rounds.
- *All D:* always choose defect no matter what the other player does.
- *All C:* always choose cooperate no matter what the other player does.
- *Random:* choose randomly (by tossing a coin) between cooperate and defect.
- *Tit-for-tat plus:* in the first round, choose cooperate; in the following rounds, if the other player cooperated in the previous round, choose cooperate with probability $1-\varepsilon$ and defect with probability ε if the other player defected in the previous round, choose defect.
- *Tit-for-two-tats:* in the first two rounds, choose cooperate; in the following rounds, choose defect if the other player defected in the last two rounds, otherwise choose cooperate.
- *Uneven:* in the first round and in all subsequent uneven rounds, cooperate; in the second and in all subsequent even rounds, defect.

Now suppose that you belong to a group of, say, ten people. You will successively play the iterated prisoner's dilemma against each of the other members of the group. That is the iterated prisoner's dilemma for many players. What is your best strategy? The answer depends on many factors:

- The pay-offs – if T (the temptation to defect in Figure 5.9) is very large, then an occasional unexpected defection could be part of your best strategy.
- The strategies of the other players – tit-for-tat-plus will perform very nicely against tit-for-two-tats, but probably not very well against permanent retaliation.
- The way you discount future pay-offs.

The iterated prisoner's dilemma has been investigated by Axelrod (1984). Axelrod invited scientists from several disciplines, from mathematics to psychology, to submit strategies for the prisoner's dilemma with pay-offs given in Figure 5.10. Note that with these pay-offs permanent mutual cooperation is better than taking turns at exploiting each other (permanent mutual cooperation gives each player 3 in each round; taking turns at exploiting each other means receiving 5 and 0 in two consecutive rounds, an average of 2.5). In most real-world situations it is better to cooperate than take turns at exploiting each other. In the iterated prisoner's dilemma, that is equivalent to assuming that $0.5(N+T) < R$.

With the pay-offs given in Figure 5.10 and no discounting, Axelrod organized two computer tournaments between the strategies he had received. In each tournament, each strategy was paired with each other strategy, with itself and with random. Both tournaments were won by tit-for-tat.

Tit-for-tat has several characteristics that may explain its success. First, tit-for-tat is *nice*. That means it is never the first to defect. If tit-for-tat is paired with itself, with tit-for-two-tats, permanent retaliation or all C, then it will receive 3 in each round.

Second, tit-for-tat is *forgiving*. That means, if the other player defects once but then starts to cooperate again, tit-for-tat will punish him only once. Thus, unlike permanent retaliation, tit-for-tat is able to restore cooperation after a single defection.

Third, tit-for-tat is *retaliatory*. If the other player defects, he is punished immediately. For that reason, it is difficult to exploit tit-for-tat.

Axelrod's results show quite nicely how two selfish and rational players in the iterated prisoner's dilemma can achieve cooperation even if they cannot make binding commitments (they cannot trust each other not to break promises). That has important consequences for the way members of an organization cooperate. Suppose the two players are Arabia and Russia and each country can choose its production level each week. The two countries then play the iterated prisoner's dilemma. Suppose, further, that they agree to have production levels observed. That mutual cooperation can arise, based on such an agreement, is not surprising. Now suppose the two players are two large firms that have formed a joint venture. To cooperate means giving your partner full access to all relevant know-how; to defect means giving away as little knowledge as possible. If both firms expect to set up similar joint ventures in the future, cooperation is likely to arise. For those firms, it now pays to invest in their *reputation* as trustworthy partners. Building a reputation is one way to show a commitment (see Box 5.8). In single-stage games it is not possible to build a reputation as the game is over after the first move. In repeated games, however, players may invest in building reputations. Reputations for trustworthiness and cooperativeness help to establish cooperation even in the adverse conditions of a prisoner's dilemma.

Box 5.8 Reputation as commitment

Dixit and Nalebuff (1991) explain the building of reputation as being a form of commitment as follows:

If you try a strategic move in a game and then back off, you may lose your reputation for credibility. In a once-in-a-lifetime situation, reputation may be unimportant and therefore of little commitment value. But, you typically play several games with different rivals at the same time, or the same rivals at different times. Then you have an incentive to establish a reputation, and this serves as a commitment that makes your strategic moves credible.

During the Berlin crisis in 1961, John F. Kennedy explained the importance of the US reputation: 'If we do not meet our commitments in Berlin, where will we later stand? If we are not true to our word there, all that we have achieved in collective security, which relies on these words, will mean nothing.'

Source: Dixit and Nalebuff (1991)

Similar situations arise when two people have to work together to accomplish a task. They can both choose between a high level of effort (which is equivalent to cooperating) and a low level of effort (defecting). If they have to work together many times, cooperation is more likely to arise than if they work together only once. If the players meet only once, then we predict mutual defection.

What happens if they know that they will meet each other 1000 times? In the last round they will surely both defect as there is no future from there on in which the other player can punish defection. In round number 999, they will also both defect as they know they are both going to defect in the last round anyway. That logic, taken to the extreme, leads inevitably to the conclusion that both players will defect in the first round. Of course, instead of 1000, any other finite number will yield the same result. Only if both players are to meet an infinite number of times or they do not know how often they will meet can we expect mutual cooperation.

5.5.3 The iterated prisoner's dilemma when players can make mistakes

What is the lesson we can learn from Axelrod's results? Does it mean that, in reality, it is always best to play tit-for-tat? Not necessarily. An important difference between the real world and a computer tournament concerns the possibility of mistakes. In computer tournaments, errors do not occur, unless programmed. In reality, mistakes are a fact of life. Therefore, we have to allow for the possibility of errors if we want to increase the usefulness of game theory's recommendations.

Suppose that the heads of two Mafia families, Antara and Brizi, are both tit-for-tat players. Suppose, too, that mistakes are possible. Thus, it is possible that, while Antara and Brizi both cooperated in a certain round (round n), Brizi incorrectly thinks Antara defected in round n. Brizi will then defect in round $n + 1$. Antara will react by defecting in round $n + 2$, which means that Brizi will defect in round number $n + 3$. That is called the **echo effect**, as the echo of a mistake can go on indefinitely. It is illustrated in Table 5.1.

Echo effect

One mistake provokes a chain reaction of punishments. Antara and Brizi now take turns at exploiting each other, which is worse than mutual cooperation. When mistakes are possible, tit-for-tat may be too aggressive. In game theory, such random errors are called **noise**. When we allow for noise in the iterated prisoner's dilemma game, we can show that it is better to play an amended tit-for-tat strategy with, for example:

Noise

Generosity
- **generosity**: make the response to a defection somewhat less than the provocation, so retaliation diminishes over time and a new basis for cooperation can be established;

Contrition
- **contrition**: show 'remorse' if you realize that you have defected by accident, which you can signal by, for instance, not responding to the other's retaliation with yet another defection, so the vicious circle of retaliations by defection can be broken.

So, introducing noise into the system requires the tit-for-tat strategy to be more forgiving than it already was. It is, however, a fine balance in an environment where other strategies may be seeking opportunities to benefit from such

Table 5.1 Two tit-for-tat players with the possibility of making a mistake

Round	Antara	Brizi
1	Cooperate	Cooperate
2	Cooperate	Cooperate
⋮	⋮	⋮
n	Cooperate	Cooperate
$n + 1$	Cooperate	Defect
$n + 2$	Defect	Cooperate
$n + 3$	Cooperate	Defect

forgiveness. As summarized by Axelrod: noise calls for forgiveness, but too much forgiveness invites exploitation.

Tit-for-tat can be observed in real-world situations, such as the trade policies pursued by various countries and regions. Box 5.9 gives an example. You may ask yourself if President Bush made a mistake in the example. You may also ask yourself if there are examples of forgiveness and retaliation.

Box 5.9 Tit-for-tat between the EU and the USA

Countries, such as the USA, and regions, such as the EU, cooperate in the World Trade Organization (WTO) to establish a 'level playing field' of common rules for international trade. In spite of the WTO rules, every now and then a 'trade war' may erupt with tit-for-tat characteristics:

- Early in 2002, President Bush slapped tariffs of up to 30 per cent on imported steel, hurting European exports, and the EU contested the tariffs before the WTO – the wait for the final WTO ruling could take two to three years.
- The EU published a list of retaliatory tariffs on such products as citrus fruit, clothing and sunglasses to be imposed in mid-2002 – the products were clearly chosen to inflict electoral pain on President Bush in states viewed as key political battlegrounds, with Senate elections foreseen in November 2002
- Moreover, the EU drew up its own steel restrictions 'to prevent cheap steel diverted from the US flooding the European market'.
- The EU delayed the imposition of the retaliatory tariffs in anticipation of a WTO ruling, which was promised in a 'fast track' process; in late autumn of 2003, the WTO came out against the steel tariffs, saying that they represented an illegal barrier to free trade.
- After receiving the verdict, Bush declared that he would still maintain the tariffs; under WTO rules, the EU threatened to now counter with the retaliatory tariffs.
- Faced with this credible threat, the USA backed down and withdrew the tariffs in December 2003.

In the context of international trade, tit-for-tat can be observed between two players (as above), between multiple players (as in the trade rounds aimed at expanding the reach of WTO rules) and in multiple rounds (the trade rounds continue over time). As we move to situations involving many players in many rounds, a branch of game theory becomes relevant, called 'evolutionary game theory'. We introduce that branch briefly in the next section by examining three types of questions that can be answered by the evolutionary game theory approach. That brief introduction will also serve to make a useful link between this chapter and Chapter 11 on evolutionary approaches to organizations.

In Sections 5.2 to 5.5 we assumed that players are rational decisionmakers who act only in their own interests. That is exactly what *homo economicus* would do. Consider, however, Box 5.10 for a result that is not really consistent with this view of human behaviour.

Box 5.10 The ultimatum game

Before we leave classical game theory, we want to discuss one other game that is rapidly becoming just as famous as the prisoner's dilemma. It is the one-stage *ultimatum game,* in which two players interact anonymously.

The first player (the 'proposer') has a sum of money available and is asked to propose to the second player (the 'responder') how to divide the money. If the responder accepts the proposal, the sum is divided accordingly. However, if the responder rejects the proposal, both players receive nothing.

The full rationality assumption of the *homo economicus* model would imply that any offer to split the money should be accepted by the responder, as receiving some money is better than getting nothing. Anticipating such rational behaviour from the respondent, a proposer should be able to get away with offering very low amounts of money.

In fact, across many cultures and with varying amounts of money involved, proposers offer very substantial amounts of money (the modal offer is 40–50 per cent) and responders frequently reject proposals below 20–30 per cent. Apparently, a notion of 'fairness' is implied in the behaviour of proposers as well as responders. Moreover, that notion is shared by the players in the ultimatum game.

These experimental results are generally interpreted to mean that the *homo economicus* model is incomplete. The model is useful to approximate human behaviour with respect to the 'economic aspect' of decisions, but it is not sufficient as a model of real-life decisions involving more than 'purely economic' aspects. Besides (full) rationality, human behaviour is also determined by notions such as reciprocity and fairness. We return to this discussion in Chapter 8 (see Box 8.3).

Sources: Güth, Schmittberger and Schwarze (1982) and Gintis (2000)

5.6 Evolutionary game theory

The iterated prisoner's dilemma is a dynamic game involving multiple players. In Axelrod's computer tournaments, different strategies were submitted and tit-for-tat came out as the overall winner. Imagine that the whole population of players in the tournament uses tit-for-tat. Would that population now be immune from attack by an alternative strategy such as 'always defect'? This is one of the oldest questions in evolutionary game theory. It is asking if an 'evolutionary stable strategy' has evolved.

Evolutionary stable strategy (ESS)

A behaviour is defined as an **evolutionary stable strategy (ESS)** if a population adopting that behaviour cannot be invaded by any competing alternative strategy. Consider an entire population playing the tit-for-tat strategy and a group of newcomers who prefer the 'always defect' strategy (they try to cheat everyone they meet) entering the population. Then the defectors will be less successful than the tit-for-tat players. If we assume further that lack of success means less offspring, tit-for-tat players will come to dominate the population. Tit-for-tat is therefore an ESS with respect to the strategy 'always defect'.

The Hawk–Dove game depicted in Figure 5.11 is a different game. In the Hawk-Dove game there are only two strategies; the first is 'always fight' and the second is 'always cooperate'. Originally developed to analyze 'the logic of animal conflict', the game refers to two types of birds (or players) competing for food (or resources):

- *hawks* use the strategy of 'always fight'; they initiate a fight, not stopping until exhausted or the opponent backs down;
- *doves* use the strategy of 'always cooperate'; they retreat immediately when the opponent initiates a fight.

		BIRD B	
		Hawk	Dove
BIRD A	Hawk	−1,−1	9,1
	Dove	1,9	5,5

Figure 5.11 Hawk–Dove game: pay-offs to Birds A and B respectively

In the game specified in Figure 5.11, the hawk wins most of the food when it meets a dove. The latter has to be content with leftovers. When two hawks meet, however, they will use more energy fighting than the food can replenish. When two doves meet, they share the food.

If better fed birds breed more, how will the bird population evolve over time? We can start by observing that any population consisting entirely of doves is not 'evolutionarily stable' as they can be successfully invaded by a hawk mutant. Initially, such a hawk invader will have an easy time winning each fight for food. The hawk proportion of the bird population will grow as the initial hawks spend their time feeding and breeding. Increasingly, however, they will be confronted with other hawks putting up a fight for their food. The end result of a population totally dominated by hawks is not attainable as they will all fight each other to starvation (each fight costing more energy than the food gives back). Each dove, however, always gains something (either 1 or 5) in its food encounters. As a result, the dove population will always have some breeding success. Doves will have higher breeding success than hawks when the hawk numbers are reaching the point where they fight each other to death. Thus, it can be seen that the bird population settles into an equilibrium of doves and hawks. If the population swings out of that equilibrium towards one type of strategy, the other strategy will become slightly more advantaged and its proportion in the population will increase to bring the balance back.

In business environments, the Hawk–Dove game may play out in aggressive environments, with fierce competition for projects. Powell (2003) gives the following example:

> some buyers demand 'fly-offs' when contracting larger projects. In a 'fly-off' bidders have to make huge risky investments to develop prototypes which are then trialed against each other with the winner taking full control of the project. One response is to put investment into this highly uncertain bidding process and take the competitors head-on. Another response is to look for small work-shares from the resulting winners, taking a smaller return, but using much less resource in the process. Contractors in these environments can be clearly seen to fall into two groups – those who fight aggressively for leadership (i.e. majority work-share) and those who act as substantial subcontractors for, say, production or specialized contributions. Often these *Doves* are as large and successful as the *Hawks* but their core competencies are very different, the latter having highly developed bidding teams skilled in fighting the *Hawk–Hawk* game.

Note that the two games analyzed above (the iterated prisoner's dilemma and the Hawk-Dove game) relate to the success of *fixed* strategies in a population. If we relax that assumption and allow the strategies to evolve over time, evolutionary game theory takes us a step further. What will happen if we model gradual change (evolution) of strategies? How much learning would we observe? Would new strategies emerge?

Such questions are addressed in a younger branch of evolutionary game theory. It allows strategies to develop over time by using the evolutionary mechanism (or genetic algorithm) of:

- **variation** (or mutation) of strategic behaviour or response to the environment;
- **selection**: testing for success (or fitness) of the variations;
- **retention** (or heredity) of successful variations.

That is the same mechanism we will encounter in Chapter 11, where we introduce evolutionary approaches to organizations. It is the mechanism operating in our genes, bringing about the evolution of humankind. It is a mechanism that can also be modelled using a computer to operate on strategies (represented as strings of bits). That is exactly what Robert Axelrod did in cooperation with John Holland.

Instead of humans proposing strategies for the prisoner's dilemma, he started with a population of strictly random strategies. He then allowed strategies to evolve on the computer and slug it out in a 'survival of the fittest'. Essentially, the genetic algorithm enables *learning*.

First, he held the environment constant by playing the evolving strategies against fixed proportions of competitor strategies. What were the results? Well, quite remarkable. From a strictly random start, the genetic algorithm evolved populations the *median* member of which was just as successful as the *best* rule in the tournament – tit-for-tat. Most strategies actually resembled tit-for-tat: 95 per cent of the time they would make the same choice as tit-for-tat in the same situation. However, the effective strategies had evolved certain variations, such as (Axelrod, 1997, p. 21):

> very effective rules evolved by breaking the most important advice developed in the computer tournament, namely, to be 'nice', that is, never to be the first to defect. These highly effective rules always defect on the very first move, and sometimes on the second move as well, and use the choices of the other player to discriminate what should be done next. The highly effective rules then had responses that allowed them to 'apologize' and get to mutual cooperation with most of the unexploitable representatives, and different responses that allowed them to exploit a representative that was exploitable.

So, in a fixed environment, it pays to learn which competitors are exploitable and which are not. Maximum effectiveness is then reached by maximizing cooperation with cooperating strategies and maximizing exploitation of the exploitable strategies. Note that that outcome crucially depends on the environment being structured as fixed proportions of competing strategies: the exploitable strategies retain their proportion despite being taken advantage of.

Then, Axelrod relaxed the assumption of a constant environment. Instead of playing against fixed proportions of competitor strategies, the environment now evolved itself. That is called an **ecological simulation**, which selection process using the average game pay-offs of the various strategies as fitness criterion determines the evolution of the population. The more successful strategies increase their proportion in the population and the less successful ones decrease their proportion. What happens now?

Ecological simulation.

Typically, cooperation first decreases and then increases:

> From a random start, the population first evolves away from whatever cooperation was initially displayed. The less cooperative rules do better than the more cooperative rules because at first there are few other players who are responsive – and when the other player is unresponsive, the most effective thing for an individual to do is simply defect ... However, after about ten or twenty generations the trend starts to reverse. Some players evolve a pattern of reciprocating what cooperation they find, and these reciprocating players tend to do well because they can do very well with others who reciprocate without being exploited for very long by those who just defect ... As the reciprocators do well, they spread in the population, resulting in more and more cooperation and greater and greater effectiveness.

So, in an ecological simulation, where the proportion of strategies in the population varies with their success, 'not nice' strategies destroy the basis of their initial success because the exploited (unsuccessful) strategies become a decreasing proportion of the environment. Now, the evolving ability to discriminate between those who will reciprocate cooperation and those who will not allows reciprocators to jointly do well and increase their proportion of the population.

Coevolution

If all strategies in a population can evolve, we are simulating **coevolution**. Strategies can learn and evolve. Their success depends on the speed of their learning versus that of the others in the population. Success is never guaranteed as new mutations continuously arise, either through random variation or recombination (when two strategies combine in a novel way).

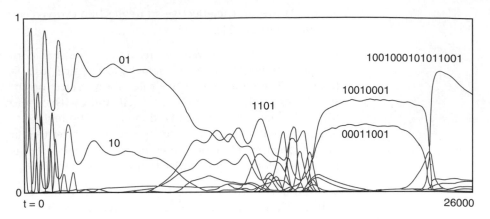

Figure 5.12 Coevolution of strategies
Source: Lindgref (1997)

While most of these will fail, a few will represent successful *innovations*. Successful innovations will spread in the population, until they meet the boundaries of their success or new competition. To get an impression of the coevolution of such populations, have a look at Figure 5.12. Without getting into the details of this simulation, it is essentially a coevolutionary simulation over 26,000 generations of strategies for the prisoner's dilemma, allowing the development of memory (longer strings have longer memories). So, in the simulation, strategies develop from simple to more complex. Notice the progression in the simulation:

1 Initially, a few simple strategies fight it out (with 01 being most successful).
2 Then, evolution creates longer memory strategies and a period of turbulence sets in (with 1101 being the most successful, but with many competitors).
3 In a next stage, two strategies emerge that coexist and together wipe out almost all competition in a period of relative stability, until;
4 A new mutant strategy develops with an even longer memory (1001000101011001) that rapidly becomes dominant but the success of which already starts to fade towards the end of the simulation.

This example of a simulation, allowing the evolution of strategies, shows how a population may develop over time, never reaching any stable equilibrium, with increased learning and new innovations popping up continuously, and periods of relative stability alternating with high levels of turbulence.

Let us sum up some of the lessons we have learned from applying the genetic algorithm to the iterated prisoner's dilemma:

■ *Evolution can be a better designer than humans* The genetic algorithm produced strategies that can be more effective than tit-for-tat in specific environments. Allowing agents to be *adaptive* (as in evolutionary game theory) can be more effective than only allowing them to be rational (as in classical game theory).
■ *Cooperation can emerge from reciprocity* That is now confirmed not only for human entries to the tournament but also emergent strategies in fixed and evolving environments.

■ *There is often an optimal balance between cooperation and exploitation* Already in the tournament setting, the introduction of noise calls for forgiveness, but too much forgiveness invites exploitation. If the environment contains exploitable strategies, it usually pays to learn how to identify them and take advantage of their exploitability.

■ *Strategies and environments interact and coevolve* Depending on the specifications of strategies, the environment can come to be dominated by one (environmentally stable) strategy, into a (dynamic) equilibrium between strategies (as in the Hawk–Dove game) and become highly turbulent as strategies continually learn and evolve (as in Figure 5.12). Alternatively, the properties of the environment determine the relative success of strategies. In Chapters 11 and 12 we will further explore how organizations and environments can coevolve.

We will not delve further into the exciting new field of evolutionary game theory here (see Gintis, 2000, for an introduction). We will, however, build on its foundations when we discuss *evolutionary approaches to organizations* in Chapter 11 and *complex adaptive systems* in Chapter 12. To summarize, evolutionary game theory primarily studies the development of **populations** rather than the rational decisionmaking of an individual. In those populations there is a variety ($N \geq 2$) of strategies to survive and compete. Interactions between players (or agents) are simulated by having the computer organize chance encounters (random pairing). In many rounds, the strategies of the different players are tested for success (or fitness). Successful strategies increase in the population and unsuccessful ones are 'selected out'. If an entire population adopts a strategy and cannot be invaded by a competing alternative strategy, we say that an 'evolutionary stable strategy' has been selected. Alternatively, two strategies may come to a (dynamic) equilibrium, as in the Hawk–Dove game. If strategies are allowed to evolve (through mutation), such an equilibrium may prove to be elusive as new innovations are continuously tested and successful ones are selected for further replication (and mutation). This latter representation of evolutionary dynamics may be close to our real-world development of organizational populations over time – a topic that we will return to in Chapters 11 and 12.

Populations (margin)

5.7 Summary: insights from game theory

In this chapter we have given an introduction to game theory. Game theory is, first of all, a powerful tool for analyzing situations in which two or more people have to make interdependent decisions.

Several types of game have been discussed. In the one-stage game for two players we distinguished between sequential and simultaneous games. In a sequential game, one of the players moves first and the other player can observe that move. In a simultaneous game, each player has to make her decision not knowing what the other player has decided or will decide. The difference between a sequential and a simultaneous game has to do with lack of information. Without observable information, coordination is difficult to achieve.

The main principle to remember in sequential games is 'look ahead and reason back'. We saw how a potential entrant can use that principle in the entry game. A threat by the incumbent firm to lower prices after entry is an empty threat if, after entry has occurred, it is in the incumbent's own interest to not lower prices.

The incumbent can make its threat credible by making a commitment that irreversibly alters the pay-offs so that, after entry, it is in the incumbent's interest to execute the threat. By applying the principle of looking ahead and reasoning back, we saw how the incumbent firm can determine whether or not it is in its interest to change the pay-offs (and, thus, pose a credible threat). Of course, it is again a necessary condition that the information about the commitment is available to the entrant. If it is, the entrant can apply the same principle of looking ahead and reasoning back to determine whether profitable entry will be possible or not. By changing the structure of the game, the incumbent can thus influence the incentives for the entrant and, thereby, the likely outcome of the game.

The role of observable information became even more apparent in the discussion of different types of auction. In open auctions, the private information of most bidders is gradually revealed. Only the winner can still possess private information that would have led him to bid substantially higher, if he were forced to. We saw how the seller may therefore consider changing the design of the auction to a two-stage process with a Dutch auction as a second stage. That was another example of when one party may change the structure of the game, the incentives for the other party and, thus, the likely outcome.

In sealed bid auctions, no information about the private valuations of bidders is revealed during the auction. In the face of this uncertainty, winners run the risk of suffering the winner's curse – that is, obtaining the prize as a consequence of making the most optimistic estimates.

For simultaneous games (such as the prisoner's dilemma), we explained the concept of a dominant strategy. A dominant strategy is one that is best whatever the other player does. In the prisoner's dilemma, each player has a dominant strategy. That strategy is to defect. Hence, if the game is played only once, we would expect both players to defect. However, mutual cooperation is better for both of them. If they can trust each other – that is, if they can both make binding commitments – then surely they will agree to cooperate.

The problem in the prisoner's dilemma is that, after such an agreement has been made, each party has an incentive to cheat. That is a problem, too, for the stability of cartels. After an agreement has been made to restrict output by cartel members, each member has an incentive to increase output. Another problem for cartels is that governments may offer incentives to defect by adopting a 'leniency policy'.

Finally, we explored the consequences of playing a game repeatedly. We saw that cooperation between individual players may then evolve even in the adverse conditions of a prisoner's dilemma. In the iterated prisoner's dilemma, a strategy consists of a set of rules that specify what action to take given the history of the game so far.

In computer tournaments, tit-for-tat has proven to be a good strategy. That is probably because tit-for-tat is nice (it is never the first to defect), forgiving (it is able to restore cooperation after a defection by the other player) and retaliatory (the other player is punished immediately for defection). However, when mistakes are possible, tit-for-tat may be too aggressive. As the strategy now includes the history of the game so far, players may invest in building reputations. It was shown that reputations can be considered to be assets that reflect commitment.

When games are played for many rounds, and the focus is more on populations than on individuals, we enter into evolutionary game theory. We examined several questions that can be addressed by evolutionary game theory, including the following.

- What is an 'evolutionary stable strategy' (ESS) – that is, one immune to the invasion of the population by another strategy?
- How can we model the mix of strategies in a population when there is not one ESS (using the Hawk–Dove game)? We saw how a population may tend towards an equilibrium balance between competing strategies.
- What happens when we relax the assumption that strategies are fixed and, instead, allow for evolution of strategies (through application of the genetic algorithm)? We saw that learning and innovation enter into the picture and the population may not tend towards equilibrium. Instead, it may be in continuous evolution and flux, just like our own human evolution, as well as the evolution of organizations, to which we will turn in Chapter 11.

This chapter completes the set of Chapters 2–5 in which we have explained the fundamental concepts and methods underlying the economic approaches to organizations. In Chapters 6–11, we will build on that knowledge to introduce economic approaches to organizations. As you will see, the approaches differ in terms of the problems addressed, concepts and language used and modes of analysis. This introduction to game theory will help you discern, first, the basic features of the settings in which the players make their decisions in each of the subsequent chapters and, second, distinguish between different levels of analysis – individual players and populations of players – that we will both further explore in subsequent chapters. In chapter 12, we return to the common perspective in these approaches and highlight their similarities and differences.

Questions

1 When corporations want to divest individual business units, they often employ the services of an investment banker, such as Goldman Sachs or Morgan Stanley. Such investment bankers often use an auction process to find the most suitable buyers for the business. It is customary that these auctions are two-stage and sealed bid.

- The first stage consists of soliciting non-binding bids from a wide range of potential buyers on the basis of general information distributed in a bid book.
- The second stage consists of a 'due diligence' procedure in which a limited set of potential buyers may investigate the acquisition candidate in depth as a basis for their final (binding) bid.
- Discuss the advantages of this procedure for the corporation selling the business unit.

2 Suppose you are a competitor of the business unit to be sold under the conditions sketched in Question 1. You have no interest or not enough money to acquire the divested company, but you would like to obtain the private information that will be available for inspection in Round 2. You contemplate the possibility of making a sufficiently high (non-binding) bid in Round 1 in order to be admitted to Round 2, only to decline making a final, binding bid in Round 2.

   Apart from legal reasons (you would not be negotiating in good faith), which economic reason could deter you from this course of action?

3 Look at the list of strategies against which tit-for-tat competed in Axelrod's tournament (Section 5.5.2). It varies from permanent retaliation to uneven. Against which individual strategies do you expect tit-for-tat to win, tie and lose? Why did tit-for-tat win the tournament?

4 Can you explain why tit-for-tat is an 'evolutionary stable strategy' in Axelrod's tournament?

Part II

Economic Approaches

6 Behavioural theory of the firm

6.1 Introduction

How does a business firm make economic decisions? That is the central question of the behavioural theory of the firm developed by March, Simon and Cyert (March and Simon, 1958; Cyert and March, 1963). Examples of economic decisions include those regarding price, output, advertising levels and investments in machinery.

In standard microeconomics it is assumed that firms are holistic entities seeking to maximize their profits. By contrast, the behavioural theory of the firm postulates the firm as a coalition of (groups of) participants, each with their own objectives. This is the subject of Section 6.2. Such a coalition of participants need not have maximization of profits as its sole objective. In fact, the process of defining the goals of the organization is the first step in describing actual decision processes within the firm. The second step is to describe how the organization forms expectations on which the decision processes are based. The third and last step is to describe the process of organizational choice. These three steps are dealt with in Sections 6.3 to 6.5.

The behavioural theory of the firm is not based on the 'full rationality' assumption of standard microeconomics (see Chapter 2), but instead uses the concept of 'bounded rationality' which emphasizes cognitive and informational *limits* to rationality. This concept is explained in Section 6.5 in the context of organizational choice. In Section 6.6 we discuss how more recent work has led to further insights into human decisionmaking and choice. In particular, the work of Kahneman and Tversky (1974, 1979) has shown that we not only have limits to full rationality, but also show some systematic *deviations* from the concept of full rationality. These insights form the foundation of Behavioural Economics. Section 6.7 provides a summary of this chapter.

6.2 The firm as a coalition of participants

The behavioural theory of the firm postulates that it is a coalition of participants. Each participant receives from the organization *inducements* and, in return, makes *contributions* to the organization. Each participant will continue to participate only as long as the inducements offered are as great as or greater

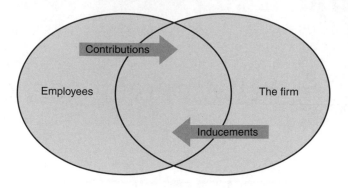

Figure 6.1 The firm and its employees in behavioural theory

than (measured in terms of the *individual's* values and the alternatives open to him) the contributions he is asked to make. Hence, the organization will continue to exist only so long as the contributions are sufficient to provide inducements in large enough measure to draw forth these contributions.

Participants in the firm are employees, investors, suppliers, distributors, consumers and possibly others. **Contributions** made by employees include not only the labour hours they put in but also their ideas for improvements, intelligence and so on. **Inducements** offered to employees include monetary payments (like pay and pensions), but also non-monetary benefits, such as self-achievement and job satisfaction. The relationship between the firm and its employees is illustrated in Figure 6.1. A similar figure can be sketched for any other group of participants. The figure suggests that the firm is more than just one group of participants (here the employees). It also suggests that employees have other roles outside the firm, such as in their families, their communities, their churches etc.

In order to illustrate the differences between the behavioural theory and standard microeconomics, we discuss the decision of an employee to continue participation. In our description of standard microeconomics, employees receive pay in return for a number of hours of work. In behavioural theory, employees receive several different inducements, including monetary and non-monetary payments. In mathematical terms we would say that they receive a vector of inducements (that is, several inducements of different types). They also make a vector of contributions. That, however, is not a fundamental difference as standard microeconomics can also handle a vector of inducements and contributions. The fundamental difference lies in the *information* that employees have concerning alternative job opportunities.

In standard microeconomics we assume that each employee knows exactly what she could earn elsewhere. As soon as an employee sees more can be earned elsewhere, she will take the other job. So, for the same work, all companies must pay the same – in a competitive labour market there can be only one price for labour of a particular type. In behavioural theory we assume that each employee has an **aspiration level** concerning the rate of pay. She will be content and not start looking for another job so long as the pay received is greater than or equal to that aspiration level. If the pay received

Contributions

Inducements

Aspiration level

continues to be higher than that aspiration level, then the aspiration level is slowly adjusted upwards. Thus, it takes some time before the aspiration level will reach the pay she regularly receives. The aspiration level is also adjusted upwards if the employee hears that another company pays more than the aspiration level for the same work. That adjustment also occurs slowly, so it takes some time before she becomes dissatisfied.

If after some time there is a large enough gap between the employee's aspiration level and the pay received, she will start to look for another job. If the employee finds another job that pays significantly more than the current job, she will leave. This process of adjusting one's aspiration level and looking for another job may take a considerable amount of time.

The situation is even more complicated than described above because inducements contain not only monetary payments but also various other benefits. Information about these other benefits may be even harder to obtain than information about levels of pay. It is, for example, usually very hard to find out what the atmosphere among colleagues in another organization is really like. The harder it is to obtain information about inducements and contributions that other firms offer and demand, the slower is the process of adjusting aspiration levels. In behavioural theory the labour market is not a market of perfect competition. Differences in levels of pay and other working conditions can exist for long periods of time because workers cannot compare the inducements offered and the contributions demanded by other firms. They simply lack that information.

For other participants we can sketch a similar picture concerning the decision to stay with the coalition or leave. Consider consumers. In the model of perfectly competitive markets, price is all that matters for a consumer (remember that in the model of a perfectly competitive market, products are homogeneous: there are no differences between the products of different producers). Moreover, we assume that consumers know exactly what prices quoted by different producers are. Naturally they buy only from the cheapest source. Thus, in the model of a competitive market, all prices must be equal. If producers quote different prices, only the one with the lowest price will sell anything; all others will cease to exist.

In behavioural theory we assume that consumers do not know exactly what prices are quoted by other producers. A consumer continues to buy from the same producer so long as the price is less than or equal to his aspiration level. If a consumer gets more information on lower prices quoted by other producers he will slowly adjust the aspiration level downwards.

This picture becomes more realistic if we allow quality differences between products from different producers. Then a consumer also has an aspiration level with respect to quality. It seems quite reasonable to assume that a consumer has only vague information about quality levels of products offered by other producers. Thus, aspiration levels with respect to quality will be adjusted only slowly.

For every group of participants we can sketch a picture like that in Figure 6.1. If we do so and combine all those pictures we arrive at a picture like that in Figure 6.2. It shows that the firm is a coalition of groups of participants and each group of participants has other roles and interests outside the firm.

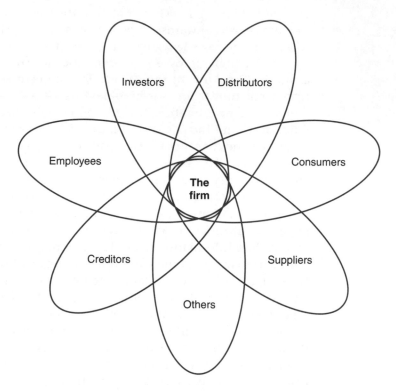

Figure 6.2 The firm as a coalition of groups of participants

The groups of participants in Figure 6.2 are often referred to as *stakeholders* (each group has a 'stake' in the firm). Stakeholders include the financial investors and creditors (the shareholders, banks providing loans, and other creditors) as well as employees, suppliers and customers. According to standard microeconomics, managers should serve only the interests of the shareholders. According to behavioural theory, however, a firm can survive only if its managers take care of the interests of all stakeholders, not just the shareholders (Box 6.1 develops this point further).

Box 6.1 Stakeholders and shareholders

One of the liveliest current debates in the management field focuses on the question of which interests the management of a company should serve: those of the shareholders (only) or of the broader set of 'stakeholders' (which includes the employees, customers, suppliers and the community as well as the shareholders)?

Economic theories give different answers to this question. In Chapter 7 we see that agency theory tends to view the shareholders as the owners of the firm. In this view the managers should act as agents of the owners of the firm, maximizing the owner's wealth. In everyday management language, this view implies that the management of a company should maximize shareholder value.

Behavioural theory of the firm has a different perspective. It views the firm as a coalition of groups of participants. In this view, management's task is not to maximize the wealth of any particular group of participants, such as shareholders; rather, it is to enhance the firm's wealth by serving all interests of participant (that is, stakeholder) groups well. (Behavioural theory leaves the question unanswered as to what should happen with any economic surplus (profit) that is left after all participants have received their necessary inducements. In agency theory, this residual value belongs to the shareholders.)

In practice, many different views exist. One clear proponent of the stakeholder model was Sam Palmisano, who stepped down in 2012 as Chief Executive of IBM after a very successful tenure of ten years:

During his tenure, IBM has been a textbook case how to drive change in a big company...Mr Palmisano said his guiding framework boiled down to four questions:

- "Why would someone spend their money with you – so, what is unique about you?"
- "Why would somebody work for you?"
- "Why would society allow you to operate in their defined geography – their country?"
- "And why would somebody invest their money in you?"

Mr Paul Polman is the Chief Executive of Unilever, the Anglo-Dutch consumer goods company:

Mr Polman makes it clear that shareholders are not exactly the first thing on his mind. "I do not work for the shareholder, to be honest; I work for the consumer, the customer," he says. "I discovered a long time ago that if I focus on doing the right thing for the long term to improve the lives of consumers and customers all over the world, the business results will come....I'm not driven and I don't drive this business model by driving shareholder value. I drive this business model by focusing on the consumer and customer in a responsible way, and I know that shareholder value can come."

Sources: 'Retired chief leaves behind a refashioned IBM', *The New York Times (global edition),* 2 January 2012; 'The outsider in a hurry to shake up his company', *The Financial Times,* 5 April 2010

It is clear from the discussion that in behavioural theory there is competition between firms in the labour market, the market for final products, the capital market and so on. However, behavioural theory focuses not on competition between firms, but on the process of decisionmaking within the firm. The competitive context in various markets is further taken as given.

6.3 Organizational goals

6.3.1 Bargaining and organizational slack

The process of decisionmaking within the firm starts with the definition of its goals. In standard microeconomics we assume that the firm has a single goal – usually profit maximization. In behavioural theory the firm is viewed as a **coalition of participants.** Each participant has his or her own goals. Ordinarily, those goals will not coincide. In general, we expect a conflict of goals from different participants. Consumers cannot be offered lower prices and employees higher pay without lowering profits (the inducements for the providers of equity capital).

Coalition of participants

Bargaining power

In behavioural theory it is postulated that the goals of a firm are arrived at through a bargaining process. During that bargaining process both the composition and the general goals of the coalition are established. The **bargaining power** of each potential participant depends on how unique the contribution is that he can offer to the coalition. So, an unskilled worker in a country where unskilled labour is plentiful does not have much bargaining power (unless there are strong labour unions). Someone possessing a highly specialized skill that is essential to the success of the coalition has much more bargaining power. For the providers of equity capital, profit maximization or maximization of the value of the firm is an important objective. The extent to which they succeed in realizing their objective depends on the relative bargaining power of the various groups of participants.

The upshot of this discussion is that a real firm ordinarily has no single goal or clearly defined objective function. Only individual participants have goals. Those goals are in the form of aspiration levels. The real achievement of the particular goal of a certain participant can be only temporarily below his aspiration level. For all participants, achievement levels will be at least equal to their aspiration levels most of the time. For some they will be above their aspiration levels.

Organizational slack

The difference between total resources and the total payments necessary to preserve the coalition is termed **organizational slack.** Participants' aspiration levels adjust to actual payments and alternatives external to the organization. Hence, in the long run, we would expect aspiration levels to be equal to actual payments *and* alternatives external to the organization. If this were the case, there would be no organizational slack. The rate of payments made to coalition members would then be analogous to factor prices in a perfectly competitive market. However, behavioural theory states that markets are imperfect. The basic reason is that information about levels of goal achievement participants can realize if they join another organization is difficult to obtain, especially concerning non-monetary payments, so aspiration levels adjust only slowly. In a world without change, aspiration levels would, after some time, equal actual payments and external alternatives. In a changing world – for example, in a world with technological progress – we normally expect to have organizational slack.

6.3.2 Operational subgoals

Operational subgoals

In a real firm, an overall goal such as profit maximization needs to be translated into several **operational subgoals.** It is often impossible to avoid a conflict between those operational subgoals.

As an example, imagine a firm making soap noodles. Soap noodles are little pieces of soap in the form of noodles. They are made in a chemical plant that uses animal fat as a basic raw material. They are sold to soap manufacturers, who press soap noodles into tablets and give the soap a colour, a scent and a brand name.

Suppose you are in charge of the soap noodle firm. You have two managers reporting to you – a production manager and a sales manager. You know that the number of soap noodles sold depends on price, level of effort of your sales manager and a random factor. You also know that the real production costs per unit depend on the number of units sold per year, number and size of changes in production levels during the year and level of effort of your production manager. The sales manager makes decisions on prices quoted to individual customers; the production manager decides how much to produce each week.

Assume for the moment that soap noodles can be stored on site at no cost. You want to give each manager an operational subgoal that is consistent with your overall goal of profit maximization. You can do this by specifying the following operational subgoals.

For the sales manager:

$$\text{maximize } N \times (P - SC)$$

where
   N = number of units sold
   P = price
   SC = standard unit cost

For the production manager you can specify the following goal:

$$\text{minimize } RC$$

where
   RC = real unit cost

This is equivalent to maximizing $(SC - RC)$ as SC is fixed.

Now, for simplicity, assume that the production cost per unit does not depend on the number of units sold (that is, assume there are no scale economies to be had in production). The production manager's goal is then equivalent to:

$$\text{maximize } N \times (SC - RC)$$

We can now combine the goals of the two managers thus:

$$\text{maximize } [N \times (P - SC)] + [N \times (SC - RC)]$$

That is equivalent to:

$$\text{maximize } N \times (P - RC)$$

As we assume inventory costs are zero, that is equivalent to profit maximization. If inventories can be stored without cost, the sales manager and the production manager can make their decisions independently. In reality, inventories cannot be stored without cost. If inventory costs are not negligible, you cannot specify operational subgoals for your two managers without creating a conflict of interests between them.

Who should be responsible for inventory costs? The inventory level depends on the decisions made by both the sales manager and production manager. If you make the production manager responsible for inventory costs, you create a conflict. The production manager will want to keep the inventory levels as low as possible, but that imposes the risk of stock-out on the sales manager. She would prefer safe levels of inventory in order to be able to satisfy customer demand at all times. However, if you make the sales manager responsible for inventory costs, you also create a conflict. Now the sales manager will want to keep inventory levels as low as possible. She will try to achieve that by frequently ordering very small lots. That means very small lots in manufacturing. The production manager would prefer large lots in order to minimize production costs. If you introduce an inventory manager, what subgoal can you specify for her? You would surely create a conflict between your inventory manager and your sales manager as well as one between your inventory manager and your production manager.

This example demonstrates that it is difficult, and often impossible, to specify operational subgoals that are consistent with profit maximization and do not lead to conflicts between managers of functional departments.

In behavioural theory we assume that operational subgoals are specified and given to managers of functional departments. With each subgoal goes an aspiration level. Managers are rewarded if they at least reach those aspiration levels. This does not eliminate conflict between managers of functional departments – it is *quasi-resolution of conflict* rather than *complete* resolution of conflict.

6.4 Organizational expectations

An important assumption of standard microeconomics is symmetrical information: everyone has the same information. In behavioural theory that assumption is relaxed: everyone does not have the same information.

In the soap noodle firm, you have a production manager and a sales manager reporting to you. The production manager decides how much to produce each week. To make that decision, he needs information on future sales. He can make a sales forecast by extrapolating historical data on shipments made. He can also ask the sales manager to make a sales forecast. It is likely that the sales manager can make the better forecast: the sales manager can make the same extrapolation as the production manager, but she can improve on it because of her knowledge of recent changes in market situations.

Suppose the sales manager makes a sales forecast each week. Will the production manager now use that sales forecast only? Empirical evidence shows that many production managers do not – they continue to make their own sales forecast. The reason is that they know:

- the sales manager is more often than not too optimistic (maybe people with an optimistic nature tend to become sales managers);
- the sales manager has an incentive to make an optimistic sales forecast in order to reduce the probability of a stock-out.

The above example demonstrates the use of expectations in decisionmaking within the firm. Expectations are the result of drawing inferences from available information. Decisionmakers within the firm may have different information. In addition, they may draw different inferences from the same set of information. Hence, even if two people within the same firm have the same information, they may still have different expectations.

6.5 Organizational choice

Another important assumption made in standard microeconomics is that behaviour of firms can be adequately described as maximizing behaviour. That itself makes two assumptions:

- at the moment of decisionmaking, firms know all the decision alternatives;
- firms are able to compare all alternatives and choose the one that maximizes the objective function.

Behavioural theory rejects both assumptions. In the real world, firms have to make decisions under conditions of partial ignorance. That is, they have to make a decision on a proposal (for example, to accept or reject a **proposal** to develop a new product) without knowing what alternatives will turn up the next day. Of course, they can also decide to devote resources to search for alternatives before deciding on the present proposal.

In the context of standard microeconomics we would have to assume that firms are able to calculate the expected marginal revenue from searching for an alternative and the expected marginal cost of searching for an alternative. Firms would then, presumably, continue searching until the marginal cost of additional searching equalled the marginal revenue of additional searching. If many alternatives were potentially available, firms would invest a lot of time (and resources) in searching. So much, in fact, that other firms could realize significant advantages in deciding more quickly. Moreover, in the real world, firms cannot possibly hope to evaluate all potential new products against each other.

In behavioural theory we therefore assume that alternatives are evaluated one at a time. Firms do not maximize an objective function. Instead, they make a rough estimate of several consequences of a decision alternative. For example, for a proposal to develop a new product, they try to estimate:

- the size of the market;
- their expected market share;
- the price and production cost of the new product;
- the development cost.

There are perhaps other variables as well. They have aspiration levels for all of these variables. If the market is 'large enough', if their expected market share is 'sufficient', if the margin between price and production cost is 'reasonable' and if the development cost is 'not too high', then they accept the proposal. They do not maximize in the sense of evaluating all possible proposals for new products at the same time. Their behaviour is better described as **satisficing** – that is, searching for a solution that meets aspiration levels and is therefore acceptable.

Satisficing

In behavioural theory, then, we assume that firms satisfice rather than maximize. One reason for this is that decision alternatives come one at a time.

Another reason is that human decision makers are simply unable to make all the calculations necessary to compare all the alternatives. The calculations often are too complex. To put it another way, the capacity of the human mind to make all the necessary calculations is often too small. In behavioural theory, therefore, we assume **bounded rationality** – we assume that human decision makers may try to maximize but are not always able to do so: they are *intendedly* rational, but only *limitedly* so. We return to the notion of bounded rationality in Chapter 8 on transaction cost economics. It has proven to be an important concept. Therefore, we sum it up here in the words of James March (1994, pp. 8–9):

> 'Studies of decision making in the real world suggest that not all alternatives are known, that not all consequences are considered, and that not all preferences are evoked at the same time. Instead of considering all alternatives, decision makers typically appear to consider only a few and to look at them sequentially rather than simultaneously. Decision makers do not consider all consequences of their alternatives. They focus on some and ignore others. Relevant information about consequences is not sought, and available information is not used. Instead of having a complete, consistent set of preferences, decision makers seem to have incomplete and inconsistent goals, not all of which are considered at the same time ... Instead of calculating the 'best possible action', they search for an action that is 'good enough' ... The core notion of limited (or bounded) rationality is that individuals are intendedly rational. Although decision makers try to be rational, they are constrained by limited cognitive capabilities and incomplete information, and thus their actions may be less than completely rational in spite of their best intentions and efforts'.

Finally, there is a third reason for firms satisficing rather than maximizing. The firm is seen as a coalition of participants, each having his own objectives. If a firm has no single objective function, how can it maximize? Instead, organizational choice is described as a process of deciding on alternatives one at a time. As soon as an alternative is found that meets the aspiration levels of all coalition members, it is accepted.

Suppose a firm wants to buy a new software package for order processing. Suppose, further, that the sales manager, production manager and controller form a three-person committee that has to make the decision. Behavioural theory assumes that each may have a different criterion for choosing the software package. For example, the sales manager wants to buy a package that provides information on inventories available for sale in real time, the production manager wants one that allows him to make a reliable sales forecast and the controller one that produces invoices as soon as the order is shipped. The three-person committee cannot maximize as their three criteria cannot be translated into a single criterion (see Box 6.2). Instead, they start to look for a package that meets certain minimum standards (aspiration levels) for each of those three criteria. As soon as they have found a package that is acceptable to all of them, they stop searching for another package.

Box 6.2 Decisionmaking by a committee

Consider a three-person committee. Suppose each person wants to maximize his or her own objective. Suppose, further, that all objectives are quantifiable and you denote them as C_1, C_2 and C_3. The three-person committee can maximize only if these three objectives can be combined into a single objective function, as follows:

$$C_0 = \alpha C_1 + \beta C_2 + \gamma C_3$$

That requires the three-person committee to:

- accept each other's objectives;
- agree on the weights (α, β, γ) assigned to each objective.

Only if the members of the committee are able to meet both conditions, can they jointly maximize an overall objective function (C_0). If either of the two conditions is not met – as will often be the case in real life – satisficing is a ready alternative procedure. It requires only that each member of the committee is able to specify his or her own aspiration level. If an alternative is found that meets all three aspiration levels, a unanimous decision can be made.

6.6 From bounded rationality to behavioural economics

Herbert Simon and James March were concerned with the limits to the 'full rationality' model of *homo economicus*. They maintained that most decision-makers were *intendedly* rational, but only *limitedly* so. Later research revealed that may be still a somewhat too generous description of human decision-making. Further limits on rationality were uncovered in the work of Daniel Kahneman and Amos Tversky. They found that many judgments and decisions, made in conditions of uncertainty, are subject to **Biases** (systematic errors) and are taken with **Heuristics** (simple rules of thumb), such as the following:

Biases

Heuristics

- *Availability* People base their prediction of an outcome on the vividness and emotional impact of recent information rather than on actual probability. For example, most people overrate the probability of airplane crashes versus car crashes, because plane accidents are reported more frequently and vividly.
- *Anchoring* The tendency to rely too heavily on one (early) piece of information when making decisions. That specific piece of information then becomes an 'anchor', an initial value from which people make their adjustments to arrive at the outcome. For instance, when you ask a group of people 'What is the success rate of acquisitions? Is your estimate higher or lower than 50%? Please indicate how much higher or lower'. you will get higher values than if you had set the anchor at 30 per cent. That is because most people adjust from the anchor given.

■ *Representativeness* Basing your prediction not on an individual case but the class of cases you think that individual case belongs to (or is representative of). That bias leads you to 'jump to conclusions' about the individual case. See Box 6.3 for an example.

Box 6.3 Who does Steve represent?

Consider the question below and assume that Steve was selected at random from a representative sample:

An individual has been described by a neighbor as follows: "Steve is very shy and withdrawn, invariably helpful but with little interest in people or in the world of reality. A meek and tidy soul, he has a need for order and structure, and a passion for detail." Is Steve more likely to be a librarian or a farmer?

Have you made up your mind?

In answering this question, most people use the **heuristic** of *representativeness,* basically using stereotypes to judge whether Steve belongs to the class of librarians or farmers. What most people ignore is that there are many more male farmers than male librarians (in the USA more than 20 times as many). In statistical terminology, people tend to ignore such differences in base rates and base their judgment far too much on the fit between the given description and their stereotypes of librarians and farmers. This leads to a systematic **bias** to overestimate the probability of an unlikely (low base-rate) outcome.

Source: D. Kahneman (2011), *Thinking, fast and slow,* London: Penguin.

Since the pioneering work of Kahneman and Tversky, quite a few deviations from the 'full rationality' model of *homo economicus* have been solidly established. Some further examples include:

■ *Loss aversion* In many decision contexts, there is an 'upside' (a chance for a gain) and a 'downside' (a chance for a loss). Loss aversion means that most people do not weight these chances equally. You can measure the extent of your own aversion to losses by asking yourself the question: What is the smallest gain that I need to balance an equal chance to lose $100? For most people this amount is somewhere between $150 and $250: technically, their 'loss aversion ratio' is in the range of 1.5 to 2.5.

■ *Endowment effect* Suppose you are a soccer fan and you have obtained a ticket to see your national team play at the World Championships. You have paid $200 for this ticket, but you would have been willing to pay up to $500. The match is sold out and you learn on the Internet that other people (perhaps richer or more desperate) are offering $2000 for a ticket. Would you sell? In fact, most of the audience at sold-out events do not sell. This is one manifestation of the endowment effect, the tendency to value goods that we already hold to consume or otherwise enjoy higher than our willingness to pay for these goods before owning them.

■ *Reciprocity and Fairness* In chapter 5 (Box 5.10) we referred to the *ultimatum game* to show that most people apply social norms like reciprocity and fairness to exchange situations. In the ultimatum game, proposers offer more money than the *homo economicus* model would predict, whereas responders reject offers that are below their threshold of fairness. See further Box 8.4.

Such experimental findings have provided a richer description of the cognitive bases of human decisionmaking. This richer description forms the foundation of *Behavioural Economics,* in which the insights of cognitive psychology are integrated with neoclassical economic theory.

In particular decision contexts, behavioural economics explains human decisionmaking significantly better than standard microeconomics and it also generates policy prescriptions for how to counter the effects of heuristics and biases. Box 6.4 gives two striking examples.

Box 6.4 Framing

Do you think it would make a difference whether we present a specific medical treatment as having:

- a 90% one-month survival rate, or;
- a 10% one-month mortality rate?

Objectively, the two statements are the same. Emotionally, they are not. Hospital patients and medical doctors alike are more inclined to choose a treatment with a 90 per cent survival rate than another treatment with a 10 per cent mortality rate. This is an example of the *framing* effect, where the phrasing of the critical question or statistic has a dramatic effect on the decision outcome. Framing is related to loss aversion: people perceive gains and losses differently.

Many countries have regulated organ donation. But these regulations produce strikingly different rates of organ donations in neighbouring countries:

- nearly 100% in Austria but only 12% in Germany;
- 86% in Sweden but only 4% in Denmark.

Again the explanation resides in the way the critical question is framed. The high-donation countries have an opt-out system where individuals must take a simple action to indicate that they do *not* wish to be a donor. In the low-donation countries, an opt-in system is used: you must check a box that you *do* wish to become a donor.

Sources: E.J. Johnson and D. Goldstein (2003), '*Do defaults save lives?*', Science, 302:1338–1339, and Kahneman (2011)

Behavioural economics has shown that we must pay considerable attention to the context in which decisions are taken. The limits to (full) rationality sometimes lead to dramatically different outcomes, dependent on the decision context provided (as shown in Box 6.4) while in other cases they are 'often irrelevant to the predictions of economic theory, which work out with great precision in some situations and provide good approximations in many others' (Kahneman, 2011, p.286). Furthermore, we have to keep in mind that we are specifically concerned with organizational contexts for decisionmaking in this book. Organizations may adopt routines to foster rational decisionmaking:

'Organizations are better than individuals when it comes to avoiding errors because they naturally think more slowly and have the power to impose orderly procedures. Organizations can institute and enforce the application of useful checklists, as well as more elaborate exercises...At least in part by providing a distinctive vocabulary, organizations can also encourage a culture in which people watch out for one another as they approach minefields. Whatever else it produces, an organization is a factory that manufactures judgments and decisions. Every factory must have ways to ensure the quality of its products in the initial design, in fabrication, and in final inspections. The corresponding stages in the production of decisions are the framing of the problem that is to be solved, the collection of relevant information leading to a decision, and reflection and review. An organization that seeks to improve its decision product should routinely look for efficiency improvements at each of these stages. The operative concept is routine' (Kahneman, 2011, pp 417–418)

The concept of organizational routines has a prominent place in Chapter 11, where we discuss evolutionary approaches to organizations.

6.7 Summary: goals and decisionmaking within the firm in behavioural theory

In behavioural theory, the firm is postulated as a coalition of (groups of) participants, such as shareholders, employees, managers, suppliers and customers. That is a major way in which it differs from standard microeconomic theory, which sees the firm as a holistic entity. Each participant receives inducements from the firm in return for the contributions he or she makes to the firm. A participant will remain within the coalition if, in his own opinion, the value of the inducements received is greater than the value of the contributions made.

In behavioural theory we assume that not all people have the same information. For example, an employee may not know exactly how much he could earn with another employer or what the atmosphere between colleagues is really like in another firm.

In behavioural theory we also assume that human beings are boundedly rational. That means human beings are unable to make all sorts of difficult calculations in a split second, nor can they process all the information they receive. It does not mean that humans do not want to maximize something, only that they are not always able to do so. The behaviour of human beings is better described as satisficing than maximizing. For example, an employee will have an aspiration level with respect to the level of pay he wants to receive. As long as the pay earned is above that aspiration level, the employee is content. Owing to lack of information he may even be content with a lower level of pay than is offered elsewhere.

In behavioural theory concerning the firm, each participant or group of participants has his own goals, usually in the form of aspiration levels. Those goals will generally not coincide. The result is that the firm will generally have several goals, which are arrived at through a bargaining process between the (groups of) participants.

The overall goals of the firm need to be translated into operational subgoals in order to be of practical value. That is usually quite complicated, even if the firm has only one goal, such as profit maximization.

Consider a firm owned and managed by one person, the entrepreneur. Why is it impossible for the entrepreneur to hire only people who just do as they are told? In a very small firm, it may be possible. Direct supervision is often the most important coordinating mechanism in a very small firm, as we saw in Chapter 3. In a larger firm, however, the decisions that have to be made become so numerous the entrepreneur has to delegate some of them. For example, one person cannot make all the decisions concerning marketing, production and inventory management. It is simply inefficient to transmit all information to a single person so that he can make all the decisions. So, we have a decisionmaking process in which two or more people participate. Those people bring their own goals to the organization.

Suppose the goal of the entrepreneur is profit maximization. If he appoints functional managers, it is impossible to specify operational subgoals without creating a conflict of interests between them. So, managers of functional departments are given an operational subgoal with a target level. Their task is to reach their target level, not to maximize or minimize something. By giving managers of functional departments a target level, the entrepreneur leaves some room for mutual adjustment. Mutual adjustment is then used in conjunction with direct supervision as a coordinating mechanism (see Chapter 3).

There are four fundamental differences between behavioural theory and standard microeconomic theory. Behavioural theory:

- postulates the firm as a coalition of participants, whereas standard microeconomics postulates the firm as a holistic entity;
- does not assume that the firm has a single objective, while standard microeconomics assumes that the firm has just one objective;
- assumes that information cannot be transmitted without cost, while standard microeconomics assumes it can;
- assumes that human decisionmakers are boundedly rational, while standard microeconomics assumes full rationality.

As we shall see in the following chapters, several of these characteristics of decisionmaking within firms have been incorporated in various economic approaches to organizations, which were developed later. That was recognized by Cyert and March when they wrote a preface to the second edition of their classic book *A Behavioral Theory of the Firm* in 1992:

> We had an agenda in 1963. We thought that research on economics and research on organizations should have something to say to each other. We thought that the theory of the firm should be connected to empirical observations of firms. We thought that empirical observations of what happens in firms should be connected to interesting theoretical ideas ... The agenda and the first steps we proposed were somewhat deviant from dominant ideas in both economics and organization theory when the book first appeared. In the years since 1963 ... a number of the ideas discussed in the book have become part of the received doctrine. In particular, a perspective that sees firms as coalitions of multiple, conflicting interests using standard rules and procedures to operate under conditions of bounded rationality is now rather widely adopted in descriptions and theories of the firm.

Similarly, many concepts from behavioural economics are now becoming mainstream in economics and organization theory. We have become much more aware of the importance of decision contexts and the framing of the issues at hand. We know that we commonly use heuristics as a short-cut to 'intuitive' judgments and that we are prone to systematic errors called biases. As a consequence, we can strive to mitigate such departures from rationality, both as individuals and in organizations. In organizations, we can adopt routines to carefully examine and challenge critical decisions. Nowadays, economic approaches to organizations encompass the full spectrum of behavioural assumptions, from full rationality in the next chapter (on agency theory) to bounded rationality in the chapter thereafter (on transaction cost economics) to organizational routines in the chapter on evolutionary approaches to organizations.

Questions

1 In a period of economic recession, most companies are able to increase production efficiency by reducing their workforce without any decrease in the level of output. Apparently, firms take action to reduce costs only when profit rates are declining. Many firms seem to be able to restore previous profit levels by taking this kind of action. Why do firms not minimize production cost in the first place, before the recession sets in?

2 Reread Box 6.1. We assume you agree with Sum Pulmisano and Paul Polman, that managers should serve the interests of all stakeholders in the firm, not just those of the shareholders. Somehow it seems morally right to do so. Now, suppose that you meet a proponent of standard microeconomic theory who tells you:

> 'Yes, I do agree with you that the interests of the employees are very important. That is exactly why managers should take into account only the interests of the shareholders. If they do just that, the result will be a Pareto-optimal allocation of resources in the economy. That is the major result of standard microeconomic theory. There can be no doubt about the correctness of that statement. The result is that the employees will be better off when the managers do not take into account the interests of their employees explicitly than when they do. If they were to do so, they would make decisions resulting in an allocation of resources in the economy that is not Pareto-optimal. For example, managers may be tempted to postpone a plant closure because by closing that plant employees would lose their jobs. The result would be that employees would have to continue working in their present job, but, if managers were constantly to close inefficient plants, people would always work in the most modern plants where they can earn the most.'

Suppose that you are invited to debate with this proponent of standard microeconomics. What would your main arguments be?

3 In behavioural theory regarding the firm, management's task is not to maximize shareholder value, but to achieve a balanced satisfaction of all the firm's stakeholders, including employees, customers, suppliers and shareholders. In the real world, a firm's top management team has a choice. It can emphasize shareholder value in its policy statements and use shareholder value as the main objective in strategic decisionmaking or it can emphasize stakeholder interests in its policy statements and use a variety of objectives, including satisfaction of major stakeholders, in strategic decisionmaking. Can you give arguments as to why firms choosing the second option might end up creating more shareholder value than would firms choosing the first?

4 Goliath Ltd is a company manufacturing bicycles. It is located in Hemel Hempstead, England. The Goliath product offering includes 20 different models with names such as Goliath-Sport, Goliath-Tourist, Goliath-City and so on. Each type comes in versions for men and women and is available in several colours and sizes. In total, Goliath's product range consists of about 600 different bicycles. It is quite difficult to make reliable demand forecasts for each of the 600 types.

Goliath sells its bicycles mainly through servicing retailers. These are quite small outlets. On average these outlets have no more than 30 bicycles in store. Very often, a potential buyer will choose a bicycle of a certain model, but in a colour or size that is not directly available in the store. In such a case, the retailer can check online whether or not the desired bicycle is available in Goliath's central warehouse in Hemel Hempstead. If it is, the retailer can order the desired bicycle with one mouse click and it will be delivered within 72 hours to any retailer in England. If the desired bicycle is not available, Goliath is likely to lose the sale.

Mrs Prime is Goliath's sales manager. She is responsible for making a new sales forecast every four weeks. She has considerable freedom in setting prices and spending money on promotions and campaigns. A substantial part of her compensation is tied to the results of her sales department. Those results are defined as sales minus cost of sales (at standard cost prices) minus selling costs (such as advertising).

Mr Griffin is production manager at Goliath. He is responsible for planning and scheduling production runs. A large part of his compensation is in the form of a bonus, which is determined by manufacturing costs per bicycle. Small production runs are extremely expensive and so Mr Griffin is very reluctant to plan them.

Mr Robbins has been recently appointed as managing director. He soon finds out that Mrs Prime and Mr Griffin have many conflicts. Very often, certain bicycles are out of stock, so Mrs Prime complains bitterly to Mr Robbins about Mr Griffin's refusal to adjust to what the market demands. In turn, Mr Griffin complains to Mr Robbins that Mrs Prime's sales forecasts are very unreliable.

What do you think Mr Robbins should do in order to improve cooperation between Mrs Prime and Mr Griffin? Discuss.

7 Agency theory

7.1 Introduction

Agency theory, in its simplest form, discusses the relations between two people – a principal and an agent who makes decisions on behalf of the principal. Here are a few examples of agency relations:

- the owner of a firm (principal) and the manager of a firm (agent), who makes decisions affecting the owner's wealth;
- the owner of an estate (principal) and her steward (agent), who makes decisions affecting the owner's wealth;
- a manager (principal) and his subordinate, who makes decisions affecting the manager's reputation;
- a patient (principal) and her physician (agent), who makes decisions affecting the patient's health;
- an insurance company (principal) and a person holding a fire insurance policy (agent), who makes decisions affecting the insurance company's cash flows;
- a lessor (principal) and a lessee (agent), who makes decisions affecting the lessor's property.

Agency relations can be found both within firms (manager and subordinate) and between firms (for example, licensing and franchising). In this chapter we shall take the agency relation between the shareholder(s) and the manager of a firm as our main example.

Within agency theory two streams of literature can be distinguished: the positive theory of agency and the theory of principal and agent.

Positive theory of agency

In the **positive theory of agency,** the firm is viewed as a nexus of contracts. The main research questions in this theory are how do contracts affect the behaviour of participants and why do we observe certain organizational forms in the real world? In general, it is assumed in the theory that existing organizational forms are efficient. If they were not, they would not continue to exist. The positive theory of agency thus sets out to explain why organizational forms are as they are. The theory is not (yet) expressed in the form of mathematical models.

Theory of principal and agent

In the **theory of principal and agent,** the central question is how should the principal design the agent's reward structure? That question is dealt with in formal mathematical models.

Both streams of literature – positive agency theory and theory of principal and agent – have their antecedents in the literature on the separation of ownership and control (see Section 7.2).

The remainder of this chapter is organized as follows. Sections 7.3–7.5 discuss three different but strongly related contributions to the positive theory of agency. Two important organizational forms in Western societies are the entrepreneurial firm and the public corporation. The entrepreneurial firm is a firm owned and managed by the same person. The public corporation is a corporation with publicly traded shares and widely dispersed ownership. In the entrepreneurial firm there is no separation of ownership and control, while in the public corporation there is.

How ownership structure affects managerial behaviour is discussed in Section 7.3. Then, in Section 7.4, we explain how team production might explain the existence of entrepreneurial firms. In Section 7.5 the existence of both entrepreneurial firms and public corporations is explained by focusing on decision processes in conjunction with residual claims. The theory of principal and agent is then discussed in Section 7.6. A summary is provided in Section 7.7.

Applications of agency theory can be found in Section 13.10 and in Chapter 15.

7.2 Separation of ownership and control

Adam Smith recognized the problem resulting from the separation of ownership and control: 'Negligence and profusion ... must always prevail, more or less, in such a company' (see quote from *The Wealth of Nations* in Box 7.1).

Box 7.1 The joint stock company

The trade of a joint stock company is always managed by a court of directors. The court, indeed, is frequently subject, in many respects, to the control of a general court of proprietors. But the greater part of those proprietors seldom pretend to understand any thing of the business of the company; and when the spirit of faction happens not to prevail among them, give themselves no trouble about it, but receive contentedly such half yearly or yearly dividend, as the directors think proper to make to them. This total exemption from trouble and from risk, beyond a limited sum, encouraged many people to become adventurers in joint stock companies, who would, upon no account, hazard their fortunes in any private copartnery. Such companies, therefore, commonly draw to themselves much greater stocks than any private copartnery can boast of ... The directors of such companies, however, being the managers rather of other people's money than of their own, it cannot well be expected, that they should watch over it with the same anxious vigilance with which the partners in a private copartnery frequently watch over their own. Like the stewards of a rich man, they are apt to consider attention to small matters as not for their master's honour, and very easily give themselves a dispensation from having it. Negligence and profusion, therefore, must always prevail, more or less, in the management of the affairs of such a company. It is upon this account that joint stock companies for foreign trade have seldom been able to maintain the competition against private adventurers. They have, accordingly, very seldom succeeded without an exclusive privilege; and frequently have not succeeded with one.

Source: Adam Smith (1776) *The Wealth of Nations,* Book V, Chapter 1

The issue of separation of ownership and control did not receive much attention from other early economic writers. The situation changed when, in 1932, Adolf Berle and Gardiner C. Means published *The Modern Corporation and Private Property*. In that book, Berle and Means describe the **separation of ownership and control** in the typical twentieth-century corporation. The large corporation, they say, is owned by so many shareholders that no single shareholder owns a significant fraction of the outstanding stock. Therefore, no single shareholder has the power really to control the actions of the officers of the corporation.

Separation of ownership and control

The officers themselves, in general, also own a very small part of the stock of their corporations. Hence, the situation may be characterized as follows:

- The bulk of the dividends goes to the outside shareholders.
- All the major decisions are made by the corporate officers.
- The outside shareholders are unable to control the corporate officers.

In that situation, Berle and Means say, the interests of the officers and shareholders diverge widely. The officers are in search of power, prestige and money for themselves, while the shareholders are interested only in profits. Senior managers, in the view of Berle and Means, are in a position to enrich themselves at the expense of the shareholders and, they fear, sometimes engage in corporate plundering.

In most but not all large corporations, the officers own only a very small percentage of all shares. In some large corporations the officers' portion is significant. Those corporations might be called owner-controlled and the corporations with widely dispersed shareholdings manager-controlled. If the argument of Berle and Means is true, we expect a significant difference in profitability between owner-controlled and manager-controlled companies. Owner-controlled companies should be much more profitable than manager-controlled companies. That is a direct implication of the work by Berle and Means. There are, however, powerful mechanisms that prevent managers from engaging in excessive on-the-job consumption. Let us examine some of those potential mechanisms.

First, there is the *stock market*. If a corporation performs badly because the managers of that corporation are incompetent, lazy or not really interested in running the corporation as well as they can, the market price of that company's stock will decline. If, moreover, it becomes clear why the market price of that company's stock is so low, a determined outsider can try to acquire a majority of the shares at a low price. The outsider can then oust the managers, install new managers and control them more tightly. Therefore, managers who perform poorly must always fear that their company can be taken over. There is a market not only for individual shares but also for whole corporations. To put it differently, there is a market for the rights to manage corporations. That market is usually called the **market for corporate control**. Competition between management teams in the market for corporate control increases the pressure on managers to perform well.

Market for corporate control

Second, there is a *market for managerial labour*. The top position in a large company usually gives a manager more power, more prestige, more money and more job satisfaction than the top position in a smaller company. Hence, we expect some competition between managers to obtain those few top positions in the largest firms. All managers, therefore, have to worry about their reputations. If they acquire a reputation for pursuing their personal interests instead of profit opportunities, it is likely that their chances of being offered a better position are small.

Third, there are *markets for the company's products.* The more intense the competition in those markets, the less opportunity there is for managers to pursue their own interests. If they do so, the company will have higher unit costs than its competitors or it will turn out products of a lower quality than those of its competitors. It will lose market share and, ultimately, cease to exist. Therefore, competition in product markets also restricts managers from pursuing their own interests. How markets can discipline managers of public companies is discussed more extensively in Section 15.6.

Finally, even if the officers of a company do not own shares in their company, their *pay package* may still include a bonus related to annual profits, an option to buy stock at a later date and so on. This can also bring the interests of top managers more in line with those of the shareholders. The role of reward structures is the key issue in the theory of principal and agent. The theory is discussed extensively in Section 7.6. The question of how to design compensation packages for managers is discussed in more detail in Section 15.3.

So let us return to the question whether owner-controlled firms are more profitable than manager-controlled firms. From the discussion above it is not clear how effective competition in various markets and managerial pay packages effectively constrain excessive on-the-job-consumption. The relationship between ownership structure and firm profitability is an important issue in the field of corporate governance. In Chapter 15 on corporate governance we shall deal with this issue in greater detail. Here we want to say that, yes, of course, managers can and should refrain from excessive on-the-job consumption because of ethical considerations. Moreover, managers do not work in isolation but in an environmental and institutional context, consisting of company law, auditing, antitrust authorities and public opinion.

7.3 Managerial behaviour and ownership structure

7.3.1 Managerial behaviour and ownership structure in a world with certainty and symmetrical information

The preceding section discussed the separation of ownership and control in quite general terms. Here we discuss the issue in more precise terms. How does the ownership structure of the firm affect the behaviour of managers in that firm? To answer that question, Jensen and Meckling in 1976 developed a theory that is explained in this section.

Consider, first, a manager who owns all the shares of the company she manages. That owner-manager has two conflicting objectives. She is interested in maximizing both the value of the firm and **on-the-job consumption**. The latter may take various forms, such as buying a company jet, furnishing the office in a luxurious way or spending fewer hours on the job (and more in expensive restaurants). This is not to say that buying a company jet is always a matter of on-the-job consumption. In order to make the point clear, consider what a manager interested only in maximizing the value of a company would do. Such a manager would first calculate the following:

■ the present value of the managerial time saved by buying a company jet (a);
■ the present value of buying tickets for regular airlines (b);
■ the present value of the cash outflows from buying and operating a company jet (c).

A manager interested in maximizing the value of the firm would buy a company jet if, and only if:

$$c - a < b$$

Now define d as $d = c - a - b$ and suppose that d is greater than zero. A manager interested in not only maximizing the value of the firm but also in prestige and personal comfort might still buy a company jet. If so, d is the amount spent as on-the-job consumption.

On-the-job consumption does take place in the real world, although not often in a way that is as conspicuous as the example given in Box 7.2.

Box 7.2 The agency costs of Casey Reginald Williams

Sometimes the agency costs of on-the-job consumption are not only substantial but also hilarious. Below are some excerpts from the interrogation of Raymond R. Williams, founder and former CEO of the Australian firm HIH Insurance Limited, about the bankruptcy of the firm.

Mr Williams was interrogated by Mr Wayne Martin, QC as follows:

Martin: *Could you tell us please if, on your frequent first-class trips to London, you booked the seat next to you for your briefcase?*
Williams: *I don't recall specifically. But that may have been the case, on some occasions.*
Martin: *That your briefcase was also travelling first class?*
Williams: *That may have been the case.*
Martin: *Did you express the view to Qantas that this briefcase should be eligible for frequent flyer points?*
Williams: *I can't recall that.*
Martin: *And were you subsequently informed that said briefcase would not be eligible for such points on the grounds that it was not, in fact, a person?*
Williams: *That may have been the airline's position on that issue.*
Martin: *Was that briefcase, from that point on, booked under the name of Casey Williams?*
Williams: *Yes, Casey Reginald Williams, AM.*

Source: HIH Royal Commission, Day 131, Wayne Martin QC examining Raymond Reginald Williams, AM (founder/former CEO of HIH) as reported in Nederlandse Corporate Governance Stichting, *Corporate Governance in Nederland 2002*, p. 63.

From the example it is clear that, if managers engage in on-the-job consumption, they are not maximizing the value of their firm. The more that is spent as on-the-job consumption, the lower the value of their firms. If a manager spent $1 million as on-the-job consumption (in our example, $d = \$1$ million), she would lower the value of the firm by $1 million.

In Figure 7.1, the present value of on-the-job consumption, C, is plotted against the value of the firm, V. It is now clear that the sum of the two variables – value of the firm and present value of on-the-job consumption – is constant. If the manager decides to consume C_4, the value of the firm will be V_4. If she decides to consume C_5, the value of the firm will be V_5. The line V_0C_0 represents all possible combinations of V and C. That line gives the set of combinations of V and C the manager can choose from and is called the **budget constraint**. In Figure 7.1, the budget constraint V_0C_0 has slope -1. Note that a manager who is interested only in maximizing the value of the firm, not in any form of on-the-job consumption, would not consume anything on the job. The value of the firm then would be V_0.

Budget constraint

The values of C and V chosen by the manager depend on her utility function. In Figure 7.1, all points on curve U_3 represent points of equal utility to the manager. All points on curve U_1 also represent points of equal utility to the manager. Points on curve U_1, however, represent a higher level of utility than points on curve U_3. Points on curve U_2 represent a still higher level of utility, but there is no way the manager can reach that level. The manager maximizes her utility

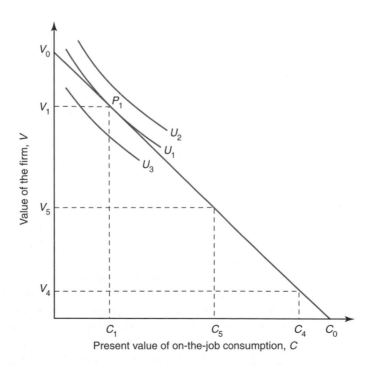

Figure 7.1 Value of the firm (V) and present value of on-the-job consumption (C). The manager owns all the shares in the firm

by choosing point P_1, where her consumption is C_1 and the value of the firm is V_1. At that point, the marginal utility of an additional dollar of on-the-job consumption is equal to the marginal utility of an additional dollar of wealth.

The curves U_1, U_2 and U_3 in Figure 7.1 are called *indifference curves* because they represent points of equal utility to the manager.[1] Thus the manager is indifferent about the points lying on the same indifference curve. As we are still dealing with a manager who owns all the shares in the firm, we need only the information in Figure 7.1 to determine her trade-off between the value of her firm and her on-the-job consumption.

Now suppose the manager sells a fraction $(1 - \alpha)$ of her shares to outsiders. The manager then owns a fraction α of the shares herself. For example, α could be equal to 0.7, which would mean that the manager sells 30 per cent of the shares to outsiders and retains 70 per cent herself. If she decides to spend an additional \$1 on on-the-job consumption, the value of the firm will be reduced by \$1. Now, however, the personal wealth of the manager will be reduced by only 70 cents and the wealth of the outside shareholders by 30 cents. The manager will now spend an amount on consumption such that the marginal utility of an additional \$1 of on-the-job consumption is equal to the marginal utility of an additional 70 cents of personal wealth. So we know that she will now spend more money on on-the-job consumption.

How much more the manager will spend on on-the-job consumption depends on the set of possible combinations of personal wealth and on-the-job consumption she can choose from. That set depends on the price she can achieve for the shares she sells to the outsiders, which depends on whether or not the outsiders know beforehand that the manager will spend more on on-the-job consumption after she has sold the shares.

Suppose they do *not* know the manager will do that. Such naïve outsiders will be willing to pay 30 per cent of V_1 for 30 per cent of the shares. The budget constraint now facing the manager must have a slope of –0.7 as the manager can trade \$1 of consumption for 70 cents of personal wealth. The budget constraint must also pass through point P_1. At that point the manager consumes C_1 and her personal wealth is V_1 (she will have 30 per cent of V_1 in cash and the other 70 per cent of V_1 in shares). So, the budget constraint now facing the manager must be line L in Figure 7.2. Line L passes through point P_1 and has a slope of –0.7.

At point P_2 there is an indifference curve (U_2 in Figure 7.2) tangential to the budget constraint L. At that point the manager consumes C_2. The value of the firm is reduced to V_2. Thus, the outside shareholders, who paid 30 per cent of V_1 for their shares, now find that their shares have a value of 30 per cent of V_2 only.

Suppose now that the outsiders were not so naïve as to assume the manager would not increase her on-the-job consumption. Suppose, instead, that they expected the manager to increase her consumption as soon as she sold the shares. Suppose, moreover, that the outsiders knew the exact shape of the manager's indifference curves. They would have a look at Figure 7.3 and try to find a point P_3 such that P_3 lies on V_0C_0 and the indifference curve passing through P_3 has, at point P_3, a slope of $- \alpha$ (that is, the indifference curve is tangential at P_3 to a line through P_3 with slope $-\alpha$).

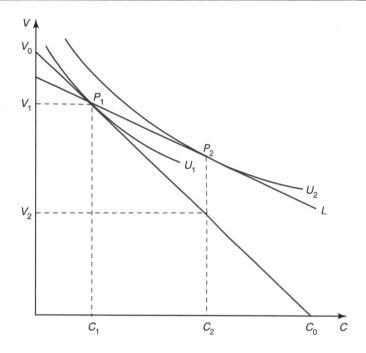

Figure 7.2 Value of the firm (V) and present value of on-the-job consumption (C). The manager owns a fraction α of the shares. The outsiders expect no increase in on-the-job consumption after the manager has sold a fraction $(1 - \alpha)$ of the shares

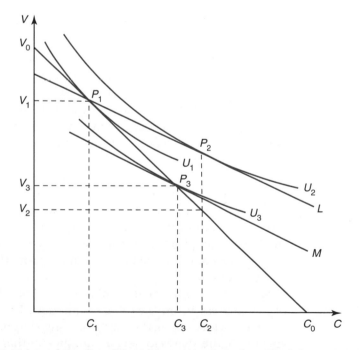

Figure 7.3 Value of the firm (V) and present value of on-the-job consumption (C). The manager owns a fraction α of the shares. The outsiders know the exact shape of the indifference curves of the manager and adjust the price they are willing to pay accordingly

The outsiders will soon find out that there is one, and only one, such point P_3. Thus, they will know that at P_3 the marginal utility for the manager of spending an additional \$1 on on-the-job consumption is equal to the marginal utility of 70 cents of personal wealth. Therefore, they are willing to pay only 30 per cent of V_3 for the shares, not 30 per cent of V_1. If they pay 30 per cent of V_3, the manager's budget constraint becomes line M with a slope of -0.7. The manager will then decide to consume C_3. The value of the firm will be V_3 and the outsiders will neither gain nor lose from buying the shares.

The personal wealth of the manager is now V_3. Of this amount she has a fraction $(1 - \alpha)$ in cash and a fraction α in shares. Her wealth has reduced by $V_1 - V_3$ and the present value of her on-the-job consumption has increased by $C_3 - C_1$. The result is a decrease in his level of utility: she is now on indifference curve U_3, having started on indifference curve U_1. So, it is clear that no manager would ever sell a fraction of the shares of her company unless there were something else, not included in the analysis presented above, that would make her do so. Three such possibilities are:

- the manager prefers to have a portion of her wealth in cash instead of shares because she can then use the cash for other things;
- the manager wants to diversify company-specific risk;
- the manager sees an opportunity for investment that she cannot finance out of her own personal wealth.

7.3.2 Monitoring and bonding

In Section 7.3.1 we discussed the case of a manager-owner who wants to sell part of her shares to an outside investor. After she has done so, she will engage in more consumption-on-the-job. Why can she not simply promise not to do so? If she can make a credible promise, she can sell a fraction $(1 - \alpha)$ of her shares for $(1 - \alpha)$. V1. The problem here is that she cannot make a credible promise. In the above analysis, we have implicitly assumed that the outside shareholder cannot prevent the manager from consuming more on the job after she has sold part of her shares. Suppose now that outsiders can monitor the behaviour of the manager. In practice, it is usually possible for outsiders to observe the behaviour of managers to a certain extent. For example, they could have the books audited by an external auditor or install a board of directors.

Monitoring

Monitoring the behaviour of a manager is not without cost. By spending money on monitoring, however, the outsiders could reduce the manager's on-the-job consumption. The more they spend on monitoring, the better they can observe the manager's behaviour and the more they can reduce her on-the-job consumption.

We know from the analysis of Figure 7.3 that the manager bears the full cost of her increase in on-the-job consumption. If the manager can convince the outsiders before selling the shares that she will consume less than C_3, she will be able to sell the shares for an amount greater than 30 per cent of V_3. If she consumes less, the value of the firm increases and it is the manager who captures that increase, not the outsiders. Hence, it is in the interests of the manager to

Bonding

bind herself – called bonding. **Bonding** and monitoring are almost the same

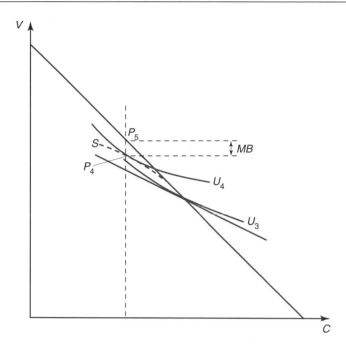

Figure 7.4 Value of the firm (V) and present value of on-the-job consumption (C) with monitoring and bonding costs

thing. *Bonding* means that the manager takes the initiative to bind herself and be monitored; *monitoring* means that the outsiders take the initiative.

Like monitoring, bonding is not without cost. It involves the same kinds of activity as monitoring: the manager takes the initiative to have the books audited or install a board of directors. Monitoring costs and bonding costs are borne by the manager. By consuming less than C_3, she increases her level of utility. By spending money on monitoring and bonding, she decreases the value of the firm. For this reason her budget constraint is no longer shown by the line V_0C_0. Rather, her budget constraint now is curve S in Figure 7.4.

Somewhere there is an optimal amount of money to spend on monitoring and bonding. That is indicated in Figure 7.4 by point P_4. At that point, the manager spends an amount MB (equal to the distance P_5P_4) on monitoring and bonding costs. Her level of utility is U_4 – higher than U_3, but still lower than U_1.

7.4 Entrepreneurial firms and team production

Entrepreneurial firm

Why do entrepreneurial firms exist? By an **entrepreneurial firm** we mean one that is owned and managed by the same person. That person (the entrepreneur) coordinates and monitors the work of several others (the employees) and receives the residual funds after fixed contractual payments (such as wages and interest payments) have been paid.

Direct supervision is the most important coordination mechanism in such a firm. An alternative organizational form is a workers' cooperative, in which the workers cooperate as peers. Then, mutual adjustment is the prime coordination mechanism. In manufacturing industries, few workers' cooperatives exist. Alchian and Demsetz (1972) explain this by using the concept of **team production.**

Team production

Team production is a situation in which two or more people can produce more when they are working together than when they are working separately. The classical example is two people loading heavy cargo on to a truck. Suppose two people have to load heavy cargo on to two trucks. They can organize their work in one of two ways. Either each person can load one truck, working on his own, or they can work together, first loading one truck and then the other. If the second arrangement is more efficient, you have team production. Some goods or services cannot be produced by one person working alone. Examples are the music made by a symphony orchestra and open heart surgery. These are also examples of team production.

Self-employed people receive the fruits of their efforts alone. If they put in more effort, they produce more and earn more money. How much effort they put in depends on their utility function. In equilibrium, the marginal utility of having an additional unit of leisure is equal to the marginal utility of earning an additional unit of money as income. Now, suppose that n people form a team and share the earnings from their production activities. Then, each person knows that if he puts in an extra unit of effort, he will receive only $1/n$th part of the additional earnings generated by his additional effort. For that reason each person will be strongly tempted to put in a much lower level of effort.

We know, then, that people working in a team and sharing the proceeds of their work will put in a lower level of effort than people who are self-employed. The phenomenon is called **shirking.** Every team member will be tempted to engage in shirking. With everybody shirking, the total output of the team will be much lower than if there were no shirking. Every member of the team is willing to put in more effort, provided that everybody else also puts in more effort.

Shirking

The members of a team can discuss this issue. Suppose the result of such a discussion is that everyone promises not to shirk. If shirking by one of the team members is easily detected by the other team members, such mutual promises can work. A team member who shirks could then be expelled. If, however, it is difficult to detect shirking, such mutual promises will not be effective. Here again we see that the unobservability of the effort put in by the team members causes an information problem.

Do you think shirking occurs in the real world? Box 7.3 gives the results of a survey examining people's propensity to shirk.

Box 7.3 What people say about shirking

In 2000, a national telephone survey was conducted with adult members of the workforce in the USA to determine their work attitudes. Slightly over 1000 interviews were completed. The survey examined people's propensity to shirk by asking the following question:

Suppose that it is almost impossible for your employer to check up on you. Would you say that you are very likely, somewhat likely, somewhat unlikely or very unlikely to work hard if you agreed to?

Of the respondents, 82.7 per cent answered that they were 'very likely' to work hard, 12.1 per cent 'somewhat likely', 1.9 per cent 'somewhat unlikely' and 1.6 per cent 'very unlikely'.
What do you think? Do those results corroborate or refute the potential problem of shirking?

Source: Minkler (2004)

Monitor

Suppose that it is difficult for other team members to detect shirking but not very difficult for someone whose only task is to detect shirking. Let us call that person a **monitor**. A team with a monitor would produce more than a team without a monitor. If the value of the additional output from having a monitor is sufficiently high, it is in the interests of all team members to have a monitor.

How should the monitor be rewarded for his effort? Suppose that the monitor just shares in the proceeds on an equal basis with the other team members. The monitor then also has an incentive to shirk. The question then becomes, who monitors the monitor? If there is a second monitor to monitor the first monitor, who will monitor that second monitor? There is only one solution: give the monitor title to the residual funds after the other team members have been given a fixed level of pay. If the monitor receives the residual funds, he will have no incentive to shirk as a monitor.

If the monitor is to be effective, he must have the power to revise the terms of the contracts of individual team members, without having to negotiate with all the other team members. The monitor must have the right to terminate contracts, attract new members and adjust the rates of pay of every team member to reflect the marginal productivity of each person. Finally, the monitor must also have the right to sell his rights as monitor. Some of the monitor's activities – for example actions to alter the composition of the team – will pay off only after a certain period of time. There would be no incentive to engage in those kinds of activities unless he sooner or later would receive the rewards of such activities. If the monitor has the right to sell his rights as monitor, that will be a strong incentive to build an effective team.

Thus we have the entrepreneurial firm. The monitor is the owner of the firm, who receives the residual funds, has the right to sell the firm, has the right to hire and fire team members and adjust their pay on an individual basis. The monitor is the entrepreneur and the other team members are his employees.

The classical entrepreneur emerges in this theory as the solution to the problem of shirking within teams. The theory rests on two vital assumptions:

■ there is team production;
■ monitoring by someone specializing in that function can reduce shirking.

The second assumption really means that, for the other team members, it is more difficult or costly to monitor other team members than it is for someone who specializes in being the monitor. If the team members can see quite easily who is shirking and who is not, they can adjust team membership without having a monitor. Therefore, the monitor must be able to detect shirking more easily than the other team members.

7.5 The firm as a nexus of contracts

In Sections 7.3 and 7.4, ownership of the firm is a concept of vital importance – it restricts on-the-job consumption and shirking by managers. How, then, can we explain the existence of large corporations, shares in which are publicly traded and the managers of which do not own (a significant portion of) the shares?

In order to answer this question we need to have a closer look at the large public company in which there is separation of security ownership and control. Note that here we introduce separation of *security ownership* and control. In the theory explained here, ownership of the firm is an irrelevant concept. A shareholder in a large public corporation owns just a number of shares. With ownership of the shares go certain well-defined rights, but that does not mean a shareholder (or all shareholders jointly) own the corporation in any meaningful sense. They just contract to receive the residual funds, just as workers contract to receive a fixed rate of pay. Shareholders are just one party in a group of many parties bound together in a nexus of contracts. Box 7.4 gives an illustration of a company that may be not much more than a 'nexus (bunch) of contracts'.

Box 7.4 Monorail Corporation as a nexus of contracts

In an excellent small book on the evolution of 'The Company', Micklethwait and Wooldridge (staff members of *The Economist*) discuss different perspectives on its future.

One perspective – particularly popular in antiglobalization circles – holds that giant corporations will come to dominate the world (economy). Empirical evidence shows, however, that big companies have been losing ground.

A second view argues the opposite – that companies are becoming ever less substantial:

> for a glimpse of the future, its proponents recommend the Monorail Corporation, which sells computers. Monorail owns no factories, warehouses, or any other tangible asset. It operates from a single floor that it leases in an office building in Atlanta. Its computers are designed by freelance workers. To place orders, customers call a toll-free number connected to Federal Express's logistics service, which passes the orders on to a contract manufacturer that assembles the computers from various parts. FedEx then ships the computers to the customers and sends the invoices to the Sun Trust Bank, Monorail's agent. The company is not much of anything except a good idea, a handful of people in Atlanta and a *bunch of contracts* (emphasis added).

A third perspective holds that the company will be increasingly replaced by networks – boundaryless firms operating together in loose-fitting alliances. Micklethwait and Wooldridge conclude that:

> none of these three futures looks inevitable. Yet, the last two visions seem more plausible than the first. The trend at the moment is for the corporation to become ever less 'corporate': for bigger organizations to break themselves down into smaller entrepreneurial units. The erosion of Coasian transaction costs will make it ever easier for small companies – or just collections of entrepreneurs – to challenge the dominance of big companies; and ever more tempting for entrepreneurs to enter into loose relationships with other entrepreneurs rather than to form long-lasting corporations.

In Chapter 14 on hybrid forms we will explore the network perspective further.

Source: Micklethwait and Wooldridge (2003)

Fama and Jensen (1983a, b) use this perspective to explain the existence of both entrepreneurial firms and public corporations. They see the organization as a nexus of contracts, written and unwritten, between owners of factors of production and customers. The most important contracts specify the nature of residual claims and the allocation of steps in the decision process of agents. Most agents receive a fixed promised payment or an incentive payment based on a specific measure of performance. The residual risk is the risk of the difference between stochastic inflows of cash and promised payments, which is borne by the residual claimants or residual risk bearers.

The decision process has four steps:

Initiation

- **initiation**, which is the generation of proposals for resource utilization and structuring of contracts;

Ratification

- **ratification**, which is the process culminating in choosing which of the initiatives is to be implemented;

Implementation

- **implementation**, which is the execution of the ratified decisions;

Monitoring

- **monitoring**, which is the measurement of the performance of decision agents and implementation of rewards.

Decision management

Decision control

Initiation and implementation are usually allocated to the same agents. These two functions are combined within the term **decision management**. Likewise, **decision control** includes ratification and monitoring.

Fama and Jensen now posit two complementary hypotheses about the relations between risk-bearing and decision processes of organizations:

- The separation of residual risk-bearing from decision management leads to decision systems that separate decision management from decision control.
- Combining decision management and decision control in the work of a few agents leads to residual claims that are largely restricted to those agents.

Fama and Jensen call an organization *non-complex* if specific information relevant to decisions is concentrated in one or a few agents. 'Specific information' is detailed information that is costly to transfer between agents. Most small organizations tend to be non-complex, while most large organizations tend to be complex, but the correspondence is not perfect.

In small, non-complex organizations it is efficient to allocate both decision management and decision control to those agents who have the specific information. When decision management and decision control are combined, residual claimants have no protection against the opportunistic actions of decision agents. Hence, in small, non-complex organizations, residual claims are also allocated to the important decision agents. An example is the small entrepreneurial firm, owned and managed by the same person. Such an example conforms to the second hypothesis.

Now, suppose that the small entrepreneurial firm (we shall call it company E) is acquired by a larger firm (company L). The managers of company E are now no longer the residual claimants of the company. It is likely, however, that they still possess the specific knowledge relevant to making decisions for company E. It is now efficient to delegate decision management to the managers of company E. Decision control, however, is exercised by the manager(s) and corporate staff of company L. The separation of residual risk-bearing from decision management makes it necessary to separate decision management from decision control. This conforms to the first hypothesis.

In the large public corporation there are many shareholders. Having many shareholders has advantages because the total risk to be shared is large and there are large demands for capital in order to be able to make fixed promises to other agents. It is very costly for all of the shareholders to be involved in decision control, so they delegate decision control to the board. While decision management is diffused within a large public corporation, decision control is exercised by the board on behalf of shareholders.

7.6 Theory of principal and agent

In Section 7.3, the agency relation between the outside shareholder and the manager was analysed in a deterministic way – risk did not play a role in the analysis. Moreover, neither principal (outside shareholder) nor agent (manager) had private information. In the theory of principal and agent, risk is introduced into the analysis. In addition, we relax the condition of symmetrical information for our discussion in this section.

The theory of principal and agent is developed in mathematical models that, even in their simplest form, are already quite complicated. The essentials of such models can be explained by giving an example.

Take the relationship between the owner of a piece of land and someone who is willing to use that land to grow strawberries. The owner is the principal and the other person the agent. The principal is willing to give the agent the right to use her land to grow strawberries for one summer. The principal's problem is that of designing the agent's reward structure.

The quantity and the quality of strawberries that are available for sale at the end of the summer depend on two factors: how well the agent cares for the strawberries and the weather. In the language of the theory of principal and agent, the pay-off (the amount of money realized from the sale of the strawberries) depends on two variables – the level of effort exerted by the agent and a random variable (the weather).

A crucial question in the theory of principal and agent is how well the principal can observe the agent's behaviour. In this respect, three cases will be discussed:

- Case 1: the principal can observe the agent's behaviour.
- Case 2: the principal has no information about the agent's behaviour.
- Case 3: the principal cannot observe the agent's behaviour directly, but can obtain a signal concerning the level of effort being put in by the agent.

In Case 1, there is symmetrical information, but in Cases 2 and 3, there is asymmetrical information. In Cases 2 and 3, the agent knows his own level of effort, but the principal does not. The agent has *private information* (about his level of effort; see Chapter 4 for more on the concepts of asymmetrical and private information).

7.6.1 The principal can observe the agent's behaviour (symmetrical information)

Assuming that the principal can observe the level of effort being exerted by the agent, what is the optimal reward structure from the principal's point of view?

The agent's compensation can be based on his level of effort. We know that the agent does not like effort. He is willing to put in more effort only if his compensation is also higher. In Figure 7.5, curve *I* represents one of the agent's indifference curves. The graph plots the agent's level of effort against his income. The higher his level of effort, the more additional income he demands for an additional unit of effort.

Curve *I* is really one of a *set* of indifference curves. Assume, however, that the agent cannot obtain a contract anywhere that gives him a positive income if his level of effort is zero. Curve *I* then represents the minimum level of utility that the agent is willing to accept. He need not accept a contract giving him a lower level of utility as he is free not to work. So, he can always choose the point at the origin, which puts him at the utility level given by curve *I*.

The higher the agent's level of effort, the higher the expected pay-off. This relation is given by line *m* in Figure 7.5 (for simplicity, we have assumed that this relation is given by a straight line).

The principal now must choose a reward structure for the agent. Before dealing with that issue, let us try to find out what, from the principal's point of view, is the optimal level of the agent's effort. For the principal, the optimal level of the agent's effort is e_0. At that point, the expected pay-off is Ey_0 The agent must receive an amount W_0 and the principal receives the difference:

$$Ey_0 - W_0 = R_0$$

At any other point, the vertical distance between line *m* and curve *I* is smaller than R_0. So, the principal wants to select a reward structure that induces the agent to choose a level of effort e_0, which also gives him a payment of W_0 if he chooses that level.

Forcing contract

A very simple contract that solves the principal's problem is a **forcing contract**.

Under a forcing contract, the principal promises to pay an amount e_0 if the agent's level of effort is at least e_0 and to pay nothing if the agent's level of effort is smaller than e_0. Under such a contract, the agent is forced to bring his level of effort up to e_0, otherwise he will not be paid. He will not increase his level of effort any further, however, as he receives no extra reward for doing so. Hence, the agent is forced to work at level e_0.

Another solution would be to give the agent the reward structure represented by line *n* in Figure 7.5. Under this reward structure, the agent would have to pay an amount *A* to the principal if his level of effort was zero. For every additional unit of effort, the agent receives an amount given by the slope of line *n*. In order to obtain the highest utility level achievable under that reward structure, the agent will again choose effort level e_0.

The point of this whole discussion is that, if the principal can observe the agent's level of effort, the principal can, first, determine which level of effort, from her own point of view, is optimal and, second, give the agent a forcing

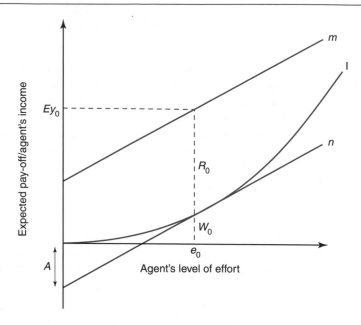

Figure 7.5 The optimal level of the agent's effort from the principal's point of view

contract that obliges him to choose that level of effort. As the principal can observe the actual level of effort chosen by the agent, she will pay W_0 only if the agent works at level e_0.

The set of Pareto-optimal solutions

In the discussion above, we have assumed that curve I represents the minimum level of utility that the agent is willing to accept. Let us call that level of (expected) utility EUA_1. EUA_1 represents the expected utility that the agent can obtain elsewhere. The principal maximizes her own expected utility by designing a reward structure, given the constraint that the agent will not accept a contract giving him an expected utility lower than EUA_1. Let EUP_1 be the principal's maximum level of utility, given EUA_1.

Now suppose that the agent perceives an opportunity to obtain a level of utility $EUA_2 > EUA_1$ elsewhere. Let EUP_2 be the principal's maximum level of utility, given EUA_2. As the principal is now faced with a tighter constraint, it follows that $EUP_2 < EUP_1$.

In Figure 7.6, the horizontal axis represents the agent's expected utility, while the vertical shows the principal's expected utility. If the minimum level of expected utility that the agent is willing to accept is EUA_1, then the principal's maximum level of utility is EUP_1 – point 1 in Figure 7.6. If, elsewhere, the agent can obtain EUA_2, then the principal's maximum level of utility is EUP_2 – point 2 in Figure 7.6. By choosing different values for EUA, we can calculate for each value of EUA the principal's maximum level of utility, EUP. All points thus found form the curve cs.

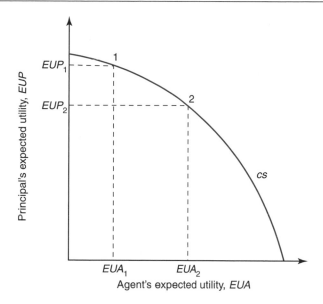

Figure 7.6 The set of Pareto-optimal solutions for the case of symmetrical information

Pareto-optimal solution

A **Pareto-optimal solution** of the principal's problem is defined as one in which it is impossible to increase one person's expected utility without decreasing the other person's. Point 1 in Figure 7.6 represents a Pareto-optimal solution as the principal can obtain more than EUP_1 only if the agent receives less than EUA_1, while the agent can obtain more than EUA_1 only if the principal receives less than EUP_1. Point 2 is also a Pareto-optimal solution. In fact, curve cs gives the set of Pareto-optimal solutions.

7.6.2 The principal cannot observe the agent's level of effort (asymmetrical information)

Let us now assume that the principal has no way to observe the level of effort exerted by the agent and, after the summer, she also has no detailed information about weather conditions during the summer. All she can observe is the pay-off – the amount of money made by selling the strawberries. If the pay-off is high, it can be the result of a high level of effort on the part of the agent and average weather conditions or an average level of effort by the agent and good weather conditions.

The principal cannot tell what contributed more to a good result – the agent's effort or the weather conditions. Those are now the conditions under which the principal must specify, at the beginning of the summer, a reward structure for the agent. How should she do that? There are two extreme solutions.

The first of these is to set a fixed salary for the agent, independent of the pay-

Wage contract

off. Such a reward structure may be called a **wage contract**. It is like an employment contract with a fixed rate of pay. The problem with a reward structure like that is the agent has no incentive whatsoever to do a good job. In the theory of principal and agent it is assumed that the agent likes to receive more money and dislikes delivering more effort, so the agent will choose a level of effort equal to zero if his income does not depend on the pay-off.

The second extreme solution is that the agent receives the pay-off minus a fixed amount to be agreed at the beginning of the summer. Such a structure may be called a **rent contract.** The agent rents the land from the landowner for a fixed amount. The rent is not dependent on the pay-off. The agent grows the strawberries and receives whatever he can make for the strawberries after he has paid the rent to the landowner. With such a reward structure, the agent has a maximum incentive to do his very best.

Rent contract

The wage and rent contracts differ not only in terms of how the rewards are distributed, but also in the distribution of risks imposed on agent and principal. Under the wage contract, the principal bears all the risk. For instance, if weather conditions ruin the strawberry crop, she still has to pay the agent, but receives no reward herself. Under the rent contract, the situation is reversed. The agent now bears all the risk. He has to pay the rent, whether or not the proceeds from selling the strawberries permit him to do so. Hence, we can see that the reward structure determines the distribution of risks between principal and agent.

What reward structures are acceptable to both parties will depend on their attitudes to risk. They may be risk-neutral, risk-averse or risk-loving. In most agency models, the principal is assumed to be risk-neutral and the agent either risk-neutral or risk-averse.

If both principal and agent are risk-neutral, the best reward structure is a rent contract. It gives the agent maximum incentive. It also imposes all the risk on the agent, but, as he is risk-neutral, he does not care about risk. To be more precise, a risk-neutral agent does not demand **compensation for risk-bearing** as he does not care about risk. As risk can be imposed on the agent without cost, a rent contract (giving maximum incentives) is the best reward structure for the agent.

Compensation for risk-bearing

Suppose that the principal is risk-neutral and the agent is risk-averse. With a rent contract, the agent has maximum incentive to put in a high level of effort, but he also has to bear all the risk. As we are now assuming that the agent is risk-averse, the agent cares about the amount of risk he has to bear. He, therefore, is willing to accept more risk only if it is offset by a higher expected income. This is illustrated in Figure 7.7. Curve U is the agent's indifference curve. It is also assumed that the agent has an alternative opportunity to accept another job. It is a job without risk and an income of W. W is the agent's **reservation wage**.

Reservation wage

If the principal wants to engage the agent, she can offer a wage contract for amount W. The principal can also offer a contract where the agent's income depends on the pay-off. The agent is willing to accept such a contract provided he remains on the same indifference curve.

The relation between the expected pay-off and the amount of risk borne by the agent is illustrated in Figure 7.7 by line I (we assume that this relation can be shown as a straight line). The higher the level of risk borne by the agent, the more incentive the agent has to do a good job and the higher the expected pay-off will be. If the agent bears no risk (a wage contract), the expected pay-off is Ey_3. As the agent will not accept a pay contract if his pay is lower than W, the

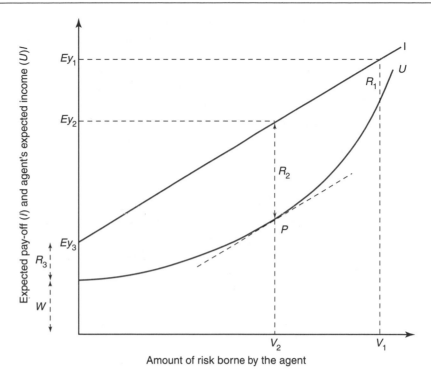

Figure 7.7 The trade-off between incentives and risk-bearing in the theory of principal and agent

maximum amount the principal can receive is R_3. If the agent bears all the risk (a rent contract), the expected pay-off is Ey_1. The principal can then charge a rent equal to R_1. If the principal charged a higher figure for rent, the agent would not accept the contract. The principal thus maximizes her expected income by choosing point P on the agent's indifference curve U, such that the slope of the indifference curve at point P is equal to the slope of line I. At that point the agent bears some risk (V_2) but not all of it (V_1).

Figure 7.7 portrays the fundamental trade-off that the principal must make. The principal wants to give the agent incentives in order to make him put in more effort, but, in order for this to occur, the agent must *also* bear risk. The agent is willing to accept risk only if he is compensated in the form of a higher expected income. So, the principal must make a trade-off between giving the agent incentives (the more incentives, the higher the expected pay-off) and having the agent bear more risk (the higher the level of risk borne by the agent, the more the principal has to pay him in the form of expected income).

As we can see in Figure 7.7, the optimal contract for the principal involves risk-sharing between agent and principal. The agent bears an amount of risk equal to V_2 and the principal bears an amount of risk equal to $V_1 - V_2$. The result is true if the principal is risk-neutral and the agent is risk-averse.

Why does the theory of principal and agent assume that the principal is risk-neutral while the agent is risk-averse? If both the principal and the agent are risk-neutral, the optimal contract is a rent contract. The theory then is not very interesting. It also seems reasonable to assume that the principal is risk-neutral and the agent risk-averse if the situation is such that the principal can diversify while the agent cannot. If, for example, the principal is the landowner and the agent the farmer, the principal may own several pieces of land in countries with different climates. The principal can then make contracts with several agents and, in so doing, diversify away most of the risk. The agent, however, can work on only one piece of land, so cannot diversify his risk. If the principal is the owner of a company and the agent is the manager of that company, we have the same situation: the principal can diversify (by owning shares in several companies) while the agent normally cannot.

In situations in which the model discussed here represents reality, there is no doubt that, for the principal, it is best to design a reward schedule based in part on the agent's performance. As shareholders can be regarded as risk-neutral and the top manager (the CEO) as risk-averse, we would expect to find performance-related pay packages for top managers. That is indeed what we find in the real world (see Section 15.3 and Box 15.2 for more details).

First-best and second-best solutions

All points on curve U in Figure 7.7 give the agent the same expected utility. Let us call that level of utility EUA_1. Associated with EUA_1 is EUP_1 – the principal's maximum level of utility given EUA_1. For each level of EUA we can calculate the associated level of EUP. That gives curve ca in Figure 7.8. Curve ca represents the set of Pareto-optimal solutions.

Curve cs in Figure 7.8 is the same as curve cs in Figure 7.6. That is, curve cs represents solutions to the principal's problem for the case of symmetrical information (the principal can observe the agent's level of effort). Curve ca represents

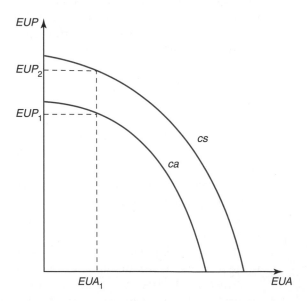

Figure 7.8 First-best and second-best solutions

solutions to the principal's problem in the case of asymmetrical information (the principal cannot observe the agent's level of effort).

The solutions represented by curve cs are called **first-best solutions** and those represented by curve *ca* are **second-best solutions**. If EUA_1 is the minimum level of utility the agent is willing to accept, then the principal can obtain EUP_1 if she cannot observe the agent's behaviour and EUP_2 if she can. The distance $EUP_2 - EUP_1$ represents the principal's loss of expected utility because of non-observability. Moral hazard is also involved, however. Recall that moral hazard refers to the *ex post* information problem owing to private information (Chapter 4). In such a case, the agent has private information on his effort level and may exploit that information asymmetry.

To see that is so, suppose for a moment the principal cannot observe the agent's level of effort and the principal can trust the agent's word. We then have the situation shown in Figure 7.5. The optimal level of effort from the principal's point of view is e_0. The principal simply asks the agent to deliver that level of effort and the agent promises to do so. There is no need for the principal to observe the agent's level of effort if she can trust him. So, the difference between a first-best and a second-best solution is caused by non-observability of information in the presence of moral hazard.

7.6.3 The principal can observe a signal concerning the agent's level of effort

Now suppose that the principal cannot observe the agent's level of effort directly but, instead, the principal can observe, without cost, a **signal** concerning the agent's level of effort. For example, the principal can observe how many hours the agent spends on his job. The number of hours worked by the agent gives the principal an indication about the agent's level of effort. The true level of effort, however, remains unobservable for the principal. This may be the case, for instance, if the agent is required to clock in when he begins work and to clock out when he stops. His real level of effort, however, still remains unobservable.

In formal agency models, one can show that the agent's reward structure should be based on such a signal if' and only if' the agent is risk-averse. To make this result intuitively clear, assume first that the agent is risk-neutral. The agent then does not care about risk-bearing, so he does not demand compensation in the form of a higher expected income if more risk is imposed on him. Therefore, there is no cost to the principal for imposing risk on the agent, if the agent is risk-neutral. In such a case, it is better for the principal to give the agent incentives by letting him bear all the risk (through a rent contract) than by giving him a reward structure based on an imperfect signal concerning his level of effort.

Suppose now that the agent is risk-averse. In that case, there is a cost to the principal of letting the agent bear more risk. In such a situation a reward structure based on both the signal concerning the agent's level of effort and the pay-off is better from the principal's point of view than a reward structure based only on the pay-off.

Hence, the information contained in the signal concerning the agent's level of effort is valuable to the principal if' and only if' the agent is risk-averse.

Consider next the situation where the principal can observe a signal through monitoring and that monitoring is not free. Assume, further, that the quality of the signal (the correlation of the signal with the agent's real level of effort) increases as the principal spends more on monitoring. Assume, too, that the principal is risk-neutral and the agent is risk-averse. In that situation the principal has to determine the optimal level of monitoring and the reward structure simultaneously.

7.6.4 Extending the model

In this section we have given an introduction to the theory of principal and agent. In its simplest form the theory concerns the relations between one principal and one agent. Moreover, that relationship is analyzed in a one-period model. What happens to our conclusions, however, when we examine the relations between one principal and several agents? What happens if we analyze the relations between one principal and one agent in a model with more than one period?

One principal and several agents

Consider first one principal with several agents. As an example, think of our landowner again who divides her land into several plots. Now there are several agents who want to grow strawberries on adjacent plots. The weather conditions are the same for all the plots. The principal does not know in detail about the weather conditions either before or after the summer, but she does know that the weather conditions are the same for each plot. That gives the principal the opportunity to make comparisons between the pay-offs of the agents.

Assume that the principal is risk-neutral and some agents are risk-averse and others risk-neutral. Consider, first, agents who are risk-neutral. Those agents do not demand compensation for bearing risk, so it is best to give them a rent contract. The principal can now give the other agents a forcing contract: 'If your pay-off is not lower than the pay-off of the risk-neutral agents, who have a rent contract, your compensation will be the same as theirs; if, however, your pay-off is lower, then you will get nothing.'

Assume now instead that all the agents are risk-averse. In that case, it is still possible to make comparisons between agents by comparing the pay-off of a certain agent with the average for all the agents. Any difference between the pay-off of a particular agent and the average pay-off for all the other agents can be due only to that agent's level of effort. For the principal, that is a signal concerning the agent's level of effort. From the principal's point of view, an optimal reward structure should be based on both the pay-off and the average pay-off for all the agents.

Several periods

Consider next one principal and one agent in a setting with several periods. Assume further that the principal cannot observe the agent's behaviour and the agent is risk-averse (if the agent is risk-neutral, the best contract is, again, a rent contract). The principal can now base the agent's reward structure on the pay-off of the present period and on that of all previous periods. From the principal's point of view, such a reward structure is better than one based only on the pay-off of the present period.

7.6.5 Applying agency theory

In the previous sections, various agency models have been described. We, the authors, hope that you have enjoyed reading about this fascinating field. In this final section on agency theory, we want to stress that care should be taken when applying agency theory to practical situations. We will discuss some factors that impede a straight 'translation' of agency concepts and solutions into the real world.

As an example, consider a corporation with several business units. It is a situation with one principal and several agents: the CEO is the principal, the managers of the business units are the agents. Suppose the CEO engages you as a consultant to devise incentive contracts for the business unit managers. How useful is the theory explained in previous sections to you in that situation? If you do not fully understand the theory's limitations, there is a real danger that the theory will be misapplied. There are several reasons for that.

First, the models we have discussed in Sections 7.6.1, 7.6.2 and 7.6.3 are one-period models. That is why we have used the example of growing strawberries during one summer. However, you are asked to advise in a situation where the business unit managers will be reviewed periodically by the CEO. That requires a multiple-period model. Multiple-period models have been described only very briefly in Section 7.6.4.

Second, you are being asked to advise on a situation with one principal and several agents. In Section 7.6.4 we briefly discussed a situation with one principal and several agents. In that model we saw several agents growing strawberries on adjacent plots of land. The weather conditions were the same for each plot, so we could assume that each agent faced the same random factor (the same weather conditions). In a setting with several business unit managers, each business unit may be affected differently by such random factors as the exchange rate or the fortunes of important customers. Another complication is that different business units may be affected by different random factors.

Third, the CEO will probably be able to collect several signals concerning the effort levels of business unit managers. As monitoring reduces the information asymmetry problem, it is quite likely that it will reduce the principal's loss of expected utility (see Figure 7.8). Monitoring is costly, however, so the real issue is not whether or not to monitor, but how and how much. It is a very complicated issue with no easy solutions. Most CEOs will evaluate the performance of a business unit manager on several financial and non-financial indicators and compare the manager's performance against those indicators with his and his colleagues' previous performance against those indicators. Those quantitative evaluations may be used to determine bonus payments. When it comes to promoting a business unit manager to a position of more responsibility, most CEOs will be reluctant to rely exclusively on such quantitative evaluations. Instead, they will tend to supplement them with a qualitative judgment of a business unit manager's qualifications and performance.

Finally, alignment of business unit managers in the real world is not only affected by their contract and pay packages but also the company culture and opportunities for promotion. There are more factors at play than mere monetary compensation!

Applying agency theory to practical situations is by no means easy. It is, however, very useful for shaping our thinking regarding, for example, the way in which public companies are (or should be) governed. The subject is discussed extensively in Chapter 15 on corporate governance.

7.7 Summary: agency relations between owners, managers and employees

Within agency theory we distinguish between the positive theory of agency and the theory of principal and agent. The positive theory of agency views the organization as a nexus of contracts. It tries to explain why organizational forms are as they are. Two important questions in this respect are how does the ownership structure of a firm affect managerial behaviour and why do we observe certain organizational forms in the real world?

In order to explain how the ownership structure of a firm can affect managerial behaviour, let us consider first an entrepreneurial firm. An entrepreneurial firm is one that is owned and managed by the same person. In such a firm there is no conflict of interests between owner(s) and manager(s).

A public corporation is one with shares that are traded on a stock market. In a public corporation there may be a real conflict of interests between the (outside) shareholders and the manager(s). Usually, shareholders are interested in a high return on their investment (in the form of dividends and appreciation of the share price on the stock market), so they would like to see managers maximizing the value of the firm on the stock market. The managers, however, may have other interests. Some of them like to have a luxury car, or travel and stay in expensive hotels, as long as the bill is paid by the company. In other words, managers may engage in on-the-job consumption that decreases the value of the firm. Even in an entrepreneurial firm, the manager will engage in such consumption. If he sells (part of) his shares to outsiders, he will increase his on-the-job consumption, thus reducing the value of the firm. The outsiders expect such behaviour and it is reflected in the price they are willing to pay for the shares.

In most manufacturing industries there are entrepreneurial firms and public corporations, but very few cooperative firms (a firm owned by the workers). Why do we observe so many entrepreneurial firms and so few cooperative firms in the real world?

The answer may have to do with the existence of team production. Team production is a situation in which two or more people can produce more when they are working together than when they are working separately. A problem with team production is that it leads to shirking. A member of a team who receives only a portion of the team's output will work less hard than a person working alone. The result is that the output of the team is greatly reduced. Thus, team members want to reduce shirking.

One solution may be to have a monitor who specializes in observing shirking. In a cooperative firm, the monitor would share in the proceeds with other team members. That would give the monitor an incentive to shirk as a monitor. If the monitor is the owner of the firm, however, he has no incentive to shirk. That may explain why entrepreneurial firms are more efficient than cooperative firms. As we would expect the most efficient organizational forms to survive, we are not surprised to see many small manufacturing firms organized as entrepreneurial firms and very few as cooperatives.

The theory of principal and agent forms the core of modern agency theory. In the theory, risk is introduced into the analysis. In its simplest form, the theory focuses on the relations between one principal and one agent. The agent performs a task and, in so doing, has to choose a level of effort. The output is determined by the level of effort but also by a random factor, such as the weather. The problem for the principal is one of determining a reward structure for the agent. If the principal can observe the level of effort of the agent, she can specify a minimum level of effort. The agent will receive nothing if he does not meet that minimum level of effort. If his level of effort exceeds the minimum, he will receive a fixed level of pay.

The principal's problem is much more interesting if she cannot observe the agent's behaviour. In that case, the agent's attitude towards risk becomes important. If the agent is risk-neutral, he is willing to take on risk without asking compensation for bearing it. The best solution then is simply to give the agent a rent contract. It allocates all risk to the agent, but also gives the agent a very strong incentive to increase his level of effort. If the agent is risk-averse and the principal risk-neutral, the principal has to make a trade-off between giving the agent incentives and having the agent bear more risk. The best solution in that case is to give the agent a reward structure that depends to some extent on the pay-off but also contains a fixed element independent of it. Such a contract involves risk-sharing between principal and agent.

In summary, we want to stress that:

1 The agency problem is a very real one in many settings.
2 Economists have started to conceptualize and model the agency problem, which has led to some insightful results.
3 There is still a gap between rather 'pure' agency models (focusing on one or a few variables only) and the rather 'messy' real world, in which many factors are at play.

Questions

1 Your car has been making a strange noise lately. You do not know what it is, but you do not feel comfortable with it, so you take your car to the garage. You take it in the morning and return in the evening to collect it. Is the relation you have with your garage an example of an agency relation? Who is the principal and who is the agent? Which kind of action is taken by the agent? Can the principal observe the actual action taken by the agent? Why do the agent's decisions or actions affect the principal's assets broadly defined?

2 Consider, in the theory of principal and agent, the case in which the principal can observe the agent's behaviour. Does the optimal reward structure from the principal's point of view depend on the agent's attitude towards risk? Explain your answer.

3 Fama and Jensen (1983a, b) describe decision processes as consisting of four steps – initiation, ratification, implementation and monitoring. Further, they introduce the terms 'decision management' and 'decision control'. Consider a small company (S) operating as a subsidiary of a larger company (L). Suppose that the managers of S are contemplating a major investment. Who will exercise decision management and who will exercise decision control? Why? Does it conform to one of Fama and Jensen's hypotheses? If yes, how did Fama and Jensen phrase that hypothesis?

4 Consider, in the theory of principal and agent, the situation in which the principal cannot observe the agent's behaviour and in which both principal and agent are risk-neutral. What is the optimal contract from the principal's point of view?

5 A definition of team production has been given on page 148. Which of the following situations represents team production? Explain your answer.
a A violin quartet playing Mozart.
b Eighteen people working in a factory that produces grandfather clocks (see Box 8.1 in the next chapter).
c Twenty engineers working on the design for a new car.

6 Ummels Services BV is a Dutch company with limited liability offering maintenance services for chemical processing plants. Ummels Services BV was founded in 1984 by Mr Stef Ummels. The company was owned and managed by Mr Ummels until he died in 1995. Since then, 50 per cent of the shares of Ummels Services BV have been owned by his son, Paul Ummels, while the other 50 per cent are owned by his daughter, Lara Ummels. Since his father's death, Paul Ummels has managed the company. Lara Ummels is a medical student and intends to become a urologist.

In March 2002, Paul and Lara talk about Lara selling her shares in the company to her brother. Lara would like to cash them in because she has little affinity with the company. Paul is interested in buying because he likes the idea of becoming sole owner. Paul is sure that he can borrow the money he needs to buy Lara's shares. Paul and Lara engage Mr Schlösser, an independent financial consultant, to estimate the value of Lara's shares.

Mr Schlösser calculates the present value of all future cash flows of the company. In estimating future cash flows, he uses the historical cash flows for the last five years. This results in a value of € 4.6 million for the company. He recommends that Lara sells her shares to Paul for € 2.3 million.

Lara is now asking you for a second opinion on Mr Schlösser's calculation. Do you see anything that Mr Schlösser may have neglected? How can Lara justify a price higher than € 2.3 million? Do you think Paul will be interested in buying at a price higher than € 2.3 million? Why?

7 Mr Howard Rothey owns an ice-cream bar at the beach in Bournemouth. He has been running it for several years. Ice-cream sales at the beach are highly seasonal: almost all sales take place in the period of May to September. For that reason, Mr Rothey has never taken a holiday during the peak season. Now, however, he wants to visit his son and daughter-in-law in Alaska in July, so wants to engage someone to run his ice-cream business during a period of three weeks in July. Alex Waterman, a 22-year-old student

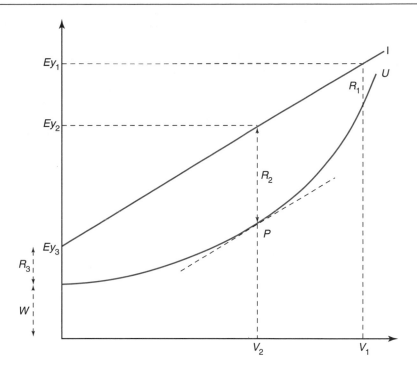

Figure 7.9 The trade-off between incentives and risk-bearing in the theory of principal and agent

from Bath University, is looking for a summer job. Mr Rothey is contemplating the kind of contract that he should offer. Mr Rothey is well aware of the fact that ice-cream sales depend, to a large extent, on the way Alex will treat customers (in the language of the theory of principal and agent, we would say that ice-cream sales depend on Alex's level of effort). Of course, the weather is quite important, too. For the English south coast, the weather in July can be very nice with lots of sun, but it can also be rainy and cold for several weeks.

a   Should Mr Rothey offer Alex a forcing contract?
b   Should Mr Rothey offer Alex a wage contract? If he does and Alex accepts, what will be Alex's level of effort?
c   What other types of contract can Mr Rothey offer?
d   What is the best contract for Mr Rothey if he and Alex Waterman are both risk-neutral?
e   Now suppose that Mr Rothey is risk-neutral and Alex Waterman is risk-averse. Figure 7.9 gives the trade-off between providing incentives and the cost of risk-bearing for that situation.
   ■   Which variable is indicated on the horizontal axis?
   ■   What does line I stand for?
   ■   What does curve U in this figure stand for?
f   Figure 7.9 also indicates the optimal solution for Mr Rothey. Indicate in the figure how much money Alex Waterman receives in the optimal solution.

8 Large multinational companies have many foreign subsidiaries. The relationship between the manager of one of those foreign subsidiaries with company headquarters is an agency relationship, with the manager of the foreign subsidiary as agent and headquarters as principal. Managers of the foreign subsidiaries can receive a bonus payment related to the financial results of their subsidiary. There is considerable variation, however, in terms of the relative importance of such financial incentives.

One factor that might explain part of the variation is industry volatility (the degree to which conditions in the foreign subsidiary's industry fluctuate: some industries are relatively stable, others show large fluctuations in levels of demand and customer preferences). How would you expect industry volatility to influence the use of financial incentives?

Which other factors could possibly explain the variation in the use of financial incentives?

Note

1   The concept of the indifference curve is explained in Section 2.3.

8 Transaction cost economics

8.1 Introduction

In Chapter 1 we laid the framework for this book, which was summarized in Figure 1.1. Essentially, the argument is that division of labour creates opportunities for specialization, which necessitates the coordination of economic decisions. There are two ideal types of coordination mechanism: markets and organizations.

In transaction cost economics the fundamental unit of analysis is the transaction. Transactions can take place across markets or within organizations. Whether a particular transaction is allocated to the market or an organization is a matter of cost minimization. Transaction cost economics emphasizes that transaction costs as well as traditional production costs should be taken into account. The term 'transaction costs' includes costs of both market transactions and internal transactions.

According to the argument we have developed so far, firms exist because, in some cases, the costs of internal coordination are lower than the costs of market transactions (see Box 8.1). That is almost a tautology. If there is a firm, then, apparently, the costs of internal coordination are lower than the costs of market transactions. That is not much of a theory. Such a 'theory' can never be empirically tested. If we really want to develop a theory, we should specify beforehand in which cases we expect the costs of market transactions to be high compared with the costs of internal coordination. If we can do that, we can hope to derive hypotheses that are suitable for empirical testing.

Oliver Williamson has almost single-handedly developed such a theory in numerous publications. This chapter is based primarily on Williamson's work, especially on his two books *Markets and Hierarchies* (1975) and *The Economic Institutions of Capitalism* (1985).

Box 8.1 A factory making grandfather clocks

Why do firms exist? Why is not everyone self-employed?

Consider a factory employing 18 people making grandfather clocks. Five of the employees specialize in sawing the wooden parts that together form the clocks' cases. Two of them assemble the wooden parts to form the cases. Another two spray the cases with paint. Two paint faces. Four

▶

assemble cases, faces and movements to form complete clocks. There are two salespeople and one general manager. The general manager is also the owner of the company.

Why are the first 17 people working as employees? Why is not everyone self-employed? The answer is transaction costs. Consider the following three situations:

- *Situation 1* 17 self-employed people working at geographically dispersed locations;
- *Situation 2* 17 self-employed people all working under the same roof;
- *Situation 3* 17 people employed by the owner of the factory.

Compare, first, Situations 1 and 2. In Situation 1, the costs of transporting semi-finished goods is high compared with 2. In Situation 2, the costs of market transactions between the 17 self-employed people may be high because of the small numbers bargaining. For example, if the two people spraying cases with paint collude, they can try to lower the prices of unpainted cases and raise the prices of painted cases. That may result in frequent interruptions of the workflow. In Situation 1, the two sprayers may have to compete with numerous other sprayers, which would restrict their bargaining power.

Compare now Situations 2 and 3. In Situation 3, there is no costly haggling over prices of semi-finished goods (no interruptions of the workflow because parties cannot reach agreement over prices of semi-finished goods). The quantities of semi-finished goods that each must produce are determined by the general manager, not negotiation between the self-employed people.

The general manager must also evaluate each person's level of effort. The three situations can be summarized as shown in the table below.

	(1) Self-employed workers in geographically dispersed locations	(2) Self-employed workers under the same roof	(3) Employeees working for an employer
Transportation costs	High	Low	Low
Costs of market transactions	Low	High	Low
Costs of internal coordination	Low	Low	High

In a market economy, only the most efficient organizational form can survive in the long run. Therefore, if we observe, in reality, there are only grandfather clockmaking factories like Situation 3, then, apparently, that is the most efficient type of organization.

Transaction cost economics as developed by Williamson is based on the assumption that human beings are *boundedly rational* and sometimes display *opportunistic behaviour*. These two behavioural assumptions are discussed in Section 8.2. Whether transaction costs for a particular transaction will be high or low depends on the *critical dimensions* of that transaction. Critical dimensions of transactions are discussed in Section 8.3. These two sections lay the basic foundations for transaction cost economics.

In the subsequent sections, we apply transaction cost reasoning. First, we discuss several organizational forms–peer groups, single stage hierarchies and multistage hierarchies. Then we discuss internal markets within firms. We examine the role of reputation and trust as countervailing forces against opportunistic behaviour in Section 8.8. In Section 8.9 we round off by paying attention to the (meso) level of analysis at which the governance of transactions is located and the interplay with the macro (institutional) and micro (individual) levels.

8.2 Behavioural assumptions: bounded rationality and opportunism

8.2.1 Bounded rationality

Bounded rationality

The concept of bounded rationality was introduced in Chapter 6 on behavioural theory. **Bounded rationality** means that the capacity of human beings to formulate and solve complex problems is limited. It was already introduced and discussed in Chapter 6. To refresh your memory, a good example is the game of chess. A chess player has all the information she needs to make her decisions: the positions of the white and black pieces at the moment that she is contemplating a move are all the information she needs. In order to evaluate a certain move, she needs only to analyze what moves her opponent can possibly make and evaluate all possible moves that she could make in answer to each possible countermove. The problem in chess is simply that the number of alternative sequences of moves and countermoves is too great even for the world's best chess players. It is not that a chess player does not want to make fully rational decisions. She does want to make fully rational decisions, but her capacity to evaluate fully the consequences of all the possible decisions is limited. So, bounded rationality refers to human behaviour that is 'intendedly rational, but only limitedly so' (Simon, 1961).

From the discussion it is clear that bounded rationality poses a problem in chess because chess is a complex game. A game such as bridge is characterized by both complexity and uncertainty. In bridge the players do not know the hands of their opponents. If they did, then the game would be much less interesting. In bridge, bounded rationality is a problem because of the combination of uncertainty and complexity.

Uncertainty/complexity

Now let us return to transactions. Bounded rationality will pose a problem only in environments that are characterized by **uncertainty/complexity**. When you buy petrol for your car, there is not much complexity or uncertainty. You know the product quite well, you do not have to worry about aftersales service and the seller does not need any information about you provided you pay directly. To buy petrol you do not need to write and sign a contract.

Now consider the case of a government that wants to buy a new weapon system. In that case it *is* necessary to write and sign a contract. Such a contract is very complicated. Product specifications should be clearly defined in the contract, but that can be quite difficult because of uncertainty about the technology. Is it feasible to develop a new weapon system that meets some clearly defined specifications? How much will it cost to develop such a system? How much will it cost to manufacture those systems? These are elements of uncertainty/complexity in the case of buying new and complex weaponry. It is likely that bounded rationality in conjunction with uncertainty/complexity makes it costly to write a contract for buying a new weapon system.

8.2.2 Opportunism

Opportunism

In Williamson's view, human beings are not only boundedly rational but they also sometimes display opportunistic behaviour. Williamson describes **opportunism** as 'self-interest seeking with guile' and as making 'self-disbelieved statements'. Opportunism may involve outright lying and cheating (which, unfortunately, happens in the real world occasionally – see Ariely, 2012), but it may also involve more subtle twists to the truth, as our Box 8.2 shows from the world of online dating.

Box 8.2 Online dating and self-disbelieved statements

Online dating has come of age in some societies. Once a seedy corner of the internet, digital romance is today nearly as commonplace as e-commerce in the USA. Of the 87 million singles in the US, nearly half of them have tried online dating, according to the US Census. Some surveys estimate that one in five new relationships, and one in six new marriages, begins online. Dating sites, like Match.com and eHarmony, bring together supply and demand on the online dating and marriage market.

When you register on these sites, you are asked to submit a profile. Of course, you can submit a profile which you believe reflects 'the truth and nothing but the truth' about yourself. On the other hand, you might be tempted to present yourself in a slightly more favourable light, perhaps twisting the absolute truth a bit in order to attract the right kind of interest. What do you think happens on this online market? Dan Ariely, a Professor of Psychology and Behavioral Economics at Duke University, reports the following:

If you suspect that most people on the site slightly exaggerate their vital and biographical statistics, you're right! When Günter Hitsch and Ali Hortaçsu (both professors at the University of Chicago) and I looked into the world of online dating, we discovered that men cared mostly about women's weight and women cared mostly about men's height and income. We also discovered, perhaps not surprisingly, that the online women reported their weight to be substantially below average while the men claimed to be taller and richer than average. This suggests that both men and women know what the other half is looking for, and so they cheat just a little bit when describing their own attributes. A fellow who is 5'9" and earns $60,000 annually typically gives himself an extra inch and a $30,000 raise, describing himself as 5'10"and making $90,000. Meanwhile his potential partner remembers her weight in college and, with a 5 percent discount, becomes 133 pounds.

Source: 'Inside Match.com', *FT Weekend Magazine*, July 30/31, 2011 and D. Ariely (2009), *Predictably Irrational,* NY: Harper Collins

---

In plain English, opportunism means trying to exploit a situation to your own advantage. Williamson does not assume that everybody behaves opportunistically. He assumes only that some people might display opportunistic behaviour *and* that it is difficult or impossible to distinguish *ex ante* (that is, before you make a deal) honest people from dishonest people. Even those who behave opportunistically need not do so all the time. Williamson assumes only that those who might display opportunistic behaviour do so *sometimes* and that it is difficult or costly to tell *ex ante* when they do or do not.

Sometimes people blame Williamson for having too pessimistic a view of human nature. It somehow does not seem right to build a theory on such a gloomy assumption. If that is your first reaction, too, consider the following examples.

Suppose you would like to spend your summer holiday in Greece. You go to a travel agent and find that almost everyone wants to go to Greece this year. You have to decide on the spot and book a holiday that is a little bit too expensive and not exactly what you want. The next day you see the perfect holiday at another travel agent – it is exactly what you want *and* much cheaper. Would you not be tempted to cancel the first reservation if you could?

Suppose travel agents did not make their customers sign contracts that were legally binding, would you not agree that sometimes some customers would deny they had already booked the first expensive holiday? Apparently, travel agents think so – that is why they have their customers sign a contract.

Consider also box 8.3 for an example of opportunistic behaviour.

Box 8.3 Opportunism: return to vendor

Retailers benefit from having good customer services and a generous returns policy. Most customers only return products that they have experienced as truly faulty. But some customers take advantage of generous returns policies, engaging in a practice that is called 'de-shopping' by some retailers and 'wardrobing' by clothing stores:

> Times may be tough, but women still need little black dresses to wear to posh parties. So some buy a fancy frock, dance the night away in it and then return it to the store, pretending that it does not fit. To ensure a refund, they may even unpick a seam and complain that the garment is faulty. This is an example of a growing problem.
>
> Return fraud… cost American retailers $14.4 billion in 2011, according to the National Retail Federation. Online stores are particularly vulnerable. The worst offenders are women returning clothes. Most do not see their behavior as fraudulent says Tamara King of Cranfield School of Management in Britain. If retailers are gullible enough to take goods back, they think, then more fool them. Few would cross the line to shoplifting, which they (correctly) regard as criminal.

Ariely (2009, p. 301) maintains that the annual losses from wardrobing are about the same amount as the estimated annual loss from home burglaries and automobile theft combined.

Source: 'Return to vendor: a dress on loan', *The Economist*, 3 March 2012; D. Ariely (2009), *Predictably Irrational*, NY: Harper Collins

---

Consider also the following example. Suppose you want to buy a second-hand car from someone you do not know. The seller tells you that the car has no defects. Do you believe him? Suppose you can have the car inspected by an independent expert. Would you pay the cost of the inspection before buying? If you are prepared to pay the inspection cost, it means that you do not believe everyone.

Suppose you can choose between two secondhand cars (A and B) from two different sellers (A and B). You can detect no difference between the two cars themselves. There is only one difference: car A has been inspected by an independent expert, who tells you that it has no defects. Car B has not been inspected. Seller B tells you that car B has no defects. Would you prefer car A? That means you do not rule out the possibility of opportunistic behaviour by seller B.

From these examples it is clear that travel agents and buyers of secondhand cars must spend a little amount of money (on drawing up a contract or having a car inspected), not because they expect all their trading partners to behave opportunistically all the time, but because *some people* might display opportunistic behaviour *sometimes*.

Box 8.4 The evolution of exchanges between strangers

Paul Seabright has written a beautiful book entitled *The Company of Strangers: A natural history of economic life* (2004). In the book he examines the evolutionary economic history of mankind. Specifically, he enquires how we have been able to build such a complex, interlinked economy in a relatively short period of time (a mere ten thousand years – equivalent to about two and a half minutes on an evolutionary clock that began ticking when our evolution diverged from the rest of the animal kingdom). Seabright shows the most remarkable feature of that evolution to be the enormous amount of (economic) interaction we have with strangers:

> *Homo sapiens* is the only animal that engages in elaborate task-sharing–the division of labour as it is sometimes known–between genetically unrelated members of the same species. It is a phenomenon as remarkable and uniquely human as language itself. Most human beings now obtain a large share of the provision for their daily lives from others to whom they are not related by blood or marriage.

This is what Seabright has to say about the behavioural underpinnings of that evolution:

> Two kinds of disposition have proved important to our evolution: a capacity for rational calculation of the costs and benefits of cooperation, and a tendency for what has been called *reciprocity* – the willingness to repay kindness with kindness and betrayal with revenge, even when this is not what rational calculation would recommend. Neither disposition could support cooperation without the other. People given to calculation without reciprocity would be too opportunistic, so nobody would trust them. People given to reciprocity without calculation would be too easily exploited by others. It seems likely that natural selection favored the evolution of a balance between these two dispositions in our ancestors. It did so because such a balance was important to the development of social life even before these ancestors ever began to deal with strangers in any systematic way. But once these dispositions were there, they could be put to work to make exchange between strangers possible.

Note that Seabright's argument is in line with Williamson's: not all people are opportunistic all of the time, but this 'disposition' does exist in the population. Particularly, as many of our dealings are with 'strangers', we have a hard time sorting out who can be trusted (when) and who not. Note also the link with evolutionary game theory (Section 5.6), showing how cooperation can evolve from reciprocity, but that it usually also pays to learn where exploitation may be applied. We return to the topics of trust, reciprocity and reputation later in this chapter.

From the two examples above, it is also clear that opportunistic behaviour can occur *ex ante* (a seller might not tell you about defects before you buy) or *ex post* (after you have booked a holiday you might want to back out of it). *Ex ante* opportunistic behaviour leads to adverse selection, a concept that was introduced in Section 4.2. *Ex ante* opportunistic behaviour can occur only when there is asymmetrical information: the seller of a used car has information that potential buyers do not have.

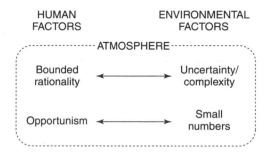

Figure 8.1 The transaction cost framework

Now suppose that there are large numbers of sellers and buyers who trade with each other on a regular basis. Suppose that in a certain town there are ten dealers in secondhand cars. Suppose you buy a secondhand car. If you have a negative experience with one of the dealers, you do not want to buy from her a second time. A dealer who behaves opportunistically will damage her reputation. The dealers know that and you know the dealers know that, so you tend to believe a dealer when he says that a car has no defects. In that way, the problem of opportunism is attenuated because there are many sellers and because reputations matter. You can therefore save the inspection costs. (Note that you can save the inspection costs only if reputations are important and information about reputations is freely available.) There is a problem only if opportunism occurs in conjunction with small numbers of trading partners, which is termed **small numbers exchange**. If there is only one seller, he does not have to worry about reputation because you do not have an alternative. In that case you would want to have the car inspected, so you have to pay transaction costs.

The argument so far is illustrated in Figure 8.1. There are two human factors and two environmental factors. Bounded rationality in conjunction with uncertainty/complexity and opportunism in conjunction with small numbers exchange lead to transaction costs.

8.2.3 Atmosphere

The mode of a transaction (that is, whether a transaction is governed by the market or an organization) is determined by minimization of the sum of production and transaction costs. There is another factor that also determines the mode of a transaction, however. It is called **atmosphere** (see Figure 8.1).

The atmosphere factor refers to the fact that participants in a transaction may value the mode of the transaction. Consider, for example, the workers making grandfather clocks in Box 8.1. Maybe they derive satisfaction from being self-employed. If that is true, they would be willing to work as an employee only if higher income compensated for the loss of atmosphere. For that reason, an employer with 17 employees might not be able to compete against a group of 18 self-employed people even if the transaction costs of the former arrangement were lower than those of the latter.

Small numbers exchange

Atmosphere

Sometimes people prefer to give away something for free. In that case, they derive more satisfaction from the act of giving than from the money they could receive. That indicates that most people value the nature of a transaction. As an example, read Box 8.5 about donating blood.

In the framework of transaction cost economics, the atmosphere factor refers to the *local environment* in which the transaction takes place. Just as in our conceptual framework (see Figure 1.1), it acknowledges the fact that economic exchange is embedded in an environmental and institutional context with formal and informal 'rules of the game'. As elaborated in Section 1.7, the informal rules of the game are norms of behaviour, conventions and internally imposed rules of conduct, such as those of a company culture. Williamson (1998, 2007) relates the atmosphere factor to the concept of 'informal organization'. He acknowledges the importance of such informal rules, but admits that both the concept of informal organization and the economics of atmosphere remain relatively underdeveloped.

Box 8.5 Blood donorship

As described in Box 4.2, there is a serious shortage of good quality blood that can be used for blood transfusion purposes. Clearly there is a demand for blood. Good quality blood should command a high price, yet we observe that blood collection is still organized on a voluntary basis. Blood donors give their blood for free. Why are blood donors not paid?

One reason, explained in Box 4.2, is adverse selection, but there is a second reason: if blood donors were to receive payment, then that would fundamentally change the nature of the transaction. As it is, blood donors derive satisfaction from the idea that they give their blood for the common good. They voluntarily give to those who are so unfortunate as to need a transfusion. To pay blood donors would transform the act of giving blood into an ordinary commercial transaction. Titmuss (1971) argued that it would be quite likely that the result would be fewer (good quality) donors instead of more. This is called the 'crowding out' effect. It is an example of 'atmosphere' being disturbed by transforming blood donation into a commercial transaction.

Mellström and Johannesson (2008) tested the crowding out effect in a field experiment in Sweden. They found that there is a significant crowding out effect for women, but not for men. In addition, they found that the crowding out effect could be fully counteracted by allowing the individuals to donate their payment to charity. Apparently, the (female) blood donors felt that this option restored the transaction to a voluntary contribution rather than a commercial transaction.

Source: C. Mellström and M. Johannesson (2008), 'Crowding out in blood donation: was Titmuss right?', *Journal of the European Economic Association*, 6(4): 845–863

8.2.4 The fundamental transformation

Suppose that an automobile company invites bids from a large number of potential suppliers for a certain part for a new automobile. Suppose that the automobile company signs a contract with one of the original bidders for a five-year period. During that five-year period the supplier learns how to produce the component efficiently. After five years, when the contract must be renewed, the original winner of the contract has a significant advantage over other potential

Lock-in

suppliers. Williamson (1975) refers to this situation as **lock-in**. Through learning by doing, the original situation, involving a large number of bidders, is transformed into a situation of monopoly: the experience gained by the supplier puts the firm in the position of a monopolist. However, the supplier can use that experience only in the manufacturing of a part for which there is only one buyer. So, the situation is again one of bilateral monopoly. See Box 8.7 for a real-world example of lock-in.

Fundamental transformation

When learning by doing occurs, an original situation of large numbers exchange is transformed into a situation of small numbers exchange. That is termed the **fundamental transformation**.

8.3 Dimensions of transactions

Critical dimensions of transactions

Transaction costs for a particular transaction depend on the critical dimensions of that transaction. There are three **critical dimensions of transactions**:

- asset specificity;
- uncertainty/complexity;
- frequency.

8.3.1 Asset specificity

Asset specificity

Transaction-specific assets

The **asset specificity** of a transaction refers to the degree to which the transaction needs to be supported by **transaction-specific assets**. An asset is transaction-specific if it cannot be redeployed to an alternative use without a significant reduction in the value of the asset. Asset specificity may refer to physical or human assets. To illustrate the concept, consider the following example, which refers to physical assets.

Imagine a town located in the centre of a very thinly populated area. Let us call the town Appropria. At present there is no local newspaper in Appropria, but there is a publisher, Mr P, who wants to start a local newspaper.

The new newspaper must be printed locally in Appropria because of transportation costs. Mr P does not have printing know-how, so he must rely on that of one of the local printers. There are several printers in Appropria but none of them has a press suitable for printing newspapers.

One of the printers in Appropria, Mrs Q, considers buying a press for printing newspapers. If she buys such a press, it will be a transaction-specific asset: she can use the press only for the transaction with Mr P as there is no other newspaper in Appropria and it is very costly to transport newspapers to other towns. To put it in the language of transaction cost economics, the transaction between Mr P and Mrs Q is characterized by asset specificity and lock-in.

For transactions with high asset specificity, the costs of market transactions are high. To see why that is true, let us return to Appropria. Suppose that the new press has an economic life of five years. Mrs Q will want a five-year contract with Mr P before she buys the press. At first glance it may not seem very difficult or costly to write and sign a five-year contract. To illustrate the difficulties in writing such a contract, however, we use a numerical example.

Assume fixed costs are $3500 per day, if the new press is depreciated over five years. Assume, further, that variable costs for operating the new press are $1500 per day. Mrs Q cannot sell the services of the press to another publisher, nor can she sell the press.

Suppose Mrs Q obtains a five-year contract from Mr P for $5000 per day and, on that basis, orders the new press. As soon as Mrs Q has committed herself, Mr P has an incentive for opportunistic behaviour. Even though Mrs Q has a legally binding contract with Mr P, he can come back to her. Suppose he tells her, 'Look, this new newspaper is not really the success I expected it to become. With a contract for $5000 a day I will go bankrupt and then your press will have no value at all. If you can help me a little by agreeing to lower the price to $4000 a day, I will be able to manage. I am very sorry that I have to say this, but really I see no other solution.'

If Mrs Q believes his story, she has no other choice than to accept the lower price. In fact, she must accept any price higher than $1500 a day. In business language, we would say that, for a price higher than $1500, there is still a posi-tive contribution margin. In the language of economics, we would say that, for

Quasi-rent

a price higher than $1500, there is still a positive **quasi-rent**. By making self-disbelieved statements, Mr P tries to appropriate (a part of) that quasi-rent. In Appropria, trying to appropriate someone else's quasi-rent is a great sport. If someone else can try to appropriate your quasi-rent, economists refer to the

Hold-up

danger of **hold-up**. Box 8.6 gives another example of the threat of hold-up (and the solution applied in that situation).

Box 8.6 Hold-up in The *Lord of the Rings*

When television series become successful the lead actors can often renegotiate their compensation before shooting the next season. A similar threat of hold-up may occur with films – for example, when a trilogy is foreseen:

All three movies in the *Lord of the Rings* series were made before the first was released to avoid just this problem. The studio clearly wanted to avoid a situation in which Elijah Wood, who played central character Frodo Baggins, could negotiate a new and highly lucrative contract on the strength of the success of the first film before completing the final part of the trilogy, *Return of the King*.

Source: Gilson et al. (2006)

If Mr P cannot go bankrupt under any circumstances, there is no problem. In that case, a legally binding contract protects Mrs Q against post-contractual opportunistic behaviour by Mr P. If, however, Mr P can go bankrupt, Mrs Q will not buy the press on the basis of a simple five-year contract. What she needs is a guarantee from Mr P's bank that, in the event of bankruptcy, the bank will pay her the fixed costs ($3500 a day, assuming no salvage value) for the rest of the five-year period. Now, though, the bank will be vulnerable to Mr P's post-contractual opportunistic behaviour. Mr P can go to his banker and say, 'Look, if you pay me $1000 a day, I will not go bankrupt and you can save your contractual obligation to pay Mrs Q $3500 a day.' So, the guarantee does not solve the problem, but transfers it to someone else.

In reality, Mrs Q might be willing to sign a contract with Mr P but, before doing so, she needs much more information about Mr P's business plan, his character, his personal wealth and so on. To acquire such information is costly. In addition, she will demand the right to have Mr P's books inspected by an independent auditor, which is costly, too. Finally, as her money will still be at risk, she will demand compensation for risk-bearing. That compensation may come in the form of a price higher than $5000 a day or a share in Mr P's profits.

Another solution to these contractual difficulties is a merger between the firms of Mr P and Mrs Q. Then, the transaction between publisher and printer would be taken out of the market and allocated to an organization. After a merger, Mr P and Mrs Q jointly own the assets and share the profits, so Mr P no longer has an incentive to behave opportunistically towards his partner.

In our example, the degree of asset specificity is so high that a series of sequential spot contracts (say, contracts for one day only and daily negotiations on the price for the next day) is not feasible (Mrs Q can never accept this, so she will not buy the press). So, there are only two options left: a merger between Mr P and Mrs Q or a five-year contract specifying in detail Mrs Q's right to inspect Mr P's business. Such a long-term contract is an intermediate form between market and organization. In the language of transaction cost economics, it is termed **relational contracting**.

Relational contracting

By the way, there may be another asset that is highly transaction-specific in the example above. A new newspaper normally suffers start-up losses during the first few years. By financing those start-up losses, Mr P invests in an intangible asset. Let us call it goodwill. That goodwill is also a transaction-specific asset. Mrs Q now also has an incentive for post-contractual opportunistic behaviour. For example, she might say, 'Look, I made a mistake in calculating the price of $5000 a day. You really must pay me $5700 a day. If you don't, I will go bankrupt and the value of your investment in goodwill will be zero.' That would pose a problem for Mr P if other printers would need at least a few months before they could start printing newspapers.

So, Mr P and Mrs Q both have to invest in a transaction-specific asset. That means, after they have invested, they will be locked into a bilateral monopoly: they both have a monopoly position towards the other with respect to certain assets.

In the introduction to this section we distinguished between physical and human asset specificity. Box 8.7 gives a somewhat finer distinction.

Box 8.7 Asset specificity and lock-in: benefits and risks

Transaction cost economics has filtered through to the managerial literature. Consider the following discussion of several types of asset specificity from the *McKinsey Quarterly*:

There are three principal types of asset specificity ... *Site specificity* occurs when buyers and sellers locate fixed assets, such as a coalmine and power station, in close proximity to minimize transport and inventory costs. *Technical specificity* occurs when one or both parties to a transaction invest in equipment that can only be used by one or both parties and that has low value in alternative uses. *Human capital specificity* occurs when employees develop skills that are specific to a particular buyer or customer relationship.

The upstream aluminum industry has high asset specificity. The industry has two principal stages of production: bauxite mining and aluminum refining. Mines and refineries are usually located close together (site specificity) because of the high cost of transporting bauxite, relative to its value, and the 60 to 70 per cent volume reduction typically achieved during refining. Refineries are tailored to process their own bauxite, with its unique chemical and physical properties; switching suppliers or customers is either impossible or prohibitively expensive (technical specificity). Consequently, mine-refinery pairs are locked together economically.

Being 'locked in' with suppliers is not without risk, however. Toyota is a company that has perhaps overstretched its supply chain by relying too much on 'sole sourcing' in a period of rapid expansion and globalization:

Toyota revolutionized automotive supply-chain management by anointing certain suppliers as the sole source of particular components, leading to intimate collaboration with long-term partners and a sense of mutual benefit…A consequence of Toyota's breakneck expansion was that it became increasingly dependent on suppliers outside Japan with whom it did not have decades of working experience. Nor did Toyota have enough of the senior engineers, known as *sensei,* to keep an eye on how new suppliers were shaping up. Yet Toyota not only continued to trust in its sole-sourcing approach, it went even further, gaining unprecedented economies of scale by using single suppliers for entire ranges of its cars across multiple markets.

This policy of global 'sole sourcing' has contributed to the scale of recalls and production stops that Toyota had to endure when certain components turned out to be defective, as summarized in Box 4.1.

Source: 'The machine that ran too hot', *The Economist,* 27 February 2010

8.3.2 Uncertainty/complexity

The second dimension of transactions, uncertainty/complexity, needs no further explanation: we learned earlier that bounded rationality is a problem only for transactions with a high degree of uncertainty/complexity (remember the examples of buying petrol and ordering a new weapon system).

8.3.3 Frequency

When asset specificity is high, we expect transactions to be carried out within organizations rather than across markets. However, to set up a specialized governance structure (such as a vertically integrated firm) involves certain fixed costs. Whether the volume of transactions conducted through such a specialized governance structure utilizes it to capacity is then the remaining issue. The costs of a specialized governance structure are more easily recovered for high frequency transactions. Hence, frequency is the third relevant dimension of transactions.

8.3.4 Competition between organizational forms

Transaction costs for a particular transaction depend on the critical dimensions of that transaction. For transactions with a high degree of asset specificity, a high degree of uncertainty/complexity and a high frequency, the costs of market transactions are extremely high–much higher than the costs of internal transactions. Such transactions tend to be carried out within organizations, at least in the long run.

In the real world, we might see certain market transactions and, at the same time, similar transactions taking place within organizations. That can indicate the costs of transacting under the two modes are about equal. If the costs of transacting under the two modes differ significantly, then the most efficient form will ultimately prevail. It might take quite a long time, however, as is illustrated in Box 8.8.

Box 8.8 Why are dairy firms organized as farmers' cooperatives?

Dairy firms are often, though not always, organized as farmers' cooperatives. Why is that?

Before trying to answer this question, let us give you some details about the emergence of the first dairy cooperatives in the Netherlands or, more specifically, in two provinces of the Netherlands: Friesland and North Holland.

In the middle of the nineteenth century, there were only three dairy products: cheese, butter and fresh milk. In those days, farmers made cheese and butter at the farm (that was usually done by women). In 1878, a centrifuge for separating cream from milk was developed. The invention provided economies of scale and led to the emergence of dairy factories.

In Friesland, the first dairy factory was established in 1879 by a private entrepreneur. Seven years later, in 1886, Friesland had seven dairy firms owned and operated by entrepreneurs. In that same year, a dairy factory was established by a group of farmers as a cooperative firm.

A dairy firm organized as a farmers' cooperative does not have shareholders, so maximizing profit is not its main goal. A farmers' cooperative has members and tries to pay its members as high a price as possible for the milk its members supply.

In Friesland, the number of dairy factories set up by farmers' cooperatives grew rapidly, but so did the number of dairy firms run by entrepreneurs. In 1898, Friesland had 46 dairy factories run by entrepreneurs and 66 run by farmers' cooperatives. In the first 25 years of the next century, however, dairy firms run by farmers' cooperatives grew faster in size and number, while some of the entrepreneurial dairy firms failed. As a result, the farmers' cooperative has been the dominant organizational form of dairy firms in Friesland since 1925.

In the northern part of North Holland, dairy firms developed in the same way as in Friesland; around 1900 there were entrepreneurial as well as cooperative dairy firms, but the cooperatives grew faster. As a result, cooperatives came to dominate that region as well.

In the southern part of North Holland, there were no farmers' cooperatives around 1900. That area is close to the cities of Amsterdam, Haarlem, Leiden and Utrecht. Milk from the area was sold primarily as fresh milk to consumers in those cities by distributors. The distributors were private entrepreneurs.

Why did the cooperative dairy firm overtake entrepreneurial dairy firms in Friesland and the northern part of North Holland? Why did cooperative dairy firms not emerge in the southern part of North Holland?

▶

The answers to those questions have much to do with the fact that milk is a perishable product. In the nineteenth century, milk could not be stored for more than a day (cooling was not available) and transporting milk over long distances was not feasible. Milk had to be processed into cheese and butter within a short time and not far from the farm. As a result, farmers who sold their milk to an entrepreneurial dairy firm were in a situation where they had only one customer. Their investment in cattle is a transaction-specific investment. The farmers had no alternative for their milk but to resume the old way of processing milk at the farm. In the early days of the dairy factories, it was probably a feasible alternative because farmers still had the equipment and the know-how for making butter and cheese. However, as economies of scale became more pronounced and farmers' equipment for making butter and cheese was no longer in a good condition, making butter and cheese at the farm ceased to be a realistic alternative. Farmers were powerless against opportunistic behaviour from entrepreneurial dairy firms, especially as butter and cheese are much less perishable than fresh milk. That prompted more and more farmers, who initially sold their milk to entrepreneurial firms, to become members of the nearest farmers' cooperative. It explains the developments in Friesland and the northern part of North Holland, where almost all milk was used for making butter and cheese.

In the southern part of North Holland, the situation was different; the distributors of fresh milk were as dependent on the farmers as the farmers were dependent on them. The investment by the farmers in cattle is transaction-specific, but so is the investment by the distributors in their customer base and their means of distribution. As fresh milk could not be stored for more than a day, the distributors needed a daily supply of fresh milk. That made opportunistic behaviour by distributors towards their suppliers unlikely.

The main difference between a distributor of fresh milk and an entrepreneurial dairy firm making butter and cheese seems to be that the former needs a daily supply of fresh milk while the latter does not. That explains why cooperative dairy firms did not emerge in the southern part of North Holland.

The example in Box 8.8 also illustrates how organizational forms compete. There was competition between cooperative dairy firms and entrepreneurial dairy firms. That points to a fundamental assumption in transaction cost economics: there is always competition between organizational forms and, in the long run, only the most efficient organizational form will survive.

8.4 Peer groups

In Sections 8.2 and 8.3 we have laid the foundations for transaction cost reasoning. In the next sections we apply transaction cost reasoning to explain the existence of different organizational forms.

Peer group

The first organizational form to be discussed is the peer group. A **peer group** is simply a group of people working together without hierarchy. In a peer group, the most important coordinating mechanism is mutual adjustment. There is no boss, so there can be no direct supervision. The peer group sells its output, the proceeds of which are shared among the members of the peer group according to some sharing rule. Examples of peer groups are small partnerships, such as lawyers, auditors and doctors.

8.4.1 Advantages of peer groups

Why do peer groups arise? For example, why do most management consultants work as partners in a partnership instead of working independently? What are the advantages of a peer group over a group of independent self-employed people?

First, *economies of scale* may be obtained. Suppose two dentists form a partnership. The partnership may then buy equipment for X-ray photography that each dentist uses for perhaps not more than half an hour per day. However, an alternative arrangement would be two dentists working independently (without pooling revenue) in the same building. They could still jointly own or lease the X-ray equipment.

In the examples, economies of scale arise because the workers (the dentists) need the services of expensive equipment on a part-time basis only. Joint ownership (as farmers sometimes have of harvesting machines) is then a viable arrangement for obtaining such economies. It may also be possible to obtain the services of such indivisible specialized physical assets by renting (harvesting equipment that can be moved easily from one farmer to the next provides an example).

Economies of scale may also arise in *information-gathering.* Imagine two consultants who specialize in marketing studies for pharmaceutical companies. Both need background information on developments in the pharmaceutical industry on a continuous basis. Suppose they both employ a young economist for desk research. By forming a partnership, they can economize on desk research.

Suppose the two consultants decide to remain independent, but still want to economize on desk research. Could one of them stop doing desk research and buy the information he needed from his competitor/colleague? Without going into details now, it seems plausible that this would be more difficult than buying the services of specialized equipment. In general, it is difficult to trade information because of the fundamental paradox of information (see Section 4.1). So, economies of scale in information-gathering are difficult to obtain for two independent consultants.

Second, a peer group may have *risk-bearing advantages* over a group of independent people. Consider a group of ten independent marketing consultants. A major risk for each of them is to have no assignments for an extended period. Forming a partnership is one way to obtain pooling of that risk. Alternatively, it is useful to ask if such risk-pooling could be obtained through a market, in this case the insurance market.

It may be possible but difficult to obtain insurance for the risk of having no assignments. Those consultants who are weak in selling their services will be especially eager to take out such an insurance policy. Also, after having obtained one, it may be quite difficult for the insurance company to check whether or not the consultant really tried hard enough to get assignments. Thus, adverse selection and moral hazard would be severe problems for the insurance company.

The partners forming a peer group may be able to mitigate against adverse selection if they can screen potential partners better than an insurance company can. It also seems plausible that a partnership can avoid the problem of moral hazard, as observability of effort is less of a problem for colleagues than it is for an insurance company.

Third, a peer group may offer *associational gains.* That is, consultants may be more productive when working as member of a partnership than when working independently. If they belong to a partnership, they may feel a responsibility to do their fair share, but, working alone, they may slack off. Also, they may value being a partner and working with peers. That is an example of atmosphere: people may simply prefer one organizational form over another.

8.4.2 Limitations of peer groups

In a small peer group (for example, two authors writing a book on economic theories of organization), shirking may not be a problem at all. On the contrary, each may take pride in doing more than his fair share. In a large peer group, however, shirking often becomes a severe problem. Very large partnerships (in auditing and/or consulting) do exist, but then some of the partners are elected managing partners. It is their duty to restrict shirking by evaluating the performance of other partners and adjusting the income-sharing rules accordingly. Such large partnerships are, therefore, more accurately described as simple hierarchies than peer groups.

8.5 Simple hierarchies

Simple hierarchy

A **simple hierarchy** is a group of workers with a boss. The boss has the right to adjust rates of pay, alter the composition of the group and tell the workers in the group what to do. Most small manufacturing firms (such as the factory making grandfather clocks) are organized as simple hierarchies, not peer groups.

In a peer group, all members are equal: they receive the same income and have the same decision rights. In a hierarchy, some people can tell other people what to do, so direct supervision is an important coordinating mechanism. Also, in a hierarchy, a person's income usually has a relationship to his or her performance–either past performance or expected future performance.

Why do we observe so few peer groups, especially in manufacturing industries? What advantages do simple hierarchies have over peer groups?

8.5.1 Team production

In Section 7.4 we explained how, in the view of Alchian and Demsetz (1972), team production leads to the emergence of a simple hierarchy. Team production, they say, will induce people to shirk. A monitor has to be brought in to reduce shirking. To avoid shirking by the monitor, the monitor must be the residual claimant.

Williamson (1975) disagrees with Alchian and Demsetz's view. Most production processes consist of several stages, he says, which are technologically separable. As an example, consider again the factory making grandfather clocks. There are several stages of production, such as sawing, assembling and painting. Those stages can be separated by intermediate product inventories, so the work

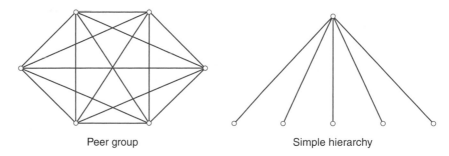

Peer group   Simple hierarchy

Figure 8.2 Number of communication channels in a peer group and in a simple hierarchy

of the sawyers and assemblers can be separated. There is no team production in this example, yet we see most such firms organized as simple hierarchies rather than as peer groups.

8.5.2 Economies of communication and decisionmaking

In a peer group, every member participates in decisionmaking. In a simple hierarchy, decisions are made by the boss. Now, suppose that information relevant for decisionmaking originates with each member. In a peer group, each member must communicate with all the other members. In a simple hierarchy, that person need only communicate with the boss. Thus, in a peer group the number of communication channels is $\frac{1}{2}n(n-1)$ while in a simple hierarchy it is $n-1$, where n is the number of individuals in the group (Figure 8.2). Transfer of information is costly because of bounded rationality (it takes time to explain things to other team members; information may become distorted when transferred). Thus, for $n > 2$, a simple hierarchy can realize **economies of communication** over a peer group.

Economies of communication

Economies in decisionmaking

A simple hierarchy can also realize **economies in decisionmaking**. Where, in a peer group, decisions are reached after discussions in the whole group, in a simple hierarchy the boss alone makes decisions, so less time is needed for decisionmaking.

8.5.3 Monitoring

As indicated in Section 8.4, shirking becomes a severe problem in a large peer group. Thus, in such a group it is not uncommon to see one or a few members designated to perform productivity audits and given the power to adjust the compensation of group members accordingly. That, however, violates the essence of a peer group. Whatever its legal form (partnership or mutual corporation), it has now been transformed into a simple hierarchy.

For the reasons explained above, we observe relatively few peer groups in the economy. Williamson stresses hierarchy as the alternative to mutual adjustment within peer groups. Most organizations are of a more complex type, involving more coordination mechanisms than mutual adjustment and direct supervision (see Chapter 3).

8.6 Multistage hierarchies: U-form and M-form enterprises

In a simple hierarchy, there is only one manager who coordinates the work of the other team members. Suppose that economies of scale are such that the size of the group is large. Then, because of bounded rationality, a single manager can no longer coordinate the work of all team members. Several managers are now needed. That creates an opportunity for division of managerial work so that each manager can specialize. One manager, for example, may specialize in managing the factory, another in managing the marketing and salespeople and so on. Thus, within the firm, departments are created along functional lines and each functional department has a manager. The work of those functional managers is coordinated by a general manager. This organization form is used widely by medium-sized firms. Williamson calls it the *unitary form,* or, *U-form enterprise.* Within a **U-form enterprise** there are at least two layers of managers. It is a **multistage hierarchy** as opposed to a single-stage or simple hierarchy.

U-form enterprise

Multistage hierarchy

Now suppose that a U-form firm expands by adding several new products. Alfred D. Chandler (1966) studied the history of several large American companies and found that, in the late nineteenth century, most of them were involved in a single activity (for example, steel, meatpacking, tobacco, oil) and were organized along functional lines.

In the early twentieth century, however, many of the large companies diversified into new products. At first, most of them continued as U-form enterprises, but, after some time, they found out that, for the large, multiproduct firm, the U-form has severe disadvantages. The disadvantages are of two kinds.

First, in a large U-form firm, there are several layers of management. Coordination of two functional departments (say marketing and production) occurs mainly at the top level. Thus, information has to be transmitted across several layers before it is used for decisionmaking. As information is transmitted, some of it is usually lost. Data are summarized and interpreted as they move upwards and instructions are operationalized as they move downwards, which leads to **cumulative control loss**, the corporate board losing control of day-to-day operations as the number of management layers increases. Cumulative control loss is a result of bounded rationality. Only because of bounded rationality do data have to be summarized and interpreted before they reach the top manager, and only because of bounded rationality is the top manager unable to give detailed, operationalized instructions.

Cumulative control loss

Second, as the U-form firm grows, the character of the strategic decision-making process alters. The top manager is involved in day-to-day operational coordination to such an extent that long-run, strategic decisions receive little attention. That is another manifestation of bounded rationality. Suppose that a management committee is formed consisting of the general manager and the top managers of the functional departments. In a large U-form firm, the top manager of a functional department may be interested more in furthering the local interests of her department than the overall goals for the enterprise. As explained in Section 6.3, it is very difficult to translate an overall goal, such as profit maximization, into operational subgoals for functional departments.

Conflicts of interest between functional departments cannot be avoided. In a small U-form firm such conflicts of interest are mitigated because the general manager is still in a position to judge how much functional managers care for and contribute to overall goals. In a large U-form firm, the top manager may find herself to be the only person attending to overall company wide goals. Thus, the tendency to pursue operational subgoals simply becomes too strong. Departmental interests voiced by functional managers enter the strategic decisionmaking process.

To summarize, the large, multiproduct U-form firm faces two problems: cumulative control loss and corruption of the strategic decisionmaking process. The solution to these two problems is to introduce the *multidivisional* or **M-form enterprise**. In the 1920s, the multidivisional structure was a major organizational innovation that occurred first in the USA. Most large American multiproduct firms adopted this structure before World War II. Most large European multiproduct firms followed in the 1950s and 1960s.

M-form enterprise

The M-form firm is divided at the top level into several quasi-autonomous operating divisions, usually along product lines. Top management is assisted by a general office (corporate staff). The main characteristics and advantages of the M-form are as follows (Williamson, 1975):

- The responsibility for operating decisions is assigned to more-or-less self-contained operating divisions that operate as quasi-firms.
- The corporate staff attached to the general office performs both advisory and auditing functions, which have the effect of securing greater control over operating division behaviour.
- The general office is principally concerned with strategic decisions, including the allocation of resources to the operating divisions.
- The separation of the general office from operations provides general office executives with the psychological commitment to being concerned with the overall performance of the organization, rather than becoming absorbed in the affairs and subgoals of functional departments.

Compared with the U-form organization of the same activities, the M-form serves to economize both on bounded rationality and opportunism. Bounded rationality is less a problem in the M-form than in the U-form firm because information needs to be transferred less often. Opportunism is attenuated in the M-form firm because goal congruence is easier to obtain: it is easier to translate an overall company goal (such as profit maximization) into operational subgoals per division (such as profit maximization for each division).

8.7 Organizational markets

8.7.1 Markets for intermediate goods and services

Within M-form enterprises, division managers are evaluated primarily on the basis of indicators of financial performance, such as return on sales, return on assets and so on. Between divisions, numerous transactions of intermediate goods and services take place. There are internal markets within the M-form enterprise for intermediate goods and services. The financial results of each division are affected by the prices (usually called transfer prices) at which those internal transactions take place. Transfer prices may be either set by corporate headquarters or negotiated between divisions. If divisions are left free to negotiate transfer prices for internal transactions, then one advantage of organizations over markets (reduction of transaction costs due to costly haggling and workflow interruptions) is seriously impaired.

Transactions can also occur between corporate headquarters and an operating division. As an example, consider a group of internal management consultants belonging to the corporate staff. Suppose the internal management consultants do not have to charge the operating divisions for their services, but are paid out of corporate funds. In that case, the marginal cost to operating divisions of an additional consulting hour is zero, so the operating divisions will demand more services until the marginal revenue to the division of an additional consulting hour is zero. The result is an oversized group of internal management consultants at the corporate level.

Now, suppose that the management consultants do have to charge the operating divisions for the full cost of their services. If operating divisions are not allowed to hire external consultants, the internal consultants have a monopoly for consulting services. The result will be monopoly pricing and shirking by the internal consultants.

Such a situation can be avoided by giving the operating divisions freedom to engage external consultants. The internal consultants now have to compete with external consultants and an internal market for consulting services with several suppliers has been created.

When, in addition, the internal consultants are allowed to offer their services in the external market, the difference between the internal and external market virtually disappears. There is then simply one market for consulting services with several suppliers (one of which is the group of internal consultants) and several customers (operating divisions and numerous other companies).

8.7.2 Internal labour markets

Internal markets also exist for human resources. Two ways to organize the internal managerial labour market will be considered.

First, managers may be rotated, working in the various divisions according to a plan devised by a corporate personnel department. Operating divisions notify the corporate personnel department if there is a vacancy and the corporate personnel department then selects a person to fill that vacancy.

Second, operating divisions may simply compete for the best managers in the internal managerial labour market. If there is a vacancy, they advertise in a corporate newsletter or on the Intranet. Managers from other divisions who are interested may apply. If they have to compete with candidates from outside companies, there is little difference between the internal managerial labour market and the external one.

8.7.3 Internal capital market

Finally, there is an internal capital market. Three ways to organize the internal capital market will be discussed:

- *Case 1* The operating divisions are not allowed to reinvest automatically the cash flow they generate. Instead, the general office reallocates the entire corporate cash flow to the divisions. Moreover, operating divisions are not allowed to raise equity capital or debt capital in the external capital market.
- *Case 2* The operating divisions are allowed to reinvest the cash flow they generate. Moreover, operating divisions are free to raise debt capital in the external capital market, but not equity capital.
- *Case 3* The operating divisions are allowed to reinvest the cash flow they generate. Moreover, they are allowed to raise both equity capital and debt capital in the external capital market.

Case 1 is the normal situation for most M-form enterprises. The general office reallocates cash flows to divisions to high-yield uses. That is a fundamental attribute of the M-form firm.

Williamson (1975) argues that the general office in an M-form enterprise is in a better position to allocate capital to the highest-yield uses than is the external capital market. His argument is as follows. Compare an M-form enterprise with, say, five operating divisions with a set of five independent comparable companies. The general office has an advantage over the external capital market in monitoring the performance of the division managers: there exists an internal relation with the division and, thus, better access to information than external investors have to independent companies. Also, the general office is in a better position to evaluate investment proposals. The manager of an operating division can provide sensitive internal information to the general office, while the disclosure of such information to outsiders (including competitors) might jeopardize the project.

In Case 2, the general office is, in essence, reduced to a clerical agency for the preparation of financial reports. The role of the general office is simply that of a large shareholder. As long as financial results of an operating division are satisfactory the general office does not interfere. Only when results of an operating division are deteriorating would the general office take steps to replace the division manager or sell the division. Williamson calls this organization form a **holding company, or H-form**.

Holding company, or H-form

In Case 3, the operating divisions are really autonomous companies forming a loose federation. An example is the Belgian Société Générale. There is a central holding company, holding majority as well as minority interests in numerous operating companies. Also, between operating companies there are several interlocking shareholdings. Other examples are venture capital companies that have majority as well as minority shareholdings in several operating companies.

8.8 Markets and organizations: are these all there is?

In the conceptual framework of this book (see Figure 1.1) markets and organizations are seen as two alternative ways to coordinate economic decisions. Markets are coordinated by means of the price mechanism; organizations by any (combination) of the six mechanisms we introduced in Chapter 3. To refresh your memory, those organizational mechanisms are repeated in Figure 8.3, together with the organizational configurations they are associated with.

In Chapter 3 we also argued that, in practice, those organizational coordinating mechanisms will often be combined. While we can distinguish the six pure types of organizational configuration that are mentioned in Figure 8.3, in practice we often observe that bundles of coordination mechanisms will govern specific transactions. Moreover, we showed in Chapter 3 that market coordination and organizational coordination often operate in conjunction–that is, within organizations markets exist and markets are always more or less organized.

So far in this chapter, organizations have been analysed from a narrower perspective. Williamson's transaction cost economics is also called the **markets and hierarchies paradigm**. In this view, markets are replaced by hierarchies when price coordination breaks down. In that sense, Williamson's ideas are direct descendants of Coase's, who also argued that organizations are characterized primarily by 'authority' (in our terminology, direct supervision). Within organizations, however, there are other coordinating mechanisms, such as mutual adjustment and standardization of norms. Mutual adjustment is the main coordinating mechanism in a small peer group (for example, a partnership of a few consultants). It is also very important in larger organizations and occurs between departments (such as marketing and product development) in a U-form firm and between divisions in an M-form firm. Mutual adjustment can also occur between two organizations, such as a supplier and a buyer.

It is hard to see how mutual adjustment can work smoothly between parties who display opportunistic behaviour. For that reason it is not surprising Williamson's version of transaction cost economics has evoked several critical comments. These critical comments pertain to two points:

- Transaction cost economics relies too much on the assumption of opportunistic behaviour. In the real world, people often cooperate because they trust

(margin note:) Markets and hierarchies paradigm

PRIME COORDINATING MECHANISM	CONFIGURATION
Direct supervision	Entrepreneurial organization
Standardization of work processes	Machine organization
Standardization of skills	Professional organization
Standardization of outputs	Diversified organization
Mutual adjustment	Innovative organization
Standardization of norms	Missionary organization

Figure 8.3 The six organizational coordination mechanisms

one another. Many commercial transactions cannot occur without a certain level of trust between the parties to that transaction. That is especially true for transactions that are conducted over a period of time.

- Markets and hierarchies should not be viewed as two mutually exclusive governance structures. In the real world, we also see organizational forms such as long-term relations between buyers and suppliers, joint ventures and various forms of network organizations. They are examples of intermediate or **hybrid organizational forms** – organizational forms that fall somewhere between markets and hierarchies. In Chapter 14 we will discuss hybrid forms in some detail.

Hybrid organizational forms

That hybrid organizational forms exist has also been recognized by Williamson. For him, they occur for intermediate levels of asset specificity. Other scholars have argued that some hybrid forms can be understood only if the assumption of opportunism is relaxed. For them, those two critical comments above are very much related.

We shall first discuss an approach in which the assumption of opportunism is partly replaced by allowing for trust. In that approach clans are defined as organizations that rely to a great extent on mutual trust. Also, a distinction is made between markets, bureaucracies and clans as three alternative ways to coordinate economic decisions and that is explained in Section 8.8.1. In Section 8.8.2, we explain in more general terms the role of trust.

8.8.1 Markets, bureaucracies and clans

One of the earliest extensions of the markets and hierarchies framework was provided by William G. Ouchi. A professor of management, he drew on organizational theory to suggest that a more appropriate framework would encompass markets, bureaucracies and clans (Ouchi, 1980; Ouchi and Williamson, 1981). In that extension, bureaucracies were substituted for hierarchies and clans were added as a third way to coordinate economic transactions.

The substitution of bureaucracies for hierarchies is in accordance with mainstream organizational sociology. It was the German sociologist Max Weber (1925, English translation 1947) who proposed that, in modern organizations, personal authority had been replaced by organizational authority. While older organizations had relied on the personal authority of the ruler, modern organizations had acquired the legitimacy to substitute organizational rules for personal authority. Such modern organizations were described by Weber as bureaucracies. Ouchi therefore argued that, in organizational coordination, prices were replaced by rules. The rules contained the information necessary for coordination. The essence of that type of coordination was therefore not its hierarchical but its bureaucratic nature.

Moreover, Ouchi argued that there was a third way of coordinating transactions. That third way relies on the socialization of individuals, which ensures that they have common values and beliefs. Individuals who have been socialized in the same way have common norms for behaviour. Such norms can also contain the information necessary for transactions. By way of example, Ouchi (1980) pointed to Japanese firms that rely to a great extent on socializing their workers to accept the company's goals as their own and compensating them according to length of service and other non-performance criteria. For those firms it is not necessary to measure the performance of their employees as the employees' natural inclination (thanks to socialization) is to do what is best for the firm.

Thus, Ouchi argued that Williamson's framework did not acknowledge the richness of organizational coordination, as summarized in Figure 8.3. The markets and hierarchies paradigm pays too little attention to the role of rules and norms. However, Ouchi's proposal of markets, bureaucracies and clans does not capture that full richness either. In our view Ouchi's proposal is subsumed in Mintzberg's typology, displayed in Figure 8.3. Ouchi's emphasis on the importance of rules corresponds with the standardization of work processes, standardization of skills and standardization of output, while socialization is equivalent to standardization of norms. For that reason, in this book we have not adopted Ouchi's proposal to distinguish between three governance structures. Rather, we argue that markets are replaced by neither hierarchies nor bureaucracies but *organizations* when the price mechanism starts to fail. Organizations do not rely on authority (direct supervision) only but employ the full set of six coordination mechanisms identified by Mintzberg.

8.8.2 The role of trust

Williamson's version of transaction cost economics is built on the assumption of opportunism. As explained in Section 8.2.2, Williamson does not assume that everyone behaves opportunistically all the time. Rather, he assumes that some people might behave opportunistically sometimes *and* that it is difficult to tell *ex ante* (that is, before you enter into a transaction) whether or not your partner will behave opportunistically. That means you do not know up front who you can trust (especially if you have not dealt with the person before).

Several scholars have attacked that assumption. It has been argued (Goshal and Moran, 1996) that the tendency of a certain person to behave in an opportunistic way depends on two things: the immediate net benefits of such behaviour and 'disposition toward the transaction partner'. This recognizes that many people will not cheat their partner in a transaction simply because they would not have a good feeling when they do so. If you like your trading partner and feel that he trusts you, you will probably not cheat on him even if that would bring you some financial gain. Also, if you trust your trading partner and he trusts you, you can develop a long-term mutually profitable relationship. Thus, many economists now recognize that trust is an important concept and several have tried to investigate under which circumstances trust is likely to develop. Box 8.9 presents some of the results.

Box 8.9 Economic research on trust

Economists have begun to measure trust in order to establish when it is present and explore the circumstances in which it increases or decreases over time. Some of the research outcomes indicate the following:

- *Different people behave differently* That has been established in experimental games such as iterated prisoner's dilemmas (see Chapter 5) in which they have to decide whether to cooperate or defect during several rounds of play. For instance, in a game set up by Clark and Sefton (2001) the first mover began by trusting 57 per cent of the time and, in 35 per cent of those cases, the second mover reciprocated by trusting also. In the other instances, the players decided to defect, thus undermining the best (trusting) outcome.

■ *To a certain extent, these differences can be traced to their personality traits and genes.* For instance, people differ in their attributions of causes for their success or failure. Some people tend to point towards external, environmental causes. Others attribute their successes and failures more to their own choices and behaviour. The former tend to prefer cooperative strategies while the latter favour competitive strategies. Other personality traits, such as sensation seeking and anxiety, also help to explain individual variations in players' behaviour (Boone et al., 1996, 1999; Fahr and Irlenbusch, 2008). These differences in personality traits may be genetically hard-wired in our DNA. There is increasing evidence that our inclination toward cooperation has a genetic component (see Christakis and Fowler, 2011).

■ *Culture may matter, too* A striking example is in the study by Henrich (2000), who showed that the Machiguenga Indians of the Peruvian Amazon strongly deviate from Western game theory predictions in a bargaining game. Follow-up studies among many different cultures indeed showed significant variety in trust levels and 'prosocial behaviour'. Interestingly, this variation may be linked to the extent these societies interact with strangers, the view brought forward by Paul Seabright in Box 8.4. (Christakis and Fowler, 2011).

■ *Over time, levels of trust can increase or decrease* In Clark and Sefton's (2001) game, the percentage of first movers trusting their counterparts went down from 57 per cent in the initial rounds to 32 per cent in the tenth round. Trust is fragile and prone to break down altogether in the event of negative experiences.

■ *Incentives matter* If, for instance, the rewards for solitary confessors are increased in the prisoner's dilemma game, defections tend to increase. Gneezy (2005) showed that people are sensitive to their gain when deciding to lie. In a setting in rural India, Andersen et al. (2011) showed that high stakes in an Ultimatum Game do matter: these lead responders to almost full acceptance of low offers.

■ *Already knowing each other helps* Glaeser et al. (2000) also played the Ultimatum Game. In their version, the first player received $15, of which he could give any part to a second player. The amount sent to the second player was then doubled by the researchers and the second player could decide how much to send back to the first player. The trusting outcome is that the first player sends all of the $15 to the second and the second sends half of the doubled sum back. That allows both players to walk away with $15. In the game, however, the first players sent an average of $12.41 to their partners, who returned an average of 45 per cent of the doubled sum. The existence of a previous acquaintance helped, however: both the amount initially sent, and the percentage returned by the second player, rose in proportion to the length of time the players had known each other.

■ *Belonging to the same 'group' helps* In the game set up by Glaeser et al. (2000), the ratio of money returned was much lower when players were of different races or nationalities. Alesina and La Ferrara (2002) found that members of racially mixed communities were less likely to trust each other than members of racially homogeneous communities.

■ *Seemingly unrelated, personal experiences play a role, too* Alesina and La Ferrara (2002) report that respondents who had recently suffered a personal setback–for instance, serious illness or financial problems–also reported lower levels of trust.

■ *And education as well?* A study by Frank et al. (1993) raised the question whether studying economics inhibits cooperation? Worryingly, the study did find evidence that economists behave less cooperatively than non-economists in a variety of settings and they found some indications that this might partly be due to their training; the other part would be selection and self-selection.

▶

Overall, these first studies show that trust is prevalent in many situations and can then help towards achieving the best collective outcome. However, trust cannot be taken for granted and people differ in the trust they have when dealing with others. Moreover, trust is fragile and can be destroyed more easily than built. Finally, trust is dependent upon context, like culture. Economic research thus supports both the view that trust is an important foundation for many economic transactions and Williamson's admonition that opportunism cannot be excluded from the outset.

Trust

Trust plays a role both *between* and *within* organizations. Between organizations very often long-term trading relations develop. Such relations are, to a large extent, based on mutual trust and often of crucial importance for the organization's success.

Within organizations it is very important that employers place a certain level of trust in their employees. Employees who feel that they are being trusted by their employer will be more inclined to 'act in good faith' than employees who feel that they are not. Employees might see very close monitoring by their boss as a sign that they are not being trusted. That will have a negative effect on their 'disposition' towards their firm and, thus, increase rather than attenuate opportunistic behaviour. An employer who installs close monitoring on the assumption that employees will behave opportunistically will indeed find that they behave opportunistically. Opportunistic behaviour thus becomes a self-fulfilling prophecy!

8.8.3 Impersonal trust: institutions and reputation

As argued above, trust is important as a condition for economic exchange. Throughout most of economic history, trust was built up in personal exchange. Repeat dealings in small groups and personal contexts allowed transaction costs to remain relatively small. As the economy expanded, however, personal exchange was increasingly replaced by exchange between 'strangers' (see Box 8.4). As a consequence, more fundamental transaction problems arose. 'Personal trust' needed to be complemented by other means of a more impersonal nature.

Two important forms of such 'impersonal trust' are the following:

- *In institutions* (See Section 1.7.) We have to be able to trust the rule of law and its enforcement. Similarly, we have to trust the Central Banks to maintain the value of our money. To return to the quote from Douglass North in Section 1.7, such an institutional framework 'must substitute effectively for the "trust" that comes with personal exchange. The failure to create the essential institutional base is the central problem of economic development'.
- *Reputation* As economies evolve, someone's reputation as a trustworthy partner for exchange transactions may increasingly involve an impersonal element as well. Originally, a trader's reputation would be built up solely in small groups. Small groups are usually able to enforce standards of behaviour via peer group pressure. When you cheat in a small group, the word will spread and your reputation will be undermined, affecting the willingness

of other parties to deal with you–see Box 8.10 for an impressive example. As exchange takes place in larger and larger groups, however, it becomes increasingly difficult to rely on small group pressure and sanctions. In our modern economy, many transactions take place with 'strangers'. Consider, for instance, the many transactions over the Internet. When you participate in an eBay auction, you may not even know the real name of the seller. How can you trust that person? Interestingly, eBay has found a way to provide you with information about sellers by using the 'feedback system' to build a reputation. By giving feedback on previous transactions, buyers collectively allow eBay to communicate a seller's reputation to prospective buyers–see Box 8.11. As a consequence, the reputation of a seller is no longer restricted to small group settings; it has become public.

Box 8.10 Enforcing honesty in diamond trading

In the New York wholesale diamond trade, dealers pass among themselves bags of diamonds worth millions of dollars, without written contracts. A handshake with the words *mazal u'brache* – 'with luck and a blessing' – creates a binding agreement. The oral contracts work in part because the dealers are mostly Hassidic Jews, sharing a common outlook. With such large sums at stake, however, individual relationships would not provide a weighty sanction. The diamond marketplace is designed so that anyone who breaches a contract loses the future business not only of the person cheated but also of all the other diamond traders. The Diamond Dealers Club organizes the sanctioning. On joining, a new member agrees to submit all disputes to the club's arbitration. Members who breach contracts may be fined or excluded from trading up to 20 days. Unpaid fines are posted for all to see. In the extreme, a member may be expelled from the club and thus from diamond dealing. To last in the business, a diamond trader must be honest.'

Source: McMillan (2002, p. 57)

Box 8.11 Reputation on eBay

In 1995, computer programmer Pierre Omidyar founded AuctionWeb, which was to become eBay. Ten years later, it had become a phenomenal success, partly because of its culture and philosophy, but surely also because of the inventive way in which it makes reputations publicly available:

> So much for the warm and fuzzy side of eBay, which is surely not enough to explain $8bn in cold cash changing hands in the latest quarter alone. For that, you need not only fellow-feeling, but rock-solid trust. And that, in the end, is the true genius of eBay: not just that it resurrects the market stalls of the Middle Ages, but that it rebuilds a pre-industrial system of trust. Everybody in the ancient souk knew who was a crook and who was honest: eBay has done its best to build that same certainty into the cybersouk. The secret is the eBay system of 'feedback': after each transaction, buyers and sellers get to rate each other–positive, negative or neutral. In that way, every eBay member builds a reputation. Beside every member's auction ID is their feedback score: mine is 786, and it is 100 per cent positive. A reputation like that is invaluable. Some day I may put it on my résumé.

> Feedback explains the fundamental mystery of eBay: why strangers buy from strangers. Buyers must pay for goods before receiving or inspecting them–without feedback, it is hard to believe they

▶

would be so foolish. In some ways, feedback is just a very old solution to a timeless problem, writes Chrysanthos Dellarocas–an academic who has studied the phenomenon of trust among strangers online. It guarantees 'good conduct in communities of self-interested individuals who have short-term incentives to cheat one another'. The eBay system is different from the reputation systems evolved over thousands of years to guarantee trust in the marketplace, however. Paul Resnick, a professor at the University of Michigan, says that, offline, we buy goods because we can see them and squeeze them and learn about the seller from our neighbours–or because we have dealt with that seller in the past or he knows our brother-in-law. Online, we cannot buy by these rules. There is much less information about merchants–eBay sellers do not even use their real names. What information there is, says Resnick, is distributed more efficiently.

As power seller Wood points out: 'When you walk into a store, you don't have comments from the last 600 buyers to go by!' On eBay, everyone will know if you cheat your customer.

Source: E. Waldmeir, 'Sold on the web', *FT Weekend,* 2004

To sum up this section, let us first return to Paul Seabright's account of the evolution of economic transactions in humankind, as summarized in Box 8.4.

Seabright was particularly impressed with how we have learned to deal not only in personal networks but also increasingly with 'strangers'. He argued that two 'dispositions' must be present in the population to enable such an evolution: the capacity for rational calculation and reciprocity. Williamson's opportunism refers to rational calculation without any regard for another person's interest. Let us emphasize again that Williamson does *not* argue that this is a universal characteristic of all human beings. He *does* argue that it is present among the population and that it is hard to tell *ex ante* where and when you will encounter it. As a result, economic institutions have to arise that are robust against opportunism.

In this section, we have examined the role of trust and the transfer of trust from personal to impersonal settings. We have also summarized what economic research has so far uncovered as factors increasing or decreasing trust. We believe that the arguments show Seabright is right: economic transactions take place in an environment that is characterized by *both* rational calculation (including outright opportunism) *and* reciprocity and trust.

In this section, we have also started to examine hybrid organizational forms, using Ouchi's introduction of 'clans' as a third way to coordinate transactions. We have contrasted it with our perspective in this book that all non-price coordination is organizational in nature. We have adopted Mintzberg's rich description of six such organizational mechanisms. As a consequence, all non-market coordination is organizational by definition in our framework. We have thus maintained Williamson's bipolar distinction between markets and 'something else'. For Williamson that 'something else' consisted of *hierarchies* (vertical coordination based on authority); for us it is *organizations* in all their possible variations.

Organizational theorists were right to argue that Williamson took too narrow a view on organizations, seeing only one form of non-market coordination: hierarchy. By allowing for rules (standardization) or trust to develop between parties to a transaction we can adopt the full set of six organizational mechanisms proposed by Mintzberg. Our bipolar distinction in this book is between markets and organizations. As repeatedly stressed, the bipolar distinction refers to ideal types of coordination. In practice, we shall encounter many mixed cases or hybrid forms. Chapter 14 discusses several examples of hybrid forms.

8.9 Governance in a three-level schema

Transaction cost economics is mainly concerned with the governance of contractual relations. It is, however, recognized that governance does not operate in isolation. It is embedded in the wider institutional environment (the macro level) on the one hand and the individual attributes of economic actors (the micro level) on the other hand. Williamson (1995) therefore proposes a three-level schema, as depicted in Figure 8.4.

Shift parameters

In the schema, the institutional environment is seen as the context from which shift parameters originate. Shift parameters cause changes in the comparative costs of governance. The macro institutional environment defines the 'rules of the game' for governance. If changes in, for example, property rights, contract laws or social norms induce changes in the comparative costs of governance, then usually a reconfiguration of the economic organization is triggered.

Behavioural attributes

Transaction cost economics operates with **behavioural attributes** that are drawn from the individual level. They are the assumption of bounded rationality and the possibility of opportunism.

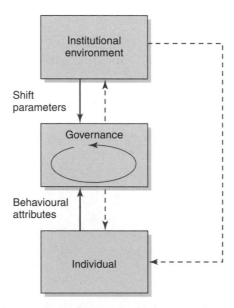

Figure 8.4 A layer schema of governance in Transaction Cost Economics

Source: from *Organization Theory: From Chester Barnard to the present and beyond,* © Oxford University Press (Williamson, O. E. 1995) p. 213.

Finally, Williamson recognizes that there may be feedback effects. For instance, economic actors may attempt to change the rules of the game, as defined in the institutional environment. Think of all the groups lobbying in the political capitals of the world. Similarly, they may try to influence individuals by, for example, advertising. Also, the individual is, of course, influenced by developments and opinions in the wider environment. These three kinds of feedback effects are shown as dotted lines in Figure 8.4. It is fair to say, however, that they are underdeveloped in the Transaction Costs Economic (TCE) framework, which is focused on governance as the central concept, with shift parameters and behavioural attributes 'imported' from the other two levels.

In Chapter 12, we will give an overview of the economic approaches to organizations as presented in this book. There, we will also distinguish (more) levels of analysis at which the various approaches operate. That allows us to compare the 'reach' of the economic approaches to organizations across the various levels of analysis (see Figure 12.4).

8.10 Summary: effect of transaction costs on choosing between markets and organizations and organizational forms

Transaction cost economics attempts to explain the governance of transactions. Which transactions will be executed across markets and which transactions will take place within organizations? Transaction cost economics is based on two assumptions with respect to human behaviour:

1 Human beings are boundedly rational.
2 Human beings can be opportunistic.

In comparison, behavioural theory also assumes bounded rationality but not opportunism, while the theory of principal and agent assumes full rationality and opportunism.

Box 8.12 Why Oliver Williamson won the Nobel prize

In 2009, Oliver Williamson received the Nobel prize for economics (together with Elinor Ostrom). *The Economist* explained how Williamson had built on the work of Ronald Coase and had made it possible to empirically test it:

'Mr Coase's theory explained why companies existed but it was not specific enough to predict the conditions under which firms, or markets, would be the superior form of organization. Clarifying this was Mr Williamson's signal contribution. In a series of papers and books written between 1971 and 1985, he argued that the costs of completing transactions on spot markets increase with their complexity, and if they involve assets that are worth more within a relationship than outside it (a rear-view mirror made to the specifications of a particular car company, for example).

Both these features make writing and enforcing contracts which take every eventuality into consideration difficult, or even impossible. At some point, therefore, it makes sense to conduct the associated transaction within a single legal entity rather than on the market. The car company might prefer to produce its rear-view mirrors in-house, for example, perhaps by buying the mirror company. This would reduce the time and resources spent over haggling over profits, because decisions would simply be taken by fiat.

Mr Williamson's theory helpfully specified measurable attributes of transactions that would make them more or less amenable to being conducted on markets. That meant his thinking could be tested against decisions by companies to integrate parts of their supply chain. It has held up remarkably well. Several studies find, for instance, that when an electricity generator can choose between the output of many nearby coalmines that produce coal of a particular quality, it tends to buy its coal on an open market. But if there is only one nearby mine that can be relied upon as a supplier, the electricity generator tends to own it. A transaction that could be done on the market moves into the firm.

Both Mr Williamson and Ms Ostrom have built on Mr Coase's idea that all transactions have costs but that these costs will be minimized by different institutional arrangements in different situations. Their work uses methods and insights from fields that many economists are not sufficiently familiar with: detailed case studies, in the case of Ms Ostrom, a political scientist by training, and insights from the law in Mr Williamson's case. Their win reminds economists that borders between disciplines, like those between the firm and the market, can be profitably crossed.'

Source: 'Economics focus: reality bites', *The Economist,* 17 October 2009

Choosing between markets and organizations depends on three critical dimensions of transactions: asset specificity, uncertainty/complexity and frequency. Transactions are said to have a high level of asset specificity when they need to be supported by assets that can be used only in those specific transactions. The higher the levels of asset specificity, uncertainty/complexity and frequency, the higher the costs of executing the transaction across a market. Thus, transactions with high levels of asset specificity, uncertainty/complexity and frequency tend to take place within organizations rather than across markets.

Transaction cost economics can also be used to explain why we observe different organizational forms, such as peer groups, simple hierarchies, U-form firms and M-form firms in different circumstances.

Providers of professional services–such as management consultants, accountants, lawyers and doctors–frequently form partnerships. They do so because forming a partnership offers advantages (economies of scale in information-gathering, pooling of risk) that are difficult to obtain through market transactions between independent professionals.

A small partnership can function as a peer group–that is, a group of equals cooperating without hierarchy. In a large peer group, however, communication and decisionmaking become quite complicated and time-consuming. That is why large partnerships usually have a managing board and thus a form of hierarchy. Hierarchy in a large partnership also helps to reduce shirking.

Small manufacturing firms are usually organized as a simple hierarchy: a group of workers with a boss. That happens mainly because a simple hierarchy offers advantages in communication and decisionmaking. If there is team production, these benefits can explain why a simple hierarchy is an efficient form of organization.

Suppose that, because of economies of scale, an efficient firm needs to employ 100 workers. Such a firm needs at least two levels of managers because one manager cannot direct the work of so many workers. In a firm of that size, it is usually efficient for the workers to specialize in one type of activity, such as manufacturing, sales or billing. That leads to the formation of functional departments, with managers also specializing in the functional activities of those departments. That is the unitary or U-form firm.

Now suppose that the firm grows by adding more and more product lines. If the firm continues to use the U-form, its top managers will experience cumulative loss of control. The firm may also face a corruption of the strategic decisionmaking process because functional top managers may display too much loyalty to their department. The solution to those problems is to create a multidivisional (M-form) firm in which the divisions are responsible for manufacturing and marketing of a more limited product range. The divisions operate as quasi-autonomous firms, responsible for all day-to-day decisions. In an M-form firm, there is a general office responsible for strategic decisions and allocating cash flows to divisions.

A major criticism of transaction cost economics is that it ignores the role of social relations and culture. Many relations between human beings are built on trust. Without trust it is difficult to understand how people can cooperate within a firm or build lasting commercial relations.

We have examined the role of trust and the factors that increase or decrease the level of trust. We have also seen that the modern economy requires trust in 'strangers' for the execution of most transactions.

Clans, built on shared norms and trust, have been proposed as a third governance structure besides markets and hierarchies. On closer inspection, we believe that clans correspond closely to organizations relying heavily on standardization of norms as their main coordinating mechanism. That is why we argue that markets are replaced not by hierarchies but by organizations. Organizations use various coordinating mechanisms. In practice, there are also many hybrid forms that combine market relations with coordinating mechanisms used within organizations (see Chapter 14).

Another criticism is that transaction cost economics is static: in comparing different organizational forms, it simply assumes that the most efficient forms have survived. That ignores the dynamic process of competition between different organizational forms, which takes centre stage in the next chapter.

Questions

1 Suppose you are Spanish and living in Sevilla. You have bought a car from a garage in Sevilla and bring it back regularly to the garage for ordinary maintenance.

Now imagine that you are on holiday in the Netherlands. Your car has been making a strange noise lately, so you decide to go to a local garage. You bring your car in the morning and return in the evening to collect it.

There is, of course, the problem of the possibility of opportunistic behaviour by the garage: the garage can misrepresent the amount of time spent on fixing your car. Do you expect that the problem will be more severe or less severe than when you take your car to the garage in Sevilla? Why?

2 Mayer GmbH is a small German company involved in car body repair. Mayer GmbH employs ten people: Gert Mayer, who owns all the shares in Mayer GmbH, and nine other people working as employees. The production process involves three stages: parts repair, painting and assembly. Four people are working in parts repair, two in painting and three in assembly. Mr Mayer takes care of marketing, sales, bookkeeping, and general management.

Autofix is one of Mayer's competitors. Autofix is a workers' cooperative and has recently been set up by ten people. Four people are working in parts repair, two in painting, three in assembly and one in marketing, sales and bookkeeping. All decisions within Autofix are being made by the general assembly, consisting of all ten worker-members. The general assembly is chaired each week by a different worker-member.

a How would you characterize Mayer GmbH in Mintzberg's typology of organizational configurations? What is the main coordinating mechanism in that configuration? Now answer the same questions for Autofix.

b How would you characterize Mayer GmbH in the language of transaction cost economics? What about Autofix? Compare, using transaction cost economics, the organizational form of Mayer GmbH with that of Autofix in terms of efficiency advantages and disadvantages.

c Suppose that competition in the car body repair industry becomes very intense. Which of the two companies is more likely to survive that competitive battle? Why?

3 In some industries, private firms compete with non-profit organizations. An example is the hospital industry in the USA, where hospitals owned and run by private companies compete with hospitals owned by foundations, charities and local governments. Private hospitals and public hospitals face the same make-or-buy decisions: services such as laundry, maintenance, restaurant, physical therapy, laboratory and pharmacy can be bought from outside suppliers or supplied inhouse.

Transaction cost economics predicts that transactions with high levels of asset specificity, uncertainty/complexity and frequency will be supplied inhouse, while transactions with low levels of asset specificity, uncertainty/complexity and frequency will be bought from outside suppliers. A recent study examined if that was really the case. The study also examined whether or not the prediction from transaction cost economics was true for both private and non-profit hospitals. Do you expect the prediction to be equally true for private and non-profit hospitals? Why?

4 Rock bands emerged in the late 1950s and early 1960s in coastal areas of the UK (Liverpool, for example) as very informal partnerships of young males. Originally bands performed in dance venues, did not produce their own songs and did not make much money. That changed with the meteoric rise of The Beatles, a band built on original songs written by the band's members. The example of The Beatles was soon followed by other bands who also integrated writer and performer functions. This created income disparities between band members according to their writing royalties.

Most rock bands were organized as partnerships. However, some were organized as hierarchies, with one band member acting as entrepreneur and the other members receiving pay as workers. What do you think are the advantages and disadvantages of partnerships versus hierarchies in the case of rock bands?

5 Renata Girndt holds a degree in business administration from a well-known Swiss university. She has three years' experience working for a major Swiss pharmaceutical firm. Her main task for the firm has been to investigate ways to enter eastern European markets.

Annamaria Schalke holds a degree from the same university as Renata and has five years' experience working for a major international consulting firm based in Frankfurt, Germany. Her main experience is in designing joint ventures between German and eastern European firms.

Renata has been considering starting her own business as a self-employed consultant. So has Annamaria. When they meet during an alumni day, a plan to form a partnership begins to emerge. In the partnership they will share all revenue and expenses. The partnership will focus on German companies willing to enter eastern European markets through strategic alliances.

For Renata, one of the main risks of starting to work as a self-employed consultant is that of having no consulting assignments during a certain period of time. As she sees it, one of the advantages of forming a partnership with Annamaria is to share that risk.

Do you think Renata would be able to buy an insurance policy for that risk from an insurance company? What kinds of problem(s) might occur for an insurance company offering such a policy? Do they occur when Renata and Annamaria share the risk by forming a partnership? Do you see other advantages of forming a partnership instead of Renata and Annamaria each setting up their own business independently?

9 Economic contributions to business/competitive strategy

9.1 Introduction

In Chapters 6–8, three different but closely related economic theories of organization (behavioural theory, agency theory and transaction cost economics) have been discussed. This chapter focuses on economic contributions to the field of strategy and strategic management. As you will see, those contributions do not (yet) form one integrated theory, although they have much in common. There are many different views and definitions of strategy. In Box 9.1 we summarize the perspective of Rumelt (2011) which is conceptually quite close to the basic framework of this book. In his view the essence of strategy is the adoption of *coherent, coordinated action* by an organization, based on a good *diagnosis* of its situation and environment and a *guiding policy* for its further development.

Box 9.1 Good strategy, bad strategy

Richard P. Rumelt has made many important (economic) contributions to the field of strategy. In 2011 he published *Good Strategy, Bad Strategy*, a book summarizing his perspective on what constitutes a good strategy, also based on his wide consulting experience. In this book Rumelt adopts a view on strategy which corresponds closely with our basic framework, as introduced in Figure 1.1:

> The kernel of a strategy contains three elements: a diagnosis, a guiding policy, and coherent action. Coherent actions are not "implementation" details: they are the punch in the strategy… The coordination of action provides the most basic source of leverage or advantage available in strategy.
>
> The idea that coordination, by itself, can be a source of advantage is a very deep principle. It is often underappreciated because people tend to think of coordination in terms of continuing mutual adjustments among agents. Strategic coordination, or coherence, is not *ad hoc* mutual adjustment. It is coherence imposed on a system by policy and design.
>
> Coordination is costly, because it fights against the gains to specialization, the most basic economies in organized activity. Good strategy and good organization lie in specializing on the right activities and imposing only the essential amount of coordination.

Source: Rumelt (2011)

Competitive strategy

Corporate strategy

There are two levels of strategy in a multibusiness firm: competitive strategy (also termed business strategy) and corporate strategy. A **competitive strategy** is a strategy for a single business unit: it specifies *how* the business unit's managers compete in a given industry. A **corporate strategy** is a strategy for a portfolio of business units: it specifies *where* (that is, in which industries and in which countries) a multibusiness firm competes.

The field of strategic management has a normative and a descriptive part (as do many other empirical fields). Normative questions deal with what firms *should* do. Descriptive questions deal with what firms *actually* do. The literature on strategic management may be further divided into contributions that focus on the *process* and the *content* of strategic management (see Table 9.1). Economics attempts to analyse the content of firms' strategies. To see whether the analysis has explanatory power, it is compared with the actual behaviour of firms. If the analysis does correspond to real firms' behaviour and, furthermore, indicates which choices are best, then we have a basis for normative recommendations. That is why it is hard to divide economic contributions to the content of strategic management into normative and descriptive contributions.

Strategic planning

The early literature on strategic management (for example, Ansoff, 1965) emerged out of a need to help practitioners with the process of strategic planning. **Strategic planning** is the component of strategic management that aims at the formulation of a firm's strategy.

An important issue in that literature is how the process of strategic planning should be structured. It is argued that the process of strategic planning should consist of a logical sequence of steps, such as the seven steps indicated in Figure 9.1. The figure is an example of a normative model of strategic planning. You might wonder why that sequence of steps is the most logical one or whether it leads to the best results. Economics has little to say on that question. As we want to focus on economic contributions to strategic management, we shall not try to answer it.

You may also wonder if, in real firms, the process of strategic planning is always as neatly structured as Figure 9.1. Descriptions of actual strategic planning processes show that it is usually not, but, again, this issue falls outside the scope of this chapter.

The economic contributions to strategic planning and strategic management focus mainly on issues of content, not of process. Economics deals with the actual information that firms need and the actual choices they have to make when formulating their strategies but hardly at all with the process they may use to arrive at those choices and implement their chosen strategy.

Table 9.1 The literature on strategic management

	Process	*Content*
Normative	Normative models of strategic management processes	Economic contributions to strategic management
Descriptive	Description of actual strategic management processes	

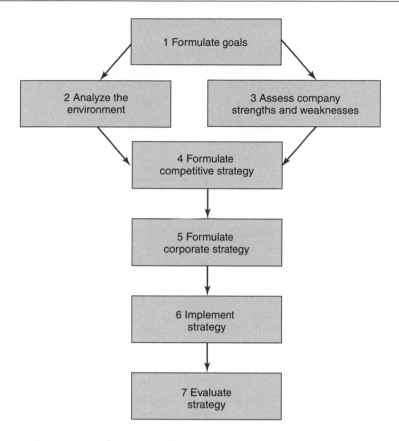

Figure 9.1 The process of strategic planning in a multibusiness firm

Important economic contributions have been made to the content of Steps 2–5 in the diagram; very few economic contributions have been made to the other three steps.

This chapter focuses on economic contributions to the field of competitive strategy (the strategy of a single business firm or the strategy of a business unit belonging to a multibusiness firm). This corresponds to Steps 2, 3, and 4 in Figure 9.1. The next chapter discusses economic contributions to corporate strategy (Step 5 in Figure 9.1).

Section 9.2 discusses Step 2 in the strategic planning process. It focuses on industry analysis. The industry in which a firm operates is an important part of its environment, and economics offers important insights to the subject of industry analysis.

Section 9.3 on competitor analysis discusses Step 3 in the process of strategic planning (assess a company's strengths and weaknesses) Competitor analysis is a way to compare a company's strengths and weaknesses relative to its competitors.

Section 9.4 discusses Step 4, formulation of a competitive strategy.

In Section 9.5 we return to Step 3 to introduce the resource based theory of the firm. This is an alternative way to assess a company's strengths and weaknesses. According to the resource-based view of the firm, a competitive advantage is sustainable if it is based on the possession of resources that other firms cannot easily obtain. This indicates that the resource-based view is also of vital importance in Step 4, formulation of a competitive strategy.

Section 9.6 on dynamic capabilities builds on the resource based view and also offers important new insights for Steps 3 and 4.

Section 9.7 discusses the formulation of competitive strategy (Step 4) in a dynamic context, drawing on concepts from game theory.

9.2 Industry analysis

Structure–conduct–performance (S–C–P) paradigm

The economic contributions to industry analysis stem from the field of industrial organization. Industrial organization emerged as an academic discipline in the 1950s and 1960s. Its main paradigm was the **structure – conduct – performance (or S–C–P) paradigm**. 'Structure' refers to characteristics of the industry, such as the number, size and distribution of firms in that industry and the barriers that impede other firms entering it. Other examples of characteristics that determine industry structure are given in Figure 9.2.

'Conduct' refers to the behaviour (or strategies) of firms in the industry. Aspects of firm conduct are collusion (that is, the extent to which firms cooperate), pricing strategy of firms in the industry and product strategy.

'Performance' refers to performance of the industry in such terms as profitability, growth in output and employment.

According to the S–C–P paradigm, the structure of an industry determines the conduct of the firms in that industry and, in turn, 'conduct' determines industry performance (see Figure 9.2). As an example of how structure determines conduct and conduct determines performance, consider the US automobile industry during the 1960s.

There were only four firms – General Motors (GM), Ford, Chrysler and American Motors (AM). General Motors and Ford were much bigger than Chrysler or American Motors. There were many buyers (dealers), so sellers were few and unequal in size, while buyers were numerous. Moreover, barriers to entry into the automobile industry were high. In this industry economies of scale are very important: you can produce cars efficiently only if you produce on a large scale. If a new competitor were to consider entering the industry, it would have to enter on a large scale. That would create overcapacity in the industry, prices would fall and no one would make a profit. Hence, in the automobile industry, economies of scale constitute a barrier to entry.

Another barrier to entry is the technological know-how required to develop a new car. In the automobile industry in the USA during the 1960s, GM and Ford were the most efficient producers, so they could set prices, while Chrysler and AM followed GM's and Ford's pricing strategy. Although the four firms probably never coordinated their pricing strategy as such, the result was coordination of prices. Such **tacit collusion** is greatly facilitated if there are only a few sellers of unequal size and there are significant barriers to entry. Collusion, whether tacit

Tacit collusion

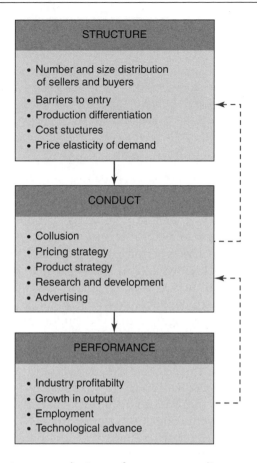

Figure 9.2 The structure – conduct – performance paradigm

or more explicitly organized, is easier to organize in concentrated, oligopolistic industries, like the US automobile industry was in the 1960s. Consider Box 9.2 for a more recent example at a global scale (with the automotive industry as a victim of price-fixing practices).

Box 9.2 Breaking a glass cartel

Four leading glass manufacturers, together controlling about 90 per cent of the European auto glass market, were found guilty of price-fixing by the European Union in 2008. For a period of five years they had held secret meetings at hotels and airports across Europe to coordinate pricing, although not all of the companies were involved for the whole of that period.

France's St Gobain will have to pay € 896m ($1.2bn). The amount is a record fine by European regulators on a single company. The penalty on St Gobain is particularly high because of its history of previous cartel offences. Pilkington faces a € 370m penalty; Japan's Asahi Glass must pay € 113.5m; and Belgium's Solivar faces a relatively modest fine of € 4.4m.

"These companies cheated the car industry and car-buyers for five years in a market worth €2bn in the last year of the cartel."said Neelie Kroes, EU competition commissioner. "Management and shareholders of companies that damage consumers and European industry by running cartels must learn their lesson the hard way – if you cheat, you will get a heavy fine."

The decision could open the way for buyers of the glass – notably car manufacturers – to pursue private damages against the companies involved on the grounds that prices were illegally inflated.

Source: 'Record EU fine for glass cartel', *The Financial Times*, 13 November 2008.

Structure (number and size distribution of sellers and buyers, barriers to entry) therefore determined conduct (pricing strategy). Pricing strategy, of course, directly affects profitability. Thus, an element of conduct (pricing strategy) affects performance (profitability). These relationships are indicated by the solid arrows flowing from the top to the bottom of Figure 9.2.

In the S–C–P paradigm, the direction of causation runs, therefore, from structure to conduct and from conduct to performance. However, it is now increasingly recognized that the conduct of firms can also affect industry structure and the performance of an industry can also affect the conduct of firms in that industry. For example, firms can change market structures by innovation, like Apple's iPod undermined the market for other MP3 players. In addition, firms can try to erect barriers to entry. They may, for instance, protect their product and process innovations by means of patents. If such patents are awarded, the firm can prevent competitors from using the latest technology. Patents are an example of strategic barriers to entry. The conduct of firms (their patenting behaviour) thus affects an industry's structure. In addition, performance may affect conduct, as when industry profitability affects the amount of R&D carried out. These relationships are indicated by the dotted 'feedback' arrows in Figure 9.2.

A crucial view in many early empirical studies was that, as structure determined conduct and conduct determined performance, one could ignore conduct and look directly at industry structure to try to explain performance. Thus, many studies sought to explain an indicator of industry performance (such as industry profitability) by using elements of structure as determinants. By comparing several industries in the same time period it became clear that, first, not all industries are equal in terms of profitability and, second, differences in profitability between industries can be explained in large measure by the elements of structure indicated in Figure 9.2. As a result, the profitability of a multibusiness firm is determined, to a certain extent, by the choice of which industries to compete in.

Five forces driving industry competition

These findings from industrial organization inspired Michael Porter's well-known model of **five forces driving industry competition** (Figure 9.3). Intensity of rivalry between existing firms depends *inter alia* on the number, size and distribution of firms, level of product differentiation and cost structures. The threat of new entrants depends on barriers to entry. The bargaining power of buyers depends inter alia on the number, size and distribution of buyers and level of product differentiation. A similar statement can be made

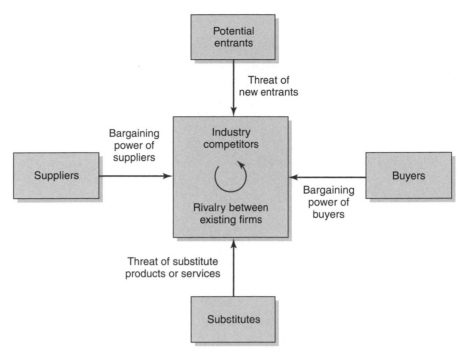

Figure 9.3 Five forces driving industry competition

Source: reprinted with the permission of The Free Press, a Division of Simon & Schuster, Inc., from (*Competitive Strategy: Techniques for analyzing industries and competitors*) by Michael E. Porter. Copyright © 1980, 1998 by The Free Press. All rights reserved.

regarding the bargaining power of suppliers. Therefore, in Porter's five-forces model, the industry's structure determines the intensity of competition and, thus, the industry's profitability.

Five-forces model

Porter's **five-forces model** has proved to be a valuable tool for analysing present and future levels of an industry's level of competition and profitability. Box 9.3 provides an illustration for the airline industry.

Box 9.3 Porter's five-forces analysis applied to the airline industry

The airline industry has historically been one of the worst performing industries. Porter (2008) showed that its average profitability (ROIC) in the period 1992–2006 had been only 5.9 per cent compared with an average of 14.9 per cent across all examined industries, not to mention the 40.9 per cent of security brokers or the 37.6 percent of soft drinks and prepackaged software. Why has the airline industry performed so dismally?

Consider the five forces as summarized below:

■ The *threat of new entrants* is high in the airline industry, since there are low barriers to entry. Countries all want their own national airline and in addition have encouraged low-cost competition. Consider the emergence of Emirates and Etihad as global competitors from the Middle East.

▶

- The *bargaining power of suppliers* is high. There are only a few aircraft manufacturers and the large jet airliner market is dominated by Airbus and Boeing. The jet engine market is dominated by GE and Rolls-Royce. In addition, airline labour union power is high in many countries, particularly for pilots.
- The *threat of substitute products* is moderate, but existent. Passengers can take the car or train for short distances. Freight can be sent by train or (container) ship.
- The *bargaining power of buyers* is relatively high, given the fragmented nature of the market. For most routes many different carriers offer alternatives. The industry finds it difficult to raise prices sufficiently when, for example, the oil price increases.
- *Rivalry* between competitors is high and is mainly focused on price. There is little room for differentiation, neither in the passenger market nor in the freight market.

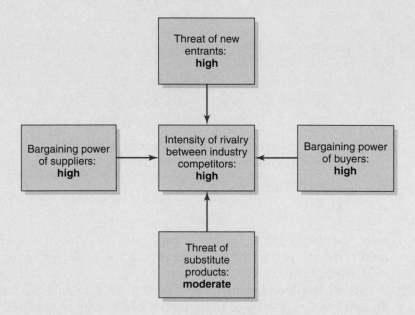

Given the nature and intensity of these five forces it should come as no surprise that very few airline companies are structurally profitable; most suffer from prolonged periods of losses.

9.3 Competitor analysis

In the S–C–P paradigm discussed in Section 9.2, the unit of analysis is the industry. In this paradigm, industry structure determines the firm's conduct, which, in turn, determines the industry's performance. If industry structure were completely to determine a firm's conduct, there could be no differences between the conduct of firms in the same industry. For example, if industry structure determines a firm's pricing strategy, all firms in the industry should follow the same pricing strategy. If, moreover, all firms in the industry have the same unit cost (they employ the same technology, are of the same size and so on), profitability differences between firms in the same industry can be attributed only to random disturbances. However, the firms in an industry are clearly not all alike. The result is that there are usually differences in profitability between firms in the same industry.

How important are differences between industries relative to differences between firms in the same industry? That important question has been examined by several researchers. Most have used large samples of business units from large (Fortune 500) firms over a period of several years and have found evidence that differences between business units in the same industry are far more important than differences between industries.

Firms belonging to the same industry can still differ in many respects. They differ along dimensions such as pricing strategy, advertising levels, R&D levels, degree of vertical integration, breadth of product line, cost position and so on. Such disparities may be due to differences in information. Firms may perceive different profit opportunities when they enter an industry, for example. So, firm A may decide to advertise heavily a high-quality product and firm B to pursue a high-volume line because they do not have the same information.

Once firms A and B have made such decisions, they become committed to a strategy. Firm A invests in building a brand name; should firm A decide to change its strategy, then its past advertising expenditures would lose most of their value. As long as it sticks to its present strategy, those past expenditures constitute an intangible asset. Similarly, firm B has to invest in facilities for high-volume production. If firm B changes its competitive strategy, its high-volume production facilities are likely to decline in value. So, both firms A and B have to invest in assets that probably decline in value if the firms change their strategies.

That is one reason firms' strategies are likely to be 'sticky' and difficult to alter radically. Another explanation is that firms use organizational routines to make strategic decisions. As long as profit performance is satisfactory, firms tend to follow the same rules of thumb (in setting advertising levels, R&D levels and so on) that they have used in the past.

Firms do not maximize but satisfice, as explained in Chapter 6. That is to say, as long as their routines lead to satisfactory results, firms have few incentives to search for better routines. In some industries (for example, those with many small firms and very low entry barriers), rivalry may be so intense that only one strategy can survive. In other industries (for example, those with a few large firms and high entry barriers), two or more different strategies may turn out to be sufficiently profitable to allow survival.

Strategic dimensions

Mobility barriers

It seems likely, then, that firms in the same industry differ along certain key variables. Those key variables are the **strategic dimensions** of that industry. In addition, it seems likely that those differences persist for several years because there are **mobility barriers** between the strategic groups. If both propositions are true, then an industry can be viewed as being composed of groups of firms, each group consisting of firms following similar competitive strategies.

The competitive strategy of a firm is that firm's choice with regard to the strategic dimensions of its particular industry. Strategic dimensions can vary with the industry studied. Examples of strategic dimensions are advertising levels, R&D levels, cost position, product differentiation, breadth of product line and degree of vertical integration.

Strategic groups

Groups of firms following similar competitive strategies are called **strategic groups**. Firms within a strategic group closely resemble one another. Profitability differences between firms in the same strategic group are likely to be small. However, profitability differences between firms in different groups (firms pursuing different strategies) may be large.

Following this line of reasoning, two empirical questions have to be answered:

- Do differences in strategies persist over time? (If they do not, the concept of strategic groups has little meaning.)
- Are profitability differences between strategic groups significant?

Several studies have examined these questions. Most have come to the conclusion that strategic groups can be identified in many industries. Moreover, they tend to be stable over time. Significant profitability differences between strategic groups are found less often. Hence, in many industries there appear to be several roads to (roughly the same kind of) success. Thus, strategic planners can use the concept of strategic groups to construct a map showing the competitive strategies of their own company and those of their competitors. As

Strategic map

an example, consider Box 9.4, which describes a **strategic map** of the European brewing industry in 2001.

Box 9.4 The European beer industry

The European beer industry consists of a large number of companies.

In Germany, there are many (several hundred) small breweries, each serving a small regional market.

Small breweries with only one brand serving a local or national market can be found in many other European countries. Heineken sells beer under a variety of brand names: Heineken, Amstel and Murphy's (which are sold in almost all countries in Europe) and a large number of national brands (for example, Moretti and Dreher in Italy).

Interbrew also uses a variety of brand names: Stella (its most international brand) and a large number of local or regional brands.

SAB (South African Breweries) has acquired several European breweries, each with its own brand name, but SAB does not have a pan-European brand.

Finally, the American brewers Anheuser-Bush and Miller are active in Europe with their flagship brands (Budweiser and Miller respectively).

Thus, on the basis of brand strategy and market share, four strategic groups emerge (Figure 9.4).

See further: McGee (2003)

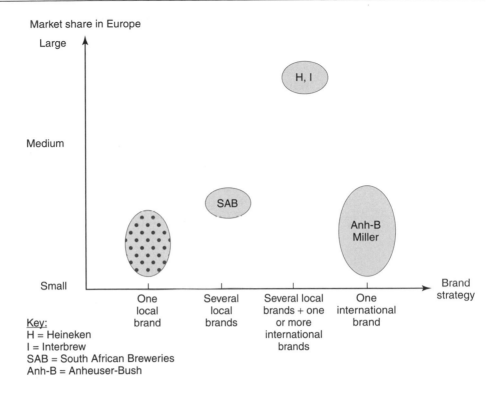

Figure 9.4 Strategic map of the European brewing industry

The strategic map shown in Figure 9.4 uses brand strategy (one local brand, several local brands, several local brands plus at least one international brand, one international brand only) and market share as strategic dimensions. Other strategic dimensions that may be important in the brewing industry (such as level of diversification, level of advertising or level of vertical integration) cannot be shown on the same map.

9.4 Competitive strategy

A competitive strategy reflects the firm's choices concerning the strategic dimensions of its industry. As there are many strategic dimensions and different industries may have different strategic dimensions, many competitive strategies are possible. In many industries, however, two successful competitive strategies can be identified: cost leadership and product differentiation. Both strategies can be applied industry-wide or to a few segments only. Such so-called **generic competitive strategies** have been discussed extensively by Michael Porter (1980, 1985).

Under a **strategy of cost leadership**, the firm tries to manufacture and distribute products at the lowest possible unit cost. Quite often, cost leadership can be attained only through large-scale production (economies of scale) or

Generic competitive strategies

Strategy of cost leadership

experience. Both economies of scale and experience are easier to obtain if the firm has a large market share.

strategy of product differentiation

Under a **strategy of product differentiation**, the firm competes by offering a product that the customers perceive as more valuable than the competitors' products. It can do so by offering a product that differs from other products in quality, safety, design, reliability, ease of repair, durability, taste or whatever. If buyers recognize the additional value, the firm can charge a higher price. For a strategy of product differentiation, brand name recognition is usually very important. Thus, advertising levels tend to be high for firms using that strategy.

As discussed above, firms' strategies are likely to be sticky as a result of the necessary commitment to a chosen strategy and because of the development of successful routines. Once a firm has chosen to pursue one of Porter's generic strategies, it is likely to continue along that path for quite some time. That may be dangerous, however.

A firm committed to a strategy of cost leadership must be aware that its customers compare the standard low-cost products with differentiated products offered by its competitors. As income levels rise or demand patterns change, customers may increasingly demand a number of differentiating features, forcing the low-cost producers to incorporate these into their product offerings. The Model T Ford and the VW Beetle are examples of very successful low-cost products. In both cases, the more differentiated cars offered by GM and others finally forced Ford and Volkswagen to develop new, more differentiated cars. Similarly, firms pursuing a strategy of product differentiation cannot remain complacent about their costs. Buyers do not simply seek high value; they seek value for money. Hence, care should be taken not to overemphasize Porter's useful distinction in generic competitive strategies.

9.5 Resource-based view of the firm

In the preceding section, two competitive strategies – cost leadership and product differentiation – have been discussed. A firm may attain cost leadership through large-scale production (economies of scale) or through experience. According to the resource-based view of the firm, a competitive advantage is always based on the possession of (or, at least, the access to) certain resources, such as a large-scale plant or experience. The extent to which a competitive advantage is sustainable depends on how difficult or costly it is for other firms to obtain the same resources.

Resource-based view of the firm

In the **resource-based view of the firm** (RBV), resources are defined quite broadly. They include human, financial, tangible (such as plants, equipment and buildings) and intangible resources (such as patents, know-how, brand names, experience and organizational routines). Some resources are easily bought and sold in (nearly) perfect markets. That is true of most financial assets, such as marketable securities. Other assets are much more difficult to buy and sell, however. For example, there are active markets for new and secondhand cars and trucks, but there is no market for 'organizational routines' (the concept of organizational routines is explained in Section 11.5).

According to the resource-based theory of the firm, a resource can be the basis of a competitive advantage *only* if that resource has certain properties. First, it must be *valuable*. That is it must enable the firm to operate more efficiently than other firms and/or it must enable the firm to deliver more value to its customers. Second it must be *rare*. That is, for other firms it should be very difficult or impossible to acquire the same resource. Third, it must be *imperfectly imitable* (that is it must be difficult to replicate) by other firms. And, fourth, it must be *non-substitutable*, that is it must be such that substitute resources are simply not available.

In summary, the original formulation of the RBV pointed to four conditions that resources have to satisfy in order to contribute towards competitive advantage. They have to be:

- valuable;
- rare;
- inimitable;
- non-substitutable.

VRIN-framework

Those conditions are sometimes thus referred to as the **VRIN-framework** of competitive advantage.

In order to understand what these conditions mean, consider a market with five firms of equal size, each having a market share of 20 per cent. Suppose that firm A has more modern equipment than the other firms and, thus, enjoys a cost advantage. If the other firms can easily buy the same equipment, the equipment is not rare and firm A's advantage will be short-lived. However, if firm A has developed its own equipment and the development of that type of equipment demands special skills or experience only firm A's employees possess, then the equipment is valuable, rare and inimitable. In this example one can also argue that it is not the equipment itself, but rather the skills and experience of firm A's employees that are valuable, rare and inimitable. In general, intangible resources (such as skills or routines) are more likely to fulfill the VRIN conditions than tangible resources.

For intangible resources, it is useful to make a distinction between resources for which property rights are well defined (such as patents, brand names and copyrights) and intangible resources for which property rights are ill defined (such as technological know-how not protected by patents, organizational routines and the know-how and experience of the top management team). It is quite difficult to trade in know-how that is not protected by patents because of the fundamental paradox of information (see Section 4.1). That type of know-how can be the basis of a sustainable competitive advantage. If several competing firms obtain a licence to use the same patented know-how in return for a royalty payment, the use of that know-how is unlikely to be the source of a competitive advantage.

We will return to the question of competitive advantage in the next section, but first wish to make some remarks evaluating the contribution of the RBV to economic approaches to organizations.

Note first that the RBV of the firm argues that the competitive advantage of a firm depends on the resources at its disposal. For a sustainable competitive advantage, it must be difficult or costly for other firms to obtain similar resources. Sustainable competitive advantage should lead to superior economic performance over a period of time. On this reasoning, there is a direct causal chain from a firm's resources to its performance. It is, therefore, very important to know which resources can lead to such superior economic performance. See Box 9.5 for a discussion of this perspective by a leading strategy consulting firm.

Box 9.5 McKinsey on 'special capabilities'

The resource-based view of the firm has become incorporated in the perspectives of leading strategy consulting firms, as the following discussion of 'special capabilities' by McKinsey shows:

'Too often, companies are cavalier about claiming special capabilities. To truly yield advantage, special capabilities need to be critical for generating profits and exist in abundance within the organization, while being scarce and hard to imitate outside. As such, they will tend to be very specific in nature and few in number. Firms often err in this regard by mistaking size for scale advantage, overestimating how they can leverage capabilities across markets, or inferring special capabilities from observed performance, often without considering other explanations (such as luck or positional advantage). Any claimed capability advantage should be carefully examined before pinning the future hopes of the company on it.

It is critical not to confuse special capabilities with best practices, which can keep you in the race but won't let you beat the market. Furthermore, best practices are often viewed in isolation, while in reality the most sustainable advantages are tough-to-copy combinations of activities across the business system.'

Source: McKinsey, *10 Timeless tests of strategy*, September 2009

In standard economic theory, the resources at the firm's disposal were traditionally classified as follows:

■ land (including natural resources);
■ labour (human resources);
■ capital (financial and physical resources).

A debate in economics is whether or not *information* should be included as a fourth type of resource (also called a 'factor of production').

As noted in Chapter 2, in standard microeconomics, the factors of production come together in firms seen as *holistic entities*. That is to say, economic theory did not look *into* firms: they were regarded as black boxes.

RBV is an economic theory that *does* look inside firms. It tries to identify which resources are the basis of sustainable competitive advantage. As noted above, it defines resources much more widely. It then examines which conditions those resources must meet in order to serve as a basis for sustainable competitive advantage.

As an economic approach to organizations, the RBV of the firm is a clear improvement over standard microeconomics. However, it had to deal with two criticisms that were levelled against its original formulation:

■ RBV is, to a certain extent, *tautological*. It attempts to explain superior performance in terms of the use of particular valuable resources. At the same time, the question as to whether or not resources are valuable has to be answered by reference to the performance they enable. In other words, the argument is circular. What is missing is an independent selection mechanism that explains which resources are valuable and which are not.

- RBV is *static*. It assumes that resources simply 'exist' and the firm's task is to choose from among the existing resources. RBV, in its original formulation, neither asked where these resources came from nor how they were developed and maintained over time.

As a response to those criticisms, the RBV has been further developed. We deal with that further development in two steps.

In the next section, we introduce the concept of *dynamic capabilities*. As the terminology already implies, the concept of dynamic capabilities addresses the development of a firm's capabilities as the basis for sustainable competitive advantage. While it therefore addresses the second criticism above, it also enquires deeper into the nature of the resources and capabilities that generate competitive advantage.

At the end of the next chapter, on evolutionary approaches to organizations, we return to the concept of dynamic capabilities. There we will show that the selection mechanism introduced to address the first criticism, is evolutionary selection. Thus, dynamic capabilities provide a bridge between strategic and evolutionary approaches to organizations.

9.6 Dynamic capabilities

Dynamic capability

A **dynamic capability** can be defined as 'the capacity of an organization to purposefully create, extend, or modify its resource base'. The 'resource base' of an organization includes tangible, intangible and human assets (or resources), as in the RBV. However, it also includes capabilities that the organization owns, controls or has access to, on a preferential basis. An example could be the process of new product development. A start-up company may have the tangible assets (plant), intangible assets (intellectual property) and human assets (researchers) to come up with good product inventions, but it may have to draw on the resources and capabilities of a partner to commercialize them. If it has preferential access to such complementary resources and capabilities through an alliance, we may say that it has extended its resource base by creating that alliance.

Operational capabilities

Dynamic capabilities can be distinguished from **operational capabilities**, which pertain to the current operations of an organization. Thus, operational capabilities are any type of capability that the organization uses in its effort to earn a living in the present. Current production methods, existing marketing policies and customary human resources (HR) recruiting campaigns are all operationally orientated. Dynamic capabilities, by contrast are aimed at change. They alter the resource base of an organization. Forging alliances or making acquisitions are typical examples. The capabilities of Starbucks to open new outlets at an amazing rate, also in foreign markets, is another example. Note, further, that through dynamic capabilities the organizational resource base is *purposefully* created, extended or modified. That means there must be some degree of intent, either on the part of top management or at lower levels in the organization (such as the country managers in the Starbucks organization). In our alliance example, there must be a search and selection process to identify the right alliance partner. Furthermore, there must be a capability to work with an alliance partner. The firm must, therefore, have some alliance management skills that can be deployed in such a situation. From this perspective, the strategic management of the organization therefore entails the purposeful application of dynamic capabilities to change the resource base of the organization.

The extension of RBV with the concept of dynamic capabilities also allows for the possibility of delving deeper into the nature of the resources and capabilities that generate sustainable competitive advantage. Economic researchers have uncovered specific factors and circumstances that contribute to dynamic capabilities being valuable, rare and/or inimitable. Some of the features identified include the following:

Co-specialization

- **Co-specialization** Consider our example of a start-up company above. Let us say that it is involved in the development of new biotech-based drugs. It has created special purpose laboratories and manufacturing facilities. It has recruited researchers at the cutting edge of a particular branch of biotechnology. It has also filed for patents that give it the exclusive rights to its new findings. We can say that all of its assets and resources are specialized. What is more, the plant, patents and researchers are *co-specialized*, meaning that they are uniquely valuable only when used in combination. It may cost a considerable amount of time and/or investment to build such a complementary combination of assets. Outside of that combination, any individual asset loses a significant amount of value. Co-specialization may therefore contribute to the value of assets.

Box 9.6 The Apple iPod as an example of co-specialized assets

Apple has shown an uncanny knack at innovation with recent successes like the iPod, iPhone and iPad. As Teece (2009) argues, such innovation nowadays often requires that co-specialized assets are combined globally:

'Steve Jobs and his colleagues at Apple combined known technology (digital music players had already been invented) with the iTunes music store (a cospecialized "asset" pioneered by Apple; CEO Steve Jobs himself persuaded key artists to provide content) and digital rights management (DRM) software developed by Apple to give artists confidence that their music would not be pirated. These key elements were combined in a superbly well-designed package (the iPod player itself) which has obliterated Sony's lead in the personal stereo market (the Sony "Walkman").

Nevertheless, the components that make up the iPod are almost all completely outsourced. As one observer noted: "take an iPod apart and 83% of the components are made by Japanese companies". In short, it was Apple's dynamic capabilities – the ability to sense a market need, and then to uniquely bring together all the necessary cospecialized assets – that undergirds Apple's success with this product, which has been sold through Apple stores around the world.'

Source: David J. Teece, *Dynamic Capabilities & Strategic Management*, Oxford: Oxford University Press, 2009

Asset orchestration

- *Asset orchestration* If capabilities are dependent on co-specialized assets, it makes the coordination task of management particularly difficult. Managerial decisions should then take the optimal configuration of assets into account. The term 'asset orchestration' is used to denote the managerial search, selection and configuration/coordination of resources and capabilities. The term attempts to convey that, in an optimal configuration of assets, the whole is more valuable than the sum of its parts.

Tacit knowledge

- *Tacit knowledge* If the capability is partly based on tacit knowledge, it is impossible to make it fully explicit. The capability can therefore not be fully articulated. It partly resides in people's heads and behaviour. That makes it difficult for competitors to fully imitate it. We return to tacit knowledge in Chapter 11.

Firm specificity

- *Firm specificity* Dynamic capabilities are often dependent on the firm's historical development and unique circumstances. They are usually developed in practice through learning-by-doing. Therefore, there is an element of *path dependence* – that is, the particular paths taken by a firm have shaped the opportunities for its specific learning-by-doing. As a consequence, its dynamic capabilities have become firm-specific. Firm specificity makes a dynamic capability rare and imitation difficult.

Box 9.7 Asset orchestration and specific capabilities to produce cellulosic bio-ethanol

In 2012, Royal DSM (a global Life Sciences and Materials Sciences company) and POET LLC (one of the world's largest ethanol producers) announced a joint venture to commercially demonstrate and license cellulosic bio-ethanol, named POET-DSM Advanced Biofuels LLC. The JV aims to demonstrate that *second generation* cellulosic ethanol from corn crop residue can be produced commercially at a par with *first generation* bio-ethanol which uses the corn itself. First generation bio-ethanol therefore introduces a 'food versus fuel dilemma', while second generation bio-ethanol would resolve this dilemma by using the waste material of corn production: the cobs, leaves, husks and some stalk left in the field after the grain harvest. The JV clearly demonstrates the principle of asset orchestration since both companies are contributing their proprietary and complementary technologies. POET already has a network of nearly thirty corn ethanol facilities and the capabilities to manage the value chain from field to fuel. DSM has a unique position in the development of cellulosic ethanol as the only company offering both yeast and enzyme solutions necessary to increase conversion rates to make the technology commercially viable.

In addition, the example illustrates the path dependence of DSM's specific capabilities. These originate in its 1998 takeover of the biotechnology group Royal Gist-brocades, a leader in the field of yeasts and enzymes. In subsequent years DSM has designated the field of Industrial Biotechnology as one of its 'Emerging Business Areas' to which it has dedicated substantial resources to develop further. Had DSM not acquired Gist-brocades or had it made different strategic decisions in subsequent years, it would not have developed the specific capabilities to make it an attractive partner for POET for the production of cellulosic bio-ethanol.

Source: 'DSM and POET to make advanced biofuels a reality by 2013', joint press release, 23 January 2012.

Isolating mechanisms

- *Isolating mechanisms* A dynamic capability is also inimitable if it is surrounded by effective 'isolating mechanisms'. Such mechanisms are to a firm what an entry barrier is to an industry: they prevent other firms competing away the profit that a firm earns from its capability. If capabilities are highly firm-specific and partly depend on tacit knowledge, there may be significant 'causal ambiguity' as to the exact way in which they contribute to competitive advantage. It may then already be difficult for the firm's managers to articulate the causal connection between capability and competitive advantage, let alone for outside managers to copy the capability easily. Moreover, companies can invest to develop further their product or service offerings and thus make them a 'moving target':

> Another broad approach to strengthening isolating mechanisms is to have a moving target for imitators...Consider, for example, Microsoft's Windows operating system. Were this to remain stable for a long period of time, there is little doubt that clever programmers around the world could, over time, create a functionally equivalent substitute. However, by continually changing the program – even if the changes are not improvements – Microsoft makes it very costly to engineer a continuing series of functional equivalents. Windows is a moving target. (Rumelt, 2011, p. 176)

The discussion in this section shows that the concept of dynamic capabilities is a useful extension of the RBV. It effectively addresses the earlier critique that RBV provided only a static perspective. Dynamic capabilities are aimed at change in the resource base of organizations. They are developed over time and may require significant managerial effort to maintain and extend. Management's task is not only to choose from among 'existing' resources but also engage in active search, selection, configuration and orchestration of resources and capabilities. The objective remains sustainable competitive advantage. How to achieve competitive advantage may well depend on the development of the specific firm so far (and thus be path-dependent) as Box 9.8 discusses.

Box 9.8 Coordination skills as rungs on a ladder

Richard P. Rumelt discusses how the development of skills (or: dynamic capabilities) has a certain sequential logic: only if certain basic skills and capabilities have become 'routines' can an individual or a firm aspire to develop the next layer:

'...I came to see skills at coordination as if they were rungs on a ladder, with higher rungs in reach only when the lower rungs had been attained. Indeed, the concept of the layering of skills explains why some organizations can concentrate on issues that others cannot. This understanding has helped shape the advice I offer clients.

For example, when I work with a small start-up company, their problems often revolve around coordinating engineering, marketing, and distribution. Asking the CEO of such a firm to concentrate on opening offices in Europe may be pointless, because the company has not yet mastered the basics of "flying" the business. Once the firm stands firmly on that rung, it can move abroad and develop international operations. But, in turn, asking that newly international firm to move knowledge and skills around the world, as does a global veteran such as Procter & Gamble, may also be pointless. It must first master the complexity of operating in various languages and cultures before it can begin to skillfully arbitrage global information.'

Source: Richard P. Rumelt (2011), *Good strategy / Bad Strategy*, New York, NY: Crown/Random House.

The concept of dynamic capabilities has allowed a deeper understanding of factors that may contribute to resources and capabilities generating sustainable competitive advantage. If resources and capabilities are co-specialized and configured well, that may contribute to their value. If they are (in part) dependent on tacit knowledge, firm-specific and surrounded by isolating mechanisms, that makes them rarer and more difficult to replicate than resources and capabilities without such features. Potentially, they can therefore contribute to resources and capabilities meeting the requirements of Barney's VRIN-framework. However, the discussion so far has only highlighted the *internal* organizational context of dynamic capabilities. If they are to have value and generate sustainable competitive advantage, an *external* dimension is required as well. The capabilities have to be applied in a competitive environment.

Competition is an environmental selection mechanism. Only dynamic capabilities that survive competitive environmental selection have value. Therefore, we return to the concept of dynamic capabilities in the next chapter, after having introduced environmental selection.

9.7 Move and counter move

In the discussion in the preceding section we have ignored the fact that, in the real world, companies choosing a competitive strategy usually take into account how competitors are likely to react.

When a firm chooses a competitive strategy, it chooses values for the strategic dimensions of its industry. For example, it chooses its levels of expenditure on advertising, R&D and so on. When a firm makes such choices, it should (and usually does) take into account how competitors will react. If it does not, it is like a chess player who, when considering a move, does not analyse the possible counter moves an opponent will make. If you have ever played chess, you will know that you will probably lose the game if you play that way.

In this section we want to show how a company, when considering a strategic move, can take into account possible counter moves by a competitor. We shall do this by discussing how a monopolist can impede entry into its industry by a potential entrant. It is a complicated subject as many moves and counter moves are possible. To make things as simple as possible we shall use a particular industry to illustrate moves by the monopolist and counter moves by the potential entrant: the ice-cream-selling business. After our analysis of the ice-cream-selling industry, we shall translate our main findings for other industries.

9.7.1 The ice-cream-selling industry

Imagine a beach with a length of 1000 meters. Potential customers are evenly distributed along the beach. There are two entrepreneurs that consider setting up ice-cream stands on the beach. Let us call them Peter and Sandra. There is another company, Rent-a-Stand, that specializes in letting ice-cream stands.

Rent-a-Stand is not interested in selling ice-cream. Ice-cream stands can be rented for $255 a day. Both Peter and Sandra can rent as many ice-cream stands as they want.

The price of an ice-cream is $3. The price has been determined by the municipality and neither Peter nor Sandra is allowed to sell ice-creams at any other price. Peter and Sandra both have to buy ice-creams from a distributor at $1 a piece, so, for each ice-cream they sell, they make a gross margin of $2. One thousand ice-cream consumers are evenly distributed along the beach. Each consumer buys one ice-cream per day and buys her ice-cream at the nearest stand.

9.7.2 Number of ice-cream stands

Peter arrives at the beach one day. He has to decide how many ice-cream stands to place on the beach. As soon as Peter has placed his stands, Sandra arrives. Sandra then has to decide if she wants to place ice-cream stands on the beach as well. That, of course, is an entry game (see Section 5.3 for another example of an entry game).

Let us return to Peter deciding how many stands to place on the beach. Suppose, first, that he chooses to have only one stand. If he has just one stand and Sandra does not enter, he will sell 1000 ice-creams. He will make a gross margin of $2000 and has to pay the rent for one stand, $255, so his profit will be $1745.

However if Peter places only one stand on the beach, there is ample room for Sandra to enter. If Peter places his stand in the middle of the beach, Sandra can place two stands at a distance of 250 metres left and right from Peter's stand. By doing so she will sell 375 ice-creams in each of her two stands, make a gross margin with each of her stands of $750, and make a nice profit. In fact she can do even better by placing two stands as close as possible left and right of Peter's stand. She will then sell 1000 ice-creams and Peter will sell nothing.

Peter is not so naïve as to place only one stand on the beach. He can deter entry by placing four stands on the beach, one at 125 metres from the left, one at 375 metres from the left, one 375 metres from the right and one at 125 metres from the right (see Figure 9.5). If Sandra now places a stand between any of his stands (for example between Stands A and B) she will sell 125 ice-creams and make a gross margin of $250. This is not enough to cover the rent. If she places a stand to the left of Peter's Stand A she will also sell not more than 125 ice-creams. So she will not enter and Peter will make a profit of 2000 − 4 × 255 = 980.

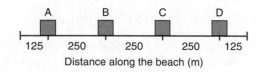

Figure 9.5 Four ice-cream stands on a beach

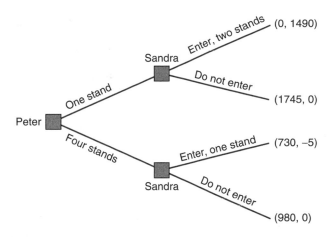

Figure 9.6 Game tree for the ice-cream-selling game. Peter moves first to determine the number and location of his stands

The results of this analysis are indicated in the game tree shown in Figure 9.6. If Peter applies the principle of looking ahead and reasoning back, he will decide to have four stands. Notice two interesting features of this game:

- Peter would choose to have only one stand if he had a legal monopoly. By choosing four stands instead of one he can effectively deter entry. The essence of this strategy is to *blanket* potential demand for ice-cream, leaving no room for Sandra to enter. We will come back to blanketing strategies in Section 9.7.6, in the context of product competition.
- It is a great advantage for Peter that he arrives on the beach before Sandra. As a consequence, he can make the first move in the game and deter Sandra from entering. If Sandra had arrived first, she could have blocked Peter and she would have pocketed all ice-cream profits. Hence, this game illustrates a situation with a significant **first mover advantage**. In Section 9.7.7 we will explore this concept more generally.

First mover advantage

9.7.3 Commitment

In Section 5.3 we introduced the idea of commitment. There we discussed a situation in which the incumbent firm can commit itself to lower prices after entry has occurred. The ice-cream example offers an opportunity to illustrate another form of commitment.

Thus far we have assumed that the future consists of only one day. Suppose now that both Peter and Sandra have a time horizon of seven days rather than one day. Suppose that Peter can choose between two types of rental contract: a fixed contract and a flexible contract. A fixed contract is a contract for seven days that cannot be cancelled by Peter. If Peter chooses a fixed contract, he has to pay the rent ($255 per stand per day) for seven days even if he does not sell a single ice-cream. A flexible contract is one that gives Peter the option to cancel the contract after one day. After Peter has signed a rental contract with

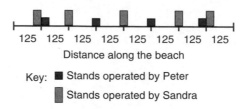

125   125   125   125   125   125   125   125

Distance along the beach

Key: ■ Stands operated by Peter

▮ Stands operated by Sandra

Figure 9.7 Nine ice-cream stands on a beach

Rent-a-Stand, Sandra has to decide whether or not she wants to rent a stand. For simplicity, we shall assume that Sandra can choose only a fixed contract.

To analyse this situation, suppose, first, that Peter decides to choose a flexible contract. He rents four stands and places them as indicated in Figure 9.5. If Sandra does not enter he will make $2000 − 4 × $255 = $980 per day. This is $6,860 during the whole week. If Sandra does enter, she will hire five stands for seven days, using a fixed contract. She will place those five stands on the beach as indicated in Figure 9.7. During the first day Sandra will sell 625 ice-creams, make a gross margin of $1250 and a 'profit' of $1250 − 5 .$255 = −$25. Peter will sell 375 ice-creams, make a gross margin of $750 and a 'profit' of $750 − 4. $255 = − $270 during the first day. After the first day Peter will decide not to renew his rental contract. So during the rest of the week Sandra will sell 1000 ice creams per day and make a profit of $2000 − 5 .$255 = $725 per day. For seven days she will make a profit of 6 .$725 − $25 = $4325. After the first day, Peter has to decide whether to cancel the rental contract with Rent-a-Stand. If he does not cancel the contract, he will make a loss of $270 for each of the remaining six days. If he cancels the contract, his loss during the whole week will be only $270. Sandra will then make a profit of $725 during each of the remaining six days, $4325 for the whole week.

If Peter chooses a fixed contract and hires four stands, and Sandra does not enter, he will make a profit of $2000 − 4 .$255 = $980 per day, or $6860 for the whole week. If Sandra enters with five stands she will sell 625 ice-creams per day and make a loss of $25 per day, or $175 for the whole week, and Peter will sell 375 ice-creams per day and make a 'profit' of $750 − 4 .$255 = −$270 per day, or −$1890 for the whole week.

This results in the game tree shown in Figure 9.8. Peter and Sandra apply the principle of looking ahead and reasoning back. So Peter chooses a fixed contract, and Sandra does not enter. That is an example of *temporal commitment*. By signing a contract for a week rather than for a day, Peter commits himself to the ice-cream-selling business and so deters entry.

9.7.4 Lessons from the ice-cream example

Two important lessons emerge from the ice-cream example. First, from Section 9.7.2, we see that Peter can block entry by employing four stands rather than one. That finding has an important analogy in product competition, as we shall explain below (in Section 9.7.6).

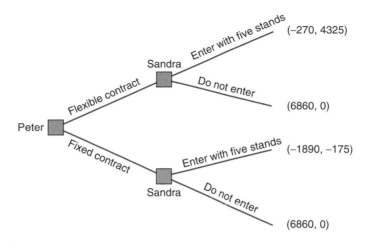

Figure 9.8 Game tree for the ice-cream-selling game. Peter moves first to choose between a flexible and a fixed contract.

Credible commitment

Second, from Section 9.7.3, we know that Peter can deter entry by making a **credible commitment**. If Peter has to choose between a fixed rent contract and a flexible rent contract, he can deter entry by choosing a fixed contract. Suppose Peter chooses a flexible contract and then simply tells Sandra that he will stay in business for seven days whether she enters or not. If he does that, however, Sandra will not believe him. The problem for Peter is one of convincing Sandra that he will not stop his business after the first day. Peter must make a credible threat not to retire from the ice-cream selling industry, and he can do so by choosing a fixed contract.

The lesson from the game in Figure 9.8 is that Peter has to make a credible threat. The simple but important point is that it is easier to convince someone of something that is true than of something that might not be true. By signing a long-term contract Peter really cannot leave the ice-cream business. Peter's threat is credible because he has committed himself. See Box 9.9 for more on commitments.

It is often thought that strategic flexibility is always an advantage. In Section 9.7.3, we analyzed situations where flexibility (the ability to leave the industry) was a disadvantage rather than an advantage.

Box 9.9 Commitments are essential to strategic management

Commitments are essential to management. They are the means by which a company secures the resources necessary for its survival. Investors, customers and employees would likely shun any company the management of which refused to commit publicly to a strategy and back its intentions with investments.

▶

> Commitments are more than just necessities, however. Used wisely, they can be powerful tools that help a company to beat the competition. Pre-emptive investments in production capacity or brand recognition can deter potential rivals from entering a market, while heavy investments in durable, specialized and illiquid resources can be difficult for other companies to replicate quickly. Sometimes, just the signal sent by a major commitment can freeze competitors in their tracks. When Microsoft announces a coming product launch, for instance, would-be rivals rethink their plans.
>
> *Source*: D. N. Sull, 'Managing by commitments', *Harvard Business Review*, June 2003, pp. 82–91

Flexibility is always an advantage when you play against Nature. Nature's moves are determined by a random process: they are not determined by whether or not you are committed to a certain strategy. If, however, you play against a human opponent, it may be better to commit yourself rather than retain flexibility. To use a military analogy, burning the bridges behind you signals a credible commitment that you are willing to fight.

9.7.5 Spatial competition

Spatial competition

Selecting locations for ice-cream stands on a beach is an example of spatial competition. A clearer example of **spatial competition** is the competition between supermarket chains for new locations. It differs from our ice-cream example in the following respects:

- It is spatial competition in two dimensions instead of one (our beach could be represented by a line and, thus, has only one dimension; an area has two dimensions: north/south and east/west).
- Zoning regulations and existing buildings exclude parts of the total area as possible sites for a new supermarket.
- Customers tend to shop at the nearest supermarket, but not everyone always shops at the nearest supermarket.
- Population, and thus demand, need not be evenly distributed over the area.
- Population shifts may occur – to be able to forecast population shifts correctly is an important competitive weapon.

9.7.6 Product competition

Spatial competition has an important analogy in product competition. Imagine two companies selling different brands of cola drink, which differ along one dimension – let us say, sweetness. If sweetness can be expressed as a number, the position of a brand can be given by a number.

To introduce a new product is then the equivalent of opening an ice-cream stand on our beach. Potential customers have different tastes. The distribution of tastes is the parallel of the distribution of potential customers along the beach. Each customer will buy the brand that comes closest to his or her taste preference.

Of course, products can differ in more than one dimension and consumer preferences may change over time. Under these conditions the game of introducing new brands is analogous to the game of selecting new supermarket sites.

In most real-life cases, firms compete in several dimensions. For example, Coca Cola and Pepsi compete not only in terms of the taste of their products, but also branding, distribution channels, price and so on. The importance of those dimensions may vary per region and change over time, which adds further complexity to the competitive game of move and counter move in the 'cola wars'.

By the way, do you think Coca Cola or Pepsi was the first to market cola drinks? Which company pioneered diet colas? Would it be an advantage to be the 'first to market' with such products? What would determine success? These questions are explored in the next section (where we will also answer those cola questions).

9.7.7   First mover advantages

First mover advantages

In Section 9.7.2, we saw that Peter enjoyed a great advantage – he was the first to arrive at the beach. In this section, we explore under which circumstances such **first mover advantages** can be expected. We will also examine why it is not always an advantage to be the first and why many pioneering firms that are 'first to market' fail to take advantage of their lead.

First mover advantages may arise in the following situations:

■ *The first mover is able to capture a resource that gives competitive advantage* That is the situation in our ice-cream example. Peter is able to monopolize the beach, by means of either a blanketing strategy of putting up two stands first or making credible commitments. Peter's location on the beach is a valuable resource that is rare, inimitable and non-substitutable (VRIN). A location on the beach thus conforms to the VRIN conditions for competitive advantage (see Section 9.5). That advantage is temporary, however, if the game is repeated after expiry of the rental contract. Sandra will have learned that it pays to get to the beach first. Mining companies acquiring the best locations to find natural resources, however, are building the resource base for sustainable competitive advantage. Similarly, a unique patented technology provides such a basis.

■ *The first mover is able to 'lock-in' customers or suppliers* An example may actually be Coca Cola, which was invented and first marketed in 1886 (Pepsi followed in 1898). Coca Cola was originally positioned as one of many medicinal drinks, offering the beneficial effects of the coca leaves and kola nuts used to make it. It may well have been that Coca Cola's initial formulation was mildly addictive for consumers (containing cocaine, until it was removed in 1903) – a very literal route to lock-in. More generally, we saw in Section 8.2.4 that lock-in may occur when large numbers exchange is transformed to small numbers exchange as a result of learning-by-doing. If Peter is able to strike an exclusive long-term deal with the rental company letting the ice-cream stands, he may be able to achieve lock-in with his supplier (locking out Sandra).

- *The first mover is able to benefit from learning* In many industries, the production costs per unit decrease over time as a result of learning. The first mover may therefore have lower costs per unit than followers.
- *The first mover is able to appropriate increasing returns* Normally, economics works with decreasing returns: demand curves are downward sloping. The first product is able to fetch a higher price than later copies. Sometimes, however, products exhibit increasing returns – namely, if your product or service becomes more valuable as the number of buyers or users gets larger. An example is Facebook. The first Facebook account was essentially worthless, as it could not communicate with anyone else, but each additional account increases the value for all other users. This is called a **network effect** (or, more formally, a **positive network externality**). Other examples are the creation of *standards* (the Windows standard for computer operating systems, for example) or *dominant designs* (such as Intel has established for microprocessors). We will come back to these concepts in Chapters 11 and 12. Suffice it to say here that it is usually very difficult for a first mover or pioneer to start a process of increasing returns *and* appropriate those returns.

Network effect, or, positive network externality

Is it, then, *always* an advantage to be the first mover, to come to market with your products first? The answer is no. In fact, it is much more often the case that 'first to market' is 'first to fail'. Among the reasons for that are the following two:

- The pioneer has to gain acceptance of the new product. That process is known to be subject to high failure rates and, even in the case of a success, to long time delays. Often, those hurdles are too high for pioneers to overcome. In the next chapter, we will see that there is a 'liability of newness', causing high mortality among firms in the early stages of establishing new markets.
- The skills and competences necessary for *invention* (discovery) are rather different from those necessary for *innovation* (commercial success of inventions). Entrepreneurial firms that are good at idea generation and prototyping (making the first version of a product) often already have difficulties working towards market adoption of those products. When they succeed in building a market, it often remains a *niche* market. They lack the competences to really build a *mass* market. To do that requires marketing and distribution skills as well as manufacturing competences and a low cost mentality, which are usually difficult to reconcile with the entrepreneurial culture. Large, established firms on the other hand, usually have difficulty combining sufficient **exploration** with their competences in **exploitation** of existing concepts and products (see also Chapters 11 and 12).

Exploration

Exploitation

As an illustration of the last point, consider the market for 'diet coke'. Which one of the large, established cola companies (Coca Cola or Pepsi) created the market? The answer is neither of them. The pioneer was Kirsch with a 'No-Cal Cola' in 1952, creating a niche market. The mass market was, however, developed by Coca Cola with its Diet Coke (1982, notice the time lag!) That is only one example among very many of an established company making an innovation success out of an invention and niche market developed by another, pioneering firm. Markides and Geroski (2005) therefore shift the original meaning of *first mover advantages* (for pioneers) to the *first movers into the mass market*, as follows:

> First mover advantages are almost permanent competitive advantages that early movers can realize and use to protect themselves against the competitive threats of later-moving, imitative entrants. They come from being first to the *mass* market, but, as we have just seen, this is not the same as being first in the market.

Fast second

Their recommendation for established firms is to follow a **fast second** strategy in the case of radical innovations – that is, allowing early movers to establish a niche market and then being the first to consolidate it into a mass market. In fact, such a strategy need not be very 'fast'. Research by Tellis and Golder (2002) showed an average time lag of 19 years between the (niche) market entry of pioneers and the (mass) market entry of consolidators.

Consolidators then leverage their existing resources (such as brands and distribution networks) and their established lock-ins (with retail chains and suppliers) to realize first mover advantages in the mass market. In that process of consolidation, the early movers into the niche market usually (but not always) lose out.

It is fair to say that the literature on first mover advantages is still in its infancy. We expect that our insights into when it is advantageous to move first and when it is better to be (fast) second will be further developed in years to come.

9.7.8   Moving lessons

Let us summarize some of the main lessons we have learned in this section on moves and counter moves:

- Given a (potential) demand for a certain product, firms may deter entry by blanketing that demand – that is, leaving no room for other firms to enter profitably. If, however, they leave certain niches open for potential entrants, they may be profitably exploited. Niches may be of a geographical or product differentiation nature.
- Incumbents may also deter entry by showing that they are committed to their (place in the) industry. In order to be an effective deterrent, the commitment needs to be observable by and credible to the potential entrant.
- As a corollary, flexibility is not always the strategic advantage it is usually assumed to be. If potential entrants interpret an incumbent's flexibility as the likelihood that it will accommodate new entries, entry may in fact be encouraged.
- Similarly, moving first can be an advantage in certain circumstances. It may be less often the case than usually presumed, however. Sometimes, it is more beneficial to wait and be (fast) second. That is specifically the case if the competences for invention/exploration are very different from the requirements for innovation/exploitation. We return to this theme in Chapters 11 and 12.

9.8 Summary: how economic analysis can contribute to the formulation of competitive strategies

Each single business firm and each business unit in a multibusiness firm needs to have a competitive strategy that specifies how that business intends to compete in its given industry.

The first requirement in formulating a competitive strategy, is to analyze the environment and assess the firm's strengths and weaknesses. Porter's five-forces model, which is based on the results of several studies in the tradition of the structure – conduct – performance paradigm, has proved to be a useful tool for assessing the attractiveness of the industry in which the firm operates. The concept of strategic groups provides a foundation for analyzing differences in performance between companies (or business units) belonging to the same industry. That gives the strategic planner a tool with which to assess a business unit's strengths and weaknesses.

In formulating a competitive strategy, the firm has many options. The options that are available depend on the industry and the firm's position within that industry. However, two successful strategies – those of cost leadership and product differentiation – have been identified in many industries. Any firm should at least consider these so-called generic competitive strategies.

The objective of a competitive strategy is to create a competitive advantage over rival firms. Preferably, that competitive advantage should be as sustainable as possible. The resource-based view (RBV) of the firm examines which resources may form the basis of such a competitive advantage. It has concluded that resources should be valuable, rare, inimitable and non-substitutable (the VRIN-framework). The RBV has been extended with the concept of dynamic capabilities, denoting the capacity of an organization purposefully to create, extend or modify its resource base. That has allowed us to delve deeper into the factors enabling resources and capabilities to provide competitive advantage. Factors noted in this chapter include co-specialization, asset orchestration, tacit knowledge, firm specificity and isolating mechanisms. In Chapter 11 we will examine the evolution and selection of dynamic capabilities.

In formulating a competitive strategy, a firm should take into account how its competitors will react. That is true especially in an oligopolistic industry – an industry consisting of a few large companies. For example, when Google decided to launch a new open-source platform for mobile phones (Android) it had to take into account how its competitors (Apple and Microsoft, among others) would react. Game theory (discussed in Chapter 5) can help in that respect. The game of selling ice-cream on a beach shows, first, how companies can try to prevent entry by other firms by offering several competing brands and, second, that by making a credible commitment to an industry, a company can discourage other firms from entering that industry.

Questions

1 Consider an industry that you know well – for example, the industry consisting of the bars in the town where you live. Use Porter's model of the forces driving industry competition to describe the intensity of competition in that industry.

2 You are managing director of a small, young electronics firm. One of your engineers has developed a specialized kind of memory chip. The new chip can be manufactured in one of two ways – by buying highly specialized equipment or buying less specialized equipment. The specialized equipment can be used to produce only the new chip. The less specialized equipment can be used to produce the new chip but could, with a minor additional investment, also be used to produce a variety of other chips. Demand for the new chip is highly uncertain. The new chip could turn out to be a bestseller or a complete failure in the market. Also uncertain is whether or not other firms are already working on the development of a similar chip. You know that it is impossible to protect the new chip by patents.

Do you see an advantage in buying the specialized equipment? Assume that the amount to be invested and unit cost for the specialized equipment are the same as for the less specialized equipment.

10 Economic contributions to corporate strategy

10.1 Introduction

In a multibusiness firm there are two levels of strategy: competitive strategy and corporate strategy. Economic contributions to competitive strategy (also termed business level strategy) have been discussed in Chapter 9. This chapter is concerned with corporate strategy (also termed corporate-level strategy).

Consider a multibusiness firm (Firm A) consisting of four business units (a1, a2, a3, a4) and a corporate office (headquarters or HQ). The business units of the multibusiness firm operate as quasi-independent firms. That is: they buy most of their inputs from external suppliers, sell most of their output to external customers and (try to) make a profit. Corporate HQ attracts capital from the capital market and allocates capital to the business units, selects and monitors the managers of the business units, may provide advice to the business units, and may buy and sell business units. Business unit a1 may sell part of its output to a2, and business units a3 and a4 may exchange knowledge.

The alternative to a multibusiness firm is a set of fully independent businesses (then a1, a2, a3 and a4 would all be fully independent companies). These independent businesses would have to buy all their inputs (including capital, managerial labour and advice) from external suppliers and would sell all of their output to external customers.

So, in the multibusiness firm certain transactions between HQ and business units (capital market, managerial labour market, market for advice) as well as certain transactions between business units (components, know-how) are taken out of the market and internalized within the firm.

From the perspective of our conceptual framework (Figure 1.1) we would ask: is organizational coordination within the multibusiness firm more efficient than market coordination? If the answer is yes, we say that the corporate form creates value. If the answer is no the corporate form destroys value.

We may also choose to focus on corporate HQ of Firm A. An important question may be whether a corporate HQ adds value. The answer can be obtained in two steps. We may first determine that the corporate HQ creates (or destroys) value if coordination within multibusiness Firm A is more (or less) efficient than market coordination. Please note that this is the same test as applied above. In our conceptual framework, the first relevant test is between organizational and market coordination. So, saying that 'organizational coordination is more efficient than market coordination' is, from this point of view, the same as saying that 'corporate HQ adds value' even though not only transactions between HQ of A and business units of A are taken out of the market, but also transactions between the business units of A. If in this first test the corporate form (or HQ) does not add value, the business units are better off as fully independent businesses, subject to market coordination with the outside world.

A next question might be whether another corporate HQ might not be a better owner for one or more of the business units of A, because it could add even more value to these business units. This is the question of 'parenting advantage' raised by Goold et al. (1994). Please note that this second test compares two potential forms of organizational coordination with each other. If, in this second test, the current corporate HQ adds less value than another potential parent, the business units are better off to be taken over by the other parent. This question is, therefore, closely related to the market for corporate control as discussed in Chapter 7.

Within a multibusiness firm transactions may take place that would be impossible in the market. An example is the exchange of know-how (or experience) for which property rights are ill defined. In such cases value is created if the benefits of the transaction exceed its cost.

Interference of HQ with the business units may also be counterproductive. Box 10.1 describes a situation where a company has come to the conclusion that it has two different businesses that would benefit from being run independently of each other, rather than as part of the same company.

Box 10.1 Kraft-ing corporate strategy over time

The corporate history of Kraft Foods shows how it has alternated between being an independent company on the market and being part of a larger corporate organization (Philip Morris). Having regained its independence in 2007, it announced in 2011 that it would break itself up.

J.L. Kraft started selling cheese from a horse-drawn wagon in 1903. By 1914, the company started manufacturing its own cheese. Throughout the 20th century the company grew strongly, also by acquisitions, and diversified into a food company with strong brands. In the 1980s, the cigarette company Philip Morris wanted to diversify itself and first bought General Foods for $5.6 billion and later Kraft for $12.9 billion, merging the two companies under its corporate ownership. Philip Morris allowed Kraft to grow, for example by acquiring Nabisco for $18.9 billion in 2000 and merging it with Kraft.

In 2007, Kraft Foods regained its full independence after having been partially listed by Philip Morris already in 2001. It continued to grow, amongst others by takeover of the British confectionary company Cadbury for £ 11.5 billion ($18.9 billion) in 2010. In 2011, Kraft Foods announced that it wanted to split itself in 'a High-Growth Global Snacks Company and a High-Margin North American Grocery Business, Each with a Portfolio of Iconic Brands':

> Having successfully executed its transformation plan, and 18 months into the Cadbury integration, the company has, in fact, built a global snacking platform and a North American grocery business that now differ in their future strategic priorities, growth profiles and operational focus. For example, Kraft Foods' snacks business is focused largely on capitalizing on global consumer snacking trends, building its strength in fast-growing developing markets and in instant consumption channels; the North American

grocery business is investing to grow revenue in line with its categories in traditional grocery channels through product innovation and world-class marketing, while driving superior margins and cash flows.

The company believes that creating two public companies would offer a number of opportunities:

■ Each business would focus on its distinct strategic priorities, with financial targets that best fit its own markets and unique opportunities.
■ Each would be able to allocate resources and deploy capital in a manner consistent with its strategic priorities in order to optimize total returns to shareholders.
■ Investors would be able to value the two companies based on their particular operational and financial characteristics and thus invest accordingly.

The history of Kraft shows acquisitions and organic growth have increased organizational coordination over time, while market coordination has been enhanced by divestitures, stock market listings and now break-up.

Source: Kraft Food press release, August 4, 2011.

Please note that, in the discussion so far, we have been careful to emphasize that the efficiency of market and organizational coordination can only be determined by mutual comparison. It will depend on the environmental and institutional context in which the trade-off is made. Kraft Foods, the example in Box 10.1, is based in a highly developed market economy, the USA. Both the capital markets and the managerial labour markets function well. This means that organizational coordination has a relatively 'tough' (market) efficiency benchmark to surpass. In other environments, with less developed markets, the (market) efficiency benchmark may be lower and organizational coordination may compare more favourably. Indeed, we see business groups and conglomerates more often in emerging economies, as we will further explore in Chapter 14. Box 10.2 already illustrates some elements of this rationale.

Box 10.2 Conglomerates valued in emerging markets

Tata, India's second largest industrial group, spans several sectors, from communications to energy via materials, engineering, services and chemicals. Fosun – China's biggest privately held conglomerate – takes in property, steel, retail and healthcare among other businesses. Tarun Khanna, professor at Harvard Business School and co-author of *Winning in Emerging Markets*, argues that groups with a wider scope make sense in markets where much of the institutional infrastructure is missing: 'For example, it is much harder to get access to risk capital in most parts of India or China than it is in Silicon Valley, New York or London' he says. 'Within a broadly based business, you can move existing cash flow from one part of the organization to another, as long as you do it with discipline and disclosure.'

Others say that, in markets where governmental supervision and control of the economy remains substantial, operations within large and diverse companies may benefit from the parent organization's experience of negotiating bureaucratic processes or network of public sector connections. As one advisor puts it, these advantages come under the euphemistic heading of 'regulatory synergies'.

A further reason why conglomerates are still in fashion is that attracting the best possible management talent can be easier in a large group with extensive opportunities for career advancement.

Prof Khanna says a big brand can also help consumers feel comfortable that they are making the right decision. 'Take the distrust of foods in China. Middle-class families are constantly worrying about whether food is contaminated. In the shops you can see people being anxious where food has come from. Without an authority like the US Food and Drug Administration, people end up relying on pre-existing companies or organizations they trust.'

Source: 'Conglomerates valued in emerging markets', *The Financial Times*, 24/25 September 2011

Given a certain institutional context, the potential benefits of organizational coordination depend on the type and degree of relatedness of the business units. If we have a corporate HQ with two business units A and B, relatedness between A and B can take different forms:

- Business units A and B are vertically related when A supplies components to B (or vice versa). This is a case of *vertical integration*.
- Business units A and B are horizontally related when A and B operate in the same industry. When A and B operate in the same industry but in different countries we have a situation of *horizontal multinationalization*.
- If A and B are neither horizontally nor vertically related, A and B can still be related in some other way, for example because they use the same technology or serve the same (type of) customer. This is a case of *related diversification*.
- If A and B are not related, we have a situation of *unrelated (or conglomerate) diversification*.

At the corporate level, the firm needs to decide in *which industries and in which countries it w*ants to operate. By acquiring new businesses, by selling businesses, by developing new businesses and by discontinuing businesses it can adjust its portfolio of businesses. This is called **portfolio management**. It is a vital element of corporate strategy, since the corporation can influence the type and degree of relatedness (and thus the potential benefits of organizational coordination) by adjusting its portfolio.

Portfolio management

We start by discussing unrelated diversification (in Section 10.2). As we shall see, even in this case corporate HQ can perform several roles; whether it can do so more efficiently than markets depends on the efficiency of those markets. We then move on to the case of related diversification (Section 10.3), where corporate HQ can perform the same roles plus a new role; that of fostering cooperation between business units. Section 10.4 focuses on horizontal multinationalization, and Section 10.5 on vertical integration. We summarize this in Section 10.6.

10.2 Unrelated diversification

Consider a corporation consisting of a corporate HQ and a number of business units that are not in any way related. Such a corporation is often called a *conglomerate*. Coordination of the actions of unrelated business units cannot yield any benefits. Indeed one may wonder why conglomerates (continue to) exist at all, However conglomerates do exist even in highly developed economies. Box 10.3 gives an example.

Box 10.3 A successful conglomerate: Berkshire Hathaway

Berkshire Hathaway Inc. is an American multinational conglomerate holding company headquartered in Omaha, Nebraska, United States. It started out as a textiles company (see Box 10.4). Today, it oversees and manages a large and diverse range of subsidiary companies. These include insurance firms, confectionery, retail, railroad, home furnishings, encyclopedias, manufacturers of vacuum cleaners, jewelry sales; newspaper publishing; manufacture and distribution of uniforms; as well as several regional electric and gas utilities.

Berkshire Hathaway ended up owning such a wide array of businesses due to the investment philosophy of its chairman and CEO, Warren Buffett. Using the '*float*' provided by Berkshire Hathaway's insurance operations (paid premiums which are not held in reserves for reported claims and may be invested) to finance his investments, Warren Buffett has applied the principles of 'value investing' to detect undervalued firms. He invests only in companies that he can understand and has therefore avoided the high-tech sector, for instance. Based on a deep understanding of the business, Warren Buffett of course applies financial criteria and calculations to his investment, but attaches at least equal weight to having the right management in place. In his 2010 letter to shareholders, he explained:

"First, we possess a cadre of truly skilled managers who have an unusual commitment to their own operations and to Berkshire... At Berkshire, managers can focus on running their businesses...They simply get a letter from me every two years and call me when they wish. And their wishes do differ: There are managers to whom I have not talked in the last year, while there is one with whom I talk almost daily. Our trust is in people rather than process. A "hire well, manage little" code suits both them and me.

Berkshire's CEOs come in many forms. Some have MBAs; others never finished college. Some use budgets and are by-the-book types; others operate by the seat of their pants. Our team resembles a baseball squad composed of all-stars having vastly different batting styles. Changes in our line-up are seldom required."

Moreover, he looks for companies with a clear and sustainable competitive advantage, calling this a 'moat': 'something that gives a company a clear advantage over others and protects it against incursions from the competition.' In economic terminology, these are the *isolating mechanisms* introduced in Chapter 9.

His investment strategy has been highly successful: Berkshire Hathaway averaged an annual growth in book value of 20.2 per cent to its shareholders for the last 46 years, while employing large amounts of capital, and minimal debt. Berkshire Hathaway stock produced a total return of 76 per cent from 2000–2010 versus a negative 11.3 per cent return for the S&P 500. It is in the top-10 of largest public companies in the world, according to the Forbes Global 2000 list of 2011. An open question is how Berkshire Hathaway will cope when Warren Buffett and his 'right hand' Charlie Munger, who are both in their eighties, will be succeeded.

Source: from http://www.berkshirehathaway.com/letters/2010ltr.pdf. The material is copyrighted and used with permission of the author.

If business units are not in any way related, HQ will treat business units as stand alone units. The question then is: 'How can corporate HQ add value through stand alone influence?' The answer is that HQ can do so by performing one or more of the following roles:

- Attract capital and allocate capital to business units.
- Appoint, evaluate and reward business unit managers.
- Offer advice.
- Provide functions and services.
- Performance management.
- Portfolio management.

10.2.1 Attract capital and allocate capital to business units

Attracting capital is almost always a role performed by the corporate HQ rather than by the individual businesses. Attracting capital centrally may reduce *transaction costs* in various ways. For debt financing, diversification across industries should reduce the chance of bankruptcy. In combination with the larger size of the conglomerate, this results in a better rating by the rating agencies, like Standard & Poor's or Moody's. Better ratings lead to lower debt financing costs. Similarly, there are usually economies of scale in equity financing, resulting from the greater stock market liquidity of companies with higher capitalizations.

HQ also receives net cash flow from business units and *allocates capital* to business units. Why could corporate HQ do a better job than capital markets in allocating capital? The answer is information asymmetries in the capital market:

- Corporate HQ may have better information than outside investors because business unit managers will be prepared to share with the corporate office confidential information that they would not like to reveal to external investors (and thus to potential competitors).
- Corporate HQ may be better equipped to assess investment opportunities than outside investors, for instance because it has specialized knowledge about its business areas.

So one could say, that the conglomerate organization arises as a solution to *information problems* in the capital market.

In countries with well-developed capital markets, especially markets for venture capital, these advantages will be less important than in countries lacking such markets.

10.2.2 Appoint, evaluate, and reward business unit managers

As the owner of its businesses, each corporate organization appoints, evaluates and rewards the managers of the business units. It is a vital role; appointing the best manager for the top position in a business unit can have a significant impact on the performance of the business. The relevant question here is: 'Is a corporate HQ better able to find and select people for the top jobs of its business units than would emerge if the businesses were independent?'

As a start, a large corporate group has a 'pool' of management resources available which it has come to know well. Performance evaluations over time will have revealed the strong and weak points of a large number of candidates who can be comparatively assessed. The information about these candidates will thus be 'richer' than is routinely available on the market. In this sense, there is an information asymmetry between internal and external candidates. Corporate organizations may have an advantage because they can access the external market for business managers *as well as* tapping their internal labour market and utilizing the superior knowledge accumulated about internal candidates. Internal candidates may also have been trained over time in company-specific knowledge and skills, an example of *human asset specificity*.

How important would such an advantage be? This will depend greatly on the environment and the situation. In an environment with few qualified candidates (e.g. a developing country, or developing industry), 'growing your own managers' may provide an important advantage. However, in many developed economies there is a well-functioning market for managerial talent, assisted by institutions like executive search firms that specialize in building their own knowledge about available candidates. As these markets develop, the comparative advantage of 'growing your own managers' may lessen and the attractiveness of exploiting the external labour market may increase.

HQ also needs to design a reward system for the business unit manager. This is the principal-agent problem. The reward system may include a bonus based on performance of the business unit. Reward may also come in the form of promotion to a more important business unit. An important part of the job of HQ is to evaluate the performance of the business unit managers.

10.2.3 Offer advice

The manager of a business unit has in most cases the best knowledge about how to run her business. She has intimate knowledge of her products, her markets and customers, and the technology she uses. Despite that, she can possibly profit from advice from others. Independent entrepreneurs often have a network of informal advisors, and may also use the services of professional management consultants. Managers of business units can do the same. In addition, they may tap into the experience managers and staff members at HQ have. Many corporate HQ do 'strategy reviews' with their business unit managers. While the business unit's manager remains responsible for her strategy, she is required to explain and defend her strategy to the board of the parent company. The business unit manager can thus benefit from the suggestions made by board members. There is a real danger, however, that advice from board members will dominate valuable suggestions made by other, informal advisors.

The question here is: 'Will the corporate board do a better job in these strategy reviews than outsiders would do if the business was independent?' The answer may be yes if board members have a deeper understanding of the business than those outsiders.

10.2.4 Provide functions and services

Corporate organizations usually have a number of central functions at HQ, such as finance, personnel, engineering etc. They aim to provide specialist functional leadership and guidance for the businesses as well as functional advice to the corporate board. In addition, central services may be provided, like pensions administration, catering or security. In principle, such functions and services might also be procured by the individual businesses market contracting.

The economic rationale for central services is simply to reach critical mass in order to provide a cost-effective service that may not be otherwise contractable for individual businesses. It also avoids duplication: for example, the interpretation of changes in pension rules or security standards needs to be done only once instead of by all business units. Thus, the efficiency depends on the economies of (collective) scale versus individual contracting. For central functions, there may be additional economies of specialization allowing, for example, to develop scarce skills or highly specialized expertise.

10.2.5 Portfolio management

By acquiring and selling business units – or by developing new businesses – a corporation adjusts its portfolio of business units. This is called corporate *portfolio management*. The question whether it is possible to add value by doing so, depends on knowledge and negotiation skills of the corporation. Box 10.4 presents the views of Warren Buffett how capital (re)allocation and portfolio management have contributed considerably to the success of Berkshire Hathaway. In Chapter 13, however, we discuss the success rate of acquisitions and show that this is generally a risky activity from the point of view of the shareholders of acquiring companies. The Berkshire Hathaway example shows that there are exceptions to this general rule. What might explain these exceptions?

Box 10.4 Capital allocation and portfolio management at Berkshire Hathaway

Continuing to explain to his shareholders the advantages of Berkshire Hathaway, next to the selection of the right management (see Box 10.3), Warren Buffett commented:

> Our second advantage relates to the allocation of the money our businesses earn. After meeting the needs of those businesses, we have very substantial sums left over. Most companies limit themselves to reinvesting funds within the industry in which they have been operating. That often restricts them, however, to a "universe" for capital allocation that is both tiny and quite inferior to what is available in the wider world. Competition for the few opportunities that *are* available tends to become fierce.
>
> At Berkshire we face no institutional restraints when we deploy capital. Charlie and I are limited only by our ability to understand the likely future of a possible acquisition. If we clear that hurdle – and frequently we can't – we are then able to compare any one opportunity against a host of others.

▶

When I took control of Berkshire in 1965, I didn't exploit this advantage. Berkshire was then only in textiles, where it had in the previous decade lost significant money. The dumbest thing I could have done was to pursue "opportunities" to improve and expand the existing textile operation – so for years that's exactly what I did. And then, in a final burst of brilliance, I went out and bought *another* textile company. Aaaaaaargh!

Eventually I came to my senses, heading first into insurance and then into other industries. There is even a supplement to this world-is-our-oyster advantage: In addition to evaluating the attractions of one business against a host of others, we also measure businesses against opportunities available in marketable securities, a comparison most managements don't make. Often, businesses are priced ridiculously high against what can likely be earned from investments in stocks or bonds. At such moments, we buy securities and bide our time.

Our flexibility in respect to capital allocation has accounted for much of our progress to date. We have been able to take money we earn from, say, See's Candies or Business Wire (two of our best-run businesses, but also two offering limited reinvestment opportunities) and use it as part of the stake we needed to buy Burlington Northern Santa Fe (a railroad).

Source: from http://www.berkshirehathaway.com/letters/2010ltr.pdf. The material is copyrighted and used with permission of the author.

In Chapter 9 we introduced the concept of *dynamic capabilities*, which are aimed at change and alter the resource base of the organization. Forging alliances or making acquisitions were presented as examples. Indeed, there is considerable evidence that some companies have a significantly higher than average success at making acquisitions and that a main reason for their success is the frequency with which they engage in such transactions. Such companies are called 'serial acquirers'(see further Chapter 13). They learn by doing more often and thus accumulate experience and 'best practices'. Similarly, a recent McKinsey study (2012) investigated differences between companies in the rate of capital reallocation across businesses (both normal capital expenditures as well as acquisitions and divestments). McKinsey found that active reallocators achieve significantly higher returns for shareholders and are also more likely to stay independent. Again, this points toward the existence of dynamic capabilities for capital reallocation as an explanation of superior performance.

The benefits of unrelated diversification must be balanced against the costs. As conglomerates grow larger and older, the general office tends to grow and corporate overhead costs tend to rise; moreover, as bureaucratic rules are installed incentives are weakened and interference of HQ tends to become counterproductive. Thus, the financial performance of conglomerates is, on average, not impressive.

It is not always easy to classify a firm's portfolio as either related or unrelated. Perhaps it is better to speak about degrees of relatedness. As an example, consider Gillette's product portfolio, described in Box 10.5.

Box 10.5 Gillette's product portfolio

Gillette was an American company based in Boston, Massachusetts, with three major product divisions: grooming, portable power and oral care. Grooming includes products for male shaving, such as razors – manual and electrical – razor blades, shaving preparations and aftershaves. Gillette's grooming business also includes hair removal products for women. Gillette's portable power business consists mainly of Duracell, a company offering alkaline batteries for use in a wide variety of consumer products. Duracell was acquired by Gillette in 1996.

Gillette's oral care products include manual toothbrushes and a variety of oral care appliances sold under the Braun brand name.

At first glance, there appears to be little possibility for economies of scope for Gillette's three divisions. If one division, say the grooming business division, has unused manufacturing capacity, then it is highly unlikely that capacity can be used by another division, simply because razor blades, batteries and toothbrushes require highly different manufacturing facilities. Thus, specialized indivisible physical assets cannot be the source of economies of scope. The same is true of technological know-how (batteries are quite different from razor blades and toothbrushes) and brand names (batteries are sold under the Duracell brand name, oral appliances under the Braun brand name).

It is possible, however, that economies of scope may be obtained by using one sales organization for the products of all three divisions, especially in certain developing countries (Gillette's products are sold in over 200 countries). In that case, economies of scope would be based on organizational know-how (local marketing know-how in countries such as China and India).

Gillette's product portfolio may be classified as related (economies of scope from the joint use of marketing and sales operations in certain countries), but only distantly related.

In 2005, Gillette was acquired by Procter & Gamble and became one of its business units.

10.3 Related diversification

This section discusses related diversification. In a firm consisting of a corporate HQ and a number of related business units, corporate HQ can perform all five roles described in the previous section:

- It has to attract and allocate capital to business units.
- It has to appoint, evaluate and reward business unit managers.
- It may offer advice.
- It may provide functions and services.
- It may conduct portfolio management, acquiring and selling businesses and developing new businesses.

In addition to these roles, corporate HQ of a related diversified firm can try to create value by encouraging cooperation between business units.

Related diversification occurs when a firm starts or acquires a new business that is in some way related to the firm's existing business. Examples of related diversification are a coffee firm diversifying into coffee creamer (market-related), a dairy firm currently producing only cheese, butter and fresh milk products that diversifies into coffee creamer (input-related) and a commercial aircraft company diversifying into military aircraft (technology-related).

Economies of scope

An important reason for related diversification is the existence of **economies of scope**. Economies of scope exist when the joint production of two goods is less costly than the cost of producing those two goods separately. As an example, which we borrow from Teece (1980), we can consider the joint production of fruit and sheep.

A fruit grower must have space between fruit trees in order to facilitate adequate growth of the trees and the movement of farm machinery between the trees. That land can be used as pasture, where sheep can graze. As the land can be used as a common input, the joint production of fruit and sheep on one piece of land is less costly than the production of fruit and sheep separately on two different pieces of land. A more industrial example is the joint use of a physical distribution system for beer and soft drinks.

The existence of economies of scope does not imply that both goods should be produced by the same firm, as has been pointed out by Teece (1980). The fruit grower can diversify into sheep and thus realize economies of scope. As an alternative, however, he may lease the land to a sheep farmer. In the latter case, a market transaction in the common input factor (land) occurs. Thus, the fruit grower can choose between two governance structures: the firm (if he diversifies) or the market (if he leases his land to a sheep farmer).The actual choice made between these two arrangements will thus be driven by the transaction costs involved. So let us have a look at which factors determine these transaction costs.

Economies of scope can always be traced to a common production factor. If market transactions in this common production factor are relatively costly, joint production of the two products in one firm may be the most efficient solution. Common production factors leading to economies of scope are:

- specialized indivisible physical assets;
- technological know-how;
- organizational know-how;
- brand names.

Specialized indivisible physical assets

The services of **specialized indivisible physical assets** may be difficult to sell (exactly because the assets are specialized). As an example, consider once again a newspaper publisher in an isolated town. Suppose the publisher prints his own newspaper. The press is used for this purpose six days a week. One day a week, then, the press is idle. Suppose that idle capacity can be used to print a Sunday paper. Suppose further that there is a small company with a well developed plan to start a Sunday paper. The newspaper company can then buy that small company in order to obtain economies on the use of the printing press. An alternative would be a long term contract with the small company for printing the Sunday paper.

Technological know-how

Technological know-how may also lead to economies of scope. Technological know-how may be difficult to trade across markets for two reasons:

- property rights may be ill defined;
- transfer of know-how within a firm may be easier than across markets.

Not all technological know-how is patentable. Also, firms often choose not to patent technological findings, even if patents could be obtained. One reason is that they have to register their findings at the patent office. By registering, they reveal their knowledge, which is not always strategically advantageous. It is usually difficult to sell technological know-how if property rights are not protected by patent law, however. Thus, a seller must try to convince a potential buyer of its value and, in doing so, must reveal some of his know-how. A potential buyer can assess the real value of the know-how only after she has received it, but then she already possesses the know-how, so will refuse to pay for it. That is the fundamental paradox of information, as described in Section 4.1: its value can only be revealed to another party by disclosing the information, while such disclosure destroys its value.

The paradox emerges because potential buyers may behave opportunistically. Suppose a buyer agrees to pay in advance for technological know-how. Now the seller may behave opportunistically by transferring only a minor part of the know-how. Thus, the possibility of opportunistic behaviour by both buyers and sellers leads to the fundamental paradox of information.

Suppose now that property rights to know-how are protected by patent law. Then a potential buyer knows what he buys. Opportunistic behaviour by buyer and seller is less of a problem.

Transfer of know-how within a firm may still be easier (and thus cheaper) than between firms. If a recipe or a blueprint is all that needs to be transferred, it is easy to realize the transfer both between firms and within a firm. Frequently, however, more than a recipe or blueprint needs to be transferred: if the know-how contains an element of learning-by-doing, then training and consulting are part of the transfer. If engineers working for the same firm have received similar training, the transfer between engineers working for the same firm may be easier than that between engineers working for different firms. In such a case, related diversification may again be efficient.

Transfer of know-how may also be facilitated by having R&D performed in one central research lab. The central research lab can work on R&D projects formulated by and paid by the business units, while researchers share ideas during seminars or simply while having lunch at the lab's cafeteria.

Organizational know-how is the third production factor giving rise to economies of scope. The term refers to the fact that organizations 'know' how to respond to external events. Organizations use *routines* to respond to external events. An important characteristic of routines is that they are, to a large extent, *tacit*: organization members find it difficult to articulate why they respond to a stimulus in a particular way. Yet, organizations seem to 'remember by doing'.

The concept of organizational routines (developed by Nelson and Winter, 1982) is discussed more fully in Section 11.5. Here, we want to state that organizational know-how is often *fungible* – that is, organizational know-how often has several kinds of application (Teece, 1982). For example, automobile companies can also use their organizational know-how to make tanks (as they did during World War II) and breweries can use their organizational know-how to produce soft drinks and so on. Box 10.6 describes how Royal DSM combined its existent market, technological and regulatory know-how to build a new business in biomedical materials.

Box 10.6 Combining know-how for biomedical materials in Royal DSM

Royal DSM is a global Life Sciences and Materials Sciences company, based in The Netherlands (see also Box 9.7). In 2012, it announced the acquisition of Kensey Nash, a US-based technology-driven biomedical company, primarily focused on regenerative medicine. For DSM, this acquisition was another milestone in its ambition to build a new business in the field of Biomedical Materials.

This strategic ambition was formulated in its corporate strategy *Vision 2010* and announced in 2005. In this strategy DSM stated that it wanted to build new Emerging Business Areas, one of which was Biomedical Materials (BMM). DSM believed that it was in an advantageous position to grow a new business in BMM because it could draw on:

- Market know-how from operating in both Pharma markets (Pharmaceutical Ingredients and Antibiotics) and markets for Engineering Materials and Coatings.
- Technological know-how because of its strong research bases in both Life Sciences and Materials Sciences.
- Regulatory know-how, for instance with respect to approval procedures required by the US Food and Drug Administration.

DSM therefore combined a number of researchers, marketeers and other business people in a new unit Biomedical Materials, which was also given a number of products that had been developed scattered across DSM's businesses. One example was a strong fibre (Dyneema Purity) that could be used within the body, for example for stitching. Another example was a hydrophylic coating that could be applied on cardiac stents.

This combination of know-how, people and products and the new organizational dedication soon started to pay off in strong organic growth. On top of that, DSM acquired the Polymer Technology Group (Berkeley, California) in 2008. In 2010 it made a joint venture with DuPont to commercialize a portfolio of products based on DuPont's biodegradable hydrogel technologies. With its acquisition of Kensey Nash, DSM showed its skill as a "serial acquirer" (see Chapter 13) augmenting the organic growth of its Emerging Business Areas with focused acquisitions.

Sources: *Vision 2010*, Royal DSM (2005); DSM press release 3 May 2012

It is nearly impossible to trade organizational know-how across a market. If one manager is transferred from one firm to another, she must learn the organizational routines of her new firm. Organizational routines are more difficult to transfer. Through diversification, organizational know-how can be exploited across different applications. Thus, organizational know-how is a fundamental reason to diversify.

Brand names

Brand names can also lead to economies of scope. That is because it is usually cheaper to introduce a new product under an established brand name than under a new one (suppose DaimlerChrysler were to diversify into motorcycles; it would then be cheaper to use the Mercedes brand name than it would to use a new name). Brand names can also be traded across markets. We shall say more on this subject in Section 10.4.

Sometimes economies of scope can be quite important. Box 10.7 describes the attack of Amazon (exploiting internet-based economies of scope) on traditional bookstores, like Barnes & Noble. The strength of such internet-based economies of scope varies per industry, as is illustrated in Box 10.7 by comparing book retailing with food retailing.

Box 10.7 Bricks and/or Clicks?

Since the advent of the internet, many companies were set up to challenge incumbents in various industries. For instance, Amazon.com challenged the traditional bookstores. Since 2002, the United States has lost roughly 500 independent bookstores – nearly one out of five. In addition, large bookstore chains went out of business (like Borders) or are struggling (like Barnes & Noble).

Both Amazon and the bookstores have to make important decisions about the scope of their business. After having originally built an infrastructure for the distribution of books, Amazon has expanded its scope also to distribute articles like toys, jewelry and clothing. Once you have the warehousing, computer systems and value chains in place to distribute books, there are economies of scope in extending your product range to articles that can be ordered and distributed in similar fashion. Amazon has also extended its business model by entering the field of digital downloading of books by introduction of its successful Kindle e-reader.

Incumbents like Barnes & Noble also had to rethink their business model. It has gone from a 'Bricks and Mortar' model (only owning bookstores) to a 'Bricks and Clicks' model (adding Internet-based services). It has also introduced an e-reader, the Nook. Barnes and Nobel now holds about 27 per cent of this market in the US, while Amazon has at least 60 per cent.

Will the book industry follow the path of the music industry, where digital downloading is wiping out the sales of CDs? Or will the bricks & clicks model be successful, like in grocery retailing where companies like Safeway, Tesco and Ahold have successfully fought off the web-based start-ups (by perfecting a 'store-picking system' under which orders placed online are mainly plucked from the shelves of existing warehouses and stores). Much of the answer will depend on who has the strongest economies of scope. Waterstones, the British bookseller, decided to strike a deal with Amazon to sell the Kindle in its stores. It is hoping to sell ebooks over newly installed Wi Fi networks in its shops.

Sources: 'The bookstore's last stand', *New York Times*, 28 January 2012, 'A page is turned', *Financial Times*, 9 February 2010; 'Waterstones in Kindle deal with the 'devil'', *Financial Times*, 22 May 2012.

The argument so far can be summarized as follows. An important reason for related diversification is the existence of economies of scope. Economies of scope always rest on use of a common production factor. Four such factors have been identified:

- specialized indivisible physical assets;
- technological know-how;
- organizational know-how;
- brand names.

Economies of scope between two businesses can be exploited through market arrangements or through coordination by corporate HQ.

If economies of scope rest on joint use of physical assets, market coordination between independent businesses will often be efficient.

If economies of scope rest on difficult to trade intangible assets (such as non-patented know-how and brand names) organizational coordination may be more efficient. Within a multibusiness firm, cooperation between business units in order to realize economies of scope may take shape spontaneously, that is without interference by HQ, if two business units see an opportunity for mutual gain (for example by sharing information about customers). This is coordination by mutual adjustment. Such mutual adjustment is more easily obtained between business unit managers knowing and trusting each other. Corporate HQ can foster cooperation between business units in various ways. For example, HQ can try to create an atmosphere where business unit managers develop personal ties and trust. Rotating employees may also help in transferring 'best practices' between business units.

In section 10.2 we identified five roles which corporate HQ may assume to create value in the case of unrelated (conglomerate) diversification. In the case of related diversification, as examined in this section, we have thus identified two more roles: HQ can play a more active role by identifying opportunities for realizing additional economies of scope (in management language: opportunities for synergy) and by persuading business unit managers to realize these opportunities. In summary, in the case of related diversification we would say that corporate HQ may also attempt to create value by:

- identifying opportunities for synergy;
- fostering cooperation between business units.

There is, however, a real danger that intervention by the corporate office is counterproductive. For example, HQ may require business unit managers to attend a meeting to identify opportunities for synergy, where such opportunities do not exist. Or, worse, HQ may force business unit managers to share a common facility (for example purchasing) and thus compromise individual responsibility. When cooperation between business units does not occur spontaneously and needs to be forced by HQ, there is a very real danger of value destruction. As a more general point: all potential sources for value creation by corporate HQs can turn into sources of value destruction, if not carefully tailored to the real business needs and opportunities.

10.4 Horizontal multinationalization

In the previous section we discussed why a firm may extend its portfolio of business units through related diversification. A firm can also extend its portfolio through horizontal multi-nationalization. By **horizontal multinationalization** we mean becoming involved in the same activities in another country. An example is the acquisition of an American truck company by a German truck company.

Horizontal multinationalization

Consider a firm operating two different plants in two different countries (say the USA and Germany). Suppose, further, that both plants produce the same product (trucks) and that there are no shipments of intermediate goods between the two plants. Suppose, also, that transportation costs or import duties make it efficient to operate two plants (in the USA and Germany) instead of one. What advantage can be realized by bringing the US plant and the German plant under one managerial hierarchy? One answer is the realization of economies of scale. Another is the application of dynamic capabilities.

10.4.1 Economies of scale

As there are no shipments of intermediate goods or finished products, the reason must be the realization of economies of scale through the joint use of intangible assets. Three types of asset are relevant here:

- technological know-how;
- organizational know-how;
- brand names.

These three types of asset have also been mentioned in the preceding section. There we discussed economies of scope; now we discuss economics of scale.

There is a strong similarity between related diversification (which is one way to exploit economies of scope) and horizontal multinationalization (which is one way to exploit economies of scale). For that reason, the discussion here closely resembles that of the preceding section.

- *Technological know-how* As an example, suppose that the German firm has an excellent capability for designing aerodynamic trucks. There are two ways in which it can exploit its technological know-how in the USA. It can try to sell that capability to US truck manufacturers or it can acquire a US truck manufacturer and transfer the know-how to the new subsidiary. Again, a market arrangement or an organizational arrangement can be used to exploit the economies of scale from technological know-how. The difficulties involved in trading technological know-how were discussed in Section 10.3.
- *Organizational know-how* Suppose a Dutch brewery, such as Heineken, has expert knowledge in the marketing of premium beers. Through horizontal multinationalization that know-how may be applied in other countries. See also Section 10.3 for the difficulties involved in selling organizational know-how across markets.
- *Brand names* Suppose an American hotel chain (Hilton or Sheraton) has invested heavily in developing a brand name. Suppose, further, that the hotel appeals especially to business people who also travel a great deal abroad. Clearly, a hotel in Beijing, New Delhi or Amsterdam would be in a better position to attract American businesspeople if it could use the Hilton brand name. Hilton now has three alternatives: it can start its own hotels in other countries (or buy existing ones), it can sell the Hilton brand name once and for all or it can employ franchising.

Suppose Hilton wants to continue to use the Hilton name in the USA but decides to sell the right to use the Hilton brand name in the Netherlands once and for all to a Dutch firm. For Hilton, that would entail a big risk: the Dutch firm may, after the sale, behave opportunistically by charging high prices (customers would book because of the Hilton name) and not delivering quality. The American Hilton hotels would, in time, be hurt because the value of the brand name would decline owing to the opportunistic behaviour of the Dutch firm.

Franchising, however, is a feasible alternative. Through franchising, the Dutch firm acquires the right to use the Hilton name for a limited period of time only. The franchisor (the American Hilton) has the right to inspect the franchisee's (the Dutch) hotel during that period. If the franchisee does not comply with specified quality standards, he loses the right to use the Hilton name in the next period. Franchising is an example of a hybrid organizational form (a form somewhere between market and organization); franchising is further discussed in Section 14.6.

10.4.2 Dynamic capabilities

A company may also start operations in another country simply because it sees an opportunity to operate profitably in that country. While some such international expansions flounder, others may be successful. Companies with successful internationalization efforts may learn by doing and over time build a *dynamic capability* to expand internationally. Such firms become truly multinational and some may even be called 'global firms'.

A prime example is McDonald's. Originally, McDonald's had devised a *business model* that had proved to be very successful in the USA. A business model defines in detail which customers a company targets, how it intends to deliver value to them, and how the company captures its share of the value (see further Section 11.7). Mc Donald's had found a very successful formula for serving fast food in the USA. In the 1960s it grew to 1000 restaurants in the USA and it made its first foray outside the country, into Canada in 1967. Experiencing success with its first international expansions in nearby markets, McDonalds cast its geographical net wider and accelerated the pace of its multinationalization strategy. In 2012, it had more than 33,000 locations serving nearly 68 million customers in 119 countries each day. It has become a truly global company, indeed almost a symbol of globalization. As Box 10.8 illustrates, it had to adapt its business model to local circumstances and thus further refine its dynamic capability of international expansion over time.

Box 10.8 McDonald's dynamic capability of international expansion

The business model of McDonald's, as originally developed in the USA, was geared toward efficient delivery of 'fast food'. It relied heavily on standardization, both of output (a standard menu) and of work processes. This business model delivered phenomenal growth in the USA and in neighboring countries, like Canada. As McDonald's reached out further into the world, however, this standardized 'American' business model started to meet with some resistance in various countries and did not prove to be conducive to further growth. In 1999, the French 'anti-globalist' José Bové attacked the company for spreading 'junk food' and ruining the French farmers. In 2002, sales actually declined by 2 per cent and in 2003 the company had to declare its first quarterly loss. As a result, McDonald's has re-examined its business model and has made various adaptations.

First of all, it has allowed local adaptations of the menu. In France, McDonald's has started using French cheeses such as chèvre as well as whole-grain French mustard sauce. McDonald's India has a menu with vegetarian selections to suit local tastes. Chicken and fish choices are offered, but no beef or pork items. Israel has both kosher and non-kosher restaurants.

Second, McDonald's has introduced new formulas, like McSalad and McCafé. McSalad is an all-salad restaurant where customers will not find any of the traditional burgers, fries or shakes. McCafé emulates the Starbuck's formula, offering higher quality coffee and a lounge-like atmosphere. In France, McCafé offers baguette sandwiches.

Third, McDonald's today emphasizes how much it is part of the local economy. In France, it has strengthened its ties with French agribusiness and proudly advertised that 95 per cent of the company's ingredients come from France, with the rest coming from the European Union. Similarly, in many countries it operates with local authorities to provide 'entry-level' jobs for young employees struggling to join the labour market.

In all such ways, McDonald's had to adjust its business model to enable further international expansion. This illustrates how its dynamic capability of international expansion has needed refinement and local adaptation over time as the environments in which it operated broadened and changed. We will return to the topic of dynamic capabilities and their environmental context in the next chapter.

Sources: 'Born in the USA, Made in France: How McDonald's succeeds in the land of Michelin stars', Knowledge@Wharton, article ID=2521, 2011

10.4.3 Summary

By way of a summary we can now state that three types of intangible asset – technological know-how, organizational know-how and brand names – may lead to economies of scale when used outside the firm's home country. In principle, both market arrangements and organizational arrangements may be used to realize those benefits. What can corporate HQ do to realize these benefits?

First, it can foster cooperation by business units. Joint use of intangible assets may take shape spontaneously, that is without interference by HQ, if two business units see an opportunity for mutual gain. This is coordination by mutual adjustment. But HQ can facilitate mutual adjustment by creating an atmosphere where business unit managers develop personal ties and trust. Rotating employees may also help in transferring 'best practices' between business units.

Second, HQ may (try to) identify opportunities for synergy and encourage business unit managers to use these opportunities.

And third, HQ may facilitate sharing of intangible assets (such as technological know-how) by centralizing certain activities (such as R&D). This list of what HQ can do should parallel the list for economies of scope.

Finally companies may seize an opportunity in another country and be successful because they sense and seize opportunities earlier than potential competitors. They may start a trajectory of international expansion by 'exporting' a domestically grown business model to other geographic markets, thus becoming multinational. As they meet with success, they start building a dynamic capability of international expansion. As Box 10.8 illustrated, such a dynamic capability will tend to require refinement and adaptation over time, as a wider range of geographical markets is targeted and environmental contexts change themselves.

10.5 Vertical integration

Most production processes consist of several technologically separable stages. The production of automobiles, for example, consists of assembling an automobile from components such as the body, engine, gearbox, wheels and so on. Each of those components consists of several other components. **Vertical integration** means moving into the production of previous stages (backward integration) or subsequent stages (forward integration).

Vertical integration

It is easy to see that no firm can be *fully* integrated. For example, for a textbook publisher to be *fully* integrated would mean that it would have not only to undertake printing, bookbinding and operating bookstores but also producing paper, ink, computers, printing presses, bookbinding equipment and all the inputs for producing paper, ink, computers and so on. So, the question is not whether or not to be fully integrated, but, rather, in *which stages* of the production process do you want to be involved? For example, an automobile company may or may not produce its own gearboxes or ignition systems, but it is unlikely to consider producing tyres or lightbulbs.

In order to analyse vertical integration, we can directly apply transaction cost economics, discussed in Chapter 8. An automobile company making its own seats and a small building contractor buying nails from a hardware shop rely on different governance structures. The first uses a managerial hierarchy, while the latter relies on the market. Between the two extremes are long-term contracts, such as a five-year contract between an automobile company and a seat manufacturer. Such long-term contracts are sometimes called *quasi-vertical integration*. Other examples of quasi-vertical integration, involving long-term contracts between firms, are franchising and licensing contracts. These are hybrid forms, neither pure market nor pure hierarchy but rather somewhere in between. We will discuss hybrid forms more extensively in Chapter 14.

10.5.1 Technological interdependence

It is sometimes thought that technological factors determine whether or not two subsequent stages in a production process will be vertically integrated. As an example, consider steelmaking.

Steelmaking involves two stages. First, iron is produced by heating iron ore in a blast furnace. Then, the iron is used to produce sheet steel in a rolling mill. Significant energy savings are realized when these two stages are located next to each other. Then, the molten iron need not cool and be reheated, but is used directly as input for the rolling mill. Thus, it is sometimes argued that the production of iron and steel should be vertically integrated because of their technological interdependence.

Williamson (1975) argues that technological interdependence alone does not necessarily lead to vertical integration. The blast furnace and the rolling mill could be owned and operated by two independent firms. Of course, they should still be located next to each other in order to capture the energy savings.

10.5.2 Critical dimensions of transactions

In order to explain why, in practice, we observe integrated iron and steelworks instead of two separate firms, we need a transaction cost argument in addition to the technological factors.

What factors determine the choice made between vertical integration, quasi-vertical integration through long-term contracts and a series of spot contracts? As discussed in Chapter 8, three dimensions of transactions are important:

- asset specificity;
- uncertainty/complexity;
- frequency.

Asset specificity and uncertainty/complexity are more important than frequency, so, for simplicity, we shall ignore frequency for the moment.

Asset specificity can be low for both parties to a transaction or it can be high for one party and low for the other party or it can be high for both parties. If asset specificity is high for one party but low for the other, the party with highly transaction-specific assets is vulnerable to opportunistic behaviour by the other party. If, however, asset specificity is high for both parties to a transaction, they are in the same position as two enemies holding hostages. If one party hurts the hostages it holds, the other party can retaliate. Such a situation encourages both parties to be careful. In military terms, there will be an incentive to aim for a truce. In economic terms, two parties with mutually high asset specificity may aim for a long-term contract. If either party violates the contract, both will be hurt. Under such conditions, a long-term contract may work quite well, provided that not too many contingencies need to be included in it.

If we say that asset specificity can be low for both parties, high for one party and low for the other or high for both parties and that uncertainty/complexity can be low or high, we have six different situations (see Figure 10.1).

We discuss each of these six situations below and analyse which governance structures are efficient in each case.

Case 1: Asset specificity low on both sides, uncertainty/complexity low

An example of such a situation is a building contractor buying nails. Spot contracts are very efficient in such cases.

Case 2: Asset specificity high on both sides, uncertainty/complexity low

As an example of this situation, consider again the relationship between a newspaper publisher and a printer in an isolated town discussed in Section 8.3.

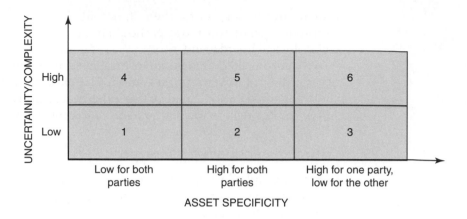

Figure 10.1 Six different cases with regard to asset specificity and uncertainty/complexity

For the printer, the press is transaction-specific as there is only one newspaper publisher in that town. The printer cannot sell the services of the press to newspaper publishers in other towns because of transportation costs. For the publisher, his investment in goodwill with subscribers and advertisers is transaction-specific because there is only one printer. Hence, asset specificity is high for both parties: they are dependent on each other for a transaction to occur.

The major source of uncertainty/complexity would seem to be whether or not the publisher will be able to pay. If the printer has no doubts concerning the publisher's ability to pay (either because she knows that the publisher has ample financial resources or because she knows that the newspaper will generate enough cash flow), a long-term contract will work quite well.

Case 3: Asset specificity high on one side, uncertainty/complexity low

As an example, consider the relations between an auto component manufacturer and an automobile company. Suppose the component manufacturer has to invest in specialized tooling for a component that can be sold to one automobile company only, while the automobile company has several suppliers for that component. Then asset specificity is high for the component manufacturer, but not for the automobile company. Suppose further that demand for the component is easy to forecast and the component is easy to produce, so uncertainty/complexity is low. In this case the component manufacturer is vulnerable to opportunistic behaviour by the automobile company. So, vertical integration can be a good solution. Another solution would be to have the automobile company own the specialized tooling and to use a long term contract.

Case 4: Asset specificity low on both sides, uncertainty/complexity high

As an example of such a situation, consider the relations between an oil company and a management consulting firm. The potential transaction might be advice about the oil company's organizational policies. Asset specificity is low on both sides: the oil company can turn to many other consulting firms for advice; the management consulting firm has many other potential clients. It may be quite difficult, however, to specify in a contract the services of the management consulting firm. Often, the specific problems that have to be dealt with only become clear as the consultancy work progresses, so uncertainty/complexity may be quite high. In that case, frequency may become an important dimension.

If frequency is very low (if the oil company seeks that type of advice only very rarely) vertical integration cannot be the solution. Somehow the two parties must agree on a contract, even in the face of high uncertainty/complexity. Perhaps the consultancy work will be split into phases, with the oil company retaining the right to reconsider the transaction after a pilot study by the consulting firm. But if frequency is high (if the oil company needs such advice regularly), vertical integration might be a good solution. The oil company then builds an internal group of management consultants.

Case 5: Asset specificity high on both sides, uncertainty/complexity high

Consider again our steelmaking example. Suppose the two stages in steelmaking (blast furnace and rolling mill) were organized in two separate firms. In order to realize energy savings, the blast furnace and the rolling mill should be located next to each other. The blast furnace would have only one customer for its molten iron and the rolling mill would have only one supplier of molten iron. That implies, for both the blast furnace and the rolling mill, most of the physical assets would be transaction-specific.

Uncertainty/complexity would also be high. One source of complexity may be the fact that the quality of the different grades of steel depends to a large extent on the quality of the molten iron, while the quality of molten iron is hard to measure. As the quality of the molten iron depends on the quality of the iron ore used by the blast furnace, and grades of iron ore differ in quality and in price, the owner of the blast furnace has an opportunity to behave opportunistically. Under such circumstances, it is very difficult to write and enforce a contingent claims contract. In this case, vertical integration is the most efficient solution.

Case 6: Asset specificity high for one party and low for the other, uncertainty/complexity high

Consider a component manufacturer who has to invest a large sum in the development of a component for which there will be only one customer. The investment in development is then highly transaction-specific. Uncertainty/complexity may come from two sources: the development costs may be uncertain and/or demand for the final product (and thus for the component) may be uncertain. If uncertainty from either source is high, it is very difficult to write and enforce a contingent claims contract. Vertical integration is the most efficient solution here.

The six cases discussed above are summarized in Figure 10.2.

So, in the Cases 5 and 6 above (where asset specificity and uncertainty/complexity are high) we know that vertical integration is more efficient than two independent companies. If we have vertical integration, what would be the role of corporate HQ? If, like in the steelmaking example, one factory 'sells' all of its output to the other factory, it makes no sense to treat these two factories as two business units. Coordination between these two stages of production is best coordinated by

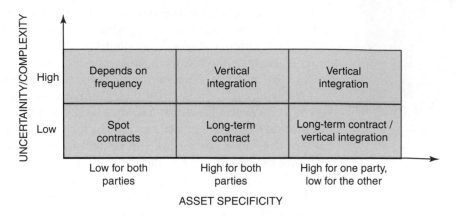

Figure 10.2 How asset specificity and uncertainty/complexity determine governance structure

the manager of the combined business unit. If, however, the first stage has several customers, only one of which is a sister business unit, then it will make sense to have two separate business units. In that case the role of corporate HQ is to settle any disputes (for example haggling over price) between the two business units. To have such disputes settled by corporate HQ may be cheaper than having interruptions of the production process and lawyers from both parties meeting in court.

The analysis summarized in Figure 10.2 is an example of comparative-static analysis: the efficiency properties of various governance structures are compared with each other at a certain point in time (hence: static). When we analyze governance structures dynamically, we may see that the boundaries between market and organization shift over time. Box 10.9 presents the example of the computer industry where technological progress has caused a transformation of the industry structure from vertically integrated firms to (horizontal) specialists. Another example would be how, in many firms and industries, we have seen a trend of 'out-sourcing' (moving activities out of the organization and into markets), while in some cases this trend has been reversed when too many disruptions in the (global) supply chains were experienced. These examples show that the boundaries between organization and market are not fixed but may shift as environmental conditions change. In the next chapter we introduce evolutionary approaches to organizations that specifically address the interplay between organizations and their environments.

Box 10.9 Vertical integration: the dynamic boundaries of the computer industry

When the computer industry came into being, it initially consisted of vertically integrated firms. A company like IBM made its own chips, assembled its own computers, wrote its own operating systems and application software and sold through its own distribution channels. Note how often the word 'own' occurs in this description. Indeed, the initial computer firms owned the whole (proprietary and vertical) chain of activities necessary to manufacture and sell their 'own' computer system. Competition was between the one proprietary chain (IBM) against the others (like HP, DEC).

In the 1980s all of this changed: the industry structure went from vertical to horizontal. Instead of large, vertically integrated firms, a number of specialist firms had emerged for each step in the value chain. Intel focused on chips and microprocessors. Dell and HP on assembling computers. Microsoft had captured a large part of the market for operating systems etc. The old vertical companies struggled (IBM) and many disappeared (Wang, Sperry Univac).

This example illustrates that the structure and boundaries of an industry may shift over time. In this case of the computer industry, the shift was caused by technological progress. The microprocessor made it possible to decouple the various stages of the computer value chain. Separate microprocessors control the various components of a modern computer and allow them to communicate in a standardized way. This has enabled a 'modularization' of the industry which, in turn, has encouraged various specialist firms to focus on the separate modules.

In terms of Figure 10.1 the situation has shifted from Case 5 to Cases 1 and 2: contractual market relationships have taken over from organizational, vertical coordination. Another way of summarizing this example is, therefore, to say that technological progress has increased the efficiency of market solutions over organizational solutions in the computer industry. In the words of Richard Rumelt (2011):

> 'What is actually surprising about the modern computer industry is not the network of relationships but the absence of the massively integrated firm doing all the systems engineering – all of the coordination – internally. The current web of 'relationships' is the ghostly remnant of the old IBM's nerve, muscle, and bone.'

Source: Richard P. Rumelt (2011), *Good Strategy/Bad Strategy* and Andrew S. Grove (1996), *Only the Paranoid Survive*.

10.6 Summary

This chapter is concerned with corporate-level strategy: strategy at the level of the HQ of a multibusiness firm. The function of HQ is to provide organizational coordination between the business units (and HQ itself). The alternative to organizational coordination is to have market coordination, which we would have if the business units operate as independent firms.

Organizational coordination by corporate HQ is more efficient than market coordination, if the benefits of organizational coordination by HQ exceed the cost of HQ. If this is true, we say that HQ creates value. If the reverse is true, we say that HQ destroys value. Given a certain institutional context, the potential benefits of organizational coordination depend on the type and degree of relatedness of the business units.

At the corporate level, the firm needs to decide in which industries and in which countries it wants to operate. By acquiring and selling businesses, by developing new businesses and discontinuing businesses it can adjust its portfolio. This is a vital element of corporate strategy, since the corporation can influence the type and degree of relatedness (and thus the potential benefits of organizational coordination) by adjusting its portfolio.

In an unrelated diversified firm (also called a conglomerate) corporate HQ will treat business units as stand alone units. Corporate HQ can add value through stand alone influence by performing one or more of the following roles:

- *Attract capital and allocate capital to business units* Attracting capital by HQ may be more efficient because it can reduce transaction costs and because the credit rating of a conglomerate firm may be better than the credit ratings of independent businesses,leading to lower cost of debt financing. Allocating capital to business units by HQ may be more efficient than allocating capital by capital markets, because businesses of a conglomerate may want to reveal private information to HQ and because HQ may have specialized knowledge about its business areas.
- *Appoint, evaluate and reward business unit managers* Corporate organizations may have an advantage in finding the best candidate for the top job of a business because they use their internal labour market and utilize the superior knowledge they have accumulated about internal candidates. In addition they can access the external market for business managers and may be able to attract better people from that market.
- *Offer advice* Corporate board members and corporate staff may be able to offer better advice if they have a deeper understanding of the business than outsiders.
- *Provide functions and services* The corporate office can provide specialist functions and services. This may prove advantageous if economies of specialization or economies of scale can be obtained.
- *Portfolio management* A corporation adjusts its portfolio of business units by acquiring and selling business units, or by developing new businesses. The question whether it is possible to add value by doing so, depends on knowledge and skills of the corporation.

Related diversification occurs when the *new* business is related to the firm's *existing* business. Through related diversification the firm may realize economies of scope. Economies of scope arise when the joint production of two products is less costly than the production of each product separately. Such instances may occur when the firm can use one input factor to produce two different products. When it is difficult or impossible to sell the services of those input factors in the market for input factors, related diversification is an efficient way to realize the economies of scope. Examples of input factors that may lead to economies of scope and are also difficult to trade are specialized machinery, technological know-how, organizational know-how and brand names. A firm that has these types of input factors and sees an opportunity to employ them in another industry may be well advised to take this opportunity. It will then lead to related diversification.

In a related, diversified firm HQ will perform the same five roles mentioned above. In addition it may foster cooperation between business unit managers and try to identify opportunities for realizing economies of scope.

Horizontal expansion occurs when the firm extends its activities within the same industry. When, in doing so, it crosses national borders, it engages in horizontal multinationalization. A firm operating plants that produce the same products in different countries may realize economies of scale if those plants share the use of intangible assets, such as technological know-how, organizational know-how and brand names. As such intangible assets are generally difficult to sell across markets, horizontal multinationalization may be the only way to capture those benefits. In addition, horizontal multinationalization may be pursued by companies who want to exploit a successfully developed 'domestic' business model in other countries, building a dynamic capability for international expansion.

Vertical integration means that the firm moves into activities that were previously performed by its suppliers or its customers. Transaction cost economics (discussed in Chapter 8), can usefully be employed to analyze when it will pay to integrate vertically. The important dimensions of transactions to be included in the analysis are asset specificity and uncertainty/complexity. Two polar cases stand out. First, if asset specificity is low and uncertainty/complexity is also low, then spot contracts are efficient. Vertical integration is not warranted in such cases. Second, if asset specificity is high and uncertainty/complexity is also high, then vertical integration is desirable.

Questions

1 Box 10.7 described how the clicks and bricks model was succesful in food retailing. Do you see potential economies of scope for traditional food retailing and Internet-based food retailing? Do you think potential economies of scope are of equal importance for other retailing businesses (for example, books)? Which production factors will probably lead to economies of scope in food retailing and book retailing?

2 During the last two decades, the big global auditing firms (such as KPMG, PricewaterhouseCoopers and Ernst & Young) have diversified into areas such as consulting, IT services, legal advice and headhunting (also called executive recruiting). The reasons for that are discussed in an article in The Economist (7 July 2001). According to The Economist, the auditing firms themselves see two reasons for transforming into professional services conglomerates.

■ The first reason is risk reduction. The risk that auditors worry most about today is the risk of being sued. Expensive settlements of shareholder lawsuits are increasing. According to *The Economist*, the best way to reduce that risk is not to offer more services, but seek incorporation as a limited liability company.

■ The second reason given by professional services firms, according to *The Economist,* is that their corporate clients want it. Again, *The Economist* is sceptical – many large global businesses use several different consulting firms.

The Economist suggests a third reason: networking: In professional-service conglomerates, old-fashioned networking is a powerful influence on business. The addition of legal (and other) services to the big firms' menu of offerings will expand their networking potential considerably. At a time when there is downward pressure on fees for professional services of all kinds, that could help explain their enthusiasm for diversification.

Compare the three reasons given above with the logic underlying related and unrelated diversification as given in the text. On the basis of your analysis, can you come up with a list of other possible reasons? In order to be able to get an idea of the relevance of those reasons, what kind of additional information would you need?

11 Evolutionary approaches to organizations

11.1 Introduction

While the preceding chapters dealt mainly with the explanation of current organizational forms, the perspective now shifts to the *development* of organizational forms over time. In economic terms, we shift from a static to a dynamic perspective. In organization theory, such dynamic, developmental perspectives are usually called *evolutionary*. We already encountered such an evolutionary perspective when we discussed evolutionary game theory in Chapter 5. A biological example (the long necks of giraffes) introduces the perspective further in the next section. Then we move on to consider the usefulness of evolutionary ideas when explaining organizational phenomena in Section 11.3.

Two examples of evolutionary approaches represent the core of the chapter. One of them is decidedly economic in nature; the other is presented as sociological. They are introduced in Sections 11.4 and 11.5 and compared in Section 11.6.

In Section 11.7, we come back to the concept of dynamic capabilities, as introduced in Chapter 9. We can now delve into the evolution of dynamic capabilities and the question of how they are selected for providing sustainable competitive advantage. These broad linkages (economics, sociology, strategy) demonstrate that the evolutionary perspective transcends the boundaries of several scientific disciplines and has the potential to integrate the contributions of various disciplines into the study of particular organizational phenomena. That potential is outlined in the final section.

11.2 Giraffes

Our biological example is a famous one: why do giraffes have such long necks? That simple question allows us to separate creationist and evolutionary arguments and, within the evolutionary strand, Darwinist and Lamarckian arguments.

The creationist answer to the question why do giraffes have such long necks is quite straightforward: because they were made that way. *Creationist* arguments involve deliberate design. Giraffes were designed with long necks. That characteristic gave them an advantage and allowed them to survive when in competition with other species. Only giraffes could reach for the leaves at the top of trees. That monopoly among the leaf eating species guaranteed them a continuing food supply.

Cumulative adaptation

Evolutionary arguments, however, emphasize **cumulative adaptation**. Giraffes were not designed with long necks, but gradually acquired them. It was a process involving many generations of giraffes. The evolutionary process consists of small steps that, over time, may make a large difference. Moreover, evolutionists argue that the cumulative effect of these changes over time amounts to adaptation of the species to its environment. It is a particular type of adaptation to its environment that allows the species to survive when in competition with other species. Giraffes survive because they occupy the 'niche' of 'high leaf eaters'. In that niche there is hardly any competition from other species.

Within the evolutionary perspective, there are several explanations that account for the process of cumulative adaptation. One explanation can be traced to Lamarck, another to Darwin.

Lamarckian explanation

Inheritance of acquired characteristics

Principle of use and disuse

The **Lamarckian explanation** is based on two principles: the **inheritance of acquired characteristics** and the principle of use and disuse. The **principle of use and disuse** states that those parts of an organism's body that are used grow larger. Those parts that are not used tend to wither away. For individual giraffes, that principle translates into a lengthening of the neck due to continuous striving for higher leaves.

The second Lamarckian principle takes care of the intergenerational effect. Characteristics acquired by individuals can be inherited by future generations. The longer necks acquired by father and mother giraffes can be passed on to their offspring. Each generation thus ends up with a slightly longer neck than its predecessor and passes that feature on to the next generation. Such evolutionary advancement continues until giraffes can reach the highest leaves.

Darwinian explanation

Natural selection

The **Darwinian explanation** emphasizes the role of cumulative **natural selection**. A Darwinist explains the giraffe's long neck as being the result of the cumulative selection, step by step over many generations, of small mutations (or variations) in giraffe genes. Consider a stage in their development where giraffes had medium/long necks. They could reach halfway up the tallest trees. At that stage, all kinds of small mutations in the genes of that generation of giraffes would have occured. Only one or a few of those mutations would have caused longer necks. The giraffes that embodied that mutation had better survival chances in the environment (other things being equal) – they could reach just a bit higher for their food. Put differently, given competition for food resources, the environment will tend to select giraffes with longer necks. The reason is that the selected animals are better adapted to their environment. Over time, mutations that cause longer necks will be increasingly passed on in the gene pool of the giraffe species. Hence, while the individual mutation is a chance process, the cumulative selection is not. Over generations of giraffes, natural selection will favour the growth of necks and will cause a better adaptation of

Variation

Selection

Retention

the species to its environment. Individual (chance) **variations**, natural **selection** as a result of environmental conditions and **retention** (in the gene pool) of the adaptive characteristics thus form the causal chain of the Darwinist explanation. In Chapter 5 we already encountered this as the evolutionary mechanism (or genetic algorithm) at work in evolutionary game theory.

Why bother with giraffes in a book on organizations? The reason is that such a biological example serves as a useful analogy for contemplating possible explanations for the evolution of organizational forms. In the next section, we consider to what extent biological explanations can be transposed to the organizational field. To conclude this section it should be emphasized that, while the analogy is useful, there is no reason to expect that it is perfect. In biology, the Darwinist explanation appears to have the best scientific credentials (although not everyone is convinced – see Box 11.1),[1] but organizations are different beasts from the species examined by biologists. Perhaps creationist or Lamarckian arguments (or still other explanations) should carry greater weight in the organizational field. Indeed, we shall see that competing explanations currently run neck and neck.

Box 11.1 The public acceptance of evolution

Darwin published his evolution theory in *On the Origin of Species* in 1859. One of its implications is that humans descended from apes. That implication has been hard for people all over the world to accept, and some incredulity remains even today. The figure below shows for a number of countries how the public responded to the question 'Human beings, as we know them, developed from earlier species of animals: true or false?' (or not sure/does not know).

PUBLIC ACCEPTANCE OF EVOLUTION

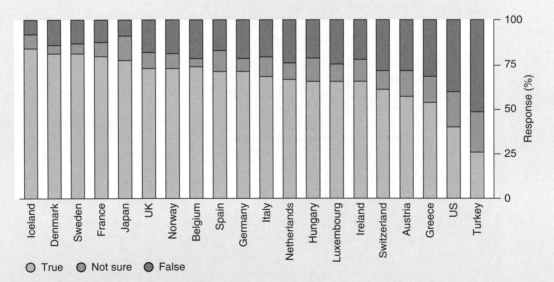

Darwin has had a more difficult time being accepted in the USA than in Europe. Figure 11.1 shows the percentages of Americans who believe in creationism (the top line), intelligent design (the middle line) and evolution (the bottom line).

Source: J.D. Miller, E.C. Scott and S. Okamoto (2006), 'Public acceptance of evolution', *Science*, vol. 313.

11.3 Organizations and giraffes

First of all, let us repeat that we are now dealing with a different set of questions from those in the previous chapters. We are now interested in explanations of the development of organizational forms over time. Of course, we may take as a starting point the question why do we observe so many different organizational forms in the present?[2] The explanation of current forms will, however, necessarily involve arguments that address their development over time, if we are to regard them as dynamic or evolutionary.

Second, the analysis now explicitly deals with populations of organizational forms (our equivalent of biological species). It is not the individual organization in which we are interested, but the class of similar organizational forms.

Third, the development of organizational forms is not analyzed in isolation from the environments in which the organizations operate. Environmental selection plays a prominent role in both of the evolutionary approaches outlined in the following sections.

What use can we make of our biological analogies? What are some obvious differences and similarities between organizational forms and biological species? We briefly discuss one cluster of differences and one cluster of similarities.

Human constructs

The differences relate to the fact that organizations are **human constructs**. To denote organizations as human constructs has two kinds of implication.

Which of the following statements comes closest to your views on the origin and development of human beings:

- God created human beings pretty much in their present form at one time within the last 10,000 years or so.
- Human beings have developed over millions of years from less advanced forms of life, but God guided this process.
- Human beings have developed over millions of years from less advanced forms of life, but God had no part in this process.

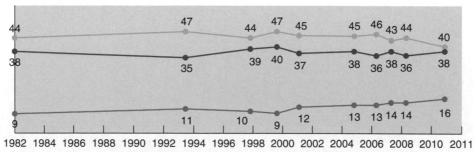

Figure 11.1 Percentages of Americans believing in creationism, intelligent design and evolution

Source: www.galluppoll.com (2012)

The first is that organizations are created and constructed by human actors. Entrepreneurs create small firms, governments create their agencies, management teams regularly redesign organizations and human decisionmakers are similarly involved in the merger or discontinuance of organizations. Giraffes cannot (re)design themselves. Organizations are, to some extent at least, purposively created and designed. Of course, they often turn out differently from how they were originally intended – organizations can lead a life of their own, to continue the biological analogy – but the element of purposive human behaviour and rational construction is always there (Scott, 2003). That means creationist arguments, emphasizing purposive design, will probably play a greater role in the organizational field than they do in the biological one.

The second implication follows from the term 'construct'. Organizations are not only constructed in the real sense of deliberate design but are also constructs in the more philosophical sense that they are products of human mental activity. That can perhaps be best illustrated by means of the anecdote of the three baseball umpires being interviewed about how they call balls and strikes. They answered as follows:

The first: I call them as they are.
The second: I call them as I see them.
The third: They are nothing until I call them.

The first umpire assumes that there are balls and strikes 'out there' and that he sorts them out correctly. The second acknowledges that there may be a difference between reality and his perception or judgement. The third shows that it is nothing but his judgement that makes them balls and strikes. The third is right, of course – in the sense that baseball rules dictate that it is only his judgement that counts. In philosophical terms, the first umpire is a realist, the third an idealist or constructionist. In the constructionist view, reality has to be constructed through human mental activity.

What about organizations and giraffes? Without delving too much into philosophical issues, it may be said that many organizational theorists would regard organizations as much more constructional in nature than giraffes. Consider the following questions:

■ What do organizations/giraffes consist of?
■ What are the boundaries of organizations/giraffes?

There is more room for differences in judgement about organizations than about giraffes. Organizations are much less 'out there': we have first to construct them in our minds before we find them. This delicate philosophical point has important consequences. One of those consequences is that it is harder to agree on the delineation of organizational forms than of biological species. Another consequence is that it is much less clear what exactly is being 'selected', 'reproduced' in the next generations and so on. There is room for choice and the choices made will depend partly on who makes them. The two approaches discussed later in this chapter also take different viewpoints here.

The cluster of similarities evolves from the recognition, first, that organizations, whatever they are, have environments and, second, that environments will play a role in explaining the development of organizational forms. In some of the previous chapters, we examined organizational phenomena without much reference to the environmental context. Agency relationships, for instance, are analyzed rather 'context-free'. In transaction cost analysis, the environment is represented as two variables: uncertainty/complexity and small numbers exchange.

In industrial economics and strategy, the environment begins to play a more prominent and complex role. That role is extended in the present chapter. It is extended in two ways. First, we explicitly analyze the development of organizational forms rather than the development of individual firms (as in most of the strategy literature). Second, the concept of the environment is broader. It includes any dimension of the environment that may influence selection processes. Those dimensions are not only economic in nature, but may also be social, political, cultural or institutional. As we shall see, the concept of legitimacy of an organizational form is important in the next section. Thus, this chapter provides the most extensive illustration of the role of the environmental context – including environmental pressure and selection – in our conceptual framework, as introduced in Chapter 1 (see Section 1.7).

By using the biological analogy, our attention is directed towards *selection* processes rather than *adaptation* processes. Most organizational theory focuses on the adaptation of individual organizations to environmental circumstances and change. Yet, it cannot be denied that selection processes are important, too. There is such a thing as organizational mortality. Organizations go bankrupt, are abandoned by their members or cease to exist in other ways (such as due to prohibition). Organizational forms also have their lifecycles: new forms come into being (often as a result of new technology), old forms wither away and die. See Box 11.2 for the fate of the largest 100 industrial companies in the world over the period 1912–1995. In many professions and industries, the medieval guilds gave way to more modern forms of organization. So, there is no question that selection, birth and death, replacement and other such phenomena are important objects of organizational study as well. The approaches to be outlined in the following sections illustrate the usefulness of the biological analogy.

Box 11.2 The largest 100 industrial companies in 1912

The list of the largest 100 industrial companies in the world in 1912 contains some familiar names. We recognize Procter and Gamble, Siemens, General Electric and Royal Dutch Shell. But who would today still know of Briansk Rail and Engineering (Russia), Hohenlohe Iron and Steel (Germany) or Central Leather and Cudhay Packing (USA)? The economic historian Leslie Hannah reconstructed the fate of the largest 100 industrial companies over the period 1912–1995. These are his findings:

Disappeared 48 of which bankrupt: 29
Survived   52 of which remained in Top 100 in 1995: 19

Almost half of the largest companies did not survive these 80+ years as independent entity. Almost a third went bankrupt. Only 28 were larger in 1995 than they were in 1912. Disappearance or decline was almost three times as likely as growth. Commenting on these findings, Paul Ormerod (2005) noted:

"I am often asked by would-be entrepreneurs seeking escape from life within huge corporate structures: 'How do I build a small firm for myself?' The answer seems obvious: buy a very large one and just wait."

Source: Paul Ormerod (2005), *Why most things fail*, London: Faber and Faber; L. Hannah, 'Marshall's 'trees' and the global 'forest': were 'giant redwoods' different? in: N. Lamoreaux, D. M. G. Raff, and P. Temin, eds., *Learning by doing in markets, firms, and countries*. (Chicago: University of Chicago Press,1999)

11.4 Organizational ecology

Organizational ecology

The first approach is labelled *population ecology* or, more appropriately, **organizational ecology**. It has been elaborated by a relatively small number of authors over the past decade, foremost among whom are Michael T. Hannan and John Freeman. In the exposition that follows, their work will feature most prominently.

Hannan and Freeman present their work as sociological, but, as will become clear, their approach uses economic concepts, such as competition, and is often likened to economic analysis. We, too, believe that this approach intersects with economic analysis and can be fruitfully integrated with it (see Section 11.6). Hence, it is included in this overview of economic approaches to organizations.

Organizational ecology distinguishes between three levels of complexity of the analysis. The first level deals with the *demography* of organizations. At that level, various rates of change in organizational populations are the central interest. Foremost are founding rates and mortality rates.

The next level concerns the *population ecology* of organizations and attempts to link vital rates between populations. How are the founding and mortality rates of organizational populations interlinked?

The third level is the *community ecology* of organizations. At that level, the central question is how the links between and among populations affect the likelihood of persistence of the community as a whole.

It is fair to say that much of the work done so far concerns the first (demographic) level. Some studies are located at the second level – for instance, the studies comparing the survival rates of generalist and specialist restaurants in different environmental situations.[3] Hardly any studies could aspire to be located at the third level of analysis.

Ecological studies use data on individual organizations. Those data are used, however, to analyze developments at the population level. Ecologists are not so much interested in explaining the founding, growth, decline and death of individual organizations but, rather, want to find out what the aggregate rates are at the population level. We, therefore, need a definition of populations and a procedure to separate one populaion of organizational forms from another.

For biologists, the main criterion for distinguishing populations of different species is interbreeding. A biological species is a collection of forms that can interbreed – that is, constitute a gene pool. No such operational definition exists for organizational analysis. An analogy of interbreeding is probably not very useful as we observe mergers and joint ventures between all sorts of firms in the real world. What should we do, for example, with conglomerate firms?

Theoretically, that is a difficult issue. In practice, most ecological studies focus on populations that are readily acceptable as distinct, such as newspapers, restaurants and labour unions. As a working definition (adopted from Carroll and Hannan, 1995), we can say that an **organizational form** summarizes the core properties that make a set of organizations ecologically similar. Thus, organizations with the same form depend in a common way on the material and social environment. A set of organizations possesses the same form in that sense if environmental changes affect them similarly.

Organizational form

An **organizational population**, then, consists of the set of organizations with a specific form within a particular time and space. A public bureaucracy and an investment bank are examples of organizational forms. The set of public bureaucracies in Japan from 1946 to 1997 and the set of investment banks in the USA during the same period are examples of interesting organizational populations.

Organizational population

An important assumption in organizational ecology is that organizations are characterized by **relative inertia**. They are rather slow to respond to changes in their environment. It is not claimed that organizations never change; rather it is argued that, if radical change is required, organizations are hard pressed to implement it. Such changes are infrequent, subject to serious delays and often unsuccessful. Therefore, organizations tend to be inert, relative to changes in the environment. That is an important assumption as it separates organizational ecology from many other organizational approaches that emphasize adaptability. Below, we explore the assumptions that form the basis of organizational ecology and indicate how the assumption of relative inertia fits into that foundation.

Relative inertia

Box 11.3 Inertia and change: outsider versus insider CEOs

There is a large, anecdotal body of literature on 'heroic CEOs' who are appointed from outside a troubled company and subsequently have successfully turned their new companies around and transformed them. Indeed, sometimes that appears to be the case, as Lou Gerstner showed at IBM. There is, however, relatively little systematic evidence that such outsider appointments and 'heroic CEOs' are in actual fact generally effective. Research by Jim Collins points towards other conclusions, including slow change and relative inertia, as summarized in *The Financial Times* as follows:

> Research by Jim Collins, formerly of Stanford Business School, found turnarounds were usually the work of insiders. In his book *Good to Great*, Mr Collins identified 11 US companies that, after 15 years of underperformance, had produced shareholder returns at least three times the market average over the next 15 years. Of the 11 chief executives responsible, 10 came from inside the company.
>
> Most of these turnaround bosses were people we have never heard of: Darwin Smith of Kimberley-Clark, for example, and Jim Herring of Kroger, the US retailer.
>
> The source of their success was not the advice of outsiders but an instinctive feel for and deep knowledge of their companies and industries.
>
> Organisations are difficult to budge. Most people resist change. Sacking their colleagues may frighten them into working harder but will not win their enthusiasm or commitment. Producing

improved performance comes from a detailed knowledge of the market and a feel for the company's culture. It also comes from knowing who in the organisation wields influence.

Mr Collins' chief executives often changed their companies substantially but they took their time thinking about it. 'We're a crawl, walk, run company', said one. Stories of heroic action and speedy deliverance appeal to something deep within us. We should not always believe them.

As Jim Collins observed himself: 'Our research across multiple studies (*Good to Great*, *Built to Last*, *How the Mighty Fall*, and our ongoing research into what it takes to prevail in turbulent environments) shows a distinct negative correlation between building great companies and going outside for a CEO.' (J. Collins, 2009, pp. 94-95).

Source: Michael Skapinker, 'Slowly does it', *The Financial Times*, 27 March 2002, p.11; J. Collins (2009), *How the Mighty Fall*, London: Random House

Why *are* organizations assumed to be inert? In most of the approaches discussed so far, efficiency arguments are used. Efficiency drives organizations to change or else they are replaced by more efficient organizations. Hannan and Freeman (1989a) take a different route. They argue that organizations have different competences. The first of these is **reliability**. Theoretically, organizational products and services could often be produced just as well by *ad hoc* groups of skilled workers. Compared with such *ad hoc* groups, however, organizations will tend to produce more reliably – that is, they will do so with less variance in the quality of performance, including its timeliness. Given uncertainty about the future, the potential members, investors and clients might value reliability more than efficiency. That is, they may be willing to pay a relatively high price for the certainty that a product or service of a minimum quality will be available when needed. Therefore, they transact with organizations.

Reliability

Within organizations, **routines** develop that direct the activities. Such routines can be retained within organizations, but not in *ad hoc* groups of varying composition. The routines play an important role in ensuring the reliability of performance. To empathize with that argument, imagine yourself as a businessperson travelling to an unfamiliar country and needing a rented car. Would you book your car with an international chain (such as Avis or Hertz) or with a local individual who has dropped a leaflet through the letterbox? Indeed, international hotel chains, car rental agencies and financial services may thrive more as a result of our need for reliable services than as a result of their being the low-cost alternative in any specific case.

Routines

Organizations are not only more reliable than *ad hoc* groups but they can also be held accountable more easily. **Accountability** is an important property in the modern world. Sociologists argue that norms of (procedural) rationality are pervasive. Decisions and actions must be explained in rational terms. For instance, investors expect reasonable and consistent accounts of the allocation of resources. The profession of accountants arose in response to such desires. Employees demand rational explanations for hiring and firing practices and will evaluate those explanations against widely held social standards (such as equal opportunities legislation). Consumers demand rational justifications of product

Accountability

performance. This can be seen most clearly in the case of litigation. If taken to court regarding product liability, producers must be able to argue their case convincingly based on full documentation of their procedures, decisions and actions.

Hannan and Freeman (1989a) argue that organizations can produce such rational accounts of their decisions and actions more readily than can *ad hoc* groups. An important factor is the existence of appropriate rules and procedures within organizations. Just like the production routines, such rules and procedures are also more easily developed and retained within organizations than within other collectives (such as *ad hoc* groups). The plethora of information that they collect and file means that they can document how resources have been used and reconstruct the sequences of decisions, rules and actions that produced an outcome. In a world that increasingly demands procedural rationality, such accountability gives organizations an advantage over *ad hoc* groups.

Hannan and Freeman (1989a, p. 74) summarize the present stage of the argument as follows:

> The modern world favors collective actors that can demonstrate or at least reasonably claim a capacity for reliable performance and can account rationally for their actions. So it favors organizations over other kinds of collectives and favors certain kinds of organizations over others, since not all organizations have these properties in equal measure. Selection within organizational populations tends to eliminate organizations with low reliability and accountability ... Thus we assume that selection in populations of organizations in modern societies favors forms with high reliability of performance and high levels of accountability.

From this summary to the conclusion that organizations exhibit high levels of inertia requires one more step. That step is the recognition that organizational reliability and accountability require that organizational structures are highly **reproducible**. The routines, rules and procedures that determine reliability and accountability must stay in place. The organizational structure – the structure of roles, authority and communication – must therefore be very much the same today as it was yesterday. That is to say, it must be reproducible from day to day. Indeed, it will be (very nearly) reproduced from day to day to ensure reliability and accountability. As one executive of a large financial services company put it (Box 11.4), that requires a tight organization.

Reproducible

Box 11.4 Reproducibility in the ING Group

The ING Group is a large banking and insurance group with its roots in the Netherlands. It was one of the first corporations to combine banking and insurance (*bancassurance*) in one group on a large scale. It globally employs more than 100,000 people. It is well known for its Internet daughter ING Direct. Below are excerpts from an interview with one of its former board members, Alexander Rinnooy Kan:

> Our activities are characterized by very high process requirements in terms of reproducibility and documentation. That is true globally, across all distribution channels and across the full range of financial products. Regulatory bodies also require this, both on the banking and on the insurance side.

Those tight process requirements are a necessary condition to be active in this sector. They are not easily compatible with an environment that is primarily focused on creativity, flexibility, and improvization. In the financial world, today's whim is not tomorrow's product.

We may not lose sight of which products the ING Group offers. Concepts such as trust, predictability and solidity are crucial. Particularly in the current hectic environment, people need dependability of financial services. Look what happens when electronic banking [*initially*[4]] turns out to be less reliable than everybody thought. We therefore have the task to retain that trust, also in times of turbulent change. It is an important part of the value we can add. That is only possible by meticulously safe-guarding the quality of all processes enabling our services. This requires a tight organization.

Source: Management Scope, October 2000 (translated by the authors)

Selection pressures will work in this direction. The conclusion that organizational structures will be (very nearly) reproduced is equivalent to say-ing that they will be (relatively) highly *inert*. Selection pressures will thus favour organizations that have structures with high inertia. Structural inertia, accord-ing to Hannan and Freeman's argument, is a *consequence* of selection rather than a precondition.

The preceding argument can be represented diagrammatically to show the interrelationships between the various basic assumptions (Figure 11.2).

We shall not attempt to spell out the entire theoretical structure that is built on these basic assumptions of organizational ecology. Rather, we shall move on to some of the more solid empirical results. They apply to the founding and death rates within organizational populations. Specifically, the ecological perspective has convincingly shown that these vital rates are dependent on the density of the population. Below, we first focus on the theoretical reasoning underlying the empirical work, then summarize some results.

What determines the size of an organizational population? In other words, how many individual organizations do we expect to find within a certain population? The answer depends on various factors. First of all, we have to know in what environmental **niche** the population resides. A niche expresses the population's way of earning a living, its role and function in a community. The niche is assumed to have a particular **carrying capacity**. There are social and material limits to the extent to which we need particular roles and functions

Niche

Carrying capacity

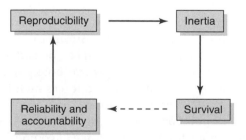

Figure 11.2 Interrelationships between the four basic assumptions
Source: derived from Young (1988)

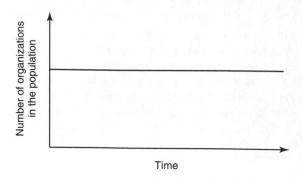

Figure 11.3 A hypothetical population over time

to be performed in society. There is only so much 'written news' that we can absorb, for instance. As a consequence, the environment will allow only a certain volume of newspapers. That volume can, however, be filled by a few large newspapers or many small ones. Thus, the carrying capacity of an environmental niche only represents an upper bound on the aggregate levels of activity performed by a certain organizational form.

The actual number of organizations inhabiting a certain niche will then depend on the founding rate, mortality rate and merger rates over time. Assume, for instance, we observe a particular population that remains constant in number over a certain period of time (Figure 11.3). How can that phenomenon be explained? If we were dealing with biological populations, there would be two answers:

- over that period of time, the population consisted of exactly the same individuals;
- or the birth rate equaled the death rate.

For organizational populations, the second explanation would remain valid in the absence of mergers. Otherwise, it should be amended to read:

- the birth rate equaled the death rate + merger rate.

In addition, the interpretation of the term 'birth rate' has to be slightly changed for organizations. It includes not only new foundings but also migrations of organizations into the population. Animals cannot change population, but organizations can. For example, the 3M Corporation was originally called the Minnesota Mining and Manufacturing Company. Whereas mining was its initial activity, now it is strong in the bonding and coating business. By changing its major activities, it can be said to have migrated to a new population.

How do *actual* organizational populations develop over time? Hannan and Freeman argue that two forces mainly account for actual developments: *competition* and *legitimation*. These two forces will both affect the **density of the population** (the number of organizations in the population), but they have opposite effects. The force of **competition** is, of course, familiar to economists. If resources within the niche are scarce, there will be competition within the

Density of the population

Competition

population for those resources. Moreover, there may be competition between populations. Think of the competition between all sorts of shops for the best locations in shopping areas.

Legitimation

The force of **legitimation** is less familiar to economists; it is a sociological concept. Essentially, it refers to the social 'acceptance' of the organizational form. New forms have low legitimacy. As they perform reliably and accountably over time, they may acquire greater legitimacy. However, if they do not conform to social norms over time, they may not acquire the legitimacy that is necessary for them to survive.

Roughly, organizational ecology assumes that both legitimacy and competition increase with the age of the organizational form. As stated above, a new form has low legitimacy. It has to acquire it over time. As the form acquires legitimacy, it becomes easier to found organizations of that form. In addition to increasing legitimacy, a variety of other factors may contribute to the self-reinforcement (or positive feedback) of the early growth of an industry. Those factors include changes in consumer tastes and habits, the development of markets, collective gains in efficiency from learning-by-doing and the emergence of supporting institutions. Hence, we expect the founding rates to increase, with the age of the form (at least initially), but competition will increase too. As more organizations come to inhabit the niche, competition within the population will increase. Competition will have a negative effect on founding rates. It will be harder to found a new organization or migrate into a more competitive environment.

Density dependence

Liability of newness

In the language of organizational ecology, the vital rates of an organizational population – the rates of founding and mortality – show **density dependence**. Legitimacy processes produce positive density dependence in *founding rates* and competition produces negative density dependence. Using similar reasoning, it is assumed that the *mortality rate* is high at first (owing to insufficient legitimacy, there is a **liability of newness**), then falls with increasing density up to a point (the neighbourhood of the carrying capacity) and then rises with increasing density (owing to competitive effects). All in all, then, organizational ecology expects:

- the relationship between density and mortality rates to have a U-shape;
- the relationship between density and founding rates to have an inverted U-shape.

The empirical work that has been done to date has largely borne out these expectations (Carroll and Hannan, 1995). The observed densities of organizational populations produce a figure like Figure 11.4. While it charts the number of newspapers in the San Francisco Bay area, such graphs have been produced for other newspaper populations, unions and restaurants, for example. The organizational ecology approach has given us empirical insight into the density dependence of founding and mortality rates. It has, therefore, also given us an approximation of 'typical' developments of populations over time. In the following sections they are compared with another evolutionary approach, developed by the economists Nelson and Winter (1982).

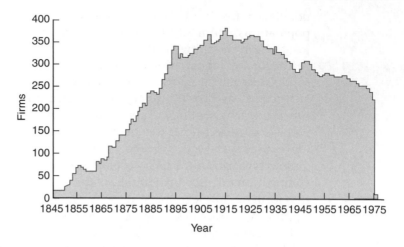

Figure11.4 Density of newspaper publishing firms by year (1845–1975) in the San Francisco Bay area

Source: Hannan and Freeman (1989a, p. 239)

11.5 An evolutionary theory of economic change

In their book *An Evolutionary Theory of Economic Change* (1982), the economists Richard Nelson and Sidney Winter outline another evolutionary perspective. That perspective shares a number of features with organizational ecology, including:

- an emphasis on organizational routines and limits to organizational adaptability;
- the population or system level of analysis;
- the importance of environmental selection.

Nelson and Winter's theory is different from Hannan and Freeman's in several respects as well. One important difference is that Nelson and Winter attempt to provide an alternative to what they label orthodox economic theory. By that they mean standard micro- and macroeconomic theory and, specifically, the standard concepts of maximizing behaviour by firms and equilibrium outcomes in markets. Instead, their alternative view stresses *routine* behaviour by firms and *development* of economic systems.

Nelson and Winter provide an alternative 'microfoundation' of macroeconomics. Their models show, for instance, the effects of technological change on macroeconomic growth. In this section we concentrate on the main features of their microfoundation: their modelling of firm behaviour and the selection process. That allows us to compare the two evolutionary approaches in Section 10.6.

Nelson and Winter conceive of organizations as being typically much better at the tasks of self-maintenance in a constant environment than they are at major change; and also much better at changing in the direction of 'more of the same' than they are at any other kind of change. Their primary concept to

Routines

denote organizational functioning is routines. **Routines** refer to all regular and predictable behaviour patterns of firms. There are production routines, advertising routines, hiring and firing routines and strategic routines. Routines rather than deliberate choice determine, in large part, how an organization functions. They explain why organizations are resistant to change. They are the organizational analogue of biological genes. In 'organizational genetics', routines are selected by the environment. Let us examine how these ideas are introduced and developed.

Skills

Organizational routines may be understood by comparison to individual **skills**, such as riding a bicycle, playing tennis or operating a computer. Such skills have two features in common. First, they require exercise. It is not enough to read how to ride a bike, it must be practised; learning-by-doing is involved. At the outset, the learning is very conscious – every detail of the performance is observed. During practice, however, the conscious attention to the performance is gradually transformed into a behaviour programme. Riding a bike becomes a capability that can be exercised automatically. Individual skills, such as organizational routines, can be usefully regarded as such automatic behaviour programmes.

Tacit knowledge

Second, it is ordinarily very difficult to fully articulate the programme. It is, for example, impossible for most people to express fully in words how to ride a bike. There is **tacit knowledge** involved – a concept introduced in Section 9.6 (see also Box 11.5). Similarly, it is often impossible in organizations to explain fully particular behaviour programmes, such as the selection of job candidates. Skills and routines share this tacit component, which may vary in importance. Skills such as computer operation and routines such as production schedules can probably be articulated more fully than the examples given above. However, such articulation is often not necessary for correct execution, is difficult to reproduce when called for and is almost never complete.

Box 11.5 Tacit knowledge

Michael Polanyi (1962, 1967) developed the concept of 'tacit knowledge'. The importance of tacit knowledge is nowadays widely recognized, as can be seen from the following excerpt from the magazine published by the consultancy company Arthur D. Little:

> When Banc One decided to grow through acquisitions, its learning challenge was at the *process* level: how to create a particularly effective process for making many successful acquisitions – identifying, acquiring, and integrating companies that would be a good strategic, operational, and cultural fit.
>
> When Mercedes-Benz opened a new factory to produce its cars in India, the Indian organization needed to learn at the *procedures* level: to acquire and use explicit knowledge from Mercedes to produce Mercedes cars.
>
> The distinction between process and procedure is essential. Procedures contain only *explicit* knowledge. Processes embed procedures in *tacit* knowledge of both the expert and the social kinds. Many of the problems of re-engineering can be traced to the treatment of processes as though they were procedures – i.e. as though people's tacit knowledge didn't matter.

Source: Nayak et al. (1995)

Organizational routines

Organizational routines are thus the analogue of individual skills. In executing those automatic behaviour programmes, choice is suppressed. When riding a bike, we normally do not consider all the choice options when we approach a red light. Instead, we automatically slow down, and come to a halt if necessary. Similarly, many behaviours in organizations are evoked automatically. The clock tells people when it is time for lunch or the weekly meeting. The calendar marks the date for closing budgets. One activity automatically leads to the next, as when a person reacts to mail in their inbox, or products reach the next stage in the assembly line. Responses to external signals can be nearly automatic, such as the prescription to match price cuts by the competition. Numerous examples can be added. In all cases, behaviour is governed largely by routine-like programmes and the role of deliberate choice is much less pronounced than 'orthodox' economic theory would have it.

Routines thus abound in organizational life. Before categorizing organizational routines, it is useful to point out two other aspects. One is that routines

Organizational memories

serve as **organizational memories**. Organizations remember largely by doing, according to Nelson and Winter. Routines that are not used for some time wither away. The organization loses the capability to perform such routines. Individuals lose the required skills to perform the routines and play the organizational role required of them. Routine-like coordination is disturbed. Memories are further endangered when there is individual turnover. Turnover is one cause of mutations in routines, as we observe later.

Organizational truce

The second aspect is that routines also serve as an **organizational truce**. By this metaphor, Nelson and Winter refer to the behavioural foundations of their concept of organizations (see Chapter 6). Satisficing takes the place of maximizing and the existence of organizational conflict is not assumed away. Routines may be seen as a stabilizing force in organizations: in that sense they represent a truce in intraorganizational conflict. Changes in routines will upset existing political balances (Nelson and Winter, 1982, pp. 111–12):

> The result may be that the routines of the organization as a whole are confined to extremely narrow channels by the dikes of vested interest ... fear of breaking the truce is, in general, a powerful force tending to hold organizations on the path of relatively inflexible routine.

Three broad classes of organizational routines can be distinguished:

- *Operating characteristics*, which relate to what a firm does at any time, given its prevailing stock of plant, equipment and other factors of production that are not readily augmented in the short run.
- The predictable patterns in the period-by-period changes in the firm's *capital stock* (those factors of production that are fixed in the short run).
- Routines that operate to *modify over time* various aspects of the firm's operating characteristics.

The last category represents 'higher-order' routines that may act occasionally to modify lower-order ones. Thus, it may be customary in a firm to review the R&D policy from time to time or change advertising agencies or make a competitive analysis. Nelson and Winter argue that such 'strategic' behaviours are often also subject to quite stringent rules within a firm. Thus, the routine-changing processes are themselves routine-guided (or guided by dynamic capabilities, as Sections 9.6 and 11.7 argue). In Nelson and Winter's terminology, organizational search is itself routine-like. It may lead to mutations in organizational routines. Just as in biological species the genetic make-up partly determines the potential mutations, so the routine make-up of firms partly determines the outcomes of their search.

Mutations of organizational routines can thus come about by chance or as a result of deliberation. An example of a chance process is the turnover of individuals in the firm. A deliberate mutation may result from organizational search. Deliberate mutations will, however, first be sought in the neighbourhood of existing routines. In that respect, Nelson and Winter again use ideas from the behavioural school ('local search', see Chapter 6). Whatever change takes place, it is expected to follow the path of least resistance. Staying close to prevailing routines minimizes the disturbance of the organizational truce. Moreover, it enhances the probability of success as firms will be able to draw largely on the (tacit) knowledge and experiences they have collected.

Environmental selection will favour successful routines. For firms, that translates into higher profit levels. If an existing routine is a success, replication of that success is likely to be desired. The point emphasized by evolutionary theory is that, when a firm is already successful in a given activity, it is a particularly good candidate for being successful if it attempts to apply its routine on a larger scale. From one period to another, that implies successful routines will be increasingly incorporated in the 'routine pool' of the particular industry concerned (Nelson and Winter, 1982, p. 19):

> Search and selection are simultaneous, interacting aspects of the evolutionary process: the same prices that provide selection feedback also influence the directions of search. Through the joint action of search and selection, the firms evolve over time, with the condition of the industry in each period bearing the seeds of its condition in the following period.

In their models, the distribution of routines is carried over from one period to the next by means of a stochastic (Markov) process. While the technicalities of such modelling do not interest us here, the basic idea is clear. It is the basic idea of all evolutionary approaches: *variations* (or mutations) of routines, environmental *selection* (according to the value of the routine for the survival chances of the firms in the population) and cumulative *retention* of successful routines.

The original contribution by Nelson and Winter has given rise to a growing body of economic literature employing such evolutionary approaches. Surveying that literature, Nelson (1991) remarked, the common element is a focus on firm-specific dynamic capabilities. Comparing *An Evolutionary Theory of Economic Change* (1982) with the current state of the literature, Nelson observed that, 'with the vision of hindsight, it is clear that our writing then was handicapped by insufficient study of the writings of Chandler, particularly his *Strategy and Structure* [1966]'.

He went on to point out that there are 'three different if strongly related features of a firm that must be recognized if one is to describe it adequately: its strategy, its structure, and its core capabilities'. The evolving insights into those three features together constitute an 'emerging theory of dynamic firm capabilities'. In that theory, the concept of *strategy* connotes a broad set of commitments made by a firm that define and rationalize its objectives and how it intends to pursue them. Some of the strategy may be formalized and written down, but some may also reside in the organizational culture and the management repertoire. Strategy tends to define a desired firm structure in a general way, but not in its details. *Structure* involves the way a firm is organized and governed and the way decisions are actually made and carried out. Thus, the organization's structure largely determines what it does, given the broad strategy. Changes in strategy may require changes in structure, but the latter are difficult to carry out. The reason is that structure involves not only the organization chart but also, much more basically, the routines governing the operating level decisions. Changing them is time consuming and costly, so it is a major task to get the new structure into shape and operating smoothly.

Core capabilities

The reason for contemplating a change in the organization's structure is to change, possibly augment, the things that a firm is capable of doing well: its **core capabilities**. Strategy and structure call forth and mould organizational capabilities, but what an organization can do well also has something of a life of its own. Nelson and Winter (1982) had already proposed that firms working well can be understood in terms of a hierarchy of practised organizational routines that define lower order organizational skills and how those are coordinated as well as higher order decisionmaking procedures for choosing what is

Hierarchy of organizational routines

to be done at lower levels. This notion of a **hierarchy of organizational routines** is the key building block of Nelson and Winter's concept of core organizational capabilities (see, further, Section 11.7 for how this line of thinking was further developed in the literature on dynamic capabilities).

This summary of the developments in the evolutionary approaches in the economic literature illustrates how influential this line of thought has been. While most people would, for instance, believe that the concept of core capabilities or core competences was developed by Prahalad and Hamel and popularized by them in their very successful book *Competing for the Future* (1994), in fact, the origins of this line of thought can be traced much further back. Similarly, just as the organizational ecologists provided a fresh, dynamic approach to the organizational literature, so the evolutionary economists have provided a healthy antidote to too much (comparative) static and equilibrium thinking in economics.

In conclusion, we therefore want to summarize the basic process of economic change that is incorporated in Nelson and Winter's models. That change starts with firms characterized with behaviourist notions. They satisfice rather than maximize, they would rather not upset intraorganizational balances and, if they have to change, they search locally for solutions (that is to say, they start searching as near to their current routines as possible). That search is modelled probabilistically, by assuming that the probability of finding a superior technique – by innovation or imitation – is a function of the amount invested in the search. The search may be induced by adverse conditions or may itself be a routine – firms often have routinized R&D and strategic planning.

Selection by market forces will favour firms that happen to find better techniques or to use better search rules than the others. Their features – the techniques or search rules that make them successful – will spread in the population of firms, partly by expansion and partly by imitation. In that process, however, new mutations of routines will be generated. Replication of routines by successful firms will often already be less than perfect, imitation by other firms probably involves a higher mutation rate and innovation will occur.

Innovation is modelled by Nelson and Winter as a routinized activity, consisting in a large part, of new combinations of existing routines (but discontinuous, radical innovation is not excluded). Through all these sources, the economic system is continually injected with new mutations of routines. It is thus in continuous flux, so equilibrium will be the exception rather than the rule. The changing economic system, however, constitutes an evolving environment for firms and routines, with corresponding change in selection pressures over time. New routines impact the economic system and the economic system impacts the selection of (old and new) routines. In Section 5.6, we introduced the concept of coevolution to denote this feature of Nelson and Winter's approach.

11.6 Comparison

As a starting point for a comparison of the two evolutionary approaches, let us return to the introductory comments we made on the biological strands of arguments. We distinguished between evolutionary and creationist arguments and, within the evolutionary branch, between Darwinism and Lamarckianism. How do the approaches discussed in this chapter relate to those distinctions? The answer is quite straightforward: Hannan and Freeman's perspective is Darwinistic, while Nelson and Winter's is Lamarckian. (We would add that both leave room for creationist arguments to play a role.)

Nelson and Winter (1982, p. 11) classify themselves as follows:

> It is neither difficult nor implausible to develop models of firm behavior that interweave 'blind' and 'deliberate' processes. Indeed, in human problem solving itself, both elements are involved and difficult to disentangle. Relatedly, our theory is unabashedly Lamarckian: it contemplates both the 'inheritance' of acquired characteristics and the timely appearance of variation under the stimulus of adversity.

Hannan and Freeman (1989a, pp. 20–2) take the following position:

> Our work approximates a Malthusian–Darwinian position on the nature of change in organizational populations over time. We think that the current diversity of organizational forms reflects the cumulative effect of a long history of variation and selection, including the consequences of founding processes, mortality processes, and merger processes ... The line of theory we develop builds on the assumption that change in core features of organizational populations is more Darwinian than Lamarckian. It argues that inertial pressures prevent most organizations from radically changing strategies and structures.

Both approaches leave room for not only organizational members to make rational plans for change but also the possibility that organizations may be founded with a rational design. In the latter sense, they both allow creationist elements. They further agree that organizations show intrinsic rigidities that hamper change. Finally, both view organizational adaptability not as an all-or-nothing proposition, but in relation to environmental change. That said, Hannan and Freeman subsequently argue that the original organizational 'imprint' will, essentially, remain intact. Inertial pressures will prevent major change and cause a major gap between individual intentions for change and organizational (inertial) outcomes (see Box 11.6). Ecologists generally regard successful adaptation as unlikely for two reasons (Carroll and Hannan, 1995). First, organizations frequently cannot make good forecasts about future states of the environment. Second, it is uncertain whether or not designed organizational adaptations will have their intended effects (if not, the cure may be worse than the disease).

The ecologists' position, therefore, in essence, states that adaptation is random with respect to the future. Nelson and Winter, on the other hand, allow for more learning, imitation and conscious adaptation through search. However, they also argue that prevailing routines will seriously constrain such processes and organizations are therefore much less adaptable than other organizational theories would have it. We will return to this important issue of relative inertia versus relative adaptability in the concluding section of this chapter (as well as in the next chapter).

Box 11.6 The last Kodak moment?

The name Kodak was almost synonymous with cameras and films for a long time. It produced the first photocamera for the consumer market in the late nineteenth century, marketing it with the slogan 'You press the button, we do the rest'. It constantly innovated its cameras, leading to consumer favorites like the Brownie and the Instamatic. Kodak's name also stood for high-quality film: in the 1930s it introduced the highly successful brand Kodachrome for its color movies. By 1976 Kodak accounted for 90 per cent of film sales and 85 per cent of camera sales in the USA. In 1996 its revenues peaked at $16 billion and in 1999 its profits peaked at $2,5 billion. In 2012, it filed for bankruptcy.

Was this due to 'missing the boat' on digital technology? Yes and no. No, because it built one of the first digital cameras in 1975 and was well aware that digital technology would undermine its traditional products and technologies. Yes, because it failed to adapt to these new realities. Among the specific reasons offered for this failure to adapt are:

- Its near-monopoly position had fostered a culture of complacency.
- It tried to avoid 'cannibalization' of its traditional products and therefore did not wholeheartedly push the new digital technology.
- Based on its chemical know-how, it attempted to diversify into production of pharmaceuticals, but this was unsuccessful and again distracted the attention from the necessary adjustments in the core business.

More generally, when technologies shift so dramatically, the odds are stacked against incumbent firms to make the required shift:

'This is especially true in consumer technology, where a Darwinian struggle keeps on punishing the pioneers, from RIM to Palm, Yahoo and Nokia, that lose an early lead.'

Note, however, that Fuji (Kodak's Japanese rival) did successfully make the required shift. See further Section 11.8.

Sources: 'The last Kodak moment?', *The Economist*, 14 January 2012 and ''The smart technology loser folds', *The Financial Times*, 11 January 2012

Care should be taken to not overemphasize the biological analogy. In both approaches, the authors are very explicit about that. Nelson and Winter (1982, p. 11) state:

We are pleased to exploit any idea from biology that seems helpful in the understanding of economic problems, but we are equally prepared to pass over anything that seems awkward, or to modify accepted biological theories radically in the interest of getting better *economic* theory.

Hannan and Freeman (1989b, p. 428) explain things in much the same manner:

We did not seek to use biological theory to explain organizational change. Nor did we propose to develop metaphors between biotic populations and organizational populations ... We relied on models from population ecology because these models appeared to clarify the social processes of interest ... We have adapted ecological models to sociological uses and have changed them in the process.

Therefore, it is inappropriate to judge these approaches on the basis of the (too) simple question, What does biology have to say about organizational or economic phenomena? The appropriate question is indeed whether the imported and adapted ideas contribute to our understanding of these phenomena. To this latter question we would suggest an affirmative answer.

We indicated earlier the main similarities between the two approaches, namely, first, the emphasis on organizational routines and limits to organizational adaptability, second, the population or system level of analysis and, third, the importance of environmental selection. It is now useful perhaps to point out some differences.

One major difference concerns the question of what it is that is selected by the environment. In organizational ecology, it is the 'organizational form'. Although a precise definition of organizational forms is lacking, it is clear that forms are collections of core properties of organizations. It is the entire collection of properties of, say, newspapers or labour unions that is selected. In contrast, Nelson and Winter propose that specific characteristics of organizations (particular routines) are selected: theirs is a 'routines as genes' approach (Winter, 1990). Owing to their Lamarckian perspective, those specific characteristics may change, while the form remains intact in other respects. Furthermore, their approach allows the possibility that particular competences are 'inherited' by other organizations – by acquisition or sharing in an alliance, for example.

A second major difference is closely related to the first. It is the observation that Nelson and Winter have more to say about intraorganizational processes. Both approaches are interested in phenomena at the population level, but only Nelson and Winter provide a microfoundation for changes at the population level. They explicitly incorporate a number of behavioural features into their models of organizations. As a result, we have an idea of the forces at the micro level that contribute to stability and change. In comparison, the organization is a relatively empty box in organizational ecology. The emphasis there is more on the external demands on organizations (demands of reliability and reproducibility) than on internal processes. Organizational ecology has relatively little to say about what goes on *inside* organizations.

A third and final difference pertains to the description of organizations and their relative success. Organizational ecology generally treats all organizations in a particular population as alike: it relies heavily on counting numbers of organizations. This research strategy tends to disregard differences between the members of that population. Evolutionary economics, however, accords particular significance to the organizations' size and their success. The two are, of course, interrelated: successful organizations are assumed to grow. The economic approaches tend to focus on the *firm* as the particular subject of interest. Hence, they can model success with a profit measure and capital accumulation. Organizational ecology, however, aspires to be a more general organization theory and empirically examines non-firm types of organization as well, such as labour unions. That makes a general approach to the modelling of success much more difficult.

11.7 The evolution of dynamic capabilities

In Section 11.5 we introduced the seminal work of Nelson and Winter, as incorporated in their book *An Evolutionary Theory of Economic Change* (1982). In that context, we noted Nelson's remark in 1991 that a 'theory of dynamic firm capabilities' was emerging. Indeed, in Section 9.6 we introduced you to the concept of dynamic capabilities as an extension of the resource-based view (RBV) of the firm. As mentioned at the end of that section, we concentrated in the previous chapter on the internal organizational context of dynamic capabilities. We had to refrain there from introducing the external context, notably environmental (competitive) selection, until we had the chance to introduce environmental selection more generally in this chapter. We can now proceed to adding the external context. More specifically, we will focus in this section on the question of environmental selection of *valuable* dynamic capabilities of firms.

Dynamic capabilities

Recall first that **dynamic capabilities** have been defined as 'the capacity of an organization purposefully to create, extend or modify its resource base'. They are geared towards change in an organization's resource base. This aspect distinguishes dynamic capabilities from **operational capabilities**, which pertain to the *current* operations of an organization. How does the concept of capabilities compare with Nelson and Winter's original concept of organizational routines?

Operational capabilities

Some of the main similarities and differences are as follows:

- Both routines and capabilities only continue to exist if practised. They are remembered by doing. If not practised, a routine or capability withers away. Consider a research capability – in semiconductor development, for instance. If Intel would consider halting R&D for several years, it would seriously erode the firm's capability to perform research. Such capabilities are subject to the adage 'use it or lose it'. In that sense, both Nelson and Winter's routines and the concept of dynamic capabilities are decidedly Lamarckian: they are acquired characteristics, that need to be maintained by active use.

- Both routines and dynamic capabilities generate 'patterned activity'. When confronted with a problem, there is a 'normal way' to seek the solution. They do not start from scratch or engage in *ad hoc* problem solving (see Winter, 2003). Rather, they start from 'the way we do things around here'. For example, some firms have developed their own 'best practices' for integrating acquisitions. When making a new acquisition, the assumption will be that the best practice will be applied, perhaps with some variation to allow for the particularities of the new acquisition. In Chapter 13, on mergers and acquisitions, we will refer to evidence that firms making acquisitions quite often (serial acquirers) have a higher acquisition success rate. Part of the explanation may be that they have developed well-honed acquisition routines or dynamic capabilities.

As noted by Nelson (1991; see also Section 11.5), with hindsight he would have liked to link the concept of organizational routines more closely to Chandler's work *Strategy and Structure*. It is fair to say that the concept of dynamic capabilities is more closely linked to the strategy literature, in particular the resource-based view (RBV). Therefore, we already introduced the concept in Section 9.6 as a further development within RBV. We will now proceed to elaborate on the environmental context and, particularly, the selection of dynamic capabilities in the remainder of this section. Thus, the concept of dynamic capabilities serves as a link, connecting evolutionary theory with strategic management.

The reason that dynamic capabilities can serve as such a link is that they emphasize more the necessity of strategic management of the firm. While routines can also involve deliberate choice, it is much less pronounced. The literature on dynamic capabilities seeks explicitly to ground this concept in a view on the strategic management of organizations (Helfat et al., 2007, pp. 20–1; see also Teece, 2009):

> executive management performs several distinctive and important roles, which help the economic system overcome special problems, problems that might otherwise result in 'market failures'. That is, but for the actions of astute managers, competitive markets wouldn't function very well. Moreover, business organizations couldn't function either. Seven particular classes of economic functions can be assigned in economic theory to management. They are: 1) orchestrating co-specialized assets; 2) selecting organizational/governance modes and associated incentive systems; 3) designing business models; 4) nurturing change

(and innovation) processes/routines; 5) making investment choices; 6) providing leadership, vision, and motivation to employees; and 7) designing and implementing controls and basic operations ... Managers are needed to make markets work well, and to make organizations function properly.

Nelson and Winter introduced the notion of a *hierarchy of organization routines*, which was already the basis for core capabilities' thinking. The distinction between dynamic and operational capabilities can be regarded as a further elaboration on this approach. Operational capabilities are the basis of a firm's ability to survive and compete in present circumstances. Dynamic capabilities provide the (higher-order) capacity for change by purposefully altering the organization's resource base. The linkage to the RBV enables the concept of dynamic capabilities to be much more specific in terms of the reasons for some changes enhancing competitive advantage and other changes not. In Section 9.6 we examined specific factors and circumstances that contribute towards dynamic capabilities being valuable, rare and/or inimitable. If resources and capabilities are co-specialized and configured well, that may contribute to their value. If they are (partly) dependent on tacit knowledge, firm-specific and surrounded by isolating mechanisms, that makes them rarer and more difficult to replicate. Potentially, such features help dynamic capabilities to meet the requirements of Barney's VRIN-framework to generate sustainable competitive advantage. If, on the other hand, dynamic capabilities can be easily bought and sold in the market or simply imitated, they will most likely not contribute much to sustainable competitive advantage. Best practices that can be acquired from consultancy firms, for example (such as state-of-the-art IT systems), will spread rapidly through the population of competing firms if they contribute to competitive advantage. Such advantages will be short-lived, however, as they will be eroded by rapid imitation. A firm with a unique innovation culture (such as Apple), though, that attracts unusually talented people and is able to protect its innovations by patents, will likely maintain its competitive advantage for a significantly longer period of time.

So far, we have compared the notion of dynamic capabilities with Nelson and Winter's original concept of organizational routines. We hope to have shown, first, that it is more firmly embedded in a strategic management view of the firm and, second, provides a better basis for understanding the potential basis for competitive advantage than their original concept. However, competitive advantage is necessarily an externally orientated concept: it has to be gained in the external competitive environment. In the language of the present chapter, environmental selection will ultimately determine which dynamic capabilities are valuable in the external context (and, hence, can provide a sustainable competitive advantage). Therefore, we now turn to the environment to examine how the external selection of dynamic capabilities that do, or do not, contribute to competitive advantage takes place.

Consider the evolution of Dell, as summarized in Box 11.7. Michael Dell created a company in 1984 that succeeded to become the market leader in the USA 15 years later and the worldwide leader soon thereafter. That success was due to an innovative business model offering personal computers for an unprecedented low cost.

Box 11.7 The evolution of Dell Inc., Part 1

In 1984, Michael Dell founded a company selling personal computers from his student room at the University of Texas. In 1999, his company had become the largest seller of personal computers in the USA and, in early 2006, it had the largest share (some 18–19 per cent) of the worldwide personal computer market. How did Dell achieve such phenomenal success?

There are several important elements:

- While most large computer manufacturers, such as IBM and Hewlett-Packard, sold via retailers or their own stores, Dell developed a direct-to-consumer sales model – initially mainly by telephone, later via the Internet. In that way, Dell 'cut out the middle man', shortened the supply chain and saved itself the retailer's margin.
- The Dell computers are assembled from standard components, but customers can order their own configuration of those components. That allows Dell to capture the benefits of standardization (of components), while offering its customers choice (of computer configurations). Dell can therefore very closely match its product offerings to consumer demand.
- Dell practises just-in-time assembly by building the computers only after customers have ordered them and taking the components from suppliers as needed. It is a pull system of lean production that economizes significantly on inventory (of both components and end products).
- As a consequence, Dell receives payment for its computers from the customers before it has to pay its suppliers for the necessary components. That is called a negative cash conversion cycle. Together with the low inventories, that means Dell needs only very low levels of working capital.
- Dell has captured the benefits of the Internet faster than its rivals – for example, economizing on ordering procedures. It has also led the way in establishing call centres for customer support and outsourcing.

In all these ways, Dell has been able to build a low-cost business model that offers consumers a range of choices for an unprecedented low cost. As the Internet became available to more and more households across the world, the target market for Dell expanded accordingly. Moreover, it was also able to penetrate the market of corporate customers and expand its range of products to include servers, printers and televisions.

Source: Dell (1999); http://en.wikipedia.org/wiki/Dell

In terms of our discussion so far, Dell was initially successful in building up the *operational capabilities* of his firm to run a low-cost direct-to-consumer business model. Later success was based on Dell's *dynamic capability* to adjust the business model (and its required resource base) with a continuous focus on remaining the lowest-cost supplier, by for instance, taking early and full advantage of the rise of the Internet.

So far, so good. We also know, however, that many more attempts at building new business models fail than succeed. Sometimes they fail for internal reasons, but Dell obviously got that part right.

More often, they fail for external reasons. What explains the success of Dell from the external perspective? Why was Dell's new business model successful in its relevant environment? Why did it succeed against the competition? Why was it not 'selected out', like so many other attempts?

We suggest that, in the case of Dell, the explanation involves a combination of the following three factors:

- The new business model offered many consumers sufficient functionality for dramatically lower costs. In more general terms, we can say that the model had excellent 'technical fitness' (see further below).
- In the fast growing market for personal computers, there was a large and growing demand for such relatively standardized low-cost products.
- The competitive environment was rather 'soft' as the established producers (IBM and HP) had difficulties matching the low-cost proposition of Dell. There were four main reasons for that:

  - the established firms were themselves vertically integrated, covering the value chain from R&D to manufacturing and sales, whereas Dell focused just on assembly and direct sales;
  - they covered inhouse the full scope of chips, operating systems, computer hardware and application software;
  - they had difficulty switching to a direct-to-customer model because of the inherent conflicts with their prime sales channel through retailers;
  - they were slow to realize that the innovation driven industry they had competed in successfully for many years had been maturing and personal computers had developed into rather commodity-like products for many customers.

The case of the rise of Dell Inc. illustrates that the answer to the question of whether or not capabilities can offer competitive advantage is context dependent. We cannot give such an answer without considering the nature of the environment in which the capabilities are executed. We need a measure of success for capabilities that accounts for that context-dependence.

External fit

For operational capabilities, that measure is **external fit**, as developed in the so-called 'contingency theories of organization'. External fit measures the match between organizational and environmental characteristics at any moment in time – hence, it measures in a *static* way.

Evolutionary fitness

For dynamic capabilities, the measure is **evolutionary fitness**. It is a dynamic concept. Evolutionary fitness refers to how well a dynamic capability enables an organization to make a living by creating, extending or modifying its resource base. It depends on the external selection environment: evolutionary fit dynamic capabilities enable a firm to survive and perhaps grow, as well as prosper in the marketplace (in changing circumstances). In line with our example of Dell, Helfat et al. (2007) suggest that evolutionary fitness is affected by three important influences:

Technical fitness

- **Technical fitness** How effectively a capability performs its intended function when divided by its costs. In shorthand, it can be denoted as quality per unit of cost. In our example of Dell, the ability of Dell's business model consistently to deliver sufficient functionality to the customers at absolute lowest cost is evidence of its technical fitness.

Market demand

- **Market demand** The (derived) demand for a capability, depending on the demand for the end product or service to which that capability contributes.

The market demand for Starbuck's ability to open new stores at amazing speed is derived from the ultimate demand for espressos, cappuccinos and café lattes in various countries.

Competition

■ **Competition** Finally, the competitive environment – including competition and cooperation with other firms – impacts on the evolutionary fitness of dynamic capabilities. As the case of Dell illustrated, relatively 'soft' competition from the incumbents allowed Dell to build and expand its business model rather rapidly. That contributed to its sustainable competitive advantage for a period of over 20 years (see, however, Box 11.8 for the second part of the story). Greater competition makes it more difficult for firms to survive and prosper.

Capturing the argument so far, we should first recall that we discussed in Section 9.6 a number of 'internal' factors that may contribute to resources and capabilities offering sustainable competitive advantage. Those factors include co-specialization, asset orchestration, tacit knowledge, firm specificity and isolating mechanisms. To those internal factors we have now added external factors. They are the technical fitness to deliver the required quality per unit of cost, sufficient market demand and the ability to survive competition. Together, these external factors determine the evolutionary fitness of firms' dynamic capabilities. Evolutionary fitness results in the survival and growth of companies and their production of economic value.

As an overall summary, we can now answer the question 'when do dynamic capabilities lead to competitive advantage?' The answer is as follows:

■ There must be differences in the technical fitness of dynamic capabilities of competing organizations. The technical fitness of our capabilities should allow us to survive the actions of competing organizations.

■ There must be market demand for the end products or services to which the capability contributes. Hence, there is derived demand for the capability itself.

■ The capability must be relatively rare in relation to that demand. This conforms to standard economic reasoning: value comes from scarcity.

In order for the competitive advantage to be *sustainable*, several further conditions should be met.

■ The capability should be inimitable and non-substitutable by the competition.

■ It should be able to cope with the rate of change in the external environment. Hence, it should not become obsolete as a result of environmental change that it cannot accommodate.

■ The capability should be maintained by continued good asset orchestration (as an element of strategic management).

Hence, sustainable competitive advantage arises from the interplay of internal and external factors. It is the outcome of both adequate strategic management and evolutionary environmental selection. Box 11.8 illustrates that sustainable competitive advantage can never be taken for granted. Internal and external factors can, similarly, work together to undermine even the strongest capabilities and best business models. After 20 years of uninterrupted success, Dell started to experience difficulties as well.

Box 11.8 The evolution of Dell Inc., Part 2

In 2004, Kevin Rollins took over as CEO from Michael Dell, who remained chairman of the Board of Dell Inc. In February 2005, *Fortune* magazine awarded Dell first place in its annual ranking of 'Most Admired Companies', but soon thereafter cracks were appearing in its business model:

- By the second quarter of 2005, Dell was missing revenue and earnings targets and that remained the case in subsequent quarters.
- Operational problems surfaced, such as faulty capacitors on the motherboards of some models, costing over $300 million to address.
- Customer complaints doubled in 2005, mainly about levels of service received from Dell's customer support.
- Dell started losing market share in personal computers as of 2006 and was overtaken as market leader by Hewlett-Packard. In 2009, it lost second place to Acer, the Taiwanese manufacturer.
- Similar problems became manifest in other parts of the product range, such as servers and televisions.

Commentary on Dell's problems suggested that internal as well as external factors played a role. Competitors had reacted to Dell's success: Hewlett-Packard had taken over Compaq and IBM had sold its PC business to Lenovo, a Chinese company. Other low-cost rivals had emerged, such as Acer. As a result, Dell was increasingly facing stronger and equally low-cost competitors. As a reaction, it may have cut costs further in ways that compromised customer service and, possibly, product quality. As *Business Week* quoted some observers, 'They are a one-trick pony. It was a great trick for over ten years, but the rest of us have figured it out and Dell has not ploughed any of its profits into creating a new trick' and 'This is when they have to be imaginative, but Dell's culture only wants to talk about execution'.

In January 2007, Kevin Rollins abruptly resigned and Michael Dell returned to the CEO role. His strategy is to continue selling PCs, particularly to small and medium sized businesses in the USA as well as in emerging economies, like China, India and Brazil. At the same time, he is shifting the company toward IT services, software, data centres, servers and network security. This is executed mainly by acquisitions, like the IT service company Perot Systems in 2009 (for $3.9 billion) and another eight companies in 2010. Basically, Dell is now emulating the successful IBM turnaround executed by Lou Gerstner between 1993 and 2002. Whether this will lead to a new period of success remains to be seen.

Based on 'It's bad to worse at Dell', *Business Week*, 1 November 2005; 'Dark days at Dell', *Business Week*, 24 August 2006; 'Transitions: Michael reinvents Dell', *Forbes*, 5 September 2011.

The more recent problems at Dell are an illustration of a theme that we will elaborate on further in the next section and Chapter 12. It is the theme of the sustainability of success. Firms such as Dell, which are on a successful strategic trajectory, will want to build on that success and expand it further. Following the standard evolutionary pathway of variation – selection – retention, they will therefore want to select, retain and extend successful capabilities. In the case of Dell, that entailed the further development and refinement of the low-cost direct-to-consumer business model. On the one hand, it is exactly what was needed to reinforce its competitive advantage. On the other, there is the threat that firms will myopically invest according to their 'dominant logic' only, which may come to haunt them when environmental conditions change. We saw in Chapter 5 how evolutionary game theory can model such changes in environmental conditions, including the learning by competitors and emergence of innovative strategies (see Section 5.6). Evolutionary approaches offer great potential to understand the basic tensions involved in those strategic choices more fundamentally. It is with a sketch of this potential that we want to conclude this chapter.

11.8 Further developments

In conclusion, we should like to observe that there appears to be great potential for the further development and integration of the evolutionary approaches we have described. The evolutionary perspective is still young in our field and is attracting increasing numbers of researchers. As a result, it is to be expected that the perspective will be developed and refined. In that process, it is to be hoped that a more integrative framework for the evolutionary analysis of organizational phenomena will emerge. Ecological and evolutionary models have great potential to incorporate insights from various disciplines. For a multidisciplinary field such as organization studies, it is to be hoped that this potential will be realized.

As an illustration of its potential, we can speculatively point to two fields of interest. The first is the further analysis of organizations as 'bundles of routinized competences' or 'bundles of dynamic and operational capabilities'. Particularly in the learning perspective of evolutionary economics, the conceptualization of the firm as a bundle of competences/capabilities may provide a unitary framework for a number of theoretical and empirical observations, including the following:

The finding that firms which have a head start (or, more formally, a *first mover advantage*) along a competence-building pathway that eventually turns out to be a success often experience significant **increasing returns** (Arthur, 1994b, 1996). Microsoft and Apple are examples. The firm that can set the standard for the development of such new environmental niches will reap a disproportionate share of the resources that the niche will provide (see Box 11.9).

Increasing returns

Box 11.9 Examples of increasing returns (or positive feedback)

The history of the videocassette recorder furnishes a simple example of positive feedback. The VCR market started out with two competing formats selling at about the same price: VHS and Betamax. Each format could realize increasing returns as its market share increased. Thus, large numbers of VHS recorders would encourage video outlets to stock more prerecorded tapes in VHS, thereby enhancing the value of owning a VHS recorder, leading more people to buy one. The same would, of course, have been true for Beta-format players. In that way, a small gain in market share would improve the competitive position of one system and help it to further increase its lead.

▶

Such a market is initially unstable. Both systems were introduced at about the same time and so began with roughly equal market shares. Those shares fluctuated early on because of external circumstance, 'luck' and corporate manoeuvring. Increasing returns on early gains eventually tilted the competition towards VHS. It then accumulated enough of an advantage to take virtually the entire VCR market. Yet, it would have been impossible at the outset to say which system was going to win, which of the two possible outcomes would be selected. Similar examples are the victory of Blu-ray over HD-DVD in the market for optical disc storage as well as Facebook and LinkedIn over their many early rivals in their particular niches of the market for social media.

One reason for success breeding success in such firms is the early accumulation of resources, which allows them to pursue dominance of their niche more aggressively. Another organizational reason may be that its early start increases the possibility that the firm will also develop the necessary supporting competences earlier. Eventually, it will need to arrive at a 'configuration' of competences that allows it to exploit the possibilities of the niche to the optimum. Think of the various competences that allowed IBM to dominate the niche of mainframe computers for several decades or, alternatively, of the competences that McDonald's needed to acquire in order to, first, dominate the US market in its niche and then internationalize successfully.

Such successful configurations often contain the seeds of their demise. Successful corporations can become simple over time, focusing exclusively on the successful repertoire of routines and becoming intolerant of deviation or variation (Miller, 1990, 1994). It is well documented how IBM underestimated the potential impact of the personal computer and has had great difficulty in catching up. Similarly, former dominant players in their industries such as Steinway pianos or Singer sewing machines have lost their dominance or even ceased to exist. Large corporations, such as ITT and Texas Instruments, have

Icarus paradox

also floundered. This phenomenon has been labeled the **Icarus paradox** after the Greek saga of Icarus, who suffered a fatal fall after achieving great success.

Successful firms may find it hard to adapt for the following reasons, among others:

- As discussed in Chapter 8, firms may invest in specific assets to demonstrate their commitment to a strategy. However, the more such specific investments are made, the more *lock-in* occurs (see Section 8.3) Lock-in is thus a two-edged sword: it demonstrates commitment, but reduces flexibility. In the terminology of this chapter, it contributes to relative inertia.

Cannibalization

- Relative inertia may be further increased in incumbent firms by the threat of **cannibalization** of their existing products. An outsider firm with no stake in the current market may expect to reap the full benefits of an innovation. An incumbent firm, with existing products that threaten to be replaced by the innovation, will also consider the lost profits from existing products. Thus, the incentives for the outsider firm to introduce the innovation, will be higher.

- success may generate a feeling of complacency (Tellis and Golder, 2002, chapter 7). For example, the potential of external innovations may be underestimated as a result of a 'not invented here' attitude. Sometimes companies may focus excessively on providing ever more functionality for their products, thus increasing their vulnerability to 'disruptive innovations' that offer basic functionality at a much lower cost (Christensen, 1997, 2003).

Exploitation

Exploration

■ In many ways, then, success fosters a focus on **exploitation** rather than **exploration** – that is, on fully exploiting the current pathway to success and to underinvesting in the exploration of new pathways.

Many firms, however, do live a long life. Some are able to persist as industry leaders during decades of economic and social change – General Electric and Shell, for example. Others completely transform themselves along the way, such as STORA, a Swedish company that has gone from copper mining to forestry operations, paper production and power generation in the more than 700 years of its existence to date (see Box 11.10).

Box 11.10 The history of STORA

STORA is probably the world's oldest limited liability company. It was officially founded in 1288, when Bishop Peter signed a deed of exchange. That was the document on which the 700th anniversary of the founding of STORA was based in 1988. The company brochure, *STORA's world*, describes its history as follows:

The world's oldest company

STORA's history commences with a copper mine, which in the 14th century produced approximately 200 tons of crude copper per year. Some 300 years later, the mine entered its golden era, producing an ore that was richer in copper content than at any time previously. During the 17th century, the mine was generating about 1500 tons of crude copper per year. In 1687, the great cave-in occurred, which signalled the end of the golden era. Operations continued after the collapse, however, with the extraction of new products, such as sulphur, vitriol, and pigment for red paint. This latter product continues to be used today to decorate many homes throughout Sweden.

The mining of copper ore based on a 'fire-setting' process required substantial quantities of wood. And to obtain wood, forests were required. Towards the end of the 18th century, the company's operations shifted increasingly towards forestry and the production of iron. In the middle of the 1870s a large iron mill and one of the largest sawmills in Europe were built near the copper mine.

At the end of the 19th century, a sulphate (kraft) and sulphite pulp mill was constructed in Skutskar in central Sweden. Around this time, the first paper mill was also built in Kvarnsveden, not far from Falun. In 1972, Kvarnsveden produced approximately 300,000 tons of newsprint and magazine paper. At the end of the 1970s, the mining and steel operations were gradually phased out.

During the next decade, the Swedish companies Billerud, Papyrus and Swedish Match were acquired and incorporated within the STORA Group. Following the acquisition of Germany's Feldmühle group in 1990, STORA could without doubt be ranked as one of the world's leading forest products companies. In 1998 STORA merged with Enso, a Finnish forest products company, to become STORA Enso.

The company continues to innovate and adapt. It is now looking into expanding into bio-energy and green construction materials, areas that it has spent several years developing. 'The next 40 years look very different from the 700 years behind us,' says Stora Enso spokesman Jonas Nordlund, emphasising the company's desire to expand outside Europe in Brazil, China and Uruguay, as well as its investment in cross-laminated timber, a building material that sequesters carbon dioxide.

Sources: Stora company brochure 'Stora's world"; 'Can a company live forever? 'BBC News, 19 January 2012

Further development of the evolutionary approaches will, it is hoped, lead to more systematic insights into the organization/environment interplay that gives rise to such pathways and the triggers of its various episodes. As will be evident from the above, a key theme will be the relative importance of *inertia versus adaptability* in various circumstances. This theme shows close correspondence with the 'commitment versus flexibility' theme in industrial organization and strategic management we encountered in Chapter 9. It is therefore very likely that cross-fertilization of these various approaches offers ample opportunities to increase our understanding of these important phenomena.

As noted above, organizational ecology is rather silent about what goes on *within* the organization. Evolutionary economics has more to say about processes within the firm. In particular, the behavioural concept of a local search near existing routines is incorporated into this theory. In terms of organizational change, the concept implies that firms will prefer to stay close to current competences. Organizational change, then, will be predominantly *incremental* (Quinn, 1982). Such change will allow a firm to keep up with slow to moderate environmental change. It does not seem to explain how firms can survive in the midst of turbulent change, however. Nor does it seem to allow for complete transformations of firms, such as in the example of STORA above.

Intraorganizational ecology and evolution

A promising avenue of enquiry that may contribute to our understanding of these phenomena relates to **intraorganizational ecology and evolution**. The basic idea here is that selection takes place *within* the organization as well as outside it. Various world views may exist among the organization's members; different analyses of the organization's challenges may vie for prominence; too many requests for resource allocations may compete for scarce resources; different strategies may be propagated and so on (Bettis and Prahalad, 1995). How do the internal selection processes of the organization operate under such circumstances?

Induced strategic processes

Burgelman (1990, 1991, 2002) has proposed a distinction in strategic processes that may contribute to an intraorganizational ecology of strategy formation: induced processes versus autonomous processes. **Induced strategic processes** fit with the current strategy, as propagated by top management, and are compatible with current routines and competences. Induced processes serve to ensure that organizational actions will remain consistent with top management preferences as incorporated in the current strategy. In that vein, induced processes are within the current strategic domain and, hence, also demarcate what the organization will *not* do. Burgelman thus identifies such processes as *variation-reducing*.

Autonomous strategic processes

Autonomous strategic processes refer to strategic initiatives outside the current strategic domain. They arise 'bottom up', from the managers who are directly in contact with new technological developments and changing market conditions and have some budgetary discretion. Such autonomous initiatives are expected to emerge unpredictably, but not completely randomly as they are rooted in, and constrained by, the evolving competence set of the organization (including newly acquired and perceived competences at lower levels of the organization). Hence, such processes tend to be *variation-enhancing* rather than variation-reducing. An important task of top management is to nurture such operational level strategic initiatives as they spur continuous strategic renewal.

Burgelman has summarized his perspective in his book *Strategy is Destiny* (2002). The book explains how Burgelman's conceptual framework was developed in close association with his work at Intel and its CEO, Andy Grove. In his own words, Burgelman's (2002, pp. 20–1) integrated view of strategy-making and organizational ecology is as follows:

> Almost all companies start small and are subject to liabilities of newness (they are unknown, untested, lacking legitimacy, and so on). The major force faced by small, new companies is environmental selection. Most do not survive external selection pressures. Organizational ecology provides a useful framework within which the evolutionary dynamics of small companies can be more clearly understood. Some companies, however, do survive and become large and established. Although large, established companies continue to remain subject to the selection force of the external environment – and many succumb to it in the long run – these companies have gained the opportunity to substitute internal for external selection. Analogous to external selection, internal selection is concerned with a company's entering new businesses and exiting from failing ones over time.

In other words, Burgelman argues that, as companies grow from small to large and established, the question of corporate strategy is added to the question(s) of business strategy. The ecological approach to corporate strategy adds the internal selection environment of firms to the external selection environment (the issue of 'external fit'). In the internal selection environment:

- *Induced* strategy processes take place within the familiar environment of the firm. They emphasize current competences, fit with the prevailing strategy, and 'alignment'. Induced processes thus favour exploitation rather than exploration and contribute to strategic inertia.
- *Autonomous* processes involve new combinations of competences that are not currently recognized as distinctive or important to the firm. They are aimed more at emerging environments than the firm's familiar environment. They do not 'fit' the current corporate strategy well, but may achieve recognition over time and then be incorporated in the new corporate strategy, almost 'after the fact' of their emerging success.

All in all, Burgelman's perspective is that the long-term survival of firms is enhanced by the balancing of variation-reducing and variation-enhancing mechanisms. One process leads to relative inertia and incremental adjustments; the other expands the organization's domain and renews its competence base. Likely propositions are that:

- the appropriate balance of the two will depend on environmental conditions;
- the episodes of organizational success and failure observed above depend on the appropriateness of the actual choices made by firms, given the then prevailing environmental conditions.

In the latter statement, our two 'speculative fields of interest' are coming together. Conceptualizing the firm as a bundle of competences allows us to analyze whether or not it makes *competent* choices with regard to its environmental challenges. That is no coincidence. We see the evolutionary perspectives as being capable of integrating theoretical and empirical contributions from various disciplines.

11.9 Summary: the evolutionary perspective

This chapter has presented two original strands of the evolutionary perspective on organizations as well as some more recent developments.

We started out by exploring the biological analogy and examining different biological explanations for the long necks of giraffes. That allowed us to distinguish creationist and evolutionary arguments and, within the latter, Lamarckian and Darwinist explanations. Those distinctions are also helpful in the organizational field. We were careful, however, to point out that there are both differences and similarities between organizational forms and biological species. The differences imply that successful biological explanations do not necessarily translate to the organizational field. While the Darwinian perspective currently has the strongest scientific credentials in biology, creationist or Lamarckian (or still other) arguments may be much more important for organizational evolution.

We saw that Nelson and Winter's evolutionary theory of economic change is decidedly Lamarckian in nature, while Hannan and Freeman's organizational ecology is Darwinist. Both, however, employ the basic process of variation – selection – retention as their main explanatory device for evolution, with competition (and legitimation in organizational ecology) as the external selection mechanism.

Evolutionary perspectives direct our attention to the development of organizational forms in the interaction with their environments. Such perspectives therefore accord more importance to environmental selection processes than most of the other organizational theories, which tend to emphasize organizational adaptability. In organizational ecology, it is assumed that organizations are relatively inert. That is to say, they have a hard time responding to changes in their environments. The reasons for this relative inertia are sought in the demands on organizations for reliability, accountability and reproducibility. Selection pressures will favour organizations with structures exhibiting relatively high inertia. Therefore, organizational ecology sees inertia as a consequence of selection. The empirical work within this approach has tended to concentrate on the vital rates for organizational populations: the rates of founding and mortality. Those rates have been found to be density dependent.

Nelson and Winter's evolutionary theory of economic change focuses on organizational routines as being the primary concept when describing organizational functioning. Routines refer to all regular and predictable behaviour patterns of firms. They often contain a component of tacit knowledge. Routines explain why organizations are resistant to change and, therefore, again relatively inert.

In this approach, routines are the organizational analogue of biological genes. Successful routines are those that have survived environmental selection. They serve as organizational memories. In addition, they may be seen as a stabilizing force in organizations, representing a truce in intraorganizational conflict.

Nelson and Winter clearly build on the foundations of the behavioural theory of the firm. Their emphasis on organizational routines has been extended to encompass firm-specific dynamic capabilities. Thus, the organization itself has increasingly come to be studied through the evolutionary lens. From the evolutionary perspective, the organization may be seen as an ecology of patterned activity.

We discussed two examples of the increasing attention on evolutionary processes within organizations. The first example pertained to the research into dynamic capabilities. These were introduced in the previous chapter as an extension of the resource-based view (RBV) relating to strategy. There, the focus was on the internal context of dynamic capabilities and the strategic management tasks required to build and maintain such capabilities. In this chapter we have added the external context. We have shown how technical fitness, sufficient market demand and the ability to survive competition determine the evolutionary fitness of dynamic capabilities. Thus, we were able to specify the internal and external conditions for dynamic capabilities to provide sustainable competitive advantage. Competitive success arises from the interplay of internal *and* external factors: it is the outcome of adequate strategic management *and* environmental selection.

As a second example, Burgelman's analysis of the internal selection environment of companies was presented. Burgelman explicitly analyses *intraorganizational* processes through the evolutionary lens of variation – selection – retention, with competition as the selection mechanism.

Variation exists within firms as, usually, a variety of strategic initiatives exist at any moment. Induced strategy processes are variation-reducing due to their emphasis on alignment with the prevailing strategy. Autonomous strategy processes, on the other hand, are variation-enhancing as they lead to strategic initiatives outside of the current strategic focus.

There is *internal competition* between the different strategic initiatives to obtain the resources necessary to grow and increase in importance in the firm. *Selection* works internally through the managerial processes that regulate the allocation of resources and attention to the various initiatives.

Retention operates on those initiatives that survive the internal and external competition. Those initiatives are enabled to grow and become more important in the company.

The evolutionary approaches to organizations thus shed light on the dynamics of organizational functioning. They also give insights into the long-term evolution of organizations. They show that, in the interactions between populations of organizations and their environments, conditions may change over time. Organizational ecology shows how the forces of competition and legitimation develop with the density of the population. That has an effect on the founding and mortality rates. All in all, the conditions for survival change substantially over the lifetime of a population.

Similarly, the analysis of firms as bundles of routinized competences or capabilities illuminates a number of formerly disparate theoretical and empirical observations. It shows how firms may have initial success by building competences along a new pathway. Success will reinforce the routinization of those competences. As competences become more routinized, the relative inertia of the firm increases. Thus, success breeds not only success but also its own demise when environmental conditions change and organizational adaptation is called for. Some firms do live a long life, however, and succeed in adapting when necessary.

A deeper understanding of the conditions leading to relative inertia on the one hand and relative adaptability on the other is one of the greatest challenges for current organizational theory. We return to this theme in the closing section of the next chapter.

Questions

1 In evolutionary approaches to organizations, biological analogies play an important role. It is argued that populations of organizational forms develop over time as a result of environmental selection, just as populations of giraffes do. Yet, a major difference between organizations and giraffes is that organizations are human constructs. That difference has two kinds of implication for the analogy between populations of organizations and populations of giraffes. Explain the two implications.

2 Skills and routines are two important concepts in the evolutionary theory of economic change developed by Nelson and Winter.
   a Give an example of a skill.
   b Name two characteristic features of skills.
   c Give an example of a routine.
   d What is the major difference between a skill and a routine? What are the major similarities between skills and routines?
   e What are the differences and similarities between routines and dynamic capabilities?

3 In a number of countries there has been experimentation with a new form of pharmacy: mail-order pharmacy. This new distribution form would allow patients to receive their regular prescriptions by post. In the Netherlands, the early experiments with this new form of pharmacy were set up by entrepreneurs. They were not successful. Many of the entrepreneurial firms failed (the experiments continue, but now under the auspices of health insurance companies). What could explain the early failures, if you adopt the perspective of organizational ecology?

4 Read Box 11.10, on the 700+ year history of STORA, again. If you look at its history from the perspective of Nelson and Winter's evolutionary theory of economic change, what may be the factors contributing to STORA's remarkably long survival as a company?

5 In 1959, almost all petrol in major Canadian cities was sold by service stations. Service stations provided simple car repair services and sold tyres, batteries and car accessories as well as petrol. They also employed 'pump jockeys', who filled up the tanks and perhaps provided other services, such as washing the windscreen. Thirty years later, that situation had changed dramatically. Less than 30 per cent of all petrol sold was sold by traditional service stations – the rest being sold in roughly equal proportions by 'gas bars' (outlets selling petrol only), convenience stores (petrol sales plus convenience retail) and car washes (petrol sales and automated carwashes). Table 11.1 provides data for the city of Edmonton in Alberta, Canada.

   Using population ecology, how would you explain the transition that occurred in Edmonton between 1959 and 1988? Which information would you need in order to know whether or not your explanation is correct from the point of view of population ecology?

Table 11.1 Number of outlets selling petrol in Edmonton, Alberta, Canada

Year	1959	1988
Service stations	262	104
Gas bars	1	73
Convenience stores	0	73
Carwashes	1	84
Other outlets selling petrol	15	40

Source: Usher and Evans (1996)

Notes

1   The second author's eldest son advanced a new hypothesis for the long necks of giraffes. According to him, giraffes were created when a baby dromedary had difficulty leaving its egg. This led its parents to pull it out. As the little dromedary was really stuck in the egg, the parents had to pull so hard that a giraffe with a long neck was born.

2   As, for instance, Hannan and Freeman (1989a) do. Their approach is outlined in the subsequent section.

3   Some studies are located between these two levels of analysis, such as the studies that use environmental variables as 'proxies' for competition by other organizational forms.

4   Added by the authors as Rinnooy Kan is referring to some early breaches in security in Internet banking.

12 All in the family

12.1 Introduction

You have now been introduced to the main economic approaches that are currently available. You are familiar with the problems addressed by each approach, the basic concepts used and the particular mode of analysis. Our task in this chapter is to provide you with an overall perspective on the various approaches included in this book.

First, we return to the basic conceptual framework laid out in Chapter 1. Having thus refreshed your memory, we proceed to discuss, in Section 12.3, what the similarities are between our family of economic approaches to organizations. In Section 12.4, we turn to the family differences. Together, these two sections should provide a balanced view of our family. Do they quarrel a lot? Are there any clear family traits? Do they have the same views or hobbies? Can we discern a family structure? Section 12.5 summarizes our findings and Section 12.6 sketches a concluding perspective before we move on to look at the applications of these approaches in the final three chapters.

12.2 The basic conceptual framework

In Chapter 1, we developed a basic conceptual framework, which is reproduced in Figure 12.1. The framework took, as its starting point, the division of labour in society. That division of labour allows economies of specialization to be gained. It is only one side of the coin, however. The other side is that coordination is necessary in a specialized economy. Without some kind of coordination, no exchange transaction could take place between specialized economic actors. Specialization and (the need for) coordination are, thus, the inseparable consequences of division of labour.

We argued that markets and organizations offer alternative solutions for the coordination of exchange transactions. We characterized markets and organizations by means of the coordination mechanisms they employed. Markets use the price mechanism. Organizations use any of six alternative mechanisms. We argued that pure market coordination and pure organizational coordination are rare. In practice, we often find a mix of coordination mechanisms. The actual mix that we find in any one situation will depend mainly on the information

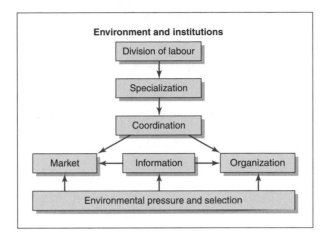

Figure 12.1 The basic conceptual framework

required to execute the transaction. Thus, information is the pivotal element of our basic conceptual framework, determining which (mix of) coordination mechanism(s) will prevail. Finally, we placed our framework in an environmental and institutional context, highlighting the environmental pressure and selection operating on both markets and organizations.

In Chapter 1, too, we showed how the basic economic perspective expressed in Figure 12.1 could be traced to some founding fathers of modern economics. Division of labour and its consequences was a main theme of Adam Smith; the efficiency of market coordination by the price system was vigorously expounded by Friedrich Hayek; and the idea that organizational coordination could arise as a remedy to flaws in market coordination was first systematically addressed by Ronald Coase. Now that we have surveyed more recent economic approaches to organizations, to what extent can we say that this basic conceptual framework underlies the spectrum of approaches that are currently available?

'To some extent', would be our answer. If anything has become clear in the preceding chapters, it should be the diversity of the approaches surveyed. In Section 12.4, we chart that diversity in more detail. Notwithstanding such diversity, we also see a common foundation to the economic approaches to organizations. Three of the common elements included in our framework are discussed below.

12.3 Family resemblances

12.3.1 Organizations and markets

The first common element in the economic approaches to organization is indeed that economists always tend to compare organizations to markets. Their background leads economists to think of markets as natural benchmarks for the appraisal of organizations. That is probably most obvious in

Chapter 8, where we discussed transaction cost economics. Williamson's initial formulation of that approach in terms of markets and hierarchies brings it out clearly.

The leading question in transaction cost economics is how to explain the relative occurrence of markets and firms as governance structures for economic transactions. It represents an extension of Coase's fundamental question, why do we observe so many firms (with internal governance of transactions) if the market functions so efficiently? Both Coase and Williamson take the market as their point of departure and explain that organizations exist as a result of 'market failure'.

Another, perhaps more implicit, way to compare organizations with markets is to analyze the boundaries of organizations. Consider the corporate strategies discussed in Chapter 10. Vertical integration, horizontal multinationalization and corporate diversification all extend the boundaries of an organization. If vertical integration, multinationalization or diversification is effected by a merger or acquisition, two firms are integrated into one. In these cases we now find one firm instead of two. The relevant comparison is between one integrated firm and two firms with a market relation between them. If the policies of vertical integration or multinationalization or diversification are pursued by internal growth (instead of mergers and acquisitions), the analytical benchmark from an economic point of view remains that a separate entity could have been created and a (cooperative or competitive) market relation established. Again, the relevant comparison is between one integrated firm and two firms with a market relation between them. This boils down to a comparative assessment of organizational versus market coordination of transactions.

Consider also the agency explanation for the existence of firms. As elaborated in Chapter 7, this explanation involves the concept of team production. Team production denotes the situation where two or more people can be more productive when they join forces than when they operate separately. Again, the (implicit) comparison is between an organizational arrangement and a market arrangement. Organizational arrangements come into being when market arrangements would be inferior.

Finally, the evolutionary approaches to organizations direct our attention to the environment in which the organization operates. A significant part of that environment will consist of markets: markets for the products and services produced by the organization, but also markets for the resources they require and even a 'market for corporate control' (see Chapter 7). In all those markets, the force of *competition* operates as an external selection mechanism. Organizations only survive if they are able to withstand such competitive market pressures and selection. In that sense, a market versus organization perspective can be discerned in the evolutionary approaches to organizations as well.

12.3.2 Efficiency

By what standards would the market arrangement be inferior? That question leads us to the second common element in the economic approaches to organization. It is the observation that the primary economic criterion for evaluating market versus organizational coordination is *efficiency*.

Efficiency

As broadly defined in Chapter 1, the **efficiency** criterion refers to the optimal allocation of scarce resources. That is to say, resources are efficiently allocated if they are directed towards their most productive use or, alternatively, if a given amount of production is achieved with a minimum of resources. If, moreover, all resources can be expressed in money terms, it translates into the 'least cost' condition that most people would intuitively associate with the term 'efficiency'. Bear in mind, however, that the economic definition of resources encompasses *all* means that may contribute to the satisfaction of human needs, broadly conceived (see Chapter 1).

Efficiency considerations abound in the preceding chapters. In the behavioural theory, organizational participants weigh up the contributions they have to make against the inducements they are offered. They compare that ratio with the alternatives available elsewhere. They strive for the most efficient allocation of their resources. A manager, according to agency theory, will wonder about the effects of buying a company jet on the objective of maximizing her utility (her utility depends on the value of the firm and on her on-the-job consumption). Will the company's resources be spent efficiently if they are spent on a jet? The strategist in another firm will consider moving from a cost leadership position to a differentiation strategy. He will conclude that this is feasible only if the increase in revenue outweighs the increase in costs.

Hence, efficiency considerations are, in part, manifest in the assumed thoughts and behaviour of economic actors. Economists tend to presume that people are not totally unaffected by the expected efficiency of the resources at their disposal. However, efficiency considerations play an additional and more important role in economic analysis. Efficiency is the economic selection mechanism. It is our main criterion for assessing which coordination arrangements have the highest survival value when selection pressures are operative. Economists usually assume that the least efficient arrangements will tend to be selected out (after some time).

That assumption is evident in Nelson and Winter's evolutionary theory of the firm. Environmental selection favours successful routines. Successful routines are indicated by the higher profit levels of the firms incorporating them. Profit is an indicator of efficiency. Hence, efficient firms will tend to be selected by the environment and inefficient firms (with less successful routines) will tend to be selected out. Similarly, in transaction cost economics, the governance structure that economizes on production and transaction costs (and is thus more efficient) supersedes the less efficient alternative. These examples refer, strictly speaking, to **Static efficiency** the commonest use of the efficiency concept – that is, **static efficiency** or *allocative efficiency*. Another question is how should resources be (re)distributed over time to adapt an economy or an organization to changing circumstances and **Dynamic efficiency** keep it efficient and growing? That is a question of **dynamic efficiency**.

In Chapter 11, we introduced the concept of 'evolutionary fitness'. We noted that dynamic capabilities that are evolutionarily fit, enable a firm to survive, and perhaps grow and prosper in the market-place (in changing circumstances). Thus, evolutionary fitness and dynamic efficiency are conceptually related criteria, both referring to adaptability. In his later writings, Williamson has come to emphasize that "transaction cost economics maintains that adaptation is the central problem of economic organization" (Williamson, 2009, P. xiv).

Efficiency, therefore, is the second common element that binds the various economic approaches to organization together. It is partly implicit in the basic conceptual framework of Figure 12.1. As discussed above, it is the primary economic criterion that determines the selection of either markets or organizations as coordination devices for particular transactions. We have also made it explicit, however, by focusing on one specific source of efficiency: informational advantages.

12.3.3 Information

The focus on information is the third and final common element that we want to discuss here. An important impetus to both agency theory and transaction cost economics was provided by the development of the **economics of information**. It was increasingly recognized that information itself was a scarce resource that could be unevenly distributed. Uneven distributions of information present opportunities for strategic behaviour. Whether the relevant information is observable to all players or not is a prime distinction in the games that people (and organizations) play, as we saw in Chapter 5. There is economic value in the possession of private information. Informational asymmetries can be exploited, whether opportunistically or not.

Agency theory and transaction cost economics share a concern for such situations. Both maintain that such informational problems pervade (economic) life and both seek efficient contractual arrangements to deal with such problems. As markets and organizations differ in the types of information problem they can handle (efficiently), a good part of the choice between them will be explained by the information requirements of particular transactions.

Although less clearly at first sight, information is a central concept in most other economic approaches to organizations as well. The behavioural theory of the firm, for instance, departs from standard microeconomics in the assumptions that, first, information is often imperfectly available to economic actors and, second, these actors are only boundedly rational in processing the information that is available.

Those behavioural assumptions spurred later developments in organizational economics, as we have seen, and have often been incorporated in later approaches. In the evolutionary approach, much information is stored in the organizational routines and capabilities. They embody **tacit knowledge**. Tacit knowledge is difficult to articulate and, therefore, communicate. It is, consequently, also difficult for third parties to acquire. In that sense, tacit knowledge embodied in organizational routines and capabilities represents a well-protected form of private information for the organization. A fundamental information asymmetry exists between firms with and without successful routines and capabilities. Just like DNA stores our (coded) genetic information, routines and capabilities store the information necessary for organizations to function and grow. As Beinhocker (2006, p. 12) has noted:

> Evolution is an *algorithm* ... Evolution can perform its tricks not just in the substrate of DNA, but in any system that has the right information-processing and information-storing characteristics.

Economics of information

Tacit knowledge

We do not want to overemphasize the commonality between the economic approaches to organizations. Each common element discussed above is probably to some extent debatable. Together, however, they represent the main binding features, as we see them. In the next sections, some important differences between these approaches are discussed and summarized, together with the similarities. Taken together, these sections should provide a balanced overall picture.

12.4 Family differences

Let us now turn to the differences between our family members. You will have noticed abundant differences while reading through Chapters 6–11. Our purpose here will not be to enumerate all those differences. Rather, we shall attempt to provide some structure by ordering the various approaches along some dimensions that we believe are particularly instructive. Three such dimensions are discussed below.

12.4.1 Process versus content approaches

The first dimension refers to the subject matter of the various approaches, which is the problems that they deal with. Here, we borrow a distinction from the strategy literature in order to classify our approaches. It is the distinction between *process theories* and *content theories* of strategy.

Process theories deal with the processes that enable strategies to come into being. *Content theories* deal with the content of those strategies: the firm's strategic posture and positioning in the market.

Similarly, we shall distinguish here between **process and content approaches to organizations**. The former deal with organizational processes, but hardly inform us about the likely outcomes of those processes. The latter focus on substantive outcomes without being very informative about the processes that lead to these outcomes.

To illustrate this dimension, let us contrast two of our approaches. The behavioural theory of the firm is a process approach. It explains the internal functioning of the firm when seen as a coalition of participant groups. It highlights the potential conflicts between those groups as well as the organizational processes that may lead to quasi-resolutions of such conflicts, such as satisficing and sequential decisionmaking. It does not tell us, however, what the specific outcome of those processes will be. That is completely dependent on the detailed decisions and behaviours of the organizational participants involved.

Contrast this with principal/agent theory. How do the principal and the agent arrive at making a choice between, say, a wage contract and a rent contract for growing strawberries (see Section 7.6)? Is it a matter of intense dispute with fierce bargaining on both sides? Is one party in a better bargaining position, maybe because of a lack of alternatives for the other party? Is it only a bilateral exchange situation or perhaps what Williamson would call a large numbers exchange situation (ex ante)?

Process and content approaches to organizations

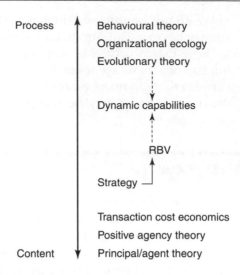

Figure 12.2 Process and content approaches

Principal/agent theory is silent on such process and content issues. It presents the expected outcomes, given the variables on which it focuses (utilities, reservation pay, effort levels and so on) and the efficiency criterion it employs.

Figure 12.2 presents our ordering of the various approaches along the process versus content dimension. Behavioural theory is a fairly pure process theory. Organizational ecology is only somewhat more content orientated. 'Content' here refers to the expected development of the population over time and the density dependence of founding and exit rates.

Nelson and Winter's evolutionary theory started out as a rather pure process theory. However, as discussed in Chapter 11, subsequently they came to realize that the theory could have benefited from the incorporation of some insights from the strategy literature. That led them, first, to explore links with Chandler's work, *Strategy and Structure*, and later contribute to the literature on *dynamic capabilities*. Winter in particular has been personally active in further developing the literature on this subject (Winter, 2003 and his contribution to Helfat et al., 2007). As a result, evolutionary theory has strengthened its microfoundations and acquired the possibility to conduct content research – into the nature of dynamic capabilities that provide sustainable competitive advantage, for example. Such research is coming to fruition now. Therefore, we classify evolutionary theory (with the incorporation of dynamic capabilities) as a process theory with more ability to generate substantive outcomes than in its original formulation.

At the other end of the spectrum, positive agency theory is slightly more process orientated than principal/agent theory because it is occasionally more explicit about the mechanisms that produce particular outcomes, such as the operation of a market for corporate control. It roughly shares this position with transaction cost economics. The latter is explicit about one particular process: the fundamental transformation that may occur as a result of increasing asset specificity (see Section 8.3). Transaction cost economics leaves the selection process, which is assumed to lead to efficient outcomes, open, however.

Finally, we turn to the classification of economic approaches to strategy. As explained in Chapter 9, traditional industrial organization is clearly a content theory. It attempts to explain the structure, conduct and performance of (firms within) an industry. In so far as industrial organization is the basis of our approach to strategic management, we are therefore applying a content theory. It informs us about the posture and positioning of firms within and across industries. Our discussion of move and counter move is only partly more process orientated, to the extent that the development of strategies over time is considered. The economic contribution to strategic management originally left the internal processes of strategy formation and development undiscussed. However, with the development of the resource-based view (RBV) and, particularly, the extension to dynamic capabilities, process considerations are entering into the economic contributions to strategy. The concept of dynamic capabilities allows a link between economic contributions to strategy and evolutionary theories, which offers exciting opportunities to narrow the gap between content and process theories. We show this link as a dotted line in Figure 12.2.

Figure 12.2 makes it clear that there still remains a gap between process and content orientated approaches. While this is true of economic theories of organization, it also reflects the more general tendencies in the field of organization studies. A fully integrated content and process model of organizational behaviour and development is still a challenge.

12.4.2   Static versus dynamic approaches

The second dimension we use to order our economic approaches to organizations is not unrelated to the first one discussed above. It is, however, sufficiently different to merit a separate discussion. It is the distinction between static and dynamic theories. This distinction allows us to make some observations about the various modes of analysis used in our theories. It also allows some remarks on the timeframe that is inherent in each theory.

In Figure 12.3, the vertical axis corresponds to that in Figure 12.2 and represents the process versus content dimension. We have now added the static versus dynamic dimension as a horizontal axis. Each axis is divided into three parts, which define regions of the figure.

Following the vertical axis, we find that the process approaches are in the top region and the content approaches in the bottom region. The rather empty middle region illustrates the absence of integrated process and content theories (but we have indicated the potential of the dynamic capabilities literature to start filling this gap).

The horizontal axis is also divided into three parts. The regions defined by the horizontal axis are discussed in turn below.

To the left we find the agency theories. They employ a mode of analysis that is known as **comparative-static** in economics. A comparative-static analysis compares one (static) situation with another. For instance, the principal/agent situation under a wage contract is compared with the situation under a

Comparative-static analysis

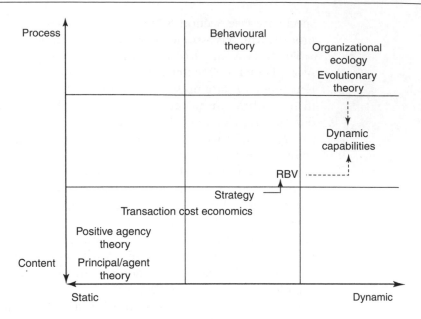

Figure 12.3 Static and dynamic approaches

rent contract. The analysis is aimed at discovering whether or not one of these situations is superior to the other (given the variables included in the analysis and the criterion of efficiency). What the analysis reveals, therefore, is a ranking of alternative situations, given the (efficiency) criterion employed. It will not tell you how the present situation may evolve or how to get from here to there if you are now in an inferior situation.

To the right, we find the ecological and evolutionary theories that are characterized by their long-term perspective. The cumulative selection and adaptation processes that are required for the theories to work clearly indicate their long-term dynamic character.

Behavioural theory and strategy occupy a middle position between these two extremes. They usually take the present situation as a starting point for the analysis and may then ask, what's next? In behavioural theory, we might analyse the effects of the rise in aspiration levels. In strategy, we may contemplate a strategic move. While, therefore, these approaches are partly dynamic in character, they certainly do not share the long-term timeframe of their neighbours to the right.

That leaves transaction cost economics to be classified. As is evident from Figure 12.3, it is not possible to classify it completely in just *one* of the three boxes along the static versus dynamic dimension. The reason is that transaction cost economics employs a mode of analysis that can be characterized as **comparative-institutional**. It compares the functioning of one institutional arrangement (such as markets) with the functioning of another (such as hierarchies). The criterion for comparison is, again, efficiency (now including transaction costs, of course). In that respect it is analogous to a comparative-static approach comparing one situation with another. It also answers some 'what's next?' questions, however. The progression of hierarchical forms – from peer

Comparative-institutional analysis

groups via simple hierarchies to more complex hierarchies – is one case in point. Another is fundamental transformation (see Section 8.3). These elements of transaction cost theory belong in the middle column. That is why we have placed this approach in both the left and middle regions of the static versus dynamic axis.

12.4.3 Levels of analysis

Level of analysis

Our third and final dimension refers to the level(s) of analysis the theories are addressing. A **level of analysis** denotes the level at which the problems that a theory is attempting to analyze is located. Psychological theories, for example, are directed mainly at the individual level of analysis: they attempt to explain individual behaviour.

Which level(s) of analysis are the economic approaches to organization addressing? A surprisingly large number, we submit. We feel obliged to distinguish the following seven levels of analysis:

- *person dyad* a pair of individuals in an exchange relationship;
- *group* a (relatively small) number of individuals bound together by a community of purpose, interest or function;
- *intergroup* the relations between organizational groups with different purposes, interests or functions;
- *organization* the nexus of contracts, the coalition of participant groups and/ or the administrative structure that forms a unity and is usually legally recognized as such;
- *organizational dyad* a pair of organizations in an exchange relationship;
- *population of organizations* all organizations of a particular type or form;
- *system* the entire set of organizational populations, environmental characteristics and their interrelationships that are relevant to the analysis of aggregate phenomena.

These seven levels form the vertical axis in Figure 12.4. The figure shows which levels of analysis are covered by the approaches included in this book. The position of each approach is discussed in turn below.

Agency theory spans the person dyad to organizational levels of analysis, while *principal/agent theory* is specifically geared to the person dyad level. That is because the latter theory formally examines agency relationships between two people. Although attempts are made to extend principal/agent theory to multiple agent and/or multiple principal settings, it proves to be very difficult. The formal analysis soon poses intractable problems when heterogeneity of principals or agents is introduced. The insights gained from principal/agent analysis, therefore, strictly apply only to the one principal, one agent level of analysis. Often they are used, however, as a paradigm for analyses at a higher level. It should be clear that considerable caution is in order when such inferences are made. At the group level, all kinds of heterogeneities and group interactions may already start to play a major role. At higher levels of analysis many environmental and institutional factors will come into play.

Positive agency theory takes the analysis up from the group to the organizational level. An example at the group level might be the analysis of the managerial

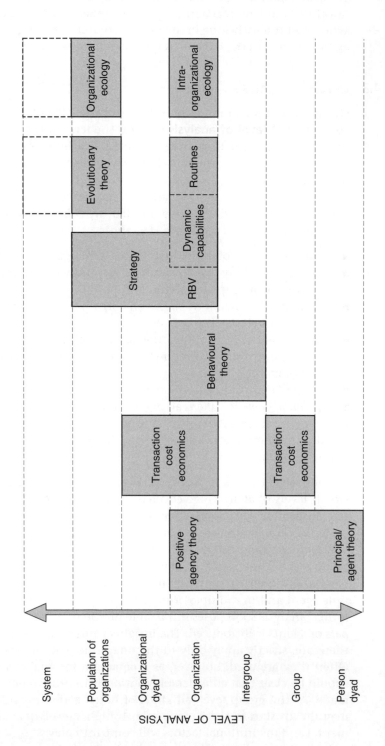

Figure 12.4 Levels of analysis

reward structures. For instance, how should managerial reward packages at the corporate and divisional levels differ? The intergroup level of analysis is reached when potential conflicts between, for instance, shareholders and bondholders in public corporations are analysed. The organizational level of analysis pertains to, for example, takeovers and the market for corporate control.

Transaction cost economics focuses at the group level when it analyses peer groups. However, most of its attention is directed at the organizational level (e.g. the comparison of U-, M- and H-forms) and the organizational dyad level (such as vertical integration). Interestingly, the intergroup level of potential conflicts between participant groups is hardly analyzed. Transaction cost analysis focuses on governance and has a rather holistic view of organizations. As discussed in Section 8.10, it 'imports' shift parameters from the institutional environment and behavioural assumptions from the individual level.

It is, of course, a major characteristic of *behavioural theory* that it explicitly deals with intraorganizational processes, particularly intergroup conflict. The organization is analysed as a coalition of participant groups and organizational behaviour is explained from that perspective.

The *economics and strategy* literature spans three levels of analysis. It analyzes individual organizations and contemplates their strategic development (such as the diversification issue). However, it also studies competition and rivalry, both at a dyadic level (the moves and counter moves of two strategic players) and at a population level (rivalry within an industry). The RBV is primarily located at the organizational level. It looks inside the firm to determine which resources are the basis of a sustainable competitive advantage. As discussed in Sections 9.6 and 11.7, the RBV has been extended to incorporate not only (static) resources but also dynamic capabilities. That extension has allowed for a very interesting 'bridge' to evolutionary theory, as originally developed by Nelson and Winter.

Evolutionary and ecological theories are both located at the population level of analysis. They both analyze the population of organizations of a particular type or form. Both also have the potential to extend to the system level. Both are silent on the interactions between two organizations, the organizational dyad level.

Nelson and Winter's evolutionary theory originally already contained some analyses at the organizational level, as the firm is conceptualized as a hierarchy of routines. Those routines can be subject to development and change, such as through learning, imitation and conscious adaptation through a (local) search. However, such change is seriously constrained by prevailing routines. Hence, evolutionary theories strongly emphasize the relative inertia of firms. Interestingly, the extension of the concept of routines with dynamic capabilities, which has provided a 'bridge' to the strategy (RBV) literature, implies that evolutionary theories now allow for more *purposeful adaptation* than in their original formulation. It also means that there is more recognition of the managerial task to build, maintain and modify the resource and capability base of an organization. Recent contributions by Teece explore the 'microfoundations' of dynamic capabilities: 'the organizational and managerial processes, procedures, systems, and structures that undergird each class of capability' (Teece, 2009, p.8).

Organizational ecology, in its original formulation by Hannan and Freeman (1989a), treated organizations as rather inert 'black boxes' (see also Section 11.6). The reason is that in their approach the 'organizational form' in its entirety was subject to selection (while Nelson and Winter selection operated at the intraorganizational level of routines). For Hannan and Freeman there was, therefore, much less reason to look inside the firm. However, in subsequent research, the ecological perspective has also been applied to the organization itself. Burgelman (2002, p. 7) conceptualizes a company as 'an ecology within which strategic initiatives emerge in a patterned way'. As a consequence, he is able to add the force of *internal selection* to the external selection forces operating on the firm. Through such contributions, the box of *intraorganizational ecology* in Figure 12.4 has become a fully fledged research stream of its own.

We may make three final observations about the levels of analysis addressed by economic approaches to organizations. The first is that they vary widely. That is probably due to the fact that economics has something to contribute as soon as there is an economic aspect involved in the phenomena that interest us (see Chapter 1). At all levels of analysis – from the two-person to system levels – economic aspects are involved.

The second, related, observation is that the various approaches tend to address quite different problems. That is, in part, due to the different levels of analysis. The evolution of organizational forms over long periods of time is a very different sort of problem from that of the short-term strategic moves that a company may make in a strategic battle. Each level of analysis has its own particular characteristics: groups are more than a collection of dyads; organizations are more than a collection of groups. Care should be taken to specify clearly the level of analysis at which certain findings apply and not make any undue inferences to other levels.

Third, even if we stay with one level of analysis, different theories tend to see different problems. Take the organizational level, to which nearly all theories apply (not surprisingly in this book). Agency theories tend to see an organization as a nexus of contracts; transaction cost economics see it as a governance structure of transactions, behavioural theory as a coalition of participant groups and evolutionary theory as a collection of routines or capabilities. Different theories look at the world through different lenses. The image of the organization that underlies any particular theory strongly shapes the kinds of problem observed and the importance attached to them.

12.5 Summary: all in the family?

We have now discussed the three major similarities we observe between the economic approaches to organizations as well as the three major dimensions of their differences. These are summarized in Table 12.1. The final question remains as to whether the similarities outweigh the differences or not. Are the approaches included in this book members of a family?

Table 12.1 Family resemblances and differences

Major similarities	Major differences
Organizations versus markets	Process versus content approaches
Efficiency	Static versus dynamic approaches
Information	Levels of analysis

In the final analysis, we should like to leave that question for you to answer. We have presented the approaches themselves, as well as our view on their resemblances and differences, in some detail. That should enable you to form a judgement. Obviously, our judgement is that they belong together in this book and, yes, we do regard them as a family. We pursue this metaphor below, offering some observations on the structure of the family as we see it.

Agency theory, transaction cost economics and industrial economics-cum-strategy and game theory are the members of the *nuclear family*. They represent the hard core of the present economic approaches to organizations. They are the fields where most of the current attention is focused and most of the research work in organizational economics is presently done.

The other approaches belong to the *extended family*. We may think of behavioural theory as being at the grandparent level. It has generated work in many areas and, within organizational economics, its strongest influence has been on transaction cost economics and evolutionary theory. There are other siblings, too, in microeconomics as well as in theories of organizational behaviour. Behavioural economics has explored the limits of rationality further by incorporating heuristics and biases in its models of human decisionmaking.

Evolutionary theory might be a cousin (perhaps once removed). One familial link is through the behavioural foundations of its concept of organizations, which connects it to organizational theory. Moreover, it has become recently engaged to the RBV member of the strategy clan. Last but not least, it has a clear lineage in economics. Such a family tree leaves no doubt about its inclusion in the family of organizational economics.

Organizational ecology, finally, may be regarded as the 'odd one out' in the family. It is clearly a relative of evolutionary theory and it is also a member of the family of organizational theories. Its links to the economic family are tenuous, however. Its clearest connection with economics is through the concept of competition but, as that concept is not well developed in organizational ecology, doubts remain. Our reasons for including organizational ecology in this book were two-fold:

1 Its relation to evolutionary theory.
2 Our expectation that it will develop more links with economics over time (see Sections 11.6–11.8). In fact, it is already quite attracted to industrial economics–cum–strategy, with which it shares some basic interests (See, for example, Barron, 2003 and Baum et al., 2006).

That rounds off our picture of the family structure. For us, the similarities discussed in Section 12.3, as well as our perception of the family structure, led us to include these approaches in the book. Some judgement is involved, however.

What is more, the family structure is not static: it develops over time. As with human families, new offspring may be generated and the family may redefine its structure as its members are perceived to grow either closer together or further apart. That is all in the family.

12.6 New developments: organizations as complex, adaptive systems

In this section, we want to sketch a theoretical perspective that we expect will have a significant impact on the future development of our family of economic approaches to organizations. It is the perspective of complexity. The **complexity perspective** spans several scientific disciplines and it is being developed by a truly interdisciplinary set of scholars. In this section we want to focus on potential implications of this perspective for the study of organizations.

Complexity perspective

As a starting point, look back to Figure 12.4. It describes a hierarchy of levels of analysis. Individuals may form dyads, dyads may cluster into groups, various groups may constitute organizations, organizations have relations with other organizations and belong to populations, populations together form a community system. At each level of analysis, the phenomena we study are usually complex. At the lowest level of our analysis, the dyad, the people concerned may already have complex relationships with one another. Organizations certainly represent complex systems.

Complexity has no generally accepted definition (See Gell-Mann, 1994), but usually refers to systems in which numerous agents are interacting with each other in a great many ways (Waldrop, 1992, p. 86):

> Whenever you look at very complicated systems in physics or biology, ... you generally find that the basic components and the basic laws are quite simple; the complexity arises because you have a great many of these simple components interacting simultaneously. The complexity is actually in the organization – the myriad possible ways that the components of the system can interact.

When scientists from different backgrounds came together to compare notes on such complex systems, they found that (Waldrop, 1992, p. 88):

> every topic of interest had at its heart a system composed of many, many 'agents'. These agents might be molecules or neurons or species or consumers or even corporations. But whatever their nature, the agents were constantly organizing and reorganizing themselves into larger structures through the clash of mutual accommodation and mutual rivalry. Thus, molecules would form cells, neurons would form brains, species would form ecosystems, consumers and corporations would form economies, and so on. At each level, new emergent structures would form and engage in new emergent behaviors.

Emergence

Emergence is thus a central concept in the science of complexity (See Holland, 1998 and Johnson, 2001). It denotes the common finding that the properties, behaviours and structures of systems cannot simply be deduced from the properties, behaviours and structures of the constituent agents. Complex systems 'lead a life of their own'. Knowledge of their parts is helpful, but knowledge of the whole requires more than knowledge of all the parts. In other words, applying this thinking to organizations, we cannot hope ever to understand organizations fully by dissecting them and examining all their parts. The reason is that the interaction of the parts and the interaction of the organization with the environment co-determine the organizational evolution. In the language of complexity, complex systems self-organize.

Self-organization

The exact form of that **self-organization** emerges from the evolution of the system. Remember Box 11.9 on the evolution of competition between Betamax and VHS in the market for videorecorders? As Brian Arthur told the story, the outcome could have gone either way. In the language of complexity, the competitive outcome emerged from the self-organization of the market.

In Chapters 3 and 8 we argued that within large organizations we often see markets for intermediate goods and services. Self-organization and decentralized decisionmaking are often superior to direct supervision and centralized planning in large complex organizations.

Insights from complexity theory can be usefully applied in that context, as illustrated in Box 12.1. The examples in Box 12.1 show that, in large complex systems, detailed top-down planning may be inferior to self-organization of the system.

Deliberate strategies

Emergent strategies

That insight, in turn, corresponds well to Mintzberg's (1985) empirical observation that strategies arise in organizations in (a mix of) two ways: deliberate and emergent. In **deliberate strategies**, pre-existing intentions or plans are realized over time. In **emergent strategies**, a strategic pattern of behaviour develops in the absence of intentions or plans (and sometimes even in spite of other pre-existing intentions or plans). Emergent strategies are thus one manifestation of the self-organization of organizational systems.[1]

Box 12.1 Complexity science in business

Complexity science has been applied with success in some business situations. In some cases, companies have moved away from centralized control of their operations – for instance, in their production scheduling. Recognizing that such centralized control is vulnerable to breaking down in circumstances of high uncertainty, companies have been experimenting with models that allow a solution (to a scheduling problem, for example) to 'emerge' from the interaction of organizational units acting as free agents. Here are two cases in point.

General Motors
In 1992, Dick Morley, one of the creators of the floppy disk, developed a factory control system based on complexity theory principles.

Morley's computer system was put to the test in the paint section of a GM assembly plant in Fort Wayne, Indiana. Morley enabled ten paint booths, previously routed by a centralized controller, to act as free agents with a simple goal: paint as many trucks as possible using as little paint as needed. Each booth electronically 'bids' for the right to paint a certain truck based on colour and the queue in front of the booth. A central computer then compares the bids and assigns a 'winner'.

This system saved $1 million per year in paint alone.

▶

Cemex
Cementos Mexicanos (CEMEX), one of the leading construction materials companies of the world, with over 50,000 employees, uses complexity principles to create order out of chaos in its home market, Mexico. Using the latest in information technology, including computers and GPS units in all their ready-mix delivery trucks, each truck operates as independently as possible – cruising Mexico's notoriously unpredictable roads as an autonomous agent, waiting for orders. There are no fixed schedules. Instead there is real-time data of customer orders, production schedules, traffic reports, even weather reports that allow operators to make decisions on the spot as to where to deploy resources. The objective of the drivers is to deliver within a twenty-minute time window, otherwise the customer receives a twenty percent discount. The results: 98 percent of deliveries occur within this time frame, whereas before only one-third of orders were on time in a three-hour time window.

Based on The Corporate Strategy Board, 'Current state of complexity science', Washington DC, October 1998; G. Seijts et al (2010), 'Coping with Complexity', *Ivey Business Journal*, May/June.

In such self-organization, small factors may make a huge difference. The reason is that complex systems can behave in a way that mathematicians describe with non-linear dynamics. One of the most striking non-linear phenomena has come to be known as **chaos**: under the right circumstances, tiny perturbations and slight uncertainties may grow until the system's future becomes utterly unpredictable. Moreover, patterns of regularity and chaos seem to alternate in the evolution of most complex systems (Waldrop, 1992, p. 66):

Chaos

> Researchers began to realize that even some very simple systems could produce astonishingly rich patterns of behavior. All that was required was a little bit of nonlinearity. The drip-drip-drip of water from a leaky faucet, for example, could be as maddeningly regular as a metronome – so long as the leak was slow enough. But if you ignored the leak for a while and let the flow rate increase ever so slightly, then the drops would soon start to alternate between large and small: DRIP-drip-DRIP-drip. If you ignored it a while longer and let the flow increase still more, the drops would soon start to come in sequences of 4 – and then 8, 16, and so forth. Eventually, the sequence would become so complex that the drops would seem to come at random – again, chaos. Moreover, this same pattern of ever-increasing complexity could be seen in the population swings of fruit flies, or in the turbulent flow of fluids, or in any number of domains.

The non-linear, dynamic behaviour of complex systems implies that their evolution can be very **sensitive to initial conditions**. Small variations in the circumstances at the start of their development may have large consequences for their direction and outcome. An organizational example may be the 'imprint' that founders leave on their companies, even long after they have retired. Sam Walton's impact on Wal-Mart and Walt Disney's lasting influence on the Disney Corporation are cases in point.

Sensitive to initial conditions

A related characteristic of non-linear, dynamic systems is **path dependence**. Path dependence means that history matters. Consider again the development of STORA over more than 700 years, from copper mining to a forest products company (see Box 11.10). If the 'fire-setting' process for copper mining had

Path dependence

not required substantial quantities of wood, STORA would not have acquired forests. Having acquired the forests, it made sense to use the forest products more widely, including the construction of paper mills. There is, thus, a 'chain of events' that explains the transformation of STORA from a mining company to a paper company. Any changes in that chain of events could have yielded a very different outcome. The sensitivity to initial conditions, together with the path dependence of non-linear, dynamic systems, makes it notoriously difficult to predict their development.

Another property of complex systems is that they seek to adapt to their environment. They do so by constantly revising and rearranging their building blocks as they gain experience. The brain will continually strengthen or weaken myriad connections between its neurons as an individual learns from experience in the world. A firm will promote individuals who do well, attempt to transfer best practice across its units and occasionally reshuffle its organization chart.

A particular set of building blocks are the internal models from which complex systems anticipate and predict the future. From bacteria upwards, every living creature has an implicit prediction encoded in its genes. Every creature with a brain has numerous predictions encoded in what it has learned. As we have seen in Chapters 3 and 11, organizations have routines that serve as internal models for prediction. Such organizational routines guide organizational behaviour. In the perspective of complexity, such routines are not passive blueprints but subject to continuous testing, refinement and rearranging as the organizational system gains experience. It is through this process of readjustment of its internal models that a complex system learns to adapt its predictions and, consequently, its behaviour. Hence, we speak of complex, *adaptive* systems.

We can model their behaviour with the tools of evolutionary game theory, as introduced in Section 5.6. You may recall the model of Lindgren (1997) in which he allowed agents (strategies) to develop memory. As a result of learning, the strategies develop from simple to complex. The interactions between agents, similarly, develop from simple to complex. The population, consisting of all strategies at any point in time, continually evolves. Sometimes it shows periods of relative stability, but then it suddenly 'tips' into turbulence. New innovations pop up and upset any seeming stability achieved for some time. Those new innovations thus also change the environment for all other strategies, thereby shifting selection pressures. As a consequence, strategies and environments coevolve.

When selection pressures are strong, success spreads rapidly as the most successful strategies are copied. The disadvantage is that variety is reduced in the population. Such variety can be required when new, better strategies need to be explored as the environment develops further. Weak selection pressure encourages such variety. Thus, the strength of selection pressures impacts the trade-off between exploitation (of success) and exploration (of innovations).

These ideas correspond closely to insights in organization theory about organizational learning (and unlearning), managerial repertoires and dominant logics. We want to illustrate the potential of applying 'complexity theory' to organizations with one example, which we borrow from Bettis and Prahalad (1995). We have chosen it because it sheds additional light on the inertia versus adaptability theme that we raised at the end of Chapter 11.

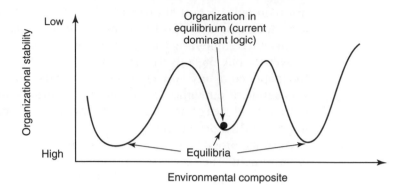

Figure 12.5 Organizational stability

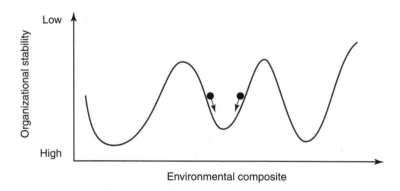

Figure 12.6 Small fluctuations return to original equilibrium

Dominant logic

As noted in Section 11.8, successful firms can become 'simple' over time, focusing exclusively on their successful repertoire of routines (or competences) and becoming intolerant of deviation or variation. Bettis and Prahalad refer to the **dominant logic** of such a firm. Its dominant logic serves an organization well so long as its predictions about the environment are largely borne out. When the environment is turbulent and conditions change rapidly, however, the organization may need to 'unlearn' its dominant logic.

Complexity theorists have shown that complex systems can achieve such unlearning when they move far from (the previous) equilibrium. Bettis and Prahalad visualize these notions with the three graphs shown in Figures 12.5 to 12.7. All three figures show organizational stability plotted against a composite environmental variable, which is assumed to be composed of the major environmental variables combined in some fashion. Hence, different points on the horizontal axis represent different environmental conditions.

The organization is shown as a small marble at rest in Figure 12.5 in one of the 'valleys', or equilibria, of the stability function. That particular equilibrium corresponds to the current dominant logic that is matched to the environment facing the firm.

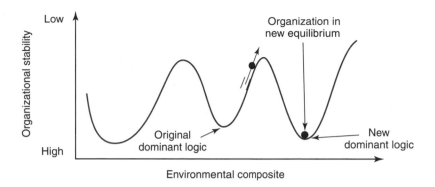

Figure 12.7 Moving far from equilibrium allows firms to establish new equilibrium

Figure 12.6 shows how small displacements from a state of equilibrium, corresponding to small changes in the environment, will result in the firm 'rolling back' into its previous repertoire, called forth by the dominant logic. That is the situation described by organizational ecology when it argues that organizations tend to be relatively inert.

Under such circumstances, the match between dominant logic and environment may deteriorate, but, because of the small differences, the current dominant logic may continue to be useful. If, however, there are large enough changes in the environment (Figure 12.7), organizations may be sufficiently shaken up to roll over an adjacent hill into a new equilibrium, based on a newly developed dominant logic.

This last proposition corresponds closely with the empirical observation that organizations often develop such new logics only in response to crises – or fail (See Schreuder, 1993b). It may also suggest why firms that recognize they must do something completely different locate new activities far away from their current activities. When IBM struggled to catch up with developments in the PC field, for example, it established a separate unit that was geographically and managerially insulated from the 'old IBM' with its mainframe mentality. Similarly, when established airlines wanted to respond to the threat of new, low-cost carriers they usually set up a separate company with a different brand name.

Finally, this proposition may explain why new competitors often displace experienced incumbents in an industry when major structural change occurs. The new entrants are, in essence, starting with a clean sheet and do not have the problem of having to climb up an unlearning curve (the 'hills' in Figures 12.5 to 12.7) before being able to run down a new learning curve.

If the steepness of the hills and/or their height were to depend on the strength of the dominant logic, we would have an explanation of the Icarus paradox discussed in Chapter 11. Continuous success would have the effect of reinforcing the dominant logic of the incumbent firm, deepening the 'valley' of its current position and, thus, making it harder to migrate over the unlearning curve to a new and more appropriate position when external change would demand so.

Competency trap

March (1994) refers to this situation as a **competency trap** – a type of lock-in produced by prolonged positive feedback on a successful competence. All in all, such a perspective explains why success carries the seeds of its own demise and successful companies so often fail after some time.

Interestingly, an analogous story can be told about the evolution of new markets, based on new technologies (See Geroski, 2003). Those new technologies are often pushed to markets from the supply side – that is, the technology has not yet developed in a way that is user-friendly. That opens up space for entrepreneurs to offer many different adaptations or applications to the market. Sometimes entrepreneurial established firms can occupy that new space (think of Apple with its iPod in the space of portable music carriers), but often it attracts many new entrants as well (think of all the new Internet-based businesses in the dot-com bubble of Box 1.6).

In fact, most new markets cannot sustain the whole population of firms that enter early or the wide range of different product variants. As a consequence, there is often a **shakeout**, of both the product variants and the firms that supply them. What emerges is a well-defined product with a **dominant design**. That dominant design is then the basis for the development of a mass market for the product.

Shakeout

Dominant design

In the shift from a new market to a mass market, the basis of the competition changes. Where, initially, the competition is between different designs, the emergence of a dominant design implies that competition shifts to differentiation within the dominant design and price. With the maturing of the market, the product becomes more of a commodity. For a totally commoditized product, only price competition remains.

Box 12.2 Xerox: dominant designs and dominant logic.

In the 1930s, Chester Carlson invented a new technology for copying: xerography. It promised much better performance than the prevailing technologies ('wet' photographic methods or 'dry' thermal processes), but initially also at a much higher price.

Carlson took his invention to many of the leading American technology firms of his day, including IBM, Kodak, General Electric, but none was interested. In the end, only the Haloid Corporation, a small manufacturer of photographic paper, was willing to develop the xerography technology further.

It took Haloid Corporation 14 years of research, at a cost of $75 million, to develop the invention into an innovation. In 1960, the first commercial model, named the Xerox 914, was shipped.

To overcome the problem of its still relatively high cost, Haloid offered customers a lease contract at $95 per month. That lease cost included service and 2000 free copies. Additional copies cost 4 cents each. The revenue from leasing alone would not be sufficient for Haloid: the Xerox 914 would have to lead to greatly increased volumes of copying for this business model to pay off.

The Xerox 914 was a huge success. Once it was installed, customers made an average 2000 copies per day, not per month, generating enormous additional revenue for Haloid by each second day of the monthly lease. Haloid's revenues started growing at an average of 41 per cent over the next 12 years. The company changed its name to The Xerox Corporation. By 1966, Xerox held 61 per cent of the copier market. The little $30 million Haloid Corporation turned into the global Xerox Corporation with $2.5 billion revenue in 1972.

Its success was built on developing the dominant copier design of that age – the Xerox 914. That design not only radically altered the market for office copying, sweeping the older technologies away, but also vastly expanded the market (the new design triggering a coevolution of company and market).

Its enormous success shaped the dominant logic of Xerox for many years to come. The 914 business model generated more revenue as more copies were made. As a consequence, Xerox was motivated to develop ever faster machines that could handle very high copy volumes, with maximum uptime and availability. As a later Xerox CEO said, 'If a copier was slow in generating copies, that was money plucked out of our pocket.'

The dominant logic of Xerox led it to focus on large companies and governmental organizations needing high volumes of high-quality copies. It was not suited to serving the needs of small businesses and individuals, requiring lower outputs and willing to trade off quality against price. Japanese firms later attacked that segment of the copier market with low-cost machines, in effect establishing a new dominant design for that particular segment.

Xerox wanted to fight for that segment, but faced great challenges. It had to ask its engineers, who excelled in developing ever faster machines, to now focus on simpler products that cost less. It had to build a distribution network to reach the home office and small business market. It had to retrain its sales force to propagate a different business model and manage sales channel conflicts. Xerox attempted all of that for over a decade. In 2001, under pressure across its copier business, Xerox abandoned that part of the market and refocused on its dominant logic.

Sources: Chesbrough (2003) and Tellis and Golder (2002). Both books also discuss how the strong dominant logic of Xerox prevented it from benefiting from many computer technology inventions in its Palo Alto Research Centre (PARC) that did not fit its prevailing business model. Only inventions, such as laser printing, which did fit its dominant logic and business model, were exploited by Xerox. Steve Jobs built the success of Apple on the graphical interface technology developed at PARC (see W. Isaacson, *Steve Jobs*, 2011, pp. 94–101)

Our discussions of the *dominant logic* of organizations and the emergence of a *dominant (product) design* that causes the shift from new to maturing markets are, of course, closely interrelated. The dominant logic of firms competing successfully in new markets should focus on creating the dominant product design. An example of this is the competitive battle between retailers and e-tailers (the new Internet-based retailers), as recounted in Box 10.7. Another example is the 'standards wars' that have raged in videorecorder markets and DVD markets between firms trying to establish their standard as dominant for these new technologies. Box 12.2 illustrates the case of the then small Haloid Corporation, which introduced the dominant design of xerography printing and was transformed into the global Xerox corporation as a result.

As soon as a dominant design has been established, however, the basis of the competition shifts and firms then need to focus more on developing a sound business strategy and business model. As commonly used nowadays, the term

Business model

business model refers to three interrelated elements:

- the *value proposition* a company wants to offer its customers;
- the *delivery system* to bring that value through its products or services to the customers; and
- the *profit model* that allows the company to capture its share of the value in terms of profit.

Young start-up firms often find it difficult to work out an appropriate business strategy and business model. They may, for example, continue to emphasize exploration and flexibility, thus showing insufficient commitment to the emerging dominant design. An example of a company that has been very successful in turning a dominant design into a winning business model is Google. Box 12.3 describes the story in the words of Teece (2010).

Box 12.3 Google: from dominant design to winning business model

Search engine development and the Google story is another interesting business model illustration. Early efforts in this field, including Lycos, Excite, Alta Vista, Inktomi and Yahoo, would find lots of information – perhaps too much – and present it to users in an unhelpful manner, with maybe thousands of results presented in no discernible or useful order. Alta Vista presented links, but without using them as aids to searching. Larry Page, one of the founders of Google, surmised that counting links to a website was a way of ranking its popularity (much like higher citation counts in scientific journals point to more important contributions to the literature), and decided to use the number of links to important sites as a measure of priority. Using this link based approach, Page and his colleagues at Google devised an Internet site ranking system – the PageRank algorithm – which went on to be their core product/service offering, and one which has proved very valuable to users. The challenge was to tune the product offering and devise a business model to capture value, which was not easy in a world in which consumers expected search to be free.

The business model developed around Google's product/service innovation required heavy investment in computing power as well as in software. Google writes its own software and (remarkably) builds its own computers. It takes advantage of its considerable computing power to count words and links, and to combine information about words and links. This allows the Google search engine to take more factors into account than others currently in the market. The Google revenue model eschewed funding from advertisers: directed search biased to favour advertisers was perceived by Google's founders as degrading to the integrity of the search process and to its emerging brand. Accordingly, it decided that the essence of its revenue model would be sponsored links i.e. no pop-ups or other graphics interfering with the search. In short, Page and Brin found a way to accommodate advertising (thereby enabling revenue generation) without subtracting from the search experience, and arguably enhancing it. However, they also adopted an integrated approach (by fulfilling their own software and hardware requirements) to keep control of their product/service offering, ensuring its delivery and its quality.

Source: D. J. Teece (2010), Business Models, Business Strategy and Innovation, *Long Range Planning* Vol. 43, pp. 172-194. See also D.A. Vise (2005), *The Google Story*, New York: Bantam Dell.

Incumbent firms, which have enjoyed success with a particular dominant logic for a long time, find it just as difficult to adjust their *modus operandi* when radically new technologies emerge that have the potential to erode their basis of competition. Again, Box 12.2 illustrates this point. Xerox found that it was unable to compete against the Japanese dominant design developed for the low-cost segment of small business and home office copying. In effect, the Japanese split the copying market in two, with different firms competing on the basis of different competences in the two segments.

All these examples show that there is coevolution between markets and firms. As markets change (in their structure and basis of competition), organizations have to adapt. Conversely, successful innovations and adaptations by firms change the market conditions.

All in all, complexity theory allows us to see the organization as a complex, adaptive system that has several levels of analysis. Each level acts as a building block for the next higher level. At the same time, each level cannot be completely explained by understanding the lower levels. In that sense, each level leads a life of its own. Each is subject to internal as well as external selection. For instance, in organizations, there is internal selection of competing views, routines, proposals and so on and there is external selection (by the environment) acting on the resulting organizational configuration of strategy, structure and capabilities.

Organizations and their relevant environments (including markets) coevolve. Organizations can adapt, but it is a process that can lead as often to failure as it does to success. We are beginning to see some of the mechanisms that underly those processes. A better understanding of these phenomena is of utmost theoretical as well as practical significance.

Questions

1 Which definitions of the firm have been given in this book? Indicate for each definition how coordination between several (groups of) people within the firm is achieved.

2 Consider Boxes 12.2 and 12.3. What relevance do these extracts have for the discussion in the text of Bettis and Prahalad's view on dominant logics and organizational adaptability (through learning)?

Note

1 In Burgelman's (2002) terminology, it is the interplay of variation-reducing induced strategic processes with variation-enhancing autonomous processes that produces the pattern of strategic behaviour.

Part III

Applications

13 Mergers and acquisitions

13.1 Introduction

On 10 January 2000, America OnLine (AOL) bid $166 billion for Time Warner in an all-stock offer. AOL was an Internet-based company offering e-mail and messenger services. As such, it was a delivery company with little content. Time Warner, however, was a formidable content company, based on the successes of *Time* magazine, the Warner Brothers movie studio and Turner Broadcasting Systems (owning cable networks).

Steven Case, CEO of AOL, argued that the companies therefore formed a perfect match. They were strongly complementary and could offer the best of both worlds: the 'old world' of content delivered by magazines, books and films and the 'new world' of Internet-based delivery of such content. Jerry Levin, CEO of Time Warner, felt that his company might have missed the Internet revolution and probably saw the merger as a fast route to catch up. Both CEOs promised substantial synergies of the merger at about $1 billion.

After the successful completion of the merger bid, the company renamed itself AOL Time Warner. Shortly thereafter, problems started to emerge.

The new business model did not work as anticipated. Cross-selling Time Warner content to AOL customers proved to be a difficult proposition.

AOL's mail system was largely based on dial-up and not yet on broadband. When the company ordered all employees to switch to AOL e-mail, Time Warner employees rebelled: they complained that the AOL system could not handle large digital files. Executives had to rescind the e-mail mandate.

Another synergy should have come from package deals for advertisers: 'space in *Time* magazine, air time on Turner cable networks, spots on AOL, and licensing opportunities with Warner Brothers film studio'. That synergy also failed to materialize.

Perhaps most importantly, the cable system executives in Time Warner resisted carrying AOL on their system, preventing the AOL switchover to broadband.

Problems accumulated to the extent that Jerry Levin stepped down as CEO in December 2001 and Steven Case as chairman in January 2003. In September 2003 the company changed its name back to Time Warner and AOL became one of its divisions. In the process, an enormous amount of 'shareholder value' was first (seemingly) created and then destroyed. (Figure 13.1 shows the development of the Time Warner share price from 1996 to 2005). On the merger

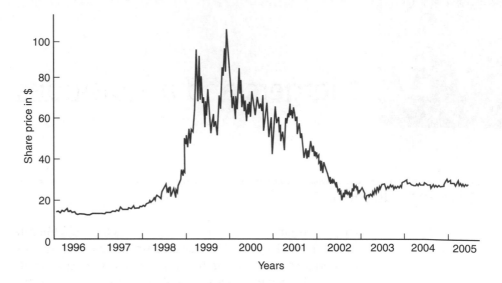

Figure 13.1 Share price, Time Warner, 1996–2005

announcement date of 7 January 2000, AOL and Time Warner had market values of $165 billion and $76 billion respectively – a combined value of $241 billion. By the end of 2004, the combined value of the two firms had slumped to $78 billion, about the same as Time Warner's standalone value at merger. This downward trend continued until 2009, when Time Warner finally decided to spin off AOL. On 9 December 2009 AOL became a separate independent company again. Jerry Levin apologized in 2010 to have 'presided over the worst deal of the century, apparently'.

From this example of Time Warner, it is already clear that mergers and acquisitions (M&A) can be a dangerous route to growth for companies. In this chapter we will examine the risks from an economic point of view, using the concepts introduced in previous chapters. At the same time, it is also obvious that many successful companies of today have succeeded in executing M&A in an effective way. General Electric (GE) has transformed itself from a lighting company into a broad service and industrial company. M&A has been a very important tool to accomplish this transformation and GE is today still regarded as a skilful acquirer.[1] In the oil industry, Royal Dutch Shell is the result of the successful merger of the Dutch firm Koninklijke Olie with the British firm Shell Transport and Trading Company, while British Petroleum (BP) acquired its American rival Amoco in 1998 and Exxon reacted by acquiring Mobil in 1999. M&A has been instrumental in these oil companies gaining the required scale to compete on a global basis. Apparently, they have also managed to handle the risks involved in such transactions. In this chapter, we will also look at some solutions that have evolved as answers to the risks inherent in M&A.

Acquisition

First, a short introduction to the terminology of M&A. An **acquisition** occurs when one company takes a controlling ownership interest in another firm (or in a subsidiary or selected assets of another firm). Acquisitions may also be called

Takeovers

takeovers.

Merger

A **merger** is a combination of two or more firms in which all but one cease to exist, and the combined organization continues under the name of the surviving firm. In practice, the terms 'mergers' and 'acquisitions' are often loosely lumped together: acquisitions are often presented as 'mergers' to give them a more equal and friendly appearance.

From an economic point of view, business combinations can also be classified as horizontal, vertical and conglomerate mergers (or acquisitions). A **horizontal merger** is between two competitors in the same industry. A **vertical merger** occurs when two firms combine across the value chain, such as when a firm buys a former supplier (backward integration) or a former customer (forward integration). When there is no strategic relatedness between an acquiring firm and its target, this is called a **conglomerate merger**. Conglomerate mergers are a case of unrelated diversification, as discussed in Chapter 10. Such a classification is used by, for example, the antitrust authorities to evaluate whether or not they can approve M&A in the context of competition policy. In principle, an antitrust authority such as the Federal Trade Commission (FTC) in the USA will disallow any acquisition that has the potential to generate monopoly or oligopoly profits in an industry.

Horizontal merger

Vertical merger

Conglomerate merger

We will discuss the broad field of M&A as follows. We start out by further indicating the significance of M&A and examining the evidence for the success and failure of M&A transactions. We then delineate the M&A process from the buyer's and from the seller's side, pointing out that many M&A transactions are structured as **auctions**. The fundamental problem in such auctions is the **information asymmetry** between the seller and the buyer(s). Such information asymmetry leads to the problems that we encountered in Chapter 4: **hidden information (adverse selection)** and **hidden action (moral hazard)**. There is also the danger that the winner of the auction will experience the **winner's curse**.

Auctions

Information asymmetry

Hidden information (adverse selection)

Hidden action (moral hazard)

Winner's curse

Some types of M&A may suffer from problems due to **transaction specificity** and the possibility of **hold-up**.

Transaction specificity

Hold-up

Finally, we also examine the **agency relationship** between managers and shareholders with respect to incentive alignment for making the right type of M&A transactions and appropriate **corporate governance** after the transaction.

Agency relationship

Corporate governance

13.2 The significance of M&A

The volume and value of M&A are enormous. For 2007, the last peak in M&A activity, estimates are that more than 10,000 M&A transactions took place with a total value of $4.83 trillion. In order to realize the magnitude of that figure let us write it out: $4,830,000,000,000 changed hands in 2007 as a result of mergers and acquisitions. Clearly, this extent to which firms change ownership is of great significance for managers, shareholders, employees and societies alike.

Figure 13.2 gives an overview of the development of M&A in the period 2003–2011. It shows that M&A activity has been cyclical, with peaks (2006–2007) and troughs. Indeed, such a pattern has been typical over time.

Value of deals (USD bn)   **Volume of deals**

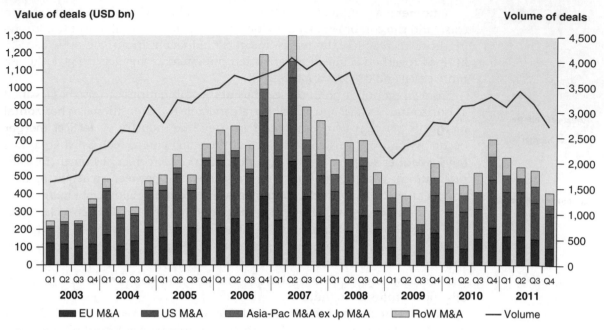

Source: Mergermarket M&A Round-up for Year End 2011, January 2012

Figure 13.2 Global M&A activity

| Merger waves |

Economists talk of **merger waves** and have identified six such waves so far. In Box 13.1 the five waves for the USA in the nineteenth and twentieth centuries are discussed and the evolving reasons for such waves over time are indicated.

Box 13.1 The merger waves of the 19th and 20th century

The first merger wave began after the worldwide depression of 1883, which left many capital-intensive industries with overcapacity, and ended in the early 1900s. This wave involved roughly one-sixth of all US manufacturing firms. Some combinations that arose at this time, such as Standard Oil and United States Steel, were able to monopolize their industries. A second, smaller merger wave occurred in the early 1920s. Antitrust laws, such as the Sherman Act and the Federal Trade Commission Act, discouraged grabs for monopoly power that failed to promote increased efficiency. As a result, many combinations stopped short of achieving 50 per cent market share, and their industries resembled oligopolies instead of monopolies. Other combinations involved vertical, rather than horizontal, integration. The formation and growth of General Motors during this time displayed both types of integration.

The reasons for the first two merger waves are easy to understand. Firms in the same market combined to reduce competition and achieve scale economies. The emergence of manufacturing giants tilted the calculus of the make-or-buy decision in favor of vertical integration. The Great Depression of the 1930s and American participation in World War II put a damper on merger activity until 1950.

By 1960, the pace of merger activity had again quickened. Unlike the previous waves, this third wave featured increased levels of unrelated diversification and produced large conglomerates selling extensive product lines in diverse markets. Mergers in the 1960s resulted in firms such as American Can, which sold cans, clothing and financial services, and ITT, whose business portfolio included life insurance, car rental, hotels and vending machines.

The mergers of the 1980s again differed markedly from their predecessors. Some cash-rich firms, lacking solid investments in their own businesses, instead attempted to grow through acquisition. Philip Morris, flush with cash from the tobacco business, bought 7-Up in 1978, General Foods in 1985, and Kraft in 1988. Some economists have argued that the fourth merger wave was a reaction to the poor performance of the conglomerations formed during the third wave. The merger wave of the 1980s also saw the emergence of the 'leveraged buy-out' in which the company was purchased by not another firm, but by a group of private investors (with heavy reliance on debt as a means of financing the transaction).

The fifth merger wave began in the mid-1990s and ended in 2001. Deals made during this period included Exxon-Mobil, Pfizer-Warner Lambert, Chrysler-Daimler Benz, Vodafone-Mannesmann and AOL-Time Warner. Drivers of this merger wave included: (1) firms desired to establish dominant market shares within specific industries; (2) firms desired access to international markets, (3) high stock market valuations and perhaps (4) a more permissive regulatory environment. Merging firms were usually 'related' businesses. This wave came to an end with the burst of the dot.com bubble and the ensuing recession in the beginning of this millennium.

Source: Besanko et al. (2012) and M. Lipton (2006), 'Merger waves in the 19th, 20th and 21st centuries, The Davies lecture, York University, 14 September 2006

As Figure 13.2 shows, a new wave started in the beginning of the twenty-first century and reached the most recent peak in M&A activity in 2006–2007. Probable reasons for this international wave of M&A include the following:

- *Globalization* Many companies found that they were increasingly confronted with global competition. They aspired to obtain global leadership in their business areas. This was also fostered by the lowering of trade barriers as a result of the cooperation in the World Trade Organisation (WTO). Therefore, industry consolidation took place not only at the national or regional levels but also on an international scale. The number of cross-border and intercontinental deals has been steadily rising. Some countries contributed to this trend by encouraging their national champions to become 'global champions'.
- *Strong cash flows* After the slump in the years 2001–2003, the global economy showed a good performance, generating strong cash flows and healthy balance sheets for many companies. Confidence was rising that this positive development would continue for some time. Strong demand from emerging economies, such as China and India, boosted consumption of many products. Commodity prices were high and companies tried to secure their resource base. Even rather mature industries, such as steel, benefited from this trend. As a result, the steel industry witnessed its own international merger wave with Mittal (India) buying Arcelor (Europe) and Tata (India) buying Corus (Europe)

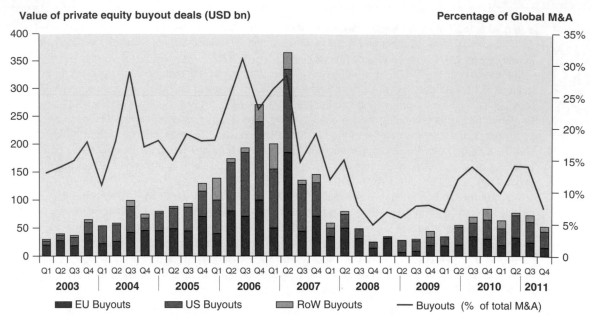

Figure 13.3 Global private equity buyout activity

- *Private equity* Financing was relatively cheap (in fact too cheap, we would find out later) and private equity funds, among others, used such sources to pursue ever more and larger deals. In 2007, Blackstone bought Equity Office Properties for $38.9 billion while the ownership of Energy Future Holdings passed to KKR, TPG and Goldman Sachs for $44.4 billion. In many industries, about 25–30 per cent of all deals in late 2006 and early 2007 were done by private equity players (see also Figure 13.3). Favourable debt markets enabled these acquirers to finance their deals with high leverage. We will come back to private equity towards the end of this chapter.

- *Hedge funds and 'shareholder activism'* In 2007, after acquiring 1 per cent of the shares of major Dutch bank ABN AMRO, the British hedge fund TCI led an attack demanding the bank split up or sell to the highest bidder to produce shareholder value. ABN AMRO was ultimately split and sold to Royal Bank of Scotland (RBS), Fortis, and Banco Santander for nearly $100 billion. The takeover was ill-timed and unsuccessful and was a major contributing factor in the downfall of both RBS and Fortis when the credit crisis of 2008 struck. Hedge funds like TCI specialized in such 'event-driven strategies' that allowed them to make handsome profits on their acquired stakes.

In view of the major significance of M&A, it is important to know how successful these transactions are. Failure of major M&A transactions can have dramatic consequences for the managers and shareholders of the companies concerned, as we saw in the AOL-Time Warner example discussed in the introduction to this chapter. The consequences may also extend to the employees of the firm, its suppliers and customers, as well as local communities and society at large, as illustrated by the RBS and Fortis bail-outs necessitated by the ABN AMRO takeover.

So, what do we know about the factors contributing to success and failure of M&A transactions? The next section attempts to summarize our present knowledge.

13.3 Success and failure of M&A transactions

The fact that not all M&A transactions are successful has not escaped the notice of the popular press. For example, *Business Week* magazine regularly reviews the success rate of acquisitions, making observations such as, '*Business Week* investigations in 2002 and 2004 showed that 61 per cent of big deals hurt the company's shareholders. Half of them also leave customers dissatisfied' ('Have dealmakers wised up?' *Business Week*, 21 February 2005). What, though, do we know about the success and failure of M&A from solid research?

Corporate finance

Industrial organization

Event studies

Most empirical M&A research has been done from the perspective of either **corporate finance** or **industrial organization**. Different research tools are used in each tradition. Below we summarize the main findings from both perspectives.

Finance researchers use the research tool of **event studies**. They investigate the movement of share prices when there is an acquisition announcement. If the share price of a company shows an 'abnormal' upward movement, that is interpreted as revealing that the shareholders regard the acquisition announcement as good news. If the share price does not move, it is assumed that the acquisition had already been anticipated by the markets. If the share price shows 'abnormal' downward movement, the acquisition is regarded as bad news.

An early survey of such event studies by Jensen and Ruback (1983) showed that the shareholders of target firms typically achieve abnormal returns of 20–30 per cent around the time of an announcement, while shareholders of the bidding companies more or less break even. Overall, the findings have been corroborated in subsequent research. The outcomes were interpreted as demonstrating that acquisitions create value by allocating the assets of the acquired firm to a more efficient management team. If that is the case, then it can be said we observe an efficient market for corporate control.

There is an obvious problem, however, with event studies that concentrate on share price movements around the announcement date. If you look back to Figure 12.1, the problem is clear: the market can be very excited about an acquisition when it is announced, but may be disappointed about the real value of the transaction as it unfolds. Finance researchers have, therefore, tried to lengthen the window of their observations to several years around the announcement date. What they have found is that bidders typically show positive abnormal returns before they make an acquisition announcement and negative abnormal returns thereafter. Tichy (2002) summarized these studies with long windows, quoting Andrade et al. (2001):

> It reveals a clear trend of declining abnormal bidder returns, starting from say +20% five years before the announcement to some –5% two years after and about –10% five years after ... These results confront the hypothesis of efficient capital

markets no less than the hypothesis of value-creating acquisitions: 'In fact, the shareholders of the acquiring firm appear to come dangerously close to actually subsidizing these transactions'.

All in all, event studies reveal that, around the announcement of a takeover, the target's abnormal returns increase steeply, while the bidder's returns remain unchanged at best. After the acquisition, increasing negative abnormal returns prevail, implying a negative wealth effect on the shareholders of the acquiring company. These findings raise the question as to what the overall net effect of M&A transactions is. Is the gain of the winners higher or lower than the loss of the losers? The overall net economic gain from M&A deals appears to be positive: almost all studies report positive returns for the investors in the combined buyer and target firms. That would imply that M&A *does* create value from an overall economic point of view, presumably by transferring assets to management teams that use them more efficiently (Bruner, 2005, M&A Research Centre (MARC), 2011).

Industrial organization researchers use a different research toolbox, named **outcome studies**. Outcome studies compare pre- and post-M&A performance of firms with other firms in their industry, with matching firms or with performance projections. While event studies use a single performance measure (abnormal returns), outcome studies use multiple measures, such as cash flow, profits or performance ratios (return on sales, assets or equity).

Summarizing the results of 36 such outcome studies, Tichy (2002) found that profits come out weaker than in the respective non-merging control group in 58 per cent of the studies and stronger in only 11 per cent. This overall result across outcome studies is consistent with the long-term result of event studies. The combined sales of the two companies are hardly affected in about half of the outcome studies, but are lower in about one third of the cases. That is in spite of the tendency for consumer prices to rise post-acquisition. Investments are not necessarily reduced, but combined R&D may be lowered. Assets are restructured. A few studies report slightly reduced labour costs, but not much is known about lay-offs. Manager turnover, however, is observed in about half of the M&A transactions.

Finally, there is increasing evidence that 'serial acquirers' are more successful with M&A than companies who only make an acquisition occasionally. For instance, McKinsey (2012) found that 'the more deals a company did, the higher the probability it would earn excess returns.' In the terminology of our strategy Chapters 9 and 10 this may be interpreted as the creation of a *dynamic capability* for making successful acquisitions as a way to extend the firm's resource base. Serial acquirers learn by doing (more often). Interestingly, Ernst & Young (2011) find that the 'serial transactor advantage' applies even more to the cross-border acquisitions than to domestic deals.

Other research results include the following:

- Acquisitions or takeovers are much more prevalent than mergers of 'equals'. Typically, a bidder – large by the standards of its industry – acquires a target that is much smaller, and small by the standards of its industry as well.
- Bidder and target are at least as profitable as their respective industries in four out of five cases, but the bidder, generally, is more profitable than the target.
- The bidder tends to grow faster than its industry and faster than the target.

- The shares of the bidder tend towards overvaluation and positive abnormal returns in the year before the acquisition, while those of the target rather tend towards negative abnormal returns.
- Focus-increasing acquisitions tend to show relatively the best results, followed by related and horizontal acquisitions, while unrelated acquisitions (diversifications) and conglomerate mergers fare worst.
- Larger deals are in general more risky than smaller deals. However, in mature industries there is value in large deals that reduce excess capacity.
- Cash offers are more likely to have positive returns than share offers.
- Returns to buyers will likely be lower if M&A markets are 'hot' (around the peaks of the M&A waves).
- All in all, the best approximation of the success and failure rates of acquisitions in general is around 50–50.

From this overview of research results with respect to the success of M&A, it is clear that shareholders of target companies stand to gain most, particularly if they receive cash. If they receive shares of the acquiring company, they may want to consider selling them as the likelihood of abnormal negative returns in the medium term is significant. For the acquiring companies and their shareholders, M&A transactions are clearly risky from the point of view of subsequent performance. For effects on other stakeholders, less robust research results are available, but some evidence suggests that consumers may suffer higher prices and employees slightly reduced labour costs.

Next to the shareholders, it is the stakeholder group of management that is affected most, given the significant likelihood of management turnover. Indications are that almost 70 per cent of target-firm's top management team members depart in the five years following completion of the takeover (Krug & Aguilera, 2005). In that sense, our opening example of AOL-Time Warner is illustrative. The transaction led to the departures of both CEOs in a relatively short period of time.

In the next sections, we will further examine M&A transactions mainly from a managerial point of view. We will first ask how buyers and sellers may come to such transactions and which M&A processes are then likely to be employed. Then, we focus on the risks involved in such transactions and the evolution of ways and means to address such risks. From the overview of the M&A research in this section, however, you may conclude that those ways and means are obviously not yet perfect.

13.4 Strategy, acquisitions and hidden information

In Chapters 9 and 10, we examined the economic contributions to the field of strategic management. We distinguished between the *competitive strategy* of single business units and the *corporate strategy* of multibusiness firms. In Figure 9.1, we showed the process of strategic planning in a multibusiness firm. In such a process, the firm will have to determine whether or not it can achieve its goals of growth and further development on its own strength. If so, we say that it can pursue a strategic course of **organic (internal) growth and development**. If organic growth and development

Organic (internal) growth and development

External growth and development (through M&A)

is insufficient, however, the option of **external growth and development (through M&A)** can be considered. In Chapter 10, we specifically looked at the strategies of vertical integration, diversification and horizontal multinationalization. While such strategies can be pursued organically, in practice they will often be executed via M&A. In such cases, firms will enter the M&A market as buyers.

Divestment

A firm may, alternatively, come to the conclusion that **divestment** is a strategic option to consider. This may apply to the whole firm, such as in the case of a family firm without family members in the next generation to succeed the present owner-managers. Another case might be the national firm that is faced with the choice to either compete with global competitors or sell out to them in time. It may also apply to a multibusiness firm that has come to the conclusion that certain activities no longer belong to its core business. In all these examples, companies enter the M&A market as sellers.

So, there are potential buyers and sellers of business assets. Does that automatically lead to a market for M&A? The answer is no. Buyers and sellers in the M&A market, in principle, face the same basic difficulty as those in the market for used cars: **hidden information**.

Hidden information

Sellers may have private information as to the assets they are selling. Buyers have private information as to the value they would be willing to attach to those assets. Such private information is unobservable by the other party. As explained in Chapter 4, such information asymmetries may have the consequence that certain transactions are impossible to execute or can only be concluded at a severe discount.

Market for 'lemons'

The classic reference on this subject is to Akerlof's (1970) article on the **'the market for lemons'**. In the article, Akerlof explained the discount that sellers of almost new used cars would have to accept because of the problem of hidden information they might have regarding the quality of the car offered for sale. That discount may be so great that it prevents the successful conclusion of a transaction.

The above problem manifests itself in exactly the same way in the M&A market. The seller of a business may also have hidden information on the quality of the business, its future prospects and its inherent risks. If buyers suspect such hidden information, a transaction will be hindered (see Box 13.2). In Chapter 4, we argued that market participants, therefore, have an incentive to come up with solutions to those information problems. In the remainder of this chapter we will introduce the solutions that have evolved for problems of asymmetrical information in M&A transactions.

Box 13.2 How M&A targets can be like used cars

In 2001, George Akerlof, Michael Spence and Joseph Stiglitz shared the Nobel Memorial Prize in Economic Sciences for their work on information economics.

The classic 'market for lemons' example offered by Professor Akerlof describes how the market for used cars can fail because of the information asymmetries between a buyer and seller that arise due to the latter's experience of the vehicle. In the absence of appropriate remedies, such as warranties, reputation and so on, buyers will discount their offer prices for all used cars and, as a consequence, the sellers of high-quality vehicles will no longer be willing to trade.

Indeed, information asymmetries crop up in an array of settings, including M&As. During M&A valuation and negotiation processes, an acquirer needs to be able to discern the value of a target and the parties need to agree on a price for the transaction. The acquiring company collects information on the target during the due diligence process, yet it often still remains at an information disadvantage in M&A negotiations. Buyers, therefore, face the risk of 'adverse selection' or overpaying and winding up with a 'lemon'.

Because M&A targets can have attributes that are only understood after purchase, costly surprises emerge during the post-merger integration process. For their part, sellers have an incentive to misrepresent the quality of the company and realize higher gains from the deal.

In short, the seller has a credibility problem that is rooted in the one-shot nature of sell-outs, so its claims will be discounted accordingly. As a result, sellers of good companies run the risk of not receiving fair value for their assets. Therefore, it is in each party's interests to address the problems posed by information asymmetries in M&As. Academics in strategic management and financial economics are now using the insights from information economics to understand when asymmetrical information can adversely affect the efficiency of acquisitions, what remedies might be available and how buyers and sellers can design deals to address these challenges.

Source: Reuer and Ragozzino (2006)

13.5 Auctions

How do the buyers and sellers meet in the M&A market?

A possibility is, of course, that a seller approaches a specific buyer (or a buyer approaches a specific, potential seller) to see whether or not a private negotiation is possible. If both parties agree, they can have an 'exclusive' discussion. That happens, for instance, when two parties want to explore the opportunity for a 'friendly merger of equals'. It is, however, usually to the advantage of sellers to organize some competition for assets to be sold. Therefore, the vast majority of M&A transactions take place through some form of *auction*.

As explained in Chapter 5, auctions are designed to force bidders to reveal their true preferences and their private information as to the valuation of the assets being auctioned. It is, therefore, a mechanism for promoting the efficient allocation of the assets to be sold to the bidder with the highest private valuation of those assets.

In the auction process, the information asymmetry between buyers and seller can be reduced in order to address uncertainties the buyers may have as to the quality of the assets for sale.

How is such an auction organized? See Box 13.3 for an indication. Usually, the seller engages the services of an investment bank to assist in the auction process. Firms such Goldman Sachs, Morgan Stanley and Rothschild are well-known examples. Together with the investment bank, the seller prepares an **information memorandum**. In the information memorandum (IM), the seller supplies basic data on the company to be sold, such as:

Information memorandum

■ historic and projected sales, cash flows and profits;
■ industry and market data;

- descriptions of assets and technologies;
- profiles of the management team.

The investment bank explores potential interest for the company to be sold (sometimes using condensed information in a 'teaser'). In the first stage of the auction, the IM is sent to potential buyers who have expressed an interest, together with a 'process letter', which outlines the rules and procedures of the auction. The IM can, of course, be understood as the first step towards reducing the information asymmetry between the seller and the potential buyers. It allows interested parties to submit an **indicative bid**.

Indicative bid

Indicative bids contain a preliminary price indication, while the buyer often also lists the further information he requires to come to a firm offer for the company (a so-called 'binding bid'). Such information may include, for instance, the content of the R&D pipeline, the specifics of the customer base, the details of the employment contract and other sensitive information not yet included in the 'teaser'. In addition the indicative bid may specify conditions that still have to be fulfilled (such as shareholder approval of the final bid).

On the basis of the indicative bids, the seller can determine which parties are admitted to the second stage of the auction.

Note, however, that an IM contains only basic data. As it may be distributed to several parties, potentially including competitors, the seller will be reluctant to supply sensitive information. Two further steps to reduce the information asymmetry are therefore included in the design of the second stage of a standard auction:

Data room

- The preparation of a **data room**, containing a much wider variety of more detailed data on the business; data rooms used to be physical (containing hard copies of relevant documents), but are increasingly 'virtual' (electronic).

Management presentations

- **Management presentations**, allowing potential buyers to interact directly with the management of the company to be sold in a question and answer session.

Box 13.3 A typical auction process

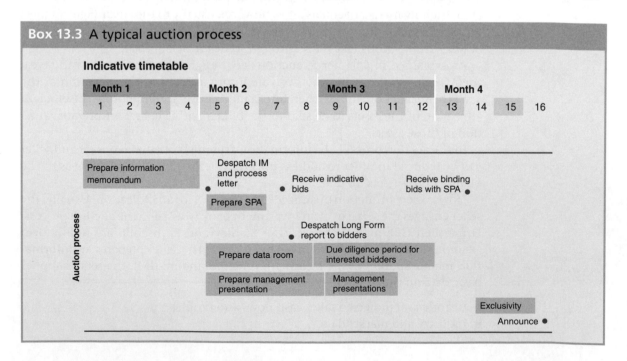

Due diligence process

The data room and the management presentations are elements of the **due diligence process** any serious buyer will have to conduct. Other elements of the due diligence process may include, for example, plant visits and expert meetings (where functional experts can delve deeply into complex topics, such as tax or environmental issues). All elements of the due diligence process together should enable buyers to reach the required 'comfort level' regarding the information obtained on the characteristics of the target company. In all these ways, the auction process is designed to narrow the information gap between buyers and seller.

Binding bid

Sales and Purchase Agreement (SPA)

At the end of the second stage of the auction, buyers submit a **binding bid**. A binding bid is usually based on a **Sales and Purchase Agreement (SPA)**[2] that has been negotiated in the meantime between buyer and seller. The SPA formulates the terms and conditions agreed between the parties in this transaction. Box 13.4 lists a number of typical clauses found in a SPA contract. Such contracts can run to hundreds of pages for complicated deals (and when American lawyers are involved).

Box 13.4 Typical clauses in a Sales and Purchase Agreement (SPA)

- *Definitions and Interpretation* To avoid confusion regarding terminology.
- *Scope* Business or assets being sold.
- *Consideration* Type and amount of payment.
- *Completion* How to proceed from signing the SPA to closing the transaction.
- *Closing accounts* How to draw up the financial statements at closing.
- *Transfer of property* Special clauses as to land or intellectual property (patents), for example.
- *Business liabilities* How to deal with identified liabilities, such as pensions or claims.
- *Contracts* How to deal with contracts with other parties, such as change of control clauses.
- *Representations* Statements about the current status of the business or its operations.
- *Warranties* Guarantees of the truth of statements made.
- *Indemnities* Promises by the seller to compensate buyers for specific damages or losses.
- *Conditions precedent* Conditions that have to be fulfilled before the contract comes into effect (antitrust clearance, for example).

Several of the clauses may further address any information problems involved in the transaction. In the 'representations and warranties', for instance, the seller will confirm the veracity of statements made during the sales process. Here the buyer has the chance to list the factors that are of particular importance to the value of the business for the buyer. The seller confirms the truthfulness of the statements made about particular aspects of the business. These clauses, therefore, counteract the potential for

Opportunism

opportunism on the part of sellers. As discussed in Chapter 8, opportunism is the possibility of making 'self-disbelieved statements'. By including such statements in the SPA and having the seller sign off on their truthfulness, the buyer has legal recourse if the statements turn out to be untrue after all. Here are two examples of such statements:

- *Tax liabilities* To the Seller's knowledge, there is no dispute or claim concerning any tax liability of the Company either claimed or raised by any authority in writing.
- *Inventories* All of the Company's inventories, materials and supplies consist of items in good condition and usable or saleable in the ordinary course of business. The values of the inventories stated in the financial statements reflect the Company's normal inventory valuation policies and were determined in accordance with generally accepted accounting principles, practices and methods consistently applied.

Breached representations and warranties are the most common causes of litigation after acquisitions. This illustrates that the problems of hidden information and opportunism are very real in M&A transactions. In an auction process, such problems can be reduced, but hardly ever completely eliminated. Nevertheless, negotiating and agreeing a SPA can give both parties sufficient comfort to proceed and complete the second stage of the auction process – the buyers submitting binding bids and the seller selecting the best bidder.

When a seller has received the binding bids of the potential buyers, accompanied by the SPAs outlining the agreed terms and conditions, this provides a basis for making the final selection of the best buyer. As a last stage in the process, a short period of 'exclusivity' may be granted to that buyer. During the exclusivity period, some last items of the most sensitive information may be shared. Examples of such commercially sensitive items are the terms and conditions of the main customer contracts.

The description of the M&A auction process in this section has served to illustrate how its design is geared toward addressing the information asymmetry between the seller and potential buyers. As the auction process proceeds, more detailed and more sensitive information is supplied to an increasingly smaller group of bidders. By gradually narrowing the information gap, buyers can reach a sufficient 'comfort level' to complete the transaction. They form an increasingly solid basis for their bids.

By addressing the specific information needs of the buyers, the seller enables them to assess their value drivers in the deal in a progressively better way. That may lead to upward revisions of their bid range.

By including sufficient competition in the auction (until the very last stage of exclusivity), there is a strong pressure on buyers to reveal their true preference for a price and submit the highest bid they can. The auction process promotes the efficient allocation of the assets to be sold – namely, to the bidder with the highest private valuation.

The widespread use of auctions for M&A transactions can be understood as a way to increase the level of competition in such transactions. Competitive bidding may help to explain why shareholders of target companies do receive abnormal returns on announcement of a deal, while shareholders of the acquiring firm do not. The competitive pressure on the acquiring firm to 'give away' a large part of that private value has been quite high. As a result, they can end up paying 'full value' for the target or more (see Box 13.5 and the next section).

Box 13.5 The Corus auction

In 2007, the UK Takeover Panel took the unusual step of deciding a bidding war for the British-Dutch steelmaker Corus by organizing an auction. The case shows the power auctions have to extract full prices from competitive bidders.

The bidding war had been started off in October 2006 by the Indian group Tata making an all-cash bid of 455 pence per share for Corus, which was recommended by the Corus Board. In November, the Brazilian company CSN announced that it was working on a bid of 475p. Before CSN had a chance to make a formal bid, Tata raised its bid to 500p. CSN struck back and launched an offer of 515p later in December, which was also recommended by the Corus Board.

Rumours circulated about Tata's next move. Worried that the battle would drag on indefinitely, the UK Takeover Panel set a deadline of the end of January and then announced that the outcome would be decided in a ten-hour, nine-round auction.

The auction started at 4.30 p.m. on 30 January and ended at 12 a.m. the next day, when both companies submitted their final sealed bids.

In the meantime, the competitive bidding had driven the price up from 515p to 585p (CSN) and 590p (Tata). CSN's final bid was that it would beat Tata's bid by 5p, up to a maximum of 603p. Tata said that it would top any offer by CSN to an undisclosed maximum above 603p. Therefore, Tata's final winning bid was 608p.

The tit-for-tat bidding war and the subsequent auction had raised the price of Corus' shares from 455p to 608p – an increase of 30 per cent and a cumulative absolute increase of £1.6 billion to £6.7 billion including debt.

Analysts were nearly universally negative about the high price paid. Tata Steel's share price dipped about 10 per cent on the Mumbai stock exchange the following day. Corus' shareholders had enjoyed a 30-fold increase in share price in a four-year period, since Corus had been battling against insolvency.

Reflecting on the process, Ratan Tata, chairman of the Tata group, said that Tata Steel was forced to pay 'very close' to its top price for Corus and almost had to decide between the good of shareholders and India's national pride.

Sources: The Financial Times, January 29 to February 3/4 and Het Financieele Dagblad, 1 February 2007.

13.6 The winner's curse and hubris

By this time, you may have been thinking about our explanation of the *winner's curse* in Chapter 5. You will recall that this phenomenon is where winners of bidding contests prevail, not because the true valuation is highest to them, but because of their optimistic expectations. We illustrated this phenomenon in Chapter 5 with the examples of MBA students bidding in the jar game and with the outcomes of the 3G mobile spectrum auctions in Europe.

The winner's curse applies in M&A transactions as well. *Business Week* on 14 October 2002, published the results of research conducted in M&A transactions announced between 1 July 1995 and 31 August 2001. *Business Week*'s major conclusion was that 'most big deals don't pay off'. Looking at the numbers, 61 per cent of buyers destroyed their own shareholders' wealth. What do the researchers think went wrong? *Business Week* contended that the bidders paid too much, which sounds a lot like the winner's curse. The bidders' CEOs offered an average premium above the target's market price of 36 per cent. 'Executives were brimming with confidence and rich stocks.' It also appears that CEOs were overly optimistic about the synergies that would result from a merger and discounted the difficulties of integrating two companies (Anandalingham and Lucas, 2004; Reuer and Koza, 2000).

Box 13.6 Hubris and 'Ebbers Rex'

Facing up to 85 years in prison for his part in the $11 billion WorldCom fraud case, former CEO Bernie Ebbers can expect to have plenty of time to read up on his Greek mythology. For the ancient Greeks, the formula of great tragedies such as *Oedipus Rex* and *Antigone* was clear: hubris (pride) leads to ate (an act of arrogance offensive to the gods), which results in nemesis (infamy and death). A more contemporary version is 'pride goes before a fall'.

Corporate fraud and the cycle of hubris, ate and nemesis are much more widespread problems than is often assumed. And the cost is much higher than people realize: from 1978 through 2002, federal regulators initiated 585 enforcement actions for financial misrepresentation by publicly traded companies, naming 2310 individuals and 657 firms as potentially liable parties. The legal penalties imposed on individuals and firms are substantial. For example, individuals were assessed $15.9 billion in fines and civil penalties, and 190 managers received jail sentences for financial reporting violations. Companies were assessed an additional $8.4 billion in fines and damages via class-action lawsuits.

This belies a widespread view that financial misrepresentation is disciplined lightly. To the contrary, the Securities and Exchange Commission historically has pursued many enforcement actions for financial misconduct, resulting in substantial legal penalties but also even higher reputational penalties. Punishment is not a remedy, of course, and it is not clear that we have found a good remedy for a complex problem. Corporate governance – at least as it is measured in corporate governance codes, codes of conduct and Sarbanes-Oxley – is not the cause of most major corporate scandals.

In a survey sponsored by the Dutch Employers' Association, I recently examined 25 cases of corporate fraud, studying incentive compensation paid to top management, the reputations of the CEOs, their growth targets, analysts' expectations and corporate governance. I also looked for evidence of overvaluation and studied price movements around the time the fraud was discovered. All cases were recent (since 2000); they were listed firms where top management was directly or indirectly involved in fraud; the fraud was substantial (at least $10 million and 5 per cent of annual profit) and so were the firms (greater than 1000 employees). Their demise accounted for $25 billion of corporate fraud. Here is what I found: surprisingly, the average governance scores for the 25 fraud firms were exactly the same as the scores of the 25 non-fraud firms they were compared to in the study. The problem, I found, wasn't so much governance, but hubris.

Companies, of course, want successful leaders. Once they find one, the new CEO gets increasingly wealthy (in 2000, the average value of stocks and options for the 25 fraud-CEOs was $1.2 billion versus $150 million for the comparison group). He also acquires icon status. He not only becomes well respected, he becomes a corporate celebrity. Precisely because they are successful, these CEOs set increasingly higher targets, for the following reasons: first, in order to remain successful in the stock market and sustain their icon reputation, they must maintain a profit growth of 15 per cent to 20 per cent per year. Second, because of increasing success and fame, the CEO starts to believe that he can make anything happen and develops 'a little bit of a God syndrome,' as a vice-president of WorldCom put it, referring to Mr Ebbers.

Indeed, one of the most interesting findings of my study was the degree to which the firms found guilty of fraud had committed themselves to unrealistic targets. On average, the 25 firms I looked at had 18 per cent yearly growth targets, that's a whopping 230 per cent growth every 5 years. Meanwhile, the non-fraud firms had on average 7 per cent yearly growth targets, or 40 per cent growth over 5 years. Not surprisingly, the CEOs who set such unrealistic targets resort to fraudulent behavior to sustain the appearance of success.

There is, however, something of a silver lining to this story. On the day the frauds I studied became public, on average 29 per cent of the value of the 25 companies vanished into thin air: $73 billion went up in smoke. Savvy investors, however, anticipated these negative effects well in advance: in the year prior to the uncovering of fraud 40 per cent of the market value of the companies had already been lost.

The moral? It's hard to hide hubris, even if you're a superstar CEO.

Source: K. Cools (2005) 'Ebbers Rex', *The Wall Street Journal,* 22 March 2005.

Managerial overconfidence as a potential explanation of the winner's curse in M&A transactions is known as the 'hubris hypothesis'. It was introduced by Richard Roll in 1986.[3] **Hubris** is a word from ancient Greek that today is used to refer to 'exaggerated self-pride or self-confidence, often resulting in fatal retribution' (see Box 13.6). Such overconfidence is not uncommon in decisionmaking, but does it also apply in the context of M&A?

Hubris

In an investment research report by the bank UBS (2004), this question is answered as follows:

One of the key findings of decisionmaking theory is overconfidence. People substantially overestimate the precision of their forecasts. A legendary example is a questionnaire in Sweden where one of the questions was: 'on your driving capabilities, compared with the people you encounter on the road, do you consider yourself to be a below-average, average, or an above-average driver?' Of the participants in the questionnaire, 90 per cent considered themselves above-average.

Overconfidence is highest when dealing with difficult tasks, and in contexts where there is a lot of, but not necessarily helpful, information. We think that M&A situations are prime examples of situations that are prone to yield overconfidence. This would cause CEOs to overestimate their knowledge and attribute excessive weight to private relative to public information. It also tends to lead to situations where risk is underestimated. Overconfidence could explain why corporate management engage in M&A deals, despite the difficult odds of generating positive returns for its shareholders.

Indeed, empirical research shows that corporate executives do show overconfidence in M&A contexts. Hayward and Hambrick (1997) investigated the premiums paid in a sample of 106 large acquisitions and found that:

four indicators of CEO hubris are highly associated with the size of the premium paid: the acquiring company's recent performance, recent media praise for the CEO, a measure of the CEO's self-importance, and a composite factor of these three variables. The relationship between CEO hubris and premiums is further strengthened when board vigilance is lacking—when the board has a high proportion of inside directors and when the CEO is also the board chair.

Malmendier and Tate (2008) use a creative approach to measure CEO over-confidence. They examine the personal decisions of CEOs with respect to the stocks and options they hold in their companies. CEOs are classified as 'over-confident' if they persistently choose to maintain a high degree of exposure to company-specific risk, even if they could diversify that risk by selling some of their company stock and in-the-money options.

Interestingly, their measure of overconfidence is strongly related to press coverage of CEOs as 'confident' or 'optimistic'. Overconfident CEOs are found to conduct more mergers and, particularly, more diversifying acquisitions that are value-destroying.

Outsiders seem to be able to recognize such CEO overconfidence. Using the 'event study' approach, Malmendier and Tate show that the negative market reaction to bids of overconfident CEOs is nearly four times greater than that for non-overconfident CEOs. John et al (2010) corroborate the findings of Malmendier and Tate on the effects of overconfident CEOs of acquiring firms. They add the interesting twist that the overpayment effect is significantly larger if also the CEO of the target firm is overconfident. Again, this seems to be recognized by the stock market: '*ceteris paribus*, the acquiring firm's market price falls on average by no less than 10 to 12% more on deal announcement when *both* acquiring firm and target firm CEO overconfidence exist, than when only one side to the deal, or neither, is overconfident'.

Empirical research therefore supports the contention in the popular press that CEO overconfidence or hubris is a significant factor in explaining the winner's curse and value destruction in M&A transactions. Overpayment is quite a common phenomenon in M&A transactions: a 2006 McKinsey analysis showed the proportion of overpayers to be above 50 per cent across the two recent merger waves.

Box 13.7 Fred the Shred: overconfidence and hubris

Fred Goodwin was the CEO of Royal Bank of Scotland (RBS) at the time this company led the consortium of three banks that took over ABN Amro (the others were Banco Santander from Spain and Fortis from Belgium). He had earned a reputation as a tough dealmaker and integrator of acquired companies. In 2000, RBS made a daring acquisition of NatWest, a bank three times its size. Goodwin's role in this acquisition secured his promotion to CEO in January 2001. He proceeded to cut 18,000 jobs by merging parts of RBS and NatWest. This earned him the nickname "Fred the Shred".

From 2001 to 2007, RBS's assets quadrupled, also due to a number of acquisitions. Moreover, both its cost-to-income ratio and its profits improved significantly. Against this backdrop, the ABN Amro acquisition was made. After it had become clear that this acquisition had turned out disastrously, the Daily Mail reported as follows:

> The arrogance of the disgraced former boss of the Royal Bank of Scotland Sir Fred Goodwin always has been his most striking feature. He was a banker who always knew better than anyone else, was contemptuous of his competitors on the High Street and had convinced himself that when it came to takeovers — whether they were in Britain, the United States, China or, finally, Holland — there was no one to match his genius. Now, we all know differently. His bank has moved from being among the world's largest lenders to corporate dunce.

The loss of £ 28 billion we now know it ran up over the past year is the biggest ever made by a British company and consigns RBS to the fate of public ownership for years, if not decades, to come. Yet to the very end, when he was finally removed from office by the Treasury in November, Goodwin behaved as if he still walked on water. The former chief executive described the process under which the Government poured in new capital in November as 'more like a drive-by shooting than a negotiation'. This despite the fact that his bank was in desperate trouble and almost certainly would have collapsed without the initial slug of £ 20 billion of taxpayers' money injected by Gordon Brown in October 2008.

Goodwin's strategy of rapid growth in the credit-fuelled years of the past decade led him confidently into a merger with ABN Amro which was doomed to failure because of its appalling timing. But he cannot take the blame alone. He was loyally supported by a board of directors which refused to put brakes on the person they regarded as financial maestro. Moreover, he was egged on by City adviser Merrill Lynch and others who earned a great payday from the takeover deal. Most significantly, however, it was his own ego which, ultimately, was his downfall. It made him delusional about the direction of the world economy and his ability to create value when everyone else was losing faith in the credit bubble. As a result of Goodwin's and the bank's hubris, the prosperity not only of the RBS but the whole nation has been betrayed.

Goodwin became *Sir* Fred Goodwin when he was knighted in 2004 for his services to the banking industry. In an exceptional decision, his knighthood was 'cancelled and annulled' by the Queen in 2012.

Source: 'Hubris, overarching vanity and how one man's ego brought banking to the brink', *Daily Mail*, 20 January 2009.

The consultancy firm Accenture published a brochure in 2005 with the title 'Making M&A Pay: Avoiding the winner's curse'. It proudly states:

> With widespread discipline and adherence to M&A best practices, the winner's curse could be stamped out.

The brochure gives a number of admonitions ('separate price from value', 'estimate synergies accurately', 'check their work', 'retain perspective') and maintains that the curse can be staved off by means of proper 'People, Processes, Perspective and Preparation'. Somehow, however, we are less than convinced that we will see no more winner's curses in M&A situations, even when these guidelines are followed.

13.7 Adverse selection: remedies for hidden information

We assume that, by now, you are convinced M&A provide ample opportunities for the problem of hidden information to occur. As a result, you may run into a situation of adverse selection, where you end up having bought a lemon. In the previous sections we outlined some remedies to the problem of hidden information that have evolved over time. In general, these remedies fall into one of the following two categories:

- Equalize access to information (or at least come close). Examples are:
  - auction design with progressive information sharing;
  - due diligence procedures, including data rooms, management presentations and expert meetings.

- Shift risk to the party with the better information. Examples are:
    - representations and warranties: the seller 'represents' the status of the business and 'warrants' the veracity of that representation;
    - indemnities: the seller undertakes to compensate the buyer for specific damages or losses that could occur in the future (such as historic product liabilities or environmental liabilities);
    - escrow accounts: buyer and seller agree that part of the purchase price is set aside (held 'in escrow') until certain conditions of the deal have been met.

These remedies have evolved as elements of M&A processes and SPA contracts. We will now focus on some other solutions to the problem of hidden information that have been examined in economic research. Interestingly, some of these solutions are organizational and some are market-based. M&A therefore, again, illustrates the basic premise of this book, that markets and organizations represent alternative coordination mechanisms for economic transactions. Also, for M&A transactions, the market/organization mix will primarily depend on the information requirements of the situation, as we will show below.

13.7.1 Organizational solutions

In the late 1980s, Philips NV had determined that its $1.55 billion domestic appliances division was no longer a 'core business'. The division was in need of restructuring. It had plants spread across five European countries. Substantial capital investments were needed to develop selected plants into world-class facilities. The division had 14,000 employees. Performance had been below Philips' standards for some time. Despite such problems, Philips' management knew that the division had potentially valuable assets, including good manufacturing skills, well-known brands, world-class design expertise and a pan-European distribution network, making it number two (behind Electrolux) in European market share.

The Whirlpool Corporation was the obvious buyer. It was looking to expand beyond its US base. It wanted to take over a European position in an industry that was rapidly becoming global. Whirlpool believed that it could radically lower the cost base of the business by rationalizing production, sourcing components globally and coordinating production, sales and distribution across countries. Furthermore, Whirlpool was willing to inject investments and technology into the European operations.

Whirlpool's executives, however, were less convinced than Philips' about the potential of the business. They had concerns about the strength of the consumer franchise behind the brands and the loyalty of the dealer network, if the business changed hands. How much time and money would be involved in turning the business around?

Both parties ran the numbers, but their widely different assumptions and information produced valuations that were not even close. A strategically sensible deal was hindered by the issue of price.

Joint Venture (JV)

A **Joint Venture (JV)** proved to be the solution. In 1989, Philips offered Whirlpool a 53 per cent majority stake in its business for $381 million, together with an option to buy the remaining 47 per cent within three years. For Whirlpool, this was an attractive arrangement as it provided an opportunity to learn about the appliances division as an insider and initiate improvement plans before taking over the division entirely.

The JV was created and Whirlpool was able to implement synergies and improvements swiftly. Indeed, the operation was turned around so successfully that Whirlpool exercised its option for the remaining 47 per cent share in 1991 for $610 million. Philips was thus able to exit the business smoothly and on substantially more favourable terms than if it had simply auctioned it in 1989. The price uplift gained by the intermediate step of the JV was estimated at $270 million.

In this example, the organizational solution to the problem of hidden information was to allow Whirlpool to become an 'insider' in Philips' appliance business before fully executing the transaction. It can thus be seen as a mechanism to equalize access to information about the division. Whirlpool was offered access to the private information Philips had about its division. The value of that private information was expressed in the significant price uplift achieved when the option was exercised three years later. To achieve this outcome, both parties were willing to take part of the risks in the JV for the first three years.

Research and case studies note that companies may use such JV-strategies in situations of significant uncertainty and asymmetric information (see Dyer, Kale and Singh, 2004; Reuer and Koza, 2000). Cisco Systems, for example, is widely known to have an acquisition-led strategy, but the company relies on small equity investments as stepping stones for about 25 per cent of its acquisitions. Many other companies have established 'corporate venturing' groups to make such initial small-stake investments in start-up companies before deciding on a full scale acquisition. These arrangements can be understood as the willingness of the potential acquirers to take some (equity) risk in order to gain access to private information about the target firm and, thus, reduce the information asymmetry.

13.7.2 Market solutions

PayPal is an Internet-based payment system, originally set up to allow winning buyers to pay sellers in online auctions. It has good antifraud capabilities. These are valuable as fraud is the major concern for participants in online auctions. For that reason, it attracted the attention of eBay.

Initial public offering (IPO)

At the time, PayPal was a privately held start-up. The two parties were, however, unable to agree on price. PayPal subsequently decided to go public in an **initial public offering (IPO)**, which was effected in February 2002. Shares were offered at $13 each and rose sharply after the IPO to levels around $20. A few months later, in July 2002, eBay made a public share offer for PayPal, which valued the PayPal shares at about $23.60. In total, eBay's offer valued PayPal at $1.5 billion.

How should we understand the PayPal–eBay case? Why could eBay and PayPal not agree on a price earlier when we now know that PayPal offered its shares for $13 to the public and eBay was willing to buy them for $23.60 a few months later? Did eBay initially just make a big mistake or is there another, more rational explanation?

Economic research has suggested a more rational explanation. While, traditionally, IPOs were merely seen as a means of financing a private company, they are now also recognized as a mechanism for reducing information asymmetries. To understand why that is so, consider the following.

Not a lot of historical, public, certified information about small, privately held firms is available, particularly younger ones. They do not publish their financial statements and they are not followed by the community of investment analysts. Moreover, they may suffer from legitimacy problems and the 'liability of newness' that we discussed in Chapter 11. Finally, the major part of the value of entrepreneurial start-up companies comes from future growth opportunities and intangible assets, which are notoriously difficult to value. For all those reasons, there is probably a significant information asymmetry between the company and potential acquirers.

Making the private company public can reduce that information gap in two ways:

- There are substantial information requirements to be met in order to obtain approval for public listing. They involve publishing an Offering Memorandum with extensive disclosures about the company. Also the requirements of stock market regulators must be satisfied. In the USA, it would entail substantial documentation to be submitted to the Securities and Exchange Commission (SEC). Those documents are also public information. Finally, investment analysts examine companies going public and publish their findings and recommendations. In all these ways, the gap between private information and public information about the company is reduced.
- By going public, the company also sends *signals* to potential acquirers. It signals that it is confident that it can pass public scrutiny. It signals that it can bear the costs of going public. It can also signal credibility by selecting reputable investment banks and underwriters to support the IPO. Such institutions then lend their reputation to the firm and bolster its legitimacy by association. All in all, the new issue market can work as a *screening* device. It helps to screen out credible from less credible private companies.

The market for IPOs of private companies thus serves as a 'market solution' for problems of hidden information and adverse selection. Through their initial public listing, companies can disseminate information in a credible way. Their willingness to do so is a strong signal to potential acquirers. In fact, the value of that signal is recognized as being so strong that many businesses are nowadays

Dual track approach

sold in a **'dual track' approach**: they are simultaneously prepared for IPO and divestment to a direct acquirer. The seller can determine at the last moment whether the bids received from interested acquirers are sufficiently high to cancel the IPO. Evidence suggests that 'dual tracking' can offer higher premiums to sellers than outright divestments. In a study by Brau and Kohers (2007) two strategies were distinguished:

- *Dual-track private harvest* The private firm files for an IPO while also courting acquirers. The firm ultimately withdraws the IPO filing and opts to be taken over directly. Firms using this strategy earned a 22–26 per cent higher premium than single-track divestments.

- *Dual-track public harvest* The private firm first completes the IPO and is then taken over as a newly public firm shortly thereafter (the PayPal case). An 18–21 per cent higher premium was achieved by firms using this strategy rather than single-track sell-outs.

Based on such evidence, we can conclude that there is substantial value in the IPO market solution to reducing information asymmetry, even if used as an option only.

In conclusion, we want to reiterate our observation that markets and organizations offer different solutions to the problem of hidden information in M&A situations. Which mix of market and organizational remedies will be optimal in any given situation will primarily depend on the information requirements of that specific situation. Is there an obvious buyer who needs to be convinced that he is not buying a lemon? Then it may be optimal to offer a JV as an intermediate step. Alternatively, are there several potential acquirers who may be concerned about the liability of newness of the target? Then, it might be optimal to go through the IPO market as a screening device. It may also be that the optimality of either route can only be determined as the M&A process unfolds. In such a situation, dual-tracking is an effective way for a seller to keep his options open.

The examples given above illustrate that markets and organizations can complement each other in lowering the M&A transaction costs due to hidden information. As discussed in Chapter 4, hidden information is the *ex ante* information problem. It exists *before* the SPA is written. We next turn our attention to *ex post* information problems, that is, hidden action *after* parties have agreed to execute a transaction.

13.8 Moral hazard: remedies for hidden action

Now you have signed a deal. There has been a ceremony where the SPA has been signed. Pictures were taken to capture the historic moment. Champagne flowed and all parties congratulated each other on the 'tough but fair' negotiations and on the 'win–win result' (and lawyers from both sides on the fees earned). It is unfortunate that you have to wait some more months before the deal can be executed (called the 'closing'), because the antitrust authorities want to examine the deal first and you also need your shareholders' approval. That evening, you feel a headache coming on. Is it the champagne or might there be another cause?

Another cause could be that there are some nagging questions in your mind. Questions such as, what will happen to your target in the months between signing and closing? Will the value you receive be the value you were expecting? Will managers be motivated to run the company in your best interests? Might they have their own agendas? Questions like these could turn your headache into a true migraine if they are not dealt with properly.

Moral hazard

Hidden action

The issues here are related to **moral hazard** – potential **hidden action** that is unobservable by you as a buyer. These issues originate from post-contractual information asymmetries. Remedies to hidden action usually fall into one of the following categories:

- *Contractual arrangements* Clauses in the SPA that specify (and sanction) post-contractual behaviour.
- *Increased observability* Taking measures to improve the information about post-contractual behaviour.
- *Incentive alignment* Putting incentives in place that align the incentives between current owners (and its management) and the new owners.

The categories are not mutually exclusive. For example, there may be contractual arrangements aimed at improving observability or aligning incentives. Below we give some salient examples of each category.

The *contractual arrangements* in the SPA, which are designed to govern post-contractual behaviour, can cover a wide variety of things. Generally, it will be stated in the contract that the seller and its management should continue to run operations 'in the ordinary course of business'. That general clause provides the norm that seller and management should refrain from exceptional behaviour and should run the business according to customary practices. For example, bonus payments should not suddenly be larger than they have customarily been. Specific clauses may deal with specific situations. Parties may, for instance, agree that investments above a certain specified amount need joint approval. Such a clause makes the behaviour of the seller with respect to the most significant investments observable to buyer.

There are further ways to *increase observability* as a remedy to hidden action. Parties will, for instance, agree to draw up closing statements reflecting the financial status of the company at the time of closing, when the ownership of the business is actually transferred. The closing statements will be audited. Through the auditor, the buyer can ascertain that no hidden action has decreased the value of the business. The purchase price will also be adjusted to allow for certain changes in financial items between signing and closing. Any value decreases that may result from the ordinary course of business can be addressed via such adjustments of the purchase price. Examples are changes in working capital or levels of bad debt.

Finally, there are many ways in which hidden action can be countered by *incentive alignment*. Consider the case of a start-up company with an owner-manager who has successfully built up the firm from scratch. He is the originator of the main technology the company has developed and patented. He has personally supervised the development of the main applications of that technology and the contacts with the main customers for those applications.

When a larger firm buys that start-up company, it can of course buy the patents and the customer contracts, but the value of the start-up resides only partially in those assets. The main asset may be the founder of the company with his **tacit knowledge**. How do you motivate him to continue to operate in the best interests of the company *and* the new owners?

Tacit knowledge

If the selling of his company has made this entrepreneur seriously rich and if he dislikes working for a larger company, there may be agency problems ahead. One remedy that has evolved in such situations is the **contingent earn-out**. Under

Contingent earn-out

this arrangement, part of the purchase price is made dependent (contingent) upon future performance. By agreeing to a contingent earn-out, the seller can signal his confidence in the future performance of the business to be sold and the buyer is assured that the seller has significant incentives to contribute to the future performance of the company.

In essence, a contingent earn-out shifts part of the risk back to the party with the best information (the seller). Ragozzino and Reuer (2009) indeed find that the usage of contingent earn-outs increases with information asymmetries surrounding acquisitions, in particular when privately held targets are young or possess knowledge bases that are dissimilar from those of the acquirers.

According to the investment bank J.P. Morgan (2011) the number of earn-out related deals has been on the rise for over a decade. The contingent earn-out is used most widely in the pharmaceutical industry where significant uncertainty surrounds the clinical trials for new drugs in the development pipeline. Large pharmaceutical firms, aiming to boost their own development pipelines, can use them to buy up smaller, innovative firms (often privately held start-ups) working on demonstrating the efficacy of their new products through such clinical trials. Next to their function as risk reduction mechanisms, contingent earn-outs may also serve as retention schemes aimed at securing the stay-on of important employees owning shares in the target company (Kohers & Ang, 2000).

In Section 13.7, we encountered another mechanism that has this virtue: the escrow account. If the buyer and seller agree that part of the purchase price is set aside (held in escrow) until certain conditions of the deal have been met, the seller also agrees to continue to bear part of the risk in the transaction until the firm's performance is clear.

The risk that the value of a target firm is materially affected between signing and closing a deal is also covered by another contractual clause: the **material adverse change (MAC) clause**. A standard MAC clause permits the buyer not to close the transaction on the occurrence of 'any change, occurrence or state of facts that is materially adverse to the business, financial condition or results of operations' of the target company. Note that such a clause creates an incentive for the seller to keep the business in good shape. By introducing the threat that the buyer may walk away if the value of the business is materially affected, the seller is encouraged to continue with value-preserving behaviour. The MAC can, therefore, be seen as a contractual clause aimed at incentive alignment (combining two of our three categories of remedies to hidden action).

Note, however, that the standard MAC clause imposes the risk of break-up of the transaction rather unilaterally on the seller. That is because the value of the business is at risk for two different sets of reasons:

Material adverse change (MAC) clause

Endogenous risk

Exogenous risk

- **endogenous risk** – risk specific to the transaction, including that from hidden action;
- **exogenous risk** – risk of a generic nature, which means that it would affect all similar transactions.

Examples of exogenous risk include major economic slowdowns, changes in applicable laws and regulations and events impacting all firms in an industry (such as the outbreak of animal diseases affecting all meat producers).

Should buyers be able to walk away from deals that are affected by exogenous risk – risks that neither buyers nor sellers could influence or prevent? Realizing that this is probably too harsh a condition for sellers, MAC clauses have come to contain such exceptions over time. Gilson and Schwartz (2005) document that:

> In 1993, only 18.33% of MAC clauses included one or more event specifications that restricted the buyer's right to exit; more than half of these stated a single event. In 1995, the percentage of clauses with an event specification had increased to 31.74% with an average of 0.67 per transaction. By 2000, event specifications had become mainstream: 83% of the acquisition agreements featured at least one MAC exclusion, with an average of 3.75 per transaction.

Modern MAC clauses (with stated exceptions) thus separate the risks of material adverse changes between sellers and buyers. Buyers can walk away from a deal if endogenous risk (including hidden action) materializes. They cannot simply cancel a deal, however, when exogenous risks arise. The spreading of the modern MAC clause is a nice example of the evolution of an institutional arrangement affecting the execution of economic transactions. Recall that, in Chapter 1, we defined institutions as 'the rules of the game in a society or, more formally, the humanly devised constraints that shape human interaction'. The modern MAC clause is such an institutional arrangement, constraining human interaction specifically to contain the risks of moral hazard.

Interestingly, the market has also developed some complementary solutions to the problems of hidden action. The insurance market has contributed some efficient remedies. It has developed a representations and warranties policy that will cover financial losses from false statements made by sellers in an SPA. Box 13.8 describes a case where this market solution contributed to the successful completion of an acquisition transaction. The example shows that a mix of market solutions and organizational solutions (the contract clauses dealing with the integration into the acquiring organization) together allow agency and transaction costs to be lowered to a level where the transaction can be executed.

Box 13.8 The market solution: M&A insurance

In most deals, buyers ask sellers to put at least 10% of a deal's value in escrow. By offsetting some risk with insurance, bidders can slash their escrow requirements, effectively offering the seller more cash up front.

Such insurance was a dealsaver for Michael Alexander, managing partner of EchoBridge Entertainment. Alexander was close to signing a deal to buy Platinum Disc. Platinum had been profitable for years and its books seemed clean. Nevertheless, Alexander was concerned: 'You worry that there's something the sellers aren't telling you – or something that they don't even know about'.

Alexander asked Platinum's owner, Dave Thompson, to set aside a chunk of the sale proceeds in an escrow account until it was clear that the conditions of the deal had been met. When Thompson balked, Alexander bought a representations and warranties policy and let Thompson put a smaller amount in escrow.

It cost EchoBridge $200,000 to cover the deal, which was worth tens of millions of dollars, and Alexander says it was worth it: 'You get millions of dollars in protection and sleep more comfortably'.

The deal closed in February. So far, there have been no surprises.

Source: 'Deal jitters?', *Inc.* magazine, October 2005. See also the topic "M&A insurance" on the website of Chubb insurance company.

13.9 Transaction specificity and hold-up

Transaction specificity of assets

In Chapter 8, we introduced the concept of **transaction specificity of assets**. An asset is transaction-specific if it cannot be redeployed to an alternative use without a significant reduction in its value. We examined the example of Mr P, who wanted to start a local newspaper in Appropria, and Mrs Q, a printer, whom he asks to buy a special printing press for this purpose. The example showed how both parties make transaction-specific investments: Mrs Q in a printing press and Mr P in start-up losses for a new newspaper. As a consequence, they are locked into their relationship.

Hold-up

If either party shows a degree of *opportunism*, it can try to take advantage of that situation by attempting to renegotiate the contract. Economists refer to this possibility as the threat of **hold-up**. Severe threats of hold-up undermine the possibility of even agreeing a transaction.

How can a hold-up problem arise in M&A transactions? For one example, see Box 13.9 where the use of a material adverse change clause to create a hold-up situation is discussed. For a more general discussion, let us return to the AOL-Time Warner deal described at the start of this chapter. This allows us to explore a potential solution to the hold-up problem: the break-up fee.

Box 13.9 A MAC as a hold-up device

A material adverse change (MAC) clause is intended to protect buyers against the (endogenous) risk that a business deteriorates significantly between the moment of signing the deal and the later moment of closing the deal. In the main text, we discuss MACs as an institutional innovation which help to execute M&A transactions because buyers and sellers can agree on an efficient distribution of risks. However, once a MAC has been agreed it can also lead to a situation of *hold-up* with buyers attempting to exploit the MAC clause to their advantage:

'The reason is the way a MAC clause works. A buyer can invoke a MAC clause to try to drive down the price of an acquisition by taking advantage of either changed market conditions or adverse events affecting the target company. In such a case, the seller usually settles at a lower price for two reasons. First, the seller does not want to litigate and argue in court how badly the MAC clause termination stinks. Second, the seller and its shareholders are typically happy to take the lower premium than risk litigation and an adverse decision resulting in no deal at all. This same dynamic also pushes a buyer to settle after invoking a MAC. The buyer also does not want to lose the litigation and be stuck buying the company at the original price. Thus, a MAC invocation is really a renegotiation tool for a lower price.'

Particularly, *private equity* companies have become adept at using MAC-clauses to their advantage. For example, Cerberus used it against Innkeepers USA Trust and Apollo/Hexion against Huntsman. During the financial crisis they often attempted to bolster their bargaining position further by negotiating a liability cap, called a *reverse termination fee*, which capped their liability to the target at about a maximum of 3 per cent of the deal price. A seller agreeing to such a reverse termination fee is effectively giving an option to the buyer to walk away for a limited amount of money. This may increase the hold-up problem, since the buyer now has an even stronger bargaining position to renegotiate the deal.

Source: 'The MAC is back, but does it kill a deal?', *The New York Times*, 23 August 2011.

Imagine that you are Jerry Levin, CEO of Time Warner. In October 1999, you receive a phone call from Steven Case, CEO of AOL, proposing a friendly all share merger of equals. You meet with Steven Case several times and, after difficult discussions, an agreement seems within reach, including the terms of the share deal. Both CEOs are to submit this potential agreement to their boards. It is uncertain how the markets will react to any announcement of the deal.

As Jerry Levin, you should be concerned that AOL could walk away from the deal, perhaps as a result of unfavourable market reactions to the announcement or other target firms offering themselves to AOL on more favourable terms. Even if AOL does not actually walk away, it could try to use the threat of doing so to

Credible commitment

Break-up fee

renegotiate the terms of the deal. Therefore, you will want AOL to make a **credible commitment** to the deal, as agreed. This can be done by agreeing a **break-up fee** to be paid by AOL, if it abandons the deal after signing. The break-up fee has to be sizable in order to be credible. It will be a contractual clause in the SPA.

Now imagine that you are Steven Case, CEO of AOL. By bidding for Time Warner you are putting that company 'in play'. Other potential acquirers will examine the terms of the deal and may decide to start a bidding war. You cannot force the board of Time Warner to stick to your deal because it has a fiduciary duty to consider more favourable bids. You do, however, want a credible commitment from Time Warner that it will not easily succumb to the attractions of a higher bid. Therefore, you ask Time Warner also to agree to a break-up fee in case it walks away from the deal.

In reality, the agreed break-up fees were $5.4 billion for AOL and $3.5 billion for Time Warner. Break-up fees in the USA generally amount to about 3 per cent of the proposed purchase price. They can be understood as a remedy against potential hold-up problems, making it more difficult for parties to renegotiate the terms of the deal or walk away altogether. It is a contractual arrangement mitigating against potential opportunism by having the firms make a credible commitment. Sometimes a break-up fee at least serves the purpose of some consolation for the party that did not see its bid ultimately win (see Box 13.10).

Box 13.10 A broken connection

In March 2011, the American telecom company AT&T launched a $39 billion bid for the US operations of Deutsche Telekom, called T-Mobile USA. In December 2011, the deal had to be called off in a telephone conversation between the CEOs, due to opposition from the regulatory authorities:

'AT&T's Randall Stephenson and Deutsche Telekom's Rene Obermann ultimately agreed the costs of continuing to fight for the deal unveiled nine months earlier were too high, given the opposition from U.S. regulators, the people said. AT&T's bid to close the year's biggest acquisition and become the largest U.S. wireless carrier was over.

Stephenson said in March, when the deal was announced, that he was confident of receiving regulatory clearance. He said the combination would help improve service, speed up investment in faster networks and drive wireless expansion in rural areas. The deal would have added T-Mobile's 33.7 million customers to AT&T's 100.7 million subscribers, surpassing Verizon Wireless's 107.7 million. Critics of the deal said it would eliminate an aggressive price competitor, driving up subscription costs. T-Mobile's monthly wireless plans are $15 to $50 cheaper than comparable AT&T plans, according to an analysis by Consumer Reports.

"I'm relieved that we are no longer at risk of concentrating such enormous power in the hands of AT&T and Verizon," U.S. Senator Al Franken said in a statement.

According to the terms of the offer, AT&T must pay Deutsche Telekom a $3 billion breakup fee in cash, transfer radio spectrum to T-Mobile and strike a more favorable network-sharing agreement. Deutsche Telekom has valued the breakup package at as much as $7 billion.'

Source: Bloomberg, 'AT&T Pulls its $39 Billion Bid for T-Mobile', 20 December 2011.

13.10 Alignment of managers and shareholders

In Section 13.8 above, we encountered the topic of 'incentive alignment' between managers and shareholders. There it was discussed as being a solution to the problem of moral hazard (hidden action) after signing the acquisition contract. Contingent earn-outs, escrow accounts and MAC clauses help to bring the interests of management and the new owners more in line with each other. More generally, the M&A context allows us to illustrate the importance of an alignment of the interests of managers and shareholder-owners by means of appropriate incentives. Such alignment is, of course, the central topic in agency theory, as explained in Chapter 7 of this book.

First, consider the risk that managers will make value-destroying acquisitions. One reason for this is that managers are free to pursue 'their own agenda' in making acquisitions. Jensen (1986) was among the first to point out that, when the interests and incentives of managers and shareholders diverge, managers may grow the company beyond the optimal level for its shareholders. They may do so, for example, to achieve published growth targets that are difficult to reach by organic growth only. They may even be interested in empire building.

Managing a large, growing company usually translates into higher salaries and bonuses and a higher standing in the business community. For such 'managerial reasons' companies may be led into acquisitions that destroy value for shareholders. How to prevent this from happening?

Free cash flow

Jensen (1986) proposes that the key concept is **free cash flow**. Free cash flow is defined as cash flow in excess of that required to fund all projects that have positive net present values when discounted at the relevant cost of capital. In other words, it is the cash that remains when managers have made all rational investment decisions, including value-enhancing acquisitions. How a firm deals with free cash flow is crucial, according to Jensen (1989):

> A central weakness and source of waste in the public corporation is the conflict between shareholders and managers over the payout of free cash flow. For a company to operate efficiently and maximize value, free cash flow must be distributed to shareholders rather than retained. But this happens infrequently; senior management has few incentives to distribute the funds, and there exist few mechanisms to compel the distribution.

Leveraged buy-out (LBO)

Jensen explains the rise of the **leveraged buy-out (LBO)** as being a reaction to the inefficiency and waste caused by insufficient disciplining of public corporations to make them distribute free cash flow.

In a LBO transaction, the public company is 'taken private' – that is, delisted from the stock exchange. It is, therefore, no longer financed by 'public funds' (publically tradable shares). Instead, its financing mix then consists of privately held shares and a much larger portion of debt: the firm's balance sheet becomes highly leveraged. This serves as the required disciplining mechanism on management: free cash flow must now be used to make promised interest and principal payments on the debt as the first priority. The private shareholders benefit from the value created by addressing the inefficiencies in the company and paying down the debt. That value can be realized at 'exit' – when the firm is sold off or again offered through an IPO to the stock market.

In the late 1970s and early 1980s, many specialized buy-out firms were established. The most well-known became Kohlberg Kravis Roberts (KKR) when it acquired RJR Nabisco at a cost of $31.4 billion with only a $3.6 billion equity investment by KKR. That transaction was made famous in the book *Barbarians at the Gate*.

Private equity

Since then, a sizable **private equity** industry has developed, with firms such as KKR, Blackstone, Carlyle and CVC. These firms address the alignment between managers and (private) shareholders differently from public corporations. Their governance model includes the following aspects:

■ High *incentives* for management that are performance driven and focused on cash generation. Often, management is also required to have some 'skin in the game' – invest its own money alongside that of the private shareholders. By means of such measures, management is offered the chance to become seriously wealthy, but only if the shareholders do well out of their investment, too. In other words, there is a much closer alignment of incentives for managers and shareholders.

- Very close *monitoring* of management. The Board of a privately held company has the direct participation of the private shareholders. By contrast, the Board of a public company often offers only indirect representation to shareholders through the election of non-executive directors. It is likely that the supervision by such directors is less intense than by active investors. Non-executive directors usually do not have any sizeable stake in the company. They are also not supposed to sit on the executives' chairs. Active investors, though, have both the motive and the opportunity to make their presence felt. Indeed, in the context of M&A, McKinsey found that 'active private equity partners devoted half of their time to the company (usually at its premises) during the first three months after the deal' (Beroutsos et al., 2007).
- Much greater use of debt financing and, therefore, of *financial leverage*. Private equity seeks the limits of financial leverage that banks and debt markets are willing to support. The more debt is financing a transaction, the lower the amount of private equity that is exposed to the risk of the transaction. As a holder of the *residual risk*, the private shareholder can also look forward to higher returns on successful transactions (as the remaining revenue, after the costs of debt have been met, accrue to the shareholders). Finally, the use of debt imposes discipline on managers in their use of free cash flow, as Jensen argued.

Governance model

These are some of the main elements of a different **governance model** applied by private equity firms to their acquisitions. Overall, it appeared to be quite successful in its first few decades, perhaps because it could address the most glaring inefficiencies among public companies. As a consequence, the share of private equity in global M&A transactions has increased significantly until it reached a share of around 25% of global M&A activity in the midst of the last decade. More specific data are shown in Figure 13.3. They show the rise of private equity financing of M&A transactions and the fact that this phenomenon has spread from the USA to Europe, Asia and the rest of the world. Figure 13.3 also shows that since 2007 the share of private equity in global M&A activity has come down to levels between 5 and 15 per cent. Among the reasons for this downward correction are the tightening of credit conditions around the world (decreasing the leveraging potential of private equity), public opposition in a number of countries, and some dissatisfaction among the investor base of private equity about the traditional 'two and twenty' earnings model (see Box 13.11).

In 1989, Michael Jensen predicted 'the eclipse of the public corporation'. While overstated, the core of his argument – that substantial value can be created by addressing the potential inefficiencies in public corporations – has proven to be true so far. The rise of the private equity industry has highlighted the choice to be made in appropriate governance models.

Governance by private owners has, of course, always existed. Entrepreneurial firms and family owned companies have always been governed by private shareholder-owners. Traditionally, however, it was thought that such firms would necessarily become public over time, as their growth and financing needs exceeded the limits of private financing. What is new is that those limits have been stretched beyond recognition by the private equity firms. In terms of financing, few large public companies can feel exempt from the pressure this brings to bear on their own performance. The private equity industry is challenging the established model of corporate governance of the public company. This situation highlights the importance of appropriate corporate governance, the subject of our next chapter.

Box 13.11 Two and twenty: for you not so much and for me plenty?

As discussed in the main text, the private equity business model aims for a better alignment between the managers of acquired firms and the owners, i.e. the private equity firms holding the shares. But what about the alignment between the managers of these private equity firms and their investors (the private and institutional investors contributing capital to the private equity funds)? Returns on such investments have come down significantly in recent years, according to various studies:

'Private equity has proved better at enriching its own managers than producing investment profits for US pension funds over the past decade, according to a study prepared for the Financial Times by academics at Yale and Maastricht University. From 2001 to 2010, US pension plans on average made 4.5 per cent a year, after fees, from their investments in private equity. In that period, the pension funds paid an average of 4 per cent of invested capital each year in management fees. On top of those, private equity often collects a variety of other fees and a fifth of investment profits. "Assuming a normal 20 per cent performance fee, this would amount to about 70 per cent of gross investment performance being paid in fees over the past 10 years" said Professor Martijn Cremers of Yale.

Private equity describes its fees as "two and twenty", a 2 per cent management fee and a 20 per cent share of profits. However, the management fee is usually calculated as a proportion of total capital committed by the investor, which takes time to invest. So, in the early years, the management fee can be a much higher proportion of actual cash invested. For instance, if a $1bn fund invests $100 m in its first year, the $20m management fee would be 2 per cent of committed capital, but 20 per cent of invested capital for that year.'

A further peculiarity about payouts to private equity managers is that they are treated favourably by most tax systems around the world because they are presented as 'carried interest'. In 2011, Henry Kravis and George Roberts of KKR each took home a payment of about $94 million, of which $30 million was 'carried interest' (taxed with 15% as a capital gain in the US against 35 per cent on ordinary income). Stephen Schwarzman, the CEO of Blackstone, received $213.5 million in pay and dividends:

'in his 2013 budget released this month, Barack Obama, the US president, proposed to "eliminate the carried interest loophole for hedge fund managers and other similar investment service providers", a move that would raise $13.4bn, the administration estimates. Previous attempts to change the treatment of carried interest and so increase the amount of tax paid by partners of financial firms have failed, including a 2010 proposal that Mr Schwarzmann compared to Hitler's invasion of Poland in 1939. He later apologized for the analogy, made privately.'

Based on Peter Morris (2010), *Private equity, public loss?*, London: CSFI and from *The Financial Times*: 'Private equity profits called into question' (23 January 2012); 'KKR founders take home $94m each' (28 February 2012) and 'Blackstone founder tops private equity pay league'(29 February 2012)

13.11 Summary: economic approaches to M&A

In this chapter, we have explored M&A from an economic perspective. We have been able to apply many concepts that were introduced more generally in previous chapters.

We have shown that problems with *information asymmetry* abound. Problems with *hidden information* may prevent transactions in the M&A market in much the same way as described in the used car market in Chapter 4. Problems with *hidden action* may plague M&A transactions after signing.

For these problems, however, remedies have evolved. In part, they are contractual clauses that attempt to address (at least partially) the problem of *incomplete contracting* – the fact that no contract can ever specify *all* potential contingencies upfront. We have seen, too, that market and organizational solutions have also been developed as remedies. Market solutions include the creation of specific insurance markets and the use of the IPO market, also as a *signalling* device. Organizational solutions include the use of joint ventures to allow a potential acquirer to first learn about the business as a JV partner.

Which mix of market and organizational solutions is appropriate for specific transactions, will primarily depend on the nature and severity of the information problems involved.

The M&A process allowed us a practical example of how *auctions* can be designed both to narrow the information asymmetries over time and promote the *efficient allocation* of assets to be sold – namely to the bidder with the highest private valuation. As a result, the winning bidder can end up paying full value for the target firm. Occasionally, the bid may even turn out to be higher than the full value, resulting in the *winner's curse*. It was interesting to review the evidence that especially overconfident CEOs, who suffer from *hubris*, are prone to suffer from this curse. As a result, they are more likely to enter into value-destroying transactions.

On balance, the net economic gain from M&A appears to be positive. It is *not a zero-sum game*: the shareholders of target firms win more than the shareholders of acquiring firms tend to lose. Effects on other stakeholder groups are, on average, not very large, with the possible exception of target firms' management teams. That would imply that M&A does create value from an overall economic perspective, presumably by transferring assets to management teams that deploy them more efficiently. In individual cases, however, the value destruction can be quite impressive, as we saw in the case of AOL-Time Warner at the beginning of this chapter and in the consequences of the failed takeover of ABN AMRO for the Royal Bank of Scotland and Fortis, which both had to be bailed out by their governments. In such cases, there is usually significant management turnover and the companies involved may be destabilized for quite some time. It clearly pays for management to be aware of such risks, take appropriate remedies and avoid becoming trapped in such a situation.

Finally, we discussed the emergence of *private equity* as an alternative governance system to that of public equity markets. Private equity firms address the *alignment between managers and shareholders* differently from that which is customary in public corporations. They restrict management's discretionary use of *free cash flow* by much greater use of debt financing.

The private equity *governance model* includes high performance-driven and cash-based incentives for management, close *monitoring* of management by the shareholders and much greater *financial leverage*. It is a different way in which to address the basic *agency problems* due to the separation of management and ownership. We have also raised some questions about the private equity model, including the alignment between the managers of private equity firms and the providers of capital to the private equity funds.

The alternative governance mechanism of private equity is one indication of the importance of *corporate governance*. Recurring problems of misbehaviour, scandal and fraud in corporations is another. We will discuss these issues in Chapter 15 on corporate governance.

Questions

1 During the first stage of an auction process an information memorandum is sent to a number of potential buyers. On the basis of that memorandum, potential buyers make a first estimate of the maximum price they might be willing to pay (they will, of course, not reveal that maximum price to the seller or anyone else).

   Do you think that each potential buyer arrives at the same estimate for this maximum price? If not, why not?

2 Transaction costs for M&A transactions are often quite high. In Chapter 8, it was argued that transaction costs depend on three dimensions of transactions (the three critical dimensions of transactions). Which of those three dimensions is, in your opinion, most important for M&A transactions?

3 This chapter argues that information asymmetry is a major problem in many M&A deals. However, the degree of information asymmetry may depend on the characteristics of the deal. Consider the following situations:

   a Two quoted companies consider a merger (such as the merger between AOL and Time Warner).

   b A quoted company is considering the acquisition of another quoted company (an example is the acquisition of Corus by Tata Steel, described in Box 12.5) by making shareholders of the target firm an offer in cash.

   c A quoted company is considering the acquisition of another quoted company by making shareholders of the target firm an offer in shares.

   d A large company wants to sell one of its divisions to another large company (an example is the sale by Philips of its domestic appliances' division to Whirlpool).

   e A multibusiness firm wants to sell one of its business units to the manager of that business unit.

   f A multibusiness firm wants to sell one of its business units to a newly formed company in which a private equity firm holds 80 per cent and the manager of the business unit to be sold holds 20 per cent.

   g A large firm in the pharmaceutical industry is considering the acquisition of a small biotech firm from the founders of that company.

   For each of the above situations, discuss if and why information asymmetry is likely to be a problem.

4 You are the CEO of a large pharmaceutical company with a substantial and stable cash flow based on several well-established prescription drugs protected by patents. You know, however, that those patents expire within the next decade. You are now looking at one small biotech firm. The firm is developing a new drug with a huge market potential. The founders and owners of the firm tell you that they need another two years to fully develop and test the new drug in order to get it approved by the authorities. They also tell you that they are prepared to sell for $800 million in cash. Your estimate of the net present value of the cash flow from the new drug is well above $800 million (it could be anywhere between $2 and 5 billion), provided you get approval from the authorities. So, you could make a deal, pay $800 million and hope for the best, or do you see another possibility?

Notes

1   See http://en.wikipedia.org/wiki/General_Electric_timeline for an overview of GE's major acquisition steps.
2   We use here the generic term Sales and Purchase Agreement for the SPA. If shares in a company are bought, the SPA may refer to the Share Purchase Agreement. In an 'asset deal' one may speak of an APA: an Asset Purchase Agreement.
3   See Roll (1986). Roll's hubris hypothesis depicts irrational (overconfident) managers operating in rational (efficient) financial markets. An alternative model is proposed by Shleifer and Vishny (2003) in which rational managers exploit inefficiencies in financial markets. In that model, managers of relatively overvalued firms have strong incentives to make a share offer for relatively less (over)valued targets.

14 Hybrid forms

14.1 Introduction

In Chapter 1 we argued that, in *ideal markets*, coordination takes place by using the price mechanism only (prices act as a sufficient statistic) and, in *ideal organizations*, various other forms of coordination are used. We also noted that ideal markets and ideal organizations hardly exist: markets are to some extent organized and within (large) organizations internal markets can exist. That however, is not the full story: there are many governance structures that fall between ideal markets and ideal organizations.

Take as an example franchising. In order to explain what franchising is, consider McDonald's. In 2011, there were more than 33,000 McDonald's restaurants in more than 100 countries. Some 6,600 restaurants are owned and operated by the McDonald's Corporation, but the rest (around 26,400) are owned and operated by local entrepreneurs. Those entrepreneurs have a contract with McDonald's Corporation giving them the right to operate under the name McDonald's. Such a contract is called a **franchise contract**. The two parties to such a contract are the franchisor (McDonald's Corporation) and the franchisee (the local entrepreneur owning and operating a McDonald's restaurant).

Franchise contract

The McDonald's Corporation has developed a formula for operating fast-food restaurants. That formula consists of a range of products (including the way those products have to be prepared), a house style (which refers to things such as the furnishing of the restaurant, the clothing of personnel and how customers are treated) and a brand name. Under the franchise contract the franchisees are allowed to use that formula in return for a fee (usually a fixed amount, plus a percentage of sales).

If we first define a hybrid form loosely as a form of governance somewhere between market and organization, then franchising fits that definition. Consider the relationship between franchisor and franchisee. We see that there is certainly an element of a market relation. The franchisee obtains the right to use a brand name owned by the franchisee in return for a fee. That is a market transaction. The franchisee is an entrepreneur who invests in his own establishment. Franchisor and franchisee are best regarded as separate organizations. Coordination between franchisor and franchisee does not take place through the market mechanism only, however. Other coordination mechanisms play an important role: standardization of work processes (for food production), standardization of norms (for the house style) and direct supervision (the franchisor monitors the behaviour of the franchisee in order to protect the value of the brand name). Between franchisor and franchisees, various organizational coordination mechanism are used, as well as the price mechanism.

Hybrid form

We can now give a more precise definition of a **hybrid form**:

> a hybrid form is a set of organizations such that coordination between those organizations takes place by means of the price mechanism and various other coordination mechanisms simultaneously.

Franchising surely fits this definition of hybrid forms. Other examples of hybrid forms are long-term relations between buyers and suppliers, joint ventures, business groups and informal networks.

That hybrid organizational forms exist has also been recognized by Williamson. For him, they occur for intermediate levels of asset specificity. As summarized in Figure 14.1 (see Ménard, 2004), Williamson sees hybrid forms as intermediate forms between markets and organizations. Hybrid forms are efficient (that is, they have the lowest transaction costs) for intermediate levels of asset specificity.

We agree with the basic line of thought behind Figure 14.1: hybrid forms are positioned between markets and hierarchies (or, in our broader approach, organizations). Thus, they can be efficient solutions in cases where neither pure market coordination nor pure organizational coordination would suffice. We find it difficult, however, to assign rather precise levels of asset specificity to the various hybrid forms. From the perspective of this book, we find it more appropriate to discuss the mix of market and organizational coordination mechanisms employed in particular hybrid forms. Some hybrid forms rely more on market than on organizational coordination. For some other hybrid forms, the mix is reversed. Hence, we can construct a picture – Figure 14.2 – in which we position the various hybrid forms somewhere along a continuum with markets at one end and organizations at the other. Towards the left of the picture, market coordination is more prominent in the bundle of coordination

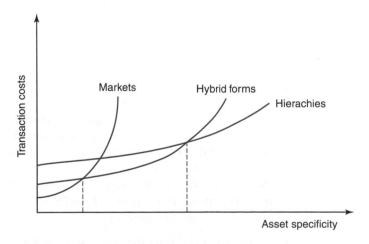

Figure 14.1 Hybrid forms are efficient for intermediate levels of asset specificity

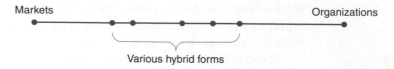

Figure 14.2 Markets, organizations and hybrid forms

mechanisms employed. Towards the right of the picture, organizational coordination is more prevalent in the bundle. In the middle, the mix of coordination mechanisms is quite balanced.

We will return to Figure 14.2 at the end of this chapter to position five examples of hybrid forms that are discussed: long-term relations between buyers and suppliers (Section 14.2), joint ventures (Section 14.3), business groups (Section 14.4), informal networks (Section 14.5), and franchising (Section 14.6). We will show how each of these forms uses market coordination and organizational coordination mechanisms. However, the relative importance of market coordination versus other coordination mechanisms differs for each of these forms. In the concluding section (Section 14.7), apart from positioning the various hybrid forms, we will also summarize some common features shared by hybrid forms. They involve pooling of resources, some joint planning and usually also a level of trust that enables the requisite level of cooperation.

14.2 Long-term relations between buyers and suppliers

Companies offering tangible products often buy materials, parts or components from suppliers. For example, an automobile manufacturer buys tyres, windows, electrical systems, spark plugs, steel and many other items on a regular basis. Some of those intermediate products (dashboards, for example) are designed for a particular car model; other parts or components are not specific to any one car model. A company making a part specifically designed for the Toyota Prius, for example, has only one customer for that part. Its investment in tooling and design for the part are transaction-specific. Because of the high level of asset specificity, transaction cost economics predicts organizational coordination as the optimal choice, which means that the part in question will be manufactured by Toyota itself. In the real world, however, we often see that such parts are manufactured by outside suppliers. The suppliers are independent (in the sense that they are not owned by the automobile company) and usually have long-term relationships, supported by long-term contracts with one or more automobile companies.

Why would an outside supplier place itself in a position where it is vulnerable to its customer(s) choosing to exhibit opportunistic behaviour? There are several answers to this question:

■ A long-term contract may offer some legal protection against opportunistic behaviour by the buyer.

- The buyer expects benefits from future cooperation with the supplier that far outweigh any short-term financial gain that may result from opportunistic behaviour.
- The buyer knows that opportunistic behaviour towards one supplier will affect his reputation *vis-à-vis* other suppliers as a dependable trading partner, so opportunistic behaviour towards one supplier will negatively affect the value of past investments in building that reputation.
- The buyer may pay for and own the design and tooling for the specific part, which reduces the level of asset specificity.

These explanations are perfectly consistent with the assumption of opportunism, which is an important assumption in transaction cost economics.

While these four answers each have an element of truth, we feel that they still fail fully to explain the existence of many successful long-term cooperations between buyers and suppliers. What is that extra element?

The benefits of cooperation are maximized when both parties really trust each other. That is especially true in a dynamic world with important technological developments and volatile markets. When both partners trust each other, they will share their technological know-how (which often means that the buyer transfers technological know-how to the supplier), the buyer and supplier will coordinate their production plans through some form of joint planning and the supplier will share cost data with the supplier and allow the buyer to visit his factory on a regular basis.

Such an intensive cooperation, built on mutual trust, has been termed **co-makership**. In a co-makership relation, buyer and supplier know that the benefits of the relationship are maximized when both of them 'act in good faith'. That means, for example, a supplier will not use technological know-how received from the buyer to produce parts for other customers. It also means that the supplier will be eager to improve efficiency because he knows that the buyer will not try to capture all the benefits of the efficiency improvements. Co-makership relies on both trust and safeguards (such as a long-term contract that can specify the buyer pays for and owns the tooling). Box 14.1 gives an example.

Co-makership

Box 14.1 A clever way to build a Boeing

In December 2009 the Boeing 787 Dreamliner – a new fuel-saving, medium-sized passenger jet – made its first flight.

The new plane was remarkable for the degree to which Boeing had outsourced development and production around the world. Boeing itself is responsible for about 10 per cent by value – the tail fin and final assembly. The rest is done by 50 partners, with the wings built in Japan, the carbon composite fuselage in Italy and the US and the landing gear in France.

One important reason for doing this was that those partners had state-of-the-art technology – for example, to build wings for commercial aircraft or to build carbon composite fuselages – that Boeing did not have. Those partners, encouraged by Boeing, have developed parts designed specifically for the Boeing 787. In doing so, they extended their expertise, which some of them may use later to develop and produce parts for others, such as the Airbus. Boeing, however, holds rights to the 787 technology.

In March 2012, Boeing had $178 billion in orders for the 787 Dreamliner, which was considered by many to be a big success. Boeing now calls itself a 'systems integrator' rather than a manufacturer.

Sources: Website Boeing, Wikipedia

In a co-makership relationship, price negotiations between buyers and suppliers are still important, so price does play a role. Mutual adjustment (through joint production planning and sharing cost data) based on trust also plays a vital role, however.

14.3 Joint ventures

Joint venture

A **joint venture (JV)** is established when two existing companies decide to pool resources to set up a new business in a newly formed company. Box 14.2 gives an example of a JV, which is, in fact, an international JV because it involves companies from different countries.

The governance structure of two (sometimes more than two) companies acting as parent companies to another company that they jointly own is called a JV. A JV consists of a subsidiary with (at least two) parent companies. Why do JVs exist?

Box 14.2 A JV between Jaguar Land Rover and Chery Automobiles

In March 2012, Jaguar Land Rover, a British car manufacturer (owned since 2008 by Tata Motors from India) and Chery Automobiles (a state-owned car manufacturer in China) announced a new joint venture to be set up in China. The aim of the new company was to develop new models tailored to the Chinese market. The new company intended to build a new plant in China (investment $1 billion), to set up a R&D centre in China (investment $1 billion) and to launch a new brand for the Chinese market (investment $ 500 million).

Chery sells relatively simple and cheap models in China. Chery will make its know-how of the local market available to the joint venture.

Source: Het Financieele Dagblad, 21 March 2012.

In order to find out why JVs exist, let us have a closer look at the example given in Box 14.2.

Apparently, in 2012 there was a business opportunity to set up a new automobile company in China. Tata Motors, through its British subsidiary Jaguar

Land Rover, and Chery Automobiles formed a JV to grab that opportunity. Tata Motors did not enter the Chinese market alone – probably because it knew that operating in a foreign country in which it had no practical experience would not be easy. To set up a new company from scratch can be quite difficult if you are not familiar with local ways of doing things, including labour relations, management practices and how to deal with local authorities. These things can be quite important as a new company needs all sorts of licences from local authorities. Further, to set up a new distribution system involving a selection of dealers can be difficult and costly without intimate knowledge of local market conditions.

So, Tata Motors needed the know-how and relations of a local partner. Why, though, did Chery not set up a new factory alone? Probably because it lacked the know-how to develop more luxurious cars. So, in order to exploit this business opportunity, one needs both technological and managerial know-how and local contacts. These are examples of intangible assets. It is quite difficult to buy such intangible assets in the marketplace.

One way to combine intangible assets is to set up a JV. The new joint venture in our example benefits from Tata Motors' dynamic capability to set up a new company in a market with established competitors and from Chery's knowledge of local circumstances.

Another way to combine such intangible assets would be a merger between the two companies or one company acquiring the other company. For example, Tata Motors could have acquired Chery Automobiles. That, however, would possibly not fit into the business strategy of Jaguar Land Rover, which aims at the top end of the automobile market. As a practical matter, it may have been impossible because Chery was a state owned company.

To put what we have learned in more general terms, a JV will be the preferred mode of organizing when the following conditions are met:

■ There is a business opportunity that requires resources from two existing companies, A and B.
■ It is difficult or even impossible to trade those resources. That is often the case with intangible assets (such as Tata Motors' dynamic capability to launch luxury brand cars in a market with established competitors or Chery's contacts with local authorities): the resources needed from company A and company B are difficult to trade (if the resource needed from A can be easily bought and sold, B can simply buy the resource from A and set up a wholly owned subsidiary).
■ An acquisition of company A by company B (or vice versa) is not viable or strategically desirable.

If all three conditions are met, a JV will be the preferred organizational form. If the first and second are met but the third is not, a merger or acquisition is an alternative solution.

Intangible assets, such as dynamic capabilities or local contacts, are difficult to trade because of opportunism. It is very difficult to specify in a contract what you buy, when you buy 'access to local contacts'. To put it differently, very high transaction costs in the markets for those intangible assets lead to the formation of joint ventures. We want to note that, after the joint venture has been formed, it is still very difficult for one partner to assess whether or not the other partner really contributes the intangible assets expected from him. This problem is attenuated if the JV is structured as an equity joint venture, as most JVs are (an equity JV is a JV established by two companies that each provide a substantial part, very often 50 percent each, of the equity in the new company). In an equity JV the equity provided by the partners operates as an exchange of hostages. The value of the JV depends on its continued operation, so each partner has an incentive to contribute to the JV. This line of reasoning assumes that both partners lose should the new company fold. We want to stress, however, that even in an equity JV, a certain level of mutual trust is necessary for the JV's success.

JVs are usually set up for an indefinite period of time. Despite that, quite often, after a couple of years, changes in the ownership structure occur. Very often one partner buys out the other and the company created as a JV continues as a subsidiary of one of the partners. That may happen if the intangible assets provided by one of the partners are no longer needed for the JV's success.

When a JV is formed, the companies involved in setting it up usually negotiate about the value of the (intangible) assets that they bring to the JV. After it has been set up, there is often a period in which the parent companies assist the subsidiary in various ways. For example, the parent companies often transfer key personnel for a limited period of time. During the period the JV is being formed and the first few years after that, prices do play a role in the relations between the subsidiary and its parents. Other coordination mechanisms, such as direct supervision and mutual adjustment, also play important roles. That is why JVs also fit our definition of a hybrid form.

14.4 Business groups

Business group

A **business group** is a group of legally independent firms that are nevertheless bound together by one or more formal and informal ties. Formal ties include reciprocal shareholding by members of the group, companies owned in part by the same shareholder (a holding company or an individual shareholder) or group of shareholders, interlocking directors, cross-guarantees of bank loans and trading of parts and supplies between group companies. Informal bonds include family ties between managers of group companies and managers of group companies belonging to the same social or ethnic group.

Business groups play an important role in most emerging markets and in many developed economies. Business groups have different names in different countries: *keiretsu* (Japan), *chaebol* (Korea), *grupos economicos* (Latin and Central America), *jituanqiye* (Taiwan) and *business houses* (India). Box 14.3 gives a description of the origin and nature of business houses in India.

Box 14.3 Business houses in India

Business groups in India (business houses) have caste and provincial origins. The initial activities of most groups can be traced back to certain parts of the country, although, in more recent times, some of the larger groups have assumed a pan-Indian operational character. Groups increased the number of companies under their fold when assets belonging to the erstwhile British companies were acquired. Traditionally, the management of most of these groups was via the *managing agency* system. Under that system, each of the participating firms signs a management contract with a managing agency owned by the group. The *managing agencies*, in turn, run these firms. Several of the largest business groups in India, such as the Tatas and the Birlas, were initially run by managing agencies owned by them. However, that system of managing groups has only historical relevance as the managing agency system was abolished in 1969 as a consequence of amendments in the statute governing corporations in India.

While firms in India are largely focused entities, the business groups tend to be diversified and have certain features similar to a typical Western conglomerate or a Japanese *keiretsu*. Similarities exist in the sense that, akin to the headquarters of a conglomerate, the controlling family sets the overall strategic direction and regulates financial transfers. An important difference, though, is that, unlike divisions of a typical conglomerate firm, each firm in India has its own unique set of share-holdings comprised of various blockholders (a promoter company, other group companies, domestic and/or foreign financial institutions, foreign corporations) and the general public. Unlike the typical Japanese *keiretsu*, though, Indian groups do not have an inhouse financial institution.

Control over these group firms is typically exercised through intercorporate equity investments (cross-equity shareholdings), holding companies (pyramidal structures) and interlocking directorates.

Group firms in India generally advertise their affiliation to a particular group and those affiliations remain substantially stable over time. Despite the institution of a takeover code in the 1990s, the practice of group firms interchanging group affiliations is relatively uncommon. Business groups also differ in the extent and diversity of their operations. The largest groups are active in a wide variety of industries, ranging from automobile production to educational publishing. They cover vast tracts of the industrial sector and contribute to a significant chunk of the country's industrial output.

Nonetheless, the bulk of the business groups can be categorized as small- and medium-sized, with the scale and scope of their activities being considerably more modest. The firms constituting business groups involve listed as well as unlisted firms. Furthermore, information pertaining to group affiliation is publicly available and it is relatively easy to identify group affiliation in India. Each firm within a group has a separate legal entity and can be listed separately on the stock exchange. Most groups have fewer than five firms listed on stock exchanges such as the Bombay Stock Exchange (BSE). More than 1000 group-affiliated firms are listed on various stock exchanges in India. They belong to a few hundred groups. About 95 per cent of those groups have five or fewer affiliates. In effect, the average business group in India has around two listed firms.

Well-known examples of business groups include Mitsubishi (in Japan – banking, insurance, cars, steel, beer, chemicals), Hyundai (in Korea – sea transport, cars, elevators) and Tata (in India – steel, cars, chemicals, tea, hotels). These three business groups display activities in a wide array of industries, as our lists and a visit to their websites will quickly reveal. That tends to be true for most business groups. Box 14.4 gives more details on the Tata group – a prominent business group in India.

14.4.1 Types of business groups

Horizontal business group

Business groups can be horizontal or vertical as far as their structure is concerned. In a **horizontal business group** there is no central holding company – the group companies are connected through various formal or informal ties, including reciprocal shareholding. Thus, a horizontal business group is a rather loose confederation of firms. Coordination between them is achieved mainly by mutual adjustment and standardization of norms. Mitsubishi is a well-known example of a horizontal business group as are many other *keiretsu*. Taiwanese and Chinese groups exhibit similar features. Horizontal business groups are also referred to as *associative business groups*.

Vertical business group

A **vertical business group** is a group of companies controlled, but not entirely owned, by a single investor. Vertical groups are often organized as pyramids of companies controlled by the main investor through a holding company. A unique feature of pyramidal holdings is that it allows the main investor to exert control with a limited amount of capital. Korean *chaebols*, Indian business houses and most European business groups are vertical in character. Vertical business groups are also referred to as *hierarchical business groups*.

Some business groups do have a main investor and also have extensive cross-holdings of shares in group companies. They thus display the characteristics of both vertical *and* horizontal business groups. One example is the Tata Group (see Box 14.4). Tata clearly has a main investor – Tata Sons – but it rarely owns more than 20 per cent of the Tata Group's companies. There is extensive cross-shareholding between the Tata Group's companies. Thus, the Tata Group displays characteristics of both horizontal and vertical business groups.

Box 14.4 The Tata Group

The Tata Group is the largest business group in India. It is comprised of more than 100 operating companies, with activities in more than 50 countries. Some of the Group's companies have a listing on a stock market (in 2011, 28 Tata Group companies had a stock market listing), while other group companies are not listed on any stock market.

The Tata Group was founded by Jamsetji Tata in the mid 19th century. In 2011, the combined revenues of the Tata Group's companies was $83 billion. Market capitalization on 8 March 2012 was $87 billion. The Tata Group's companies are active in a wide range of industries, including chemicals, steel, telecom, cars, tea, watches and hotels.

The Tata Group has three important holding companies – Tata Sons, Tata Industries and Tata Investment Corporation (earlier named the Investment Corporation of India). Those companies hold shares in the Group's companies and offer advice and assistance to them. They also take the lead in setting up new companies, which is why they are often referred to as 'promoter' companies. Tata Sons is the main promoter company of the group and can be considered the group headquarters. There is considerable cross-shareholding between the Group's companies. There are also numerous personal ties between Tata companies: Mr. R.N. Tata chairs the board of Tata Sons and Tata Industries as well as the board of several operating Tata companies. Other board members of Tata Sons also serve on the board of several Tata operating companies. Two-thirds of the equity of Tata Sons is held by various philanthropic trusts endowed by members of the Tata family.

Source: www.tata.com

14.4.2 Coordination within business groups

In vertical business groups there is a main investor who exercises control over group companies. Control in a vertical business group involves authority and hierarchy and comes close to the kind of control exercised in an M-form enterprise (see Section 8.6). Coordination between group companies is achieved through a variety of coordination mechanisms, always including direct supervision. The main investor in a vertical business group frequently uses pyramidal structures and/or differential voting rights to exercise control.

Pyramid

To explain the concept of a **pyramid** consider the following example. Suppose a holding company (H) holds a fraction a of the shares of a group company α which in turn holds a fraction β of another group company (B). If α and β are smaller than 1, but large enough to exert control, we have a pyramid – in this case, a two-stage pyramid. If, for example α = .51 and β = .52, then holding company H owns, indirectly, only 26.52 per cent of the shares of company B and still has full control over B. A pyramid allows a single investor to control many firms that, collectively, are worth substantially more than his actual wealth. Pyramids effectively lead to a separation of ownership and control.

Pyramidal structures are widely prevalent in several East Asian and European economies. Box 14.5 and Figure 14.3 give an example of a pyramidal construction from Italy. In particular, firms in Indonesia, Singapore, Taiwan and Korea use pyramids extensively.

Box 14.5 Who controls Fiat?

Fiat and Fiat Industrial are two very important industrial groups based in Italy. Fiat is well known for its automobiles (brand names include Fiat, Alfa Romeo, Lancia, Ferrari and Chrysler); Fiat employs 197 000 people and has revenues of € 60 billion (in 2011). Fiat Industrial manufactures agricultural and construction equipment, trucks (Iveco) and various other products; Fiat Industrial employs 67,000 people and has revenues of € 24 billion (in 2011).

Fiat and Fiat Industrial are both quoted companies that are controlled by the Agnelli family through another quoted company, Exor (see Figure 14.3). Giovanni Agnelli & C is a limited partnership formed by descendants of Fiat's founder. The partnership controls, indirectly, 30.5 per cent of the shares in Fiat and 33.7 per cent of the shares in Fiat Industrial.

The partnership Giovanni Agnelli & C is effectively controlled by John Elkann, a grandson and main heir of Gianni Agnelli. Elkann controls a holding company called Dicembre, which has 31.2 per cent of the votes in the limited partnership. None of the other partners/family members has more than 5 per cent of the votes, so one could argue that Dicembre (Elkann) controls Fiat, although it has an effective economic interest of only 5 per cent.

Source: The Economist, 17 March 2007, and Fiat, Fiat Industrial and Exor web sites.

Differential voting rights

Another way to exert control without (full) ownership is to use shares with different voting rights. They can take the form of two or more classes of shares having the same cash flow rights but with different voting rights. Such **differential voting rights** lead to a considerable separation of ownership and

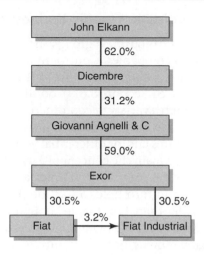

Figure 14.3 The Agnelli's empire (April 2012)

control. The main advantage lies in the controlling shareholders being able to raise capital without having to relinquish control, as long as the practice is allowed by law and other shareholders are willing to give up their control rights. Shares with differential voting rights are extremely potent devices, enabling the controlling family to allocate all voting rights associated with a fraction of shares assigned to them, while assigning no, or limited, voting rights to other shareholders. Such dual-class voting rights are extensively utilized in a number of countries, particularly Brazil, Canada, Denmark, Finland, Germany, Italy, Norway, Korea, Mexico, Sweden and Switzerland. **Dual-class equity**, therefore, can serve as an ideal device for controlling group-affiliated firms. Shares with superior voting rights usually trade at higher prices than ordinary shares – the premium being 30 per cent or even more.

Dual-class equity

In horizontal business groups there is no main investor who exercises control over group companies. Coordination in such business groups is achieved mainly by mutual adjustment and standardization of norms. Mutual adjustment is facilitated by cross-holdings between group companies and director interlocks.

When company A holds shares in company B and vice versa, we say that there is **reciprocal shareholding** between A and B. When company C owns shares in company D, company D owns shares in company E and company E owns shares in company C, we say that there is **cross-holding of shares** between C, D and E. When there is reciprocal shareholding between A and B, A and B have a clear economic motive to cooperate. In such a case we will often see that one of the managing directors of company A sits on the board of company B and vice versa. Equally, someone may sit as a non-executive board member on the boards of A and B. In both cases, we say that there is a **director interlock** between A and B. Such a director interlock between A and B facilitates information sharing between them and helps to build trust between the two companies' top management teams. The same mechanisms apply to cross-holdings combined with director interlocks between three or more group companies. Cross-holdings and

Reciprocal shareholding

Cross-holding of shares

Director interlock

director interlocks between group companies belonging to a horizontal business group help to reduce opportunistic behaviour and, thus, the cost of transacting between group companies.

Standardization of norms and mutual adjustment in both vertical and horizontal business groups is furthermore fostered by family ties between key managers of group firms or managers having the same cultural or ethnic background. This also facilitates transactions between group companies.

14.4.3 Why do business groups exist?

Business groups will continue to exist if they offer some advantages not available through other organizational arrangements. Alternatives to business groups are a set of independent companies cooperating through market transactions and a set of business units cooperating in a multibusiness firm. If we want to know why business groups exist we have to compare them with these alternatives.

Comparing a business group with a set of independent companies

A business group may have several advantages not available to a group of independent companies cooperating through market transactions.

First, business groups offer opportunities for *reducing transaction costs*. When the quality of institutions (such as intermediaries) or the efficiency of the judicial system is poor, transaction costs may be very high indeed. That may occur in capital markets, markets for consumer goods and managerial labour.

If the rights of minority shareholders are not well protected (which is the case in many countries), investors may prefer to invest in a new company backed by a business group with a reputation for honesty over investing in a similar independent company. In such environments group companies will enjoy a lower cost of capital than independent companies. That situation applies in many developing countries. In many such emerging markets, security analysts, stockbrokers and investment banks are absent or do not offer the same quality as their counterparts in more developed nations. Consequently, potential investors may hesitate to invest in new ventures because they have little reliable information. A business group may develop a reputation for honesty with respect to information disclosure to potential investors. That will help to reduce information asymmetry and lead to a lower cost of capital for that business group's companies.

When consumer protection is poor, a business group may build a reputation for quality of consumer products and a common brand name (the Tata Group has done this). A company belonging to a business group can use the common brand name. Consumers will have more confidence in products under such a business group brand name because the business group puts its reputation at stake if it delivers poor quality. An independent company offering the same quality will have to spend much more to convince potential customers. Thus, business groups may help to overcome a problem of hidden information. This explanation is borne out by the fact that business groups play a very important role in most developing countries.

When well-trained managers are scarce, business groups may hire young management trainees and educate them through a management development programme including a job rotation programme. Independent companies have fewer opportunities for job rotation and weaker incentives to invest in educating management trainees. Business groups may offer more opportunities for promotion and, thus, stronger incentives to young professional managers. At the same time, transaction costs in the managerial labour market are largely avoided by rotating young managers from company to company in the group.

Second, business groups may possess *political clout* that facilitate interaction with key government officials, which often leads to preferential access to permits and licences and the preemption of their use by potential entrants. This is an important factor in most emerging markets as, despite liberalization initiatives in several emerging markets, the level of regulation continues to be high, with companies requiring permission for activities such as exiting a business, changing prices and importing raw materials. Bureaucrats exercise a considerable amount of discretion in the application of rules concerning such decisions. Realizing this, the largest business houses in India maintain 'industrial embassies' in the capital New Delhi. The embassies serve the purpose of lobbying with the political elite. Independent companies may lack the political clout of such business groups.

Third, business groups may possess *dynamic capabilities* in setting up new ventures. Business groups in emerging markets may have developed dynamic capabilities in setting up joint ventures with foreign partners. The capabilities those groups possess cover the entire spectrum of skills associated with obtaining requisite licences, technology, training of personnel and setting up distribution networks. As that dynamic capability is embodied in the group's owners, managers and routines, it is difficult to trade. Moreover, once a new venture is up and running, that capability lies dormant. There is, therefore, a strong urge for business groups possessing that capability to diversify into a wide range of industries.

While that generic capability represents a vital ingredient in explaining the scope of the activities engaged in by such groups, it is not sufficient to maintain the long-term sustainability of their competitive advantage. To do that, the capability needs to be inimitable as well. Such inimitability could come from the prevailing institutional environment in which these business groups operate. Specifically, the sustainability of the competitive advantage of business groups is hypothesized to be greater in emerging economies with asymmetrical trade and investment conditions as, under these conditions, business groups (*vis-à-vis* groups of independent companies) are uniquely positioned to exploit their superior ability to combine foreign and domestic resources for repeated industry entry.

Comparing a business group with a multibusiness firm

In the previous section, we mentioned three advantages that a business group may have over a group of independent companies (lower transaction costs, political clout and dynamic capabilities in setting up new ventures). Those advantages are also available to a multibusiness firm. So, why do we observe (at least in many countries) so many business groups and so few multibusiness firms? The answer is that, in certain environments, business groups can have advantages over multibusiness firms.

Business groups offer controlling owners an opportunity to appropriate certain **private benefits of control**. Those private benefits involve the transfer of value from firms in which the controlling owners have low cash flow rights to those firms in which they have higher cash flow rights. This phenomenon is referred to as **tunnelling**. Value transfers can take place through transactions of intermediate products at non-market prices, provision of capital at artificial prices and inflated payments for intangibles such as patents, brand names and insurance.

Propping (or negative tunnelling) is a related phenomenon wherein controlling owners prop up lower-performing or struggling firms for the benefit of the controlling owners.

Tunnelling and propping can be especially potent devices in countries with low protection of minority shareholder rights. Empirical evidence supports the view that business groups are particularly conducive to practices involving tunnelling, propping or related party transactions, leading to the detriment of the welfare of minority shareholders of the various firms in the group.

The private benefits of control also include providing members of the controlling family with suitable employment opportunities. While it can be argued that a single firm could potentially resolve this problem, the use of multiple firms enables the patriarch to allocate separate businesses to each of his progeny, thereby minimizing thorny control issues in individual firms.

Business groups that extract such private benefits of control make themselves vulnerable *vis-à-vis* competition from independent companies. They will not be able to build or maintain a reputation for honesty and, thus, will lose certain advantages that they might otherwise have over a group of independent companies.

Business groups do have another advantage over multibusiness firms. They tend to be highly diversified, perhaps because they possess the dynamic capability to set up new ventures quickly and effectively. Highly diversified firms in developed economies tend to perform less well than more focused firms. That is probably because managing a set of business units in widely different industries is a very difficult task for corporate headquarters. At the very least, it requires a control style involving strong incentives for business unit managers. Ideally, those incentives should be tied to creating shareholder value, which is exactly what is achieved by giving the managers an ownership stake. In business groups, managers of group companies often do have an ownership stake. Thus, business groups may be an effective vehicle for obtaining some benefits of cooperation not available to a set of independent companies, while, at the same time, giving strong incentives (through partial ownership) to managers of group companies. To put it differently, just as the private equity governance model competes with the public corporation as an alternative governance model (see Chapter 13), business groups may be regarded as an alternative governance model to that of widely diversified firms. Which governance model is more successful in varying circumstances is an empirical question. Next, we discuss how developments in the institutional context may have an impact on the competitiveness of business groups.

Private benefits of control

Tunnelling

Propping

14.4.4 The development of business groups

In the USA and UK, business groups hardly exist, but, in many other countries, they play an important role. Will business groups gradually disappear as a result of globalizing capital markets and institutional reforms in non-Anglo-American countries? To answer that question, let us first discuss recent developments with respect to business groups in one particular country – India.

Developments in the institutional environment in India

When India gained its independence in 1947, it intended to have a planned economy, where all aspects of economic life were controlled by the State and licences to run companies were given to a select few. Under that system – often referred to as the '**Licence Raj**' – the functioning of markets was severely restricted. First, competition in domestic markets for products was restricted by the Industrial Development and Regulation Act of 1956 and the domestic market was shielded from import competition by very high tariff barriers.

Second, a significant proportion of Indian corporations were managed by family members. Professional managers appointed to the highest echelons of the corporate hierarchy were the exception rather than the norm. As a result, the market for managerial labour hardly existed.

Third, M&A were looked on by the Monopolies and Restrictive Trade Practices Commission with disfavour and there were restrictions on the acquisition and transfer of shares. Financial institutions remained dormant and were instructed by their principal shareholder – the government – not to destabilize existing management. A market for corporate control did not exist under this system.

In this institutional environment, business groups – many of which had existed already under British rule – were able to fill the voids created by those missing markets.

In 1990, India faced an economic crisis and, in 1991, a process of liberalization of the economy began. It entailed the repeal of the Industrial Development and Regulation Act, the Capital Issues Control Act, the Monopolies and Restrictive Trade Practices Act and significant amendments were made to the other acts. This resulted in a more open market ambience. In addition, new bodies and regulations, strengthening investor protection measures and furthering the external governance measures, were adopted. They included the creation of a Securities and Exchange Board of India (SEBI), along the lines of the Securities and Exchange Commission (SEC) in the USA, the setting up of depositories to facilitate speedier share transactions and mitigate fraudulent ones and the enactment (in 1997) of extensive guidelines for M&A.

Thus, the post-1991 period marked a dramatic shift in the institutional framework in India. Inflow of foreign capital increased dramatically. Financial institutions lost their privileged access to funds from the government and were forced to tap domestic and international markets, which, in turn, fostered a greater sense of accountability with regard to their monitoring roles in Indian corporations. Within the firms themselves, Indian companies realized

Licence Raj

the necessity to foster professionalism in their management if they were to remain competitive in both product and financial markets, domestically as well as internationally. That led to a new breed of professional managers at the helm of corporate affairs and the beginnings of a vibrant market for managerial labour.

This gradual dismantling of the 'Licence Raj' and the progressive reduction in import tariffs ignited competition in the product market and exposed firms formerly used to a cocooned existence.

As a result of these developments, business groups in India have lost some of their erstwhile advantages. Whether business groups continue to have an advantage in reducing transaction costs, in acquiring capital or managerial labour is doubtful. Many private standalone forms have been founded in India since the process of economic liberalization began in 1991. These firms have taken market share from state owned firms, but not from business groups. Whether this will happen in the future remains to be seen.

Developments in some other countries in Asia

In 1997, several countries in East Asia were affected by what has been termed the 'East Asian crisis'. Countries such as South Korea, Malaysia, Indonesia and Thailand faced a major economic crisis and a fall in the value of their currencies against the dollar. The IMF offered to step in on the condition that important institutional reforms would be made.

In South Korea, the government promised to dismantle business groups (the *chaebols*) in accordance with the IMF-instituted restructuring guidelines. However, the years since the crisis have demonstrated the resilience of business groups as an organizational form and several Korean business groups continue to prosper.

Malaysia, Indonesia and Thailand have not seen the total disappearance of business groups post-crisis either. Instead, business groups that possessed the requisite political connections with the ruling elite have been able to avoid losses and benefited by acquiring failed businesses.

Japan was not affected to the same degree as the other East Asian economies and, in any case, its government made no serious attempt to break up business groups.

Developments in the EU

In the EU, business groups continue to play an important role in many countries (such as France, Spain, Italy, Belgium, Sweden). Very few restrictions on competition in product markets remain. Also, there is an increasingly active managerial labour market. As we will discuss more extensively in Section 15.7, however, the market for corporate control is not well developed in many of the EU countries. Despite the adoption of an EU Directive on takeover bids by the EU in 2004, important differences in takeover codes between EU countries still exist (see also Box 15.11). At the time of writing (2012), there is no indication that the role of business groups in the EU will decrease in the near future.

14.5 Informal networks

Informal network

An **informal network** may be thought of as a group of firms bound together by informal ties only. An informal network consists of essentially equal members that have informal relations with one another. The basis of those relations is trust. A network is characterized more by cooperation than competition:

> If it is price competition that is the central co-ordinating mechanisms of the market and administrative orders that of hierarchy, then it is trust and co-operation that centrally articulates networks (Frances et al., 1991, p. 15).

Interlocking directorates

An example of an informal network may be **interlocking directorates** – members of a relatively small number of organizations serving on each others' boards as outside directors. Such contacts may build an atmosphere of mutual trust and cooperation. Another example is the informal networks that exist in Italy between small and medium sized firms, which work together in a subcontracting mode.

Coordination within informal networks is through mutual adjustment and standardization of norms. Standardization of norms (through self-selection, selection or socialization) probably plays an important role in the case of interlocking directorates. People who come from the same region, who went to the same university or know each other well from 'the old days' sometimes form a closed group, sitting on several boards and exchanging favours and information **Old boys' networks** with each other. Where such **old boys' networks** exist, outsiders may find it very difficult to penetrate such a network. Companies on whose boards they sit interact through markets, so market coordination still also plays a role. In our second example, of Italian networks of small and medium sized firms, the mechanisms of mutual adjustment and standardization of norms operate as well, combined with market coordination (prices are involved in subcontracting).

Networks are important in countries where the rules and institutions that are used to settle disputes are less well developed. That may explain, to some extent, why networks based on personal relations are more important in China, as suggested by the text in Box 14.6.

Box 14.6 *Guanxi*, transaction costs and rules

Many countries in Eastern Europe and Asia are making a difficult transition to more market-based economies. In Eastern Europe these are mostly replacing former (communist) planning-based systems. In Asia, the economies have often been characterized as more network- or relations-based. Economists around the world have been impressed by the difficulties that such a transition encounters. In particular, the extent to which market-based economies rely on clear and transparent rules, as well as on institutions that safeguard and enforce those rules, has become evident. One particular analysis by Professors Li Shuhe and Li Shaomin of the City University of Hong Kong was summarized as follows in a survey of Asian business in *The Economist*:

> The familiar word used to describe the old (Chinese) system is *guanxi*. Usually translated as 'connections', *guanxi* conjures up images of karaoke outings with officials, nods of understanding in

smoke-filled rooms, and the invisible hand not of the market, but of influence. *Guanxi* is a cliché, but is only too real.

Western investors tend to assume that Asian tycoons turn to *guanxi* for deep-seated cultural reasons, but in fact they do so out of necessity. Both a rules-based and a *guanxi*-based system of governance incur expenses. For both, these are made up of the fixed costs of keeping the system running – say, training and paying judges, regulators and auditors – and incremental costs, such as the effort and expense of signing one more contract, sealing one more transaction, and so on.

Developed economies have rules-based governance systems that incur enormous fixed, but negligible incremental, costs. The fixed costs, however, are spread over huge numbers of transactions and business relationships, so that the average cost of any single deal is quite low. By contrast, the poor countries of Asia so far have not been able to afford the investment in the high fixed costs of such a system, and have therefore settled on the large incremental costs of a *guanxi*-based system. As long as the number of transactions and business relationships remained comparatively small, the average cost of transactions was bearable.

As *guanxi* economies grow and become more complex, however, the incremental costs of doing business shoot up. What worked with a hundred clients, a dozen suppliers, two creditors and one shareholder no longer works with thousands of all of these. So there comes a point, Messrs Li reckon, when the average cost of doing business in a *guanxi*-based system of governance exceeds that in rules-based systems. When this happens, companies and countries that rely on *guanxi* can no longer compete. Market forces initiate a transition to a rules-based system. This is probably the largest and riskiest step that countries and companies ever have to take.

Source: 'In praise of rules: a survey of Asian business', *The Economist,* 7 April 2001

14.6 Franchising

A franchise is a contract between the owner of a production process and a brand name (the franchisor, such as McDonald's Corporation) and a local businessman (the franchisee). The franchisee operates a local unit under the brand name of the franchisor and uses the processes developed by the franchisor. Franchising is typically found in industries such as fast-food restaurants (McDonald's, Kentucky Fried Chicken), hotels (Hilton, Sheraton, Holiday Inn) and retailing. These industries have two characteristics in common:

- They provide services that have to be 'produced' locally while the customer is present;
- There are large advantages in developing and maintaining a business formula and a brand name.

14.6.1 Why does franchising (continue to) exist?

There are two answers to the question of why franchising exists. The first answer is called the **resource scarcity thesis**. According to this thesis, a firm that has developed a highly successful formula is faced with resource constraints (scarcity of capital and talented managers) if it wants to expand rapidly. Franchising is seen as a means to overcome those constraints.

Resource scarcity thesis

Administrative
efficiency thesis

The second answer is the **administrative efficiency thesis**. In this thesis, franchising is analyzed from an agency theory and transaction cost perspective. According to this view franchising, in certain industries, is a more efficient governance structure than either a pure hierarchy or a pure market.

14.6.2 Resource scarcity thesis

Suppose that the owner of a restaurant develops a highly successful formula and she sees an opportunity to open many other restaurants operating with the same formula. If she wants to do so through full ownership, she has to set up, and subsequently manage, many local units. That requires large amounts of capital and many motivated and capable managers. If she lacks those resources, she is faced with the problem of resource scarcities. That problem can be overcome, it is argued, through franchising.

The franchisee invests in her own local unit, which means that the level of investment by the franchisor is greatly reduced. The franchisee also manages her own local unit. If we suppose that talented, highly motivated people with an entrepreneurial spirit, willing to work long hours are eager to work as franchisees, and less motivated people preferring an easy life prefer to work as salaried managers, then franchising also solves the problem of adverse selection in the managerial labour market.

The resource scarcity thesis can explain why a small company that happens to find a successful formula in the service sector has little choice but to grow through franchising. It may be very important to grow quickly and a small company may face serious difficulties in attracting large amounts of capital and many talented managers for new local units.

The resource scarcity thesis cannot explain, however, why a large company such as McDonald's Corporation continues to use franchising when it expands still further. Consider first the problem of obtaining additional capital. McDonald's Corporation is a large and highly profitable company. Its shares are listed on the New York Stock Exchange. Such a company is surely not faced with the problem of scarce financial resources. On the contrary, it is quite likely that McDonald's Corporation can acquire additional capital (in the form of both equity and debt) on better conditions than local entrepreneurs.

Let us now consider the problem of hiring talented young managers. It is hard to see why a company like McDonald's Corporation could not attract talented managers working for a salary (and offer them a pay package with strong incentives), while other large multinational companies, such as Unilever and Nestlé, are able to recruit hundreds of talented young managers every year.

To summarize, the resource scarcity thesis can explain why small companies that have found a highly successful formula start to grow through franchising, but it cannot explain why large, established companies continue to use franchising when they expand still further. That brings us to the second view of franchising – the administrative efficiency thesis.

14.6.3 Administrative efficiency thesis

According to the administrative efficiency thesis, franchising exists because, in certain industries, it is a very efficient organizational form. Recall that franchising is found primarily in service industries, where production occurs in many local units and there are significant advantages to be gained from operating many local units under the same formula and brand name.

There are, in principle, three organizational arrangements that could be used in that type of industry:

- one company owning and operating all units (a hierarchy);
- franchising;
- a set of independent companies using a common brand name.

In comparing these three arrangements two problems play an important role. The first problem is *shirking by local operators*. In a large company with many dispersed units, shirking by local managers is an important problem. Suppose, first, that local managers receive a fixed level of pay (not related to the sales or profit of the unit they manage). In the language of the theory of principal and agent, that is a wage contract. The theory then predicts that the agent will choose to exert a low level of effort. One way to reduce shirking by local managers is to monitor them. That requires frequent visits by the district manager to the local units in the district. Another way is to give local managers a share in the profits of their units or offer them career prospects within the company.

In a franchising arrangement, the franchisor usually receives a franchise fee consisting of a percentage of the sales of a local unit plus a fixed annual payment. The profits of the individual unit, after payment of the franchise fee, are for the franchisee. Thus, although the franchise fee is not a fixed payment (it depends on sales), the risk of variations in profitability is borne by the franchisee. That comes very close to a rent contract. The franchisee, then, has very strong incentives to run her unit efficiently. Shirking by the local manager (the main problem in a hierarchy) is not at all a problem here. Shirking by local managers is of course not a problem, if these manager are in fact entrepreneurs operating their own company as part of a set of independent companies.

Free riding by a franchisee

The second problem is **free riding** on the common brand name. This is a major problem for a set of independent companies using a common brand name. If one company invests in advertising and offers consistent, high levels of quality, other companies can free ride on those investments. This problem can be solved only if there is a central authority monitoring quality levels and thus restricting free riding on the common brand name. Then we have franchising instead of a set of independent companies. In franchising, free riding on the common brand name is still a major problem. The franchisee may be tempted to use cheaper inputs for her products. That lowers the quality level. If there are very few repeat customers anyway, perhaps because the restaurant is located at an airport, that can increase local profits. The result, however, is that the value of the general brand name deteriorates. The point is that the decrease in the value of the brand name is borne by the franchisor and all franchisees together. If all other franchisees continue to deliver high quality, then one individual franchisee can deliver a low quality and free ride on the common brand name. In order to reduce this problem, the franchisor usually monitors quality very closely. Doing so is much cheaper than monitoring all aspects of a local operation.

Since a set of independent companies is not a viable alternative is (the problem of free riding cannot be solved), we have only two alternative arrangements: a hierarchy and franchising. The choice between these two arrangements depends mainly on the costs of shirking versus the cost of free riding. Company ownership (hierarchy) will be preferred when the free riding costs of franchising exceed the shirking costs of company ownership, and *vice versa*. Empirical work shows that firms use more franchising when the cost of monitoring outlets is high (in rural areas and foreign markets where the travelling costs of monitors is high and where it is difficult to assess managers' efforts. When local market knowledge is important it is also more difficult to assess a manager's level of effort; empirical work has shown that we see more franchising when this is the case (see Michael, S.C. and Bercovitz, J. E. L., 2009).

Inefficient risk-bearing

There are two other factors that may influence the choice between hierarchy and franchising. The first factor is the problem of **inefficient risk-bearing**. As there are so many restaurants, McDonald's shareholders do not worry about the risk of an individual restaurant. In the agency relationship between franchisor and franchisee, the principal is (almost) risk-neutral and the agent probably risk-averse. We know from Section 7.6.2 that, in that case, the agent should not bear all the risk, yet it seems that in most franchising contracts almost all risk *is* borne by the agent (the franchisee).

Appropriability of quasi-rents

The second factor concerns the **appropriability of quasi-rents**. Suppose that the franchisee has to invest in a building that is designed as a McDonald's restaurant and the resale value of that building – should the franchisee's contract with McDonald's Corporation be terminated – is much lower than the original investment. The building is then a transaction-specific investment for the franchisee. The difference between the original investment and the resale value is a quasi-rent that could be appropriated by the franchisor. The problem vanishes if the franchisor owns the building and lets it to the franchisee (as does McDonald's Corporation in many cases). The franchisor can also make transaction specific investments, such as support for site selection and construction management, and training the potential franchisee in operating the production process. Transaction specific investments on both sides (franchisor and franchisee) makes a long-term contract between franchisor and franchisee a viable solution.

By way of a summary we can conclude that the choice between hierarchy and franchising is determined mainly by the costs of shirking versus the cost of free riding and inefficient risk bearing.

Finally, we want to note that McDonald's Corporation uses a bundle of coordinating mechanisms to organize the actions of the managers of the restaurants it owns: direct supervision, standardization of outputs (products in this case), standardization of work processes and probably also standardization of norms. In its role as franchisor, the McDonald's Corporation uses exactly the same bundle of coordinating mechanisms for the franchisees. The main difference is that, with respect to its franchisees, direct supervision focuses on quality levels, whereas with respect to the managers of its own restaurants, direct supervision includes all aspects of the local manager's job. Another important difference between 'owning' and 'franchising' is the market relation between McDonald's Corporation and its franchisees: the McDonald's Corporation sells the right to use its business formula at a price (the franchise fee). In addition, the franchisee is sometimes required to buy ingredients and equipment from the franchisor.

14.6.4 The plural form symbiosis

The administrative efficiency thesis can explain why a large company, like McDonald's, continues to use franchising. However it cannot explain why company owned outlets and franchised outlets are found in the same city, where monitoring costs should be the same. The answer to this may be that there is some merit in having both company owned outlets and franchised outlets. Franchisees, it may be argued, foster innovation and local market adaptation by solving operational problems and identifying profitable new products. Company ownership promotes standardization. So, one can argue, to have both company owned outlets and franchised outlets offers advantages not available to a firm that uses one of these modes only. This symbiosis of two forms has been termed 'the plural form symbiosis'.

14.7 Comparing several hybrid forms

From the discussion in the previous sections, it is clear that there are large differences between hybrid forms. There are, however also some common features. The most important common feature is that hybrid forms are based on the necessity to pool resources in order to achieve something. In a co-makership relation, supplier and buyer share know-how, production plans and cost data. JVs are established when two (sometimes more than two) companies pool resources – often intangible as well as tangible assets – to set up a new company. Companies belonging to a business group often use the same brand name, exchange know-how, support an industrial embassy and rotate young managers. In informal networks, information is shared between participating organizations. In franchising, franchisees use the formula, including the brand name, developed and supported by the franchisor. These are all examples of pooling of (intangible) resources.

With pooling of resources often comes joint planning. In a co-makership relation, buyer and supplier often jointly plan production schedules. In a JV, the two parent companies jointly make decisions on the strategic direction of their joint subsidiary. Companies belonging to a business group discuss their strategic plans with other group companies. In franchising, the franchisor develops new products in close cooperation with (a selection of) the franchisees.

Pooling of resources and joint planning introduces organizational coordination mechanisms, such as direct supervision, mutual adjustment and standardization of work processes, skills, output and norms. We would place a hybrid form, for which these organizational coordinating mechanisms are much more important than the price mechanism, to the right side of Figure 14.2. Conversely, when the price mechanism is more important than the

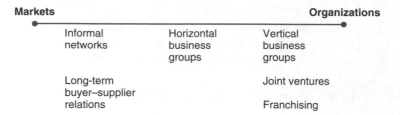

Figure 14.4 Hybrid forms placed on the line between markets and organizations

organizational coordination mechanisms, we would place a hybrid form to the left side of Figure 14.2. Where exactly each hybrid form should be placed on that line is dependent on the specific arrangements made in particular hybrid forms. Broadly speaking, however, we would say that:

- informal networks should be on the left side;
- long-term buyer–supplier relations (co-makership) should be on the left side;
- vertical business groups should be to the right of horizontal business groups;
- JVs, franchising and vertical business groups should be on the right side.

This leads us to the overview as presented in Figure 14.4.

14.8 Summary: hybrid forms as governance structures between ideal markets and ideal organizations

There are many types of hybrid forms. They may be seen as intermediate forms between markets and organizations, employing different mixes of market and organizational coordination mechanisms. That conclusion builds on our observations in Chapter 3:

- It is important analytically to distinguish carefully between market and organizational coordination to determine which is the most efficient in which circumstances;
- When we move from the analytical world (with its sharp distinctions) to the messy real world, we often find bundles of coordination mechanisms operating together.

In previous chapters we often highlighted that many markets are, to a certain extent, 'organized', while many organizations employ internal market mechanisms next to organizational coordination. As this chapter further elucidates, ideal markets and ideal organizations are two ends of a continuum. Between those two ends, many different bundles of coordination mechanisms can be observed. As we move from left to right in Figure 14.4:

- We start with an 'ideal market', utilizing only the price mechanism.
- Then markets become increasingly 'organized' (by being regulated, for example).
- They give way to hybrid forms that are first still 'market-like' and then increasingly become 'organization-like'.

- Organizations then take over – initially with the price mechanism still playing a role (in the form of transfer pricing, for example).
- Finally, we reach 'ideal organizations', entirely utilizing organizational coordination mechanisms.

It is certainly a fascinating world of markets and organizations out there!

Questions

1 Box 14.1 describes how Boeing outsources production and development to its partners around the world. Referring to the discussion on vertical integration in Section 10.5, how would you classify the situation of Boeing and its partners in terms of Figure 10.1? Do you think Boeing is now vulnerable to opportunistic behaviour by its suppliers? If not, why?

2 In 2012 Tata Motors, through its affiliate, Jaguar Land Rover decided to form a JV with Chery Automobiles for the Chinese market. Do you think that Tata Motors, after a couple of years, may want to buy out its Chinese partner? If it does, would you interpret this as the failure of the JV?

3 In Section 14.4.3, a business group is compared with a set of independent companies. One advantage of a business group mentioned is that business group firms may use a common brand name. What kind of problem could arise when, say, ten companies belonging to a business group use a common brand name? What could be done to mitigate that problem? How easy (or difficult) would it be to do that if those ten companies offered widely different products?

4 Box 8.8 describes competition between two organizational forms – entrepreneurial firms and farmers' cooperatives. Do you think that the farmers' cooperatives described should be considered as hybrid forms according to the definition of hybrid forms given in this chapter?

5 Box 8.8 describes how competition between two organization forms (entrepreneurial firms and farmers' cooperatives) led to a situation in which one form (farmers' cooperatives) became the dominant form in certain parts of the country, while the other (entrepreneurial firms) came to dominate other parts of the country. According to the scheme presented in this book (Figure 1.7 and 12.1), this should be the result of one or more differences in the environments in which these firms operated. Which difference played a vital role in this respect?

6 Section 13.7 describes how a joint venture can be used as an intermediate stage when overcoming the problem of hidden information at times when a company wants to sell one of its subsidiaries to another company (Section 13.7 discusses how Philips sold its domestic appliances business to Whirlpool in two stages, first forming a joint venture and then selling the remainder of the shares). What differences do you see between the Philips-Whirlpool joint venture and the Jaguar Land Rover - Chery joint venture described in Box 14.2?

15 Corporate governance

15.1 Introduction

Corporate governance

Corporate governance is the system by which business corporations are directed and controlled. The corporate governance structure specifies the distribution of rights and responsibilities to different participants in the corporation, such as the board, managers, shareholders and other stakeholders (like employees, customers, suppliers, creditors and society at large). It spells out the rules and procedures for making decisions on corporate affairs. By doing this, it also provides the structure through which the company objectives are set and the means of attaining those objectives and monitoring performance.

In this chapter, we want to focus our attention on the relationship between shareholders and managers. In companies with a separation of ownership and control, there is an agency problem between the shareholders as the principal and the company's top manager or CEO as the agent. The separation of ownership and control noted by Berle and Means in 1932 (discussed in Section 7.2) has been a dominant feature of large companies in the Anglo-American world ever since.

The agency problem arises because, first, there may be a lack of alignment between the desires and objectives of the CEO and those of shareholders (see Section 7.3 for the consequences of such a lack of alignment) and, second, because there is usually information asymmetry between a CEO and the shareholders. Such a lack of alignment may occur for several reasons. Shareholders are interested primarily in obtaining a return on their investment. They will want to make sure that the CEO always makes decisions that maximize shareholder value. A CEO, however, will make decisions that maximize his own utility function, which will not always coincide with maximizing shareholder value.

Free cash flow

First, there is the problem of **free cash flow**. A CEO aiming to maximize shareholder value should invest only in projects with a positive net present value (NPV). If the firm generates more cash flow than the amount it can invest in projects with a positive NPV, the difference is called *free cash flow*. Firms in mature industries often have cash-generating operations and few opportunities to invest these often significant levels of cash in their own industry, simply because, in a mature industry, there are few projects with a positive NPV. According to financial theory, free cash flow should be returned to shareholders, but the CEO may wish to retain it in order to diversify into other lines of business. That may be because managers overestimate their ability to select and subsequently run other companies (a phenomenon referred to as *hubris*: see Section 12.6), their reward scheme is tied to the size of the firm or simply the pure pleasure that comes with empire building. There are many examples of firms in mature industries that have invested heavily in other industries, only to find out much later that those investments did not succeed. One of the problems here is that the *real* NPV of an investment project (such as the acquisition of another firm) may be difficult to determine both *ex ante* and *ex post*.

Second, there is the problem of a possible difference in *attitude towards risk*. Many shareholders typically invest only a small proportion of their total wealth in any one firm. If one of their investments fails, that is probably offset by the good performance of their other firms. A CEO, by contrast, works normally for one firm only. The CEO's human capital depends on how well that single firm performs. If the firm fails, the value of the CEO's human capital declines and that human capital (earning power) is probably a large proportion of his or her total wealth. Consequently, the CEO of a widely held firm may be more risk-averse than the shareholders. Of course, this means that a difference in the degree of risk aversion between CEO and shareholders may lead to a situation in which projects that are attractive to shareholders are rejected by the CEO.

Third, there is the problem of *different time horizons*. Shareholders are entitled to all the company's future cash flows, without any time horizon. Managers, however, serve only for a limited period of time. That may give them a bias for investment projects with high accounting returns in the short term, even if the NPV of such projects is negative. Conversely, they may have a bias against projects with a positive NPV and low or negative accounting returns in the short term. An example of the latter might be investments in R&D.

Finally, there is the problem of *on-the-job consumption*. This problem has been analyzed extensively in Section 7.3.

Any agency problem arises because, first, the principal and agent have different interests and, second, there is information asymmetry between the agent and principal. Consequently, solutions for agency problems aim at:

- narrowing the gap between the interests of principal and agent;
- reducing the information asymmetry between principal and agent.

The gap between the interests of principal and agent can be narrowed by offering the agent an incentive contract (which we would call an organizational solution), but also by improving the functioning of the market for managerial labour and/or the market for the corporate control.

Information asymmetry can be reduced by monitoring. Monitoring can be done internally (by a large shareholder and/or by the (supervisory) board), which is an organizational solution. Monitoring can also be done by various parties external to the company in question, such as stock market analysts, credit-rating agencies, private equity firms and other parties possibly interested in acquiring the company. External monitoring helps to reduce information asymmetry in markets, such as the managerial labour market and the market for corporate control. Such measures will improve the functioning of those markets and, consequently, help to reduce the agency problem.

So, we see that the agency problem can be reduced by means of organizational solutions (incentive contracts, internal monitoring) and market solutions (external monitoring and the functioning of various markets). That leads us to the scheme presented in Figure 15.1.

The root of the agency problem between shareholders and managers lies in the separation of ownership and control, as identified by Berle and Means. In a firm led by one owner-manager, agency problems do not exist at the top. However, in many modern firms, management has become a specialized function and ownership is widely dispersed, shared between many shareholders.

Incentive alignment

In such a modern firm, the first agency problem to be addressed is how to narrow the gap between the interests of the CEO (or top management) and the shareholders. It is a question of **incentive alignment**.

Monitoring

The second agency problem is how to reduce the information asymmetry between the shareholders (as principal) and the CEO (as agent). That is a question of effective **monitoring**.

Monitoring can be done and incentives can be given internally (organizational solutions) or externally (market solutions). Information, again, plays a crucial role in this scheme as it facilitates both organizational and market solutions. Corporate governance may be seen as part of the institutional environment in which corporations operate. It consists of rules set by the government or other public bodies (such as the Securities and Exchange Commission – SEC) and companies themselves in their statutes and internal regulations.

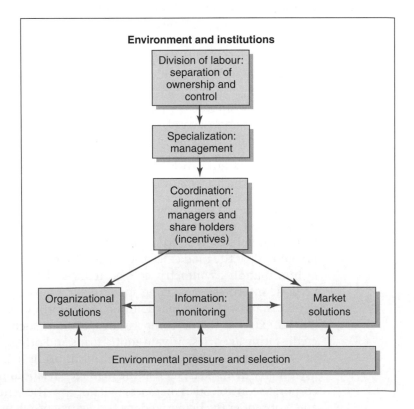

Figure 15.1 The corporate governance framework

The scheme found in Figure 15.1 has a strong resemblance to the scheme of this book, as presented in Figure 1.1. That is no coincidence: corporate governance, in our view, is a special case of the governance of transactions. Figure 15.1 describes corporate governance, while Figure 1.1 portrays the governance of transactions.

In practice, the corporate governance system used in a certain country will most likely involve a mixture of organizational and market solutions. Also, as we will see, it will be influenced by environmental pressure and selection.

In this chapter, we start by examining the evolution of corporate governance from its early beginnings in the first public company to the modern day struggles to develop and amend corporate governance codes in many countries. We do this by using the United East India Company, or Verenigde Oost-Indische Compagnie (VOC) – arguably the first public corporation in the world – as an example. This historic example highlights many corporate governance issues that are still prevalent today, especially the divergence of interests between shareholders and managers. We explore the nature of this agency relationship in Section 15.2. We then discuss how the design of incentive contracts can help to reduce (though not eliminate) the agency problem today (Section 15.3). In Section 15.4, we describe how internal monitoring in actual corporations takes place and how it can help to reduce the agency problem. After having discussed organizational solutions, we turn to market solutions – first, to external monitoring (Section 15.5) and then to how markets constrain the size of the agency problem (Section 15.6). Section 15.7 looks at institutional frameworks in different parts of the world. Section 15.8 shows how, in different parts of the world, different corporate governance systems have evolved, using organizational and market solutions in different proportions. In the concluding section, we give our views on future developments in corporate governance systems. We also illustrate the relevance of this topic for both organizations and the development of societies. First, though, let us witness the birth of the public corporation and the birth pains of corporate governance issues.

15.2 The first public company

Project financing

The (VOC),[1] was established in 1602 in the Netherlands. Its purpose was to conduct trade with 'East India' (the area we would now describe as South-east Asia), in competition with the Spanish and Portuguese fleets. It was not the first such trading company to be created, but its predecessors were usually financed in a way that we would nowadays call '**project financing**'. That is to say, entrepreneurs and investors combined in a 'company' to invest money in buying a ship and financing a round trip. On its safe return, the ship and its cargo were sold and the investors were repaid their money together with a handsome profit. If the investors were satisfied with the entrepreneurs, they would consider financing their next project. If not, they would seek alternative projects to finance. Today, we would say that the capital market was acting as a 'disciplining mechanism' on the entrepreneurs' activities.

Those projects were not without complexities and risks. A ship had to be built, a crew recruited, a destination in 'The Indies' selected and reached, trade conducted and a safe return accomplished. Risks included pirates underway, shipwrecks and fraudulent behaviour on the part of the captain and/or the crew, who sometimes sold cargoes to parties other than those who had financed the project. In the language of agency theory, the project could be considered as a nexus of contracts (see Section 7.5) between financing parties and project management. Hence, we can observe agency problems such as shirking, which requires monitoring (see Section 7.4). In modern terms, however, we would regard such agency problems as being typical of the contractual relationship between managers and providers of temporary capital. Agency problems were relatively limited because of the financing on a project-by-project basis. Entrepreneurs who built up a doubtful reputation would find the financing of their next project difficult.

The VOC started out this way in 1602, combining 70 entrepreneurs (merchants/shareholders who took the initiative for a trip and had managerial responsibility) with more than a thousand participants/investors with only a passive interest. Gradually, the merchant-shareholders came to feel that it was better to finance the company on a more permanent basis. They sought the approval of the authorities to replace the temporary nature of the financing arrangements with a more permanent structure, allowing participants to trade their shares with each other, so, in effect, creating a stock market.

In 1609, the required approval was granted and trading in the shares started. Through the transformation that resulted, the VOC achieved a permanent, anonymous capital base. It became a **public company**, with a clear separation between (public) ownership and (managerial) control, as later analysed by Berle and Means (see Section 7.2).

Public company

The public invested the enormous sum of 6,424,588 Dutch guilders. The last investor was the 'maid-servant' Neeltje Cornelis, who invested 100 guilders in the shares being issued on 31 August 1602, the day the 'participants book' was closed. Today, we would say that the IPO of VOC shares had been a tremendous success.

Participation in the VOC proved, however, not to be a fast route to high financial returns. The costs for the first fleets exceeded the revenues, partly because they also had the mission to attack the Portuguese in Asia in order to decrease their 'market share' and make room for increasing the share of the Dutch. Only in 1610 were the first dividends paid, albeit largely in kind – the participants received quantities of nutmeg and pepper! Of course, they would have preferred to receive cash. The managers, however, preferred to reinvest the proceeds of projects into the next projects and increasing their market share of the East Indian trade.

The 'outside' shareholders slowly became dissatisfied with this state of affairs. At the same time, they became wary of potential other conflicts of interest between the managers and shareholders. It was rumoured that the managers sometimes sold goods from the cargoes privately and realized substantial private benefits that way. There were also questions about supply contracts: were they sometimes awarded to parties 'befriended' by the managers? Moreover, the remuneration of the managers included fee structures that were not conducive to cost control. Finally, the managers obtained private information on the timing, quality and price of the trade flows that could be very valuable for trading on the domestic goods market. Today we would say that the managers received **inside information** (asymmetrical private information) that created the risk of insider trading.

Inside information

The 'outside' shareholders grew increasingly unhappy. In particular, one shareholder by the name of Isaac le Maire became a vocal protester. Today, we would call him an **activist shareholder**. One of his main objections to the VOC's policy was that it made insufficient use of the charter it was granted by the Dutch government. It focused on the trade with Bantam (Java), the Banda islands and Ambon (all in the present Indonesia), but neglected opportunities in South America, even though its charter permitted it to exploit the Strait of Magellan.

Activist shareholder

The agency problem here was later formulated by Jensen and Meckling (1976) as follows:

> Indeed, it is likely that the most important conflict arises from the fact that, as the manager's ownership claim falls, his incentive to devote significant effort to creative activities such as searching out new profitable ventures falls. He may in fact avoid such ventures simply because it requires too much effort on his part to manage or to learn about new technologies. Avoidance of these personal costs and the anxieties that go with them also represent a source of on-the-job utility to him and it can result in the value of the firm being substantially lower than it otherwise could be.

Le Maire calculated that the VOC only generated profits of 2.3 million guilders in the first seven years of its existence. That was insufficient to cover the cost of capital, including a risk premium, set at 8 per cent by Le Maire. Today, we would say that the VOC was destroying **shareholder value** in the first years of its existence.

In 1622, this led to a published protest containing *inter alia* the following demands for:

- transparent information on, for example, trading flows, investments and proceeds;
- the right to appoint managers;
- time limits to the managers' tenure;
- adjustments to the remuneration of managers;
- limits to the possibilities of insider trading (for example, with supply contracts).

By threatening to withhold financing for similar companies and exerting pressure on the Dutch government, the outside shareholders achieved extensive adjustments in the corporate governance of the VOC by December 1622, when its charter had to be renewed. This shows how shareholder and environmental pressure led to the adaptation of the institutional framework in which the VOC had to function.

As one can see from the above list of demands, some of the main topics of the discussion regarding corporate governance have remained remarkably constant for the last 400 years. At the same time, the institutional framework has continually evolved to protect the rights of 'outsiders' versus 'insiders' and of minority shareholders versus majority shareholders. Frentrop (2003) shows that stock market crashes and corporate scandals have provided the main triggers for improved protection mechanisms throughout history. The 1720 South Sea Bubble in the UK and the 1873 Panic in the USA were such episodes that led to improved legislation and regulation.

Throughout history, corporations have failed, the reasons for their failure have been examined and those investigations have provided input for adaptations to be made to security laws and regulations. In the USA, for example, the Interstate Commerce Act was adopted in 1887 to bring the American railway companies under federal supervision after several scandals involving fraud and corruption (the directors of the companies were called the *robber barons*). The stock market crash of 1929 led to the Securities and Exchange Act of 1934. Corporate scandals such as Enron and Worldcom triggered renewed legislative efforts, leading to the Sarbanes-Oxley Act (corporate governance) in 2002, while the crisis in the financial system led to the Dodd-Frank Act (regulation of Wall Street and consumer protection) in 2010. From an evolutionary perspective, in developed economies such as the USA, the institutional framework has therefore been frequently adapted to incorporate the lessons generated by such episodes and scandals. In Section 15.7, we will examine which evolutionary pathways were taken in different environments. Box 15.1 is a reminder of the importance of proper corporate governance for the development of emerging economies and trust in their institutions.

Box 15.1 Corporate governance (or, rather, the lack of it) in Russia and China

Corporate governance is shaped by the institutional framework of the country in which the corporation is domiciled. In some countries, that institutional framework is still inadequate because, for instance, the reorientation of the economy towards a market economy is not yet complete. That is the case in Russia and China. The Financial Times reports on the situation in Russia as follows:

"Russia: Laws do exist but enforcement is patchy"

Valued almost any way, Russian companies are cheap – their shares, on average trade at about seven times earnings, compared with 13 for Brazil, 15 for China, and 20 for India, writes Charles Clover in Moscow. But before running out to load up on Russian shares, one should ask why. Brokers and analysts almost in unison say the country's notoriously politicised and malfunctioning legal system, along with the perception that investors are vulnerable to powerful local interests are, in a sense, priced into the stock market. "What holds investors back is concern about enforcement of contracts and corporate governance", says Peter Ghavani, head of global markets for Troika Dialog, the Moscow investment bank. The government, meanwhile, is making a concerted effort to do something about the bad reputation Russia has in the business world. Legislation is planned and there has already been some progress. Changes to the insolvency laws last year gave shareholders the ability to pursue managers and other shareholders who strip assets, although no big cases have yet tested this, lawyers say. But the laws are not the main problem, say most experienced investors. "The biggest problem is not the law itself, it is the implementation of the law", says the president of a big investment bank in Moscow.

The Economist concludes an article on corporate governance in China as follows:

'China's biggest corporate governance issue is not its laws, but its government's willingness to enforce them evenhandedly. William McGovern of Kobre & Kim, a lawyer and former SEC enforcement official, argues that aggressive action by American regulators after the Enron debacle restored confidence to American markets. China risks a similar crisis of confidence now, but Mr McGovern observes that its regulators have yet to act decisively at home or to cooperate with foreign agencies such as the SEC. Not all Chinese firms are crooked – but until China gets serious about regulating its companies, investors should remain wary'

In both countries, improvements in enforcing corporate governance laws seem necessary to allow their companies to participate fully in the global economy.

Sources: 'Russia: Laws do exist but enforcement is patchy', Financial Times, October 6, 2010. "Seeing the forest for the trees" The Economist, February, 4, 2012.

15.3 The use of incentive contracts

One way to deal with the agency problem described in Section 15.1 is to offer the CEO an incentive contract. That is, of course, an organizational solution. In the real world, we see three elements in managers' compensation packages that encourage them to act in the interests of shareholders: cash bonuses, share plans and option plans. Many corporate governance codes stipulate that managers should have temporary contracts, allowing a renewal of the contract to be based on performance evaluation. We will first describe the elements of managers' compensation packages and the reasons for offering temporary contracts. We then discuss a few reasons for the fact that offering incentive contracts or temporary contracts can only partially solve the agency problem.

15.3.1 Cash bonuses

Managers often receive an annual cash bonus if certain specified goals have been met. Those goals are often based on the level or size of the improvement in ratios, such as the earnings per share, return on capital employed, return on assets, sales growth or market share. To do so rests on the belief that realizing improvements in these ratios is in the interests of shareholders.

15.3.2 Share plans

A more direct way to ensure that managers will be interested in increasing the share price is to make sure that they own shares. This can be done by giving them shares (or allowing them to buy shares at a reduced price) when they start. That is what private equity firms do (in most cases) when they buy a company and install a new management team. The aim is then to restructure the company and sell it at a later date. It is an effective way to align the interests of the private equity firm (as shareholder and principal) and the manager (as agent).

The remuneration of top managers in listed firms often includes a long-term bonus in the form of a share plan. Under such a plan managers receive shares as part of their compensation package. In a very simple plan, a manager can, for example, receive a salary of $500,000 plus 40,000 shares. That gives the manager an incentive to take actions that increase share price. If the share price goes up, the manager's remuneration increases. In a more complicated plan, a manager may receive a fixed salary plus a *conditional* number of shares. Then, the manager will receive the shares only under certain conditions – when, after three years, a clearly specified goal has been reached, for example. When that goal is an increase in share price of at least X per cent or an increase in earnings per share of at least Y per cent, the manager has a very strong incentive to reach that goal.

We know from the discussion in Section 7.3 that a manager's on-the-job consumption will decrease as a function of α where α is the fraction of shares he owns. So, there is a clear reason to give the manager, or require the manager to buy, a substantial number of shares. If the manager owns a controlling block (more than 50 per cent is a controlling block in any case, but 20 per cent can be

Managerial entrenchment

if the rest is widely dispersed), however, the problem of **managerial entrenchment** may arise. This occurs when a manager performs poorly and shareholders want to get rid of him. If the manager is also a shareholder, he can use his voting power as a shareholder to prevent the dismissal. Thus, while some share ownership by the manager may be beneficial, too much share ownership may result in managerial entrenchment.

15.3.3 Stock options

Stock options

Another possibility is to award **stock options** to managers. A stock option is a right to buy shares at a specified moment in the future against a fixed price. The value of that right will increase when the share price increases, creating a stimulus for managers to maximize the share price.

Stock options can be given to managers as a part of the total compensation package without any further conditions. Options can also be given under the condition that, after a certain specified time lag, a precise goal has been reached; for instance, share price performance as compared to a reference group (see Box 15.2). That creates very strong incentives for managers.

15.3.4 Temporary contracts

Many corporate governance codes stipulate that contracts with directors, including the CEO, should be of limited duration. That means their power is limited to a certain timespan, often to a term of four years. After the term has elapsed, the director is up for re-election. The number of times a person can be re-elected may also be limited. This system limits the power of a CEO in a significant way, because she cannot be sure of being re-elected. If the CEO ignores the interests of shareholders, the chances of being re-elected decrease. Offering temporary contracts only also mimics the managerial labour market. A disadvantage is that offering temporary contracts increases the problem of different time horizons (see Section 15.1).

15.3.5 Factors outside a manager's control

In order to ensure that a cash bonus gives the manager an incentive to act in the interests of shareholders, the (size of) the bonus should be tied to (the size of) the improvement in one or more (financial) ratios. Share plans are often conditional – tied to improvements in share price or (a number of) ratios. In fact, many corporate governance codes explicitly require that this should be the case. The same is true for stock option plans.

In the real world, profits, financial ratios and share prices are not only determined by managers' actions and decisions but also many other factors outside of a manager's control. Factors such as general macroeconomic developments, currency rates and oil prices are at least as important, perhaps more important for share prices, than management performance. Considering that, tying managerial compensation to profits and share prices may produce unsatisfying results. For example, in the general economic peak at the end of the previous century, profits and share prices of almost all companies rose sharply. It meant that even managers who had shown only mediocre performance received bonuses and realized huge options profits. In the recessionary years that followed, managers who performed well and limited the decrease of profits and share prices were not rewarded accordingly, as the value of their options suffered under the general economic climate.

Not only does this situation produce unsatisfying results, it also weakens the incentives that variable compensation schemes are designed to give. If managers realize that their level of effort has only a limited influence on their total compensation, they might be motivated only slightly more than if they had just a fixed salary. If that is true, the money spent on the additional variable compensation may be a waste of money from the shareholder's point of view.

To cope with this problem, firms have looked at various ways in which to make a more direct link between management performance and executive compensation.

One of these ways is to measure the performance of the company relative to some of its competitors, or companies similar in size and structure. The group of similar companies is called a **reference group**. The performance of the companies in the reference group will be influenced by the same outside factors. This creates an opportunity for a realistic comparison of each company's performance at the end of each period. Managers of company's that have performed better than those in the reference group are rewarded accordingly. Box 15.2 gives an example of such a compensation scheme. See also Box 15.5.

Reference group

Box 15.2 Home Retail Group's performance share plan

Home Retail Group, a British company operating more than 1,000 stores in the UK and Ireland under the brand names Homebase and Argos, offers its executive directors a pay package consisting of:

- a fixed salary;
- an annual bonus subject to achievement of profit and cash generating targets;
- a performance share plan with an earnings per share target and a relative total shareholder return target.

The performance share plan gives executives shares, which vest after a period of three years if certain conditions with respect to growth in earnings per share and relative total shareholder return are met. In order to determine relative total shareholder return a reference group consisting of 18 other British companies is used.

Source: Home Retail Group Annual report 2011.

15.3.6 Incentives that are too strong

In recent years, we have seen several cases in which managers of very large and respected companies have engaged in fraud. Companies such as Enron, Worldcom and Ahold have been on the front pages of newspapers worldwide, after it was discovered that managers had manipulated revenue and profit figures and misled their shareholders in order to increase the share price. In all three cases, criminal charges were brought against those responsible.

What happened? Although it is not exactly clear what triggered the behaviour of those managers, some point at the aggressive reward structures they had. They had a strong incentive to increase the share price in the short term in order to maximize the value of their shares and options. That might have been one of the reasons the managers artificially pumped up the share price by manipulating the figures. Even when the relationship between such behaviour and reward structures cannot be proved, it is clear that the risk of managers giving misleading information can be triggered by their own personal interest in achieving a higher share price. This results in a need for more intensive monitoring of such managers and, ultimately, higher agency costs.

15.3.7 Incentives that lead to wrong decisions

Cash bonuses and share and option plans are often tied to an increase in something – usually a profitability ratio. To show that this can lead to wrong decisions being made, consider the following example.

Suppose a firm has a regular profit level of $1 million. To stimulate management to increase that figure, the firm promises managers a bonus when profits are higher than $1 million in the next year.

Suppose, further, that managers face a decision as to whether or not to undertake a project that, if successful, could result in profits of $2 million. If the project were to fail, it would result in a loss of $5 million. The probability of the project succeeding is 50 per cent. Clearly, it is not in the interests of shareholders to undertake the project: its expected value is negative. For management, however, it might be an attractive prospect: a probability of 50 per cent of a bonus and a probability of 50 per cent of no bonus. If they do *not* undertake the project, they are certain that they will *not* get a bonus, because the net profit will, once again, be $1 million.

Clearly, a bonus tied to an increase in net profit can give a manager the wrong sort of incentive. The problem here, of course, is that the manager is rewarded when the project is a success, but is not punished when it fails.

15.3.8 Ubiquity and usefulness of incentives

Performance pay is now widely used in many parts of the world. Box 15.3 an example of the level of pay, and the proportion that is sometimes given as incentives. Box 15.3 also outlines initiatives to give shareholders more 'say-on-pay'.

Box 15.3 Overpaid bosses are back

In 2010 Ray Irani, CEO of Occidental Petroleum took home a total compensation of $76.1 million. Whether Irani really deserved so much money or not is difficult to know. To some, the amount of compensation paid to American top executives is an indication of corporate plundering. Others may point to the market for managerial labour and argue that managerial compensation is simply the result of supply and demand for managerial talent. Still others argue that one of the ways to motivate middle managers is to let them compete for promotions. To make such competition effective, a promotion should be rewarded with a large increase in compensation. That, too, could explain why the top manager receives such a large amount.

Mr. Irani received $40.3 million of his pay in 2010 in stock awards, and $35.9 million as cash incentives,

In an attempt to curb excessive pay for company executives, the UK introduced in 2002 'say on pay', giving shareholders the right to vote on managerial pay packages. This has resulted in several rejections of pay schemes proposed by the board. In the USA shareholders also have the right to vote on executive pay since the adoption of the Dodd-Frank act in 2010. This new law also requires firms to publish the ratio of CEO pay to that of the median worker, although details have still to be worked out by the SEC. In the US this ratio is far higher than in other parts of the world.

Source: 'Pay up, overpaid bosses are back', The Economist, June, 16, 2011, and 'Occidental CEO Ray Irani's pay more than doubled in 2010', Los Angeles Times March24, 2011.

With compensation schemes based to such a great extent on performance, we would expect that performance related pay schemes lead to the best results for shareholders. Although there is wide agreement on this in many boardrooms, some doubt remains, as illustrated in Box 15.4.

Box 15.4 Pay without performance?

In 2004, Lucian Bebchuk and Jesse Fried published a book titled: 'Pay without performance: the unfulfilled promise of executive compensation'. In this book they criticize the optimal contracting view: the view that executive compensation schemes are the result of contract negotiations between a principal (the shareholders) and an agent (the CEO). Instead they argue that executives control, to a certain extent, their own boards and, thus, are able to set their own remuneration (the managerial power view).

In the principal-agent problem, a principal delegates a task to an agent whose incentives are not perfectly aligned with those of the principal. The principal will not pay more than is necessary to offer the agent a package that (1) gives the agent incentives to act in the interests of the principal and (2) compensates him for risk bearing.

▶

This may be a good model, if there is only one shareholder acting as principal. In large public corporations, however, there are many shareholders, who do not contract directly with the CEO. Instead they delegate the task of setting a compensation scheme to the board. Unless the board acts perfectly in the interest of shareholders, contracts will differ from those negotiated by a single shareholder as principal.

There are several reasons why the board may consider the interests of the CEO rather than the interests of shareholders.

First, board members may be interested to keep their job; they are well paid, and opposing the CEO may decrease the likelihood that a board member will be nominated for another term. Second, a CEO can provide board members several benefits, such as donations to charities. Third, CEO's often serve as board members for other companies and, thus, help their own board members in getting additional board memberships.

Bebchuk and Fried offer several pieces of evidence to substantiate their claim. First, they state that compensation schemes, aimed at giving the CEO an incentive to create shareholder value, have almost always used raw (that is unadjusted) share options. In the bull market of the 1990s this has resulted in large capital gains for top managers, even if their firms had average or even below average performance. They see this as a deviation from an optimal compensation scheme (an optimal compensation scheme will filter out factors that are out of the manager's control, so the exercise price of options given to a manager should be tied to a stock market index), and thus as proof that executives set their own remuneration. Further, when stock markets declined, as in the early 2000s, options were commonly 'repriced', that is the exercise price was lowered, to adjust for overall market movements. Adjusting for bear markets and not adjusting for bull markets is seen as evidence supporting the managerial power view.

Another 'piece of evidence' offered is that executives are not prevented from 'unwinding' their incentives. The idea behind options and restricted shares is to give managers incentives. Options and restricted shares give incentives only if managers are unable to sell them during the period in which the incentives are relevant, or to engage in hedging transactions that undo the effects the incentives options were supposed to give. Babchuk and Fried offer evidence that the latter frequently happens. They see this as additional support for the managerial power view.

Source: Weisbach, M.S. (2007) "Optimal executive compensation versus managerial power: a review of Lucian Bebchuk and Jesse Fried's *Pay without performance: the unfulfilled promise of executive compensation*', Journal of Economic Literature, 419–428

15.4 Internal Monitoring

By using incentive alignment, as discussed in the previous section, agency problems may be reduced, but not totally eliminated. Separation of ownership and control remains. Shareholders remain relative 'outsiders', with less information than the managerial 'insiders'. It remains necessary, therefore, to seek ways to reduce the information asymmetry between shareholders and managers. This can be achieved through monitoring. Monitoring can be done either internally (the subject of this section) or externally (the subject of the next section).

15.4.1 Monitoring by shareholder(s)

Internal monitoring can be done by shareholders themselves. It can be very effective if a firm has one or a few large shareholders, as is often the case for privately held companies (companies owned by members of one family or private equity firms) and for companies belonging to a business group. For public companies with widely distributed shareholding, the situation is different.

Suppose that the largest shareholder (let us call her Mrs Navratilova) owns 6 per cent of all outstanding shares, while the remaining 94 per cent are owned by many smaller investors. Mrs Navratilova knows that if she invests time and money in monitoring, only 6 per cent of the benefits will accrue to her, while **Free rider problem** 94 per cent of the benefits will go to the other shareholders. This is a **free rider problem**. As a result of this problem, Mrs Navratilova will surely invest less time and money in monitoring than if she were the sole owner of the company.

In large public companies it may well be that the largest shareholder owns less than 5 per cent of the shares. The incentives for individual shareholders to invest in monitoring in such cases are quite weak. Internal monitoring is then done mainly by the board.

15.4.2 The role of the board of directors

In most countries, including the USA and the UK, companies are controlled by a board of directors that consists of inside directors and outside directors. The **Inside directors** **inside directors**, also called executive officers, are full time managers of the company. The firm's top manager is always a member of the board. In the USA, the title given to the top manager is chief executive officer or CEO.

Outside directors The **outside directors**, also called non-executive directors or non-executive officers, are mostly senior managers of other large firms. The board's chair may be one of the outside or inside directors. Thus, one person can combine the functions of CEO and chair of the board.

In certain countries in continental Europe (Germany, Switzerland, the **Executive board** Netherlands), large companies are controlled by two boards: the **executive board**, which is simply the firm's top management team, and the **supervisory** **Supervisory board** **board**. The supervisory Board consists of outside members only. Such a system **Two-tier board system** of corporate governance is called a **two-tier board system**.

In a two-tier system there are two boards with a complete separation of executive and supervisory duties. By contrast, the system used in the USA, the UK and many other countries, in which there is only one board, is called a **one-tier** **one-tier board system** **board system**.

15.4.3 Monitoring by non-executive board members in a one-tier board

In companies with a one-tier board, all board members are appointed by the shareholders' general assembly. They can also be fired by (a majority of) the shareholders. In many countries, including the USA and the UK, board members are regarded by public opinion and law as fiduciaries for the shareholders. Their main responsibility is to run the company on behalf of the shareholders.

The board usually consists of executive and non-executive members. While the board as a whole is responsible for running the company, the non-executive board members have the additional task of monitoring their executive colleagues. In a typical Wall Street firm, shareholding is widely dispersed and board members tend to own very few shares in the company on whose board they sit.

So, why would they spend time and energy monitoring management? They may want to protect their reputation and be re-elected by the shareholders. For shareholders, however, it is often very difficult to determine how well non-executive directors perform their monitoring role.

If the CEO is also chair of the board, he or she controls the agenda and the flow of information to the members of the board to a large extent. That can make it very difficult for board members, especially outside board members, to perform their duties effectively as monitors. For that reason, many corporate governance codes require that the roles of CEO and chair of the board be separated. Separating the two jobs is commonplace in the UK, Canada, Australia and much of continental Europe, but not in the USA. In Britain 95 per cent of companies in the FTSE 350 list have an outside chairman. But in the USA 53% of Standard and Poor's top 1,500 companies combine the two jobs (*The Economist*, 15 October 2009).

15.4.4 The two-tier board system

In a two-tier board system, there are two boards with a complete separation of executive and supervisory duties. The main role of the executive board is to run the company – that is, to set the strategic direction for the firm, make and implement operational decisions and closely monitor lower level managers.

The main roles of the supervisory board are to monitor the (members of) the executive board and advise it on a broad range of subjects, including the firm's strategic direction. Important decisions, such as large investments, acquisitions, stock issues and choice of the firm's auditor, require the prior approval of the supervisory board.

Thus, there is a separation of decision management and decision control (see Section 7.5). The executive board is responsible for decision management, the supervisory board for decision control. In a one-tier board system, the board is responsible for decision management *as well* as decision control.

In large companies in Germany, 50 per cent of the members of the supervisory board are designated by the employees, the other 50 per cent by the shareholders. This composition of the supervisory board recognizes explicitly that the firm's top management team acts as agent for two groups of principals – the employees and shareholders. The members elected by the employees are often union leaders; the members elected by the shareholders are often bankers or (recently retired) executives from other large companies. The members designated by the shareholders elect the chair of the supervisory board. In the case of a tie in the supervisory board, the chair may cast a decisive vote. The members of a supervisory board can ask for all the information they need to perform their duties as monitors. They are paid by the company to perform the task of monitoring. Does that mean that members of supervisory boards in the German system have strong incentives to perform their duties as monitors effectively? Do recently retired executives from other companies have strong incentives to monitor closely the firms' executives? Some would say yes, because their reputation may be at stake. Some would say no because they do not personally reap the rewards of their additional efforts as monitors.

The main tasks of a supervisory board are to monitor the members of the executive and to ratify certain decisions. In the Netherlands, members of a supervisory board are appointed by the shareholders; that is shareholders have to approve candidates proposed by the supervisory board. In large companies employees have the right to nominate candidates for one third of all the members of the supervisory board. Setting pay schedules and individual pay levels is a responsibility of both shareholders and supervisory board. Box 15.5 gives details of a typical listed company incorporated under Dutch law.

Box 15.5 Remuneration policy at Accell Group NV

The Accell Group NV is a multinational company listed on the Euronext stock exchange. The company makes and sells bicycles, parts and accessories related to bicycles and fitness equipment. Accell group has operations in the Netherlands, Belgium, Germany, France, Finland, Hungary, Turkey, Italy and the USA. The company's HQ are in the Netherlands and the company is incorporated under Dutch law.

The Accell Group has a two-tier board structure: there is a managing board (MB) and a supervisory board (SB). The reward structure of the members of the MB is determined jointly by the SB and the general meeting of shareholders (GMS) as follows. The SB proposes a remuneration policy, including a reward structure (consisting of a base salary and a bonus scheme), for the members of the MB to the GMS. The GMS has to approve the remuneration policy proposed by the SB. If it does not, the SB has to make a new proposal. This new proposal needs approval by the GMS, but it cannot be discussed nor voted on in the same meeting as the original proposal. The GMS normally takes place once per year only (at Accell in April), so it may be necessary to have a special GMS to vote on the new proposal.

At Accell (as in most other public companies in the Netherlands) the remuneration policy aims at attracting the best people for the job and to reward them at 'market rates'. More specifically: at Accell and most other companies the policy is that reward should be at the median found in the market for comparable jobs. To find out what market rates are for comparable jobs the SB hires a consultant specialized in executive pay.

The remuneration policy at Accell approved by shareholders further specifies that total remuneration should consist of the following elements:

- a fixed salary;
- a short term bonus, tied to clearly specified targets;
- long term incentives in the form of share options and a share bonus plan;
- other benefits including a pension scheme to be paid by the company and a company car.

Given this remuneration policy the SB then determines (1) the level of managing board member's fixed salary, (2) the criteria and the target levels for each of the criteria for the short term bonus, (3) the criteria for allocating share options and conditional shares to members of the MB, and (4) for each board a maximum amount that the company will pay for pensions, company car, etc.

▶

In February of each year, after the financial statements of the preceding year have been approved by the SB, the SB applies the criteria specified earlier to determine the short term bonus and the allocation of share options and conditional shares.

Members of the MB are selected and appointed by the SB and can also be fired by the SB. If there is a vacancy on the SB, the SB selects a candidate for that vacancy and proposes the person to the GMS. The GMS appoints the person as a member of the SB. If the GMS refuses to appoint the candidate, the SB has to come up with another candidate. This new candidate also needs to be approved by the GMS. This cannot be done in the same meeting, so if this happens it may be necessary to call a special shareholders' meeting for this purpose.

The GMS can fire all members of the SB simultaneously, but cannot fire an individual member of the SB. If the GMS does fire all the members of the SB, a court of justice in Amsterdam will seek and appoint new members of the SB.

Members of the SB receive a fixed salary (not dependent on profit, share price or anything else), the level of which is set by the GMS. The main task of the SB is to monitor the members of the MB, ratify certain important decisions (such as acquisitions) and advise the MB regarding the strategic direction of the company.

Sources: Annual Report of Accell Group NV, Dutch company law, minutes of GMS, and company web site.

15.5 External monitoring

External monitoring is carried out by parties outside the firm, such as auditors, stock analysts, debt holders and credit-rating agencies. External monitoring helps to reduce information asymmetry in markets and, thus, improves their functioning.

15.5.1 Monitoring by auditing firms

Auditing firms play an important monitoring role. They audit the firm's financial statements and compliance with the law and other regulations. They are appointed (or should be appointed) by the shareholders or perhaps (in a two-tier board system) by the supervisory board. Auditors give their stamp of approval on companies' financial statements. For companies and CEOs that is very important because, without approval by an auditor with a good reputation, the firm will soon find access to new capital blocked. It is important that auditing firms are really independent from the companies they audit. Corporate governance codes in many countries as well as the Sarbanes-Oxley Act in the USA require that they do no (or very little) consulting assignments for the firms they audit; and also that auditors report not to CEOs but to boards as a whole or committees from those boards (**audit committees**). Both requirements help to make auditors less dependent on CEOs. Auditors play a vital role in certifying financial statements and, thus, contribute significantly to the functioning of capital markets.

Audit committees

Auditors, however, also assist board members in their monitoring task. They
Management letter do so through the annual **management letter**, in which an auditor makes suggestions for various improvements, including improvements in the company's internal bookkeeping systems. So, the activities of auditing firms contain an important element of *internal* monitoring in addition to *external* monitoring.

15.5.2 Monitoring by stock analysts

Stock analysts analyze a company's performance and make predictions of the firm's future performance. Reports made by analysts can significantly influence share prices. If the share price drops, the shareholders will start to ask questions. If they are not given satisfactory answers, they may sell their shares (sending the price even further down). Alternatively, they may challenge management and even consider firing the CEO. So, stock analysts play an important role, but it is an indirect one: they help to reduce information asymmetry between shareholders and CEO and overcome the free rider problem mentioned in Section 15.4.1.

15.5.3 Monitoring by debt holders

In companies in mature industries, there is often the problem of free cash flow (Section 15.1). One way to reduce this problem is to take up large loans and distribute the cash thus obtained to shareholders. That, of course, changes the capital structure of the firm. With a large amount of debt, the cash generated by the firm is necessary to service the debt (interest payments and amortization). Thus, managers can no longer invest in projects with a negative NPV.

Providers of debt will often attach conditions to the loans they make. Such
Debt covenants **debt covenants**, as these conditions are called, often require that the company should maintain a number of financial ratios at or above a certain level. Providers of debt will be keen to monitor management on this point.

15.6 How markets constrain agency costs

Agency costs may be constrained by organizational arrangements such as incentive contracts and monitoring, but also by markets. Each firm deals with many markets – for example, buying raw materials and components, hiring staff and selling products. In such markets, the firm buys inputs or sells its output.

Competition in those markets forces companies to be efficient. In this section, we will discuss how and to what extent competition in markets serves to discipline managers.

15.6.1 Competition in the product market

Consider first the *product market*, which is the market for the firm's products. A firm that sells its products in a perfectly competitive market cannot make an economic profit, as we argued in Section 2.4.3. This also means that the manager cannot engage in on-the-job consumption, simply because that would result in negative profits and the firm would go bankrupt. In a perfectly competitive market, firms have to minimize costs, including agency costs, if they want to survive.

Why does this market mechanism not solve all our problems? The answer is that very few markets are perfectly competitive. Remember that a perfectly competitive market assumes, first, a large number of small buyers and sellers, second, no entry or exit barriers and, third, standardized products. In the real world, those assumptions are very often violated: many markets are concentrated and protected by entry barriers. Also, there are few markets with standardized products: most products are branded, so (at least some) buyers do care which company they buy from. Competition in very many markets is far from perfect, which means that companies can make profits without entrants being able to step in and take a share of the market. In such an environment, managers can engage in on-the-job consumption. That will mean lower profits, but, as long as there is sufficient profit left, the firm can continue.

15.6.2 Competition in the managerial labour market

A firm's top manager may also be disciplined by competition in the market for her own services – that is to say, the *managerial labour market*.

The CEO of a small firm who creates substantial wealth for her shareholders may be asked to become CEO of a bigger firm. Large firms can offer their CEOs more compensation. Competition between CEOs of small firms for top positions in large firms can possibly motivate CEOs of small firms to act in the interests of shareholders. Consequently some people argue that competition in the managerial labour market also disciplines managers.

For managers it is undoubtedly worthwhile to build up a reputation of successful performance. We submit, however, that competition in the managerial labour market is far from perfect, for the simple reason that, for outsiders, it is very hard to judge a CEO's performance. The CEO acts as an agent for the firm's shareholders. How well she does that job is difficult to determine, for both the firm's shareholders and other firms that might be looking for a new CEO. There is some evidence that only the very poorest performing managers lose their jobs and it takes several years of poor performance before that occurs (Warner et al., 1988; Weisbach, 1988).

15.6.3 Competition in the stock market

Now consider a firm with shares that are traded on the *stock market*. Through this market, investors will put pressure on firms to operate efficiently and maximize the value of the firm. Fast growing firms in new industries have to attract additional equity capital by issuing new shares. The pricing of new shares is heavily dependent on the firm's prospects, but potential investors also take a good look at its past performance.

15.6.4 Competition in the market for corporate control

Shares held by investors not only represent their right to a certain portion of the firm's profits but also give their owners voting rights. This give shareholders an opportunity to change the management of the firm by, for example, nominating one or more people for the Board even against opposition from incumbent board members (at least in the USA and many, but not all, other countries). Many such attempts fail, however. Box 15.6 gives an example.

Box 15.6 An activist shareholder seeking control

Bill Ackman is founder and CEO of Pershing Square, a hedge fund based in New York. In 2009 Ackman initiated a proxy fight at Target, the second largest discount retailer in America behind Walmart. Ackman had earlier launched a plan for Target to form a real estate investment trust (REIT) to own the land under Target's stores, and then to spin off 20 per cent of that REIT through an initial public offering (IPO). The REIT would lease back the land to Target for a period of 75 years. Target would retain 80 per cent ownership of the REIT and use the capital raised through the IPO to reduce debt.

After Target had made it clear that it opposed this plan, Ackman announced he would seek board representation at Target. He proposed five new candidates for Target's board, including himself. This proposal was rejected at the shareholders meeting of 28 May 2009, with 70 per cent of the shareholders supporting the existing board. Ackman, owning at that date 7.8 per cent of the shares of Target through Pershing, had failed to convince the existing shareholders of the merits of his plan.

Sources: 'Target wins proxy fight with Ackman, Pershing Square' Minneapolis St Paul Business Journal, 28 May 2009 and *'Ackman targets a proxy battle' Forbes, 16 March 2009*

Managers who perform poorly – perhaps because they do act too much in their own interests as opposed to the interests of the shareholders – must always fear that they may lose their job after the company has been acquired by another firm, as we explained in Section 7.2. Thus, every management team risks being ousted after a **hostile takeover** or, to put it differently, faces the discipline of the market for corporate control (Box 15.7 gives an example).

Hostile takeover

Box 15.7 The hostile takeover of RJR Nabisco

For this case we go back to 1988. Then, RJR Nabisco was a giant food and tobacco company listed on the New York Stock Exchange and one of America's 20 largest companies.

CEO F. Ross Johnson was famous for his luxurious lifestyle, at the expense of the company. At one point, RJR Nabisco owned ten corporate jets, employed 36 pilots and had its own hangar near corporate headquarters in Atlanta, Georgia. This fleet of planes was made available by Johnson to a range of friends, celebrities and even to Johnson's pets. Meanwhile, RJR Nabisco's shares were valued much lower than those of its competitors.

▶

Investor Henry Kravis of the famous investment company Kohlberg, Kravis and Roberts (KKR) saw an opportunity and launched a bid to gain control of RJR Nabisco through a hostile takeover. Johnson himself launched a competing bid and soon a bidding war started. Eventually, KKR's final bid turned out to be just higher, implying a premium on the initial share price of around 100 per cent and producing the largest buyout so far, with a transaction value of about $25 billion.

Johnson was forced to leave the company after the buyout by KKR. Do not worry about his well-being, though. Before the end of the bidding war, he had arranged a golden parachute for himself should he lose the battle. Under this settlement, Johnson received more than $53 million.

Source: Burrough and Helyar (1990)

If one investor buys all the shares, he is simply the owner of the company and, as such, is in a position to fire the top managers of the firm. Depending on the institutional context, that can also be true if one investor holds the majority of the shares.

Now, let us wonder in what cases an investor would be interested in purchasing all the shares in one firm. Note that, in the case of a public bid on all the shares, the buyer usually pays a price higher than the current share price (the premium usually amounts to at least 20 per cent and can be as high as 100 per cent, as in the hostile takeover of RJR Nabisco by KKR). Certainly, an investor would not be willing to pay such a premium if the company was run in an efficient way by managers who acted in the shareholders' interests. The investor would not then be able to do a better job managing the company and could not earn back that premium.

Now consider a company that is run in an inefficient way. The value of such a firm on the stock market will be low. An investor who buys all the shares, fires the inefficient managers and starts to run the company himself can create a lot of value. If the gap between the actual value (of the inefficiently run firm) and the potential value (of the efficiently managed firm) is large enough, he might be tempted to have a go, even if he has to pay a premium over the current stock price.

Thus, there is a market for not only individual shares but also whole corporations or, to put it differently, for the right to manage corporations. That is the *market for corporate control* introduced in Section 7.2. Please note that it does not have to come to a hostile takeover in order to create an incentive for managers to pursue the right goals. The mere threat of a hostile takeover, or even the threat of getting very critical outside directors elected after a proxy fight, may be enough, as managers know what can happen to them if they do not perform.

What can managers do to avoid the dangers of hostile takeovers, yet still engage in on-the-job consumption? They can, for example, sign a contract with another party that says, in the case of a hostile bid on the company, that party will have the right to buy the firm's most valuable asset (perhaps the firm's most profitable subsidiary) at a price way below the market price. That will certainly prevent an investor from trying to assume control of the firm. In the financial press, such contracts are referred to as **poison pills**.

Poison pills

Another anti-takeover method that works out extremely well for managers is the so-called **golden parachute**. That is a clause in a manager's employment contract holding that, if he is fired because of a takeover of the firm, he will

Golden parachute

receive a large amount of money. That sum can vary greatly in size, but in some cases, as we have seen, it has amounted to millions of dollars.

Sometimes managers try to avoid a hostile takeover by arranging a *friendly* takeover by another bidder. The friendly bidder, who has been invited by the managers of the target company, is often referred to as a white knight. For example, when, in 2007, the German pharmaceutical firm Merck KGaA made a 'hostile' offer of € 77 per share to acquire its rival Schering AG, the management of Schering turned to Bayer AG to be its white knight. Bayer subsequently bid € 86 per share and succeeded in a 'friendly' takeover of Schering when Merck walked away.

The methods mentioned above are contractual forms of protection against hostile takeovers. In some countries, there are also legal restrictions that can make it more difficult for a bidder to take control of a company, such as the limitations on voting powers attached to certain types of shares or rules aiming at protecting minority shareholders against the majority. Those regulations vary strongly from country to country, as we will illustrate in the next section.

15.7 Institutional frameworks: market-orientated and network-orientated systems of corporate governance

We can observe that there are rather different corporate governance systems used in various parts of the world. These can be explained by:

- the features of the societies they are embedded in;
- the economic and political developments that have been incorporated in their institutional frameworks.

For the sake of convenience, we can divide these different systems into two broad categories: *market-orientated systems* and *network-orientated systems*. We introduce both systems below – first by describing their characteristics and then by pointing to some environmental factors that have contributed to their divergent paths of development.

15.7.1 Market-orientated systems of corporate governance

The main characteristics of market-orientated systems of corporate governance are the existence of large, efficient stock markets, widely dispersed shareholding, strong legal protection of the interests of minority shareholders and separation of ownership from control. In a typical market-orientated system of corporate governance, all large companies are listed on a stock exchange. Those listed companies have many shareholders and no shareholder holds a controlling block. Managers tend to own only a small percentage of the companies they manage.

Moreover, legal rules, designed to protect small individual shareholders, limit companies from discussing strategic plans with just a few large institutional investors. That would give those investors inside knowledge about the firm not available to small individual shareholders, which would violate the laws on insider trading. So, in market-orientated systems of corporate governance, long-term relationships between a company listed on a stock exchange and a few institutional investors hardly exist.

That description more or less fits the situation in Anglo-American countries (the USA, the UK, Canada, Australia, New Zealand). In the USA more than 50 per cent of the shares of listed companies are owned by households. The rest are owned mainly by financial institutions, but a single financial institution rarely owns more than 10 per cent of the shares in a non-financial company. Commercial banks in the USA are simply not allowed to hold corporate equity. Mutual funds generally cannot own controlling blocks. Insurance companies can put only a small proportion of their investment portfolio into the stock of any single company. Pension funds are less restricted, but most pension funds are quite small and rarely own more than one per cent of a Wall Street firm. Thus, the major financial institutions in the USA (commercial banks, investment banks, mutual funds, insurance companies and pension funds) tend to hold widely diversified portfolios of shares in a large number of companies.

In a typical market-orientated system of corporate governance, each single investor owns a small percentage of a firm's stock. Consequently investors have only weak incentives to monitor the company's managers: they would capture only a very small portion of the benefits thus achieved, other shareholders would be free riders. Thus, investors who are dissatisfied with the financial performance of a company they have invested in tend to sell their shares rather than use their voting power to influence managerial decisions. If many investors do the same, the firm's stock market value will decline and the firm will be an attractive candidate for a takeover, not only by strategic buyers, who can aim to realize synergies, but also by private equity firms. That is what happened to RJR Nabisco in 1988 as we saw earlier and VNU, a media research company, now known as The Nielsen Company, in 2005 (see Box 15.8).

VNU was taken over by a consortium of private equity firms, which immediately started to restructure the company. The consortium probably planned to improve its profitability and growth and then either sell the company to a strategic buyer or float the company again on the stock market. Private equity firms can be said to compete in the market for corporate control for the right to restructure and manage companies. Managers in countries with market-orientated systems of corporate governance know that what happened to VNU's CEO can happen to them. That is why we say that, in a market-orientated system of corporate governance, managers are disciplined mainly by the market for corporate control.

Box 15.8 How VNU lost its independence

In 2005, investors in VNU NV were dissatisfied with the company's management. VNU was a Dutch company, with headquarters in New York and almost all of its activities concentrated in the USA. Its two most important subsidiaries were ACNielsen (it researches consumer behaviour through the collection of data from retailers) and Nielsen Media research (it collects data concerning the behaviour of people using media such as TV and radio). Both Nielsen companies were market leaders in their respective industries, but both were facing difficult times. ACNielsen lost the Wal-Mart account and Nielsen Media research was lagging behind competitors in installing the latest technology. VNU's share price had performed poorly in the years prior to 2005.

When Rob van den Bergh, VNU's CEO, announced plans in July 2005 to acquire IMS Health (a company that collects data about the use of pharmaceutical products in many countries) for $7 billion, shareholders began to revolt. After a group of shareholders led by Knight Vinke, and including Fidelity and Templeton, had made it clear that they would not support the plan to acquire IMS Health under any circumstance, Rob van den Bergh had to abandon it, which he did in November 2005.

In March 2006, a consortium of six private equity firms made a public offer to buy all the shares in VNU NV for € 28.75 (equivalent to $35 at that time). Rob van den Bergh had to step down and was succeeded by David Calhoun. Calhoun started by cutting the number of jobs from 42,000 to 38,000.

Rob van den Bergh received a severance payment of € 4.5 million. He soon found other employment as a member of the supervisory boards of several companies.

In January 2007, VNU decided to change its name to The Nielsen Company.

Sources: Press Release from VNU, Alp Invest, The Blackstone Group, The Carlyle Group, Hellman & Friedman LLC, KKR and THL Partners, Haarlem, the Netherlands, 8 March 2006; Bloomberg.com, 17 January 2006

As the example of VNU shows, hostile takeovers do take place. Even in the USA, however, some managers of public companies are well-protected from the market for corporate control. One example is Google Inc., where a group of three top managers has a controlling block (see Box 15.9).

Box 15.9 Google's corporate governance

Larry Page and Sergey Brin first met when doing a PhD in computer science at Stanford University. They worked on a project called: 'The anatomy of a large-scale hypertextual web search engine'. In 1998, after having developed a search engine that was more efficient than other search engines available at that time, they quit their studies and founded Google Inc. In the beginning they relied on their own funds, but soon had to attract private investments to finance Google's rapid growth.

In 2000, Google introduced advertisements alongside search results. In that same year, Google made its first profit. In 2001 Eric Schmidt joined the company as chair of the board and CEO. In 2004, Google became a public company through an IPO. In that IPO, 19.6 million shares were sold to investors, 14.1 million newly issued shares and 5.5 million shares from selling shareholders.

Google has two classes of common stock: class A and class B. The two classes of shares differ only with respect to their voting rights: class A shares have one vote per share while class B shares carry ten votes per share. Class A shares were offered to investors, class B shares are held only by Google's officers and employees. When class B shares are sold, they are automatically converted into class A shares; an exception to this rule is when Page sells to Brin or *vice versa*.

Immediately after the IPO, Google had 33.6 million class A shares and 237.6 million class B shares outstanding. The investors who bought 19.6 million class A shares obtained an economic interest in Google of 7.2 per cent, for which they paid $1.7 billion, associated with 0.8 per cent of the voting power. Page, Brin and Schmidt, who 'run the company as a triumvirate', controlled 37.6 per cent of the voting power, while the executive management team and directors as a group controlled 61.4 per cent of the voting power.

In a letter to potential investors included in the IPO prospectus, Page makes a comment on the dual class structure: 'Google has prospered as a private company. We believe a dual-class structure will enable Google, as a public company, to retain many of the positive aspects of being private. We understand some investors do not favor dual-class structures. Some may believe that our dual-class structure will give us the ability to take actions that benefit us, but not Google's shareholders as a whole. We have considered this point of view carefully, and we and the Board have not made our decision lightly. We are convinced that everyone associated with Google – including new investors – will benefit from this structure. However, you should be aware that Google and its shareholders may not realize these intended benefits.' In the same letter, Page stresses that Google will optimize for the long term rather than trying to produce smooth earnings for each quarter. Google will support high-risk, high-reward projects and, thus, will be run more like a private company than a public company. That is why a dual-class structure benefits all shareholders, according to Page.

In 2004, shortly before the IPO, Google attracted three additional outside board members and separated the roles of CEO and chair of the board.

In April 2012 Google announced a stock split of the class A shares; every shareholder will receive for each class A share one new class C share. Class C shares have the same rights to dividends as class A and class B shares, but class C shares have no voting rights. Initially the number of votes will not change as a result of the stock split. In the 'Founders letter', written by Larry Page in April 2012, Page writes: 'These non-voting shares will be available for corporate uses, like equity-based employee compensation, that might otherwise dilute our governance structure'. So, an important purpose of the stock split was the wish of Larry Page, Sergey Brin and Eric Schmidt, who together at that point in time had 66 % of the voting power, to retain control of Google. As the company's legal counsel wrote in a letter to shareholders: 'Given that Larry, Sergey and Eric control the majority of the voting power and support this proposal, we expect it to pass'.

In April 2012 Google's class A shares, which had been sold to investors for $85.00, traded at around $640 per share. Both Larry Page's and Sergey Brin's (then aged 38 and 37 years respectively) net worth at that time was estimated by *Forbes* at $18.7 billion.

Page and Brin continue to work for Google and are regarded by many as technology gurus. They are still too busy to finish their PhDs.

Source: Prospectus issued by Morgan Stanley and Credit Suisse First Boston, 18 August 2004, Founders letter by Larry Page and Sergey Brin, April, 12, 2012.

The example of Google with its dual-class shares illustrates that the environment and institutions (in the case of Google the American environment) co-determine corporate governance but do not completely determine it. Within one institutional environment, degrees of freedom remain for companies to choose their own corporate governance structure.

15.7.2 Network-orientated systems of corporate governance

Network-orientated systems

The main characteristic of **network-orientated systems** of corporate governance is the presence of blockholders. In a typical network-orientated system of corporate governance, large companies may or may not be listed on a stock exchange.

Many listed companies have one or a few large shareholders. Those large shareholders do not actively trade their shares. The free float (the number of shares actively traded on the stock market) is significantly less than 100 per cent – for many companies it is even less than 50 per cent. Large shareholders (or their representatives) sit on the board. They monitor managers and use their voting power if they are dissatisfied with a manager's performance. Managers are disciplined much more by these large shareholders, than by the market for corporate control.

This description more or less fits the situation in most non-Anglo-American countries, in both emerging markets and more developed countries (such as Japan and countries in continental Europe). In those same countries, business groups play an important role, as we noted in Section 14.4.

In a network-based economy, the typical firm has a small number of large shareholders who have a long-term relationship with the firm and its management and are represented on the firm's Board. Those shareholders often have other interests besides maximizing the value of their shares, such as strategic or family ties. If a shareholder is a bank, maybe it has some debt outstanding that it wants to protect. Such shareholders are not very likely to sell their shares to a hostile bidder. In countries with a network-orientated system of corporate governance, the effectiveness of the market for corporate control is limited not only by the institutional setting but also by the typical ownership structure in such countries.

In countries such as Germany, France, Italy, Spain, Japan, Korea and India, shares in large corporations are not as widely distributed as in the USA and UK. In the UK, for example, much more of the country's 100 largest firms are listed on a stock exchange than in Italy. Moreover, for those Italian companies that do have a listing on a stock exchange, shareholdings tend to be more concentrated than in British firms.

In Germany, the so-called universal banks (such as Deutsche Bank, Commerzbank and Dresdner Bank) used to provide not only debt capital to large industrial enterprises, but also equity capital. Since 2008, however, German banks have reduced their industrial shareholdings substantially. The universal banks in Germany also advise their clients on which shares to buy or sell. Most private investors deposit their shares with one of these universal banks and allow the bank to vote for them at shareholder meetings. This gives the universal banks considerable voting power at shareholder meetings. Institutional shareholders other than banks play an important role. Box 15.10 provides an illustration.

Box 15.10 Shareholders of Daimler AG

Daimler AG is a very successful automotive company (cars, trucks, vans, buses) marketed under the well known brand Mercedes-Benz. In 2011, 67 percent of its shares were owned by institutional investors owning 3 percent or more. The two most important shareholders were Aaber Investments PJSC (from Abu Dhabi) and Kuwait Investment Authority. Deutsche Bank owned less than 3 per cent, down from 11.8 percent in 2004.

Source: Daimler AG Annual Report 2011

In the Latin countries of the EU (Italy, Spain, Portugal, France and Belgium) many large companies, even those listed on a stock exchange, have one or a few owners of large blocks of shares. Examples of such large blockholders are financial holding companies, rich families, banks, other industrial corporations and the State. In many listed companies in these countries, one or a few large shareholders together can exercise more than 50 per cent of the voting rights. Those large shareholders may use their power to achieve their own goals, sometimes at the expense of the small private shareholders.

In Japan, there are many large industrial groups, the so-called *keiretsu*, such as Mitsubishi and Mitsui. These groups are centred on a bank or insurance company that provides the companies belonging to the group with debt capital as well as equity capital. Companies belonging to the group also commonly hold significant portions of shares in other companies belonging to the group. Thus, a large part of the shares of the companies belonging to a *keiretsu* is held by other companies belonging to the *keiretsu*.

Keiretsu

Chaebol

In Korea and India, business groups are also of paramount importance. In the typical industrial group in Korea (called a *chaebol*), companies belonging to the group hold shares in other companies belonging to the group and provide guarantees for bank loans taken up by sister companies. The business groups are not structured around a bank. Many business groups are controlled by people belonging to the same family, often the offspring of the founder of a group.

In summary, while there are important differences between the corporate governance systems in the countries mentioned above, there is also a common feature. That is, many companies have one or a few owners of large blocks of shares. Companies having the same person or institution as owner of a large block of shares may be seen as forming a network. It is for that reason, the term network-orientated systems of corporate governance has been coined.

In countries with a network-orientated system of corporate governance, laws designed to prevent insider trading are generally not very strict. That allows owners of large blocks of shares to confer with management and, thus, influence managerial decisions. Quite often they sit on the board. If they are dissatisfied with a top manager's performance, they have the power to fire the manager. Thus, in a network-orientated system of corporate governance, managers are disciplined mainly by organizational arrangements.

15.7.3 A comparison of the two corporate governance systems

In market-orientated systems of corporate governance, severe underperformance by managers is restricted mainly by the fear of a hostile takeover. The board of directors is probably less important in this respect because outside directors may lack the incentive to perform their functions as monitors well. That may be especially true when the CEO is also chair of the board. Thus, the market for corporate control is the most important mechanism for reducing the agency problem between shareholders and managers.

Incumbent managers may spend large amounts of money in the form of fees for lawyers and investment bankers in order to resist a hostile takeover bid. That is a waste of money for the shareholders of the target firm, who may be content with the bid (and the premium above the current share price). To put it differently, transaction costs in the market for corporate control may be very high indeed. As a consequence, incumbent managers have some leeway regarding on-the-job consumption. The market for corporate control is far from frictionless, which is the major disadvantage of market-orientated systems of corporate governance.

In network-orientated systems of corporate governance, monitoring of top managers by outside board members is probably the most important mechanism for reducing the agency problem. In network-orientated systems, owners of large blocks of shares have the incentives to perform their monitoring role in an effective way. The market for corporate control is of little importance in terms of disciplining managers.

A disadvantage of network-orientated systems is that markets for equity capital, including venture capital, are less well developed. That may hinder the optimal allocation of equity capital in countries in which network-orientated systems prevail. Another disadvantage may arise when the main private shareholders in a company do not act in the best corporate interests for private reasons, such as retaining family influence or prestige.

In a typical network-orientated system of corporate governance, there are virtually no hostile takeovers. This more or less fits the situation in Germany and Japan. In France, Italy and Spain, hostile takeovers are also very rare. The main reason for this is probably that a hostile bidder has to convince owners of large blocks of shares, who are also board members or are represented on the board, that selling their shares is in their best interests. It may be quite difficult for General Motors to convince the Agnelli family that selling their shares in Fiat is in their own best interest!

Another reason is that important differences exist in the institutional environment with respect to takeovers. Even within Europe, there are large differences – the UK having the most active market for corporate control. In most countries in continental Europe, corporations have been able to shield themselves from unfriendly takeover threats. Within the EU, there is a lively debate on the need to harmonize the legal framework concerning takeovers. A proposal made by the European Commission has been rejected by the European Parliament, meaning that differences between the UK and other European countries are likely to persist (see also Box 15.11).

Does that mean the managers of companies in continental Europe need not worry about the valuation of their company's stock on the stock market? Not necessarily. So long as the companies have to issue new shares from time to time, they have an interest in the valuation of their shares on the stock market. Moreover, also in Europe the role of 'private equity' has risen, as we discussed in Chapter 13.

Box 15.11 The European market for corporatism or corporate control?

In Europe, the notion of a 'market for corporate control' has always been controversial. It is quite readily accepted in the UK, but, on the Continent, the idea generally prevails that corporations lead a life of their own, aimed at continuity and serving all stakeholders equally – not primarily the shareholders. It actively seeks a dialogue with its various stakeholder groups in order to balance their competing claims on the corporation optimally. This idea is referred to as the *stakeholder model* (see also Box 6.1), the Rhineland model or corporatism.

The European Commission worked for 15 years to harmonize takeover codes in Europe in a European directive that would regulate the European market for corporate control. This directive aims to create favourable regulatory conditions for takeovers and to boost corporate restructuring within the EU. However, the directive's main provisions, which would restrict the possibilities of companies to defend themselves against bidders – for example by subjecting 'poison pills' to shareholder approval or by making share transfer restrictions unenforceable against the bidder – are not mandatory. Furthermore, the directive allows member states to exempt their companies from applying these provisions, if the bidder is not subject to the same obligations. A large number of member states have used these options and exemptions, and some have even strengthened the role of management with regard to using takeover defences against a bidder. Thus a really competitive market for corporate control in the EU had not been realized in 2012, when this box was written.

Sources: The Economist, 7 July 2001 and Press release IP/07/251, 27 February 2007 from the European Commission.

15.8 The evolution of different corporate governance systems in the world

What explains the development of these different systems of corporate governance in the world? In the descriptions above, some environmental and institutional factors have already been mentioned. If we try to group some of the important factors, though, they would include the following:

- *Social and cultural values* Social and cultural values differ substantially from one country to another. For example, Anglo-American countries tend to have a more individualistic value set than many other countries. As Hofstede (2001, p. 251) discusses, that translates into social and political systems in which individual interests prevail over collective interests. It may explain why markets (and market-orientated systems of corporate governance) are more important in Anglo-American countries.
- *The concept of the corporation* Is the corporation viewed from the perspective of the 'stakeholder model' or the 'shareholder value' model? In Germany, for instance, the participation of employees in the supervisory board is explicable from the stakeholder perspective. In the USA and UK, on the other hand, it would be inconceivable as the fiduciary duty of corporate boards is towards the shareholders as owners.
- *Institutional arrangements* As indicated above, the institutional arrangements in the USA prevented the rise of large institutional blockholdings in individual corporations. In Germany and Japan, however, the large banks were expected to be the major equity investors in large corporations. Whether large blockholdings exist or not is a major determinant of corporate governance, as explained above.
- *Lessons from evolution* The institutional arrangements we observe today have been developed over time and incorporate the lessons of the past. They are path-dependent. As different societies have taken different paths and have accumulated different lessons along the way, we would expect to see those

differences reflected in their current institutional frameworks. An extreme example is the learning in many formerly communist nations that State ownership of corporations is usually not a productive and efficient arrangement.

The factors listed above highlight reasons for there being differences in corporate governance systems. Another question is whether such differences are becoming larger or smaller. In other words, do we observe a convergence or divergence of corporate governance systems?

On balance, we would argue that the factors favouring convergence are strong. Those factors are mainly a result of globalization. They include:

- the vast increase in cross-border mergers and acquisitions;
- international standardization of disclosure requirements (such as the International Financial Reporting Standards);
- harmonization of securities regulation and the merger of stock exchanges (the merger of the French, Belgian and Dutch stock exchanges into Euronext and the subsequent merger between the New York Stock Exchange (NYSE) and Euronext, for example);
- the development of corporate governance codes – while these are usually still country-specific, they do tend to incorporate lessons and features from other codes, thereby promoting convergence.

Thus, we would see the environmental and institutional setting as evolving towards further convergence of corporate governance systems of the major economies around the world.

15.9 Summary: how the agency problems of corporate governance can be reduced by organizational and/or market solutions

This chapter has focused on the agency relation between shareholder(s) as principal and manager(s) as agent. This agency problem (as any agency problem) arises because, first, principal and agent have different interests and, second, there is information asymmetry between agent and principal. Consequently, solutions to agency problems aim at:

- narrowing the gap between the interests of principal and agent;
- reducing the information asymmetry between principal and agent.

The gap between the interests of principal and agent can be narrowed by organizational solutions (offering the agent an incentive contract) and/or market solutions (improving the functioning of the market for managerial labour and/or the market for corporate control).

Information asymmetry can also be reduced by organizational solutions (internal monitoring by shareholder(s) and/ or a (supervisory) board) and/or by market solutions (the managerial labour market and the market for corporate control). The functioning of those markets is improved by external monitoring by, for example, auditors, stock market analysts, credit-rating agencies, private equity firms and other parties possibly interested in acquiring the company.

So, the subject of corporate governance provides an excellent illustration of the framework of the book by showing that the agency problem between shareholder(s) and managers(s) can be reduced by means of organizational solutions (incentive contracts, internal monitoring) and market solutions (external monitoring and the functioning of various markets).

In different parts of the world, different corporate governance systems have evolved – mainly as a result of differences in social and cultural values and historical background. This has resulted in market-orientated systems of corporate governance, which tend to prevail in Anglo-American countries, and network-orientated systems of corporate governance, which tend to prevail elsewhere. We expect that these two systems of corporate governance will converge in the long run as a result of globalization.

Questions

1 Suppose you are a HR consultant specializing on the design of compensation packages for CEOs. Your clients are the remuneration committees of large public companies. You may assume that those remuneration committees act strictly in the best interests of shareholders. You currently have two different clients. Client A is a large brewery in a Nordic country (Sweden, perhaps) serving the local market only. Demand for beer in that market is relatively stable and so is the company's market share. Profits depend mainly on the efficiency of the production process for the beer. Would you recommend to client A a compensation package including a large or a small amount of variable compensation?

  Client B is a trading company, trading in electronic components and consumer products. Company B buys the products in various countries in East Asia, including China, Vietnam, India and Japan, and sells them in Europe. Profits for the company depend on many factors, including exchange rates, changing consumer tastes and the general economic conditions in Europe. Would you recommend to client B a compensation package including a large or a small amount of variable compensation?

2 What do you see as being the main advantages and disadvantages of a two-tier board system as opposed to a one-tier board system?

3 Suppose a company has one shareholder and one CEO – shareholder and CEO being two different people. What would be the main functions of the shareholder as principal, according to the theory of principal and agent discussed in Chapter 7?

4 Consider then Accell Group NV (discussed in Box 15.5). The Accell Group's shares are traded on a stock exchange and there are many shareholders. The company has a two-tier board structure, with a supervisory board and an executive board. Who performs the functions you identified in your answer to question 3? Which agency relations do you see? Who monitors whom?

Note

1   The primary source for this section is Paul Frentrop (2002), *Ondernemingen en hun aandeelhouders sinds de VOC*, Amsterdam: Prometheus. Translated as (2003) *A History of Corporate Governance, 1602–2002*, Amsterdam: Deminor.

Bibliography

Akerlof, G. A. (1970), 'The market for "lemons": qualitative uncertainty and the market mechanism', *Quarterly Journal of Economics*, vol. 84, pp. 488–500.

Alchian, A. A., and Demsetz, H. (1972), 'Production, information costs and economic organization', *American Economic Review*, vol. 62, pp. 777–95.

Aldrich, H. E. (1979), *Organizations and Environments*, Englewood Cliffs, NJ: Prentice Hall.

Alesina, A., and La Ferrara, E. (2002), 'Who trusts others?', *Journal of Public Economics*, vol. 85 (2), pp. 207–34.

Alvesson, M., and Lindkvist, L. (1993), 'Transaction costs, clans and corporate culture', *Journal of Management Studies*, vol. 30, pp. 427–52.

Amit, R., and Shoemaker, P. J. H. (1993), 'Strategic assets and organizational rent', *Strategic Management Journal*, vol. 14, pp. 33–46.

Anandalingham, G., and Lucas Jr, H. C. (2004), *Beware the Winner's Curse*, Oxford: Oxford University Press.

Andersen, S. Ertaç, S., Gneezy, U., Hoffman, M. and List, J. A. (2011), 'Stakes matter in ultimatum games', *American Economic Review*, vol. 101, pp. 3427–3439.

Andrade, G., Mitchell, M., and Stafford, E. (2001), 'New evidence and perspectives on mergers', *Journal of Economic Perspectives*, vol. 15 (2), pp. 103–20.

Ansoff, H. I. (1965), *Corporate Strategy*, Harmondsworth: Penguin.

Ariely, D. (2009), *Predictably Irrational: The Hidden forces that Shape our Decisions*, New York: Harper Collins.

Ariely, D. (2012), The (Honest) Truth about Dishonesty, New York: Harper Collins .

Arrow, K. J. (1963), 'Uncertainty and medical care', *American Economic Review*, vol. 53, pp. 941–73.

Arrow, K. J. (1973), *Information and Economic Behavior*, Stockholm: Federation of Swedish Industries.

Arrow, K. J. (1985), 'The economics of agency', in Pratt J. W. and Zeckhauser R. J. (eds), *Principals and Agents: The Structure of Business*, Boston, MA: Harvard Business School Press.

Arthur, W. B. (1994a), *Increasing Returns and Path Dependence in the Economy*, Ann Arbor, MI: University of Michigan Press.

Arthur, W. B. (1994b), 'Positive feedbacks in the economy', *McKinsey Quarterly*, no. 1.

Arthur, W. B. (1996), 'Increasing returns and the new world of business', *Harvard Business Review*, vol. 74, July/August, pp. 100–9.

Augier, M. and Teece, D. J. (2009), 'Dynamic capabilities and the role of managers in business strategy and economic performance', *Organization Science*, Vol. 20, no 2, pp. 410–421.

Axelrod, R. (1984), *The Evolution of Cooperation*, New York: Basic Books.

Axelrod, R. (1997), *The Complexity of Cooperation*, Princeton, NJ: Princeton University Press.

Axelrod, R., and Cohen, M. D. (1999), *Harnessing Complexity: Organizational Implications of a Scientific Frontier*, New York: Free Press.

Bachmann, R., and Zaheer, A. (2006), *Handbook of Trust Research*, Cheltenham (UK), Edward Elgar Publishing.

Bagchi, A. K. (1972), *Private Investment in India 1900–1939*, Cambridge: Cambridge University Press.

Barney, J. B. (1989), 'Asset stocks and sustained competitive advantage: a comment', *Management Science*, vol. 35 (12), pp. 1511–13.

Barney, J. B. (1991), 'Firm resources and sustained competitive advantage', *Journal of Management*, vol. 17 (1), pp. 99–120.

Barney, J. B. (1997), *Gaining and Sustaining Competitive Advantage*, Reading, MA: Addison-Wesley.

Barney, J. B., and Hesterly, W. (1996), 'Organizational economics: Understanding the relationship between organizations and economic analysis', in Clegg, S. R. Hardy, C. and Nord W. R. (eds), *Handbook of Organization Studies*, London: Sage.

Barney, J. B., and Ouchi, W. G. (eds) (1986), *Organizational Economics*, San Francisco, CA: Jossey-Bass.

Barron, D. N. (2003), 'Evolutionary theories', in Faulkner D. O. and Campbell, A. *The Oxford Handbook of Strategy*, Oxford: Oxford University Press.

Baum, J. A. C. (1996), 'Organizational ecology', in Clegg, S. R. Hardy C. and Nord W. R. (eds), *Handbook of Organization Studies*, London: Sage.

Baum, J. A. C., Dobrev, S. D., and Van Witteloostuijn, A. (eds) (2006) *Ecology and Strategy,* Amsterdam: Elsevier.

Bazerman M. H., and Samuelson, W. F. (1983), 'I won the auction but don't want the prize', *Journal of Conflict Resolution*, vol. 27, pp. 618–34.

Bazerman, M. H. (2006), *Judgment in Managerial Decision Making*, 6th edn, New York: John Wiley.

Bazerman, M. H. and Moore D. (2009), *Judgment in Managerial Decision Making*, New York: John Wiley.

Becker, G. S., and Elias, J. J. (2003), 'Introducing incentives in the market for live and cadaveric organ donations', at http://home.uchicago.edu/~gbecker/ MarketforLiveandCadavericOrganDonations_Becker_Elias. pdf

Beinhocker, E. D. (2006), *The Origin of Wealth: Evolution, complexity and the radical remaking of economics*, Boston, MA: Harvard Business School Press.

Berle, A. A., and Means, G. C. (1932), *The Modern Corporation and Private Property*, New York: Commerce Clearing House.

Beroutsos, A., Freeman, A., and Kehoe, C. F. (2007), 'What public companies can learn from private equity', *McKinsey Quarterly, web exclusive, January 2007*.

Bertrand, M., Metha, P., and Mullainathan, S. (2002), 'Ferreting or tunneling: an application to Indian business groups', *Quarterly Journal of Economics*, vol. 117, pp. 121–48.

Besanko, D., Dranove, D., Shanley, M. and Schaefer, S. (2010), *Economics of Strategy*, 5th edn, New York: John Wiley.

Besanko, D. A. and Braeutigem, R. R. (2010), *Microeconomics,* New York: John Wiley.

Bettis, R. A., and Prahalad, C. K. (1995), 'The dominant logic: retrospective and extension', *Strategic Management Journal*, vol. 16 (1), pp. 5–14.

Birchler, U., and Bütler, M. (2007), *Information Economics*, London: Routledge.

Boone, C., de Brabander, B., and van Witteloostuijn, A. (1996), 'CEO locus of control and small firm performance: an integrative framework and empirical test', *Journal of Management Studies*, vol. 33, pp. 667–99.

Boone, C., de Brabander, B., and van Witteloostuijn, A. (1999), 'Locus of control and strategic behavior in a prisoner's dilemma game', *Personality and Individual Differences*, vol. 27, pp. 695–706.

Bose, P. P. (1992), 'Commitment: an interview with Pankaj Ghemawat of the Harvard Business School on new directions in strategic thinking', *McKinsey Quarterly*, no. 3, pp. 121–37.

Bowles, S. (2004), *Microeconomics: Behavior, institutions, and evolution*, Princeton, NJ: Princeton University Press.

Bowman, E. H., and Helfat C. E., (2001), 'Does corporate strategy matter?', *Strategic Management Journal*, vol. 22 (1), pp. 1–23.

Bradbury, Drinner (2006), 'The Designated Hitter, Moral Hazard and Hit Batters: New Evidence from Game-Level", *Journal of Sports Economics*, 2006 (Aug), Vol 7(3). pp.319–329

Brandenburger, A. M., and Nalebuff, B. J. (1995), 'The right game: use game theory to shape strategy', *Harvard Business Review*, vol. 73, pp. 57–71.

Brau, J. C., and Kohers, N. (2007), 'Dual-track versus single-track sell-outs: An empirical analysis of competing harvest strategies', forthcoming in: *Journal of Business Venturing*.

Brickley, J. A., and Dark, F. H. (1987), 'The choice of organizational form: the case of franchising', *Journal of Financial Economics*, vol. 18, pp. 401–20.

Brown, S. L., and Eisenhardt, K. M. (1998), *Competing on the Edge: Strategy as structured chaos*, Boston, MA: Harvard Business School Press.

Bruner, R. (2004), *Applied Mergers and Acquisitions*, Hoboken, NJ: John Wiley.

Bruner, R. (2005), Deals from Hell: M&A lessons that rise above the ashes, Hoboken, NJ: John Wiley.

Burgelman, R. A. (1990), 'Strategy-making and organizational ecology: a conceptual integration', in Singh, J. V. (ed.) *Organizational Evolution: New Directions*, Newbury Park, CA: Sage.

Burgelman, R. A. (1991), 'Intraorganizational ecology of strategy making and organizational adaptation: theory and field research', *Organization Science*, vol. 2, pp. 239–62.

Burgelman, R. A. (2002), *Strategy is Destiny: How strategy-making shapes a company's future*, New York: Free Press.

Burrough, B., and Helyar, J. (1990), *Barbarians at the Gate: The fall of RJR Nabisco*, New York: Harper & Row.

Burt, R. S. (1992), *Structural Holes: The social structure of competition*, Cambridge, MA: Harvard University Press.

Cameron, S., and Collins, A. (1997), 'Transaction costs and partnerships: the case of rock bands', *Journal of Economic Behavior and Organization*, vol. 32, pp. 171–83.

Carney, M., and Gedajlovic, E. (1991), 'Vertical integration in franchise systems: agency theory and resource explanations', *Strategic Management Journal*, vol. 12, pp. 607–29.

Carroll, G. R. (1987), *Publish and Perish: The organizational ecology of newspaper industries*, Greenwich, CT: JAI Press.

Carroll, G. R. (ed.) (1988), *Ecological Models of Organizations*, Cambridge, MA: Ballinger.

Carroll, G. R., and Hannan, M. T. (1995), *Organizations in Industry: Strategy, structure, and selection*, Oxford: Oxford University Press.

Carroll, G. R., and Hannan, M. T. (2000), *The Demography of Corporations and Industries*, Princeton, NJ: Princeton University Press.

Casson, M. (1997), *Information and Organization: a new perspective on the theory of the firm*, Oxford: Oxford University Press.

Caves, R. E. (1992), *Multinational Enterprise and Economic Analysis*, Cambridge: Cambridge University Press.

Chandler, A. D. (1966), *Strategy and Structure*, New York: Doubleday.

Chang, S-J., (2006) 'The future of business groups in East Asia', in Chang S-J. (ed.) *Business Groups in East Asia: Financial crisis, restructuring and new growth*, Oxford: Oxford University Press.

Chang, S-J, and Singh, H., (2000), 'Corporate and Industry Effects on Business Unit Competitive Position', *Strategic Management Journal,* vol. 21, pp. 739–752.

Chesbrough, H. W. (2003), *Open Innovation: The new imperative for creating and profiting from technology*, Boston, MA: Harvard Business School Press.

Christakis, N. and Fowler J. (2011), *Connected: the amazing power of social networks and how they shape our lives*, NY: Harper Collins

Christensen, C. M. (1997), *The Innovator's Dilemma: When new technologies cause great firms to fail*, Boston, MA: Harvard Business School Press.

Christensen, C. M. (2003), *The Innovator's Solution*, Boston, MA: Harvard Business School Press.

Claessens, S., Djankov, S., and Lang, L. H. P. (2000), 'The separation of ownership and control in East Asian corporations', *Journal of Financial Economics,* vol. 58, pp. 81–112.

Clark, K., and Sefton, M. (2001), 'The sequential prisoner's dilemma: evidence on reciprocation', *Economic Journal*, vol. 111, pp. 51–68.

Clarke, R., and McGuinness, T. (eds) (1987), *The Economics of the Firm*, Oxford: Basil Blackwell.

Clegg, S. R., Hardy, C., and Nord, W. R. (eds) (1996), *Handbook of Organization Studies*, London: Sage.

Coase, R. H. (1937), 'The nature of the firm', *Economica*, vol. 4.

Coleman, J. S. (1990), *Foundations of Social Theory*, Cambridge, MA: Harvard University Press.

Coles, J. W., and Hesterly, W. S. (1998), 'The impact of firm specific assets and the interaction of uncertainty: an examination of make or buy decisions in public and private hospitals', *Journal of Economic Behavior and Organization*, vol. 36, pp. 383–409.

Collins, J. C. (2001), *Good to Great*, New York: HarperCollins.

Collins, J. C. (2009), *How the mighty fall*, London: Random House

Collins, J. C., and Porras, J. I. (1994), *Built to Last: Successful habits of visionary companies*, London: Century Business.

Collis, D. J., and Montgomery, C. A. (1995), 'Competing on resources: strategy in the 1990s', *Harvard Business Review*, vol. 73 (4), pp. 118–28.

Cools, K. (2005), 'Ebbers Rex', *The Wallstreet Journal*, 22 March 2005.

Cronqvist H., and Nilsson, M. (2003), 'Agency costs of controlling minority shareholders', *Journal of Financial and Quantitative Analysis,* vol. 38, pp. 695–719.

Cyert, R. M., and March, J. G. (1963), *A Behavioral Theory of the Firm*, Englewood Cliffs, NJ: Prentice Hall (2nd edn, 1992).

d'Aspremont, C., Gabszewicz, J., and Thisse, J. F. (1979), 'On Hotelling's "stability in competition" ', *Econometrica*, vol. 47, pp. 1145–51.

David, P. (1985), 'Clio and the economics of QWERTY', *American Economic Review*, vol. 75, pp. 332–7.

Davis, L. E., and North, D. C. (1971), *Institutional Change and American Economic Growth*, Cambridge: Cambridge University Press.

Dawkins, R. (1986), *The Blind Watchmaker*, Harlow: Longman.

Day, J. D., and Wendler, J. C. (1998), 'The new economics of organization', *McKinsey Quarterly*, 1998, no. 1, pp. 4–17.

DePamphilis, D. M. (2012), *Mergers, Acquisitions and Other Restructuring Activities,* 6th edn, Amsterdam: Elsevier.

DeAngelo H., and DeAngelo, L. (1985), 'Managerial ownership of voting rights: a study of public corporations with dual classes of common stock', *Journal of Financial Economics,* vol. 14, pp. 33–69.

De Jong, A., Kabir, R., Marra, T., and Roëll, A. (2001), 'Ownership and control in the Netherlands', in Barca F. and Becht M. (eds), *The Control of Corporate Europe*, Oxford: Oxford University Press, pp. 188–206.

Dell, M., with Fredman, Catherine (1999), *Direct from Dell: Strategies which Revolutionized an Industry*, New York: HarperCollins.

Demsetz, H. (1995), *The Economics of the Business Firm: Seven critical commentaries*, Cambridge: Cambridge University Press.

DePamphilis, D. (2005), *Mergers, Acquisitions and Other Restructuring Activities*, Amsterdam: Elsevier, 3rd edn.

Dharwadkar, R., George, G., and Brandes, P. (2000), 'Privatization in emerging economies: an agency theory perspective', *Academy of Management Review*, vol. 25 (3), pp. 650–69.

Dierickx, I., and Cool, K. (1989), 'Asset stock accumulation and sustainability of competitive advantage', *Management Science*, vol. 35 (12), pp. 1504–11.

Dixit, A., and Nalebuff, B.(1991), *Thinking Strategically*, New York: Norton.

Dobbs R., Goedhart, M., and Suonio, H. (2006), 'Are companies getting better at M&A?', *The McKinsey Quarterly*, December 2006.

Doeringer, P., and Piore, M. (1971), *Internal Labor Markets and Manpower Analysis*, Boston, MA: Heath & Co.

Donaldson, T., and Preston, L. (1995), 'The stakeholder theory of the corporation: Concepts, evidence, and implications', *Academy of Management Review*, vol. 20 (1), pp. 65–91.

Douma, S. W. (1997), 'The two-tier system of corporate governance', *Long Range Planning*, vol. 30 (4), pp. 612–14.

Douma, S., George, R., and Kabir, R. (2006), 'Foreign and domestic ownership, business groups, and firm performance: evidence from a large emerging market', *Strategic Management Journal,* vol. 27, pp. 637–57.

Dyer, J. H., Kale, P., and Singh, H. (2004), 'When to ally and when to acquire', *Harvard Business Review*, vol. 82 (7/8), pp. 108–15.

Dyer, J. H., and Nobeoka, K. (2000), 'Creating and managing a high-performance knowledge-sharing network: the Toyota case', *Strategic Management Journal*, vol. 21(3), pp. 345–67.

Encarnation, D. (1989), *Dislodging Multinationals: India's Comparative Perspective,* Ithaca, NY: Cornell University Press.

Ernst and Young (2011), *The rise of the cross-border transaction: the serial transactor advantage*, London.

Faccio, L., and Lang, L. H. P. (2002), 'The ultimate ownership of Western European corporations', *Journal of Financial Economics,* vol. 65, pp. 365–95.

Faccio, L., Lang, L. H. P., and Young, L. (2001), 'Dividends and expropriation', *American Economic Review,* vol. 91, pp. 54–78.

Fahr, R. and Irlenbusch B. (2008), 'Identifying personality traits to enhance trust between organizations: an experimental approach', *Managerial and Decision Economics*, vol. 29(6), pp. 469–487

Fama, E. F. (1980), 'Agency problems and the theory of the firm', *Journal of Political Economy*, vol. 88, pp. 288–307.

Fama, E. F., Fisher, L., Jensen, M. C., and Roll, R. (1969), 'The adjustment of stock prices to new information', *International Economic Review*, vol. 10 (1), pp. 1–21.

Fama, E. F., and Jensen, M. C. (1983a), 'Separation of ownership and control', *Journal of Law and Economics*, vol. 26, pp. 301–26.

Fama, E. F., and Jensen, M. C. (1983b), 'Agency problems and residual claims', *Journal of Law and Economics*, vol. 26, pp. 327–50.

Ferguson, T. D. (2000), 'Do strategic groups differ in reputation?', *Strategic Management Journal*, vol. 21 (12), pp. 1195–214.

Finkelstein S., Whitehead J. and Campbell A. (2008), *Think Again: Why good leaders make bad decisions and how to keep it from happening to you*, Boston: Harvard Business Press

FitzRoy, F. R., Acs, Z. J., and Gerlowski, D. A. (1998), *Management and Economics of Organization*, Harlow: Prentice Hall.

Frances, J. et al. (1991), 'Introduction', in Thompson, G. Frances, J. Levacic R. and Mitchell, J. *Markets, Hierarchies and Networks*, London: Sage.

Frank, R. H., Gilovitch, T. and D. T. Regan (1993), 'Does studying economics inhibit cooperation?', *Journal of Economic Perspectives*, vol. 7(2), pp 159–171

Freeman, R. E. (1984), *Strategic Management: A stakeholder approach*. Boston, MA: Pitman.

Friedman, E., Johnson, S., and Mitton, T. (2003), 'Propping or tunneling', *Journal of Comparitive Economics,* vol. 31, pp. 732–50.

Frentrop, P. (2003), *A History of Corporate Governance, 1602–2002*, Amsterdam: Deminor.

Galford, R., and Drapeau, A. S. (2003), 'The Enemies of Trust', *Harvard Business Review*, Feb., pp. 89–95.

Gell-Mann, M. (1994), *The Quark and the Jaguar: Adventures in the simple and the complex*, London: Little Brown.

Geroski, P. A. (2003), *The Evolution of New Markets*, Oxford: Oxford University Press.

Gerstner, L. (2002), *Who Says Elephants Can't Dance*, HarperCollins.

Ghemawat, P. (1991), *Commitment: The dynamic of strategy*, New York: Free Press.

Ghemawat, P. (1997), *Games Businesses Play*, Cambridge, MA: MIT Press.

Gibbons, R., and Katz, L. F. (1991), 'Layoffs and lemons', *Journal of Labor Economics*, vol. 9 (4), pp. 351–80.

Gilbert, X., and Strebel, P. (1988), 'Developing competitive advantage', in Quinn, J. B. Mintzberg H. and James R. M. (eds), *The Strategy Process*, Englewood Cliffs, NJ: Prentice Hall.

Gilson, R. J., and Schwartz, A. (2005), 'Understanding MACs: Moral Hazard in Acquisitions', *The Journal of Law, Economics and Organization*, vol. 21, pp. 330–58.

Gilson, R. J., Goldberg, V., Klausner, M., and Raff, D. 'Building foundations for a durable deal', *Financial Times* (Supplement), 13 October 2006, reprinted in Mayer, Colin, and Franks, Julian, *Mastering Transactions*, Financial Times/Ernst & Young, 2006.

Gintis, H. (2000), *Game Theory Evolving*, Princeton, NJ: Princeton University Press.

Glaeser, E. L., Laibson, D. I., Scheinkman, J. A., and Soutter, C. L. (2000), 'Measuring trust', *Quarterly Journal of Economics*, vol. 115 (3), pp. 811–46.

Gleick, J. (1987), *Chaos*, New York: Viking.

Gneezy, U. (2005), 'Deception: the role of consequences', *American Economic Review*, vol. 95(1), pp. 384–394

Goergen, M. (2012), *International Corporate Governance*, Prentice Hall.

Goetzmann, W. N., and Rouwenhorst, K. G. (2005) *The Origins of Value*, Oxford: Oxford University Press.

Goold, M., Campbell, A., and Alexander, M. (1994), *Corporate-level Strategy*, New York: John Wiley.

Goshal, S., and Moran, P. (1996), 'Bad for practice: a critique of the transaction cost theory', *Academy of Management Review*, vol. 21 (1), pp. 13–47.

Goswami, O. (1989), 'Sahibs, babus and Banias: Changes in industrial control in Eastern India 1918–1950', *Journal of Asian Studies*, vol. 48, pp. 289–309.

Gould, S. J. (1989), *Wonderful Life*, New York: Norton.

Granovetter, M. (1985), 'Economic action and social structure: The problem of embeddedness', *American Journal of Sociology*, vol. 91 (3).

Grant, R. M. (1991), 'The resource-based theory of competitive advantage: Implications for strategy formulation', *California Management Review*, vol. 13, pp. 114–35.

Grant, R. M. (2003), 'The knowledge-based view of the firm', in D. O. Faulkner, and A. Campbell (eds), *The Oxford Handbook of Strategy*, Oxford: Oxford University Press.

Grant, R. M. (2009), *Contemporary Strategy Analysis*, 7th Ed, New York: John Wiley.

Grove, A. S. (1996), *Only the Paranoid Survive*, New York: Doubleday.

Guillén, M. F. (2000), 'Business groups in emerging economies: a resource-based view', *Academy of Management Journal*, vol. 43 (3), pp. 362–81.

Güth, W., Schmittberger, R., and Schwarze, B. (1982), 'An experimental analysis of ultimum bargaining', *Journal of Economic Behavior and Organization*, vol. 3, pp. 367–88.

Hall, R. (1992), 'The strategic analysis of intangible resources', *Strategic Management Journal*, vol. 13, pp. 135–44.

Hall, R. (1993), 'A framework linking intangible resources and capabilities to sustainable competitive advantage', *Strategic Management Journal*, vol. 14, pp. 607–18.

Hannan, M. T., and Freeman, J. (1989a), *Organizational Ecology*, Cambridge, MA: Harvard University Press.

Hannan, M. T., and Freeman, J. (1989b), 'Setting the record straight on organizational ecology: rebuttal to Young', *American Journal of Sociology*, vol. 95 (2), pp. 425–35.

Harrigan, K. (2003), *Joint Ventures, Alliances, and Corporate Strategy*, Washington, DC: Beard Books.

Hatten, K. J., and Hatten, M. L. (1988), *Effective Strategic Management: Analysis and Action*, Englewood Cliffs, NJ: Prentice Hall.

Haugland, S. A. (1999), 'Factors influencing the duration of international buyer–seller relationships', *Journal of Business Research*, vol. 46, pp. 273–80.

Hayek, F. A. (1945), 'The use of knowledge in society', *American Economic Review*, vol. 35 (4).

Hayward, M. L. A., and Hambrick, D. C. (1997), 'Explaining the premiums paid for large acquisitions: evidence of CEO hubris', *Administrative Science Quarterly*, vol. 42 (1), pp. 103–27.

Hazari, R. K. (1967), *The Structure of the Corporate Private Sector: A study of concentration, ownership and control*, London: Asia Publishing House.

Helfat C. E., Finkelstein, S., Mitchell, W., Peteraf, M. A., Singh, H., Teece, D. J., and Winter, S. G. (2007), *Dynamic Capabilities: Understanding strategic change in organizations*, Oxford: Blackwell.

Helfat, C. E. and Winter, S. G. (2011), 'Untangling dynamic and operational capabilities: strategy for the (n)ever-changing world', *Strategic Management Journal*, 32: 1243-1250

Henrich, J. (2000), 'Does culture matter in economic behavior?: ultimatum game bargaining among the Machiguenga of the Peruvian Amazon', *American Economic Review*, vol. 90, pp. 973–79.

Hennart, J. F., and Reddy, S. (1997), 'The choice between mergers/acquisitions and joint ventures: the case of Japanese investors in the United States', *Strategic Management Journal*, vol. 18 (1), pp. 1–12.

Hill, C. W., and Jones, G. R. (1995), *Strategic Management Theory: An Integrated Approach*, Boston, MA: Houghton Mifflin.

Hillman, A. J., and Keim, G. D. (2001), 'Shareholder value, stakeholder management, and social issues: what's the bottom line?', *Strategic Management Journal*, vol. 22 (2), pp. 125–39.

Hofstede, G. (2001), *Culture's Consequences*, London: Sage.

Holland, J. H. (1998), *Emergence: from Chaos to Order*, Cambridge, MA: Perseus.

Holmstrom, B. R., and Tirole, J. (1989), 'The theory of the firm', in R. Schmalensee and R. Willig (eds), *Handbook of Industrial Organization*, vol. 1, Amsterdam: North Holland.

Hoskisson, R. E., and Hitt, M. A. (1990), 'Antecedents and performance outcomes of diversification: a review and critique of theoretical perspectives', *Journal of Management*, vol. 16 (2), pp. 461–509.

Hotelling, H. (1929), 'Stability in competition', *Economic Journal*, vol. 39, pp. 41–57.

Hurley, R. F. (2006), 'The Decision to Trust', *Harvard Business Review*, Sept., pp. 55–62.

Hymon, D. N. (1986), *Modern Microeconomics: Analysis and applications*, St Louis, MI: Times Mirror/Mosby College Publishing.

Imai, K., and Itami, H. (1984), 'Interpenetration of organization and market', *International Journal of Industrial Organization*, vol. 2, pp. 285–310.

Irvin, R. A., and Michaels III, E. G. (1983), 'Core skills: doing the right things right', *McKinsey Quarterly*, Summer, 4–19.

Isaacson W., *Steve Jobs.*, (2011): Simon & Schuster.

Jacobides, M. G., and Croson, D. C. (2001), 'Information policy: shaping the value of agency relationships', *Academy of Management Review*, vol. 26 (2), pp. 202–23.

Jensen, M. C. (1986), 'Agency costs and free cash flow, corporate finance, and takeovers', *American Economic Review*, vol. 76, pp. 323–9.

Jensen, M. C. (1989), 'The eclipse of the public corporation', *Harvard Business Review*, September/October, pp. 61–73.

Jensen, M. C. (1998), *Foundations of Organizational Strategy*, Cambridge, MA: Harvard University Press.

Jensen, M. C. (2000), *A Theory of the Firm: Governance, residual claims, and organizational forms*, Cambridge, MA: Harvard University Press.

Jensen, M. C., and Meckling, W. H. (1976), 'Theory of the firm: managerial behavior, agency costs and ownership structure', *Journal of Financial Economics*, vol. 3, pp. 305–60.

Jensen, M. C., and Ruback, R. S. (1983), 'The market for corporate control: the scientific evidence', *Journal of Financial Economics*, vol. 11, pp. 5–50.

John, K., Liu, Y. and Taffles, R. *It takes Two to Tango: Overpayment and Value Destination in M & A Deals*, Working Paper (version 16.1), 15 November 2010.

Johnson, S. (2001), *Emergence: The connected lives of ants, brains, cities and software*, New York: Scribner.

Johnson E. J., and Goldstein D (2003), *'Do defaults save lives'*, Science, 302, 1338–1339.

Johnson, S., La Porta, R., Lopez-de-Silanes, F., and Schleifer, A. (2000), 'Tunneling', *American Economic Review Paper and Proceedings*, vol. 90, pp. 22–7.

Johnson, G., Scholes, K., and Whittington, R. (2005), *Exploring Corporate Strategy: Text and cases,* Harlow: FT Prentice Hall.

Jones, G. R., and Hill, C. W. L. (1988), 'Transaction cost analysis of strategy–structure choice', *Strategic Management Journal*, vol. 9, pp. 159–72.

Kahneman, D. (2002), *Maps of Bounded Rationality*, Nobel Prize Lecture, reprinted in *American Economic Review*, vol 93 (5), pp. 1449–75, 2003.

Kahneman, D. (2011), *Thinking, fast and slow*, London: Penguin.

Kahneman, D. and Tversky, A. (1979) *'Prospect theory: an analysis of decision under risk'*, *Econometrica*. vol 47, no. 2, pp. 263–292

Katz, M. L., and Rosen, H. S. (1998), *Microeconomics*, Boston, MA: Irwin/McGraw Hill.

Kauffman, S. (1993), *The Origins of Order: Self-organization and selection in evolution*, New York: Oxford University Press.

Kauffman, S. (1995), *At Home in the Universe: The search for laws of complexity*, London: Viking.

Kaufman, A., Wood, C. H., and Theyel, G. (2000), 'Collaboration and technology linkages: a strategic supplier typology', *Strategic Management Journal*, vol. 21 (6), pp. 649–63.

Kay, J. (1993), *Foundations of Corporate Success: How business strategies add value*, Oxford: Oxford University Press.

Kay, J. (1996), *The Business of Economics*, Oxford: Oxford University Press.

Kay, J. (2003), *The Truth about Markets: Their genius, their limits, their follies*, London: Penguin

Kessel, R. A. (1974), 'Transfused blood, serum hepatitis, and the Coase theorem', *Journal of Law and Economics*, vol. 17 (2), pp. 265–89.

Khalil, E. L. (2003), *Trust*, Cheltenham: Elgar.

Khanna, T. (2000), 'Business groups and social welfare in emerging markets: existing evidence and unanswered questions', *European Economic Review,* vol. 44, pp. 748–61.

Khanna, T., and Palepu, K. (1997), 'Why focused strategies may be wrong for emerging markets?', *Harvard Business Review,* vol. 75 (4), pp. 41–54.

Khanna, T., and Palepu, K. (2004), 'The evolution of concentrated ownership in India: broad patterns and a history of the Indian software industry' *Harvard Business School, NBER Working paper W10613.*

Khanna, T., Palepu, K., and Bullock, R. (2010), *Winning in emerging markets: a road map for strategy and execution*, Boston, MA: Harvard Business Press.

Khanna, T., and Rivkin, J. W. (2001), 'Estimating the performance effects of business groups in emerging markets', *Strategic Management Journal*, vol. 22 (1), pp. 45–74.

Klein, B., Crawford, R. A., and Alchian, A. A. (1978), 'Vertical integration, appropriable rents and the competitive contracting process', *Journal of Law and Economics*, vol. 21, pp. 297–326.

Klemperer, P. (2002), 'What really matters in auction design', *Journal of Economic Perspectives*, vol. 16 (1), Winter 2002, pp. 169–89.

Klemperer, P. (2004), *Auctions: Theory and practice*, Princeton, NJ: Princeton University Press.

Kohers, N and Ang, J. S. (2000) 'Earnouts in mergers: agreeing to disagree and agreeing to stay'. *Journal of Business*. vol. 73 (3). pp. 445–476

Kreps, D. M. (2004), *Microeconomics for Managers*, New York: W. W. Norton.

Krug, J. and R. Aguilera (2005), 'Top management team turnover in mergers & acquisitions', *Advances in Mergers & Acquisitions*, vol. 4, pp. 121–149

Lafontaine, F. (1992), 'Agency theory and franchising: some empirical results', *RAND Journal of Economics*, vol. 23 (2), pp. 263–83.

Lewin, R. (1995), *Complexity: Life on the edge of chaos*, London: Phoenix.

Li, Shaomin, Li, Shuhe and Zhang, Weiying (2000), 'The road to capitalism: competition and institutional change in China', *Journal of Comparative Economics*, vol. 28 (2), pp. 269–92.

Lieberman M. B., and Montgomery, D. B. (1998), 'First-mover (dis)advantages: retrospective and link with the resource-based view', *Strategic Management Journal*, vol. 19 (12), pp. 1111–25

Liebowitz, S., and Margolis, S. (1990), 'The fable of the keys', *Journal of Law and Economics*, vol. 33 (1), pp. 1–25.

Lindgren, K. (1997), 'Evolutionary dynamics in game-theoretic models', in Arthur, W. B. Durlauf S. N. and Lane, D. A. *The Economy as an Evolving Complex System II*, Santa Fe Institute, Reading: Addison-Wesley.

Lokanathan, P. S. (1935), *Industrial Organization in India*, London: Allen and Unwin.

M&A Research Centre (MARC), (2011), *The Economic Impact of M&A: Implications for UK firms*, London: City University

Macaulay, S. (1963), 'Non-contractual relations in business: a preliminary study', *American Sociological Review*, vol. 28 (1).

McColgan, P. (2001), 'Agency and corporate governance: a review of the literature from a UK perspective', part of unpublished PhD dissertation, University of Strathclyde, Glasgow.

McKinsey (2009), '10 Timeless tests of strategy', *McKinsey Quarterly*, September 2009.

McKinsey (2012), 'Taking a longer-term look at M&A value creation', *McKinsey Quarterly*, January 2012.

McGee, J. (2003), 'Strategic groups: theory and practice', in Faulkner D. O. and Campbell, A. *The Oxford Handbook of Strategy (vol. 1)*, Oxford: Oxford University Press.

McMillan, J. (1991), *Games, Strategies, and Managers*, Oxford: Oxford University Press.

McMillan, J. (2002), *Reinventing the Bazaar: A natural history of markets*, New York: W. W. Norton.

Magretta, Joan (2002), *What Management Is*, New York: Free Press.

Maher, M. E. (1997), 'Transaction cost economics and contractual relations', *Cambridge Journal of Economics*, vol. 21, pp. 147–70.

Malmendier, U., and Tate, G. (2008), 'Who makes acquisitions? CEO overconfidence and the market's reaction', *Journal of Financial Economics*, vol. 89, pp. 20–43.

March, J. G. (1994), *A Primer on Decision Making: How decisions happen*, New York: Free Press.

March, J. G., and Simon, H. A. (1958), *Organizations*, New York: John Wiley.

Markides, C. C., and Geroski, P. A. (2005), *Fast Second: How smart companies bypass radical innovation to enter and dominate new markets*, San Francisco, CA: Jossey-Bass.

Marshall, A. (1890), *Principles of Economics*, London: Macmillan. (Reprinted 1949).

Masten, S. E., Meekan Jr, J. W., and Snyder, E. A. (1989), 'Vertical integration in the US auto industry: a note on the influence of transaction specific assets', *Journal of Economic Behavior and Organization*, vol. 12, pp. 265–73.

Maynard Smith, J. and Price, G. (1973), 'The logic of animal conflict', *Nature*, vol. 146, pp. 15–18.

Mellström, C. and M. Johannesson (2008), 'Crowding out in blood donation: was Titmuss right?', *Journal of the European Economic Association*, vol. 6(4): 845-863.

Ménard, C. (1995), 'Markets as institutions versus organizations as markets? Disentangling some fundamental concepts', *Journal of Economic Behavior and Organization*, vol. 28, pp. 161–82.

Ménard, C. (2004), 'The economics of hybrid organizations', *Journal of Institutional and Theoretical Economics*, pp. 345–76.

Ménard, C. (2010), 'Hybrid organisations', in: P. G. Klein and M. E. Sykuta (eds), *The Elgar Companion to Transaction Cost Economics*, Aldershot, UK: Edward Elgar.

Michael, S. C. (2000), 'Investments to create bargaining power: the case of franchising', *Strategic Management Journal*, vol. 21 (4) pp. 497–514.

Michael, S. C. and Bercovitz, J. E. L., (2009), 'A strategic look at the organizational form of franchising', in J. A. Nickerson and B. S. Silverman (eds), *Economic Institutions of Strategy,* Bingley, UK,: Emerald.

Micklethwait, J., and Wooldridge, A. (2003), *The Company: A short history of a revolutionary idea*, London: Weidenfeld & Nicolson.

Milgrom, P., and Roberts, J. (1987), 'Informational asymmetry, strategic behavior, and industrial organization', *American Economic Review*, vol. 77, pp. 184–93.

Milgrom, P., and Roberts, J. (1992), *Economics, Organization and Management*, Englewood Cliffs, NJ: Prentice Hall.

Miller, D. (1990), *The Icarus Paradox*, New York: Harper.

Miller, D. (1994), 'What happens after success: the perils of excellence', *Journal of Management Studies*, vol. 31 (3), pp. 325–58.

Minkler, L. (2004), 'Shirking and motivations in firms: survey evidence on worker attitudes', *International Journal of Industrial Organization*, Vol. 22 (6), pp. 863–84.

Mintzberg, H. (1979), *The Structuring of Organizations*, Englewood Cliffs, NJ: Prentice Hall.

Mintzberg, H. (1983), *Structure in Fives*: *Designing effective organizations*, Englewood Cliffs, NJ: Prentice Hall.

Mintzberg, H. (1985), 'Of strategies, deliberate and emergent', *Strategic Management Journal*, pp. 257–72.

Mintzberg, H. (1989), *Mintzberg on Management*, New York: Free Press.

Mintzberg, H. and J. B. Quinn (1991), *The Strategy Process*: *concepts, contexts, cases*, Englewood Cliffs, NJ: Prentice Hall.

Moerland, P. W. (1995), 'Alternative disciplinary mechanisms in different corporate systems', *Journal of Economic Behavior and Organization*, vol. 26, pp. 17–34.

Morck, R., Wolfenzon, D. and Yeung, B. (2004), 'Corporate governance, economic entrenchement and growth', *Harvard Business School, NBER Working paper W10692*.

Morgan, G. (2006), *Images of Organization*, London: Sage.

Morgan, J. P., *Contingent consideration*, J. P. Morgan Mergers Insight, 4 March 2011.

Moschandreas, M. (1997), 'The role of opportunism in transaction cost economics', *Journal of Economic Issues*, vol. 31 (1), pp. 39–57.

Nair, A., and Kotha, S. (2001), 'Does group membership matter? Evidence from the Japanese steel industry', *Strategic Management Journal*, vol. 22 (3), pp. 221–35.

Nam, S. W. (2001), 'Business groups looted by controlling families, and the Asian crisis', *ADB Institute Research Paper 27*.

Nanda, A., and Williamson, P. J. (1995), 'Use joint ventures to ease the pain of restructuring', *Harvard Business Review*, vol. 73 (6), pp. 119–28.

Nayak, P. R., Garvin, D. A., Maira, A. N., and Bragar, J. L. (1995), 'Creating a learning organization', *Prism*, 3rd quarter.

Nelson, R. R. (1991), 'Why do firms differ and how does it matter?', *Strategic Management Journal*, vol. 12 (special issue), pp. 61–74.

Nelson, R. R., and Winter, S. G. (1982), *An Evolutionary Theory of Economic Change*, Cambridge, MA: Harvard University Press.

Nenova, T. (2004), 'A corporate governance agenda for developing countries' *World Bank working paper*.

Nickerson, J. A., Hamilton, B. H., and Wada T., (2001), 'Market position, resource profile and governance: linking Porter and Williamson in the context of international courier and small package services in Japan', *Strategic Management Journal*, vol. 22 (3), pp. 251–73.

Noorderhaven, N. G. (1995), 'Transaction, interaction, institutionalization: toward a dynamic theory of hybrid governance', *Scandinavian Journal of Management*, vol. 11 (1), pp. 43–55.

North, D. C. (1990), *Institutions, Institutional Change and Economic Performance*, Cambridge: Cambridge University Press.

North, D. C. (2005a), *Understanding the Process of Economic Change*, Princeton, NJ: Princeton University Press.

North, D. C. (2005b), 'Corporate leadership in an uncertain world', New York: Conference Board Annual Report.

O'Donnell, S. W. (2000), 'Managing foreign subsidiaries: agents of headquarters, or an independent network?', *Strategic Management Journal*, vol. 21 (5), pp. 525–48.

OECD (2004), Principles of corporate governance, OECD.

Ormerud, P. (2005), *Why Most Things Fail*, London: Faber and Faber.

Oster, S. (1982), 'Intraindustry structure and the ease of strategic change', *Review of Economics and Statistics*, vol. 64 (3), pp. 376–83.

Ouchi, W. G. (1980), 'Markets, bureaucracies and clans', *Administrative Science Quarterly*, vol. 25, pp. 129–41.

Ouchi, W. G., and Williamson, O. E. (1981), 'The markets and hierarchies perspective: origins, implications, prospects', in Van de Ven A. and Joyce W. F (eds), *Assessing Organizational Design and Performance*, New York: John Wiley.

Oxley, J. E., (2009), 'Appropriability hazards and governance in strategic alliances: a transaction cost approach', in Nickerson J. A. and Silverman B. S. (eds), *Economic Institutions of Strategy,* Bingley, UK,: Emerald.

Pagano, M. and Volpin, P. (2001), 'The political economy of finance', *Oxford Review of Economic Policy,* vol. 17, pp. 502–19.

Park, S. H., and Luo, Y. (2001), 'Guanxi and organizational dynamics: organizational networking in Chinese firms', *Strategic Management Journal*, vol. 22 (5), pp. 455–77.

Parsons, T. (1960), *Structure and Process in Modern Societies*, Glencoe, IL: Free Press.

Perloff, J. M. (2001), *Microeconomics*, Boston, MA: Addison-Wesley.

Peteraf, M. A. (1993), 'The cornerstones of competitive advantage: a resource-based view', *Strategic Management Journal*, vol. 14 (3), pp. 179–91.

Pfeffer, J. (1982), *Organizations and Organization Theory*, Marshfield, MA: Pitman.

Pigou, A. C. (1920), *The Economics of Welfare*, London: Macmillan.

Polanyi, M. (1962), *Personal Knowledge*, New York: Harper.

Polanyi, M. (1967), *The Tacit Dimension*, Garden City, NY: Doubleday.

Polisiri, P., and Wiwattanakantang, Y. (2004), 'Restructuring of family firms after the East Asian financial crisis: shareholder expropriation or alignment?', Working paper, Center for Economic institutions, Institute for Economic Research, Hitotsubashi University, Japan.

Porter, M. E. (1980), *Competitive Strategy: Techniques for Analyzing Industries and Competitors*, New York: Free Press.

Porter, M. E. (1985), *Competitive Advantage: Creating and Sustaining Superior Performance*, New York: Free Press.

Porter, M. E. (2008), 'The five forces that shape strategy', *Harvard Business Review*, vol. 86 (1), pp. 1–17

Porter, M. E. (2008). 'The five competitive forces that shape strategy', *Harvard Business Review*, vol. 861(1), Reprint R0801E, pp. 1–17.

Powell, J. H. (2003), 'Game Theory in Strategy', in Faulkner D. O. and Campbell, A. *The Oxford Handbook in Strategy (vol. 2)*, Oxford: Oxford University Press

Prahalad, C. K. and Hamel, G. (1994), *Competing for the Future*, Boston, MA: Harvard Business School Press.

Prigogine, I. and Stengers, I. (1984), *Order Out of Chaos*, New York: Bantam.

Putterman, L. (ed.) (1986), *The Economic Nature of the Firm*: A reader, Cambridge: Cambridge University Press.

Quinn, J. B. (1982), *Strategies for Change: Logical incrementalism*, Homewood, IL: Irwin.

Quinn, J. B., Mintzberg, H., and James, R. M. (eds) (1988), *The Strategy Process*, Englewood Cliffs, NJ: Prentice Hall.

Ragozzino, R. and Reuer, J. J. (2009), "Contingent earnouts in acquisitions of privately held firms", *Journal of Management*, vol. 35(4), pp. 857–859.

Raiffa, H. (1968), *Decision Analysis: Introductory lectures on choices under uncertainty*, Reading, MA: Addison-Wesley.

Rasmusen, E. (1989), *Games and Information: An introduction to the theory of games*, Oxford: Basil Blackwell.

Reuer, J. J. (2001), 'From hybrids to hierarchies: shareholder wealth effects of joint venture partner buy-outs', *Strategic Management Journal*, vol. 22 (1), pp. 27–44.

Reuer, J. J. (2005), 'Avoiding lemons in M&A deals', *MIT Sloan Management Review*, vol. 46 (3), pp. 15–17.

Reuer, J. J. (2009), 'Organizational economics insights from acquisitions research' in: Nickerson, J.A. and Silverman, B.S., *Economic Institutional of Strategy*, *Advances in Strategic Management*, vol. 26, pp. 241–265.

Reuer, J. J., and Koza, M. P. (2000), 'Asymmetric information and joint venture performance: theory and evidence for domestic and international joint ventures', *Strategic Management Journal*, vol. 21 (1), pp. 81–8.

Reuer, J. J. and Ragozzino, R. (2006), 'Using IPOs to prove the value of M&A targets', *Financial Times (Supplement),* 6 October 2006, reprinted in Mayer, Colin and Franks, Julian, *Mastering Transactions*, Financial Times/Ernst & Young, 2006.

Reuer, J. J., and Shen, J. C. (2004), 'Sequential divestiture through initial public offerings', *Journal of Economic Behavior and Organization*, vol. 54 (2), pp. 249–66.

Roberts, D. J. (2004), *The Modern Firm: Organizational design for performance and growth*, Oxford: Oxford University Press.

Roll, R. (1986), 'The hubris hypothesis of corporate takeovers', *Journal of Business*, vol. 59 (2), pp. 197–216.

Rumelt, R. P. (1974), *Strategy, Structure, and Economic Performance*, Boston, MA: Harvard Business School Press.

Rumelt, R. P., (1984), 'Towards a strategic theory of the firm', in Lamb, R. B. *Competitive Strategic Management*, Englewood Cliffs, NJ: Prentice Hall.

Rumelt, R. P. (1991), 'How much does industry matter?', *Strategic Management Journal*, vol. 12 (3), pp. 167–85.

Rumelt, R. P. (2011), *Good Strategy / Bad Strategy,* New York: Crown/ Random House.

Sako, M., and Helper, S. (1998), 'Determinants of trust in supplier relations: evidence from the automotive industry in Japan and the United States', *Journal of Economic Behavior and Organization*, vol. 34, pp. 387–417.

Samuelson, P. (1976), *Economics* (10th edn), Tokyo: McGraw-Hill/Kogakusha Ltd.

Saussier, S. (1999), 'Duration: an empirical analysis of EDF coal contracts', *Recherches Economiques de Louvain*, vol. 65 (1), pp. 3–21.

Schelling, T. C. (1960), *The Strategy of Conflict*, Cambridge, MA: Harvard University Press. (Reprinted 1980.)

Schleifer, A., and Vishny, R. W. (1997), 'A survey of corporate governance', *Journal of Finance*, vol. 52, pp. 737–83.

Schleifer, A., and Vishny, R. W. (2003), 'Stock market driven acquisitions', *Journal of Financial Economics*, vol. 70, pp. 295–311.

Schoenberg, R. (2006), 'Measuring the performance of corporate acquisitions: an empirical comparison of alternative metrics', *British Journal of Management,* vol. 17, pp.361–370

Schreuder, H. (1993a), 'Coase, Hayek, and hierarchy', in Lindenberg S. and Schreuder, H. *Interdisciplinary Perspectives on Organization Studies*, Oxford: Pergamon Press.

Schreuder, H. (1993b), 'Timely management changes as an element of organizational strategy', *Journal of Management Studies*, vol. 30 (5), pp. 723–38.

Schreuder, H., and van Witteloostuijn, A. (1990), *The Ecology of Organizations and the Economics of Firms*, Research Memorandum, University of Limburg.

Schumpeter, J. A. (1934), *The Theory of Economic Development*, Cambridge, MA: Harvard University Press.

Scott, W. R. (2003), *Organizations: Rational, Natural, and Open Systems* (5th edn), Englewood Cliffs, NJ: Prentice Hall.

Seabright, P. (2004), *The Company of Strangers: A natural history of economic life*, Princeton, NJ: Princeton University Press.

Simon, H. A. (1961), *Administrative Behavior* (2nd edn), New York: Macmillan.

Simon, H. A. (1991), 'Organizations and markets', *Journal of Economic Perspectives*, vol. 5 (2), pp. 25–44.

Slater, M. (2003), 'The boundary of the firm', in Faulkner D. O. and Campbell, A. *The Oxford Handbook of Strategy*, Oxford: Oxford University Press.

Soeters, J., and Schreuder, H. (1988), 'The interaction between national and organizational cultures in accounting firms', *Accounting, Organizations and Society*, vol. 13 (1), pp. 75–85.

Spence, M. (1973), 'Job market signaling', *Quarterly Journal of Economics,* vol. 87(3), pp. 355–74.

Stacey, R. D. (2011), *Strategic Management & Organisational Dynamics* (6th edn), Harlow: Financial Times/Prentice Hall.

Stigler, G. J., and Friedland, C. (1983), 'The literature of economics: the case of Berle and Means', *Journal of Law and Economics*, vol. 26, pp. 237–68.

Stiglitz, J. (2002), *Globalization and its Discontents,* London: Penguin.

Stuckey, J. and White, D. (1993), 'When and when not to vertically integrate: a strategy as risky as vertical integration can only succeed when it is chosen for the right reasons', *McKinsey Quarterly*, pp. 3–27.

Sull, D. N. (2003), 'Managing by commitments', *Harvard Business Review*, June 2003, pp. 82–91

Takeishi, A. (2001), 'Bridging inter- and intra-firm boundaries: management of supplier involvement in automobile product development', *Strategic Management Journal*, vol. 22 (5), pp. 403–33.

Tallman, S. (2003), 'Dynamic capabilities', in Faulkner D. O. and Campbell, A. *The Oxford Handbook of Strategy*, Oxford: Oxford University Press.

Teece, D. J. (1980), 'Economies of scope and the scope of the enterprise', *Journal of Economic Behavior and Organization*, vol. 1, pp. 223–47.

Teece, D. J. (1982), 'Towards an economic theory of the multiproduct firm', *Journal of Economic Behavior and Organization*, vol. 3, pp. 39–63.

Teece, D. J., Pisano, G. and Shuen, A. (1997), 'Dynamic capabilities and strategic management', *Strategic Management Journal*, vol. 18, pp. 509–33.

Teece, David J. (2007), 'Explicating dynamic capabilities: the nature and microfoundations of (sustainable) enterprise performance', *Strategic Management Journal*, 28: pp. 1319–1350.

Teece, David J. (2009), *Dynamic capabilities and strategic management,* Oxford: Oxford University Press.

Teece, D. J. (2010), 'Business Models, Business Strategy and Innovations', *Long Range Planning* vol. 43, pp. 172–194.

Tellis, G. J., and Golder, P. N. (1996), 'First to market, first to fail? Real causes of enduring market leadership', *MIT Sloan Management Review*, vol. 37 (2), pp. 65–75.

Tellis, G. J., and Golder, P. N. (2002), *Will and Vision: How latecomers grow to dominate markets*, New York: McGraw-Hill.

Thompson, G., Frances, J., Levacic, R., and Mitchell, J. (1991), *Markets, Hierarchies and Networks*, London: Sage.

Tichy, G. (2002), 'What do we know about success and failure of mergers?', *Journal of Industry, Competition and Trade*, vol. 1 (4), pp. 347–94.

Titmuss, R. M. (1971), *The Gift Relationship: From human blood to social policy*, New York: Pantheon.

Tversky, A., and Kahneman, D. (1974), 'Judgment under uncertainty: heuristics and biases', *Science*, vol. 185, pp. 1124–31.

UBS (2004), 'Are you prepared for the next wave?', Jullens, D., Cooper, S., and Stillit, D., August. See: www.ubsinvestmentresearch.com.

Usher, J. M., and Evans, M. G. (1996), 'Life and death along gasoline alley: Darwinian and Lamarckian processes in a differentiating population', *Academy of Management Journal*, vol. 39 (5), pp. 1428–66.

Vaaler, P. M., and McNamara, G., (2009), 'Changing Corporate effects on US Business Performance since the 1970s', *International Journal of Strategic Change Management,* vol. 2.

Volberda, H. W. (2003), 'Strategic flexibility: creating dynamic competitive advantages', in D. O. Faulkner and A. Campbell (2003), *The Oxford Handbook of Strategy*, vol. 2, Oxford: Oxford University Press.

Waldrop, M. M. (1992), *Complexity: The emerging science at the edge of order and chaos*, New York: Simon & Schuster.

Warner, J. B., Watts, R. L., and Wruck, K. H. (1988), 'Stock prices and top management changes', *Journal of Financial Economics*, vol. 20, pp. 461–92.

Weber, Max (1947), *The Theory of Social and Economic Organization* (original edition 1925), A. M. Henderson and T. Parsons (trans.), New York: Free Press.

Weick, K. E. (1979), *The Social Psychology of Organizing* (2nd edn), Reading, MA: Addison-Wesley.

Weisbach, M. S. (1988), 'Outside directors and CEO turnover', *Journal of Financial Economics,* vol. 20, pp. 431–60.

Williamson, O. E. (1975), *Markets and Hierarchies: Analysis and antitrust implications*, New York: Free Press.

Williamson, O. E. (1985), *The Economic Institutions of Capitalism*, New York: Free Press.

Williamson, O. E. (1995), 'Transaction cost economics and organization theory', in O. E. Williamson, *Organization Theory: From Chester Barnard to the present and beyond'*, Oxford: Oxford University Press.

Williamson, O. E. (1996), 'Economics and organization: a primer', *California Management Review*, vol. 38, pp. 131–46.

Williamson, O. E. (1998), 'Transaction cost economics: how it works, where it is headed', *De Economist*, vol. 146 (1), pp. 23–58.

Williamson, O. E. (1999), 'Strategy research: governance and competence perspectives', *Strategic Management Journal*, vol. 20 (12), pp. 1087–108.

Williamson, O. E. (2007), 'An interview with Oliver Williamson', *Journal of Institutional Economics*, vol 3 (3), pp. 373–386.

Williamson, O. E. (2009), 'Foreword to economic institutions of strategy', in: Nickerson J. A. and Silverman B. S. (eds), *Economic Institutions of Strategy, Advanced in Strategic Managemnet*, vol. 26, New York: Emerald.

Winter, S. G. (1990), 'Survival, selection, and inheritance in evolutionary theories of organization', in Singh, J. V. *Organizational Evolution: New Directions*, Newbury Park, CA: Sage.

Winter, S. G. (2003), 'Understanding dynamic capabilities', *Strategic Management Journal*, vol. 24, pp. 991–5.

Wu, J., and Axelrod, R. (1995) 'How to cope with noise in the iterated prisoner's dilemma', *Journal of Conflict Resolution*, vol. 39 (1), pp. 183–9.

Young, R. C. (1988), 'Is population ecology a useful paradigm for the study of organizations?', *American Journal of Sociology*, vol. 94 (1), pp. 1–24.

Index

Pages numbers in **bold** refer to marginal definitions